FASHION FORECASTING

FASHION FORECASTING

Evelyn L. Brannon
and
Lorynn Divita

FOURTH EDITION

Fairchild Books
An imprint of Bloomsbury Publishing Inc

BLOOMSBURY
NEW YORK · LONDON · NEW DELHI · SYDNEY

Fairchild Books
An imprint of Bloomsbury Publishing Inc

1385 Broadway	50 Bedford Square
New York	London
NY 10018	WC1B 3DP
USA	UK

www.bloomsbury.com

FAIRCHILD BOOKS, BLOOMSBURY and the Diana logo are trademarks of Bloomsbury Publishing Plc
Second edition published 2004
Third edition published 2010
This edition published 2015

Library of Congress Cataloging-in-Publication Data
Brannon, Evelyn L.
  Fashion forecasting / Evelyn L. Brannon, Lorynn Divita. — Fourth edition.
    pages cm
  Includes bibliographical references and index.
  ISBN 978-1-62892-546-3 (alk. paper)
1. Clothing trade—Forecasting. 2. Fashion—Forecasting. I. Divita, Lorynn. II. Title.
  TT497.B69 2015
  746.9'20684--dc23
                            2014049253

ISBN: PBK: 978-1-6289-2546-3
          ePDF: 978-1-6289-2548-7

Typeset by Saxon Graphics Ltd, Derby
Printed and bound in China

TO MY STUDENTS—PAST, PRESENT, AND FUTURE.

CONTENTS

EXTENDED CONTENTS

PREFACE

Since the new millennium, the fashion industry has undergone a complete upheaval, the likes of which could not have been predicted even 50 years ago—the advent of the Internet making entire retailers obsolete, the importance of brand names and logos trumping the attractiveness and quality of the clothing they are attached to as motivating factors for consumers, the growth of disposable fast fashion retailers that can replicate a runway look so quickly that people are tired of it before the original makes it to the designer's store, and the rise of celebrities with no discernable talent other than being themselves being held up as fashion inspirations and even designers—that would make the idea of trying to forecast fashion an impossible proposition. When even trend sociologists such as Henrik Vejlgaard say that the speed of trends is as fast as it can possibly be, and so many trends exist simultaneously, it would be understandable that one might wonder what the point is in even trying to forecast trends.

The truth is that trends matter now as much as they ever did. Despite rapid technological change that has infiltrated every aspect of modern life, people's wants and needs have not changed. A sizeable portion of consumers still crave novelty in their wardrobes, want to convey a sense of self through their appearance, and are looking for affiliation with other people who share their sense of style and taste. With an overwhelming array of styles to choose from, in many cases the simple act of shopping can be overwhelming for consumers and they are looking for guidance. An understanding of forecasting and the flow of trends allows apparel manufacturers and retailers to continuously anticipate and fulfill their consumers' wants and needs.

ORGANIZATION OF THE FOURTH EDITION

In order to keep pace with the rapidly changing fashion industry, instructors will find several changes to the structure and format of the fourth edition of *Fashion Forecasting* that my editors and I feel make a stronger textbook. While the depth of material from the previous edition is unchanged, the structure of each chapter has been revised to streamline content and improve the flow of information. Through this streamlining process, there has been sufficient space to add a new chapter (Chapter 5), entitled "Popular Culture and Forecasting," which connects the influence of fields such as television, music, and movies as well as new online media on the dissemination and adoption of trends. A thoroughly updated Chapter 4, now entitled "Modern Forecasting Methods," replaces the profiles of forecasters who are no longer active in the field with current forecasters, all of whom have published works on the subject in the last 2 years and are taking the discipline into the future.

These two new and revamped chapters now complement the previously existing chapters, which retain their basic structure from the third edition. The first chapter of this edition offers an overview of the forecasting process and introduces the concept of the Zeitgeist (or spirit of the times) as an organizing principle for forecasting. The chapter also includes a summary of fashion change in the twentieth and early twenty-first centuries and provides students with the context for forecasting, including a section on forecasting as a career to offer guidance for students who want to pursue one of the forecasting disciplines professionally.

Part One, *Forecasting Frameworks*, covers the theoretical and historical basis for forecasting. Chapter 2 describes the diffusion of innovation. Chapter 3 discusses theories of fashion change and fashion cycles. Chapter 4 explains the strategies and techniques of forecasting by looking at social, political, and technical influences as well as other external forces, and Chapter 5 discusses the influence of popular culture in particular.

Part Two, *Fashion Dynamics*, describes how forecasting impacts various segments of the apparel and retailing industry, including color (Chapter 6), textiles (Chapter 7), and style forecasting (Chapter 8).

Part Three, *Marketplace Dynamics*, explores the methods of consumer research (Chapter 9) and sales forecasting (Chapter 10) to identify and analyze the connection between consumer preferences and product.

Part Four, *Forecasting at Work*, looks at the final stages of the forecasting process and illustrates the usefulness of forecasting as a way to locate, organize, and communicate information. Chapter 11 covers competitive analysis through gathering and analyzing competitor and industry information, while Chapter 12 focuses on presenting the forecast and includes a checklist for avoiding forecasting traps. All twelve chapters have been enhanced through the addition of many new current industry examples to which students will readily relate.

LEARNING FEATURES

The fourth edition of *Fashion Forecasting* includes several previous features together with some new additions to engage students and encourage mastery of chapter content. Every chapter now contains:

- ❖ industry profiles that illustrate the types of job opportunities that exist for students;
- ❖ "You Be the Forecaster," a new feature that encourages the student to implement the information from the chapter in scenarios that simulate real-world career situations;
- ❖ chapter summaries that synthesize the main topics of each chapter;
- ❖ activities at the end of each chapter which reinforce student learning through information gathering and creative application;
- ❖ discussion questions to engage student participation and an exchange of ideas.

These new features have been added to the existing learning features, including revised learning objectives which clearly convey the main message and goal of each presented topic; updated images which provide engaging visual examples to support concepts; key terms and concepts at the end of each chapter and a corresponding glossary at the end of the text which provide concise definitions of relevant terms specific to forecasting; and reorganized resource pointers which give students contact information for specific companies and agencies referenced in the text. By retaining these existing learning features that have proven to be successful for educating students and adding new features, educators will find this to be the strongest edition of *Fashion Forecasting* yet.

To further aid educators, a variety of Instructor's Resources accompany the text; these have been modernized in correspondence to the changes in the text. These resources include PowerPoint slides that provide lecture outlines, with images from the book, an Instructor's Guide that offers helpful tips for using the text in your course—including guides for using the You Be the Forecaster exercises in class, Discussion Question responses, and suggestions for further student reading and research—and a Test Bank with sample exam questions. Used in tandem, the text and Instructor's Resources provide a strong course foundation for a forecasting course at any student level.

FASHION FORECASTING STUDIO

New for this edition is an online multimedia resource—*Fashion Forecasting STUDIO*. The online *STUDIO* is specially developed to complement this book with rich media ancillaries that students can adapt to their visual learning styles to better master concepts and improve grades. Within the *STUDIO*, students will be able to:

❖ Study smarter with self-quizzes featuring scored results and personalized study tips
❖ Review concepts with flashcards of essential vocabulary
❖ Watch videos to see real-life examples of chapter topics and then test their knowledge

STUDIO access cards are offered free with new book purchases and also sold separately through Bloomsbury Fashion Central (www.BloomsburyFashionCentral.com).

✦ INSTRUCTOR RESOURCES

❖ Instructor's Guide provides suggestions for planning the course and using the text in the classroom, supplemental assignments, and lecture notes
❖ Test Bank includes sample test questions for each chapter
❖ PowerPoint® presentations include images from the book and provide a framework for lecture and discussion

Instructor's Resources may be accessed through Bloomsbury Fashion Central (www.BloomsburyFashionCentral.com).

ACKNOWLEDGMENTS

There are a number of people without whom this book would not have been possible, and I would like to take a moment to acknowledge their contributions. First and foremost, I would like to thank Evelyn Brannon for authoring the first three editions of the text, and for laying such a strong foundation upon which I hope to continue to build in this and future editions. I still can't believe my good fortune to work with such a talented team of people at Bloomsbury; editors are indeed amazing people. Special thanks to Amanda Breccia for having confidence that I could complete this project, to Joe Miranda, Edie Weinberg, and Gail Henry for their kindness and encouragement, and particularly to fellow music aficionado Corey Kahn for consistently striking just the right balance between cheerleader and taskmaster. Cheers to Caroline Richards for her top-notch copyediting skills and wonderful attention to detail. I would also like to thank the many people who gave their time and shared their expertise in the field by graciously allowing me to interview them, which greatly helped me shape my approach to this project.

This book also would not have been possible without the guidance of several strong, accomplished and brilliant women I have been fortunate to know throughout my career who shaped my image of what it means to be an academic through their time spent with me and their insight, but most importantly through their actions. They are, in the order in which they entered my life: Dr. Gail Goodyear, Dr. Kitty Dickerson, Dr. Betty Dillard, Dr. Nancy Cassill, Dr. Judith Lusk, Dr. Rita Purdy, and Dr. Rinn Cloud. I can only hope to inspire students and contribute to the apparel studies discipline in a manner that reflects the standards you have instilled in me.

While I owe all of my family and friends (especially Miki Romo, who listened more frequently and longer than anyone else) a note of gratitude for their interest and care in my success, the biggest thanks of all must go to my husband, Dr. David Smith, and the two great lights of my life, my children Evan and Charlotte Smith. This project has been an exercise in patience and endurance for them as well as for me, and I am grateful for their understanding and support during what was, at times, a seemingly overwhelming process.

> As a fashion designer, I think I play a role in reflecting society rather than in changing society.
>
> —*Giorgio Armani*

1

THE FASHION FORECASTING PROCESS

OBJECTIVES

◆ Establish the multifaceted character of fashion

◆ Analyze the trajectory of fashion change

◆ Identify the concept of Zeitgeist, or spirit of the times, as a framework for understanding and interpreting fashion change

◆ Comprehend the breadth and depth of the forecasting process

◆ Define the role of forecasting in the textile and apparel industries

"This … stuff? Oh. Okay. I see. You think this has nothing to do with you. You go to your closet and you select … I don't know … that lumpy blue sweater, for instance because you're trying to tell the world that you take yourself too seriously to care about what you put on your back. But what you don't know is that that sweater is not just blue, it's not turquoise. It's not lapis. It's actually cerulean. And you're also blithely unaware of the fact that in 2002, Oscar de la Renta did a collection of cerulean gowns. And then I think it was Yves Saint Laurent … wasn't it who showed cerulean military jackets? I think we need a jacket here. And then cerulean quickly showed up in the collections of eight different designers. And then it, uh, filtered down through the department stores and then trickled on down into some tragic Casual Corner where you, no doubt, fished it out of some clearance bin. However, that blue represents millions of dollars and countless jobs and it's sort of comical how you think that you've made a choice that exempts you from the fashion industry when, in fact, you're wearing the sweater that was selected for you by the people in this room from a pile of stuff."

— Actress Meryl Streep as fashion editor Miranda Priestly in *The Devil Wears Prada*

TREND FORECASTERS—WHO, WHAT, WHERE, WHEN, WHY, AND HOW

Trend forecasters locate the source of **trends** and use their skill and knowledge to identify emerging concepts. Forecasters' observations are shared with product developers, marketers, and the press, setting off the chain reaction that is fashion. The result is a continuous flow of products with new styling, novel decoration, and innovative uses. Saks Fifth Avenue fashion director Jaqui Lividini uses the services of forecasters combined with her own staff's predictions to anticipate her shoppers' preferences. "You want to have what she wants before she knows she wants it. If you're behind her, you've lost her. If you're in step, she's not excited. We try to be one step ahead. If you're two steps ahead, she's not interested in it" (Blair, 2013).

Trend forecasters work in many kinds of firms—for designers, advertising agencies, fiber producers, trade organizations, retail chains, and apparel brands. These professionals have job titles that range from Manager of Trend Merchandising to Creative Director, and their backgrounds are varied ("The next," 2003).

❖ Roseann Forde, Fordecasting. Forde studied to be a buyer, but found her calling when she became the manager of a fabric library. She was Global Fashion Director for INVISTA (formerly DuPont) for a decade before starting her own trend forecasting agency.

❖ Andrea Bell, editor of retail and consumer research at WGSN. Andrea started her career in fashion journalism, and has had work featured in *Elle*, *Maxim*, and *The Hollywood Report*. Based in Los Angeles, her position at WGSN involves communicating retail and market intelligence for the US (Henken, 2014).

One thing all forecasters have in common is frequent travel. Forde makes quarterly trips to London, Paris, and Milan. For Bell, "My role is part-social anthropologist, part-researcher, and part-forecaster, with lots of travel and airport dinners involved. Despite airplane cuisine, I'm very fortunate to have the opportunity to travel for my work. Whether it's covering fashion weeks in Peru or Brazil, attending conferences in San Francisco, Honolulu, Park City, and Las Vegas (seriously, I'm in Sin City quarterly), or visiting our corporate office in London – I can't complain" (Wang, 2014). Color forecasting dates from the early twentieth century and trend merchandising from the 1950s. For decades trendspotting meant reporting on the runways and what stylish people wore in Europe. Today, finding trends means looking worldwide and the search is incomplete without analyzing their market potential (Zimmerman, 2008) (Figure 1.1).

Forecasters also work in trend analysis firms that consult with companies in apparel, cosmetics, and interior design. Each firm develops a distinctive approach (Loyer, 2002). Compare how two Paris firms characterize their mission on their websites:

❖ Nelly Rodi looks for "new consumer behavior patterns" and applies "creative intuition" to shape insights for clients.
❖ Peclers Paris analyzes trend evolution from inception to confirmation and serves as "innovation catalysts" for clients.

Trend analysis firms publish books to illustrate their forecasts about 18 months ahead of the fashion season. The books include color chips, textile samples, fashion sketches, and photographs to illustrate trends. Increasingly the trend books are being supplemented or replaced with websites offering video, photographs, downloadable sketches, color swatches, print and fabric designs, and software tools. These subscription-only, business-to-business sites provide real-time trend forecasting. For example, Stylesight (www.stylesight.com) has a library of three million images—not just clothes but also stores, inspiration shots like graffiti, and streetwear from around the world. Images are tagged and indexed for easy retrieval. A yearly subscription to the site costs $15,000 and allows access to twenty users in an apparel firm. Other forecasting services offer similar services (see Resource Pointers). The new sites substitute for the work formerly done by fashion scouts, although firms still use fashion scouts who travel the world to find fashion inspiration (Miller, 2008).

Not all forecasters live in the fashion capitals. Many retailers and manufacturers base forecasters in their corporate offices, close to buying and product development teams. By traveling to fashion centers, covering trade shows, seeking out emerging retail concepts, and tracking consumer behavior, these professionals bring inspiration and direction to companies with a fashion-based strategy.

Trend forecasters enable companies to execute a strategy based on determining the right timing to launch an innovation. Called **strategic windows**, this strategy involves timing the firm's product offerings to the customer's readiness and willingness to accept and adopt the products (Abell, 1978).

Figure 1.1

Finding trends means looking beyond the best-known fashion capitals. Sydney hosts Australian Fashion Week.

✦ DEFINING FASHION

In the simplest terms, **fashion** is a style that is popular in the present or a set of trends that have been accepted by a wide audience. Fashion is a complex phenomenon from psychological, sociological, cultural, or commercial points of view.

✧ Fashion as a Social and Psychological Response

Defining fashion means dealing with dualities because clothing simultaneously conceals and reveals the body and the self. Clothing choices express personal style and individuality but also serve to manipulate a person's public image to fit situations and the expectations of others. The drivers of fashion are the dual goals of imitation and differentiation, of fitting in and standing out, of following the leader and being distinctive (Flugel, 1930; Simmel, 1904). Human ambivalence—conflicting and contradictory yearnings—finds an outlet in a capitalist marketplace as "appearance-modifying" goods. Through a process of negotiation between elements of the fashion industry and between the fashion industry and the consumer, ambiguous styles become accepted as fashionable (Kaiser, Nagasawa, & Hutton, 1995). Duality exists even in the buying of fashion because the process is both cognitively challenging (as when people evaluate price and value) and emotionally arousing (as when people react positively or negatively to the symbolic meaning in the products) (Brannon, 1993).

✧ Fashion as Popular Culture

Defining fashion means operating within the domain of popular culture. Unlike high culture (fine art, classical music, and great literature), popular culture often seems trivial and transient. Popular culture invites skepticism because it sometimes seems extreme and frivolous. For the same reasons, it is difficult to take fashion seriously. Fashion change is never entirely arbitrary, but ugly things are sometimes in vogue (Laver, 1937; Simmel, 1904). Most people invest their time, interest, and dollars in popular culture. The study of popular culture—the content and people's relationship to that content—has attracted the attention of scientists and scholars. Serious anthropologists, psychologists, and sociologists have written about fashion and theorized about its mechanisms of change.

✧ Fashion as Change

Defining fashion as change captures the charm of novelty, the responsiveness to the spirit of the times, and the pull of historical continuity (Blumer, 1969; Simmel, 1904). Fashion is not a phenomenon restricted to apparel. It is present in the design of automobiles and architecture, the shifting popularity of cuisine, the development of technology, and the buzzwords of business management strategies. Every few years a new management strategy is touted as a breakthrough only to be replaced by another one a few years later. The Internet was once solely an information network for scientists; now it reaches into offices and homes everywhere. Understanding fashion helps explain how these transformations happen.

✧ Fashion as Universal Phenomenon

By the mid-fifteenth century, the French duchy of Burgundy became the center of fashion for a number of reasons. It was a crossroads of international trade with exposure to foreign styles. It had the beginnings of a fashion trade in materials, ideas, and artisans, and the members of the court desired to display wealth through elaborate costumes. Finally, Burgundy had a new style made visible by its duke and duchess. The style—a long, lean silhouette in black cloth with fur—was copied by aristocrats from other parts of Europe, establishing fashion as part of the lifestyle of the elite (Rubinstein, 2001). The excitement of fashion can apply to any area of life. In the 1630s, the tulip, an exotic import from central Asia, became the focus of desire. Wild speculation among the normally sober Dutch people drove the price up until a single rare bulb could cost as much as a house (Dash, 1999). Many examples across cultures and time periods illustrate that fashion is not restricted to any era or group. Fashion is the natural outcome of markets and consumers' wish for expression.

✧ Fashion as a Transfer of Meaning

Meaning exists in the cultural environment. Designers, marketers, and the press transfer the meaning to a consumer product and increase its visibility. The consumer collects meaning out of the marketplace in the form of goods and constructs his or her own personal world (McCracken, 1988b). Not all products catch the attention of or find favor with consumers. Some meanings are rejected initially and are then taken up later. Some meanings are recycled over and over. Obsolescence is designed into the process. Fashion in its many guises plays a constant role in the evolving cultural environment. As Georg Simmel said at the beginning of the twentieth century, "The very character of fashion demands that it should be exercised at one time only by a portion of the given group, the great majority being merely on the road to adopting it" (Simmel, 1904, p. 138).

✧ Fashion as an Economic Stimulus

More than an abstract concept, fashion is an economic force. A writer in *The New Yorker* summed up the issue thus: "If clothes can not be relied on to wear out fast enough, something must be found that will wear out faster; that something is what we call fashion" (Gopnik, 1994). **Planned obsolescence** powers the economic engine of fashion. Wearing clothes until they wear out or wearing the secondhand clothes of more fickle buyers are acceptable strategies for dressing, but they omit the pleasure in new clothes and the novelty in new looks. Creating fashion goods requires the ability to mix aesthetic concerns and market mindfulness—that is, mass-produced fashion is the product of negotiation within and between the segments that make up the fashion industry (Davis, 1991).

✧ Fashion and Gender Differences

Where apparel is concerned, men and women have not been playing on the same field. The modern men's suit began its evolution with a move away from decoration in the late 1780s during the post–French Revolution period. A split arose between the design and the manufacturing modes of men's and women's clothing beginning around 1820. By the mid-1800s, the prototype of the modern men's suit—matching pieces, a sack coat, simple and undecorated, designed for ease and action—had evolved. Women's clothes continued as colorful, ornamented, and restrictive (Hollander, 1994).

Men had rejected the social distinctiveness of dress in favor of "occupational" clothing with similarity in cut, proportion, and design (Flugel, 1930). Women, in a relatively weaker social position than men, used fashion as a field where they could vent their "individual prominence" and "personal conspicuousness" (Simmel, 1904). By the 1930s, fashion commentators were seeing a change—the breakdown of social hierarchies and the "ever-increasing socialization of women" (Flugel, 1930; Laver, 1937). These commentators began asking if the changes in the lifestyle and economic status of women would lead to the same reduction in clothes competition that had occurred among men. Fashion's future may bring reconciliation between the sexes, with men having more access to color, ornament, and self-expression and women having less reliance on extraneous accessories, painful footwear, and constricting styles.

But fashion itself will continue to be available to all—for example, wristbands started as functional (to wipe sweat) and ended up as fashion for professional and college football players. Some players wear them high on the arm because with "all sorts of biceps and triceps busting out of there, it's a good look" (Branch, 2008). Some players wear fat two-inch wristbands, other cut them down for a thin look, a few wear two on each arm. Worn in the crook of the elbow or above (one player wears his over the sleeve on his shirt), wristbands have "no benefit from a performance standpoint, it's purely a fashion statement"—a fashion that has trickled down to middle school players (Branch, 2008).

✦ FORECASTING DEFINED

In the narrowest sense, forecasting attempts to project past trends into the future. A **trend** is a transitory increase or decrease over time (Makridakis, 1990). Some trends have lasted for millennia—human population growth, for example. But all trends have the potential to eventually slow down and decline. Spotting trends is not that difficult for people who immerse themselves in popular culture and trade news. Forecasters pluck emerging trends out of public information by becoming sensitive to directional signals that others miss. Faith Popcorn, the founder and CEO of the marketing consulting company BrainReserve and one of the first forecasters to gain name recognition in the media, calls this "brailing the culture"—looking for the new, the fresh, and the innovative, and then analyzing the whys behind it (1991).

Forecasters vary in the methods they use, but all are looking for signs that help them predict the mood, behavior, and buying habits of the consumer. Because trends signal the emerging needs, wants, and aspirations of the consumer, astute manufacturers and retailers capitalize on their potential for turning a profit. As Isham Sardouk, chief creative officer of Stylesight, says, "We are always hunting for what's cool, and that could be anything—a color, a song, a pair of sneakers, or a piece of art" (Grimberg, 2013). The whole idea of coolness is central to forecasting, but there are different kinds of cool. One definition of cool can be described as a set of common meanings within a peer group that signifies group affiliation (Runyan, Noh, & Mosier, 2013), and what is considered cool varies between groups and changes with time. Being a trendsetter who is always one step ahead of popular fashion is one type of coolness, and the researchers Collier and Fuller (1990) believe that cool style falls approximately 12–18 months ahead of mainstream style. Another way to view coolness is that it typically signifies rebellion, and one of the biggest powers to rebel against is consumerism—by being defiantly anti-fashion. Fashion leaders are often considered to be rebels, but it is understood that once the fashions they wear that are considered rebellious are duplicated and mass produced by the fashion industry, they cease to be cool. Brownie (2014) sums up these two viewpoints by stating that

there are two kinds of cool: either keeping up with the latest fashions, or by shunning the fashion system altogether. The challenge for apparel designers and retailers is to predict what cool people will be wearing next, which then forces the cool people to adopt new styles, and the cycle repeats itself.

Forecasting is not magic practiced by a talented few with a gift for seeing the future. It is a creative process that can be understood, practiced, and applied by anyone who has been introduced to the tools (Figure 1.2). A professional does not proceed by rule of thumb or trial and error but by mastery of the theory and practice of the field. Forecasting provides a way for executives to expand their thinking about change, anticipate the future, and project the likely outcomes (Levenbach & Cleary, 1981).

Executives use forecasting as input for planning. Marketing managers position products in the marketplace using short- and long-term forecasts. Planners of competitive strategies use forecasting techniques to look at market share and the position of competitors in the marketplace. Product developers, merchandisers, and production managers use the short-term trend forecasts of color, textiles, and style direction to shape collections.

✧ Steps in Developing a Forecast

Forecasting consists of tools and techniques applied systematically. Just as important are human judgment and interpretation (Levenbach & Cleary, 1981). The steps in developing a forecast are:

Step 1 Identify the basic facts about past trends and forecasts.

Step 2 Determine the causes of change in the past.

Step 3 Determine the differences between past forecasts and actual behavior.

Step 4 Determine the factors likely to affect trends in the future.

Step 5 Apply forecasting tools and techniques, paying attention to issues of accuracy and reliability.

Figure 1.2

Forecasters use the language of fashion—color, pattern, texture, and photographs—to communicate a forecast to clients.

Profile: Jodi Arnold, Creative Director, Eloquii

A society's dominating attitude is one of the key aspects of the Zeitgeist and one such attitude that has been steadily growing in popularity is the attitude of body acceptance for people of all sizes. The popularity of celebrities such as Lena Dunham, Mindy Kaling, Melissa McCarthy, Rebel Wilson, and the comedian Retta on television and in films is a strong indication of how society has come to broaden its idea of attractiveness. As more people feel comfortable embracing their own unique size and shape, there is a bigger demand than ever before for fashionable plus-sized clothing, a market that has long been underserved by most designers. That is where the brand Eloquii fills a void in the market, by bringing current fashion trends to its plus-sized clientele. In the words of Eloquii's creative director, Jodi Arnold, "as society has changed and social media has evolved there is much more acceptance" (Feldman, 2014).

Originally launched as a brand owned by The Limited, Eloquii was closed when the retailer chose to focus on their core lines, and then relaunched in 2014 as an independent online retail brand aimed at women ages 20 to 40 who wear sizes 14 to 24 (the line will be expanded to include sizes 26 and 28 as of spring 2015). As chief operating officer Mariah Chase says, "We want to be a leader in fashion—period. It just so happens we are making clothes sizes 14 to 24" (Moin, 2014).

Eloquii offers a full collection of dresses, skirts, tops, sweaters, coats, belts, pants, denim, jackets, and jewelry with a focus on trendy merchandise, at prices ranging from $18 to $189. All merchandise is designed in-house under the guidance of Jodi Arnold, who shares that the company operates on a 6- to 8-month design cycle "like a fast-fashion scenario … we will give her whatever the trends are without really thinking about the sizes. It's all in the execution and how it fits." Because of this design cycle, Arnold is able to execute trends in a manner similar to retailers such as Zara and Forever 21—by watching the runways and reading style.com to see what is trending in the ready-to-wear markets and then interpreting it for Eloquii customers. "One of the biggest misconceptions people have about plus-size women is that there are only certain things that look good on her. We want her to know that she can wear every trend, as long as it is cut for her specific body and proportions" (Feldman, 2014). Because of this open-minded approach, Eloquii featured crop tops in their product line, and a cropped sweater became a best-seller for the brand. When she first saw them on the runways, it did not occur to Arnold at first that this would be something for the Eloquii customer, but as she saw the trend continuing through fall, she thought it would be something she should include. While she does not feel the Eloquii woman will be the first to launch a new trend, the brand definitely introduces trends while they are still on the upswing and not in the decline.

Although she is not plus-sized herself and did not have prior experience in the plus-sized market, Arnold sees this as a positive: "When you're going into it, don't have anything in your mind about what can and can't be done. We start with the fashion, and we go into the fittings and then make tweaks and changes" (McCall, 2014). Arnold regularly reads blogs and pop culture magazines in order to stay on top of what is going on in culture, and as she reads, she compiles different stacks of what she sees in different areas. For example, she may have a collection of floral prints from many different sources which she then filters and interprets for her own designs.

The growth of Eloquii is proof of its success. The brand announced in October 2014 that in addition to online sale through its own website, www.eloquii.com, it would also be available online through Nordstrom, and the retailer would feature exclusive items (Moin, 2014; Young, 2014). In addition to her professional success, Arnold has enjoyed a personal sense of satisfaction from her newest role: "Three years ago, I would have never said I would be designing contemporary, plus-size clothing, and I have never been more fulfilled with what I am doing" (Cooper, 2014).

Sources:

Arnold, Jodi (2014, March 13). Personal interview.

Cooper, Meryl Weinsaft (2014, June 20). *Tips from the trenches: Jodi Arnold of Eloquii on seeing opportunity in adversity*. Retrieved from Forbes.com.

Feldman, Jamie (2014, March 19). How one online retailer is changing the world of plus-size fashion. Retrieved from huffingtonpost.com.

McCall, Tyler (2014, April 8). How plus-size brand Eloquii was revived by its most devoted employees. Retrieved from fashionista.com.

Moin, David (2014, February 20). Eloquii to be relaunched online. Retrieved from wwd.com.

Young, Vicki M. (2014, October 30). Eloquii heads to Nordstrom. Retrieved from wwd.com.

Step 6 Follow the forecast continually to determine reasons for significant deviations from expectations.

Step 7 Revise the forecast when necessary.

A trend forecast should identify the source, underlying pattern, direction, and tempo of the trend.

The most valuable currencies in today's competitive climate are information and learning. Decisions are enhanced in an information-rich environment. However, obtaining information is only the first step in the process of organizing, analyzing, understanding, and learning from it. Information is easy to find but difficult to sift, frame, and integrate so that learning can take place. Forecasting is the process that translates information into a form that allows learning to occur.

✦ FORECASTING SPECIALTIES

Forecasting is more than just attending runway shows and picking out potential trends that can be reinterpreted at lower prices (although that is part of it). It is a process that spans shifts in color and styles, changes in lifestyles and buying patterns, and different ways of doing business. What appears to be near-random activity is in fact a process of negotiation between the fashion industry and the consumer, and among the various segments in the supply-side chain.

By education and training, executives develop a specialty, one that restricts their view of information. By focusing exclusively on their specialty categories such as "women's knit tops" or "junior dresses," these professionals tend to restrict themselves to only a narrow scan of information generated within a specialty or within an industry segment. In doing so, they risk developing tunnel vision by focusing on information internal to the company and industry to the exclusion of the broader cultural perspective. Tunnel vision reduces the flexibility that is so essential for decision making under conditions of high-velocity change.

Even though they become experts in an information domain bounded by their placement on the supply chain, product category, or job description, all apparel executives share the same problem—how to make the right product, introduce it at the right time, distribute it in the right channels, and capture the attention of the right consumers. Collaborative forecasting within a company and among companies in partnership encourages communication across domain boundaries.

Strategic decisions in the apparel and retail industry are supported by past experience— fashion history, sales history, and traditional ways of doing business. To keep their balance, fashion industry members need a window on the future—new innovations, cultural change, and alternative ways to do business. **Environmental scanning** opens that window on the future. Professionals gather useful external information when they scan a daily newspaper, watch TV news, listen to the radio while commuting to work, chat with people at a dinner party, and log on to the Internet. The difference between information gathered in this informal way and environmental scanning is a more systematic

approach and use of information management tools (Figure 1.3).

✧ Fashion Scan

Fashion professionals eagerly follow the latest fashion news to spot emerging fashion and lifestyle trends. Environmental scanning for trends includes:

* traveling to the fashion capitals (New York, Paris, Milan, and London) and to other trendsetting spots to observe firsthand;
* scanning print, broadcast, and online sources for clues;
* networking with people in creative fields such as the arts, architecture, interior design, cosmetics, and entertainment.

Supplementing the individual's effort, forecasters and trend analysis firms gather information and present summaries in trend books, newsletters, and seminars.

✧ Consumer Scan

Consulting firms, market research organizations, advertising agencies, the government, and individual companies are constantly conducting consumer research. Whereas this research usually belongs to the organization that funded

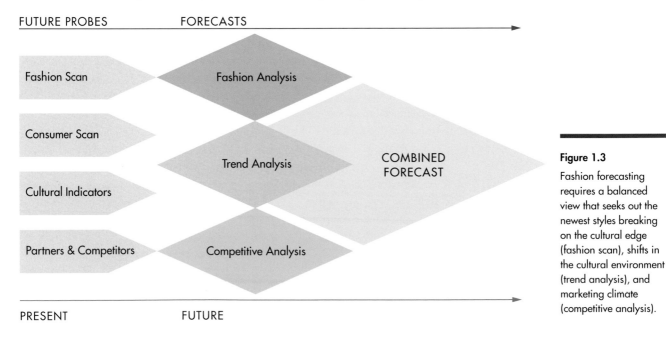

FUTURE PROBES   FORECASTS

Fashion Scan

Consumer Scan

Cultural Indicators

Partners & Competitors

Fashion Analysis

Trend Analysis

Competitive Analysis

COMBINED FORECAST

PRESENT   FUTURE

Figure 1.3

Fashion forecasting requires a balanced view that seeks out the newest styles breaking on the cultural edge (fashion scan), shifts in the cultural environment (trend analysis), and marketing climate (competitive analysis).

it, summaries are often available in trade publications or other print, broadcast, and online sources. Journalists, sociologists, psychologists, and others write about their observations of consumer culture and hypothesize about its underlying structure. Locating these sources using environmental scanning helps the apparel executive to identify shifts in consumer lifestyles, preferences, and behavior that impact store design, merchandise assortments, and fashion promotion.

✧ Fashion Analysis

Combined, the fashion scan and consumer scan provide input for fashion analysis—what is likely to happen next. Fashion is really a dialogue among the creative industries—fashion, interior design, the arts, and entertainment—that propose innovations and consumers who decide what to adopt or reject. As one forecaster put it, "Nothing will succeed in fashion if the public is not ready for it" (O'Neill, 1989). Fashion analysis brings together the expertise of a fashion insider and insights on consumer behavior to provide support for executive decisions in the supply chain from fiber to fabric to apparel manufacturing to retailing.

✧ Social and Economic Trends

The fashion story is part of larger shifts in the culture, including the fragmentation of the marketplace. Fashion forecasting requires a wide scan to encompass cultural, economic, and technology issues that have an impact on consumer preferences and spending. Some forecasters and forecasting firms focus on large-scale shifts in cultural indicators. These **megatrends** cross industry lines because they involve shifts in lifestyles, reflect changes in generational **cohorts**, or mirror cycles in the economy. Trends of this magnitude may be felt over the period of a decade, from the first time that they surface to the time that they influence purchasing decisions on a mass scale. An example of a social trend would be the shift to green marketing (positioning products, their manufacturing processes, and distribution as sensitive to environmental concerns) as a

manifestation of deep cultural changes in society. The most important economic trend is consumer spending. After the recession began in 2008, consumers modified their spending habits and lifestyles. According to a study by Pew Research, in order to make ends meet, consumers bought less expensive brands, cut back or canceled vacation plans, cut back on alcohol or cigarette consumption or moved back in with their parents. Forecaster John Zogby took this economic necessity and combined it with his observation that people were expressing a preference for a simpler, yet more meaningful lifestyle. Based on this hard data together with his observation, Zogby named this trend Secular Spiritualism—"a broader wish for a simpler life that includes hobbies, volunteering and, perhaps most important, finding that elusive 'quality time' with family and friends" (Zogby, 2008). For the fashion industry and related categories such as interiors and automobile styling, monitoring these cultural indicators is essential for strategic planning and to provide a backdrop to short-term forecasts. Environmental scanning allows any executive to monitor cultural indicators that alter the business environment and change consumers' purchasing behavior.

✧ Trend Analysis

Drawing on fashion and consumer scans, and on identification of social and economic trends, trend analysis detects short- and long-term trends that affect business prospects. Trends start as experiments, self-expression, and reactions to changing circumstances. Many vanish almost as soon as they are created but some gain adopters and gain popularity. When they are recognized by the gatekeepers of fashion—designers, journalists, merchants, and forecasters—the trends start to appear in media coverage. Trend analysis looks at the interaction of shifts in fashion, consumer lifestyles, and culture.

✧ Competitive Analysis

Space in stores is limited, and apparel competes for consumers' attention and dollars with many other alternatives, including electronics and entertainment. To be competitive in such a business environment, companies must observe competing firms through regular tracking of key information. Over time this effort allows a company to benchmark its activities against competitors and to develop "what if" scenarios about competitor initiatives. Whether it is called competitive analysis, competitive information, or competitive intelligence, business survival and growth depends on using public sources to monitor the business activities of partners and competitors. New businesses depend on this kind of information in the start-up stage; established businesses use it to help them scout out new markets; and large corporations treat it as input for senior managers coordinating activities across markets and product lines.

◇ Integrated Forecasting

No organization should rely too heavily on a single forecasting discipline or on an individual forecaster for decision support. The information environment is so rich, no one person can possibly locate and interpret all the signs and signals across multiple time horizons. Yet little effort or attention has been given to integrating information across forecasting specialties—fashion trends, shifts in consumer culture, megatrends, and competitive analysis. Information must be processed to form a forecast. A team approach to forecasting means continuous information sharing between functional groups with the goal of increasing the quality of the forecast. A multifaceted outlook benefits a company by providing both a better general picture of developments and a more fine-grained interpretation.

The best forecasts blend quantitative and qualitative components, the wide view of cultural indicators and the close focus of sales forecasting, and short-range and long-range timescales. Interpretations must be keyed to specific consumer segments and a competitive niche. Strategies that work for teens experimenting with identity and style, those that work for mainstream working people, and those for active retirees are very different. Change produces different effects according to the target consumer and the industry segment.

Intelligent use of forecasting keeps an executive from focusing narrowly on a specialty instead of how that specialty integrates with others in the decision-making chain. Integrated forecasting provides a combined forecast targeted to consumer preferences, a company's marketing niche, the competitive environment, and cultural shifts. Forecasts do not provide "the one correct answer." Instead, forecasting gives perspective on the possibilities and probabilities of the future.

UNDERSTANDING THE ZEITGEIST

Fashion is a reflection of the times in which it is created and worn. Fashion responds to whatever is modern—that is, to the spirit of the times or the **Zeitgeist**, a German word used to describe the general cultural climate of a specific period in time. According to Blumer (1969), individuals in large numbers choose among competing styles those that click or connect with the spirit of the times. This **collective selection** forms a feedback loop between the fashion industry and the consumer, a feedback loop that can be read in sales figures. The problem with this concept in terms of forecasting is that it offers little advance warning. Only **fast fashion** firms—those set up to deliver new styles in weeks instead of months—are able to capitalize on the fast-changing trends as they are revealed in the data. Other companies act only after fashion converges on the styles symbolic of the times.

All cultural components respond to the spirit of the times. The power of the Zeitgeist is its ability to coordinate across product categories. Fashion and other consumer categories such as cuisine exhibit the same trends and cycles. In the mid-1980s, the newest trend in cuisine was Tex-Mex, but that was replaced by Cajun only a few years later. Once, all "fashionable" sandwiches were served on pitta bread; a few years later it was the croissant; after that it was multigrain peasant-style bread; and then wraps, panini, and flatbread. Fashion affects all product categories—

food, sports, architecture, interiors, and automobile styling. Soccer was once an obscure sport in the United States, whereas today it is an avid passion of many Americans. Sports such as cycling and snowboarding were once the province of a small niche market. Today they are covered on television sports channels and the performance apparel worn by participants has been adapted to mass fashion. Even things like college majors are influenced by trends. Before the debut of *Project Runway*, it was believed that people perceived fashion as an insider's industry, and people who did not work in the industry would not be interested in the show. Not only did that assumption prove to be incorrect, but the show's popularity was responsible for a huge increase in enrollment in fashion schools and programs around the country ("10 Ways," 2012). Toys, professions, pastimes, and consumer products all respond to the same cultural currents that fashion does.

Media not only report on the culture, they are shaped by it. Watching network television was all important until the coming of hundreds of cable and satellite channels, the Web, streaming services such as Hulu and Netflix, and gaming systems pushed the networks off the cultural front burner. The Internet and gaming systems

You Be the Forecaster: Staying One Step Ahead of Change

Taylor is a product developer for a moderately priced junior denim line that is sold at department stores. The styles her brand has been offering for the past few seasons are still selling well with their customers, but they are starting to seem boring to Taylor, and she and the design team feel that a shift in consumer tastes is right around the corner. Before Taylor and the design team take their line in a new direction, they need to be confident that their designs for next season are going to align with what their **target market** will want, or even inspire their customers to make a fashion change they didn't know they wanted. In order to know if their instincts are correct, they are going to need to spend time looking around at what is going on in other fashion categories, in other consumer categories, and in society at large.

Fashion industry professionals are always looking at the world around them in terms of how any shift in culture and society will impact their target market's future preferences. How would Taylor and her team use the different concepts outlined in this chapter to best appeal to their customers?

Forecasting Specialties: What are some sources Taylor could use to conduct a fashion and consumer scan that is relevant to her product category and target market? What social and economic trends might impact her target market's purchase habits?

Zeitgeist: If Taylor's target market consists of junior customers, when were they born? What would the Zeitgeist consist of for today's teens in terms of dominating events, ideals, social groups, attitudes, and technology?

Fashion Directions: Which of the fashion directions in the chapter would have the most influence on Taylor's product category of jeans and her target market of juniors? How might these directions influence product development?

changed the entertainment landscape. Magazines are like any other product; they have natural life cycles connected to the spirit of the times. New magazines start up to reach new audiences. Existing magazines reinvent or refresh their look and their focus in response to the spirit of the times. Often this process involves a change in editors. New editors replace old ones because they have a vision, one that is in touch with the times, and they can shape the magazine to reflect this change.

✦ NYSTROM'S FRAMEWORK FOR OBSERVING THE ZEITGEIST

What factors should a forecaster monitor? What external factors shape the spirit of the times? In 1928, Nystrom attempted to list factors that guide and influence the character and direction of fashion. His list still provides a framework for observing the Zeitgeist.

✧ Dominating Events

Nystrom listed three kinds of dominating events: (1) significant occurrences such as war, the death of world leaders, and world fairs; (2) art vogues (the Russian Ballet and modern art in his day); and (3) accidental events (the discovery of the tomb of Tutankhamen in the 1920s). Historical examples such as the effect of pop, op, and psychedelic art on the fashions of the 1960s and 1970s extend Nystrom's analysis on the relationship between dress and art. Although world fairs no longer serve to set trends, other international events still pull in huge audiences. One such event is the Academy Awards ceremony with its celebrity fashion parade, along with film festivals (Figure 1.4). Another is the influence of the Olympic Games on activewear for athletes and on casual wear for the mainstream consumer. An updated list of significant occurrences would include the 1990s bull market on the stock exchange; Internet culture; the terrorist attacks on September 11, 2001, followed by military action in Afghanistan and Iraq; Hurricane Katrina; and the economic downturn in the United States beginning in late 2007. Lynch and Strauss (2007) propose

performance as an instigator of fashion change whether the performance is by professionals (concerts, film, the red carpet, runway shows, or sports events) or through consumers enacting a role through their apparel. Fashion is not merely a reflection of the spirit of the times but part of its creation (Vinken, 2005).

✧ Dominating Ideals

Nystrom listed dominating ideals such as patriotism and the Greek ideal of classical beauty. An updated list would include ideals of multiculturalism, environmental and humanitarian issues, equality of men and women, and the connection among health and wellness, beauty, and youthfulness. The ideal of a multicultural society is not new in the United States, but it is being reshaped by the changing demographics of color within the population. Census figures show the Hispanic and Asian populations growing much faster than the nation's population as a whole. Some cities such as Baltimore and Detroit are becoming predominately African-American; others, such as San Antonio and Miami, predominately Hispanic. Asian influence is becoming stronger in cities such as Los Angeles, San Francisco, and New York. Because some of these cities are also important as style centers and as the starting points for trends, the impact on American fashion could be considerable. One way this demographic trend is already becoming apparent in the fashion industry is the popularity of several prominent Asian-American fashion designers, including Jason Wu, Prabal Gurung, Phillip Lim, Alexander Wang, Peter Som, and Derek Lam.

✧ Dominating Social Groups

Nystrom identified the dominating social groups as those with wealth, power, and leadership positions. Although the groups themselves would have changed, the criteria still apply to today's culture. Today, the power of celebrities in popularizing fashion trends can hardly be overemphasized. Stars in the music world are directional for younger customers, actors for the older customer (Kletter, 2003). Designer Narciso Rodriguez explains:

Figure 1.4
Cate Blanchett's appearance at the Cannes Film Festival in an organza gown tells a color story (salmon), a styling story (pleats and ruffles), and an accessory story with a romantic mood—all with potential for trendsetting.

From a designer's perspective, each house represents a certain style or aesthetic—a look that has its own following. That's where a designer's power lies. It's not to say that designers don't influence fashion today, but I would imagine that music, performers, and actors have much more impact on the way people might dress, especially younger people. They are just much more visible to the mainstream population. (Wilson, 2003a)

Celebrities as presented through the multiple media channels—music videos, movies, TV series, interview programs, photographs in magazines and newspapers, on websites, social media and YouTube—have become the highly visible and highly influential "new" elite.

✧ Dominating Attitude

Nystrom's list must be extended to capture today's spirit of the times. Add to the list the dominating attitude of the times. The interplay between an individual's desire to fit in and to stand out, between imitation and differentiation, affects the Zeitgeist (Brenninkmeyer, 1963). When the desire for differentiation is the dominant attitude in an era, new fashions arise, the changes are revolutionary, and the pace of fashion change is swift. The flapper era in the 1920s and Youthquake in the 1960s are examples of eras when the dominant attitude was differentiation. When social conformity and imitation is the dominant attitude, fashion innovation slows down, the changes are evolutionary, and the pace of fashion slows down. The depressed 1930s, conforming 1950s, and dominance of casual styles beginning in the 1990s are such eras.

✧ Dominating Technology

Today more than ever, Nystrom's list must be expanded to include the dominating technology of the times. When he was writing in the late 1920s, the harnessing of the atom, the space race, the power of television, and advent of the computer were all in the future. Today, technology is deeply intertwined in everyday life,

especially in the realms of communication, entertainment, and computers. Cell phones, digital media players, GPS, and wireless connectivity make wearable technology an essential fashion accessory. Fitbit is a fitness tracker that allows the wearer to track their activity, log their food intake, monitor their weight, and measure their sleep. Designer Tory Burch teamed up with Fitbit in 2014 to design bracelets and a necklace featuring the Fitbit Flex that look like stylish jewelry instead of a standard fitness tracker (Wood, 2014) (Figure 1.5).

Technology impacts not only the Zeitgeist but also the production methods. Without computers and rapid worldwide communication, quick response strategies and global apparel production would not be possible. Instant information exchange, computer technology, robotics, and automation are driving the paradigms of production on a mass scale and production of customized products for a market of one (mass customization).

Figure 1.5

Designer Tory Burch's collaboration with Fitbit merged function and fashion by allowing the wearer to monitor their health with trackers that look like ordinary jewelry.

Together, the dominating events, ideals, social groups, attitudes, and technology exemplify and influence the spirit of the times. Together they illuminate the structure of society with fashion illustrating variations on the cultural theme (Brenninkmeyer, 1963).

✦ DEFINING FASHION ERAS

A problem for forecasters is the difficulty in recognizing the spirit of the times while living in them. In hindsight, the distinguishing characteristics of an era become clear. Although there are some limits on newness in fashion—the shape of the human body, cultural theme of the times, and production technology available—there is still an enormous range of possibilities for experimentation. A fashion era can be characterized by:

* ❖ *a designer's signature style*—Halston in the 1970s, Christian Lacroix in the 1980s, Tom Ford in the 1990s, Marc Jacobs for the 2000s;
* ❖ *a style leader*—Jacqueline Kennedy in the early 1960s, Sarah Jessica Parker in the 1990s, Kate Middleton in the 2010s;
* ❖ *a fashion look*—the flapper of the 1920s, Cardin's and Courrèges' space-age short white dresses and boots in the mid-1960s, the 1977 "Annie Hall" look, Ugg boots with denim miniskirts in the early 2000s;
* ❖ *a bohemian element*—the Beats, the hippies, hip-hop;
* ❖ *a market segment*—the middle class in the 1950s, the youth movement in the 1960s, tweens in the 2000s;
* ❖ *a celebrity icon*—Clara Bow in the 1920s, Marilyn Monroe in the 1950s, Madonna in the early 1980s, the *Sex in the City* stars in the 2000s, Taylor Swift and Anne Hathaway in the 2010s;
* ❖ *a model*—Jean Shrimpton and Twiggy in the 1960s, Lauren Hutton and Christie Brinkley in the 1970s, the supermodels of the 1980s, Kate Moss in the 1990s, Gisele Bündchen in the 2000s, Kate Upton in the 2010s;
* ❖ *a fiber or fabric*—Chanel's jersey in the 1920s, the polyester of the 1970s, Lycra in the late 1990s, organic cotton in the 2000s, scuba in the 2010s.

Whereas others merely participate in fashion change, forecasters attempt to understand the process, trace the evolution, and recognize the patterns. To do this, they must be participants, but they must also be spectators interpreting what they observe. The Zeitgeist is an expression of modernity, of the current state of culture, of the incipient and unarticulated tastes of the consuming public. Forecasters monitoring the Zeitgeist pay special attention to:

* ❖ style interactions among apparel, cuisine, sports, architecture, interior design, automobile design and innovation, toys, professions, pastimes, and play because all these fields respond to the same cultural currents;
* ❖ the content of media, the celebrities covered in the media, and the members of the press who decide what stories to cover;
* ❖ the events, ideals, social groups, attitudes, and technology that characterize the spirit of the times.

These cultural patterns define the present. Even slight shifts in these patterns act as directional signposts to the future.

✦ FASHION DIRECTIONS

To look forward, a forecaster must have an image of the past—the way styles responded to and were shaped by the spirit of the times. People who envisioned the future at the turn of the twentieth century looked forward with an optimism buoyed by the success of the Industrial Revolution. They had faith that technology would create a bright, prosperous future. As with all forecasts, there were hits and misses (Leland, 2000). One educator wrote of homes connected by cameras and telephones so that the occupants could see around the world from their living room—a dream clearly realized with television and the Internet. An economist predicted that women would have more control over their family budgets and that men would adopt an ornamented look including tights—a vision that foresaw the arc that would take women from gaining the vote to entering the workforce in huge numbers, but only glimpsed changes that would loosen the rules of appropriateness for both sexes.

Forecasts are always vulnerable to the unexpected event or the unanticipated outcome. The optimistic view of technology at the turn of the twentieth century was shaken with the sinking of the *Titanic* in 1912, the symbol of technological achievement that proved all too fragile. World War I opened occupational doors for women who became nurses, office workers, and drivers, a situation that was repeated in World War II when women became factory workers and pilots, roles formerly reserved for men. World War II galvanized US manufacturing, laying the foundation for postwar prosperity. Technology such as Redbox, Netflix, and Amazon resulted in thousands of video stores and bookstores closing and people losing their jobs.

The marketplace is shaped by constant negotiation between the apparel industry and consumers over which styles represent the spirit of the times. It is not only the styles that change but also the marketplace dynamics. Looking back over the last century reveals the changes in the marketplace that will affect the future.

✧ Rising Aesthetic Standards

Author Virginia Postrel, in her book *The Substance of Style* (2003), examines how the modern lifestyle has resulted in increased expectations of aesthetic standards. She gives the example that now that most health issues related to teeth have been eliminated as a part of standard dental care, and braces are so commonplace that straight teeth are now part of our basic expectations, dentists have turned to promoting teeth whitening as the new heightened aesthetic standard. This same increase in aesthetic expectations can be seen in something as unglamorous as bathrooms. Postrel cites a *Vogue* article that discusses an opulent New York high rise by saying, "Luxury of the bathroom is terrific—marble floor and walls and

nicely designed chrome fixtures." In today's society, such features can be options in a standard tract home, and chrome fixtures available to anyone who wishes to visit a home center and purchase them off the shelf. So those are now baseline expectations and our new standards for luxury are even higher.

Generally speaking, that which is difficult to attain is considered attractive. Consider the West African country of Mauritania, where being overweight is considered to be a sign of wealth in a nation that struggles with oppressive poverty. In order for women to be desirable to a husband, they must be fat in a society where it is difficult to be so, because skinny women are considered to be poor and unable to procure food. As a result, women who can do so force-feed themselves large quantities of camel milk, bread crumbs soaked in olive oil, and goat meat just to gain weight in a practice referred to as "gavage" — the term used to describe the force-feeding of ducks to make foie gras (Engel, 2013). By contrast, in the United States, where we have an abundance of food to the point that obesity is considered a national health epidemic, the opposite is true and the beauty ideal is thin.

Our standards of beauty just keep getting higher. Many people still hold up Marilyn Monroe's curvy figure as a beauty ideal and lament that she would be considered too heavy in today's society. In its day, Marilyn's physique was attainable for most women, and those who lacked her curves could pad themselves in the appropriate places to achieve her hourglass figure. Then, in the 1960s the skinny, boyish look became popular through models like Twiggy and Jean Shrimpton, a shape far more difficult to obtain if it was not your natural body type. Then in the early 1980s, with the rise in popularity of aerobic workout videos from celebrities such as Jane Fonda and Olivia Newton-John, being thin wasn't enough, one had to be thin and toned. The rise in popularity of aesthetic surgery among non-wealthy people increased the standards again and the ideal woman was expected to be thin, toned, and have large breasts. In the late 2000s, the rise in popularity of Kim Kardashian brought another requirement for beauty standards that added a small waist and round backside to what was already a very long list. Very few women possess those natural attributes (including the celebrities who inspire these standards), but their bodies are celebrated on television and in popular magazines, and eventually, some women feel that they themselves are not attractive because they cannot live up to these extremely high standards.

◇ Ethical Consumerism

Our purchases reflect our priorities and values, and a segment of consumers have chosen to take the concept of "voting with dollars" very seriously by spending their money only on products made by manufacturers that share the same value system that they do. A large number of ethically minded companies have sprung up over the past 20 years. Examples of these include organic clothing companies such as Synergy clothing, which uses predominantly organic cotton from India, dyed with low-impact dyes, and their clothing is produced in Nepal using fair-trade practices (www.synergyclothing.com, 2014). Other examples include Feral Childe in New York City, a small design duo that makes garments using sustainable fibers that are manufactured locally in New York. Production waste is disposed of by either donating remnants to schools or sending them to a textile recycling facility. They only produce merchandise that is made-to-order to prevent excess inventory and will provide transparent reports about their sourcing and manufacturing techniques upon request by customers (Phelan, 2012). Such companies allow consumers to feel good about themselves even when indulging in fashion.

Even the best of intentions can have drawbacks, though. TOMS shoes, with its one-for-one business model in which, for every pair purchased, a pair of shoes is donated to a developing country, seems like it would have no drawbacks, until it was revealed that their donations were putting local shoe manufacturers in these nations out of work. Consumers can now weigh the ethical implications of their purchase along with other more traditional criteria such as fit, attractiveness, and price.

◇ Shift from Appropriateness to "Anything Goes"

A woman, recalling the way she dressed for a day out in New York City in the summer of 1929, says that the ensemble began with a full set of underwear including a full-length slip and stockings, and finished with gloves and a hat. Today summer attire for a young woman in the same city might be shorts, tank top, and rubber flip-flops (Trebay, 2002a). The strict social rules governing fashion ended in the mid-1960s. Gone were the traditions of no white shoes after Labor Day, no patent leather in the winter, no suede in the summer, velvet and taffeta only between Thanksgiving and New Year's Eve, and shoes matching handbags. Instead fashion professionals and consumers took a more permissive approach, relying only on their eye to decide what looked right (Turk, 1989).

Where designer clothes in the 1950s looked as finished on the inside as the outside, by the 1990s clothing went from unconstructed to deconstructed—raveled edges, ragged, wrinkled, and faded on both sides. Replacing worn-out, bedraggled clothing with crisply new versions was once a principle driver for shopping. By agreeing that "anything goes" in terms of fashion and appropriateness, the fashion industry removed the incentive to update wardrobes and disrupted its own fashion cycles (Agins, 1995). According to one designer, "Watching a reality TV show just enforces the notion that it is OK to wear anything, while high fashion to them seems like it is becoming more elitist" (Wilson, 2003b). By the early 2000s forecasters identified the saturation of dressing down as a signal that the pendulum would swing back to something less "scruffy" (Jones, 2002). After a decade of dressing down, the news in both men's and women's fashions was not a "return to dressing up" but a cleaner, more pulled-together look that crossed boundaries between work and leisure. Tailored clothing borrowed details from sportswear and used softer fabrics and less structure to create a look that could go to the office or dress up jeans (Thomas, 2007).

✧ Shift from Fashion Seasons to Seasonless Dressing

Changing seasons once marked the fashion calendar for stores and consumers—fall, winter, spring, summer. The universality of environmental controls in building and transportation, changes in rules of appropriateness, and new fibers and fabrics made seasonless dressing possible. This shift was reinforced by volatile weather sometimes attributed to global warming—which doesn't mean warmer weather overall but more unpredictable weather. As one outerwear manufacturer put it, "I have been in this industry for 40 years, and during that time, we always knew it got cold in December and stayed that way through January and February. … Now, it's a crap shoot." In fact, a government panel found that the length of seasons had changed over a 50-year span—spring began arriving earlier and fall later, taking 2 weeks off the coldest period. Some large companies have added a climatologist or "climate merchant" to their design team to help time shipments of season-specific garments (Barbaro, 2007b). The overall changing weather patterns reinforced the shift to seasonless fabrics and styles, removing the incentive for consumers to replace their wardrobe according to the changing seasons.

The change from definite fashion seasons to seasonless has the potential to revolutionize the marketplace. As Beppe Modenese, the founding father of Milan Fashion Week, sees it, "You can't have everyone showing four times a year to present … the same fabrics at the same weight. The fashion system must adapt to the reality that there is no strong difference between summer and winter any more" (Trebay, 2007).

✧ Shift from Fashion Experts to Consumer Opinion

Miniskirts in the 1960s, bell-bottom jeans in the 1970s, and shoulder-padded power suits in the 1980s—fashion once consisted of clear directional signals about what was "in" and "out," and the desire to be "in" still motivated shopping (Pressler, 1995). By the early 1970s, a women's magazine could declare in bold type: "Fashion is going out

of fashion" ("Creative," 1971). The reasons listed included a rejection of the image of beautiful people who wear the latest thing in favor of an expanded definition of beauty and individuality—a shift from "what's in" to "what works."

Selling women's wear and menswear depends on the connection between the consumer's self-image and the narrative presented by the designer or brand. But consumers lose faith in the message when the narrative doesn't jibe with lifestyle aspirations. This occurred in the mid-1980s, when the fashion industry pushed youthful fashions just when women entering the workforce in large numbers needed conservative work clothes—the women's sportswear market collapsed ("From stupidity," 1988). Designers, merchants, and the press lost credibility as style guides. One fashion commentator summed up the situation: "In fashion … we have witnessed the abdication of the experts. Everyone's opinion matters now, and no one's opinion matters any more than anyone else's" (Brubach, 1994).

The loss of fashion leadership by the experts—designers, merchants, and journalists—led to an alienation among grassroots consumers who demoted fashion's importance on their shopping priority list in favor of other product categories such as new technology. Those still placing a high priority on fashion kept an eye on fashion news scripted by the fashion press and on websites where consumers chat with each other about styles and trends, as well as on fashion blogs where a self-appointed "expert" provides commentary. Other sites are completely consumer controlled: at Threadless.com anyone can submit designs that are voted into production by users who then can order the resulting products (Walker, 2007). A report on the WWD/DNR CEO Summit concluded: "Providers of goods and services will have to scramble to meet the needs of an increasingly educated, tech-empowered and self-service oriented consumer who will no longer wait to be 'sold' by a biased source" ("Outlook," 2008).

✧ Emergence of Cheap Chic

Over time, retailers trained consumers to wait for markdowns before buying. Constant markdowns and markdowns early in the season upset the existing relationship between consumers and stores. Gone was the stigma of wearing cheap clothes and shoppers became less loyal to a brand or a designer and more focused on finding a bargain.

During the same time period, price for mainstream fashion plummeted while prices for luxury goods inflated. Price deflation was caused mainly by the shifting of apparel production to countries with cheap labor. The change set up price competition among specialty chains, department stores, mass merchants such as Kmart and Wal-Mart, and fast-fashion firms. Eventually the question became "How low can prices go?" Bud Konheim, CEO of Nicole Miller, said, "I think we've exploited all the countries on Earth for people who really want to work for nothing." When consumers view price as a deciding factor rather than desire, then the fashion industry has lost a central driver for fashion purchasing (Wilson, 2008c). The occurrence of two tragic accidents at Bangladesh garment factories just 5 months apart (a fire where more than 100 people were killed and a building collapsed) made consumers uncomfortably aware that cheap apparel comes with a steep price—the safety and well-being of the people who make their clothes. Costs of production offshore could increase with higher energy expenditures, making it harder to compete on price alone. Although price will always be an important consideration, consumers may modify their selection process to include other considerations such as environmental impact, humanitarian issues, and the reputation of the producing country.

✧ Power of Fashion Trends Dissipates

Today trends are not as broadly influential as they once were. When Yves Saint Laurent introduced his 1977 collection based on Russian themes, every product category and price point took part in the "folkloric" look. As forecaster David Wolfe commented, "The sort of creative ideas that used to be are now just flashes-in-the-pan. They come and go very quickly. … Today trends are little snapshots of style, not the big picture."

Time lags between the introduction of an innovation and its availability worked to the advantage of the industry. It allowed time to explain the innovation and increase its visibility and desirability. The less adventurous consumer who makes up the majority of the market needed that time to become familiar with the innovation before seeking to purchase it. And companies needed time to source and produce the new look as it trickled through the marketplace. Today those time lags have all but disappeared. Trends showcased on the runway can appear in moderate-priced stores before designer labels can deliver the look to high-priced boutiques. If a new style is simultaneously available at all levels of retail from department stores to specialty chains to mass merchants, there is less time to make money on the trend ("Direction," 1999).

Fragmentation in the marketplace also helped diminish the power of trends. The fashion industry itself became "too diffuse, with too many separate points of view, for anyone to pay the attention one once did" (Horyn, 2003b). Similar to the music industry, the fashion industry had a few superstars, a few rising stars, and many others whose names were barely known even to insiders. How can reporters (much less the consumer) locate a core when "fashion has exploded into 1,000 tiny particles of style?"

When consumers changed the way they shopped—buying basics and replacement items as needed, purchasing fashion looks for immediate wear—it became more difficult for apparel companies to figure out which trends would be in and for how long, given a product development cycle of almost a year. To adjust to these changes, apparel companies cut their development schedule and moved the process closer to the store delivery dates (Larson, 2003a).

Trends, once the motivation for shopping, can die before they reach the store. As one retail buyer put it, "You don't have enough time to create volume. By the time it gets onto the floor, kids are already tired [of it]." According to a retail analyst, trends now have a life span of 8 to 12 weeks instead of 5 months or more as they did in the late-1990s (D'Innocenzio, 2001). Trends that do catch on tend to influence a specific consumer segment. Without a time lag to introduce, explain, and promote the trend, it fails to spread to other consumer categories. For fashion firms, these factors make it harder both to predict trends and to exploit them for profit.

✧ Shift from Style Evolution to Fast Fashion

Until Dior's New Look in 1947, fashion change had been evolutionary, but Dior introduced a new look each season—the H-line, the A-line. People came to expect seasonal newness (Cardin & Charney, 1992). Still, fashion forecasting was relatively simple. The fashion press and merchants focused on a short list of new trends—which were by definition "in"—and the looks appeared in stores after a relatively short time lag. Meanwhile consumers' appetite for the new looks was building through the fashion leadership of women who wore the fashions first and through visibility in the media.

The driver was seasonal change—the expectation among consumers that a change in the season required new clothes with the latest colors, silhouettes, and decorative details. Over time the number of seasons increased from four to six or more. What had been a stately progression from one new look to the next became instead a continuous flow of new trends, each crowding on the heels of the one before. The acceleration of change promoted an appetite for newness among designers, the press, and consumers.

Traditionally, delivering newness took from 9 to 11 months—the product development cycle for sportswear went from sketches to samples to orders to production and delivery to stores. With the help of technology, most companies were able to cut that timeline to 5 or 6 months ("The Cycle," 2003). Then, the fast-fashion chains—Spain's Zara and Sweden's Hennes & Mauritz (H&M)—revolutionized fashion retailing by collapsing the time between the runway and the store into days rather than months. The idea was to deliver a large assortment of runway-inspired trends rapidly at a temptingly low price for young trend-hungry consumers. By monitoring sales, these companies can stop production on

styles that fail, increase deliveries of hot items, and adjust colors and other aspects in time for the next shipment (Barker, 2002). Forever 21, an American chain, expanded fast fashion from teens to women, men, and children. Using "design merchants" rather than designers (a design process that is proprietary), the company turns out adaptations of runway hits that are almost "indistinguishable from designer clothes" in 6 weeks (La Ferla, 2007a) (Figure 1.6).

In the late nineteenth century, articles referred to "the style problem," which had three symptoms: rapid change in fashion, the increasing number of styles available each season, and availability of the styles to more people simultaneously (Parsons, 2002). Perhaps today's fast fashion is the tail end of a trend toward making fashion available to consumers at all price ranges.

While fast fashion is clearly ascendant, a countertrend emerged—slow fashion. Like the slow food movement, which seeks to counter a fast-food lifestyle, slow fashion offers respite from constantly chasing trends and fast cycle times. Focusing on a concern for where materials came from and how they were produced, use of well-paid workers, and longer use by consumers, slow fashion can take many forms: classic jeans, couture gowns that hold their value, vintage and classic silhouettes, and neutral colors. The Alabama Chanin line considers itself to be just such a company, as each item is made by hand by artisans who live and work near Florence, Alabama. They use a combination of new, organic and recycled materials and stress the importance of sustainability. Their "slow design" takes into account a wide range of material and social factors as well as the short- and long-term impacts of the design (Phelan, 2012). Slow fashion may not appeal to fashionistas who are quick to buy and just as quick to discard, but it may appeal to customers looking for clothing that expresses personal style (Tran, 2008c) (Figure 1.7).

What drives fashion today? In the past, drivers included newness associated with seasonal change, the desire to wear the latest "in" looks, the wish to be appropriately dressed for any occasion, and the desire to impress others with

Figure 1.6

When young fashion-forward consumers wanted access to runway trends faster than traditional stores could react, Zara pioneered production and distribution methods that made it possible to satisfy that demand—an example of a co-evolving marketplace.

Figure 1.7

Slow fashion seeks a more eco-conscious, long-term view compared to the disposable approach of fast fashion. Uluru's hand-embellished tunic produced with Alabama Chanin exemplifies the values of the movement.

our chic clothes—in a word, to be "cool." One thing is sure: fashion will always be around. In down times, fashion can be therapeutic. In up times, fashion lets people flaunt their good fortune and enjoy their rewards (Kermouch, 2002). Another sure thing is the co-evolving nature of the marketplace between buyers and sellers. The current era has been characterized as postindustrial or postmodern—a label that sounds like the end of something. Perhaps such characterizations are a prelude to change, to a new era with its own new innovations.

✦ FORECASTING IN THE TEXTILE AND APPAREL INDUSTRIES

Even fast-fashion companies need a picture of what consumers will see as new and exciting, which fashion forecasting provides. Whereas fast fashion may meet the needs and interests of some consumers, it cannot cater to all consumer segments, tastes, or price points. Most companies will continue to operate on a longer product development cycle. Fashion forecasting coordinates the efforts of fiber producers, yarn manufacturers, fabric and print houses, apparel manufacturers, and retailers. As Li Edelkoort, forecaster for Trend Union in Paris, explains, "Trends are meant to have a sense of timing. If you bring them in too early, people just won't get them" (Horton, 2003).

The forecaster translates ambiguous and conflicting signals to provide support for business decisions. Although they work with textile fabrications, colors, and styles, their real job is to predict the preferences of consumers in the future. Forecasters work at all stages of the textile/apparel supply chain and on timelines that vary from a few months in advance of the sales season to 10 years ahead of it. Each type of forecast and timeline has its place in providing decision support.

Every apparel executive in the fields of product development, merchandising, marketing, and promotion is also a forecaster, because those executives make decisions about an uncertain future with incomplete information. In companies today, forecasting must be a team effort, with information shared between design, merchandising, marketing, sales, and promotion, so that the right product gets produced and distributed at the right time to a target consumer. In the world of fashion, improving the success rate of new merchandise, line extensions, and retailing concepts by only a few percentage points more than justifies the investment of time and money in forecasting. Fashion forecasters believe that by keeping up with the media, analyzing shifts in the culture, interviewing consumers, and dissecting fashion change they can spot trends before those trends take hold in the marketplace. By anticipating these changes, forecasters allow companies to position their products and fine-tune their marketing to take advantage of new opportunities. Major companies are becoming more and more dependent on this kind of forecasting because traditional forms of purely quantitative forecasting are less applicable to an increasingly volatile and fragmented marketplace.

Short-term forecasting involves periodic monitoring of the long-term vision and revisions as circumstances dictate; it acts to coordinate the operations of a company within the context of the industry and the marketplace. Forecasting keeps the momentum going because it forces a perspective of the future on the day-to-day business decisions. The short-term forecasting process begins 2 to 3 years before the arrival of merchandise in the retail store. This simultaneously collaborative and competitive process allows the segments of the textile/apparel pipeline to coordinate seasonal goods around looks that can be communicated to the customer through the press and stores. The process includes textile development, color forecasting, and style development as showcased in the international fashion shows and manufacturers' showrooms. These sources provide directional information necessary to the timely and successful introduction of seasonal fashion.

The 2- to 3-year timeline of short-term forecasting allows executives to take advantage of developments and position products in the marketplace. However, this timeline is not sufficient for decisions related to repositioning or extending product lines, initiating new businesses, reviving brand images, or planning new retail concepts. These decisions require other forecasting approaches with longer time horizons. **Long-term forecasting** (5 years or more) is a way to explore possible futures and to build a shared vision of an organization's direction and development. A compelling vision draws people toward a preferred future. Long-term forecasting can be more significant for an organization because it looks at social change and demographics. Demographic forecasts are among the most stable types of forecasts. Forecasting social change and technological developments is more difficult (Mahaffie, 1995).

Many people worry that they will not recognize a trend early enough to capitalize on it. Why spend the effort on trendspotting without the expectation of a payoff? Faith Popcorn (1991) says that a shift in lifestyle triggers trend cascades that take about 10 years to work through the culture, affect related industries, and reach all market levels. Forecasters working in apparel fields need an early warning system so that trends can be fine-tuned for a specific product category and market segment. Although timing is important, trend information is useful wherever the trend is in its life cycle. Sometimes it is just as important to know when something is on its way out. If a fashion is nearing its termination point, then it is a good time to survey the trendsetters to identify the next big thing. Together, short- and long-term forecasting approaches furnish the textile/apparel executive with access to information and the tools to shape it for decision support.

✧ Forecasting within the Manufacturing Cycle

Short- and long-term forecasting have a more specific time horizon within the **manufacturing cycle** (Figure 1.8). The lynchpin in apparel planning and scheduling is the manufacturer (Michaud, 1989). The forecast is developed by the sales and merchandising managers using input from retailers, marketing representatives, sales history analysis (1 to 3 years of data), and market research. This working, long-term forecast mirrors the manufacturer's business expectations in terms of lines and styles to be produced each month. The short-term forecast includes both basic and fashion goods detailed down to weekly production by style, color, and size. Proper forecasting ensures the timely delivery of merchandise to the retailer.

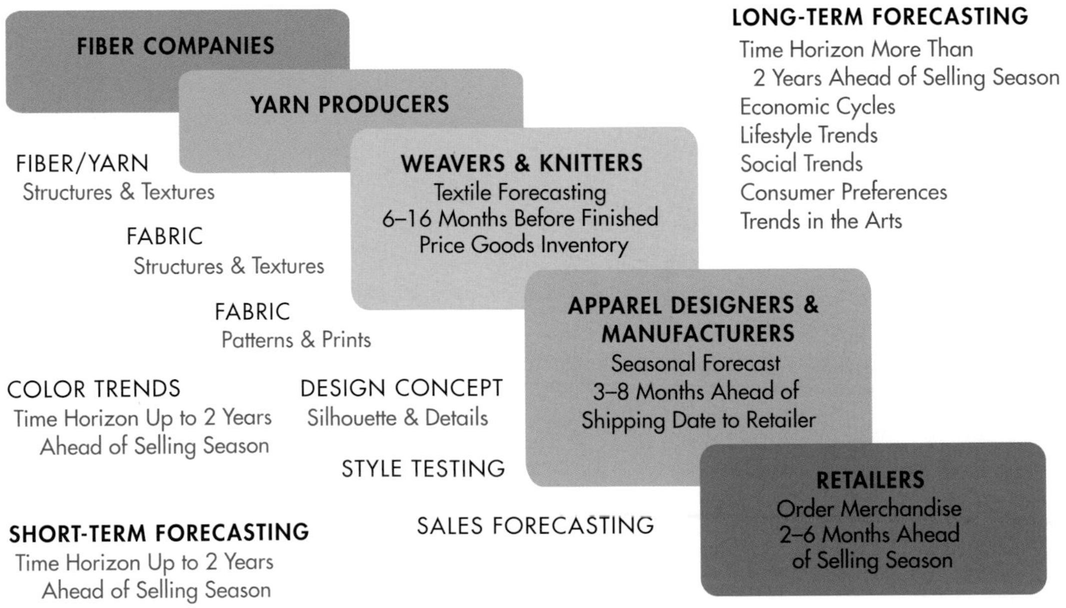

FIBER COMPANIES

YARN PRODUCERS

WEAVERS & KNITTERS
Textile Forecasting
6–16 Months Before Finished
Price Goods Inventory

FIBER/YARN
Structures & Textures

FABRIC
Structures & Textures

FABRIC
Patterns & Prints

APPAREL DESIGNERS & MANUFACTURERS
Seasonal Forecast
3–8 Months Ahead of
Shipping Date to Retailer

COLOR TRENDS
Time Horizon Up to 2 Years
Ahead of Selling Season

DESIGN CONCEPT
Silhouette & Details

STYLE TESTING

RETAILERS
Order Merchandise
2–6 Months Ahead
of Selling Season

SHORT-TERM FORECASTING
Time Horizon Up to 2 Years
Ahead of Selling Season

SALES FORECASTING

LONG-TERM FORECASTING
Time Horizon More Than
2 Years Ahead of Selling Season
Economic Cycles
Lifestyle Trends
Social Trends
Consumer Preferences
Trends in the Arts

Figure 1.8

Short- and long-term forecasting operate on different timelines within the manufacturing cycle.

The apparel manufacturer's long-term forecast traces the planning and scheduling process forward to the retailer because it is prepared before orders are received. Orders are shown as input to the short-term forecasts. The quality of the long-term forecast can be measured by comparing expected orders with orders received.

Tracing the planning and scheduling process backward, forecasts and orders feed back to the textile manufacturer. A process very similar to the one in apparel manufacturing occurs at the textile manufacturing level. The time period from initial forecast to delivery of finished piece goods to the apparel manufacturer is between 6 and 16 months. Tracing the process backward one more step leads to the yarn and fiber manufacturers, where a similar forecasting process takes place.

Industry fashion trends enter the model as input for the retailers' decisions and as part of planning at the other stages of apparel, textile, yarn, and fiber manufacturing. Color forecasting is typically done 20 to 24 months ahead of the target selling season. Textile development is typically done 12 to 24 months prior to the target selling season. International fabric fairs show new trends in fabrics one year ahead of the target selling season. All these forecasting activities are aimed at having the right product at the right time to meet customer demand.

✧ Scouting for Fashion Trends

The segments of the fashion industry synthesize information into color and textile forecasts anchored by themes that reflect the spirit of the times. These forecasts serve to coordinate the supply chain for the product development process.

Many organizations and services are available to alert executives to industry fashion trends:

* *To-the-trade only shows* showcase fabrics and prints for each season.
* *Fashion-reporting services* deliver news from the runway and street by subscription on websites, through presentations, and in print reports.
* *Color forecasters* present seminars at industry functions and deliver palettes to members or subscribers.
* *Industry trade associations* maintain fabric libraries for fashion research and present updates for apparel executives.
* The *trade press* covers industry events and reports forecasting information.

Members of product development teams, merchandisers, marketers, and retailers participate in events and read the trade press to gather trend information. Some team members are delegated specifically to scout for trend information and locate sources for the latest in fabrics, trims, and findings.

Most apparel companies subscribe to one or more trend services whose job it is to scout the market and report on developments. These services deliver trend information up to 2 years in advance of the selling season. Sometimes forecasting services are part of a buying office—either an independent organization or a division of a retailing corporation whose role is to scout the market and make merchandise recommendations to stores or chains. Because they serve as coordinating points for trend information, forecasting services exert a considerable influence on the fashion industry (see Resource Pointers for a listing of these firms).

FORECASTING AS A CAREER

Business creativity has similarities and differences with creativity in the arts. Both kinds of creativity are practiced by people who see potential in new combinations of existing ideas, products, and processes, and by people who persevere during slow periods, especially in the business cycle. But new business ideas must be appropriate and actionable—that is, they must somehow enhance the way business gets done. Creativity in business is based on expertise. Expertise consists of everything a person knows about his or her work domain. The larger the intellectual space that comprises this expertise, the more chance to discover new possibilities, new connections, and new combinations that solve problems. Working in supportive but diverse teams builds expertise by introducing different perspectives into the dialogue.

Solving problems is the essential element in business: Which new products to introduce? How to put products and likely consumers together in a space conducive to buying? How much to spend on new tools or processes? How to prosper given changing technology and a dynamic marketplace? The first step is to realize the difference between "tame" and "wicked" problems (Pacanowsky, 1995). Tame problems are those that are manageable, easy to define, and lead to a solution that can be applied consistently across time. Wicked problems (meaning in this case, "harmful and damaging") are so complex that they are very difficult to solve (Figure 1.9).

Because tame or simple problems are straightforward and manageable, it is relatively easy to gather relevant information and apply traditional methods to discover the solution. The solution to these types of problems requires **thinking inside the box** or normal practices. Wicked, or more complex problems are so difficult that they require **thinking outside the box**. Such problems defy easy definition. Forecasting, planning, and strategy development

involve complexity. The process for solving complex problems begins by generating the greatest possible understanding of the problem from diverse viewpoints. The trick is to avoid seeking closure too quickly or getting bogged down in a polarizing argument between two positions. Instead, generate a large number of questions that start out:

* "What if …" (questions about possibilities).
* "What is …" (questions about fact).
* "What should …" (questions requiring judgment and opinions).

Sort through the questions and look for those that need to be explored further, and look for relationships and patterns.

Forecasting, with its many disciplines and multiple time horizons, focuses on business creativity. Forecasting professionals are hired by a company for their expertise. Some build on their knowledge of fashion with an insider's view of color, textiles, or styles. Still others are futurists who look at long-term cultural shifts. Some bring the ability to bridge the gap between the corporation and a particular market segment, such as consumers under 30. As one partner from a research firm that uses young correspondents to track their peers explains: "A trend is a shift in the prevailing thought process that eventually manifests itself in a range of

THINKING INSIDE THE BOX

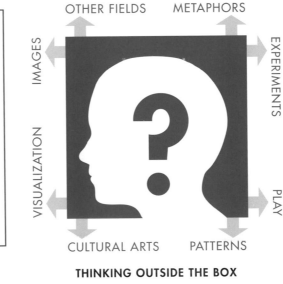

THINKING OUTSIDE THE BOX

Figure 1.9

Solving tame, or simple problems requires thinking inside the box. Solving wicked, or complex problems necessitates thinking outside the box.

popular tastes and, ultimately, consumer goods" (McMurdy, 1998). These professionals work in fashion, but also in related industries such as cosmetics, fragrance, and even cell phones. Lori Smith, a trend forecaster for one of the world's largest makers of perfume, puts it this way: "What I do is bring the outside world in" (Green, 1998). Reports from forecasters—whether working inside the company or as consultants—affect the way a product is designed, the way it is sold, or where it is sold. Salaries are on the low end for entry-level jobs for trend reporters gathering information, but forecasters with 7 to 10 years' experience can make in the low six figures working for a manufacturing, retailing, or established consultancy (Sahadi, 2005). Highly competitive, the field consists of around 1,000 to 1,500 professionals who combine training in fashion, business insight, and a wide-ranging curiosity (Zimmerman, 2008).

One of the best ways to discover if you are a person with the natural gifts and skills required for business creativity is to do an internship with a forecasting company. Consider trade organizations such as Cotton Incorporated, professional organizations such as the Color Association of the United States, retail corporations, buying offices, fashion reporting services, and forecasting agencies and consultancies. Internships are offered on the basis of a company's staffing needs at a particular time. Even if a company has never offered an internship in forecasting, it might offer one to the right applicant at the right time.

To explore your interest in forecasting, hone your skills by creating a portfolio. Developing a forecast is only the first step; communicating a forecast is an essential skill. In the portfolio you can demonstrate both these facets. Use the activities in the following chapters as a starting point for the portfolio. Use the portfolio to show your skills in an interview for a forecasting position.

Forecasting professionals are media **mavens**—sponges for soaking up news that relates to change. Begin your profession by reading the kind of sources that are important to forecasters. By beginning your environmental scanning now, you will build a base for communicating with other forecasters and business executives. A basic media scan would include:

❖ *The Wall Street Journal* or a more extensive scan of business news such as *The Economist*.
❖ A national newspaper such as *The New York Times* or another daily from an urban center or a more expansive news scan including regional newspapers from fashion centers such as Miami.
❖ The key trade papers that cover the fashion and apparel industry, including *WWD* (*Women's Wear Daily*) for women's wear and menswear.
❖ *Advertising Age* for coverage of marketing trends.
❖ Fashion and lifestyle magazines such as *Entertainment Weekly* for coverage of popular culture and opinion leaders that influence fashion trends.
❖ Online resources such as *Business of Fashion* for an overview of global news and topics related to the fashion industry.

Use the Internet to locate profiles of forecasters. Few if any started as forecasters. Instead, these professionals gained experience in retailing or product development, moving into forecasting as their talents and expertise became valuable enough to support the specialization. By beginning your career with an interest in forecasting, you can choose positions that help deepen and broaden your knowledge of the fashion industry—the kind of background essential to a forecasting professional.

Chapter Summary

Fashion is a multifaceted concept that has social, psychological, popular culture and economic implications. Fashion forecasting is a dynamic profession that involves finding social, economic, and cultural patterns and interpreting them in a meaningful way for members of the fashion and other consumer industries. Forecasts can be developed through processes such as environmental and consumer scans which form the basis for fashion, trend, and competitive analyses. Understanding the Zeitgeist, or spirit of the times, is integral to the process of fashion forecasting. One aspect of the Zeitgeist is an identifiable fashion era that can be characterized by a style leader, a fashion look, or other criteria. Several emerging fashion directions give us an accurate depiction of fashion's present, and a strong indication of what the industry's future has in store.

Key Terms and Concepts

Cohorts	Planned obsolescence
Collective selection	Point-of-sales (POS) data
Environmental scanning	Short-term forecasting
Fashion	Strategic windows
Fast fashion	Target market
Forecasting	Thinking inside the box
Long-term forecasting	Thinking outside the box
Manufacturing cycle	Trend
Megatrend	Zeitgeist

Discussion Questions

The public often considers fashion to be the trivial pursuit of a few people. Instead, fashion is a pervasive process in human culture that plays out in an infinite number of ways. The diversity produces many meanings for words such as *fashion*, *trends*, and *forecasting*. Executives in the apparel industry must be sensitive to the subtle significance of these meanings in order to successfully blend aesthetic concerns with market mindfulness. Use the following questions to summarize and review this chapter.

Defining Fashion: What mechanisms in society power fashion behavior? What psychological traits of an individual power fashion behavior? How is meaning transferred in culture?

The Spirit of the Times: Because it is difficult to recognize the spirit of the times while you are living them, how can forecasters sensitize themselves to cultural patterns? What product category interactions are indicative of the Zeitgeist?

Defining Forecasting: What is the role of forecasters inside corporations? What special forecasting disciplines apply to the apparel industry? Is there value to be derived from integrating forecasting disciplines within a company? What kinds of information are useful to forecasters and where do they find that information?

Forecasting Activities

Cover Stories. Track fashion evolution by looking at the covers of a fashion magazine over the past decade. Libraries often have bound volumes going back decades for the most popular and long-lived magazines. Some magazine websites have a section with covers by decade. Because looking at all the covers would take too long, sample the issues by deciding which month or months to examine in each year. Then, systematically look at those covers. Imagine the editor and art director carefully considering the clothes, model, makeup, background color, and all the other elements making up the cover. The cover is the billboard for the magazine and has important implications for newsstand sales. How have cover design and content evolved over the decade? What directional signals for fashion change can you derive from this study? How are fashion magazines changing in the ways they showcase fashion?

Mapping the Zeitgeist. It is difficult to recognize the spirit of the times as you are living through them. To sensitize yourself to this concept, map the Zeitgeist using the categories of dominant events, ideals, social groups, attitude, and technology for the decades from the 1920s to the 1990s. How do these categories define what is remembered about each decade?

Discovering the Zeitgeist. Use Nystrom's framework to map the spirit of the current times. Because each market segment will have its cultural identity within the cultural environment, try mapping the dominating events, ideals, social groups, attitudes, and technology for your own generational group. How important does an event have to be to affect multiple groups? What does this suggest in relationship to product development and marketing? How are such maps useful to forecasters?

Forecasting as a Career Path. Clip articles from trade and popular publications profiling forecasters in all the specialties. Note which work for companies or corporations and which work for consulting firms. Analyze the aspects that are common across all forecasting fields. What courses in your curriculum map to these competencies? Analyze the differences between the forecaster's focus and responsibilities depending on the product category, price point, and target market. What courses in your curriculum encourage the development of specialized knowledge useful in the forecasting process?

Resource Pointers

Business-to-business trend forecasting sites:

Fashion Snoops: www.fashionsnoops.com

StyleSight: www.stylesight.com

Trendstop: www.trendstop.com

WGSN (World Global Style Network):
www.wgsn.com

Trend forecasters:

Li Edelkoort: www.trendtablet.com

Nelly Rodi: http://nellyrodi.com/en

PeclersParis: www.peclersparis.com

PromoStyl: www.promostyl.com

PART ONE

FORECASTING FRAMEWORKS

The essence of fashion is changeability. It satisfies the curiosity, the human drive towards what is new.

—Karl Lagerfeld

2

INTRODUCING INNOVATION

OBJECTIVES

◆ Identify diffusion of innovation as a framework for understanding and predicting fashion change

◆ Analyze current fashion within a theoretical framework

◆ Establish theoretical models as tools for analysis and communication

◆ Describe the characteristics of a trend

◆ Summarize the diffusion process—how innovations diffuse within a social system, the kind of consumer who participates in each stage, and the social process involved in transmitting fashion innovation

DIFFUSION OF INNOVATION

Because clothing is an expression of ourselves, many consumers get bored with their clothing after they have had it for a period of time and crave novelty. Something new—an innovation—is proposed. Innovations occur in all industries—automobiles, interior design, music, or restaurants—and fashion is no exception. In fashion, an innovation isn't limited to clothing; it can be an accessory, a hairstyle, or cosmetics. It may emerge from the fashion runways, appear in a hit movie, television show, or music video, and ultimately influence the buying decisions of millions. After the innovation arrives on the scene, individuals consider it for adoption. In the book *Mad World* (Majewski & Bernstein, 2014), one English musician perfectly explains how an innovation is spread, with the idea "Now this is interesting. And it's different. I'm inspired! I might be able to do something like this"—that same internal conversation is held by thousands of consumers, who then choose to adopt the trend to their own specific tastes. The cumulative effect of those decisions can be tracked in sales and visually on the street.

Sometimes innovation redefines what is appropriate, as in the case of wearing lingerie as outerwear. At first the idea of exposed bras, lacy teddies, and corsets was socially unacceptable. Then it became rebellious when artists such as Madonna wore the look in music videos and on stage, and finally the style appeared in modified form in stores everywhere. For example, elements of the lingerie look became part of a female executive's power suit—a lace-edged camisole showing at the neckline of her business suit. The lingerie look was extended in the 1990s with the introduction of the slip dress—a style that moved from models on the runway to stores in the mall. The slip dress morphed into layers of transparency with underwear showing (Horyn, 2007), and the lingerie look continues to be new with each reinvention, such as the popularity of bandeau tops in spring 2014.

Fashion innovations may take many forms, such as a new fiber, a new finish for denim or another fabric, introduction of an unusual color range, a modification in a silhouette or detail, a different way to wear an accessory, or a mood expressed in a distinctive style (Figure 2.1). When introduced, it diffuses through the population as more and more consumers have a chance either to accept or reject it. This pattern

Figure 2.1

Dior's New Look was considered to be a radical innovation when it first appeared after World War II. The tradition is continued in the house today by Raf Simons.

Profile: Stephen Sprouse and Louis Vuitton

Although millions can recognize his work, even many fashionistas aren't aware of the influence of Stephen Sprouse, one of the most innovative designers of New York in the 1980s and the inspiration for one of the most iconic handbags of all time. Born in Dayton, Ohio in 1953, Sprouse showed an early talent for design and was offered an internship with the designer Bill Blass at age 14. He left the Rhode Island School of Design during his freshman year, went to New York and quickly got a job as Halston's main assistant. He left after 2 years to go out on his own, and that is when his legacy began.

Sprouse became known as the first fashion designer to combine rock and roll and urban street culture with high fashion, dressing Debbie Harry of Blondie when the band was still a member of New York's underground punk scene. He became known for his bright, Day-Glo colors, shift dresses, and his graffiti prints, which were meant to show the gritty energy of downtown New York, home at the time to struggling artists and musicians and not the shopping and restaurant area it is today. In addition to sending models down the runway with words like "rock" and "love" spray-painted on their dresses, Sprouse created textile prints based on his own handwriting, which consisted of bold capital letters, which became instantly recognizable when they were made into sheath dresses and other garments.

Even though his clothing was a big hit with celebrities like Mick Jagger and with fashion editors and cutting-edge boutiques, Sprouse's refusal to compromise his vision resulted in his first business closing. He had a few other clothing lines during the 1990s, but they too went out of business. It appeared that Sprouse's fame would never equal the level of talent he displayed in his early years.

However, it took another innovator to get Sprouse the recognition he deserved. Marc Jacobs was hired by Louis Vuitton in 1997 as creative director (after being fired by Perry Ellis for his controversial Grunge collection, which also merged street fashion with high fashion) so that he could make the brand more modern. Marc knew that it would take something completely novel to make a statement that this wasn't the same old Louis Vuitton, and to do that, he turned to Stephen Sprouse. Marc invited Sprouse to collaborate on Louis Vuitton's spring 2001 collection, and together they came up with the idea to graffiti the words LOUIS VUITTON over the traditional Monogram canvas print in Stephen's signature handwriting. The revamped print was an instant hit, and sold out entirely before the bags even made it into stores. Together, two innovators managed to make a 146-year-old brand the coolest label in fashion.

True innovators don't just limit themselves to one innovation; they are constantly pushing new boundaries, and Stephen Sprouse was also one of the first designers to do something that is taken for granted today—a Target collaboration. In 2002, capsule collections were not the common collaboration between designers and retailers that they are today, but Stephen Sprouse led the way with his Americaland collection of skateboards, bathing suits, and beach balls. He also was at the forefront of the designer-as-spokesperson phenomenon, appearing on billboards, subway posters, and TV commercials for the brand. This type of collaboration has been replicated numerous times, not only by Target but by other retailers such as H&M, but Stephen was among the first.

Sadly, Stephen Sprouse died in 2004 due to lung cancer at the age of 50, but his role as an innovator in the fashion world will always be remembered.

Source:
Padilha, Roger and Padilha, Maurico (2009). *The Stephen Sprouse book.* Rizzoli New York.

of acceptance or rejection determines the innovation's life cycle. The **diffusion process** maps the response to the innovation over time.

The **diffusion curve** illustrates how a trend starts slowly, peaks, and then declines among consumers, in a process that resembles a bell-shaped curve (Rogers, 1962). The far left side of the curve represents early adopters and early diffusion of innovation, the center section, majority adoption, and the right side, laggards (Figure 2.2). The shape—horizontal time axis and vertical axis for number of adopters—was retained as the component of a theoretical model that came to express many aspects of diffusion.

The most critical stage of the diffusion process comes during the initial introduction. Diffusion requires both **innovators**, people who wear new fashions and expose others to the look, and **opinion leaders**, who endorse a style to those who seek guidance, in order to happen. For the forecaster, the diffusion model provides a framework for analyzing the movement of an innovation through a social system. The framework helps to answer questions about:

❖ The innovation—Why do some innovations diffuse more rapidly than others? What characteristics of an innovation help or hinder its adoption?

❖ The **consumer adoption process**—What is the mental process used by individual consumers in deciding between adopting or rejecting an innovation?

❖ The diffusion process—How do innovations diffuse within a social system? What kind of consumer participates in each stage? What is the social process involved in transmitting fashion innovation?

✦ CHARACTERISTICS OF AN INNOVATION

For something to be considered an innovation, the consumer must perceive the newness or novelty of the proposed fashion—it must seem different when compared to what already exists in the wardrobe, across the social group, or in the market environment. This degree of difference from existing forms is the first identifying characteristic of an innovation.

Rogers (1983) identified characteristics that would help or hinder the adoption of an innovation:

❖ **Relative advantage**—the perception that the innovation is more satisfactory than items that already exist in the same class of products.

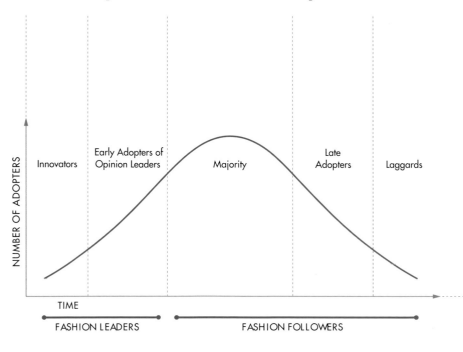

Figure 2.2
The diffusion curve is a theoretical model that depicts the spread of innovation through a social system.

- **Compatibility**—an estimate of harmony between the innovation and the values and norms of potential adopters.
- **Complexity**—a gauge of the difficulty faced by a consumer in understanding and using the innovation.
- **Trialability**—the relative ease of testing out the innovation before making a decision.
- **Observability**— the degree of visibility afforded the innovation.

An innovation will be more readily accepted if it is conspicuous, clearly better than other alternatives, easy to understand, simple to try, and congruent with the value system of the consumer.

Marketing and merchandising focus on educating the consumer about an innovation and lowering barriers to its adoption. Spraying consumers with fragrance as they enter a department store increases trialability; an ad showing how to wear an accessory reduces complexity; a fashion show illustrating how to coordinate new items demonstrates compatibility. Many other marketing tactics are aimed at lowering the barriers to the adoption of a fashion innovation.

One other characteristic inhibits or encourages adoption of innovation—**perceived risk** (Robertson, Zielinski, & Ward, 1984). A consumer, when considering something new and novel, imagines beyond the purchase to the consequences (Venkatraman, 1991). The consequences may involve:

- **Economic risk**—the risk of performance problems after the purchase, that the purchase price may reduce the ability to buy other products, and that the price will fall after purchase.
- **Enjoyment risk**—the risk of becoming bored by the purchase or not liking it as much as expected.
- **Social risk**—the risk that the consumer's social group will not approve.

Lowering the perception of risk is a powerful element in encouraging the adoption of an innovation.

One apparel retailer that tries to lower perceived risk as much as possible is Stitchfix. After creating a style profile of their personal preferences, customers receive a monthly delivery of five garments selected for them based on their profile. Clients are able to try on the garments in their own home and ask their friends' opinions, eliminating both enjoyment and social risks, and then only pay for the items they really like, reducing economic risk.

Sometimes forecasters support a trend even though it does face perceived risk. Said Sarah Rutson, fashion director of Lane Crawford: "A lot of the time it is about genuine gut instinct. Maybe a trend didn't work before, but this time you know it is right for now. There might not be data to tell you what to do, but you just instinctively know it will be strong and it's absolutely worth the perceived risk to get behind it" (Banks, 2013).

✦ THE CONSUMER ADOPTION PROCESS

The diffusion curve is a theoretical model of group dynamics because it captures many individual decisions. In each individual case, a consumer decides to accept or reject a proposed innovation. The consumer's adoption process— the private decision—is performed with consideration of how the adoption will affect the way the consumer presents himself or herself to others and how others will react to the result. There are several versions of the steps in this mental process (Figure 2.3). The original formulation of the adoption process by Rogers (1962) included the stages of:

- *Awareness*—the stage at which a consumer first realizes that an innovation has been proposed.
- *Interest*—the period when the consumer seeks information about the innovation.
- *Evaluation*—the time required to evaluate the information and form an attitude toward the innovation.
- *Trial*—the testing of the innovation before adoption.
- Adoption or rejection of the innovation.

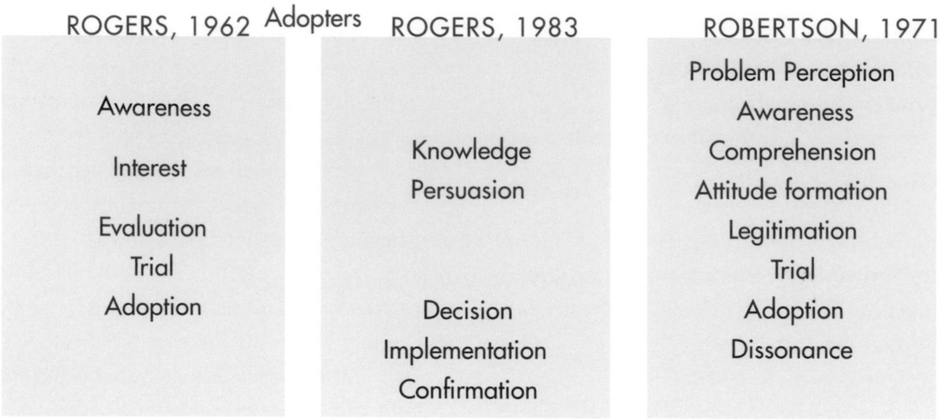

ROGERS, 1962 Adopters	ROGERS, 1983	ROBERTSON, 1971
Awareness		Problem Perception
		Awareness
Interest	Knowledge	Comprehension
	Persuasion	Attitude formation
Evaluation		Legitimation
Trial		Trial
Adoption	Decision	Adoption
	Implementation	Dissonance
	Confirmation	

Figure 2.3

A comparison of the steps proposed by different researchers for the consumer adoption process.

The most recent version of the process as outlined by Rogers (1983) included the following stages:

❖ *Knowledge*—a stage similar to awareness at which a consumer first learns of an innovation.

❖ *Persuasion*—the period when a consumer forms a favorable or an unfavorable attitude toward the innovation.

❖ *Decision*—the process of weighing the advantages and disadvantages of the innovation resulting in adoption or rejection.

❖ *Implementation*—actually using the innovation.

❖ *Confirmation*—the stage after adoption when a consumer seeks validation that the decision was correct.

Robertson (1971) proposed another model of the adoption process with the following stages:

❖ *Problem perception*—the time when a consumer recognizes a need for change.

❖ *Awareness*—the stage at which the consumer becomes aware of the innovation.

❖ *Comprehension*—the learning period during which the consumer explores the characteristics and function of the innovation.

❖ *Attitude formation*—the result of a period of evaluating the innovation.

❖ **Legitimation**—an optional stage during which the consumer seeks additional information about the innovation.

❖ *Trial*—the stage of trying on or experimenting with the innovation.

❖ *Adoption*—the ownership stage.

❖ **Dissonance**—a stage that occurs only when the consumer questions the adoption decision and seeks reassurance.

The Robertson model (1971) recognizes that consumers may skip steps, double back to an earlier stage, or reject the innovation at any point in the process.

The later Rogers version (1983) and the Robertson version both go beyond the adoption stage to what happens afterwards. This after-the-sale stage is crucial in determining consumer satisfaction and increasing the potential for repeat purchases. However, marketers and forecasters frequently ignore this crucial post-purchase evaluation.

Combining the models gives a view of the total process from initiation to purchase to post-purchase assessment. A consumer must first recognize a need—for something new or a replacement when a possession reaches the end of its usefulness, or boredom with their current wardrobe. In the awareness and interest stage, the consumer finds a possible solution in the marketing environment. By learning about the innovation, trying it, and evaluating it, the consumer forms a positive or negative attitude about the innovation. The consumer decides to buy or not buy the innovation. After purchase the consumer verifies the decision by seeking more information or reassurance from other people. Satisfaction or dissatisfaction with the decision affects the adoption process on future decisions.

One of the most critical stages in the adoption process is the learning phase (Wasson, 1968). If an innovation requires that an adopter learn a new habit pattern, that will slow down its adoption. If an innovative product merely replaces an old one and uses the same set of procedures, or even a simplified set, it will gain ready acceptance. An innovation may trigger three kinds of learning: learning a new sequence, learning to perceive new benefits, or learning to perceive the consumer's role in the use of the product. The rare "overnight success" comes when the innovation fills a missing link in a system that has already been adopted. All other innovations must negotiate a learning phase.

For the forecaster, the model points out several opportunities. The process begins when a consumer becomes dissatisfied with the current situation. If a number of consumers feel the same dissatisfaction, forecasters may pick up on that feeling and report it as a void in the market—an opportunity to solve the problem with a new product, process, or service.

The forecaster can trace consumer acceptance through the stages of awareness, exploration, and learning to gauge the eventual acceptance rate for the innovation. By monitoring consumers who discontinue the process or reject the innovation at an early stage, the forecaster can suggest ways to package or modify the innovation to overcome barriers to adoption. An early warning about the failure of an innovation to capture consumers can prevent losses by curtailing marketing efforts and by preventing overproduction of the item.

Observing the end of the adoption process— the stages after adoption when the consumer evaluates the decision—often reveals a lack of satisfaction. Products rarely deliver the full set of tangible and intangible attributes sought by the consumer. This reality initiates a new cycle with the identification of a problem. The forecaster's function is to recognize the new problem, identify possible solutions, and report to clients on the new opportunity.

✦ FASHION CHANGE AGENTS

Rogers' 1962 original model shows a very small group of innovators who begin the diffusion process followed by a larger group of opinion leaders. Together these consumers are **change agents**, and they perform several important roles in the spread of innovation in their social group:

❖ They communicate fashion trends visually and verbally.
❖ They are relatively more knowledgeable and interested in fashion compared to others in their group.
❖ They have the aesthetic taste and social sensitivity to assemble a stylish look. (King & Ring, 1980)

When others recognize them for their abilities, they become **influentials**—group members who establish the standards of dress for others in the group. Change agents are effective because they represent the ideal within the social group.

Fashion change agents are important to marketers because they control the diffusion of an innovation. A small group of **mavens**— people with knowledge about some aspect of lifestyle, a passion for newness, and the desire to share their interest with others—produces the word-of-mouth to power the spread of an innovation. Journalist Malcolm Gladwell's 2002 book *The Tipping Point* explains the influence such people have to spread an idea to a larger audience. As a panel member talking to marketing executives, he said, "These people are not necessarily the best educated or wealthiest, but they do have a special social power" ("Marketing," 2003). Edward Keller and Jonathan Berry, in their book *The Influentials*, estimate that 10 percent of consumers determine the consumption behavior of the other 90 percent, a figure based on their findings from 60 years of Roper polls (2003). Using interpersonal networks, these change agents or influentials act in the early stages of adoption and lay the foundation for later mass acceptance of a trend.

Retailers play a role as change agents in fashion diffusion (Hirschman & Stampfl, 1980). Designers and manufacturers propose many more innovations in a season than can be merchandised in the retail space available. Retailers control the flow of innovation into the social system by selecting among the proposed innovations the ones that will appear in the stores. Some high-fashion stores and avant-garde boutiques are willing to present new fashion innovations based on their own judgment and clientele. Customers rely on these retailers to curate their merchandise so they know they are picking only from the "best of the best" of available styles. These retailers are analogous to the fashion innovators. Other more mainstream retailers are like opinion leaders because consumers turn to their assortment, sales associates, and visual merchandising for informed advice and fashion direction.

✧ Innovators

Marketers usually identify innovators as people who buy new product innovations relatively earlier than others in their social group. To target such customers for product introductions, marketers need a profile of such early adopters. The usual profile is of a young, educated, affluent consumer who is very interested in the particular product category. Innovativeness, the desire for new experiences, is also a personality trait (Hirschman, 1980). Personality traits affect general behaviors more than specific purchases, but they underlie the ways consumers approach, modify, simplify, and react to their marketing environment (Horton, 1979).

Innovative people can be segmented into three groups, each with a different profile (Venkatraman, 1991):

❖ *Cognitive innovators* prefer new mental experiences and enjoy novelty when associated with thinking and problem solving.
❖ *Sensory innovators* prefer experiences that stimulate the senses, have an easygoing attitude toward life, take risks, participate in pleasurable activities without thinking too much, and engage in dreaming and fantasy.
❖ *Cognitive–sensory innovators* prefer both cognitive and sensory experiences.

Fashion apparel has both cognitive and sensory components. Purely stylistic innovations such as a new silhouette, color, or detail make their appeal on sensory grounds (Figure 2.4). Innovativeness in clothing is related to enjoying dressing just for the positive feelings created and for the excitement of experimentation (Pasnak & Ayres, 1969). New fibers and finishes, new ways to wear accessories, and novel coordination strategies are more cognitively appealing as problem solvers.

Although all three types of innovative consumers buy new products and visit new retail stores earlier than other consumers, they vary in other ways. Consumers who prefer new mental experiences monitor more mass media channels, pay more attention to ads, and do more exploratory shopping such as browsing window displays than other consumers. Sensory innovators prefer visual to verbal information, whereas cognitive innovators are the opposite (Venkatraman & Price, 1990). Innovator types

Figure 2.4
Innovators respond early to the sensory appeal of new silhouettes, details, and style combinations, and they have the confidence to wear them ahead of others in their group.

interact with the characteristics of the innovation—relative advantage, compatibility, complexity, trialability, observability, and risk—to determine marketing strategies (Venkatraman, 1991). Relative advantage will be important to all consumers considering a new product but different innovator types will vary in other preferences:

❖ Cognitive innovators are problem solvers who can figure out product complexity and analyze economic risk, but they are not risk takers. Because they closely monitor mass media and pay attention to advertising, the most effective strategy is to present ads that emphasize the relative advantage, provide the information for assessing economic risk, and reduce concerns about enjoyment risk.

❖ For sensory innovators, the most effective strategy is to reduce complexity and perception of risk while emphasizing the uniqueness of the product and the pleasures associated with it as a visual presentation.

Consumers who are first to make fashion purchases and wear new styles often pay a premium price. They are thought to be less price sensitive and more affluent than those who buy later in the season. Researchers found another factor that influences early sales—the degree of confidence the early shopper has in the economic conditions (Allenby, Jen, & Leone, 1996). By comparing sales data from five divisions of retailer, researchers were able to show that consumer confidence about the future state of the economy was a strong predictor of pre-season sales. The best predictor for in-season sales was the financial ability to purchase.

Discovering the factors that drive early sales of a fashion item is critical in business planning and forecasting. Fashion stylist Shelly Bishop, a stylist who works in Houston, Texas, shares that "innovative people start trends and are very important to a buyer, as they add legitimacy, and drive that trend to continue which equates to more sales. Innovative people are featured in magazines often in street style columns meant to inspire the every-day gal looking for fresh ideas"

(Bishop, 2014). Early warning about the potential success or failure of a look, line, or stylistic innovation allows managers to adjust pricing and production schedules. (See Chapter 10 for a more extended discussion of consumer confidence and forecasting.)

✧ Fashion Leaders

If innovators are change agents who first adopt a new fashion and make it visible within their social groups, how are fashion leaders described? Katz and Lazarsfeld (1955) sought to answer this question by interviewing women. If the women reported being asked for advice about clothes or believed they were more likely than others to be asked for advice, interviewees were classified as **fashion leaders**.

Katz and Lazarsfeld (1955) identified two kinds of fashion leaders: the glamorous woman who first displays expensive fashions and the woman who is influential face to face. When the characteristics of these self-identified fashion leaders were compared to others, the fashion leaders were found to be highly interested in fashion, sensitive to their impression on others, gregarious, and recognized as having qualities appropriate for leadership. The researchers found that single, unmarried women with a high interest in fashion had more opportunities for fashion leadership than women at other points in the life cycle. Unexpectedly, findings showed very little difference in the incidence of fashion leaders in different social classes. However, women in the lower class were more likely to seek leadership outside their class. Influence takes place mostly among women of similar circumstances and real-life groups—that is, in naturally occurring groups of friends, colleagues, neighbors, and acquaintances.

Almost 20 years later and with young, single women, Schrank (1973) confirmed the earlier findings about fashion leadership. She administered a fashion leadership scale and a clothing interest inventory to college women and interviewed them about 15 clothing or accessory items with varying degrees of diffusion. Respondents indicated which of the items they owned and when they had been purchased. Schrank found there was a significant relationship between fashion leadership and clothing interest and that fashion leadership is evenly distributed through all social classes.

If people have similar attitudes toward fashion, the difference between leaders and followers is a matter of intensity and speed of adaptation (Brenninkmeyer, 1973). In this view, fashion leaders are more susceptible to change and more interested in differentiating themselves from others. In terms of self-concept, fashion leaders consider themselves more excitable, indulgent, contemporary, formal, colorful, and vain than followers (Goldsmith, Flynn, & Moore, 1996). A fashion leader must be able to sense the spirit of the times and anticipate change in tastes, be self-confident enough to make her own fashion choices, and influential within her social group.

Leaders also differ from followers in terms of information seeking. Leaders and followers all use the same sources of fashion information, but leaders use a greater number of sources more frequently and more often prefer marketer-dominated sources—window and in-store displays, fashion magazines, and fashion shows (Polegato & Wall, 1980).

✧ Fashion Followers

Fashion followers include both the majority adopters who push the diffusion curve to its highest point as well as those who adopt after that. After the peak, the number of new adopters decreases until all people who are interested in the innovation have had the opportunity to possess it or at least try it.

If the innovation is a major trend affecting a large number of consumers over several seasons or even several years, manufacturers and retailers still have an opportunity for profit at the peak of adoption and as the innovation reaches the late adopters. If the trend is a short-lived fad, the timescale is much shorter and the potential for profit is better for manufacturers and retailers participating in the early stages. For the forecaster, the waning of a trend signals the potential for adoption of a new innovation, one that probably already exists and is beginning its diffusion cycle.

✦ MODELING THE DIFFUSION PROCESS

The theoretical model of diffusion for the Rogers model (1962) shows a two-step flow (Figure 2.5). The first step involves transmission of new ideas through the impersonal influence of mass media and marketer-based information to innovators and opinion leaders. The second step depends on the personal, face-to-face influence within social groups as new ideas move from fashion leaders to fashion followers.

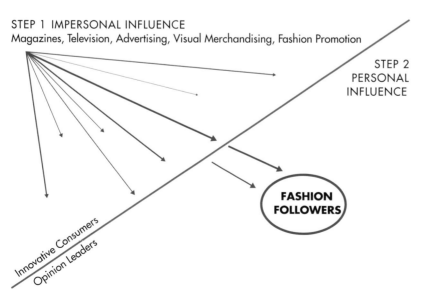

STEP 1 IMPERSONAL INFLUENCE
Magazines, Television, Advertising, Visual Merchandising, Fashion Promotion

STEP 2 PERSONAL INFLUENCE

Innovative Consumers
Opinion Leaders

FASHION FOLLOWERS

Figure 2.5

Diffusion occurs in the flow from mass media and marketer-based information to the innovators and opinion leaders and finally to fashion followers through personal influence.

An alternative diffusion model—the Bass model (1969)—makes this point even more explicitly. Instead of defining adopters only by the time period, the Bass model differentiates between the kinds of influence that most contribute to the decision. The Bass theoretical model shows that most consumers at the beginning of the diffusion process adopt the innovation based on impersonal influences such as the mass media (Figure 2.6). Most subsequent adopters make the decision based on interpersonal influence. But some adopters, even at the later stages, rely mostly on external, impersonal influence.

The bell curve of the Rogers diffusion process can be redrafted into a cumulative form—the **S-curve**—which more clearly mirrors the growth phase of the product cycle (Brown, 1992). Using this theoretical model, it is easy to see how an innovation could spread between social groups and market segments (Figure 2.7). For example, a series of S-curves could represent the spread of

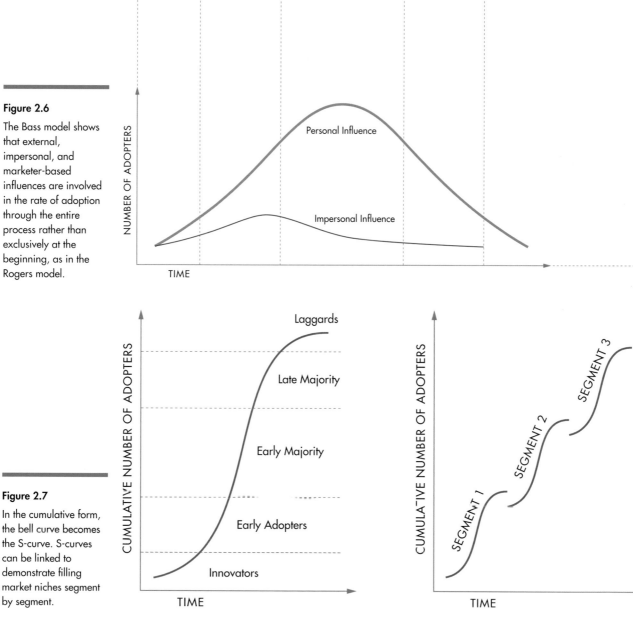

Figure 2.6

The Bass model shows that external, impersonal, and marketer-based influences are involved in the rate of adoption through the entire process rather than exclusively at the beginning, as in the Rogers model.

Figure 2.7

In the cumulative form, the bell curve becomes the S-curve. S-curves can be linked to demonstrate filling market niches segment by segment.

an innovation from a younger, hip, edgy consumer segment to one that is more educated and affluent, and then to one that is older and more mainstream. Or, the series of S-curves could represent the transmission of the innovation from one company to another, each targeting a different consumer segment. At the first stage, when an innovative product is introduced, a company targeting early adopters sells it. If successful with that first audience, the innovation is picked up by a second company targeting the next group of adopters, and finally by a third company targeting the volume market. Theoretical models of the S-curve provides a complex understanding of the diffusion of innovation and a finer-grained framework for forecasting.

Modis (1992) suggests an even more intriguing elaboration on diffusion of innovation. He argues that the S-curve can be used to describe all forms of market growth. He then links a series of curves as Brown did. Finally, using data from a number of industries, he introduces the idea of chaos at the point where the curves overlap (Figure 2.8). In this theoretical model, the innovation is introduced and goes through the growth cycle until that market niche is filled; then begins a period of chaos during which a new niche is identified. When identified, another growth cycle begins, and so on.

The bell curve describes the process of diffusion within a social system. Its cumulative form, the S-curve, linked in sequence, shows the process of diffusion as it spreads from one social system or market segment to the next. Failure to fill a niche in this progression signals the end of the innovation's life cycle. Success in filling the next niche indicates the potential for continued diffusion of the innovation to a wider audience. For the forecaster, this theoretical model holds out the tantalizing idea that such patterns of niche filling could be identified in sales data and be used to predict future patterns.

The chaotic phase between S-curves can be seen as a period during which the innovators in another social system experiment with the innovation. If these innovators adopt the innovation, it is passed to the opinion leaders and continues until that niche is filled.

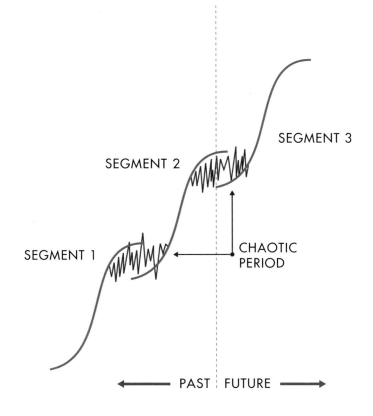

SEGMENT 3

SEGMENT 2

SEGMENT 1

CHAOTIC PERIOD

◀── PAST ┊ FUTURE ──▶

Figure 2.8

As an innovation moves from one market niche to another, the period of instability during the change can be observed as a period of chaos between periods of stable growth.

The idea of a chaotic phase between growth cycles is intriguing. It raises the possibility that a chaotic phase is a precursor to a more stable and predictable growth curve. It is during a chaotic phase that the forecaster's job becomes important to a company. By evaluating the innovation's characteristics, possible barriers to consumer adoption, the influence of change agents, and any self-limiting factors, the forecaster helps a company anticipate the future spread of the innovation to other consumer groups and other markets.

Theoretical models provide the forecaster with a way to structure observations, determine potential markets for the innovation, and estimate the timing when the innovation will reach new consumer segments. Analysis of diffusion in terms of the curves allows the forecaster to take a snapshot of the current situation, backcast to explain past events, and forecast future developments.

✧ Monitoring Change Agents

By monitoring the acceptance of a given style by change agents, the forecaster has a window on the innovation's level of visibility and the likelihood it will be widely accepted. But change agents are not a stable segment that can easily be targeted. A change agent may be influential regarding the performance of one role, in one product category such as activewear, or only at certain times, and a follower on other occasions (King & Ring, 1980).

By positioning new fashion innovations as consistent with the fashion leader's self-concept, designers, manufacturers, retailers, and marketers can attract the attention of these important consumers. Although they may not be the very first to adopt the innovation, leaders are early adopters who are very influential within their social groups. Followers do not monitor marketer-dominated information sources to the same degree as innovators and fashion leaders do. For the fashion follower, personal influence from a leader within the social group is much more compelling as an incentive to change.

Similar to individuals, social groups can act as fashion leaders. If a social group has a high proportion of leaders and frequent interaction with other groups, that group is more likely to export leadership to the other groups. Membership in one group may overlap another, allowing some individuals to serve as links between two or more cliques (Rogers, 1983). Understanding this between-group exchange suggests that adoption of an innovation will be enhanced if marketers target influential social groups and individuals who act as liaisons between groups.

The transfer of meaning from the cultural universe to the construction of an individual's lifestyle has implications for forecasting. As we will see in Chapter 5, celebrities function as advisors, role models, and ego ideals on two levels—as themselves in interviews and editorial coverage, and as the fictional roles they play. For innovations in which celebrity leadership is a factor, the forecaster can map celebrity influence to the consumer segment most likely to be influenced. The visibility and desirability of the celebrity image may be a determining factor in the diffusion of some innovations.

✧ The Observation Target

The idea that fashion leaders—influential individuals, social groups, celebrities, and retailers—adopt an innovation and transmit it to others provides the forecaster with an observation target. The forecaster can monitor the second stage of the diffusion process by monitoring fashion leaders. They may choose to watch for fashion leadership in particular geographic markets where innovations are most likely to be introduced and then predict the potential diffusion to other locales with an estimate of the timing. Another method is to watch for fashion leadership in a particular market segment and predict the potential diffusion of an innovation within that segment and as a crossover innovation for other segments. Forecasters may monitor the retailers who perform as change agents and estimate the path of an innovation from avant-garde retailers to more mainstream or mass-market clients (Figure 2.9). They may also watch celebrities and the looks and behaviors they are likely to popularize with a particular audience.

Figure 2.9

Collette in Paris is a popular trendspotting location for fashion-forward consumers, stylists, designers, and forecasters.

You Be the Forecaster: Influencing the Adoption Process

Lizzie is a marketing manager for a new clothing label that wants to bring fashion-forward clothing to an underserved market—women aged 35 and up. While some of the styles might at first seem too innovative for this audience, the brand uses cuts that flatter a more mature figure and easy-care fabrics that are conducive to the busy life of professional women and mothers who still want to be fashionable, so the line has the perfect level of novelty, if consumers will accept it. In order to make the brand successful, Lizzie knows she needs to get their styles into the hands of the right people and remove any reservations they may have about trying such fashion-forward apparel.

To encourage adoption of the fashion-forward styles her company produces, Lizzie has become familiar with how innovations are adopted and the things she can do to help her line be accepted by her target customer. Consider the different aspects of the adoption process and how Lizzie can use this knowledge to her advantage.

Diffusion: Who should Lizzie target for her line—innovators, opinion leaders, change agents, or all three? What distinguishes these types of consumers from one another, and how do they overlap? How might she locate these types of consumers and persuade them to try her brand?

Helping or Hindering Adoption: What are some specific actions Lizzie can implement to help her line's adoption, and remove perceived risk so that customers have a high level of embracing the new trend?

The Adoption Process: Which of the stages of adoption are the most critical for influencing consumer perception and purchase behavior?

Innovators: What types of innovators are the easiest to target for this new line? How could Lizzie target each kind of innovator?

Fashion, Fads, and Classics: What is the best strategy for an apparel line—to create fashion, fad, or classic merchandise? What are the advantages or disadvantages to each? Is it possible to have more than one strategy for the same line?

Trend Success Factors: How do concepts such as labeling, coattail, flow, memes, buzz, hype, and **contagion** impact the relative strength, speed of adoption, and duration of a trend? Can any of these factors be influenced? If so, give some examples of how Lizzie can establish them and use them to her company's advantage.

Trends even affect the profession of "trendspotting." In the late 1990s, "cool hunting" was a popular approach to identifying the next new thing. The idea was to watch the edgiest, most fashion-forward young people as an early warning system for developing trends. The problem was that trends identified in this way failed to generate much business. It was more important to track the most popular people—teens, celebrities, designers—rather than the edgiest ones because trends must click with the mainstream to generate high-volume sales (Seckler, 2002b). Today, the forecasting industry recognizes the importance of the combination of analyzing data together with instinct. On one hand, Julia Fowler, owner of fashion forecasting firm Editd, feels that "Industries like the financial sector have used big data for many years. The logical step for us was to apply a scientific approach to the apparel industry." From the other perspective, Isham Sardouk, chief creative officer at Stylesight in New York and once a design director at Victoria's Secret, feels that "Right now data is the buzzword. But for me, data is not everything. It's just a portion of the information that's out there. I think that intuition is underrated, and when people think of a trend forecaster they imagine a crazy guy in a room experiencing visions of salmon pink" (Banks, 2013).

FASHION TRENDS

An innovative look appears in the street, on the runway, or in the media thanks to a trendsetter's ability to stay ahead of current fashion, ignoring trends and yet anticipating them (Furchgott, 1998). The look has the appeal of "newness" because it has been missing or scarce in the marketplace. A trend is characterized by a building awareness of this new look and an accelerating demand among consumers (Perna, 1987). A study of fashion change shows that new looks rarely come out of the blue. Instead, fashion is a logical evolution from a precursor, the next step in building on a successful trial

balloon, a response to social change, or an expression of cultural drift.

✦ EVOLUTION OF A TREND

Lawrence Samuel, co-founder of the marketing consulting firm Iconoculture, Inc., spelled out the predictable and unpredictable stages in the evolution of a trend ("Will cigars," 1997). The three stages are:

- ❖ *Fringe*—a stage when an innovation arises and the trendiest consumers and entrepreneurial firms begin to participate.
- ❖ *Trendy*—a stage when awareness of the trend grows because early adopters join the innovators to increase the visibility of the trend and the most fashion-forward brands and retailers test the concept.
- ❖ *Mainstream*—a stage when more conservative consumers join in, visibility continues to increase, and corporations and brands capitalize on the growing demand.

One example of how the evolution of a trend occurs is through the rise in popularity of "extreme sports" and their impact on mainstream culture. Surfing, skateboarding, and snowboarding all started at the fringe of the sports world among a small group of enthusiasts. Each group evolved an identifying style and entrepreneurial firms sprang up to supply the look. When more people became aware of these sports, as participants or fans, their styles became trendy. Fashion journalists and forecasters began to identify these styles as fashion forward and some large brands began to test the looks in small collections in wide distribution. Top surf, skate, and snowboarding brands expanded their range into more classic looks as the sports gained recognition and acceptance. As one executive explained, "skateboarding sport has become so large and has such a following that anyone can find their style" (Weisman, 2008).

These sports and their characteristic styles moved from fringe to trendy to mainstream but with some interesting variations. Urban influences like hip-hop became directional for surf, skate, and snowboarding apparel and accessories—a fusing of two trends. Graphic T-shirts and hooded sweatshirts, or "hoodies," key items for skaters, were easily assimilated into mainstream fashion. But more extreme styles like pipe jeans remained niche products. Extreme-sports-influenced looks lost their prominence in the 1990s to more conservative looks with classic polo shirts and V-neck sweaters with discreet logos in the mid-2000s. At any stage, a trend can meet resistance, merge with another trend, be deflected in a way that changes the course of the trend, or fragment into **microtrends**, which may be countercultural twists on the trend, a reinvention, a **countertrend** (the opposite of the original trend), or a **backlash**—all create a new trend back at the fringe stage.

✧ Fashions, Fads, and Classics

The terms *fad* and *classic* are frequently used in discussing fashion, but they have a precise meaning. Fads have been defined in different ways:

❖ as involving fewer people, of shorter duration, and more personal than other fashion changes (Sapir, 1931);

❖ as outside historical continuity—each springing up independently with no forerunner and no successor (Blumer, 1969);

❖ as satisfying only one main need, the need for a new experience, and having little value after the newness wears off (Wasson, 1968).

Fashions are themselves of short duration when compared to long-term social changes. Fads are fashions of even shorter duration. The difference between fads, fashions, and classics can be depicted using variations on the diffusion curve (Figure 2.10). Classics are enduring styles that seem to reach a plateau of acceptance that endures for a long period of time.

Fashion and fads share many of the same characteristics. Meyersohn and Katz (1957) offer a comprehensive natural history of fads, identifying these distinctive characteristics:

❖ Fads are typically confined to particular segments in society.

❖ Unlike new social movements that create a new social structure, fads move swiftly through a subgroup but leave the subgroup itself stable.

❖ Fads offer a simple substitution for some predecessor item.

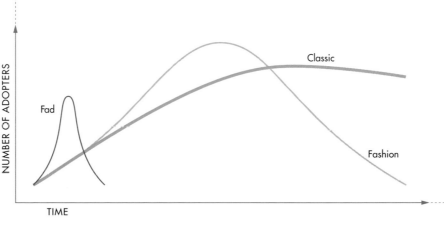

Figure 2.10

Short-lived fads versus classic clothes that stay in style for longer periods can be visualized by graphing their popularity and duration.

❖ Fads are trivial, not in terms of the emotional or functional significance of the item, but in terms of its life expectancy—a fad is susceptible to being outmoded.

Meyersohn and Katz (1957) assert that fads are not born but rediscovered from a style that existed all along in the lives of some subgroup. Likely beginning points for fads include the upper classes and bohemians because these groups represent a special kind of laboratory where experimentation can take place without threatening society as a whole. Many other observers of fashion recognize the same source for fashion ideas—the elite and the outsiders.

Innovative ideas are discovered by fashion **scouts** and moved from source to marketplace by **tastemakers**. Scouts—journalists, fashion directors, forecasters, and merchants—have the ability to recognize and transmit fads from the subgroup to the mainstream because they have a unique understanding of both. Tastemakers—celebrities, models, fashion stylists, and fashion leaders—increase the visibility of the innovation and make it acceptable to more consumers. Exporting a fad to a wider audience usually involves modifying the idea in ways that make it more acceptable to a broader audience.

The classic is a style that changes minimally over time. It remains within the acceptable range in terms of attributes offered and expenditure in terms of time and money. Classics represent midpoint compromises that deliver at least the core attributes desirable to the consumer (Wasson, 1968). Additionally, classics appeal to a special kind of personality seeking to avoid extremes in styling.

Forecasters seeking to visualize the way trends move through culture have several alternatives. The movement can be seen as an information cascade, a coattail effect, trickling, or contagion. Each alternative adds to forecasters' ability to spot and track trends.

❖ Information Cascades

Rarely do consumers make decisions in a situation in which all relevant information is available. Imitating a fashion leader is a strategy frequently used in uncertain situations. Fashion followers presume that the fashion leader has more accurate and precise information (Bikchandani, Hirshleifer, & Welch, 1992).

When an innovation is introduced and a fashion leader acts to adopt or reject the innovation, frequently others imitate the action, beginning an **information cascade** of decisions from fashion leaders to followers. Information cascades can be positive, when all individuals adopt the innovation, or negative, when all individuals reject the innovation. If these important leaders do in fact have more accurate and precise information and make a good decision initially, then the information cascade will continue. However, if that initial decision was faulty, the information cascade will be fragile and prone to fall apart. Additional information or a slight value change can shatter a cascade.

The idea of cascade reactions reinforces the disproportionate effect a few early individuals may have on the life span of an innovation. These cascade reactions explain fads, booms, and crashes, as well as other short-lived fluctuations that appear to be whimsical and without obvious external stimulus.

❖ Label, Coattail, and Flow

Of the many ideas on the runway, only a few are successfully adopted. In the first 100 years of modern fashion, adoption came from clients. Some fashion counts from that period show that only one-tenth of the designs were produced for clients (Lipovetsky, 1994). The rest were neglected, forgotten, and replaced by a new crop of proposed fashion ideas in the next season. **Gatekeepers** filter the many ideas proposed by designers and determine which will be disseminated widely and which will be discarded. The gatekeeper role initially played by clients was taken over by merchants and by the fashion press. The merchants decide which fashion ideas will be available to consumers, which will be made in small numbers, and which in volume. The fashion press defines trends by deciding which of the many ideas on the runway will be promoted in the pages of trade publications and fashion magazines.

In the past, collections could be categorized as either "editorial" (providing a hook for telling a story or creating a fantasy) or "retail" (wearable, targeted for a consumer segment). Now, the press and the merchants tend to be in sync on the looks that will be tested further in the marketplace (Socha, 1998b). Editors know that readers buy merchandise because it is featured in a magazine and that everything shown must be available at retail. Both magazines and stores cover established designers and new talents. More than ever, editors and store executives share information—key fashion stores invite editors to see what they are buying and creating in private label merchandise for a season; store fashion directors carefully analyze the press approach. Designers have to be realistic about appealing to the needs of both retailers and the press.

Once they are identified, trends must be given a label—a name or slogan that can be used as a popular identifier (Meyersohn & Katz, 1957). If the name is compatible with the spirit of the times, original, and catchy, it will speed the trend on its way. With this **labeling** comes a surge in interest in the trend. This surge of interest catches the attention of people in the industry who recognize the trend's potential and rush to produce it in their own lines. This phenomenon is called the **coattail effect** (or the bandwagon effect) during which the trend builds among the most fashion forward. Popular at first with a relatively small sphere of fashionistas, the trend will pass from group to group across social boundaries of age, income, and lifestyle—a process called **flow**.

Dior did not call his post-World War II rediscovery of close-fitting bodices, small waists, and full skirts "the New Look." A journalist used that term in a review of the designer's collection. The term stuck because it captured the spirit of that time, the radical change in silhouette that resonated with change in all aspects of life. With the labeling comes a surge in interest. Then a coattail effect begins when industry people recognize the potential of the fad and produce it and other related products. Flow results when the fad passes from group to group across social

boundary lines. If the innovation has broad appeal and staying power, the fad transforms into a fashion. With Christian Dior's post-World War II "New Look" this process took less than one year.

Jumping on the bandwagon (or catching the coattail) of a fad is tricky, but there are some guidelines for this maneuver (Reynold, 1968). Greater staying power is achieved if the innovation meets a genuine need or function, is associated with other long-term trends and concurrent trends in other industries, is compatible with the values of society, and has high visibility. The problem for designers in assessing a fad is that they may see trends where none exist—that is, their point of view tends to exaggerate the importance of fads. The problem for managers is that they may delay to the point where they miss an opportunity to participate.

Purchase decisions are the result of an approach–avoidance reaction. When the buyer sees potential satisfaction of a need, want, or aspiration in the possession of a good, then the buyer makes the purchase. If the satisfaction sought is thwarted by price, by the effort of searching, or by some compromise in product design, the purchase will not be made. Every purchase is a compromise between the attributes desired and the product that is offered.

✧ Trickling Up, Down, Across

As we will learn more about in Chapter 3, trends may trickle down from the elite, up from the streets, or across consumer segments. Tracking trend movement may require only a few points to plot a line and detect a direction. The trend may be moving up from the street through levels of consumers from the most avant-garde to the more mainstream or down from an extravagant one-of-a-kind couture creation worn by a celebrity to a **knockoff**, or copy, at the local mall. Horizontal movement occurs when more and more people progressively adopt a style as that innovation diffuses through the market segments.

The cyclical nature of fashion can be seen in the recycling of fashion ideas—such as the popularity of early 1960s dress styles in the late

2000s. Fueled partly by nostalgia among generations old enough to remember and partly by the younger generation's desire to experience the music and fashions of another era, pop culture seems to circle back, picking up speed each time (Wolcott, 1998). Looking for these movements, placing observations within a theoretical framework, and visualizing the shape and direction of the change enables forecasters to predict fashion direction and the speed of change.

✧ Contagion

The transmission of trends from person to person has been likened to the spread of a virus such as the flu. Malcolm Gladwell, a writer for *The New Yorker*, used this metaphor when he spoke to the International Design Conference about creating design trends that are "contagious"—spreading quickly through the consumer population to reach "epidemic" proportions. He urged manufacturers to aim for "sticky" looks with flu-like staying power because consumers do not want looks that quickly disappear (Feitelberg, 1998a). Authors Chip and Dan Heath (2007) extend Gladwell's ideas by identifying the key principles for turning ordinary ideas into those with "stickiness": simplicity, unexpectedness, concreteness, credibility, emotionally involving, and easily communicated through stories.

Gladwell's comments parallel the concept of **memes**—self-replicating ideas or bits of behavior that move through time and space without continuing support from their original source (Gelb, 1997; Kauffman, 1995). Memes can be advertising slogans, catchy bits of dialogue from a television show, or any concept that establishes its own repetition by appearing in many formats. The more copies of the meme, the more likely that it will replicate through time and space. A product, a look, or a brand can become a meme. The characteristics of a meme are very similar to a trend: novelty and vividness. A meme has one additional important characteristic: it must catch on in a way that favors the leaping of the meme from format to format at a rapid speed.

One example of a meme that has had widespread and enduring appeal is the "Keep Calm and Carry On" poster, one of a series of three propaganda posters commissioned by the British government to reassure its citizens during World War II. While the other two posters in the series were distributed, the one we know today never was posted during wartime. More than 50 years later, one of the unused Keep Calm and Carry On posters was found by the owner of secondhand bookshop Barter Books, and framed and put over the cash register. Customers liked it so much they began printing and selling new versions of the poster. Since then, the original poster has become recognizable to millions of people, and has been parodied with new slogans such as "Keep Calm and Eat a Cupcake." The popular lifestyle website The Chive has adopted "Keep Calm and Chive On" as its own theme, and put the slogan as well as the abbreviation "KCCO" on products such as T-shirts, swimming trunks, towels, and flip-flops.

Although memes can be anything that people recognize—everything from the McDonald's Golden Arches to Shepard Fairey's iconic "Hope" poster that gained prominence during the 2008 presidential election are examples—one particular form of meme is the Internet meme. Websites such as Meme Generator allow users to add their own captions to images such as "Condescending Willy Wonka" or "The Most Interesting Man in the World" in new and original ways that can be specific to a particular person or group, while sites such as Know Your Meme help keep track of the origin of Internet memes and how they evolve. The popularity of Vines has taken memes from photographic stills with written text to short video clips. One such popular meme is "Ryan Gosling Won't Eat His Cereal," which features short dramatic clips of actor Ryan Gosling appearing to reject a spoonful of cereal as it approaches him, to humorous effect.

Trends must be visible to possible adopters in order to spread. Trends spread through word of mouth among personal networks when one person visually or verbally recommends a new fashion to friends and acquaintances (Figure 2.11). **Buzz**—defined as excitement about something new—is created when trends

Figure 2.11

Music festivals are a good event for generating buzz about new styles, because so many of the participants have similar tastes in both music and fashion.

pass through media networks, moving from one format to another (from news magazines to talk shows, from the morning shows to late-night shows). Receiving information on a trend in this way gives the consumer a feeling of being "in the know" because of insider information from the media elite (Marin & Van Boven, 1998). Buzz lifts whatever people in the media are currently talking about to a new level of awareness. The Internet speeds up the transmission of buzz by pre-empting traditional media—that is, by breaking news about celebrities, new products, new shopping venues, upcoming movies, and other such happenings before the items can appear in traditional channels (newspapers, magazines, television, radio, and movies). As consumers rely more and more on non-traditional channels for information, **hype**—the artificially generated PR form of buzz—becomes less influential and buzz more influential for trendsetters and early adopters. Public relations (PR) executives know this and try to create buzz by planting information in "under the radar" kinds of campaigns—that is, campaigns disguised as consumer-to-consumer exchanges such as those at social networking and blog sites.

✧ Trends End

Forecasters can anticipate the life expectancy of fads by looking at a fad's "self-limiting" factors, because those are more predictive than merely visual or aesthetic considerations (Reynold, 1968). For example, take low-rise jeans—how low could they go? Five-inch rise for the young, toned consumer was moderated to eight-inch rise for more mainstream consumers. Contoured waistbands to reduce the exposure of derrière extended the look to a broader audience (Malone, 2002). Stylistic, technological, or functional modifications can lengthen the life of the fad.

Paul Poiret, a great couturier of the early twentieth century and master of fashion change, said that "all fashions end in excess"—that is, a fashion can never retreat gradually in good order but instead collapses (Robinson, 1958). Look at the craze for embellishment that recurs every few years. The idea of lace appliqué or embroidery or beading begins as a bit of novelty and ends by being a head-to-toe feature. At that point, the trend collapses in favor of less decorated or even minimal looks.

To make the jump from fashion-forward consumers to the mainstream, a trend must be modified to make it more acceptable by a large number of people. In doing so, the process sometimes dilutes the look so much that it loses its stylistic integrity. The novelty disappears, taking with it the original appeal.

In the case of a fad that has been identified and labeled, demand can become frenzied. If the coattail or bandwagon effect is too successful too fast, overproduction can result in rapid saturation of the market. The fad runs its course and collapses, leaving inventory but no buyers. Saturation can occur with any trend—when a trend moves into the mainstream and is seen widely, fashion-forward consumers have already moved on. Eventually most consumers have had a chance to see, accept, or reject the trend, and begin looking for something new.

Self-limiting factors, excess, loss of stylistic integrity, and saturation signal the end of a fad (or the longer-lived fashion) (Meyersohn & Katz, 1957). To anticipate the end, look at:

❖ *the function the fad or fashion serves.* Yogawear builds on the popularity of this form of fitness but easily translates to the lifestyles of all comfort seekers;

❖ *the fad or fashion as symbolic of the spirit of the times.* Love beads symbolized hippie times, wide-shouldered suits identified women entering the workplace, and low-rise jeans signaled a toned sexiness. When times change, so does the symbol.

Recognizing barriers to acceptance, assessing possible modifications to extend the fad, and judging the effect of those modifications on stylistic integrity are part of trend management.

✧ Trend Management

Consumers develop relationships with style, products, and brands based on habit, familiarity, and satisfaction. For a new trend to succeed, it must often replace a current purchase pattern. Managers act on both sides of the process—one set attempting to shore up the established trend with new and improved versions, the other attempting to break the old pattern and start a new one. In both cases, managers must be sensitive to consumer and media networks, understand how they work, and recognize when they must be stimulated to gain competitive advantage (Farrell, 1998).

Managerial decisions are affected by three classes of change:

❖ *Short-term variations*, such as the path of trends as they emerge, evolve, and dissipate.
❖ *Cyclical variations*, as when style features repeat over time in response to an underlying trend.
❖ *Long-term trends*, when there are fundamental and continuous changes in the pattern of culture.

Understanding how trends develop and move through society provides the perspective that managers need to shape the decision-making process.

Chapter Summary

Fashion innovations can take many forms, and whether or not they are adopted by the masses can depend on the relative advantage and the perceived risks associated with the innovation. Theories help explain how the world works, and behavioral theories such as the diffusion models by Rogers, Robertson, and Bass can help forecasters anticipate how quickly an innovation will pass from early adopters to the majority, and then ultimately be discarded. By understanding these models and related ideas such as perceived risk, forecasters don't just watch a trend disseminate through the population, they can actually help speed up its acceptance by the mainstream and even prolong its life span.

Certain people in society play a role in the introduction of trends—these mavens, influentials, tastemakers, and gatekeepers can aid a trend's popularity through visibly embracing and promoting the trend, then continually moving on to the next big thing once the majority of the population have caught on. Trends can either trickle down from the runways, up from the street, or across social groups, similar to how a virus spreads from person to person, but marketers can aid this process by encouraging buzz or hype through media. By knowing how trends spread throughout the populace, forecasters can tell when it is time to start identifying the next innovation that consumers are always looking for.

Key Terms and Concepts

Backlash	Innovation
Buzz	Innovators
Change agents	Knockoff
Coattail effect	Labeling
Compatibility	Legitimation
Complexity	Mavens
Consumer adoption process	Memes
Contagion	Microtrends
Countertrend	Observability
Diffusion curve	Opinion leaders
Diffusion process	Perceived risk
Dissonance	Popular culture
Economic risk	Positioning
Enjoyment risk	Relative advantage
Fashion leaders	S-curve
Flow	Scouts
Gatekeepers	Social risk
Hype	Tastemakers
Influentials	Trialability
Information cascade	

Discussion Questions

Introducing a new product, ways to combine apparel pieces, or sensibility about clothing is an incredibly risky and complicated business. Consumers play many different roles and have many decision points in the process. Understanding how an innovation spreads provides a framework for forecasting because it suggests what to watch and where to do the observing. Use the following questions to summarize and review this chapter.

Diffusion of Innovation: What filters do forecasters use in evaluating the potential of an innovation based on its characteristics? How does the consumer adoption process interact with the characteristics of an innovation to produce an approach or avoidance behavior? What risks does a consumer face when deciding to adopt an innovation? What is the life cycle of a fad? How does that differ from the life cycle of a fashion or a classic? Who acts as fashion change agents? What is the role of a fashion change agent?

Defining Trends: How do trends evolve and move in society? How have trends evolved to shape fashion at the beginning of the twenty-first century?

Forecasting Activities

Small Changes. Trace the evolution of the men's suit in the twentieth century. Working within a narrow band of allowable fashion change, men's suits have still displayed the influence of fashion trends on silhouette, fabric, and details. Use primary sources or publications from the time when the clothing was new. Collect examples including photographs of celebrities, newspaper ads, and offerings in mail-order catalogs. Identify the aspects of the suit that vary across time. How much variation is there between extremes? Do any aspects vary together as a recognizable pattern? Observing the details in the evolution of men's suits helps sensitize the eye to subtle variations in styles.

Naming Names. Labeling an innovation can mean the difference between rapid diffusion and failure to adopt the innovation. Forecasters are often part of the process of giving an innovation a label. A catchy name or slogan becomes part of the language and increases the visibility and desirability of a fashion product. Begin with the term "bikini" as an identifier for a two-piece swimsuit or "little black dress" for a simple, unadorned, basic black sheath. Look back in fashion history and research some of the fashion labels we take for granted. How did they originate? What effect did they have on the rate of acceptance? What labels are being applied to today's fashion innovations?

Mapping Innovation. Take a current trend such as hemlines, waistlines, necklines, color, fabric, or pattern and plot the trend on Rogers' diffusion of innovation: Who is wearing the trend right now—the innovators, early adopters, majority, late adopters, or laggards? Do this for several trends and observe the different stages they are at—what innovations do you think will replace them?

Resource Pointers

Consumer Research:

Cassandra Daily: www.cassandradaily.com

Nielsen (consumer segmentation): www.nielsen.com

The Futures Company (consumer segmentation): www.thefuturescompany.com

> I try to translate what I sense from the street.
>
> —Jean Paul Gaultier

3

THE DIRECTION OF FASHION CHANGE

OBJECTIVES

◆ Identify the directional theories of fashion change—their source, basic tenets, and predictive power

◆ Analyze current fashion within a theoretical framework

◆ Apply theoretical models as tools of analysis and communication

FASHION MOVEMENT

Even a casual trend watcher will develop the ability to identify discernable patterns. At some point in time, people begin to feel that wearing colorful clothes is unsophisticated and that black is "in." Closets fill up with neutrals until, seemingly overnight, black looks drab and monotonous. Street fashion or a runway fills up with pink and suddenly color seems fresh and inviting. Every aspect of fashion, from color to the length of skirts, the shape of the silhouette, or the placement of pockets, is in constant motion.

Anyone can pick up on a trend when it lands in their mailbox broadcasted in magazine headlines complete with an eight-page photographic spread. For the fashion professional, recognizing a trend at that stage means that it is too late to use the information for competitive advantage. Instead, fashion executives look for competitive advantage by identifying trends early. To do that, they must position themselves in the most likely spots to watch for emerging trends. With experience, a trend watcher becomes skilled at spotting the elusive and subtle shifts that signal fashion change.

Observation is not enough. If the trend watcher is to take advantage, they need a framework for explaining how the trend began and its likely path within a social system. The directional theories of fashion change make prediction easier by pointing to the likely starting points for a fashion trend, the expected direction that trend will take, and how long the trend will last.

As with fashion itself, the theories that explain fashion movement are constantly revised and refined. These theories show us the recognized patterns that have explained past fashion and can be used to arrange and order current observations. Social scientists continue to seek better explanations and to suggest new theories of fashion change. The forecaster uses these theories by matching observations with the explanation that best fits and then projecting the next stage.

Recognizing the most likely pattern of change is the first step toward prediction. Abstracting a theory into a visual representation clarifies the situation and aids in analyzing what comes next. Theoretical models help explain the concepts and communicate the logic of predictions to others.

Trend watchers move in the social world observing, categorizing what they see, and matching that to the preferences and behavior of consumers. These fashion professionals may seem to make their decisions "from their gut" in a mysteriously intuitive process. Actually, that intuitive response is the result of a highly developed sensitivity to the social environment plus the almost instant application of one of the forecasting frameworks. Experience and application of the best explanations cannot guarantee success—the situation is too complex for absolute accuracy in prediction. However, preparation and practice can improve the odds for professional trend watchers.

THE DIRECTION OF FASHION CHANGE

The three directional theories of fashion change predict that fashion will either trickle down, trickle up, or trickle across consumer segments. Introduced at different times during the twentieth century, these theories reflect not only a general understanding of fashion dynamics but also the specific marketplace conditions at the time they were proposed. Each theory has evolved since its introduction but remains a valuable guide in explaining fashion leadership and predicting fashion movement. The directional theories of fashion change help fashion professionals determine important factors such as where fashion innovations begin, who leads and who follows, how quickly a fashion moves through society, and when a style reaches the end of its popularity.

✦ TRICKLE-DOWN THEORY

At the turn of the twentieth century, a fashion observer would see that past fashion was dictated by the nobility who were leaders in all areas of fashionable behavior by birthright, rank, and wealth. Fashion spread slowly downward through the class structure but never reached all levels. The lower classes did not have the income, access, or freedom to follow fashion's dictates. Looking around at their own time, the observer notices that fashion is still restricted to those at the top of the class structure—the rich and socially prominent. The Industrial

Revolution made possible the building of great fortunes and the display of wealth through fashionable possessions including homes, furnishings, art, and handcrafted fashion. This period, roughly 1900 to 1914, is known as *la Belle Époque* in France, the Edwardian period in England, and the Gilded Age in America. It was characterized by women wearing extravagant, elaborate fashions that required devotion, attention, and seriousness at both the acquisition stage and in wearing the clothes in everyday life.

Economist Thorstein Veblen (1899) was one such observer at the turn of the twentieth century. He described the upper level of the social system as the leisure class. Members of the leisure class displayed wealth in two distinctive ways, through **conspicuous leisure** and **conspicuous consumption**. A person who does not have to work for a living and participates in an extravagant lifestyle of travel, entertainment, and the pursuit of pleasure demonstrates conspicuous leisure. Philanthropy, art collecting, acquisition of homes and furnishings, and wearing haute couture garments demonstrate conspicuous consumption. In both these models, wealth serves as the background for the activities that were the hallmark of the times.

✧ The Origins of the Theory

Explaining fashion movement in such an era is relatively easy: fashion moves downward from the elite class to the lower classes in stately and slow progression. But the explanation is not complete until it explains not only what happens but why. Georg Simmel (1904), a sociologist, identified the engine of fashion change in the opposing human tendencies toward conformity (fitting in) and individuality (standing out). As J. C. Flugel said, "the paradox of fashion is that everyone is trying at the same time to be like, and to be unlike, his fellow-men." No aspect of life can satisfy the demands of these two opposing principles, but social life and fashion offer a perfect battleground where striving for social adaptation and the need for differentiation can be played out.

These dual tendencies can be displayed when one person's style is toward imitation and another's is toward differentiation. The imitator believes in social similarity, in acting like others. The individual seeking differentiation constantly experiments with the new, relying in large part on personal convictions. These dual drives can also function in social groups where fashion simultaneously functions as a means of class distinction and as a badge of group uniformity.

Simmel observed three stages: (1) the elite class differentiated itself through fashion; (2) the adjacent lower classes imitated the look; and (3) the elite class moved to adopt a new fashion in an attempt to maintain the differentiation. These stages occur in social forms, apparel, aesthetic judgment, and the whole style of human expression—a view that expands consideration of fashion change from simply apparel to a broader range of activities and behaviors.

Because the motivation to both fit in and stand out simultaneously can never fully or finally be gratified, fashion change is inevitable for the individual and for the social group. Simmel explained that the distinctiveness afforded by newness in the early stages of a fashion is destroyed by its spread to imitators until the fashion wanes and dies. Simmel concluded that the charm of fashion lay in its novelty coupled with its transitory nature.

The views of Veblen and Simmel form the framework for the **trickle-down theory** of fashion change. The theory identified:

❖ the source of fashion ideas—designers who catered to wealthy clients with a taste for conspicuous consumption and the leisure to pursue fashion;
❖ the fashion leaders—those fashionable and highly visible individuals who served as models for the new looks;
❖ the direction of fashion change—downward from the elite class to the next adjacent class;
❖ the speed of change—regulated by the ability of the lower classes to see, obtain, and copy the fashion;
❖ the dynamics of change—the pursuit of the dual drives for differentiation and imitation.

✧ Evolution of the Theory

Fashion observers in the latter half of the twentieth century have criticized the trickle-down theory as being flawed. The chief criticism is that the elite did not consistently set prevailing styles any time after the introduction of mass production and mass communication (Banner, 1983; Blumer, 1969; Lowe & Lowe, 1984). McCracken (1988a) points out that the theory oversimplifies the social system. Instead of just two or three social classes with the elite at the top, the social system actually has many social classes simultaneously engaged in differentiation and imitation.

McCracken also questioned characterizing the process as trickle down, because the impetus for change comes from the subordinate classes as they hunt for the status markers of the upper class. He proposed replacing trickle down with **chase and flight**—chase because fashion change was driven by the imitators who chased the status markers of the elite in a drive toward upward social mobility; flight because the elite responded to imitation by flying away toward new forms of differentiation. Although this new characterization neatly captures the dynamics of the process, the phrase did not catch on with fashion writers, who still use the earlier trickle-down theory.

Along with the criticism came some proposed revisions to the theory. Dorothy Behling (1985 / 1986) identified a new, highly visible upper class made up of those occupying power positions in business, politics, and media. As she points out, "they are Veblen's new conspicuous consumer … from whom, under particular circumstances, fashion trickles down."

François Simon-Miller (1985) pointed out that the fashionable elite in the latter half of the twentieth century practiced a kind of status denial—people with the wealth and status to wear anything they wished chose to dress down. Instead of conspicuous consumption, this variation was called **reverse ostentation** or **conspicuous counter-consumption**, but it served the same purpose—differentiation. Dressing down by the fashionable elite became news in 1993 when magazines lambasted

Profile: ABS by Allen Schwartz

When Thorstein Veblen established his trickle-down theory over a hundred years ago, he stated that fashion was established by members of the elite class, but he could have no way of knowing the impact that celebrities hold today as style icons. And to see this effect at its most powerful, one needs look no further than the Academy Awards. According to Hal Rubenstein, *InStyle* magazine editor at large, an Oscar nominee doesn't "look good because they're wearing Oscar [de la Renta]. They look good because of a certain detail. Those are the elements that become influential to the consumer. Then the consumer takes it to a shop in their price point and finds some resonance" (Barker, 2013). Examples of Oscar gowns that had a major sway over popular fashion include Gwyneth Paltrow's 1999 pink Ralph Lauren dress that she wore when she received her Best Actress Award for *Shakespeare in Love*, Halle Berry's 2002 burgundy Elie Saab dress that she wore when she won Best Actress for her role in *Monster's Ball*, and Cate Blanchett's 2005 pale yellow silk taffeta Valentino gown that she wore when she won Best Supporting Actress for *The Aviator*. Gowns such as these influence what is popular in eveningwear color, silhouette, and embellishment for seasons after they are worn.

Trickle-down theory is such a well-established concept that it is not surprising that some very successful companies are dedicated to fulfilling this need. Founded in 1982 as a partnership between designer Allen Schwartz and former Guess, Inc. executive Armand Marciano, ABS by Allen Schwartz was founded when "I was watching the red carpet and got into the dress business. I'm a sportswear guy. I starting thumbing through photos of these $4,000 to $5,000 dresses that no one could afford to wear. So I started making and selling these affordable dresses. Oprah saw the dresses, *Entertainment Tonight* featured them. It's what I became known for" (Liddane, 2013).

Because trademark protection in the United States only extends to logos, brand names, and distinctive patterns such as Burberry's signature check, it is completely legal for the brand to produce such reinterpretations. Schwartz views his company as filling a niche for people who want high fashion but don't have the funds to afford designer gowns. "My job is to bring trends to the consumer at a fair market price. Few people can spend $4,000 on a dress" (Winograd & Tan, 2006). He does not listen to critics' charges that he is stealing designs from other designers. "That's ridiculous. Everyone's inspiration comes from somewhere. And remember, I am not trying to do exact copies. I'm interpreting their designs to meet the demand of my customer. The fashion industry [is] just upset that I can do it so quickly" (Redding, 1999).

For example, when reinterpreting Paltrow's pink Ralph Lauren gown, he knew that it would not work for his customer exactly how it was shown on the runway. "It looks prettier in a frostier shade of pink—with more white in it" (Redding, 1999). In order to retail the dress for a customer-friendly price of $290, the taffeta fabrication was still used, but rather than making it in silk, ABS used a rayon fiber. After the awards on Sunday night, four pattern makers started developing the dress on Monday morning. One week later the finished dresses were in the ABS showroom and retailer buyers were already placing orders (Redding, 1999).

But a celebrity alone will not guarantee that a dress will become a big hit with the masses. "It's less about, 'Ooh, I want that dress from X celeb,' and more about the vibe," according to

Seventeen fashion director Gina Kelly (Barker, 2013). Schwartz understands this and chooses which designs his company will reproduce accordingly. "We're looking for who really looks pretty. But also a dress that is wearable, that is forgiving. We think about a broader audience. Not everyone looks like J.Lo!" (Marinelli, 2010).

Because of his success in spotting which gowns will be in demand, Schwartz has earned himself the name "Master of the Trend." Mark Roberts, eveningwear buyer at Bloomingdale's, says, "A lot of people can produce quickly. But the real talent is knowing what to produce. Allen has the ability to recognize what women will want, and then jump on the trend faster than anyone else. He reacts to what is going on in the market at that time—in terms of color and silhouette, and the price point is excellent" (Redding, 1999).

The revelation of which Oscar gowns ABS will interpret has become news itself. For the 2010 Oscars, Schwartz announced that ABS would reinterpret five gowns from the red carpet: Cameron Diaz's Oscar de la Renta, Jennifer Lopez's Armani Prive, Sandra Bullock's Marchesa, Kate Winslet's Yves Saint Laurent, and Penelope Cruz's Donna Karan, saying "They all looked amazing." Schwartz's teams finished their reinterpretations of the dresses less than 48 hours after the awards show, and the dresses were anticipated to be in stores by May, less than 3 months after they were first seen by the public and just in time for prom season. Unlike the originals, they would retail at $200–$345 instead of the $20,000–$30,000 price tag of the originals (Marinelli, 2010). Schwartz does not see consumers' desire to wear replicas of Oscar dresses changing anytime soon. "Who doesn't want to look like a movie star?" (Redding, 1999).

Sources:

"About Us." ABS: http://www.absstyle.com/about-us.

Barker, Olivia (2013, February 22). Style details spill over from the red carpet. *USA Today*. Retrieved from http://www.usatoday.com/story/life/people/2013/02/20/oscar-dress-influence-kim-basinger-jennifer-lawrence/1930213/.

Liddane, Lisa (2013, December 13). A chat with designer Allen Schwartz. Orange County Register. http://www.ocregister.com/articles/abs-594711-stores-dresses.html?page=1.

Marinelli, Jill (2010). Allen Schwartz of ABS announces his Oscar picks! http://jmstylist.com/2010/03/08/allen-schwartz-of-a-b-s-announces-his-oscar-picks/.

http://www.racked.com/archives/2011/05/02/abs-allen-schwartz-knocks-off-kate-middletons-mcqueen-dress.php.

Redding, Marie (1999, April 1). Knockout knockoffs rip-offs of Oscar night dresses are bound to become best sellers. http://www.nydailynews.com/archives/lifestyle/knockout-knock-offs-rip-offs-oscar-night-best-dresses-bound-best-sellers-article-1.838980.

Winograd, Ben, & Tan, Cheryl Lu-Lien (2006, September 11). Can fashion be copyrighted? *The Wall Street Journal*. Retrieved from http://online.wsj.com/articles/SB115793222354058948.

celebrities about "style-free" dressing in shapeless T-shirts and denim, thrift shop finds, and "farm-wife dresses." As one actress put it, when you see people with real power dressing down, it must be the thing to do.

Interestingly, Simmel (1904) described the same phenomenon in his time. He characterized two distinctive fashion types:

❖ The fashion victims in whom "the social demands of fashion appear exaggerated to such a degree that they completely assume an individualistic and peculiar character."

❖ The anti-fashion individual, whose "conscious neglect of fashion represents similar imitation, but under an inverse sign."

In both these types Simmel saw a commonality—both types are paying homage to the power of fashion, one in the form of exaggeration, the other by consciously attempting to ignore it. Simmel said that both these types exhibit a "tendency toward individual conspicuousness."

More recently, economists have used seeking status as the basis for explaining fashion change. Wolfgang Pesendorfer (1995, 2004, 2005) sees fashion as having no intrinsic value other than its power to signal status. High-status items remain "in" only so long as their signal strength is strong. Pesendorfer's novel contribution is to point out the active role of manufacturers and retailers who manipulate the price (either to maintain the high status with high prices or to take advantage of weakening strength by lowering prices to increase sales to wider audiences) and who time the introduction of new high-status items. Phillip Coelho and James McClure (1993) emphasized that fashion professionals recognize status-seeking behavior and use "prestige pricing" to create "snob" appeal for a product. Paul Fritjers (1998) did not place the power to create high-status goods in the hands of the producer but instead in the status seeker. Not every high-priced, limited-production item becomes a status symbol—only those selected by the wealthy, fashion-forward consumer. That buyer selects those items likely to maintain a high price and power as a status symbol for some time in the future. Like others seeking to explain the trickle-down movement of fashion, these theorists see desire for conspicuousness as expressed in status symbols as the beginning and widespread availability as the end of an item's life cycle.

✧ How Forecasters Use the Trickle-Down Theory

The trickle-down theory underscores the self-perpetuating cycle based on people's basic human tendencies toward imitation and differentiation. Can the trickle-down theory of fashion movement be useful to a fashion forecaster today? People's motivations to participate in fashion remain essentially the same no matter the century. People still feel pressure to adapt to their place in society's structure and to the rules of their narrower circle, while simultaneously seeking to affirm their individuality. And the field of fashion is still an excellent battleground for these two opposing tendencies to be played out.

✧ Status Symbols: "In" or "Out"?

Veblen's observations about the need that some people have for conspicuous consumption continues to be part of the fashion picture even if this is more prominent in some decades than in others. Conspicuous consumption was "in" when yuppies were ascendant in the 1980s, but a stock crash late in the decade ushered in a period that shunned ostentation during the popularity of the Grunge movement in the early 1990s. By mid-decade consumers were once again in the mood to treat themselves to status symbols. That feeling ended with a downturn in the economy that coincided with the national trauma of 9/11 (Bird, 1995; Seckler, 2002a). The economy rebounded for a time, but by the mid-2000s high energy costs and slipping home prices once again sent the economy reeling. Fashion responded with "the reassurance trend," defined as classic styles and appropriateness, and consumers became careful spenders (Beckett, 2007).

The accessory category is most immune to the ups and downs of the economy. Shoppers can be segmented into true luxury shoppers who shop exclusively for name brands in upscale stores, aspirational shoppers who seek status by buying a piece of a designer label, and the brand-centric who, like trophy hunters, buy a particular brand wherever they find it (Daswani, 2008). But dropping consumer confidence can reduce the appeal of even status handbags—those with designer labels, recognizable styling, and prices around $1,000. In a down economy even luxury shoppers feel "It bag" fatigue (Wilson, 2007e). The desire for status symbols follows the cyclical nature of the economy and brands that are strong in one upturn may not be preferred in the next.

✧ The Shifting Power of Status Markers

The theory predicts that status markers can lose power when they become too available to all consumers. Take, for example, the Van Cleef & Arpels Alhambra line—quatrefoil, clover-shaped charms introduced in the 1960s but not discovered and popularized by celebrities until the early 2000s. Original earrings retail for $1,200, but necklaces with diamond-covered clovers can sell for over $60,000. Attempting to stave off saturation of the market, Van Cleef extended the line by combining large and small clovers and by adding heart, leaf, and butterfly shapes. But by the mid-2000s, knockoffs of the designs appeared in stores and online for as little as $50. To each woman, the clovers are a badge of status and inclusion, but when that badge is seen on celebrities and in the street, real and fake, ubiquity becomes the kiss of death (Kuczynski, 2007).

✧ Quality Issues in Conspicuous Consumption

Nystrom (1928) constructed a business rule based on Veblen's ideas: "to succeed as a fashion, [a style] must have qualities that advertise either conspicuous leisure or conspicuous consumption for the user." He also elaborated on the description of those exercising fashion leadership to include not only people with wealth and the power to use it but also those who know how to use it artistically and recognize this artistic ability in others. These extensions of Veblen's ideas provide the fashion forecaster with more specification in applying the ideas of the trickle-down theory to observations of today's marketplace.

Fashion leadership is tied to more than price; it is about taste and quality. To uninterested consumers, the $99 "It bag" knockoff is indistinguishable from the $1,000 original. To buyers with more discriminating tastes, the workmanship, quality of the leather, findings, and finishes on the expensive bag make it authentic and worth the price. Just as some buyers appreciate the beauty and heft of a gold Alhambra necklace at $12,900, others are content with having the look in yellow gold-plated metal for $50. After the style is usurped by those without the ability to recognize the artistry, the style then becomes less appealing to the connoisseurs who were early adopters of the look (Agins, 1994).

✧ Groups Worth Watching

There are two problems for the fashion forecaster in applying the trickle-down theory to today's society: (1) the increase in the number of social classes in the social system since the theory was first proposed; and (2) the difficulty in identifying the elite. Simmel's formulation specified only two social classes—an elite striving for differentiation, and a lower class imitating that elite. The twentieth century has produced a rising standard of living for many more people and stratified society into many more social classes than in Simmel's day. Each of these classes undertakes fashion change for the purposes of imitation and differentiation (McCracken, 1988a). The result is a much more complex dynamic. The upper class is concerned only with differentiation, the lowest class only with imitation, but the middle classes simultaneously imitate the class above and seek differentiation from the class below. McCracken sees this complexity as raising additional questions, such as: Are some groups more imitative than others are? Are there aggressively imitative groups that move so fast that differentiation is not a concern? Are some groups more concerned with differentiation? Are some groups so concerned about differentiation that they create fashion rather than imitate a higher-level group?

At first McCracken's questions seem to complicate the forecaster's job because it seems logical that a system with several social classes requires more monitoring than a simpler one. However, identifying groups most likely to generate fashion change actually directs the forecaster's attention and narrows the job of monitoring the system. Because the forecaster cannot watch every social class, they watch instead for instabilities where fashion activity is intense and fast-paced.

✧ Fast-Paced Differentiation

Fast-paced groups are more likely to feed the system with fashion change because they are most concerned with using fashion for differentiation. They may be the elite, high-status group in a particular stratum of the society or part of the new visible elite highlighted by media attention. As a group, these fashion innovators are likely to create ripples through surrounding groups, setting off a chain of fashion changes.

Take, for example, the niche "upscale streetwear" that appeals to "style-conscious young men with an aversion to mall culture." Looking for self-expression and self-invention through distinctive styling, hard-to-replicate details, quality construction, and trends with a short life span, they hunt for little-known labels in trendy stores, alternative magazines, fashion blogs, and specially targeted websites. In this world, "talk of coveted new merchandise races like a current" through the network. Much of the payoff comes from "owning something you had to hunt down." For this group of fashion devotees, exclusivity and scarcity is the key: "We all know what Ralph Lauren does, what Tommy Hilfiger does. What we want is an artist's piece" (La Ferla, 2006).

✧ Aggressive Imitation

Although some groups specialize in rapid style differentiation, feeding ideas into the fashion system, of equal interest to the fashion forecaster are the fast-moving imitative groups. Some teens and young adult groups imitate sports figures or other fashion icons, rapidly picking up on fashion looks or product identification and just as rapidly moving on to the next big thing. In such groups, fashion interest is high. Individuals are highly sensitive to the symbolic nuances of products, use them artistically, and recognize their artistic use by others. Groups that adopt these same looks after they have been discarded by the fast-moving imitative groups are much less likely to be as sensitive to the details.

✧ Fashion and Social Instability

Fashion exists where there is "fluidity" in the social system (Flugel, 1930). Susan Kaiser (1990) suggested updating the theory by examining the underlying instabilities that exist in society. She identified the source of these instabilities in tensions among cultural categories, specifically in areas of gender, ethnicity, age, and attractiveness.

Gender

Androgyny, gender bending, and gender blending have been potent sources for fashion. From the pants-wearing athleticism of Amelia Earhart in the 1930s to the gender ambiguity of a movie and now Broadway play like *Kinky Boots* (2005), the line between masculine and feminine in fashion has blurred. In 2011, gender bending was at the center of fashion week when model Andrej Pejic, a Bosnian-born model who had already found success modeling menswear became a sensation modeling women's wear at the Paris couture shows, even wearing a wedding dress for Jean Paul Gaultier, then going on to model women's wear at the London shows for designers such as Vivienne Westwood (Figure 3.1).

Harriet Quick, *Vogue* fashion features director, believes the appeal of Pejic (who in July 2014 announced that he had undergone sex reassignment surgery and had transitioned to a female named Andreja) goes deeper than his beautiful looks. "For the past decade, fashion has concentrated on the alpha male and alpha female stereotype. Now it's all about questioning

Figure 3.1

Model Andreja Pejic's androgynous appearance made her a popular model for both menswear and women's wear.

sexuality and blurring the boundaries. Andrej is reflecting our times—he's what's out there; he's reflecting culture. It's the same look we're now seeing in music and with teenagers and twentysomethings on the street. He makes people open their eyes; makes them question how one presents one's image. It's attention-grabbing—it's all about looking twice and asking questions. How? Why? And a good fashion image should hold your attention" (Haché, 2014; Williamson, 2011).

Ethnicity

Although the debate about the salability of fashion magazines that feature African-American models seems dated, the controversy arose again in 2008 when the July issue of Italian *Vogue* reversed the general pattern and used only black models. Steven Meisel, the photographer, cast the approximately 100 pages of photographs

using well-known faces from earlier fashion eras (Pat Cleveland, Naomi Campbell, Tyra Banks) and current models. The editor, Franca Sozzani, who has steered the magazine toward coverage of art and ideas, said she was aware that the lack of diversity on runways and in magazines had created a debate within the industry (Horyn, 2008). At the same time, runways, advertising campaigns, and editorial pages of fashion magazines featured a wide range of models from other ethnic groups.

Fashion designer Rick Owens made headlines with his spring 2014 fashion show, which featured choreographed step shows featuring black step dancers from four black colleges (Figure 3.2). The show was universally well received for both its racial diversity and use of real, full-figured women to show the line, and the designer was recognized for his innovativeness by the Design Museum in London ("Rick Owens Paris", 2013).

Age

With the aging of a large generational cohort, the baby boomers, definitions of attractiveness as they relate to age will be more open to redefinition than in previous decades. Brands use celebrities in their forties, fifties, and sixties as spokeswomen in ads, sometimes replacing faces in their twenties. Michael Kors explained that the fashion ideal didn't resonate with the real women who buy clothes—"the simple truth is, financially, you will have more customers who are over forty," and the market can't ignore a large demographic group with high discretionary income (Karimzadeh, 2006).

American Apparel caused a stir in February 2014 by using 62-year-old model Jacky O'Shaughnessy as a lingerie model on its official Facebook page with the tagline "sexy has no expiration date." O'Shaughnessy had previously modeled clothing for the brand, but this was the first time she had appeared in underwear. Response to the photo was very positive (Figure 3.3).

Attractiveness

Women with exaggerated features and idiosyncratic styles who would not previously

Figure 3.2

In spring 2014, Rick Owen's fashion show was praised for bringing diversity of ethnicity to the runways.

Figure 3.3

62-year-old model Jacky O'Shaughnessy's American Apparel ads redefined attractiveness for many viewers.

have been considered attractive enough for modeling assignments achieved prominence. Billed as edgy and modern, these models became symbols in a time of multiculturalism. Models and actresses were also breaking other stereotypes of attractiveness such as thinness. Thinness itself became a global controversy in the mid-2000s. Reacting to criticism about the use of ultra-thin models, the fashion industry began setting guidelines based on body mass index that excluded some models from the runway (Jones, 2007b). On the other end of the scale, Steven Meisel cast a full-figure model in the all-black Italian *Vogue* issue, saying, "What's the deal with her? She's great and she's sexy" (Horyn, 2008).

Just as the instability of a more rigid class structure and the quest of lower classes for upward mobility led to the dynamics observed by Veblen and Simmel at the turn of the twentieth century, cultural instabilities surrounding gender, ethnicity, age, and attractiveness fuel fashion change today. Simmel's engine of fashion change—imitation and differentiation—is still at work in the twenty-first century as it was at the beginning of the twentieth century.

✧ Linking the Visible Elite to a Target Audience

There is no longer a single source of fashion leadership even among the fashionable elite. Instead, there are many highly visible public figures, some using the strategy of conspicuous consumption, some using conspicuous counter-consumption. The fashion forecaster can use this phenomenon to their advantage by linking particular celebrity cohorts with the audience most likely to admire their style and imitate at least some of their characteristics.

A few celebrities, such as Sarah Jessica Parker, are perennial favorites appealing to a broad audience. Many are influential only for a short time, depending on their current roles. Some celebrities are influential to only a niche market that, although smaller, may be termed a desirable demographic. Buyers in their teens and twenties are considered desirable demographics because they are at an acquisitive stage in life with discretionary dollars to spend. Today's fashion forecaster has to be smart about segmenting celebrity influence, monitoring it for fashion direction, and mapping its impact on consumers.

✧ Applying the Theory in Today's Marketplace

The real predictive power in a theory derives from its ability to clearly establish the source, the mechanism, the tempo, and the direction of fashion change. The trickle-down theory (Figure 3.4) provides the fashion forecaster with a system for identifying the next new thing and a paradigm for mapping out the direction and speed of fashion change. The system involves identifying and monitoring:

- ❖ the visible elite;
- ❖ the status markers most likely to be imitated;
- ❖ the consumer segments most likely to imitate;
- ❖ the feeder groups for fashion ideas—that is, groups so concerned about differentiation that they create fashion rather than imitate a higher-level group;
- ❖ the aggressively imitative groups moving so fast through looks that differentiation is not a concern because others often imitate these groups;
- ❖ the instabilities in the social system in terms of economic conditions, gender, ethnicity, age, and attractiveness.

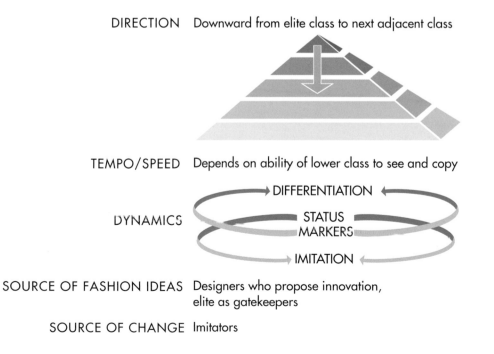

DIRECTION Downward from elite class to next adjacent class

TEMPO/SPEED Depends on ability of lower class to see and copy

DYNAMICS DIFFERENTIATION · STATUS MARKERS · IMITATION

SOURCE OF FASHION IDEAS Designers who propose innovation, elite as gatekeepers

SOURCE OF CHANGE Imitators

Figure 3.4

Trickle-down theory of fashion change.

Step one is observation: identifying potential fashion change. Step two is analysis: mapping the potential change to consumer segments most likely to adapt the change to their own fashion purpose. The paradigm calls for imitation to begin in adjacent groups and spread from group to group. The speed of change can be inferred from the power of the elite and the desirability and visibility of the status marker to the imitating group.

The environment is a complex one, but the trickle-down theory of fashion change helps the forecaster visualize the interactions. By tracking the new fashionable elite, feeder groups for fashion ideas, and aggressively imitative groups, the forecaster becomes sensitized to the ways fashion trickles down in today's marketplace.

✦ TRICKLE-ACROSS THEORY

A fashion observer in the early 1960s would see that nearly every characteristic of *la Belle Époque* had changed. Women gained the vote in 1920 and now have more access to education and the world of work than ever before. The United States fought two world wars, weathered the Great Depression of the late 1920s and 1930s, and fought to a standstill in the Korean conflict. In the early 1960s, the United States is involved in a civil war in a far-off place called Vietnam. Civil rights and integration are social issues being dealt with in the courts and in the streets. Mass communication has come of age. Television is a potent influence on the behavior of American consumers. The great development era of department stores has ended, but the stores and other retail outlets have expanded the fashion market. Mass production has matured and provides fashion apparel at all price points.

For the first few years of the 1960s, the trickle-down theory of fashion change seemed as relevant as ever. John F. Kennedy was in the White House and his wife, Jacqueline, born into the affluent upper class, was an international style setter. Jacqueline Kennedy wore clothing from American and European designers and her hairstyles, clothing, and accessories were widely copied by American women in all classes. With

President Kennedy's assassination in late November of 1963, that era came to an end. Jacqueline Kennedy would continue to be a style setter, but not on the same scale as during those early White House years.

Looking backward at the previous decades, a fashion observer would remember that fashion in the 1920s through the 1950s had an authoritarian flavor—one or two looks were considered fashionable and all other looks were not. In the late 1950s, the youth culture began to be felt and the teenager had been discovered as a market segment. With the baby boom generation in its teen years, there was a shift away from traditional forms and establishment dictates. The original form of the trickle-down theory of fashion change did not provide sufficient explanations for the fashions of the 1960s. Charles King (1963) said this in an article titled "A Rebuttal to the 'Trickle Down' Theory." He argued that society had changed in profound ways including:

* the "leveling influences" that had changed the profile of the consumer market;
* the accelerating spread of fashion awareness brought on by mass media;
* the accelerated transitions from season to season, resulting in almost nonexistent time lags such as those required for imitation and differentiation under the trickle-down theory.

King contended that the trickle-down theory of fashion change did not help the sophisticated marketer understand fashion behavior in the 1960s. Instead, he proposed a rival theory, the **trickle-across theory** of fashion change (also called the **mass market** or **simultaneous adoption theory**). Simply stated, the theory holds that fashion information trickles across horizontally *within* a social class rather than vertically *across* a class (Figure 3.5). According to King, within a given fashion season, consumers in all socioeconomic groups simultaneously have the freedom to select from a range of styles, and this range is sufficient to satisfy personal taste. Rather than an elite introducing fashion ideas

DIRECTION   Horizontal across strata

TEMPO/SPEED   Rapid and simultaneous

DYNAMICS   FASHION   MASS MEDIA   ALL
IDEAS   MARKET
LEVELS

SOURCE OF FASHION IDEAS   Couture with selection by professional gatekeepers

SOURCE OF CHANGE   Innovators and influentials in each market strata

Figure 3.5

The trickle across theory of fashion change.

into society, King saw leadership within each social stratum and within each social group. In this view, personal influence plays the key role in the transmission of fashion information and two kinds of consumers are influential in popularizing new looks:

❖ The *innovators*—people who buy early, the earliest visual communicators of a season's styles.

❖ The *influentials*—those who are frequently asked for advice and define appropriate standards within their interpersonal networks.

Three factors were essential for the emergence of a mass market: mass communication, mass production, and a growing middle class. Mass communication—in the form of magazines, newspapers, television, and movies—made style information available to all simultaneously. Mass production made more looks available in any given season, offering the possibility of individual selection from among the many resources. Imitation and differentiation were still part of the dynamic because others would imitate innovators and influentials within their social strata and those fashion leaders would move to new looks.

Just as in the trickle-down theory of fashion change, designers play an important creative role. However, the gatekeepers had changed. In the trickle-down theory of fashion change, the gatekeepers were the fashionable and affluent elite who could afford the time and effort to view and select from the designers' collections. With mass media and mass production, a new set of gatekeepers rose to prominence— journalists, manufacturers, and retailers. The professional gatekeeper's job was to view the designers' collections and select the styles to be featured in the media and produced in mass quantities (Figure 3.6).

The efficiency of mass production now enabled fashion ideas to be "knocked off" at all market levels within the same season, but that was not a new idea. In 1931, *Life* magazine reported on copies of the "Wally" dress, the $250 Mainbocher wedding ensemble worn by Mrs. Wallis Warfield Simpson when she married the Duke of Windsor (Figure 3.7). The dress appeared as a sketch in *Women's Wear Daily* on May 26 and by June 13 was available in the upscale Bonwit Teller store on New York's Fifth Avenue for $25. By early July it was featured in the window of a more moderately priced department store for $16.95. One week later, it was on the racks of a cash-and-carry store for

Figure 3.6

The press and buyers are the gatekeepers in a mass-production fashion system because they decide which looks are made available to the public at all price points.

Figure 3.7

The "Wally" dress, a $250 Mainbocher design worn by the Duchess of Windsor at her wedding, was quickly knocked off at lower price points.

$8.90 ("The descent," 1931). History repeated itself some 80 years later when Banana Republic released its own interpretation of the famous Issa London dress that Kate Middleton wore in her 2011 engagement photos (Figure 3.8). However, this time the fashion industry has now adapted to the idea knockoff, and the Banana Republic dress was part of a 2013 collaboration with Issa London, who essentially knocked off their own dress. While the original Issa London dress sold in the US for around $615, the price of the Banana Republic version was just $130 ("We tried", 2013).

By 1960, the knockoff had become the normal way to do business in the fashion industry. The practice began in earnest after World War II when discounters like Ohrbach's purchased couture fashions at a prearranged price and made line-for-line copies in the exact fabric, even advertising them with the name of the original couture house. The practice of copying became a common practice within the industry. Communication and production technology continued to speed up the process until, by the 1990s, manufacturers could pre-empt designers by making a sample of a dress shown on the

Figure 3.8

The $615 Issa London dress that Kate Middleton wore in her engagement photos exemplified the changing times when Issa collaborated with Banana Republic to produce a $130 reinterpreted dress.

runway overnight and deliver it to the stores 10 days later, a feat that the designers could not duplicate (Betts, 1994). Under these conditions, the trickle-across theory seems the ideal explanation of fashion change.

✧ Evolution of the Theory

One principle of the trickle-across theory is that mass communication and mass production sped up the process so much that time lags between introduction at the highest price points and availability at the lower price points practically disappeared. But is that how the process actually plays out?

Behling (1985/1986) agrees with King that design piracy or knockoffs play an important part in today's fashion system. But she disagrees that this process occurs with the speed suggested by King's theory, which depends on fashion looks being simultaneously available at all levels of the marketplace. Instead, she identifies a time lag of at least a year between the point when the style has been identified through a trickle-down process, is manufactured and stocked by the retailer, and when it becomes available for purchase by the majority of consumers.

Behling attributes some of this time lag to the unwillingness of consumers at all levels to adopt the new look. What may seem the inevitable next step in fashion change to fashion insiders may not be accepted readily in another social setting. It often takes time for the consumer to build a comfort level with a proposed fashion, taking into account the mores of a particular locality or social group. For example, models who wore actual lingerie slips as dresses introduced the slip dress of 1994. Picked up by designers as a trend, it traveled from the runways to the editorial pages of fashion magazines to stores and to the more avant-garde consumers (Betts, 1994). But it continued to appear on the runways for several years as acceptance of the look grew across consumer segments. Behling was making her points before the time of fast-fashion stores like Zara, H&M, Forever 21, Mango, and Mexx. These chains offer of-the-moment trends, runway-inspired styles, and prices that make clothing disposable when the trend passes. The fast-fashion chains are much nearer the ideal envisioned in the trickle-across theory because of their speed to market, rapid turnover of merchandise, and masterful use of mass communications and mass-production techniques.

Although it is undeniable that mass communication and mass production sped up the process of moving fashion ideas from the runway to the store, Behling points out exceptions to the functioning of the theory. Fashion change does not depend merely on mechanical and technological expertise. The speed of fashion change is regulated by the willingness of people to accept that change in numbers sufficient to make it profitable.

✧ How Forecasters Use the Trickle-Across Theory

The trickle-across theory of fashion change operates in an environment where designers propose fashion and gatekeepers such as journalists, manufacturers, and retailers determine which looks are reproduced in quantity at all price points. By providing a wide variety of looks at all price points simultaneously, the industry provides customers with the means to differentiate themselves from others through individual selection and the means to demonstrate group membership. Although the fashionable elite are still influential through mass communication, the key element in acceptance of a new look lies within the personal network and through the influence of innovators and influentials.

The real predictive power in a theory derives from its ability to clearly establish the source, the mechanism, the tempo, and the direction of fashion change. As in the trickle-down theory, the trickle-across theory of fashion change provides the fashion forecaster with a system for identifying the next new thing and a paradigm for mapping out the direction and speed of the fashion change. The system involves monitoring the interaction of designers' introductions of fashion ideas; the response of journalists, manufacturers, and retailers; and the acceptance or rejection reaction of consumers in different market segments. By being sensitive to the time lag inherent in the consumer acceptance of a new fashion, the fashion forecaster can predict when different market segments are most likely to move from awareness of a proposed fashion to interest in that fashion, to trying the look on, to purchase and repurchase.

✦ TRICKLE-UP THEORY

A fashion observer in the late 1960s would see that the focus is not on the apparel industry as in the trickle-across theory, but that fashion change comes from a new source of inspiration and fashion leadership. "Youthquake" is under way on both sides of the Atlantic as young people discover the expressive qualities of fashion. The symbol of the decade—the miniskirt—emerges at the midpoint of the 1960s. It is a time when music, art, television variety shows, and movies all move to the youthful beat. The Beatles revolutionize music, men's fashion, and the movies, along with the scruffier The Rolling Stones. A new youthful sensibility emerges and is expressed in the hippie and flower child looks. Women become more militant in their demands for equality and express their frustrations with social restrictions by burning bras and demonstrating in the streets. Long hair, bare feet, and nudity become socially acceptable. Unisex and ethnic looks are highly valued badges of changing attitudes. Adults, the former arbiters of fashion, now take their fashion cues from the young.

Against this backdrop, George Field (1970) proposed a new theory of fashion change that he called the **status float phenomenon** (now commonly known as the **trickle-up theory** of fashion change). According to this theory, higher-status segments with more power imitated those with lower status—that is, status markers were floating up the status pyramid rather than trickling down or across it (Figure 3.9). To support this view, Field cited specific examples from the culture. Some of his examples sound quaint and condescending today but were relevant and groundbreaking at the time:

❖ *Influence of African-American culture*—African-American music, dance, and speech patterns have long had a strong influence on popular culture. In relationship to fashion, Field pointed out the increasing use of African-American models, actors, and celebrities on television, in magazines and advertising, and as spokespersons for products aimed at a broad audience. African tribal-inspired prints in fabrics were featured in fashion magazine editorial pages. The popularity of hairstyles associated with African-Americans could be seen in wigs that allowed anyone in society to emulate the styles. Field suggests that the channels of jazz and youth culture moved African-American fashion into the consciousness of a wider audience.

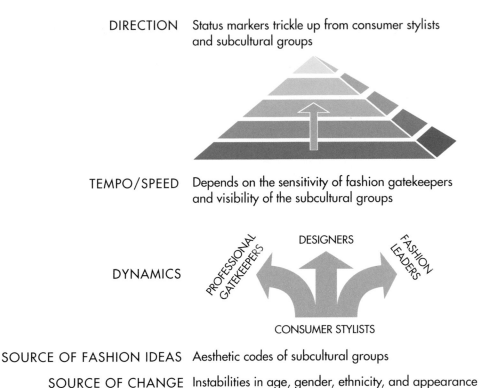

DIRECTION   Status markers trickle up from consumer stylists and subcultural groups

TEMPO/SPEED   Depends on the sensitivity of fashion gatekeepers and visibility of the subcultural groups

DYNAMICS

PROFESSIONAL GATEKEEPERS   DESIGNERS   FASHION LEADERS

CONSUMER STYLISTS

SOURCE OF FASHION IDEAS   Aesthetic codes of subcultural groups
SOURCE OF CHANGE   Instabilities in age, gender, ethnicity, and appearance

Figure 3.9

The trickle-up theory of fashion change.

✤ *Emphasis on youth culture*—Extremes in fashion originally adopted by youth to express their rebellion against the older generation were adopted and worn by the middle-aged. In a specific example, he cited the case of formerly ultraconservative automotive executives who were "sporting sideburns, square-toed buckled shoes, short, cuffless pants, wide, flashy polka-dot ties, sport coats, colored shirts, and even sport shirts" by 1969. Field suggested that these executives were wearing fashions pioneered by the teenaged and college-aged crowd.

✤ *Mixing of the classes*—Field saw the camping craze and the buying of pickup trucks by middle-class consumers as a case of typically blue-collar pursuits trickling up the status pyramid. Additionally he cited the use of garish male clothing and bright colors on automobiles as a shift from the conservative tastes of the upper class to the tastes of the lower class. He cited the adapting of work clothes—jackets, jeans, boots, and the sleeveless undershirt—into more widely

popular casual clothing styles for men as another case of status float.

✤ *Gender fluidity in fashion*—Women had freely borrowed from men's fashion at least since Coco Chanel popularized the look in the 1920s. Field cites a reverse case of borrowing: by 1969, college men and entertainers had adopted flare pants, a style originally worn by women earlier in the decade.

✤ *Style leadership by prostitutes*—Field cited the high heels, the use of rouge and lipstick, and women smoking cigarettes as examples of customs that originated in the subculture of prostitutes and spread over the decades to middle- and upper-class women.

The trickle-up theory provides the cornerstone of today's view that street fashion is a laboratory for fashion change. The concept carries with it the essence of outsider sensibility. Simmel (1904) was aware of the connection between prostitutes and fashion, except that he used the more refined term "demimonde" to refer to these fashion pioneers. He pointed out that an uprooted existence outside the bounds of acceptable society produced a "latent hatred against everything that has the sanctions of law" and that this hatred found expression in striving for new forms of appearance. It is this context of being dressed up, hanging out, and oozing attitude that finds expression in clothes, hairstyles, makeup, tattoos, body piercing, and accessories.

Today's fashion world takes the importance of street fashion for granted. Again, the motivation for differentiation drives **subcultures** where new looks are created. Members of these subcultures adopt specific aesthetic codes that differentiate them from other subcultures and from the mainstream (Blumberg, 1975). Imitation may occur between social groups but the importance of street fashion for the fashion industry is in the visual inspiration it provides for designers and other fashion gatekeepers such as journalists, stylists, and photographers.

Saint Laurent has been credited with reversing fashion's directional flow (Betts, 1994). He showed street-inspired trends on the runways as early as his 1960 collection for Dior. Later in the 1960s he was inspired by New York's army-surplus shops and by Paris student protesters. It did not take other designers long to catch onto street fashion, the youthful club scene, vintage fashion, and flea market finds as the source for fashion change. Inspired originally by the surf-oriented lifestyle, today's streetwear looks to DJs, skateboarders, artists, and musicians for trends with context, affiliation, and meaning. Authentic streetwear is restricted to those with contacts and is acquired specifically for "the thrill of standing out and being different," but when the looks reach chain stores and become part of mainstream culture they "lose the feel" for the original audience (Pallay, 2007).

In his book *Streetstyle: From Sidewalk to Catwalk*, Ted Polhemus (1994) traces the appeal of street-inspired fashion to the quest for authenticity. As the author sees it, streetstyle represents hanging out on the wrong side of the tracks with "nohopers [who] have none of those things that our society officially decrees to be

important (money, prestige, success, fame)" and yet represent something real and genuine. Polhemus sees street-style garments as radiating the power of their associations. He traces the chain of events, beginning with a genuine street-style innovation that is picked up and popularized through music, through dissemination to street kids in other locales, until it finds its way into an upscale version in a designer's collection. He calls the process **bubble up**, the opposite of trickle-down fashion. The groups whose fashions are appropriated may react in an unexpected way: they may be insulted rather than flattered because the appropriation waters down the significance of the objects, robbing them of their power and magic as symbols of differentiation.

✧ How Forecasters Use the Trickle-Up Theory

Forecasters applying the trickle-up theory of fashion change look to consumers as the source of creativity, as naive designers who propose new looks. Such people are not waiting on every street corner. Two sources serve as signs for trickle-up fashion—the alternative fashion neighborhoods and the fashion scouts.

✧ Fashion Neighborhoods

A conduit from street culture to the fashion system exists in almost all large cities—a neighborhood where young outsiders come to hang out, shop, and keep up with each other. The entrepreneurs and retailers who set up shop in these areas are the first to pick up on new trends because, in many cases, they participate directly in the social life and street culture their stores service. Often these colorful neighborhoods are a bit run down and seedy, but they serve as a playground for free-spirited experimentation in lifestyles and dress. For the fashion forecaster, these neighborhoods offer the chance to see fashion-forward consumers starting the next new fashion.

Finding emerging trends means mounting an expedition to neighborhoods where young people congregate with the aim of observing people with unconventional style of dress.

Fashion neighborhoods have shifting boundaries and a life cycle of their own. When established by boutiques and independent retailers, such areas become a target for fashion chains and designer stores. The Meatpacking District in New York was pioneered by boutiques that were replaced by luxury brands when their leases were up and owners couldn't pay the higher rent (Edelson, 2008). Chinatown replaced the Meatpacking District as "a very underground, indie thing"—an area for style seekers where fashion boutiques moved into affordable spaces scattered through the area (La Ferla, 2008c). In Los Angeles, major companies are buying out leases in the destination shopping streets of Melrose Place and Robertson Boulevard. Meanwhile the independent retailers began staking out new areas in Echo Park in Los Angeles and Bushwick in Brooklyn (Vesilind, 2007). Now, trendy neighborhoods where artists and other fashion-forward creative types congregate can be found in most metropolitan areas, such as the South Congress in Austin (Figure 3.10), Roosevelt Row in Phoenix, or Collinwood in Cleveland. Fashion forecasters find these neighborhoods good locations for scouting new trends in merchandise and observing the fashion-forward shoppers.

✧ Fashion Scouts

Because forecasters cannot watch the globally diverse subcultures that may be the origin of an emerging fashion look, they must rely on scouting reports from other professionals. The cues may come from the creative director for a fashion-forward retailer, the pages of an avant-garde publication, the windows of a shop on the side street of a fashion center, the reports of a forecasting service, or the articles of a cultural journalist. These scouts patrol the edges of culture, recognizing the potential and power of a subcultural style and transmitting it into the fashion system.

Figure 3.10

Fashion neighborhoods like South Congress in Austin give forecasters the opportunity to scout new trends.

You Be the Forecaster: The Movement of Fashion

Magali is a casual dress buyer for a middle-tier department store chain. She is looking for new trends in dresses before her next buying trip to New York City. She knows that she needs to look at trends from different sources in order to have the right merchandise mix of products.

Fashion industry professionals need to be aware of all sources of trends in order to have a complete picture of what is going on in fashion at all levels. Buyers such as Magali must know what is going on at each level and pick from among emerging trends in order to best meet the demands of their customer base.

Trickle-Down: Who are the influential designers today? How do their innovations get reinterpreted and influence fashion at lower price points? Other than designers, who are the high-status trendsetters who cause trends to trickle down?

Trickle-Up: What kinds of trends in a category such as dresses can come from street fashion? How might trends that originate on the street be reinterpreted for acceptance by a mass market?

Trickle-Across: How can the movement of a trend within a group and across groups give a buyer an idea of its overall popularity?

Subcultures: What subcultures (such as punk) have had an impact on mainstream fashion in recent memory? How did their style and symbols get reinterpreted for more popular appeal? What happens to these symbols once fashion scouts identify them and they lose their original meaning because of mass adoption?

Shifting Erogenous Zones: How could knowledge of Laver's theory (see below) of shifting erogenous zones help a dress buyer like Magali make better decisions? If high hemlines are in, based on Laver's theory, what should we expect the neckline to be like—high or low?

Retro and Vintage Fashion: Which bygone fashion era is currently in style? What elements of that fashion era are being used in new and modern ways, and which ones are still not being embraced? What do you think the next era to come back into fashion will be?

The Pendulum of Fashion: Consider a typical pair of jeans. Where on the fashion pendulum is ankle circumference—wide, narrow, or in the middle? What direction is ankle circumference moving in? What about rise on the waistband—are waistband rises high, low, or in the middle? Where do you think they are going? What are some other product categories and attributes that you can place on the pendulum?

◇ Applying the Theory in Today's Marketplace

The real predictive power in a theory derives from its ability to clearly establish the source, the mechanism, the tempo, and the direction of fashion change. As with the trickle-down and trickle-across theories, the concept of time lag plays an important part in the dynamics of fashion as it trickles up from the street corner to a mall store. Looks developed as aesthetic codes for members of subcultural groups are usually too radical to be accepted instantly into mainstream fashion. It takes time for consumers' sensibilities to adjust to the proposed look and incorporate it into their own social setting. This time lag may be as short as a year or as long as several decades. The forecaster can estimate the path and time sequence by evaluating the degree of adjustment required, the visibility of the innovation to consumer segments, and the match between the symbolism of the look and the attitudes of the target consumers.

✦ DIRECTIONAL THEORIES OF FASHION CHANGE IN TANDEM

A comparison of the fashion theories reveals the interplay between the directional theories of fashion change. Simmel's article from 1904 not only contained the seeds of the trickle-down theory but pointed to the trickle-up theory through references to the conspicuously anti-fashion consumer and the demimonde as a source for fashion innovation. The instabilities of gender, ethnicity, age, and physical attractiveness that serve to update the trickle-down theory play an important part in the fashion statements of subcultural groups. In a complex social system, it may take more than one theory to explain how a particular fashion moves from a starting point to widespread acceptance in everyday life.

◇ A Model for Vertical Flow

Behling (1985 / 1986) saw common underlying themes in the two vertical theories of fashion—trickle down and trickle up—and sought to integrate them into a single predictive model.

The model attempts to explain fashion change between 1920 and 1985 using the median age of the population and the economic health of the country as factors. When she arrays the decades on the horizontal axis and median age of the population in years on the vertical axis, a regular pattern appears. During time periods when the median age was low—the 1920s, and the mid-1960s to mid-1970s—fashion looks trickled up from youthful consumers to the market as a whole. During time periods when the median age was higher, fashion tended to trickle down from the older, wealthy, and influential strata. Behling's model shows a relationship between the median age of the population, fashion role models, and the direction of fashion flow. Events that can alter this directional flow are a depressed economy or curtailment of fashion by governmental decree, as in rationing (Figure 3.11).

Can this model be applied to current demographic conditions? Because the median age is expected to rise as baby boomers enter middle age, the model suggests that fashion influence should trickle down from an older, affluent, and visible class. Median age may be irrelevant in the late 2000s. Projections indicate that 71.4 million people will be age 65 or older in 2029. This means that the elderly ages 65 and older will make up about 20 percent of the US population by 2029 (Pollard & Scommegna, 2014). The baby boomers are closely matched in population by the millennials, or Generation Y-ers, who were born between 1977 and 1994. By 2030, Gen Y-ers will be ages 36–53 and make up 22 percent of the total population. For a while, fashion marketers will have to pick their targets and watch for fashion change both down from the affluent and up from the street. But older consumers are less interested in fashion than younger consumers and, as the boomers leave the equation, median age may again be an indicator of fashion direction.

◇ Time Lags and Idea Chains

The concept of time lags, apparent in each of the directional theories of fashion change, is an important issue in fashion forecasting. The

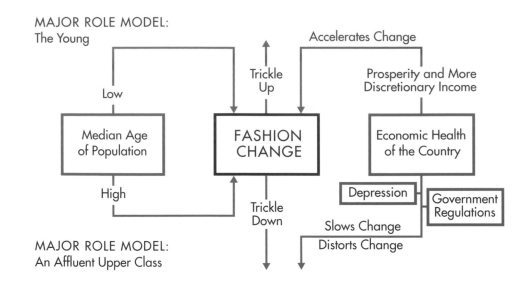

Figure 3.11

The direction of fashion changes depends on several factors: the median age of the population, the economic health of the country, and the presence or absence of government regulation.

technologies of mass communication and mass production that make possible the simultaneous adoption of a fashion across all market segments do not ensure such an outcome. Instead, the process often includes a time lag during which consumers become more aware, interested, and receptive to the new fashion—a trickle-down process. Street looks go through stages of modification that lead to wider acceptance.

Polhemus (1994) traces the path of the black leather motorcycle jacket from a functional beginning to a World War II designation of bravery and daring when worn by pilots, to a symbol of rebellious youth produced primarily by small, family-owned shops in off-Main Street locations in the late 1950s. Immortalized in the movie *The Wild One* by screen icon Marlon Brando, the jacket was still not acceptable in Main Street society. Only gradually did the black leather motorcycle jacket become normal everyday wear through the 1970s and 1980s. Helping the look gain in popularity was its adoption by visible fashionable elites—rock musicians from Jim Morrison to Bruce Springsteen to George Michael. Fashion-forward designers known for street-inspired fashion, such as Katharine Hamnett and Jean Paul Gaultier, first introduced the look to the runway. Designers such as Claude Montana, Thierry Mugler, and Gianni Versace further appropriated it into high fashion. In the designer version, the look was then available to professional

gatekeepers for dissemination through mass media and mass production.

In the history of this one style, all three directional theories of fashion change act at different stages. First, the style moves from a street fashion for a particular subculture to diffusion among other outsider groups. Then it is adopted by the visible elite of rock musicians, appropriated by designers, and presented on the runway. Knockoffs make it available to all market segments. Mass communication aids its acceptance by mainstream consumers. At each stage there were opportunities for fashion forecasters to recognize and map the process. The evolution of the "anti-hero's anti-sports coat" continues even when the original images— pilots, motorcycle gangs—are anachronistic. Today's softer version merges many stylistic characteristics to create a look that can be worn with jeans or with shirt and tie (Colman, 2008a).

In a 1992 *Newsweek* magazine cover story (Alter, 1992) on the cultural elite, an accompanying graphic introduced the concept of an **idea chain**—a set of linked events that move a phenomenon from a subculture to mainstream. The subject of the article's exercise was rap music. The chain began in 1968 when a West Bronx disc jockey invented hip-hop. The style was elaborated on during the 1970s with the addition of break dancing and the first small record labels specializing in this form of music. By 1981, the new wave band Blondie had a song,

"Rapture," featuring the artist Fab 5 Freddy, as a No. 1 hit. During the mid- and late 1980s, collegiate rappers, corporate record companies such as Columbia, and MTV took rap to the middle-class consumer. The 1990 film *House Party* further popularized the hip-hop idiom, and the sitcom *Fresh Prince of Bel-Air* brought rap to weekly primetime television. No single event or influential celebrity or corporate sponsor was sufficient to move the idea along the chain. Instead, it took the entire chain of events played out over time. In the same way, a single directional theory of fashion change is sufficient only to explain particular links in the chain, not the whole timeline, as an idea moves from source to wide public acceptance.

LONG-WAVE PHENOMENON AND FASHION CYCLES

Forecasters do their best to anticipate the size and duration of a style's popularity in order to determine if it will be a short-lived fad or a sustained trend. If a forecaster can estimate these factors, then that gives a designer, manufacturer, or retailer a chance to capitalize on change. Part of that estimate involves recognizing **fashion cycles**—fashion ideas that return periodically to popularity.

✦ RECYCLING FASHION IDEAS

Designers raid fashion's closet for inspiration, returning fashions from every decade to the runways. Recycling fashion ideas is part of **historic continuity**—the steady evolution of clothing including the continual recurrence of symbolism, styles, and elements of decoration (Brenninkmeyer, 1973). When some style is neglected for a period of time, it is ripe for revival. In the early 1980s an era of conservatism aligned with "preppy" fashion—an "old money" style borrowed from the New England prep school wardrobe of chinos and polo shirts, print dresses with ribbon belts, cardigans and madras blazers. The style revived in the mid-2000s in an

era of uncertainty and war as nostalgia for better times and as a "buttoned up" response to a period when fashion showed a lot of skin (Jackson, 2005). Although never revived exactly in form or with the same companion elements, the style is recognizably retro (from the prefix meaning backward). **Retro fashion** carries with it the nostalgia for other periods when that look was the prevailing fashion (Figure 3.12). Several theories of fashion change deal with the recurring nature of fashion.

✧ The Theory of Shifting Erogenous Zones

One of the key characteristics of eveningwear in the 1930s was the bare back look. Laver (1973) noticed these sexy dresses and compared them to short skirts in the previous decade, when the emphasis was on the legs. From this and other examples, he suggested that fashion changed systematically by covering one part of the body while uncovering another. As he explained, parts of the female body, which are exposed by a fashion, lose their erotic power to attract over time. When this happens, the fashion goes out of style. Another part of the body, one that has been hidden or de-emphasized during the previous period, becomes the focus of attention for the next fashion cycle. The newly emphasized part of the body becomes an **erogenous zone**. Any part of the female body may become the focus of erotic attention, and the erogenous zone is always shifting. Laver (1973, p. 383) said, "it is the business of fashion to pursue it, without ever catching up."

Other scholars (Wilson, 1985) disputed Laver's theory of shifting erogenous zones by saying that it applies only to female fashion, that his examples can be explained in other ways, and that the meaning of any apparel item is too complex for so easy an interpretation. Although Laver's theory may not offer a sufficient explanation of fashion cycles, it does point to an important element of newness that can be part of fashion trends. Fashion does play an important part in seduction and attracting sexual attention. Even in the use of cosmetics, the emphasis shifts—sometimes to the eyes, other times to the

Figure 3.12

Mod styles such as short minidresses recall the swinging sixties. Styles reminiscent of that time in fashion history recycle every few years, whenever the spirit of the times make people nostalgic for a more upbeat era.

mouth or the cheeks. In the same way, different parts of the body are emphasized during different fashion eras.

In discussing the history of the bathing suit, historian Lena Lencek (1996) described changes in styles in terms of shifting erogenous zones. In the early part of the century, bathing suits were very concealing; the only uncovered parts of the body were the ankles and wrists. By the 1920s, the bathing suit was beginning to shrink in size, but the torso was still mostly covered, so the emphasis was on the legs and arms. Similar to the evening dresses of the 1930s, the swimsuits of that era put emphasis on the bare back. New fabrics and bra technology made possible more structured suits in the 1940s and 1950s and the emphasis was on the bosom. When the bikini was introduced in the 1960s, emphasis shifted to the navel (Figure 3.13). Very revealing suits were seen on the beaches in Brazil and St. Tropez (in southern France) but arrived in other places with the fitness craze in the 1970s and 1980s. The new look emphasized a part of the body that had not previously been visible—the toned and muscled upper thighs and hip, which were revealed by high-cut swimsuits. For the daring in the 1990s, thong suits bared a new part of the female body, the derrière. The changes in swimsuit styling through the decades are reminiscent of Laver's theory of shifting erogenous zones.

✧ How Forecasters Use the Theory of Shifting Erogenous Zones

Although the theory of shifting erogenous zones may explain only a small percentage of fashion change, it is still a useful concept. The area above the breast—collarbones and upper chest—has rarely, if ever, been considered an erogenous zone until it became a badge of thinness. In a period when dresses covered as much as they revealed, prominent collarbones signified a thin body underneath and radiated an uncontroversial sex appeal (Jesella, 2007). Laver's theory helps explain the underlying mechanism that makes revealing or emphasizing one part of the body over all others seem new. It also explains how, after a time, the look no longer has the same effect. When this occurs, designers change the

silhouette, the cut, the fit, the detail, and the emphasis to create a new fashion look.

✦ RETRO AND VINTAGE FASHION

When people look back at fashions recently past, they find them at best amusing, at worst distasteful. As Laver (1973) put it:

> Most women … will give as their opinion that the fashions of yesterday were indeed ridiculous, and that the fashions of the present day are both beautiful and practical. Women were probably always of this opinion, and all that can be said about it is that it is a complete delusion. (p. 381)

Laver did more than just notice this trait; he established a timeline of acceptability (Figure 3.14). Looking backward, fashions closest to the present he said look dowdy. He developed a stepwise rehabilitation of a look, from frumpy and ridiculous for recently past fashion to beautiful for fashion 150 years in the past. On a somewhat shorter timeline, he suggested that innovative looks being introduced into the fashion mix were likely to be considered audacious and brazen. Only as they moved closer to full acceptance were they deemed appropriate attire. Laver called this trick of seeing current fashion as exemplary when compared to past and future fashions the "gap in appreciation" and suggested that it exists in all matters of taste.

As a style, look, or lifestyle moves further into the past, it becomes a candidate for revival because the perception of it changes. Fashion change is often the result of revising an obsolete style or reinventing an outdated trend.

✧ How Forecasters Use the Fashion Timeline

Laver's ideas about recycling fashion provide a timeline that forecasters can use in gauging probable reactions to fashion revivals. But not everything gets revived. Women's dresses have never become as ubiquitous as they were in the

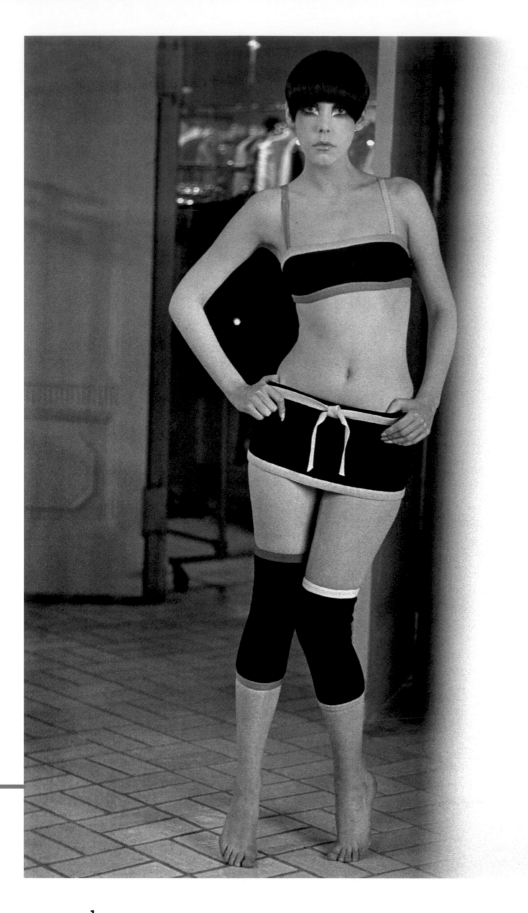

Figure 3.13

Rudy Gemreich's 1968 bikini illustrates this era's shift in emphasis to the navel.

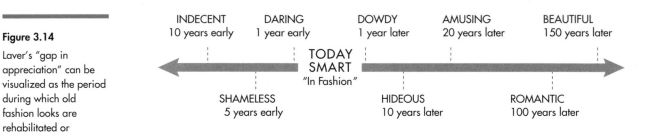

Figure 3.14

Laver's "gap in appreciation" can be visualized as the period during which old fashion looks are rehabilitated or consumers become comfortable with an innovative look.

1920s through the 1950s. Miuccia Prada, Ralph Lauren, Marc Jacobs, and Madonna (for H&M) all showed turbans and cloche styles in spring 2007, at the same time as the Fashion Institute of Technology exhibited the hats of Lilly Daché, a famous milliner of the 1950s. But it wasn't enough to overcome the old-fashioned stigma of hats (Wilson, 2007a). Whatever is selected for revival tends to be something nostalgic or a campy novelty or some guilty pleasure that is currently forbidden.

The 1950s were first revived in the early 1970s ("Back to the 50s," 1972), as Laver's timeline predicts—about 20 years after the original and just enough time to be considered amusing. Not revived were the political upheavals, bomb tests, and civil rights issues that had plagued the decade. Instead the revival concentrated on the fun of hula hoops, rock and roll, early Elvis, and the return to classic looks in fashion. Bits and pieces of the 1950s continue to be revived. In their turn, the 1970s were revived in the 1990s. According to Laver's timeline, this occurred when the fashions of the 1970s could be defined as amusing. At the end of the 1990s, it was possible to sample many eras from super-wide bell-bottoms reminiscent of the 1970s to clam-diggers and capri pants, signature looks of the late 1950s.

Prices at fashion auctions and secondhand shops echo Laver's idea of a gap in appreciation. Caroline Reynolds Milbank, a fashion historian and consultant to an auction house, says that prices depend on the age of the item (Browne, 1994): "It takes a while for people to get far enough away. Clothes from the '50s and '60s will sell for three to four thousand dollars. The '70s are at a tenth of these prices." Similar to the theory of erogenous zones, Laver's timeline of acceptability explains only one aspect of fashion

change, but even a partial explanation can represent potential profits for a forecaster and his or her clients.

Like the 1950s styles, some looks are constantly recycled. Menswear looks for women first made an appearance when Coco Chanel began borrowing tweeds from the closet of her aristocratic English lover. From the mid-1940s to mid-1950s (Figure 3.15), high school girls appropriated blazers, crewneck sweaters, Oxford shirts, and blue jeans from brothers and boyfriends as their casual uniform (Feitelberg, 1996). Diane Keaton's *Annie Hall* look of 1977 had the same borrowed-from-boys élan.

The 1990s saw waves of revivals of past fashion eras—revivals of the tailored suits of the 1940s, the club scene of the 1950s, the psychedelic 1960s, the bell-bottoms and platform shoes of the 1970s, and hints of the extravagant, colorful, affluent 1980s. In the early 2000s, "the vintage craze" was a force in fashion. Celebrities wearing vintage on the runways generated media coverage because vintage represented the ultimate in luxury given its rareness, and marked the star as an individualist and trendsetter (Jones, 2003). A popular vintage resource is Doris Raymond, who owns The Way We Wore on Los Angeles' La Brea Avenue—a popular destination for vintage-wearing actors. Her 4,000 sq. ft, two-story store is merchandised according to current fashion dictates, but her huge inventory in the warehouse next door offers inspiration to designers such as Michael Kors, Zac Posen, and Tory Burch, as well as wardrobe solutions to costume designers for period movies and television (Medina, 2007). If the clothes themselves are not available, the fashion insiders buy vintage magazines (Trebay, 2001).

Menswear also looks to vintage style for inspiration. Two leading menswear firms were

Figure 3.15

High school girls from the mid-1940s to the mid-1950s appropriated looks from the closets of their brothers and boyfriends and made them their own.

among the most prominent bidders at the auction of the Duke of Windsor's apparel (Vasilopoulos, 1998). Even the window of Marc Jacobs on Bleecker Street features an occasional treasure trove like vintage military coats from Copenhagen for a mere $59 (Colman, 2008c).

✦ THE PENDULUM OF FASHION

Just as a pendulum in a clock swings back and forth keeping time, so the pendulum of fashion swings from a point of exaggeration and then moves in the opposite direction (Robinson, 1975). In this kind of fashion cycle, a trend terminates when all possibilities have been exhausted (Blumer, 1969). When short

skirts get as short as possible, the pendulum swings toward longer skirts. When the fit gets too body conscious and cannot fit any tighter, the pendulum swings toward looser cuts. When black dominates the market for a time, brighter or lighter colors move in to relieve the gloom.

In an idealized version of this kind of cycle, a fashion look would evolve to a point of exaggeration in one direction, move toward the opposite direction, pause at the compromise point on a classic form, and then swing in the opposite direction (Figure 3.16). Such cycles can be traced in historic fashion (Young, 1937), but modern fashion tends to take a more abrupt path between extremes.

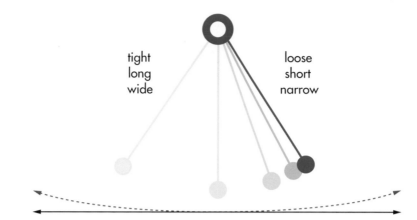

Figure 3.16

The pendulum swing of fashion can be visualized as moving from a point of exaggeration in one direction toward one in the opposite direction. The midpoint represents the classic form as a compromise between the two extremes.

tight
long
wide

loose
short
narrow

Hemline changes epitomize this kind of fashion cycle. The thigh-high miniskirt, which dates from about 1965, was new to fashion and lifted all skirts to the knee or just above it by the early 1970s. Attempts to lower hemlines by the introduction of midi (mid-calf length) and maxi (floor length) were unsuccessful. But skirts did eventually come down. Change in the opposite direction marked 1989 when, after seasons of knee-length or below-knee-length skirts, designers reintroduced short skirts. The quick change alienated working women who refused to buy the garment. Retailers were left with stock to mark down and the press reported the short skirts as a failed trend. But skirt lengths did rise in the early 1990s, and the fashion-forward customer did wear miniskirts again and, eventually, microminis. By 1997, short skirts had gotten very short. Then designers found a way to go even shorter by adding slits. But by the fall of 1998, Kal Ruttenstein, senior vice president of fashion direction at Bloomingdale's, thought that short skirts looked stale. Runways for the fall 1998 season showed floor-sweeping long looks (Schiro, 1998), and maxi dresses have since enjoyed an extended run as a fashion item.

Whereas modern fashion does not follow the idealized pendulum swing between extreme points, the cycle does manifest itself in fashion change. The pendulum action can act on hemlines, fashion colors, looks, and even lifestyles. In 1995 IBM dropped its dark-suit dress code, introducing an era of casual clothing at the office. A survey by Levi Strauss showed that, 2

years later, nine out of ten white-collar workers could take advantage of Casual Fridays, and about half could wear office casual all week (Loftus, 1999). By 2002, some corporations were reinstating business dress codes; a move was justified as a way to reassure clients in difficult economic times. Five years later, men had again embraced the striped dress shirt in oxford or broadcloth and tie, but the style was adapted— pared-down, button cuffs instead of French, a soft collar, and no breast pocket. The more edgy customer chose the Bengal stripe (classic ⅛-inch wide) but with an extra-slim fit (Colman, 2008b). Dressing up looked new again (Figure 3.17).

David Wolfe, creative director for the fashion trend forecasting division of the Donegar Group, invoked the pendulum swing in a speech to the National Retail Federation (1998). Wolfe explained: "Think of fashion as moving slowly from sloppy casual to dressed up. It's going to take a long time. What's in the middle? What fills the gap? Classics are as comfortable as casual wear but they are a bit more traditional, tend to look a little more polished. They are halfway between casual and formal." The designer collections for fall 2008 shifted from baby-doll dresses and miniskirts to sculptured feminine silhouettes, good tailoring, and sedate colors in the style of Grace Kelly or Jacqueline Kennedy. Even the bras and corsets women once burned were again on display along with satin-panel girdles—necessary undergarments for structured silhouettes. Some viewed the shift as a rebuke to the dishevelment of young Hollywood (La Ferla,

Figure 3.17

Ties, once out, returned when young men discovered dressing up as a countertrend to casual for all occasions.

2008a). For fashion professionals and forecasters, the concept of fashion's pendulum swing helps to define fashion direction and aids in predicting the next fashion change.

✦ WAVE DYNAMICS

People look for patterns in everyday happenings such as the weather and the stock market. Why not look for cyclical patterns in fashion change? Is there an inner logic peculiar to fashion? Is some aspect of fashion immune to exogenous factors (external influences)? Is there a rhythm underlying the seemingly random fluctuations in fashion? Is there a discernible pattern that recurs over time? Researchers in the twentieth century searched for such a pattern (see Table 3.1). Such research tends to use similar methods.

Researchers doing these rigorous **fashion counts** did find regularities and recurring patterns. Kroeber (1919) found evidence for a recurring pattern in skirt length of 35 years and skirt width every 100 years, 50 years for the pendulum swing from wide to narrow and 50 years for the swing back to wide. Young (1966) found a recurring pattern among back fullness, tubular, and bell-shaped skirts, with steady evolution between the styles of 30 to 40 years. However, these findings all apply to fashion before 1935.

The long-term cycles identified by Kroeber and Young and verified by other researchers are of little use to forecasters because the cultural institutions that created them no longer exist. Changes in women's status, the development of the automobile, and drastic shifts in culture terminated such cycles. Instead of slow evolution in styles, after 1935 there were increasing numbers of different styles available in the market at any given time (Belleau, 1987; Carman, 1966). More consumers became fashionable in their style because of increasing levels of income, education, and leisure. With mass production, designers shifted from selling to individuals to selling to professional buyers representing large-scale retailers. Mass media increased coverage of the role of celebrities and their part in setting fashion. These cultural and industry changes meant that style options were more numerous and changed more frequently after 1935.

Researchers are fascinated by the idea of discovering evidence of long-term cyclical fashion change. Robinson (1975) was interested in economic cycles and saw potential in Kroeber's findings. He decided to do his own research to see if men were just as prone to following fashion as women. He analyzed the styles of men's whiskers—sideburns, sideburns

Table 3.1

How to find a pattern in fashion fluctuations.

Step 1	Find a suitable source for fashion images—fashion periodicals are frequently used.
Step 2	Because not all images can be included in the sample, develop a systematic way to decide which images will be excluded (e.g., images where the model is not pictured full length and facing forward).
Step 3	Standardize a set of measurements or observations to be taken on every image in the sample.
Step 4	Sample time as well as images by developing a systematic way to decide which issues of a periodical will be used and for what span of years (e.g., April and September issues from 1920 through 1990).
Step 5	Gather the data and analyze to reveal patterns of fashion change.

with mustache, mustache alone, beard, and no facial hair—between 1842 and 1972. He found that a wave of beard wearing started about the beginning of the study and disappeared around 1940. The mustache began a sharp rise in popularity in 1870 but bottomed out in 1970. He also found a long-term cyclical wave for men wearing some form of whiskers rising between 1842 and 1885 and declining until 1970. He also charted the swings in automobile styles between 1927 and 1974. He found that, inch by inch, the car roof had come down, necessitating numerous and costly redesigning as if "fashion were a heavy hammer, pounding the car body ever flatter" (p. 125). He concluded that there is a master force that he called "the style of life" that acts like Adam Smith's "invisible hand" in economics to guide fashion change. He concluded that long-term fashion cycles involve so many years that they are outside the influence of external events such as wars, technological innovation, and economic shifts.

The search for long-wave cycles in fashion change is fueled by the desire to improve the accuracy in predictions. The idea is that just as long-term trends in lifestyles exist, so does an underlying logic in fashion evolution. In this view, seasonal fluctuations are the visible short-run phenomena that move fashion along from a precursor style to the current look, and beyond.

But these jumps and starts are part of a larger wave of change (Figure 3.18). With new computer technology, improved research facilities, and new methods, it may be possible for researchers today to carry on this line of research. Computer software now exists to search large databases of numbers for patterns that are not discernible to humans. Perhaps these new research tools hold the opportunity to study the multiplicity of looks after 1935 and discover more evidence of long-term cycles in fashion.

✧ How Forecasters Use Long-Wave Cycles

Robinson's master force, the "style of life," can be a useful concept for product planners who need to forecast long-range change. He advised them to seek revelations among the most outrageous minority forms of conventional taste. These forerunners of change should be taken seriously when a few thousand consumers have bought into the form. Both the long- and short-term prognosticator should consider not only what the professionals are doing but also what the amateurs in a field are doing. The amateurs, enthusiasts, hobbyists, and buffs are often a compass for coming fashions in terms of dress and home decor. Producers no longer dictate fashion direction and consumers themselves often point the way to the next big thing, but

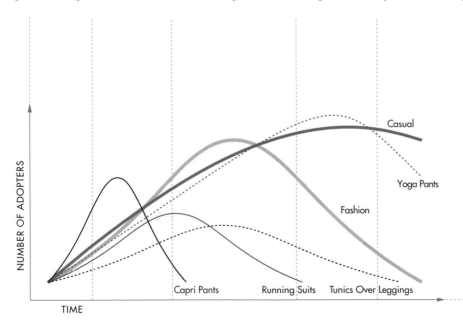

Figure 3.18

The long-wave change toward casual attire is made up of many other trends of shorter duration and different levels of acceptance.

only if a product planner is attuned to the signal. Finally, Robinson suggested that even the long fashion cycles are bounded by extremes, and a 50-year design shift is accomplished with an average yearly adjustment of 2 percent. This small incremental change gives the product planner a chance to decide what the consumer will want next year and 10 years from then.

Chapter Summary

Fashion inspiration can start in a variety of places: starting on the runways and trickling down to the masses, or trickling up from the streets to be imitated at the higher end, or within groups. The work of Thorsten Veblen and Georg Simmel form the basis of the trickle-down theory, which tells how trends spread from the elite down to the next social class through conspicuous consumption and conspicuous leisure. In response, the ideas that fashion spreads across a social class rather than between classes, and then the idea that fashions were inspired by members of lower social classes, were promoted by other theorists. By knowing how trends flow, forecasters can look for their source and anticipate how the trend will spread through the populace. Many sources of inspiration exist for fashion forecasters. Through visiting fashion neighborhoods and making idea chains, fashion scouts can find the source of the next fashion influence. Retro and vintage fashion as well as Laver's theory and the theory of shifting erogenous zones can help forecasters identify what from the past will become popular again in the future as the pendulum of fashion swings from one extreme to another.

Key Terms and Concepts

Bubble up

Chase and flight

Conspicuous consumption

Conspicuous counter-consumption

Conspicuous leisure

Erogenous zone

Fashion counts

Fashion cycles

Historic continuity

Idea chain

Retro fashion

Reverse ostentation

Simultaneous adoption theory

Status float phenomenon

Subcultures

Trickle-across theory

Trickle-down theory

Trickle-up theory

Discussion Questions

Direction of Fashion Change: How does the trickle-down theory explain fashion movement today? Who are the visible fashionable elite today? Who are the people who exercise fashion leadership through their ability to use fashion artistically to create a style? How does the trickle-across theory explain fashion movement today? What happens to fashion in the long run if the knockoff is the usual way of doing business? How does the trickle-up theory explain fashion movement today? Do the sources for trends today parallel those identified by Field in 1970? Why are there time lags in fashion change?

Fashion Cycles: What two frameworks deal with recycling fashion ideas? What is the difference between the pendulum effect of fashion in the first part of the twentieth century and the latter half? How can long-term cycles act like an "invisible hand," guiding fashion change? How useful are long-term cycles to a fashion forecaster?

Forecasting Activities

Conspicuous Examples. Make a visual dictionary of examples of (1) conspicuous leisure, (2) conspicuous consumption, and (3) reverse ostentation or conspicuous counter-consumption. Use as a timeline of the entire twentieth century or one decade. How will they be expressed in the future? Will one be more dominant than the others?

Classic Compromises. Study classics like the blazer, pleated skirts, trousers, five-pocket jeans, and the sheath dress as representations of midpoint compromises in the fashion pendulum. Using the fashion pendulum visualization, illustrate the extreme versions of the style. Analyze the cycle length between fashion extremes and the classic midpoint. Predict the future of these classic styles. Will they continue basically unchanged? What elaboration and d•etails are likely to be grafted onto these classics to create the perception of newness?

Group Identity. Identify a group that embodies the definitions of a new, visible elite or a fast-moving social group with a penchant for differentiation. Use visuals and descriptive words to describe the group's current look. What consumer segments are most likely to imitate the group's taste? Use the visualization of the trickle-down theory of fashion change to predict the next stages of fashion change. Prepare a presentation to communicate your prediction.

Who Are the Gatekeepers? Learn the names and affiliations of the fashion executives who attend and the fashion press who report on the fashion shows. Each has an individual take on the world of fashion. These fashion insiders decide what looks are selected from the designers' collection to be disseminated more widely. Find out who they are by reading trade papers for reports on seasonal fashion shows. Some fashion journalists have blogs where they comment on what they are seeing and what is happening in up-to-the-minute detail. Watch fashion on television. Who is interviewed? What point of view do they represent? Develop an insider's map of the world of fashion and know the names and positions of the key players.

Idea Chains. Select a fashion item—the T-shirt, denim jacket, stiletto heels, sneakers—and develop an idea chain. Show the origin of the item and trace its path into mainstream fashion.

What celebrities, social movements, movies, music, or other cultural shifts were involved? Sources for this investigation include:

◆ magazine or online articles on specific fashion items because they often include a brief history of how the item evolved;

◆ books on the history of fashion in the twentieth century because they often integrate the evolution of particular looks into a more complex timeline.

Find pictures to illustrate stages in the idea chain. Prepare a presentation as a visualization of your findings.

Resource Pointers

Vintage clothing sites on the Web, many with links to other sites, including those that deal with retro lifestyles:

www.ballyhoovintage.com   www.poshgirlvintage.com
www.coutureallurevintage.com   www.vintagevixen.com
www.fashiondig.com

> I don't believe that clothes can start a revolution, but I do believe that fashion is often a manifestation of a sociological or political climate.
>
> —Tom Ford

4
MODERN FORECASTING METHODS

OBJECTIVES

◆ Identify the characteristics of long-term forecasting

◆ Explain how long-term forecasting supports the decision making of executives in the textile and apparel industries

◆ Understand the methodology and evaluation of long-term forecasting

◆ Review current forecasting authors and experts

NAVIGATING CHANGE

The signals for change are present long before the results begin to be evident to most people. Most people worry that they will not recognize a trend early enough to capitalize on it. Trend forecaster Faith Popcorn (1991) wrote that a trend takes about 10 years to work through the culture and reach all market levels. She was not talking about style trends, because those move very quickly through culture, aided by media and the Internet. She was talking about lifestyle trends that reorganize consumer priorities and influence decisions in every aspect of life. As these long-term trends play out over time, people in many industries participate in translating the new priorities and preferences into many short-term style trends.

In the apparel field, companies need a system so that specific product categories can be fine-tuned to trends within a market segment. Although timing is important, an agile, responsive company will be able to capitalize on trends whenever they are spotted—sometimes just as a glimmer of something far in the future, sometimes as a phenomenon in the building stage. Waning trends are another signal. When some avocation, interest, or lifestyle loses cultural power, it is a good time to survey the information landscape for the next big thing.

Working on a long timeline—5 years, 10 years, or even longer—forecasters anticipate the future by linking breakthroughs in science, technology, and medicine to the likely course of demographic trends. Then they examine the likely results of those changes on the economy, political system, and environment. Most large businesses utilize long-term forecasters as consultants or subscribe to trend reports published by their companies.

TRENDSPOTTING AND MEGATRENDS

In 1968, John Naisbitt was reading a history of the Civil War when he realized that the author was using newspapers of that period as primary sources. Thinking of newspapers as a "first draft of history," Naisbitt began methodically sifting through newspapers for the fleeting hints of developing trends. He founded a business consulting firm and began publishing a newsletter based on this idea (Dougherty & Hoover, 1990). When Naisbitt's book *Megatrends* was published in 1982, a new word

Profile: CEB Iconoculture, Inc.

When Iconoculture, a cultural-trend research company, was founded in 1992 in Minneapolis, Minnesota, the founders envisioned the firm as "a cultural weathercaster, reading the prevailing trendwinds to forecast marketing dewpoints" (Abrahamson, Meehan, & Samuel, 1997). The goal of the company is to help clients understand "what's now" and to anticipate "what's next." The company's team includes former advertising executives, entrepreneurs, market researchers, and media professionals who are multilingual and multicultural. In 2007, *Inc.* magazine named Iconoculture one of the top fastest-growing private companies in the United States ("Iconoculture introduces," 2008). The company was acquired in May 2010 and changed its name to reflect its ownership by Corporate Executive Board Co. ("Company Overview," 2010). Today, the company has corporate members consisting of 16,000 senior leaders from more than 10,000 organizations across 110 countries ("About Us," 2014). The company counts apparel companies such as Hanesbrands among its clients.

Using proprietary observational techniques, CEB Iconoculture, Inc. seeks to understand value shifts and their effect on consumer behavior. The staff provides decision-making support to clients through presentations, reports, podcasts, workshops, and as collaborators on projects. The company offers clients the following options:

❖ Consumer Insights are reports that combine in-depth, culturally informed consumer research with tailored advisory support to give members a real-time picture of their consumers. Recent reports include *The Millennial Ties That Bind*, about the diverse millennial generation, and *Growing Up Grows Up*, about marketing to today's children.

❖ IconoIQ is an online consumer-trend database covering current and emerging trends that allows subscribers to connect their business interests with 16,000 searchable consumer-trend and observation articles.

❖ IconoCommunities are consumer panels offering clients the chance to explore attitudes and opinions, test new products, and gain insights into the moods and mindsets of people across demographic and psychographic categories using the interactivity of popular social-networking formats.

❖ CEB Blogs provide a snapshot analysis of current events and relevant topics in the context of marketing and strategic initiatives.

To identify "macrotrends" (another term for megatrends), CEB Iconoculture, Inc. begins with wide-ranging observations of unique products, services, business concepts, or cultural happenings looking for connections. Sorting those connections into categories (entertainment, sports, technology, etc.) reveals trends. If the observations and trends show value clusters that cross lifestyle categories, demographics, and geographical regions, they are classified as macrotrends—cultural shifts so wide, deep, strong, and long-lived that they are likely to have an important impact on consumer culture. Iconoculture tracks 45 macrotrends. One of these is SustainAbilities℠—the evolving mindset among consumers that they are stewards of Earth and its resources.

According to CEB Iconoculture, Inc., the macrotrend SustainAbilities^{SM} is moving mainstream in fashion by "seamlessly merging style with environmentally sensitive fabrics, manufacturing, production processes and ethical concerns" to create "eco-chic" (Daniels & Casasus, 2008). Participants in eco-chic fit four general profiles:

❖ Consumers who live a green lifestyle, take wellness seriously, value purity in what they put into and on their bodies, and are sincerely concerned about Earth and their personal carbon footprint.

❖ Trendsetters with a strong interest in fashion-forward looks who, while eco-conscious, have only begun to implement life changes; they see eco-chic as cool and innovative.

❖ Fashion followers seeking affinity with the cool, eco-conscious group by paying lip service to environmental concerns but making few lifestyle changes.

❖ Customers in an eco-luxury niche who hunt for designer labels, exclusivity, high status, and unique products beyond the means of the merely eco-chic.

Eco-chic lifestyles are likely to appeal to the Gen Y and millennial generations who will drive the trend (Mahoney, 2008). Designers like Stella McCartney, brands like Levi, and retailers like H&M are finding ways to marry environmental concerns with style. Consumers will be asking, "What are the social and environmental costs of this garment?" Better information—including more transparency about sourcing, production, and distribution—will enable consumers to identify the brands that are actually green and to align themselves with companies that share their values.

Sources:

Abrahamson, V., Meehan, M., & Samuel, L. (1997). *The future ain't what it used to be: The 40 cultural trends transforming your job, your life, your world.* New York: Riverhead Books.

Daniels, D., & B. Casasus (June 2008). "About Us" Retrieved from www.executiveboard.com/.

"SustainAbilities in style: The fashionable faces of the eco-chic consumer." Cultural Hotdish. Available at iconoculture. com.

"Iconoculture introduces annual cultural research report." (2008, June 2). *PR Newswire.*

Mahoney, S. (2008). "Gen Y demands it: Green fashion that's chic." *MediaPost Publications.* Retrieved April 7, 2008, from iconoculture.com.

Corporate Overview of CEB Iconoculture, Inc. Retrieved from Bloomburg Businessweek.

entered the vocabulary—a "megatrend" is a critical restructuring that defines a new direction for society.

Megatrends, the first trendspotting book to become a bestseller, is considered to be one of the most influential trend books. In the book Naisbitt identified ten megatrends including:

* the move toward an information-based economy;
* the dual compensations of "high-tech" and "high-touch" products—high-touch products have soft contours and cozy, handmade, or artsy attributes;
* the shift to a global economy;
* the shift away from hierarchical structures in favor of informal networks;
* the shift from an either/or to a multiple-option society.

Careful readers of trend books and subscribers to trend reports need to pay special attention to the methodology used to make predictions. In *Megatrends*, the methodology is clearly spelled out in the introduction. Data were gathered by continually monitoring 6,000 local newspapers each month to "pinpoint, trace, and evaluate the important issues and trends" (Naisbitt, 1982). The idea was that trends and ideas began in cities and local communities rather than in urban centers like New York and Washington, DC. Content analysis of local papers revealed those issues and trends that were competing for the scarce resource of space in the newspaper. Over time, these issues and trends could be observed emerging, gaining importance, and then losing space as interest declined. Naisbitt's approach of identifying emerging trends through a close inspection of media has become standard practice for trend watchers.

THE PROCESS OF LONG-TERM FORECASTING

The best way to understand the process of long-term forecasting is to look at the approach and predictions of professionals in the field. Forecasters and futurists can be characterized by the approach they use to arrive at a long-term forecast. The approach has four elements:

* the *time frame* for predictions—5 years ahead, a decade, or more;
* the *techniques* used for capturing signals;
* the *methods* used to interpret the signals and make the forecasts;
* the *range* of the forecasts, whether general or restricted to certain countries or economic systems, particular cohorts, or specific industries.

Following are three profiles of forecasters, chosen because they represent the spectrum of techniques generally used by professionals in the field.

✦ HENRIK VEJLGAARD: STYLE ERUPTIONS

Henrik Vejlgaard (Figure 4.1) describes himself as a pioneer of trend sociology, the "study of the trend process." In his books *Anatomy of a Trend* (2008) and *Style Eruptions* (2013), he defines trendsetters as "the first to adopt a *new* innovative product, design or style." He then classifies several groups as having an "overrepresentation" of trendsetters (meaning that not everyone in the group is a trendsetter, but most trendsetters tend to be a member of at least one of these groups). The trendsetter groups are:

* *The young*—examples include punk singer Patti Smith in the 1970s, hip-hop culture, and the Japanese Harajuku Girls.
* *Designers*—examples include Charles Frederick Worth, Christian Dior, and former Dior Homme and now current YSL designer Hedi Slimane.
* *Artists*—examples include painters, sculptors, composers, authors, and movie directors.
* *Wealthy people*—examples include high-society women like Babe Paley in the 1950s and 1960s and Jemima Kahn in the mid-1990s.

Figure 4.1

Sociologist Henrik Vejlgaard.

❖ *Gay men*—examples include gay men as early adopters of such now-mainstream products as Absolut vodka and common practices such as tattooing.

❖ *Celebrities*—examples include members of what Vejlgaard calls the "celebrity hierarchy" of icons, megastars, superstars, stars, minor celebrities, and wannabes.

❖ *Other style-conscious subcultures*—examples include groups of people who are different from mainstream culture and are preoccupied with style and taste, such as bodybuilders, drag queens, and chefs.

Vejlgaard also describes how trends spread through **polysocial** behavior—the behavior of individuals who mix and mingle among a wide variety of people and places, rather than just stay among people like themselves, which he describes as **monosocial** behavior. Trends spread through the mingling, observing, and imitating of polysocial groups, while trends rarely spread from monosocial groups.

Using a diamond-shaped trend model that is similar to Rogers' innovation curve (Figure 4.2), Vejlgaard profiles how trends spread from Trendsetters to Trend followers, Early mainstreamers, Mainstreamers, Late mainstreamers, and Conservatives, and Anti-innovators. Although they do not participate in the popularization of trends like the other groups, he includes Trend creators, and Anti-innovators (such as the Amish) in the model and describes them as "the 1 percent who are the most creative in coming up with new ideas and the 1 percent who are the least likely to buy anything new" (Vejlgaard, 2008).

The speed of the trend process also varies by product category. Vejlgaard estimates the approximate duration for how long it takes for a

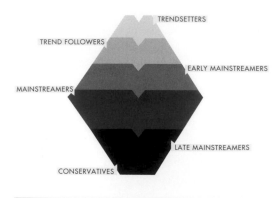

Figure 4.2

Vejlgaard's Diamond-Shaped Trend Model.

trend to go from the trendsetters to the mainstream for the five following product categories:

❖ Cosmetics: 1–2 years.
❖ Clothes: 2–3 years.
❖ Accessories: 2–3 years.
❖ Home design: 5–7 years.
❖ Sports equipment: 6–8 years.

Trendsetters tend to cluster in certain cities, which makes locations such as Los Angeles, San Francisco, New York, Paris, London, Milan, and Tokyo among the most likely to influence style and taste, in part because they are among the most connected to other locations through domestic and international flights, so a large number of people visit these cities, become inspired and take what they see back home with them. However, Vejlgaard also states that as transportation, travel, and communications have become faster, trends last for a shorter duration. He feels that while the trend process in the clothing industry cannot go any faster than it currently does, if other industries start imitating the fashion industry, the rate of trends spreading in those industries will surely increase. To appeal to the Trendsetters and keep their interest, companies must make regular product innovations a part of their strategy, or the Trendsetters will simply lose interest and move on to the next big thing. One company that does a great job of product innovation is Apple, which has several generations of its iPod that keep people coming back for the newest version.

✦ JONAH BERGER: CONTAGIOUS

In his book *Contagious: Why Things Catch On* (2013), Jonah Berger addresses why people talk about certain products and ideas more than others, and what makes online content go viral. Berger says that two main factors contribute to whether something will catch on: social influence and word of mouth. Word of mouth is more persuasive than advertising because hearing something from a friend is more credible than from a paid advertisement, and word of mouth is more targeted toward an interested audience, rather than aimed at everyone who happens to be watching a particular television program or reading a certain magazine. Berger shares six principles of contagiousness that can actually encourage the diffusion of a trend from person to person via social influence and word of mouth. The six principles are:

❖ *Social currency*—We share things that make them look good to others. Knowing about cool things makes people seem sharp and in the know.
❖ *Triggers*—Top of mind, tip of tongue. Triggers are stimuli that prompt people to think about related things.
❖ *Emotion*—When we care, we share. Some emotions increase sharing while others actually decrease it.
❖ *Public*—Built to show, built to grow. Making things more observable makes them easier to imitate.
❖ *Practical value*—News you can use. People like to help others, so if a product can demonstrably save time, improve health, or save money, it is more likely to be shared.
❖ *Stories*—Information travels under the guise of idle chatter. Stories are vessels that carry things such as a moral and lessons.

Berger contracts these principles into an acronym known as STEPPS, which can be used

Figure 4.3

Burberry's "Art of the Trench" website has received millions of page visits.

to increase the contagion of products, ideas, and behaviors. Examples that he shares of how apparel retailers have encouraged contagion include Burberry's "Art of the Trench" website (Figure 4.3), which encourages people to send in photos of themselves or friends wearing the brand's iconic trench coat. Burberry picks a select few winning images to post on the site, which reflects personal style from users everywhere.

Those people who had photos selected for the site in turn told their friends, making the Art of the Trench website contagious. The website has now received millions of views, and Burberry sales have since risen by 50 percent.

Another example Berger cites is Rue La La, the high-end designer good flash sale site that offered members deals for a limited time only. Access to Rue La La originally was by invitation only from an existing member. Members proved to be the website's best ambassadors. By combining the urgency factor of limited availability with the membership-only model that made the site's users feel like insiders, Rue La La has fostered an image of desirability that resulted in its sale, together

with its less-successful sister site Smart Bargains, for $350 million.

✦ WILLIAM HIGHAM: THE NEXT BIG THING

Author William Higham defines **trend initiators** as "those things a consumer reacts to" in his book *The Next Big Thing* (2009). This reaction can be either positive or negative. Trend initiators can be segmented into four different categories, which the author identifies with the acronym PEST. The four categories of trend initiators are:

- ❖ *Political Initiators*—government actions such as laws, or changes in the political climate domestically or internationally. Includes policy, legislation and events; for example, laws banning smoking have resulted in some consumers visiting bars less often.
- ❖ *Economic Initiators*—consumers' relative wealth and disposable income affecting how they think and behave. Includes Maslow's hierarchy of needs (physiological and safety through self-actualization), personal and national needs; for example, the Great

Depression of the 1930s led to a drive for escapism, resulting in the high point for Hollywood glamour.

❖ *Sociocultural Initiators*—factors that relate to human society and its modes of organization. Includes population, age, health, employment and education rates, and less-quantifiable topics such as lifestyle choices, media and public opinion; for example, trends like Conscious Consumption were initiated by social and environmental drivers and encouraged by media editorial.

❖ *Technological Initiators*—introduction of a technological innovation can drive consumer usage of it, but a difference exists between product availability and consumer adoption, because many technologies are introduced that do not get used. Includes communications, transport, and leisure; for example, the invention of the jet engine not only created a trend for travel abroad, but, as travel was featured more in the media, it led to a broader interest in other countries, including a growth in ethnic cuisine.

After a trend is initiated from one of the PEST initiators, it can unfold in different ways. Once a trend is determined, it can be further defined by its typology. Higham shares three sets of typologies that can be used to classify a trend:

Behavioral trends vs. Attitudinal trends: Behavioral trends include consumers changing what they do, how much they do something, when they do it, and where they do it. Behavioral trends can have a direct impact on sales, because if consumers substitute one product for another, sales will fall. For example, sales of fast fashion have had a negative impact on designer clothing sales. By contrast, attitudinal trends do not have as direct an impact on sales, as consumers may change their attitude toward something without changing their behavior. But attitudinal trends are important to identify in order to craft a marketing strategy that appeals to consumer preferences. Also, changes in attitudinal trends often precede changes in behavioral trends, such as the trend toward healthy eating.

Microtrends vs. Macrotrends: Microtrends only affect a relatively small number of consumers, and are larger than fads, of regional or national origin, and generally based around only a single sector or behavior. These trends are helpful for targeted or short-term marketing, but also can help predict future trends, because they usually do not occur in isolation, but rather are the earliest indicators of a larger trend. Microtrends such as a renewed interest in knitting, combined with related trends such as the popularity of folk music and the revival of poker, can be viewed together as a larger trend that Higham called "Traditionalizing." Macrotrends are the most powerful trends, as they represent shifts that influence a wide range of sectors, markets, and demographics. Since they appeal to a large number of people, they can be characterized by a broad, simple theme, such as "greed is good" to encapsulate the 1980s, or the recent "YOLO" (you only live once) philosophy that encourages people to enjoy life, even if that means taking risks. One macrotrend the author identifies is what he calls the Great Outdoors—a renewed interest in outdoor pastimes and the countryside that has impacted everything from housing trends to fitness trends to leisure time and even the rise in popularity of farmers' markets.

International trends vs. National trends: International trends spread between countries that share similar socioeconomic traits or are on the same societal level developmentally. If a trend spreads through several nations, it can be called a global trend. International trends share the same traits as macrotrends in that they are based on overarching behavioral drivers like the trend toward safety. These trends may occur simultaneously in several countries at the same time, but most of the time the trends start in one or two countries and then spread to others, such as the trend for renting bicycles as a means of transportation, which is spreading across Europe and is now taking hold in Canada. By studying trends in other nations, companies can decide whether they think the trend will occur in their own country, and based on how it has played out in other locations, how they can best respond. National trends can thrive in some countries without expanding into other nations. This is because each country has its own identity that influences consumer attitudes and behaviors, based on their environment, climate, moral codes, laws, infrastructure, foreign policy, and other factors. If the right environmental or social conditions exist in a country, a trend can grow there. Even a global trend may have a different twist in different countries; for example, the Green movement is a global phenomenon, but in some countries it has shown up through purchase behavior of buying environmentally friendly products, while in other countries it has shown up as a behavioral trend like recycling. Trends do tend to spread more slowly in larger countries, and also spread more slowly in nations with limited physical, media, or communications infrastructures. Trends will spread more rapidly in countries with consumers with greater disposable incomes, and in those nations who are at the later stages of sociopolitical development. Much like microtrends, national trends are useful as predictors of future global trends.

Higham notes that it is possible for two opposing trends to exist at the same time, usually among different kinds of consumers. If, for example, some consumers adopt a traditionalist trend while others adopt a future-oriented trend,

marketers will have to pick the group they feel makes up most of their customer base and try to appeal to them. However, one consumer can feel the influence of two trends at the same time, and in that case a marketer will have to figure out how the situation will be resolved in order to best meet their needs.

FORECASTING REPORTS

There are many useful resources that exist to help anyone who is interested in forecasting stay on top of what is going on in the world and that explain how seemingly separate events can all come together to form a trend. Trend Tablet by Lidewij Edelkoort combines articles about cities, artists, and movements that will impact our future. In one recent article, connections are drawn between an artist who converts traditional caravans into guest houses, how smartphones and tablets have enabled us to work anywhere, and the fashion inspiration of the Bedouin people all work together to form the basis of a rising trend the site calls "Nomadism."

Forecaster Perclers Paris has its Future Insights section, which shares its own trend forecasting themes based on its research. For their trend "Overview," their editors base their assertions that people want a clear, concise overview from the information deluge available to them online. They cite emerging signs such as the rise of the "guide-curator" to help sort out what is special, the interest in unitasking rather than multitasking to make sense of chaos, and the importance of visual ergonomics—delivering complex data visually, designed in a manner to increase readability.

Trend forecaster Nelly Rodi, in their online publication Nelly Rodi Lab, breaks its trend research into several sections, including Lifestyle, Fashion, Beauty, Inspiration, Color, Talents, Communication, and Retail. One recent post was on the topic of accessorizing with highlights, and it said that highlights would take two new forms: "Splashlight, which frames the face with a streak of highlights sandwiched between the main color," and "Painted hair, applied to look like clips or headbands, for a raw, punk look reminiscent of the 1980s." Fashion forecasting resources such as these make it easy to stay informed about how industry professionals find connections between seemingly unrelated events and sources to define the trends that will ultimately influence our future behavior.

LONG-TERM FORECASTING

When analyzing trends, it is easy to see links between the forecasts made by different people at different times and using various methods. Compare how different trends have been embraced by Vejlgaard's Trendsetter groups with how other trends have employed one or more of Berger's STEPPS. Finally, determine if any of the trends you have discussed had any of Higham's trend initiators influencing the public's adoption of them. See how the various methods work together to show the many different forces that work together to make a product or behavior a true trend. Long-term forecasting points to the future importance of customized products for consumers and businesses to make those products widely available.

Long-term forecasting looks for **cultural drift**, directional pointers for the way society is moving (Popcorn, 1997). Although major events such as war, political turmoil, and economic downturns can interrupt or even reverse such drifts, a company cannot plan for such unexpected disruptions. What it can plan for is continuation of the drift at the same rate, acceleration of the drift, or tapering off of the drift—three scenarios of alternative but possible futures. Long-term forecasts provide:

❖ insights that are valuable in evaluating current business practices;
❖ indications that a business needs to reposition the product or the way of relating to customers;
❖ input for a company's strategic planning;

❖ a backdrop for understanding and evaluating short-term forecasting.

Forecasters charge customers thousands of dollars for a seminar at a national sales meeting, a 1-year subscription to a trend report, or a concept development project. Companies find the price reasonable when the trends reported point to a new business or an investment opportunity. Learning about trends can be useful in other ways, such as expanding an executive's time horizon, encouraging creative thinking, or explaining behaviors that previously seemed insignificant. For companies that overemphasize number crunching and linear analysis, trendspotters can provide balance by showing other measures of consumer reality. Obscure events signal change at the fringes, and these changes can move toward the mainstream. Most executives are blind to such signals because, as specialists in their fields, their expectations limit their vision—they see what they expect to see. Trendspotters interpret soft data, are more receptive to change, and make connections using imaginative thinking.

Most trendspotters look for trends by scanning media and through observation. Critics of trendspotters wonder why companies would pay for a service that anyone can do. Although the techniques of media content analysis, interviewing, and observation seem simple, they must be carried out continuously and systematically to be effective. Trendspotting depends on being able to filter the trends from the stream of information. The forecaster is looking for:

❖ shifts in demographics that can restructure society;
❖ changes in industry and market structure (Figure 4.4);
❖ differences in consumer interests, values, and motivation;
❖ breakthroughs in technology and science;
❖ changes in the economic picture;
❖ alteration in political, cultural, and economic alliances between countries.

You Be the Forecaster: The Future of Information

Cheyenne has held several merchandising positions with an apparel company manufacturing branded and private label lines for men and women. Recently she has been asked to head the e-commerce division of her company. She and her staff will be responsible for the website. The issues they will consider include the look of the site and the degree of interactivity necessary to interest savvy online shoppers.

Cheyenne and her staff need to develop a long-range vision for the way that this division should relate to customers. They want to discover what forecasters and futurists are saying about the evolution of the marketplace over the next 5, 10, or more years and anticipate how these changes might impact them. Cheyenne is also interested in the concept of consumer tribes—groups with an affinity based on similar interests and lifestyles.

Her staff will need to design their own environmental scanning system to detect consumer tribes, identity trends, and monitor the technology of the twenty-first-century village marketplace.

Use the following discussion questions to review and summarize the strategies and techniques presented in this chapter.

Megatrends and Their Influence: How will identifying relevant megatrends help Cheyenne and her colleagues prepare for the future? How can employing the techniques used in the *Megatrends* book help her stay on top of changes in the marketplace?

Trendsetters: How will knowing the six types of trendsetters help Cheyenne's company improve their chances of targeting and keeping trendsetters as their key customers?

Contagion: Is there anything that can be done to motivate social influence and word of mouth? Which is more important for Cheyenne and why?

Trend Initiators: What are the four categories of trend initiators? How does understanding those categories as well as understanding the classification of trends help identify what is going on in society?

Research Strategies: Which of the research strategies are most effective and efficient for forecasters when researching trends? How do the different strategies complement each other? What are the advantages and disadvantages of each?

Figure 4.4

Even luxury brands that once feared tarnishing their image by becoming available on the Web are now seeing it as essential to grow their consumer base. Multibrand fashion and accessories e-tailer Net-a-Porter provides the link between brands and buyers.

A plan for systematic environmental scanning enables the forecaster to find signals of change and signposts to the future in today's media. Every executive already casually samples media and tracks trends by clipping attention-grabbing items or discussing news stories with colleagues. Expanding those efforts and using a more systematic approach to collecting and analyzing observations is the first step in creating an environmental scan for cultural indicators. The skill comes in recognizing the link within seemingly unrelated bits of information, and the talent in recognizing the implications. The following summary of research strategies and analysis techniques provides a toolbox for those who want to emulate the techniques used by long term forecasters.

✦ RESEARCH STRATEGY 1: MEDIA SCAN

A magazine writer who reports on emerging trends says she lives by the maxim "three's a trend"—if she sees, hears, or reads about something three times, that signals a trend (Greco, 1994). Scanning media for clues to change is a method many trendspotters share. No individual can match the efforts of an entire forecasting company. So, how can an individual be successful at spotting cultural indicators? By building on personal observations of friends and family and media habits (magazines, movies, television, music, books), any individual already has a start on forecasting. Although an executive (or even a company) cannot devote the time and energy to scanning that the professional forecaster does, it is wise to include some provision for this kind of broad-based scanning in the workday.

Collecting bits and pieces from a broad spectrum of sources, seeing hints and glimpses of possible futures, and hearing about new directions is only a first step. These signals must be linked, shaped into a vision of what the future may be, and logically supported before being dubbed a trend. Even a minimum level of environmental scanning will produce a wealth of information for analysis. How do forecasters decide what things to pay attention to and what things to ignore? They pay careful attention to the following signals of the future:

- ❖ new and unusual businesses;
- ❖ innovative and novel products;
- ❖ unusual travel destinations;
- ❖ new, rediscovered, or redesigned leisure-related activities;
- ❖ shifts in the workplace and the way people do their jobs;
- ❖ new shopping locations, store designs, and services for customers;
- ❖ stories about people and their unique adjustments to life's challenges;
- ❖ stories about neighborhoods with an interesting mix of people, shopping, or ethnic cultures.

Most trendspotters begin with lists of themes or issues that capture their attention. Trends require labels. At first, the label may be general and descriptive—for example, new music, financial issues, cult movies, and unusual jobs. Trendspotters often move from lists into a set of file folders representing major categories of interest. When something interesting and attention-grabbing comes along, forecasters capture it and add it to a "trends" folder—either an actual folder or a computer disk. When reviewing the folders, the forecaster begins to see links. If three or more items seem related, the forecaster may start a separate folder with a label that captures the trend—for example, "Cyberstyle" or "Asian Influence" or "GenNesters." When the trend begins to emerge, the next step is to think about how the trend relates to a specific product category or target market.

Reviewing, editing, and organizing the trend folders is part of the process of making connections. To keep the job manageable, Merriam and Makower (1988) suggest the following guidelines:

❖ Restrict the process to about ten major topics with possible subsets for each. Discard folders from time to time—a trendspotter can manage only about fifty major and minor categories and still be able to see the subtle relationships between the categories.

❖ Include both objective and subjective views of an issue (e.g., downsizing of a corporation from the financial viewpoint of the company and the personal stories of workers who are losing their jobs).

❖ Include intuitive categories—those where the forecaster sees a glimmer of meaning or a subtle connection but is unsure whether the matter will evolve into a trend.

✦ RESEARCH STRATEGY 2: INTERVIEWING

When trying to understand a shift in social rules or a change in lifestyle among a cohort group, a forecaster may decide to conduct a number of interviews—sometimes 100 or more. When the findings show a cultural drift that has gone unnoticed or the significance of the change has not been fully appreciated, the studies may be published in a book or article. Disseminated to a larger public, the trends can be discussed and evaluated for their impact on a particular product category or industry.

✧ Ask People

Forecaster Faith Popcorn once said she got some of her best signals about lifestyle trends by talking to people in airports. By simply asking them what was making them happy or unhappy, she opened up a discussion about lifestyle changes they were contemplating. Forecasting executives have been known to recognize social change in the conversation at a dinner party. People engage in conversation every day but fail to discern underlying trend indicators. Merely becoming aware that ordinary conversations hold deeper meaning is a first step to tapping into this rich source of cultural information.

Focus groups take the dynamic of the dinner party conversation into a more formal interview setting. The moderator uses a predesigned set of questions to guide the discussion to topics of interest to the research sponsor. Still, it is not unusual for focus group interviews to yield unexpected richness in terms of directional information (see Chapter 9 for a more detailed discussion of focus group interviewing).

In contrast to group interview situations, the **in-depth interview** is conducted one-on-one in an attempt to gain a deep understanding of a consumer's relationship to a product or product category. The interviews can last several hours, and many involve more than one session. A researcher conducting a number of in-depth interviews can use the insights gained in earlier interviews as questions and probes in subsequent interviews. Often the person interviewed reveals something interesting and unexpected. The researcher is free to pursue this new topic if it seems to hold promise. This flexibility is the chief advantage of one-on-one interviews.

✧ Ask Experts

One way to scan for hints about the future is to listen to experts in the field when they appear on panels and participate in the question-and-answer period. An alternative is to conduct a method of research called the Delphi method. The Delphi method was devised in a "think tank" environment in California in the early 1960s (Gordon, 1994). The reasoning was that experts, when they agree, are more likely than others to be correct on questions related to their field of expertise. The goal of the Delphi method is to encourage debate by making the interaction independent of personality. The following list shows the stages in using the Delphi method:

❖ *Identify the experts*—Experts are often quoted in articles or cited in the literature of the field. When a few such people have been identified and recruited, other experts are added in a "daisy chain" fashion through recommendations of those already on the panel. Expert participants are assured of anonymity—that is, comments made in the debate are not identified with the individual expert.

❖ *Introduce an issue for debate*—The researchers conducting the Delphi method pose a question to the experts. The question may involve the size of a future market, what policy will bring about a particular business goal, or the likely outcomes of a particular action.

❖ *Round 1; obtain initial response from experts*—Participants state their positions, the reasoning behind those positions, and provide supporting materials if they exist. The responses can be communicated back to the researchers in a letter, fax, or e-mail.

❖ *Summarize the responses*—The researchers summarize the responses, identifying the range of opinions. Usually there are a few extreme opinions on either side of the issue. Most responses are likely to fall in the moderate range. All comments are given equal weight and are not identified by the expert's name or title.

❖ *Report on Round 1; initiate Round 2*—The researchers present the summary to the group. They ask people holding extreme opinions to reassess their views given the group's more moderate response. Often those with extreme opinions will be asked to provide additional reasons for their positions. Once again responses are returned to the researchers.

❖ *Report on Round 2; initiate Round 3*—The researchers report on the group judgment and the reasons for the extreme opinions. Each expert is asked to reassess his or her opinion. They may also be asked to refute the reasons given for the extreme opinions using information known to them as insiders. The experts return their responses to the researchers.

❖ *Report on Round 3; initiate Round 4*—Researchers summarize the arguments and the evolving group consensus. In this final round, the experts are once again asked to reassess their opinions if the arguments of others on the panel are compelling.

Because personalities are removed from the situation, the Delphi method is like a debate but without the anger, spin, bias, or rancor that a face-to-face debate can engender. Often experts reach consensus. When they do not, at least the reasons for different opinions become clearer. The researchers and planners now have insights to use in making decisions on the issue. The value of the Delphi method is in the ideas it generates and the clarification that comes from experts debating a complex issue.

✦ RESEARCH STRATEGY 3: OBSERVATION

In the late 1980s, a group of consumer behavior researchers set out to illustrate the power of observation (Wallendorf, Belk, & Heisley, 1988). Two dozen researchers participated in the Consumer Behavior Odyssey—a trip from coast to coast in a recreational vehicle observing consumers in naturalistic settings while conducting qualitative research. The researchers stopped at fairs, swap meets, flea markets, and festivals—anywhere consumers congregated to

Figure 4.5

Every shopping trip offers the forecaster a chance to observe consumer behavior and recognize emerging trends.

shop. They used photography and interviews along with participating and observing the interactions. What they discovered was a rich and virtually untapped reservoir of relationships between people and their possessions.

New products in the grocery store, new services offered by the phone companies, an art show at a new gallery in a quaint part of town—all offer the chance to become a participant observer of change. The essence of the participant observer method is the way it provides access to the "insider's viewpoint" (Jorgensen, 1989). Being an insider provides the opportunity to understand the meaning of everyday happenings and the reality of situations as defined by the participants (Figure 4.5).

The methodology of participant observer invites involvement in concrete activities in natural settings as a way to understand people's behaviors, attitudes, and belief structures. The actual methodology has a long history, and practitioners follow careful protocols in collecting and reporting on their experiences. However, to a lesser extent, any person interested in forecasting can become a participant observer when he or she explores a

new offering in the marketplace. A forecaster is constantly aware of the potential for discovery in any and all daily activities.

✦ LOOKING INTO THE FUTURE: SCENARIO WRITING

Long-term forecasts contain optimistic predictions about amazing advances and pessimistic warnings about eroding quality of life caused by population pressures on the environment. Often predictions from different futurists seem contradictory because each predicts large-scale change and effects on large population groups and many industries. Just as an executive may have multiple color forecasts to work with, so will the executive have multiple long-term forecasts—some internal from strategic planners and consultants and others external from newsletters, books, industry groups, government reports. A professional needs a framework that will highlight the niche each forecast fills, conflict or agreement between forecasts, and voids in the forecasts. In 1928, Nystrom proposed a list of the elements that compose the "spirit of the times"—a list updated and expanded on in Chapter 1. Nystrom's framework provides a way to evaluate and organize cultural indicators.

In addition to applying a framework, it is important to use research strategies such as environmental scanning, interviewing, and observation to customize predictions to the textile and apparel industries and to specific target audiences. Customized long-term forecasts can provide meaningful guides to decision making if they focus on the effect of change on consumer cohorts (groups of consumers who share similar demographic and psychographic characteristics). The goal of long-term forecasting is to translate broad directional tendencies into an understanding of how they will affect consumer preferences and behaviors. The process begins with environmental scanning, interviewing, and observation, but it becomes meaningful only when the information is analyzed and the implications assessed through **scenario** writing.

Futurists do not predict the future (Tanaka, 1998). They look at data, identify trends, and extrapolate the trends into the future. To do this they consider alternative futures and lay out paths of probability as to which is more likely— the scenario. Looking at alternative futures can encourage executives to think more creatively about long-range planning.

The term "scenario" was borrowed from the theatrical arts, where it refers to the plot of a story or a summary of the action in a movie. In the business world, a scenario describes the evolution from the present situation to one or more possible futures (Fahey & Randall, 1998). There are many variations on how to write scenarios. One approach is to start with a vision of the future and work backward to discover the path to that future. Another is to project

present forces into the future, plotting their likely evolution.

The process usually begins when industry professionals identify an issue or decision that will influence future business decisions. The next step is to identify forces and trends in the environment that influence the issue. Then, rank these influences in terms of their importance and the degree of uncertainty associated with each. With this outline in hand, locate any quantitative data that can be used to support scenario writing (e.g., demographic data, consumer statistics, and economic indicators).

A single scenario is useless because it fails to consider alternative futures. Instead, futurists recommend a minimum of three scenarios (Kania, 1998):

* the "surprise-free" scenario—a scenario projecting the continuation of current conditions;
* the "best-case" scenario—a scenario that takes an optimistic view toward technological breakthroughs and economic conditions; and
* the "worst-case" scenario—a scenario built using more negative possibilities and a pessimistic view.

To be effective, the scenarios must be vivid and plausible.

Together, these three alternative futures provide executives with the basis for discussion of long-term plans. Scenarios lead to actionable decisions if they are tracked and monitored as the future unfolds. The final step in scenario writing is to decide on some key indicators and signposts to watch. Writing and discussing scenarios helps executives make decisions that lead to a particular and preferable path into the future.

Chapter Summary

Long-term forecasting methods allow trend forecasters to envision what the future will hold for society 5 or even 10 years from now. Forecasting authors such as Henrik Vejlgaard and his research on Trendsetters show how a trend has a greater likelihood of catching on if it is adopted by one or more of the six Trendsetter groups that he describes, and if polysocial mixing occurs, the chances are even better. Companies interested in maximizing their product's chances of going viral can use Jonah Berger's STEPPS (social currency, triggers, emotion, public, practical values, and stories) to best encourage word of mouth among consumers. William Higham's four categories of PEST (political, economic, social, technological) trend initiators can help identify the source of trends while classifying the trend into a typology that can help marketers best anticipate how to respond to the trend. Forecasting services such as Trend Tablet, Perclers Paris, and Nelly Rodi Lab offer excellent trend reports free online which make it easy to stay informed and watch the forecasting process unfold. Finally, the process of long-term forecasting is outlined so that anyone who is interested in deciphering the trend process may conduct their own research similar to that done by industry professionals.

Key Terms and Concepts

Cultural drift

In-depth interview

Monosocial

Polysocial

Scenario

Trend initiators

Discussion Questions

Trendsetter Groups: Do you agree with Vejlgaard's choice of groups that have an overrepresentation of trendsetters? Why do you think that members of those particular groups have such influence over consumers in the adoption of trends? What commonalities do the various groups share with one another, if any? Which single group do you feel has the most influence?

STEPPS and Contagion: In your opinion, which of the six STEPPS motivates people the most to spread a trend via word of mouth? How could a fashion brand influence each of the STEPPS to increase the likelihood that their trends will become contagious? How is social currency valuable to an individual compared to wealth, job title, or owning luxury brands? Is it possible to change or enhance social currency? If so, how could that be achieved?

PEST and Trend Initiators: How could each of the four PEST initiators influence fashion trends today in society? What are some current examples of each initiator that you can think of? Which is more important to a brand, a behavioral trend or an attitudinal trend, and why? Is it possible for a microtrend to become a macrotrend, or a national trend to become an international trend, and how could a fashion brand help make this happen?

Research Strategies: How do media scans, interviews and observation provide a forecaster with a complete picture of the environment? What crucial information would a forecaster miss if any one of the three were missing from their analysis? What skills does a forecaster have to have in order to draw meaningful conclusions from the information they accumulate? Why is it necessary to conduct all three research strategies on a continual basis?

Forecasting Activities

Forecaster's Motto—Be Aware. Make a Pinterest folder dedicated to the topic of Forecasting. Begin pinning directional items from newspapers and magazines. Add one or more items to your folders every day for the next 21 days. About halfway into the process, stop and organize your pins into specific folders, giving each folder a label that stands for a topic or trend name. At the end of the 21 days you will have become more aware of the signals of change in the cultural environment and established the habits of a trendspotter.

Classic Products of the Twenty-First Century. Select a long-term trend. Look for one that relates to fashion, interior design, architecture, retail stores, or other consumer culture. Do any research you need to understand the trend and to find connections to other trends. Then write two scenarios—one optimistic about the future of this item in the twenty-first century and one pessimistic. Discuss the plausibility of each scenario in class.

Check Out the Forecasters. Make an online folder for collecting long-term predictions. When you have several sets of predictions, identify the items where there is general agreement and items where there is disagreement between forecasters. If possible, check into the background and credentials of those making the predictions. Which predictions seem overly optimistic or pessimistic? Which predictions are likely to impact the textile and apparel industries? Synthesize your own customized set of predictions related to your career in the industry.

E-Commerce and the Future of Stores. Locate articles online about the future of e-commerce and about the future of store retailing, including department stores, specialty stores, discount stores, malls, outlet malls, and independent stores. Organize the projections stated in these articles for a side-by-side comparison of these forms of retailing. Analyze the sources for each prediction and the level of uncertainty each represents. Evaluate which predictions seem to project current conditions into the future and which take an optimistic or a pessimistic view. This type of content analysis helps an executive clarify a seemingly confused and contradictory set of predictions about future directions.

Resource Pointers

Trend identification and forecasting:

Iconoculture: http://www.executiveboard.com/iconoculture-blog//

Nelly Rodi Lab: http://www.nellyrodilab.com/

Perclers Paris: http://www.peclersparis.com/

Trend Tablet: http://www.trendtablet.com/

Fashion:

Burberry's Art of the Trench: http://artofthetrench.burberry.com/

Rue La La: www.ruelala.com

Forecasters and authors:

Jonah Berger: http://jonahberger.com/

William Higham: http://next-big-thing.net/

Faith Popcorn's BrainReserve: www.faithpopcorn.com

Henrik Vejlgaard: http://www.henrikvejlgaard.com/

> It used to be that we had six months to show something and then manufacture it. Now it only takes a week to copy something from an image on the Internet. So creatively, you have to be more and more unique.
>
> —Michael Burke, CEO of LVMH

5

POPULAR CULTURE AND FORECASTING

OBJECTIVES

◆ Understand fashion as a part of the cultural Zeitgeist

◆ Identify the different types of artistic and cultural influences on fashion

◆ Demonstrate how media impacts the flow of fashion trend dissemination

◆ Describe how forecasters utilize media in fashion forecasting practices

KEITH HARING—ARTIST AND STYLE ICON

When Rihanna's video *Rude Boy* dropped in 2010, one of the most visually arresting scenes featured the artist in a bodysuit, seated on a zebra with bold black-and-white graphics in the background. To most of her fans, the scene simply looked cool and interesting, but to a few culturally aware people, it was a tribute to the pop artist Keith Haring, who died in 1990 of AIDS-related complications at the age of 31. Rihanna had shown a fondness for Haring before, when she was photographed wearing a Haring-designed graffiti-print leather jacket in 2009 (Borrelli-Persson, 2014). Other pop artists referenced in the *Rude Boy* video included Haring's friends and collaborators Jean-Michel Basquiat and Andy Warhol. Four years later, in 2014, the Japanese fashion retailer UNIQLO launched its SPRZ NY collection, a self-described launching pad for "mind-blowing innovations in pop culture" ("SPRZ NY," 2015). Products like T-shirts, sweatshirts, tunics, shorts, blankets, and tote bags featured the work of several prominent pop artists including Jean Michel Basquiat, Andy Warhol … and Keith Haring.

During his life, Haring gained notoriety as an artist working on unused advertising space in the New York City subways, which he described as his "laboratory" for developing his signature style of simple line drawings ("Bio," 2014). Haring's work became popular quickly with a large number of people, in part because he wanted his work to be accessible to as many people who wanted it. To make this possible, he opened his Pop Shop in 1986 where he sold T-shirts, posters, and magnets with his drawings on them at a low cost. He also designed a series of Swatch® watches that can sell for as much as $1,000 on eBay and designed several record covers for charity compilations. References to Keith Haring's artwork are still around today; one of his drawings was made into a balloon in the Macy's Thanksgiving Day Parade and on May 14, 2012, on what would have been his 54th birthday, Google honored him with a Google Doodle (Google.com, 2012).

Haring's work still influences artists and other creative people in multiple fields. He was referenced in the Macklemore song "10,000 hours" in the lyrics, "I love Basquiat, I watched Keith Haring / You see I studied art / The greats weren't great because at birth they could paint / The greats were great 'cause they paint a lot." The artist Shepard Fairey, who became famous for designing President Barack Obama's famous "Hope" campaign poster, cites Haring as a major influence, which motivated him to collaborate with Haring's foundation to use the artist's designs on the first capsule collection that Fairey's clothing brand OBEY sold at Urban Outfitters. As Fairey said: "Inspired by Keith Haring's achievements, I pursued my art career with the optimism that my goals could be attained" ("OBEY x Keith Haring," 2012).

Haring embraced the connection between art, music, and fashion during his brief lifetime; one of his earliest collaborations was with Sex Pistols' manager Malcolm McLaren and designer Vivienne Westwood on a "pirate" textiles print shown in Westwood's fall 1983 collection and worn onstage by singer Annabella Lwin from the band Bow Wow Wow, also managed by McLaren. Haring continued to work with fashion, by designing costumes for singer Grace Jones and prints for New York designer Stephen Sprouse. It is no surprise that someone so influential on fashion during their life continues to inspire designers—Sibling's spring/summer 2015 collection included graffiti prints that reviewers noted showed clear inspiration from Haring's work (Borrelli-Persson, 2014).

CULTURE INFLUENCING CULTURE

More and more, fashion is being viewed as a significant cultural medium. When Mercedes-Benz fashion week opened in 2009 at Lincoln Center, a performing arts complex, the center hired a director of fashion and has incorporated fashion into its lineup of featured arts such as opera, theater, dance, and music by showing fashion films and photo exhibits and holding fashion lectures, which sent a strong signal that the center considered fashion to be just as worthy a cultural vehicle as their other forms of art (Postrel, 2010). The Metropolitan Museum of Art's exhibit *Savage Beauty*, showing the work of Alexander McQueen, brought in more than 650,000 people and was one of the ten most popular exhibits of all time in the museum's history (Cardwell, 2011). The McQueen exhibit has been joined by others such as *The Fashion World of Jean Paul Gaultier: From the Sidewalk to the Catwalk* and *Maison Martin Margiela: 20 Years The Exhibition* which have brought new audiences to museums.

When thinking about the different segments of art and culture, such as film, television, music, and fashion, they are usually considered separately; however, collaborations such as Vivienne Westwood's famous association with Malcolm McLaren and the Sex Pistols—which defined the look of the entire punk movement in the 1970s—and the many others since then show that the relationship between the different creative areas is much more fluid than in other industries such as business or finance. Part of the reason for this is geographic; particularly in large cities such as New York, creative people tend to attend the same parties, concerts, museums, restaurants, and nightclubs, which leads to shared inspiration and the desire to work with other like-minded creative people (Currid, 2007).

Fashion designers have much in common with artists in other creative industries such as music, including facing creative challenges like the problem of knockoffs, or copying, which was the case when critics charged that the animations in the *Rude Boy* video were too similar to the artist M.I.A.'s video for her song *Boyz*. Director Melina Matsoukas was quick to respond to the allegations: "We're all inspired by similar elements and it came together in that way" (Vena, 2010). This inspiration is exactly how the fashion industry works as well. Designers find creative stimulus in many ways, such as nature, travel, or architecture, but inspiration from popular culture is different from these in that people on a global scale can have access to the exact same product at the same time.

The fashion industry is unlike the music industry, however, in its willingness to acknowledge its sources of inspiration, and the embarrassment associated with not giving credit where credit is due, such as the criticism Nicholas Ghesquière received in 2002 when he was the creative director of Balenciaga and included an embroidered patchwork vest in the spring collection that was found to be a replica of a design from a vest made in 1973 by San Francisco Chinese-American designer Kaisik Wong. Mr. Wong had been dead for over 10 years before the incident, so although legal action was not a concern, the damage done to Ghesquière's reputation has lingered in the industry. Rather than this social enforcement, the music industry has instead chosen to establish a system of intellectual property protection that ensures that artists receive compensation for their work, but this system limits a musical artist's creativity to take existing ideas and rearrange them in new and innovative ways (Sinnreich & Gluck, 2005). United States' law provides trademark or copyright protection for things such as original textile prints and surface designs, creative jewelry and accessory designs, unique sculptural or ornamental items, or proprietary fabrics or fibers; however, the design of a garment is not protected. This allows designers to gain inspiration from other designers' works and reinterpret those styles in new and interesting ways. So far, all attempts to enact legal protection for fashion designs have failed, and several scholars feel that the American fashion industry is the better for it, because the constant need to innovate in order to stay ahead of knockoffs is what keeps American fashion fresh and creative (Jimenez, Murphy, & Zerbo, 2014).

WHY CULTURE MATTERS

Appropriation is the basis of fashion—in the same way that consumers see a style they like on the street, or on television or in a movie, and copy it for themselves, fashion designers appropriate ideas that they then translate into their collections. According to Lisa Armstrong, fashion editor for the *Telegraph* group, "The very essence of fashion is that you follow something, or someone. There has to be influence for something to be fashionable—it can't happen in isolation" (Grimond et al., 2014). Artists consistently influence other artists, and, like other types of design, fashion inspiration can come from "cross-sensory" interpretation, in which designs that appeal to one sense (such as music and the auditory sense) can inspire a design for another sense (such as fashion and the visual and tactile senses) which then in turn may inspire another design (such as perfume and the olfactory sense) (Davis, 1996).

Because creativity is influenced by everything the designer is exposed to, it is important that they regularly attend cultural events in order to continually renew their creative inspiration from these related areas. As previously discussed in Chapter 1, the Zeitgeist reflects the spirit of the time, and trends, including culture, reflect that mood. Because of this, forecasters have to know what is going on in all areas of culture because preferences in one area of art can be paralleled in another. Trend forecaster Nina Stotler calls the South by Southwest music festival in Austin, Texas one of her favorite events for researching trends: "South by Southwest provides a great insider view of the music scene, as thousands of bands from around the globe descend on Texas. This year I was able to speak with a number of young artists about their style inspirations, all of which were an indication of upcoming trends" (Halpern, 2010).

GOOD TASTE, COOLNESS, AND SUBJECTIVITY— CHALLENGES FOR FASHION

Fashion, art, and music are fun, but they are also businesses. What makes culture different from other consumer items like durable goods such as kitchen appliances is that, unlike a consumer item like a dishwasher, there is no way to evaluate its performance based on how well it works. Instead people consume culture simply because they like it (Currid, 2007). The fact that fashion is completely subjective means that what one person thinks is classic and refined can be seen instead as old-fashioned and boring by another person, and they both can be "right," based on their own personal tastes. In a famous survey conducted by sociologist Pierre Bourdieu, he found that middle- and upper-class people consider taste to be more than just personal likes or dislikes, but instead a way to differentiate one's self from people we consider below us socially, while trying to affiliate ourselves with the status level we want to achieve. In this way, taste functions kind of like a social hierarchy, by mocking people who are less cool or artsy than you are, and admiring people you think are cooler or more knowledgeable about art and culture (Wilson, 2014).

Like other forms of culture, there is both a critical and a commercial aspect of fashion, but critics and consumers often don't agree. There are no *Consumer Reports* for fashion that test different styles based on set criteria and has a definitive ranking—fashion shows are evaluated each season by critics, but frequently designs that are critically praised for being challenging do not become popular, such as the work of avant-garde designers like Gareth Pugh, Comme des Garçons' Rei Kawakubo, Dries Van Noten, or Viktor & Rolf. When the average viewer sees the work of these designers, they are quick to dismiss their work as "weird" or say things such as "I'd never wear that, why is that on a runway?" without recognizing the artistry of fashion. On the other hand, fashion critics couldn't understand why in 2009, sales of Ed Hardy-

branded merchandise exceeded $700 million, despite the fact that the brand was universally panned by critics, and style bloggers and other media figures made fun of the brand and its fans (Alabi, 2013).

Forecasters are *not* critics and it is their job to spot the trends and translate them for their clients, not to pass judgment on what is "good taste" and "bad taste" since those concepts are only in the eye of the beholder. In the wonderful film *Bill Cunningham New York*, about the fashion photographer for the *New York Times* and father of street style photography, the story is told of how Cunningham quit working for *Women's Wear Daily* because his photographs were being used for pieces that dictated whether certain styles were either "in" or "out," a philosophy that Cunningham himself does not believe in. Harold Koda, Curator of the Costume Institute of the Metropolitan Museum of Art, summed up Cunningham's sentiment that "it's all equally in, that's the reason he's documented it" (Koda, 2010), while Cunningham himself says that his job is not to judge, but to report: "I don't decide anything, I let the street speak to me … It isn't really what I think, it's what I see" (Cunningham, 2010). This unbiased opinion should be the standard for all fashion forecasters.

Even though Simon Doonan, Creative Ambassador for Barneys New York, is a respected fashion authority, he feels strongly that "good taste does not exist" (he even has this phrase embroidered on the back of a Moschino jacket) and embraces all styles, even ones he does not personally wear. As he says, "Criticizing Ed Hardy for being cheesy is like saying that Elvis was 'flashy' or that Liberace was 'tacky.' It's a giant case of DUH! Of course it's cheesy! That's the whole point, you doo-doo heads. Ed Hardy is fromage-y and hedonistic and naughty and badass and—the ultimate crime in the world of haute fashion—Ed Hardy is FUN!" Doonan supports his viewpoint by quoting former editor-in-chief of *Vogue*, Diana Vreeland, who said that "A little bad taste is like a nice splash of paprika. We all need a splash of bad taste—it's hearty, it's healthy, it's physical. No taste is what I'm against" (Doonan, 2009).

Like the idea of good and bad taste, the concept of what constitutes *cool* is subjective to each person, but being cool is how both people and brands want to be perceived. The term "cool" dates back to the African-American jazz culture, but has come to represent youth culture in general and now is as much a marketing term as it is an attitude, meaning something that is stylish, innovative, original, authentic, desirable, and unique, all positive attributes to consumers, although different people think different things are cool, and the idea of what is cool changes with time (Runyan, Noh, & Mosier, 2013; Tapp & Bird, 2008). Consumers can attain a cool lifestyle to a large extent through their purchases—the brands and products that they buy can quickly indicate their status and insider knowledge—so staying on top of what is cool is vitally important to forecasters, designers, and marketers of fashion. Businesses try to target early adopters or opinion leaders because their role in spreading an innovation is crucial, since the knowledge they have in their role as a style leader involves designer labels, brands, and advertising (Nancarrow, Nancarrow, & Page, 2002).

Young consumers also reject things that are not cool, which include the passé, older generations, or other people or things that "try too hard" to be cool, which means something backfires in its attempt to be cool. This is difficult for companies, because the message of marketing is usually the antithesis of cool. So in order to actually be perceived as cool, brands have to appear like they don't care about being cool (just like people). In order to avoid being perceived as passé, fashion brands also always have to innovate so that they can stay a step ahead of what people consider cool, and get out of a style when it becomes obvious it has been played out. Marketers need to understand what is cool so that they can speak the language of their target audience, especially if that target is teenagers (Tapp & Bird, 2008). If brands can know what their target audience thinks is cool in other areas of culture, it can help them more effectively reach them through use of the right music or product tie-in, or celebrity endorser.

SOURCES OF CULTURE

According to author Faith Popcorn (1991), cultural trends arise from three sources:

❖ **high culture**—fine and performance arts;
❖ **low culture**—activities pursued locally by special interest groups, outside mainstream awareness; and
❖ **popular culture**—advertising, movies, television, music, magazines, and celebrity news.

Each of these sources of culture has influenced fashion at a mainstream level, and there can be some overlap between sources. For example, the 2013 film *The Great Gatsby* (Figure 5.1) took a high culture work of literature by F. Scott Fitzgerald and made it into a popular culture movie that influenced fashion through details such as the popularity of beaded headbands in spring 2014 and a capsule collection of menswear inspired by the movie that was available at the retailer Brooks Brothers. High culture frequently influences the work of high-end ready-to-wear and haute couture designers. One of the most famous examples of this is the inspiration Yves Saint Laurent drew from the abstract paintings of the Dutch De Stijl artist Piet Mondrian, known for his use of intersecting black lines and blocks of primary colors. Saint Laurent's Mondrian collection from fall 1965 included shift dresses that featured blocks of colored jersey. His designs were so popular that they were copied by mass marketers everywhere. A more recent use of high art as inspiration comes from Oscar de la Renta's resort 2012 collection that drew heavily on the artist Pablo Picasso during his Cubist period (Figure 5.2a and 5.2b).

Low culture can also inspire fashion trends. In the early 2000s, trucker hats (a style of baseball cap also known as mesh caps) became a trend for a period of time. The hats were originally worn ironically as a response to the popularity of designer brands and logos because of their association

Profile: Janie Bryant, Costume Designer, *Mad Men*

When the television show *Mad Men* premiered in 2007, it quickly gained popularity with affluent, educated viewers not only for the high quality of writing and acting, but also for its historical authenticity and its visual style, in particular its costume design. Set in the 1960s, the female characters of *Mad Men* were shown wearing styles such as fitted sheaths, floral print cinched waist dresses, plaid capes, calf-length pencil skirts, leopard print kitten heels, and structured ladylike handbags with matching shoes, and the look caught on with women viewers, then with the public at large, and fashion designers and retailers responded.

The show was credited with raising the sales of everything from tortoise shell glasses to fedoras, and the term "*Mad Men* effect" was used to describe the surge in these items' popularity (Allister, 2008). The show's retro styling resonated with more than just consumers; it also influenced culturally aware designers like Miuccia Prada, whose fall 2010 collection featured models styled with their hair in high buns wearing updated cat's eye glasses, fur-trimmed princess line coats, shorter jackets, shell tops, and full skirts. Prada showed dresses in black wool, and fifties-style patterns in shades of reds, mustards, and browns came with fitted bodices and full round skirts—or "classic, forever shapes," as Miuccia Prada described them, and reviewers were quick to note the show's influence (Long, 2010). Even Louis Vuitton designer Marc Jacobs was caught up in the show's aesthetic, showing "high, bouncy B.B. ponytails; clean makeup; and square-toed, block-heeled pumps trimmed with flat bows—another angle on the *Mad Men* era but this time with a charming Frenchified accent," for his own fall 2010 collection (Mower, 2010).

Mad Men's influence has extended to men's fashion as well. When the show premiered, the character of Don Draper's "very tailored, streamlined and minimal look" gray two-piece suits struck the audience as modern and cool, in comparison to the super-skinny suits that Hedi Slimane had made popular years earlier when he was creative director at Dior Homme, and they have been credited with inspiring a return to dressing up for work among young men (Ellsworth, 2010; Heaf and Cochrane, 2014).

The *Mad Men* aesthetic is the vision of costume designer Janie Bryant, who designs for the show's principal cast using a mix of new garments, bought vintage pieces (and sometimes redesigning them), and rented garments from Los Angeles costume houses (Gan, 2013). Bryant has received four Emmy nominations—in 2007, 2009, 2010, and 2011—for her work on the show (her only win to date, in 2005, was for her previous work on the television show *Deadwood*). Her work on *Mad Men* has also received four Costume Designer's Guild nominations, which she won in 2009 and 2010 ("Janie Bryant: Awards," 2014).

Bryant's attention to detail is renowned, as well as the depth of thought that she puts into each character's dress. For example, she understood that in 1960, when the show begins, most people at the time kept their clothing for several years, so in reality, the characters would not be wearing up-to-the-minute fashions from that year: "I had brought research from the mid to late 50s because the first season started in 1960 and he [show creator Matthew Weiner] said, 'this is perfect, this is exactly what I was thinking'. So we just really connected on that level" (Elsworth, 2010).

Like traditional forecasters, Bryant cites research as the first step of doing her job: "I start my research process by going through catalogs, old photographs, all different kinds of magazines—anything from a *Sears* catalog to a *Vogue* fashion magazine from the period and everything in between. That's why I particularly love old photographs, because you truly get a sense of what people were wearing and how they wore it and where each wrinkle was. I will research newspapers. I'll watch old movies. I do a lot of research because it's always that visual inspiration of, 'Oh! This reminds me so much of the character Betty,' or 'This photograph reminds me so much of Don'" (Gan, 2013).

Thanks to the show, Bryant has become a celebrity herself, with plans for her own television show, a "reality design competition that merges costume design with fashion design. I love this whole idea because fashion designers are truly inspired by costume designers. I wanted to bring costume designers more to the forefront, but also about how the garments that we see in film and TV really do show up on the runway" (Gan, 2013).

Her own work as a costume designer has crossed over into fashion design thanks to numerous collaborations with Mack Weldon, Maidenform, and her most famous collaboration, the *Mad Men*-influenced "Back to Work" capsule collections that Bryant created for Banana Republic in August 2011, March 2012, and spring 2013. She also designed a limited-edition suit created for Brooks Brothers that sold out immediately.

Sources:
Allister, Graeme (2008, August 1). How Mad Men became a style guide. Retrieved from http://www.theguardian.com/culture/tvandradioblog/2008/aug/01/youdonthavetowatchmadmen.
Ellsworth, Catherine (2010, October 10). Janie Bryant: The woman behind the *Mad Men* wardrobe. Retrieved from http://fashion.telegraph.co.uk/article/TMG8051535/Janie-Bryant-the-woman-behind-the-Mad-Men-wardrobe.html.
Gan, Vicky (2013, September 4). Go behind the styles with *Mad Men*'s Emmy-nominated costume designer. Retrieved from http://www.smithsonianmag.com/smithsonian-institution/go-behind-the-styles-with-mad-mens-emmy-nominated-costume-designer-3802088/.
Heaf, Jonathan and Lauren Cochrane (2014, April 15). How *Mad Men* changed the way men dress. Retrieved from http://www.theguardian.com/fashion/2014/apr/15/mad-men-changed-way-men-dress-don-draper.
Janie Bryant: Awards (2014). Retrieved from imdb.com.
Long, Carola. (2010, February 26). Prada turns back clock with return to "Mad Men." Retrieved from http://www.independent.co.uk/life-style/fashion/news/prada-turns-back-clock-with-return-to-mad-men-1911330.html.
Mower, Sarah (2010, March 10). Louis Vuitton fall 2010 ready-to-wear. Retrieved from http://www.style.com/fashion-shows/fall-2010-ready-to-wear/louis-vuitton.

Figure 5.1
Films based on classic novels such as *The Great Gatsby* can inspire fashion trends based on the era in which they are set.

(a)

(b)

Figure 5.2
Oscar de la Renta was frequently inspired by art, including cubism (a) which he referenced in his resort 2012 collection (b).

with rural or blue-collar workers (the caps are also known as "gimme caps" because they frequently have advertising on the crown and are given away to customers). They were worn by young trendsetters in hip neighborhoods in Brooklyn such as Williamsburg and in Los Angeles' Silverlake, and then became a trend among suburban young people after they were popularized by celebrities such as Ashton Kutcher and Justin Timberlake. Flannel shirts experienced a similar spike in mainstream popularity. Popular with loggers in the Pacific Northwest, flannel shirts were embraced by trendsetters in the 1990s after seeing them worn by Grunge artists such as Nirvana and Pearl Jam. The influence of Grunge even trickled up to fashion runways when Marc Jacobs, who was then creative director for Perry Ellis, created a Grunge-inspired collection for spring/summer 1993 that featured Doc Martens, beanie caps, and plenty of flannel shirts. The collection did not fit with the brand's preppy image and promptly got him fired, although the look did connect with a mass audience and gained widespread popularity for a short time. Flannel shirts had a more recent revival among young women in fall 2013, when blogs such as WhoWhatWear and Buzznet featured articles such as "Top 20 Flannel Shirts for Fall" (Baker, 2013) and "30 Ways to Wear a Flannel Shirt" (Knight, 2013).

However, of the three, it is the third source, popular culture, that has the most obvious and direct impact on what the majority of consumers choose to wear at any given time. Popular culture serves as a source of new meanings and as a conduit to transmit those meanings to people (McCracken, 1988b). Slang expressions, lifestyles, sports and pastimes, personality and mood—popular culture is a visual dictionary of meanings. Mass media constantly revise the meanings of old goods and give meaning to new goods. In this way popular culture acts as innovator and as a **distant opinion leader** for consumer culture. The consumption of fashion goods and related products such as fragrance is more involved than mere purchase behavior. Consumption is a cultural phenomenon and the

designers, advertising executives, and fashion press participate in creating our cultural universe by connecting meaning to consumer goods. Consumers construct their personal worlds by choosing the products that have meaning for them (McCracken, 1988b). In this process, pop culture has both direct and indirect influence on the consumer's ideas about appropriateness, beauty, and fashion.

TYPES OF POPULAR CULTURE

✦ PRINT MEDIA

Although there has been some outcry that print journalism is in its sunset phase, fashion magazines such as *Vogue*, *Elle*, and *Harper's Bazaar* still hold tremendous influence over consumers' tastes. According to Lisa Smosarski, editor of *Stylist* magazine, which has a circulation of over 435,000 copies weekly in cities across Britain, "The two-page 'StyleList' we run at the front of the magazine shifts a lot of product: a big department store told us if we ever feature anything in the magazine they sell out" (Grimond, et al., 2014). However, magazines today don't influence trends as much as present them to their readers. Lucinda Chambers, fashion director at *British Vogue*, says, "I prefer to inspire rather than influence; influence sounds like bending someone to your will, and *Vogue* is not a catalogue—I don't expect people to buy slavishly off the page. But I understand women who are unsure of themselves, and I hope I can help them digest and simplify what's going on in fashion" (Grimond, et al., 2014).

In order to keep their reputation as arbiters of fashion when the world of media is changing so quickly around them, print magazines have had to change with the times. *Vogue* keeps its profile as the fashion world's foremost magazine through its partnerships with the Council of Fashion Designers of America (CFDA). The CFDA/*Vogue* Fashion Fund was founded in 2004 to promote American design and is now one of the most influential prizes in the fashion industry, having helped found the careers of previous winners such as Proenza Schouler, Alexander Wang, and Joseph Altuzarra. The Fashion Fund is also a video series on *Vogue*'s website, so readers can get to know the competitors, which makes them feel like insiders. *Vogue* editor Anna Wintour has been the co-chair of the Metropolitan Museum of Art's annual Costume Institute Gala since 1995 (although the event itself dates back to 1948), and has turned it into a celebrity-filled event that has raised $125 million for the institute, which was officially renamed the Anna Wintour Costume Center in January of 2014 (Shewfelt, 2014). Anna Wintour herself is a universally recognized trendsetter both in publishing and in style: in the movie *The September Issue* (2009), creative director Grace Coddington notes that Wintour was the first fashion editor to put celebrities on the cover of *Vogue* before any other publications were doing so. Sales of the magazine went up, other magazines followed *Vogue*'s lead, and celebrities effectively replaced models as the subject of fashion magazine covers. Likewise, when Wintour adopts a new trend, it makes news. When photos of the editor using a flip phone at the 2014 US Open were released, despite her having owned an iPhone since at least 2012, headlines were made and she was regarded as cool for not being a slave to technology and not caring about being constantly reachable—and, as we learned earlier in this chapter, not caring is the ultimate form of coolness (Stoefel, 2014).

Other print magazines have strengthened their position in consumers' minds as fashion tastemakers by becoming fashion brands themselves. *Elle* magazine has a licensed-clothing business, which got its start in Japan over 25 years ago and now operates in eighty countries, including more than 250 free-standing *Elle* stores and an exclusive line of *Elle*-branded women's clothing sold at Kohl's stores (Covert, 2007). *Harper's Bazaar* has chosen to go the e-commerce route with its *ShopBazaar* website, in which items come from past issues of the magazine, or just missed the cut. The magazine partnered with Saks Fifth Avenue for the launch, and about 80 percent of the merchandise is sourced, held, and shipped by Saks and other partners, but everything can be purchased through a shopping basket on *ShopBazaar* (Wicks, 2012). Magazines have taken a cue from loyalty programs from retailers and now reach out to their readers through programs such as *Elle* Inner Circle, *Harper's Bazaar* Style Ambassadors, *Allure* Beauty Enthusiasts, and *Lucky* magazine's Lucky Ones. With online quizzes, contests, product giveaways, Facebook and Twitter posts, magazines now can have direct contact with their audience and can share their fashion advice in a real-time format, making sure they are always on top of a breaking trend.

✦ MOVIES

Movies have been responsible for some of the most iconic fashion moments in history. A big-screen image can be influential for decades— Marlon Brando in a white T-shirt from *The Wild One*, John Travolta's white suit in *Saturday Night Fever*, or Jennifer Beals in a shoulder-baring sweatshirt in *Flashdance*.

In the 2000s, movies as different as the *Pirates of the Caribbean* series with its romantically disheveled chic look and the *Ocean's Eleven* series showing off slick Las Vegas styles appealed to consumers and retailers. More recently, *The Hunger Games* movie series inspired a slew of online tutorials instructing how to create a "fishtail" braid similar to the one worn by the character Katniss in response to consumers demanding the trend.

Historically, movie costume designers have both reflected trends and set them. Early standouts included Adrian, who worked on MGM productions like *The Philadelphia Story*, in which he dressed Lauren Bacall as a rich socialite. Adrian worked with the actress Joan Crawford twenty-eight times and created her signature look of big shoulder pads, which became a trend, and most famously designed the ruby slippers that Judy Garland wore in *The Wizard of Oz*, for which he was the costume designer ("Adrian," 2014). Edith Head, of Paramount and later Universal, who designed costumes for Grace Kelly in *Rear Window* and *To*

Catch a Thief and Audrey Hepburn in classics such as *Roman Holiday*, *Sabrina*, and *Funny Face*, won eight Academy Awards (Meltzer, 2013).

However, the influence that movies have on fashion appears to be dwindling. According to Simon Doonan, the Creative Ambassador-at-Large for Barneys New York, it's rare to find real fashion in films or have them influence fashion in a meaningful way: "These days the inspiration of film is never very apparent … what those viewers take away is often a single wardrobe item, a talisman. It's like they're getting a holy relic" (La Ferla, 2010). Even successful movie costume designers like Catherine Martin, who did the designs for *The Great Gatsby*, and Trish Summerville who is doing the next *Hunger Games* movie with a tie in line, Capitol Couture by Trish Summerville, on Net-a-Porter, are less well-known than their television counterparts, who are becoming brands in their own right (Meltzer, 2013).

✦ TELEVISION

Even though the Internet and mobile devices have received the majority of the attention recently as platforms for raising consumers' brand awareness, television is still a more effective medium for impacting consumer behavior through creating an emotional connection and introducing novelty. The main factor that makes television more effective than more recent forms of media is that a larger screen creates a more engaging environment, in which emotional triggers such as facial expressions are more easily perceived. Television's immersive environment results in higher emotional engagement, commercial recall, and intent to purchase, so television is still crucial in introducing new trends to a mass audience (Crupi, 2009).

The impact of television on influencing trends has resulted in a relatively new type of behind-the-scenes trendsetter: the costume designer. Costume designers do not fill the same role as celebrity stylists. "I work with the script, the director, the writer and the actor to figure out what the costume needs to do to help the actor

inhabit that person. Stylists are about satisfying the needs of the actor on the red carpet. They're telling a story, too, but it's really the story the actor wants to tell," said Audrey Fisher, the costume designer of *True Blood* on HBO. As television shows have gained critical respect as a medium due to the improvement in writing quality and production values, costume designers now say that working for television gives them greater opportunity to influence the culture at large than films provide. Previously, these professionals worked anonymously behind the scenes, but in the 1980s Nolan Miller gained widespread fame as the costume designer for the television show *Dynasty*, with a weekly wardrobe budget of $35,000, and by designing 3,000 costumes over the series' run from 1981 to 1989 (Cowles, 2012). Using television as his medium, Miller defined the over-the-top look of the 1980s through his use of gold lamé fabrics, furs, leather, and especially shoulder pads, which made the wearer appear bigger and more substantial, and were particularly popular with working women who were achieving more authority in the workforce than ever before and viewed their business attire as their own professional "armor" (Ryssdal, 2012). Ultimately, Miller made the jump from designing for television to having his own fashion line sold on QVC prior to his death in 2012.

As Miller defined the look of the 1980s, costume designer Patricia Fields defined the look of the 1990s, and became a celebrity in her own right. Fields opened her boutique in Greenwich Village in 1966, but it was as the costume designer for the HBO series *Sex and the City* where she gained her reputation. Her work on the show made household names out of brands such as Manolo Blahnik and Prada, and spawned trends including tutus, nameplate necklaces, and large silk flowers as accessories. For her creativity on the show, Fields earned five Emmy nominations and a win in 2002. In addition to her television work on *SATC* and other shows such as ABC's *Ugly Betty*, Field also designed costumes for a number of fashion-forward films, such as *Confessions of a Shopaholic* and *The Devil Wears Prada* (Figure 5.3), for which she received an

Figure 5.3

Stylist Patricia Fields is best known for her trend-inspiring work on the television show *Sex and the City*, but has also worked on such style-conscious films as *The Devil Wears Prada*.

Academy Award nomination ("Bio," 2014; "Honorary Clio," 2013).

In the 2000s, the show *Gossip Girl* emerged as a major source for trends which, according to Eric Daman, the show's costume designer, was always the goal: "We tried to launch trends from the get-go" (La Ferla, 2008d). Daman learned from the best, having spent time working on-set with Patricia Field on costumes for *Sex and the City*. In addition to igniting trends such as piped blazers, tiny kilts, plaid-mixing, argyle sweaters, knee socks, high boots, headbands, and layers of jewelry, *Gossip Girl* set trends in how fans could purchase the fashions they saw on screen. By charging some brands to be featured on the show and through point-and-click shopping on its website, the show didn't just generate trends; it also generated profit from its fashions.

Just as *Sex and the City* made certain brands household names in the 1990s, *Gossip Girl* put designers such as Nanette Lepore and Tory Burch in the spotlight. Lepore did not pay to have a character inquire, "Do you like my new Nanette Lepore?" in one episode or have her clothes featured, but she enjoyed the benefits of inclusion when, "within days after one of

our dresses appears, the store gets calls … Younger girls come in, they know which piece was featured and they look for it." Designer Tory Burch said that having an item on the show "translates to sales." As she said, "We have girls coming in with magazine tear sheets of Blake Lively or Leighton Meester, from location shootings or from everyday life" (La Ferla, 2008d).

Gossip Girl's strategic use of fashion as a show focal point was the blueprint for more recent shows such as *Pretty Little Liars* on ABC Family. According to costume designer Mandi Line, "I said, 'If you let me make fashion the fifth character on this show, people will watch it just for the clothes.'" She was correct, and "Every single day I get tweets, Facebook messages and Instagrams from girls who line up their clothes next to photos of the characters … I have seen feather earrings and black-and-white-stripe dresses in stores" (Meltzer, 2013).

Because of this newfound attention, costume designers are now represented by agents and becoming brands unto themselves, much like the celebrities they dress on the shows where they work. The Matchbook Company represents

House of Cards costume designer Tom Broecker, Dan Lawson of *The Good Wife*, Jenn Rogien, costume designer for both *Girls* and *Orange Is the New Black*," and Lyn Paolo of both *Shameless* and *Scandal*. Linda Kearns, Vice President for Brand Development at Matchbook, says, "We want the public to recognize them as people, not just behind the scenes …We are focusing on the TV designers because there's a bigger attachment when the characters of the show enter your home and life each week" (Meltzer, 2013).

Costume designers have a unique challenge, since each character has to have a distinctive style that reflects their personality, as opposed to just wearing whatever looks good on television. This can require a lot of thought and psychology on the part of the costume designer, particularly when there are considerations a fashion designer would never have to make in regular life. As Audrey Fisher, who dressed the cast of the HBO television show *True Blood* explains, "The supernatural creatures' costumes have to reflect their history or their special powers, just like the humans, in a way! For instance I always put Sam Merlotte in a snap-front Western shirt, the back story being that he's accustomed to shifting, and is sick of ruining button shirts, so he starts wearing only snaps so he could rip out of clothes easily when shifting. It's fun to try to humanize the supernatural details with practical choices like that!" ("True Blood Costume Designer," 2014).

But as with any form of media with unpredictable audiences, there is risk associated with a television tie-in campaign, which Saks Fifth Avenue learned with their first television promotion, Fox Broadcasting and 20th Century Fox Television's *Girl's Club*. The match seemed ideal: "Saks is a lifestyle brand that speaks directly to the young, upscale women who represent the core of the *Girl's Club* (target) audience," said 20th Century Fox Television Vice President of Advertising, Publicity and Promotion Steven Melnick (Rose, 2002). Unfortunately for Saks, the show was canceled after only two episodes and the stores' tie-in window displays were left up for weeks after its cancellation, an embarrassing reminder of its failed collaboration (Brownfield, 2002).

✦ MUSIC

On the Burberry website, the menu includes the standard categories for a fashion retailer—Men, Women, Children, Beauty—but one tab stands out: "Acoustic." Visitors to the site who click on this tab can view more than seventy-five videos of acoustic performances by musicians, some of whom are emerging and some of whom are more established in their careers. In June 2014, in addition to showcasing its spring 2015 menswear collection, Burberry used its show to also introduce the public at large to British singer Josh Record, who performed an acoustic set at the show and gave media interviews sharing his gratitude to the brand: "It's so creative and it's such art that it's amazing to collaborate with fashion, because you're both creating something" (Record, 2014). Burberry is no longer only a trendsetter in fashion; it is now a trendsetter in music as well.

Popular music today is totally image driven, and as singer Kevin Rowland of Dexy's Midnight Runners says, "To me, they always go together— the look somehow has to match the music" (Rowland, 2014). Dexy's Midnight Runners got their start dressing like dock workers with their first UK hit "Geno," but as their music began to change, he felt their look should change too, so he consulted with costumer designer Debbie Williams, who based the band's "dustbowl" image for the "Come On Eileen" video from a cover she had seen on a copy of Steinbeck's *The Grapes of Wrath*, because she saw economic and social similarities between Depression-era America and early-1980s England, and ended up creating a look so iconic that the band was cited as a reference when overalls once again became a trend for young women in spring 2014 (Friedman, 2014; Rowland, 2014).

As stated earlier in the chapter, there are similarities between music and fashion, both serving as a kind of shorthand for expressing our social identities, although, in addition to the absence of a copyright system for fashion, a few other major differences separate the two. The first is that music is invisible, requiring only our auditory senses, and fashion is primarily visible. The second is that, unlike music, fashion is utilitarian, so it must be functional at the same time it is creative (Sinnreich & Gluck, 2005). But both fashion and music are so much a part of the average person's daily life that many people don't even consider them as works of art in the same way they would a painting or sculpture.

The BBC television documentary *Oh You Pretty Things* traces the strong ties between music and fashion, from the style tribes of England such as the Mods, Rude Boys, Punks, and Skinheads, which were originally made up of rebellious British youths, but are now regularly used as inspiration for mainstream fashion. Leather, skulls, ripped jeans, Doc Martens boots—all of these were once associated with outcasts who were defined by the music they listened to and the clothes they wore to show their conspicuous outrage at society. At the same time, mainstream pop music is one of the biggest drivers of trends among teenagers, with Taylor Swift named as one of *People* magazine's Best Dressed of 2014, and also recognized (with model Cara Delevingne) as one of the "reigning queens of style" by *Vanity Fair* magazine in September 2014 for her Instagram expertise, the way the fashion world has embraced her, and how relatable she is (Dubroff, 2014).

✦ ONLINE MEDIA

In the distant past, trends spread via people who had gone somewhere that was a recognized fashion capital such as London or Paris. Then, beginning in the twentieth century, movies, television, and magazines accelerated the spread of trends. Now, with the Internet, blogs, and social media, trends have an instantaneous reach. Viral marketing (also called guerrilla marketing) builds on the power of word-of-mouth in personal networks and buzz in media networks. The idea is to spread a message to a wide population by beginning with a few key carriers.

Because many people have grown up with traditional marketing, they may become resistant to its ploys. Viral marketing gives them the feeling that they are discovering products through personal or media networks in a way that makes them "in the know" when compared

to the rest of society. Practitioners of viral marketing may:

* field "street teams" of young people who visit clubs, sporting events, concerts, and other hot spots in urban markets and distribute stickers, posters, or other promotional freebies to encourage word-of-mouth on a product or brand (Knight, 1999);
* create an event such as an unfolding drama acted out on adjacent billboards placed in a prime urban location (Lloyd, 2007);
* give away next season's designs to editors, stylists, artists, DJs, Internet entrepreneurs, writers, and other cultural creatives who may be seen and photographed wearing the designs as a way to build buzz—a process called product seeding (Socha & Ozzard, 2000).

Whatever its form, viral marketing usually includes something free, cross-linking influences (e.g., fashion and music, art, or sports), piggybacking on other events, using multiple channels (e.g., an event plus a website and media coverage), and meshing promotion with natural occurring behaviors (e.g., street teams and stencil campaigns).

As consumers get more aware of viral marketing, retailers are getting more creative in their approaches. JC Penney received a huge amount of press coverage for two garbled tweets sent from the company's Twitter account during the Super Bowl that gave the impression that the sender was inebriated. After many retweets, it was revealed that the tweets were sent by its social media team to promote the retailer's "Go USA" mittens. For the stunt, JC Penney got more media attention than most of the companies who paid for Super Bowl advertisements (Heine, 2014). Another viral marketing ploy that garnered a huge amount of attention was the short film *First Kiss*, which showed twenty strangers meeting for the first time on camera and then sharing their first kiss within seconds of meeting (Figure 5.4). "I had no idea it was going to be so huge. I mean we had an idea it could go viral—when I looked at it I knew it was

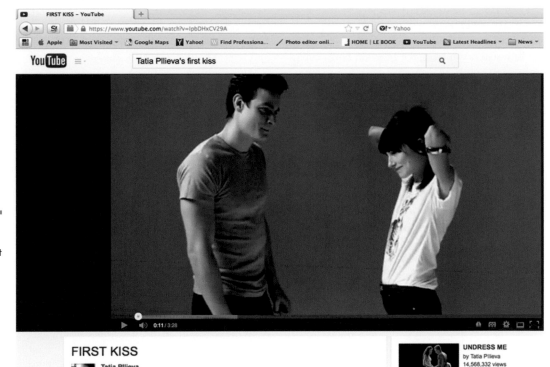

Figure 5.4

The *First Kiss* video went viral before the public realized it was for the clothing brand Wren. The video was viewed over 82 million times after its release, getting far more attention than a typical advertising campaign would.

something really special and everyone who saw it really responded to it. But when I looked at it this morning it was at 1.7 million views … now it's at more than 6 million!" says Wren designer and founder Melissa Coker. With the brief message "presented by Wren" and tweeted from the company website, the video, featuring models, singers, and actors wearing Wren clothing, amassed over 82 million YouTube views within the first 2 months after it was released (Holmes, 2014). We can only imagine what the next great viral marketing campaign will be, but what is less certain is whether all of this media attention translates into increased sales for the retailer.

Now, with worldwide access to the same media, consumers in all parts of the country and even the world can be attracted to and adopt trends simultaneously. Firsthand experience is no longer an elemental part of the process. Online media can be divided into several distinct categories, which will be discussed below.

✧ Fashion Blogs

A few fashion blogs emerged in the mid-2000s as important enough for their creators to receive invitations to designer shows ("Memo Pad," 2007). They are much faster at disseminating news when compared to traditional media like magazines—bloggers can see a runway show, comment on it, and provide video feeds within an hour, compared to 3 months or longer for magazines (Britten, 2007). Professional fashion journalists also create popular blogs giving instant commentary on runway shows and revealing insights on their lives as industry insiders ("Defining Moments," 2007). This combination of high visibility and the sentiment that a trend which meets bloggers' approval is a desirable status marker leads to speedy diffusion of a trend. The trend ends when the fashion has moved from group to group until almost anyone who wants the product has the product or a knockoff.

Fashion blogs focus on a domain—street fashion relaying sightings almost instantly to readers, a particular category like status bags, celebrity shopping venues, personal fashion quests, or criticism (Britten, 2007). The problem for forecasters is finding the relevant blogs using traditional search engines. Google takes as long as 3 weeks to index the Web and orders results by popularity. Blogs update daily and may be important for a small but important community of readers (Crow, 2007).

Fashion blogs written by independent writers not associated with magazines or corporations range from celebrity sightings to street style, shopping guides to runway reviews (Figure 5.5). A more recent category, local style blogs, focuses on identifying the fashion signature of the area and the best sources for that look. Blogs are more current because their reaction time is faster than traditional media (fashion magazines work 3 or more months in advance of release). Print media reacted to the quick response of fashion blogs by adding blogs to their websites (Britten, 2007). Today, every print fashion magazine has a blog that is updated daily with content that complements the articles found in the magazine. Designers reacted by inviting the new media to join the old media at the runway shows in New York, London, Paris, and Milan—of the approximately 3,500 journalists, 10 percent write for blogs (Thompson Smith, 2007).

Along with the proliferation of user-generated content came questions about its reliability. Iconoculture, a trend advisory service, cited a swing back to expert opinion and professionally edited content for consumers seeking credible sources ("Iconoculture," 2007). One Internet entrepreneur, linking content with the potential for premium audiences and advertising money, said, "The more trusted an environment, the more you can charge for it" (Dokoupil, 2008).

✧ Types of Fashion Blogs

The sheer variety of fashion blogs means that readers can find a blog that caters to their specific preferences. A general list of some of the types of blogs and the most popular examples include the following:

Informational Blogs. A new wave of fashion blogs is bringing up-to-the-minute trend and industry information to readers, making them feel like fashion insiders. *Racked* was founded in New York in 2007, and in addition to

Figure 5.5
Today, the definition of fashion journalism has expanded to include bloggers, some of whom have as much power as fashion editors to start new trends.

disseminating fashion trends, the site shares information with readers such as sample sales and store openings. *Racked* features focused coverage of the fashion markets in New York, Boston, Philadelphia, Chicago, Los Angeles, and San Francisco and general nationwide news. The *Racked* reader profile is that for a true trendsetter: 70 percent of readers are 21–34 years old (with a median age of 29), 85.3 percent have graduated from college, 35.9 percent earn $100,000 or more, 83 percent are female, 82 percent frequently provide advice on fashion and 85 percent have gone to a sale listed on *Racked* ("Audience," 2014).

With the stated mission of becoming "the #1 new-media brand for smart, creative and stylish women everywhere," *Refinery29* is currently the fastest growing independent fashion and style website in the United States. Started with an initial investment of $5,000 in 2005, the blog is a lifestyle platform that connects over 10 million monthly visitors and 1.25 million e-mail subscribers with content covering fashion trends, shopping, beauty, wellness, and celebrities. *Refinery29* currently publishes 1,800 stories per month, and was named the fastest-growing media company in the United States ("About," 2014; "Corporate," 2014).

Personal Blogs. One of the earliest fashion blogs was *BryanBoy*, which was begun in 2004 by Bryan Grey-Yambao, who set the standard for the bloggers who made a name for themselves by sharing their shopping hauls and posting glamorous images of themselves. *BryanBoy* also was among the first bloggers to receive presents from designers, a practice known as "gifting," and to include full disclosure of those gifts to readers, as well as generate income by receiving extensive personal appearance fees (Sauers, 2012).

Leandra Medine, founder of *Man Repeller*, was voted the top fashion blogger on the Web by fashionista.com. Medine started *Man Repeller* in April 2010, after coming up with the name during a trip to Topshop with a friend who told her that all of the items in the store that she was drawn to were designed to repel men. As her profile has grown, so has her business. She is

now author of a book, sells advertising space on her blog, and has three employees (Koski, 2013). Unlike many fashion blogs, what sets *Man Repeller* apart is Medine's self-deprecating sense of humor.

LOLO Magazine is an online lifestyle magazine that "unites all things fashion, beauty and health" through the distinctive worldview of its founder, Lauren Scruggs (Figure 5.6). Scruggs's personal history is both compelling and inspiring to her readership. Born in southern California and raised in the Dallas area, her work experience in the fashion industry made her well suited to her current position: she interned in the wardrobe department of the television show *Gossip Girl*, and in the Michael Kors showroom in New York City, and her career also included modeling and reporting on fashion week in New York, Paris, and Montreal. Scruggs became a household name for a tragic accident that

Figure 5.6

Model Lauren Scruggs parlayed her fashion industry experience and sense of personal style into her own lifestyle blog, *LOLO Magazine*.

occurred in December 2011 in which she lost her left eye and hand after accidentally walking into the spinning propeller of a small plane at night. Her recovery was chronicled in her book, *Still Lolo: A Spinning Propeller, A Horrifying Accident, and a Family's Journey of Hope*, which was published in August 2013. "I have gained a new perspective of life and I feel like I need to use my message of hope and healing to help others, [and] inspire others, just like people have inspired me."

LOLO Magazine has several categories of lifestyle-related content, including "Fashion," which provides trend information and suggestions on how readers can incorporate key looks in their own wardrobe; "Inspired," a section that provides encouragement for physical activity and personal growth; "Eats," which is devoted to sharing recipes, and reviews of restaurants, products, and food-related Web services; "Beauty," a combination of tutorials and product recommendations; and "Shop," links to websites where readers can purchase the same products and looks featured in the magazine. While the overall content of the magazine is diverse, communicating new trends is at the heart of the magazine: "To continuously network in the world of fashion as well as educate myself on upcoming trends and industry insight, I attend New York Fashion Week seasonally" (LOLO, 2014).

In keeping with its modern outlook, *LOLO Magazine* embraces all forms of social media, with a presence on Facebook, Twitter, and Instagram. On the magazine's Facebook page, fans can find additional style inspiration that complements the website content, frequently featuring looks put together by Dallas editor Lauren Sims. Scruggs's Twitter and Instagram accounts add a personal side to the website content, since she sends her own tweets. As part of a community of bloggers, Scruggs also enjoys a supportive relationship with other fashion and lifestyle bloggers, and they frequently appear in one another's blogs as interview subjects or guest commentators.

Street Style Blogs. The best known street style blog is *The Sartorialist*, founded in 2005 by Scott Schuman, a photographer who has gone on to shoot professionally for *GQ, Vogue Italia, Vogue*

Paris, and *Interview*. He has also done advertising campaigns for Nespresso, DKNY Jeans, Gant, OVS, Crate & Barrel, and Absolut vodka, and he shot the groundbreaking Art of the Trench project for Burberry ("Biography," 2014). Although Schuman shoots subjects with excellent style sense, "I'm not reporting on a bag; who's carrying what bag and who's wearing what dress. I'm not reporting on people," he says, "What I am looking for is a certain grace" (Amed, 2011). Schuman has made himself into a brand himself, with work in the permanent collections of the Victoria & Albert Museum and the Tokyo Metropolitan Museum of Photography, and is currently working on his third book ("Biography," 2014).

Another well-known street style blog is *Street Peeper*, founded by Phil Oh in 2006. Oh finds inspiration from street fashion found in fashion capitals such as New York, London, Paris, Melbourne, and Tokyo, but also secondary fashion markets such as Copenhagen, Amsterdam, Berlin, Buenos Aires, and Chicago, as well as from the runways during fashion weeks around the world. The blog spotlights trends for its readers, showing the trend on many different wearers to indicate its breadth (Swash, 2011).

Interestingly, just as fashion bloggers once upended the balance of power held over magazines through their use of new media, the field of blogging is now in the process of upheaval. After several seasons of bloggers receiving star treatment at fashion week (even receiving preferential seating over buyers in some situations), in December 2013 IMG fashion, which runs New York fashion week, announced that they would be cutting media guest lists by 20 percent and the majority of cuts would consist mostly of fashion bloggers (Wang, 2013). Part of the reason for the decision was to reduce crowds at Lincoln Center, which IMG says "has been swarmed with fashion bloggers, street-style photographers and fashion fans ... in addition to the hundreds of journalists and scores of celebrities" (Davis, 2013). One of the reasons that bloggers are not as influential now is that fashion editors and magazines have now embraced the same technologies that once set the bloggers apart and now have their own Instagram accounts, plus the credibility that comes with an established print journal's reputation. But while there may be a shakeup that results in smaller blogs folding, the most popular blogs will still find a place at the runway. Bloggers such as *BryanBoy* have shifted to branding themselves, and are making their money from collaborations, their own collections, and appearance fees, which can now reach $50,000 for one event. All of these activities combined earn top bloggers over $1 million annually. As Bryan Grey-Yambao himself put it, "I've made enough to live comfortably and be able to not wear samples and buy my clothes retail" (Strugatz and Yi, 2014).

Fan Blogs. Some of the current style icons have inspired blogs that facilitate how others can replicate their favorite stars' looks for themselves. The blog *What Kate Wore* has not only a blog, but also a Facebook and Tumblr page that chronicles all of the outfits (categorized by clothing/footwear/handbags) worn by the Duchess of Cambridge, tells what brand each piece of the garment is made by, gives prices, directs readers to where the items can be purchased and tells if there are any units left. The site has helped familiarize American audiences with UK brands such as Temperley London and LK Bennett. Fans of Middleton's fashion are loyal and have the money to spend to get her look: when Middleton wore a purple and white floral design of wool and silk by Prabal Gurung during her trip to Singapore in September 2012, the dress sold out from MyHabit.com (a subscriber fashion sale site owned by Amazon.com) in less than an hour, even with a price of $599 (Goldwert, 2012).

The Rihanna fan blog, *Haus of Rihanna,* was founded in 2011 as a way for fans to keep up with style icon Rihanna's fashion both on and off the red carpet. Because Rihanna is known for blending both high and low fashion in her looks, recent posts have featured items that the singer's fans can obtain for themselves, such as the Hunter original tall boots or a Victoria's Secret "The Angel" T-shirt, each worn by her in recent photos and identified by the site. Even though many of the items she wears are not within the price range of the typical fan, equal attention is given to Rihanna's designer clothing, such as a Balmain blue denim jumpsuit from the spring/summer 2014 women's wear collection she was photographed wearing at LAX International Airport, or a black parka by Chanel that she wore to Giorgio Baldi restaurant in Los Angeles.

✦ SOCIAL MEDIA

Social media has been a big step for fashion brands, but if done right, it pays off. As Jenna Lyons, president of J.Crew puts it, "We were late to the game with social media, but the results on Pinterest have been unbelievable: there's been tremendous excitement and a real desire to put up our images. We've had events where people have turned up in a head-to-toe look from our catalogue, or the 'Looks We Love' section from online" (Grimond et al., 2014). Ann Watson, Club Monaco's VP of marketing and communications, says, "Our goal is to use Facebook as a portal to share additional content that's not available anywhere else." Facebook is the place where Club Monaco news, content, and lookbooks are shared first, along with exclusive giveaways, such as concert tickets and original art. "The messaging is what differentiates it. We drive sales by humanizing the message around it—literally! We promote our product in a way that we hope fans feel is authentic, because we display it via real people on our team and the real way they wear our collections, offering genuine styling tips" (Indvik, 2011).

Because the types of social media change so quickly, here is a brief overview of the currently most popular social media platforms:

* *Facebook*—Founded in 2004, Facebook now has 1.23 billion users, and 757 million people log on to the site every day. The average number of friends among adult Facebook users is 338 (Sedghi, 2014).
* *Instagram*—This photo and video sharing app was established in October 2010 and purchased by Facebook in April 2012 and now has 200 million monthly actives, 65

percent of which are from outside the US. Twitter users share an average of 60 million photos per day, for a total of 20 billion photos to date ("Our Story," 2014).

❧ *Twitter*—Created in 2006, Twitter has 271 million monthly active users who send 500 million tweets per day. Twitter is a truly global platform; 77 percent of accounts are outside the US, and Twitter supports more than 35 languages ("About Twitter, Inc.," 2014).

❧ *Tumblr*—Since February 2007, Tumblr has hosted 206.3 million blogs with 76.2 million daily posts for a total of 93.1 billion posts to date. Tumblr is available in thirteen languages, and 42 percent of its traffic is from users in the United States ("Press Information," 2014).

❧ *Pinterest*—Founded in March 2010, Pinterest has "helped millions of people pick up new hobbies, find their style and plan life's important projects" ("Press," 2014).

The growth in popularity of social media is extraordinary: In a February 2014 survey of luxury brands, 93 percent of the 249 brands surveyed reported having an Instagram account, up from 63 percent in July 2013. Of these brands on Instagram, 43 percent of brands post more than once per day and 72 percent of brands are now producing Instagram videos. Although fashion brands and retailers currently dominate the platform, beauty brands have the fastest growing communities (McCarthy, 2014).

✦ CELEBRITIES

Celebrities act as influentials in their lifestyle choices and public appearances. A magazine editor explained that the red carpet at an awards show "is a runway show for us. The pickup pictures are the most important thing. Put [a star in a designer's dress] and the pictures turn up over and over again. Designers love the exposure. It's the equivalent of $10 million in free advertising" (La Ferla, 2003). A survey of 2,500 women (sponsored by a firm that covers celebrities) found that consumers look beyond the A-list to up-and-coming stars for fashion inspiration and beyond the red carpet to candid photos of the stars in real-life situations where styles are more accessible ("Celebrity," 2008).

Fashion brands rely on a celebrity to cut through the clutter of ad messages (Figure 5.7)

(a)

(b)

Figure 5.7

Fashion brands have increasingly used celebrities in their advertisements in the hope that the consumer will associate the brand with the celebrity's positive characteristics, like being trendy or likeable: (a) Lady Gaga, (b) Jennifer Lawrence.

with their recognition factor and expect the likeability of the celebrity to transfer to the product, but the relationship between viewer and celebrity is as psychologically complex as any other relationship. For example, designers will compete to dress Academy Award nominees, but that doesn't mean that the exposure will translate into higher sales. According to Lily Hollander, the former editorial director of StyleSpot.com, "For the most part, celebrities that drive sales aren't necessarily the ones that get nominated." At the 2010 Academy Awards, nominees like Sandra Bullock, Meryl Streep, and Gabourey Sidibe were all considered to be influential because of Bullock's ability to relate to women, Streep's appeal to the older consumer with money to spend, and Sidibe's favor with the plus-sized market. One nominee who didn't make the list was Carey Mulligan, although she most closely resembles the runway models the designers' clothes are shown on, because she doesn't motivate viewers to buy clothes in the same way as regular attendees Kate Hudson and Drew Barrymore, who appeal to Internet shoppers who have money (Binkley, 2010).

However, as the public becomes more aware of how celebrities are used to gain publicity for a brand or designer, more people are becoming skeptical of whether celebrities' style is showing their own personal taste or if it is just another form of paid advertisement. One designer, Nicole Farhi, spoke negatively about the practice of paying celebrities to attend fashion shows: "It is so unprofessional. I have never paid a celebrity and I will never do it. It's stupid. What do they show you in the papers after a fashion show? Not the clothes, but the celebrities who are paid to sit at the show" (Lusher, 2012). Even just paying for a celebrity's travel costs and expenses can add significantly to a designer's budget. Abe Gurko, a fashion talent services and public relations manager said, "The most I paid was about 18 months ago: $25,000 for flights for two people for a European star— the hotel, clothes, makeup, the car and driver— for three days. She was worth every nickel." But even he was opposed to appearance fees: "I

wouldn't give a dime. All this back-room dealing cheapens the whole business. And I don't think it's going to stop" (Lusher, 2012).

The connection between celebrities and endorsements is not new. As early as the 1860s, popular New York stage star Adah Isaacs Menken allowed the designer Madame Marguerite to advertise that she was the star's dressmaker, and in exchange, Menken was compensated with a new wardrobe. Fifteen years later, Dr. Gouraud, a purveyor of cosmetics, pioneered celebrity endorsement with advertisements that featured testimonials from actresses and singers popular at the time (Banner, 1983). In 1927, the Thompson advertising agency launched a campaign in which Hollywood stars praised the skin-care qualities of Lux soap (Fox, 1984). The practice of star endorsement was well established by the early 1940s.

The question of celebrity credibility was already a topic of concern in the 1920s. Starlet Constance Talmadge appeared as an endorser in eight ads for eight different products in a single national magazine in 1927—an early case of celebrity overexposure. By the 1950s, the public's attitude toward celebrity advertising had changed from one in which a celebrity could sell just about anything to a rejection of testimonials as insincere (Fox, 1984).

Features in weekly celebrity magazines such as *Us Weekly* or *Life & Style* create the illusion of interpersonal relationships with viewers. In today's media-rich environment, relationships of this imaginary sort are intertwined with media experiences (Horton & Wohl, 1956). The real social world consists of a few hundred relatives, friends, and acquaintances a person actually knows. The artificial social world consists of celebrities and the characters they play. Although the relationship takes place in the imagination, people identify with celebrities and feel as if they know them (Caughey, 1978). Social behavior and consumer purchasing can be influenced by media personalities because they act as advisors, role models, and ego ideals.

Today, television audiences are so fragmented, and there is so much competition with other forms of media that brands have new and different ways of getting their name out to consumers, even if consumers aren't aware that they are viewing a paid transaction. Teri Agins, author of *Hijacking the Runway: How Celebrities Are Stealing the Spotlight from Fashion Designers*, discusses the frequency of paid celebrity endorsements: "Covering the industry since 1989, I watched celebrities evolve from being a part of culture to being the spokesmen for everything." Although designers have had celebrities wear their clothes for promotional purposes for decades, it was always the designers themselves who were considered to be, as Agins puts it, "the gods, the arbiters of fashion. People were enamored with designers like Pierre Cardin, Dior, and Chanel and consumed these big brands because of their fascination. In the '70s, they told you what to wear because then you'd feel like a part of Paris. That mystique has now transferred to celebrities" (Lieber, 2014). Formerly, celebrities lined up to have the right designer dress them, but now it is the brands who pay for the celebrity to wear their products in public. Even a contract is not a guarantee that a celebrity will wear the product as they are supposed to. Agins gives the example of Charlize Theron, who had to pay an undisclosed sum of money for wearing a Dior watch after violating an exclusive contract she had with Raymond Weil (Lieber, 2014).

Today's media culture has given rise to a new type of fashion industry professional—the celebrity stylist. Because of the power that comes from dressing the world's most famous women, stylists such as Cristina Ehrlich, Erin Walsh, Leslie Fremar, Kate Young, Elizabeth Stewart, and the most famous celebrity stylist of all, Rachel Zoe, have major influence in setting trends. These stylists can start a trend just by having one of their clients wear it on the street and be photographed for a weekly magazine, and at the same time, they have enough clout to make a designer alter a runway garment based on what they think will look best on their client. As Leslie Fremar says, "I've been doing this for 10 years, and it's become relevant as a business during that time. A big business" (Grigoriadis, 2014). The business aspect extends to the stylist

becoming a brand themselves: Leslie Fremar has a collaboration with Fruit of the Loom selling T-shirts at Bloomingdale's. Kate Young had a limited-edition line of women's apparel and accessories at Target. Rachel Zoe, the stylist for Jennifer Lawrence, Anne Hathaway, and Kate Hudson, has her own fashion line sold through retailers such as Piperlime, and filmed five seasons of her reality show, The *Rachel Zoe Project*. Top stylists are aware of the power they hold. Leslie Fremar shares, "People don't understand that I collaborate with [Dior creative director] Raf Simons. This never would have happened before. Giorgio Armani would not have known who I was 10 years ago. He would only have known [*Vogue's*] Grace Coddington and Carlyne Cerf [de Dudzeele, fashion editor-at-large at *Lucky*]. If I run into [Lanvin's] Alber Elbaz, he says hi to me" (Grigoriadis, 2014).

Some celebrities such as Grace Kelly, Audrey Hepburn, or Jacqueline Kennedy Onassis influence fashion for decades. Marilyn Monroe was the muse for designer Jenny Packham's spring 2015 ready-to-wear line, which she researched by visiting Monroe's bungalow at the Beverly Hills Hotel and traveling to Jersey to view a private collection of the actress's dresses. "It's blatantly Marilyn Monroe … She's been there all my life, but I've rediscovered her again." Packham acknowledged Marilyn's enduring appeal: "She's still so relevant … What she wore doesn't date" (Sherman, 2014). However, like fashion, the idea of celebrity is constantly changing, and today's teens have a different concept of celebrities than they did even 20 years ago because of new media such as YouTube and Vine. In a survey of 1,500 Americans between the ages of 13 and 18, conducted for *Variety*, respondents answered a series of questions to measure how twenty well-known personalities ranked in terms of approachability, authenticity, and other criteria considered to be an indicator of their overall influence. Half the twenty were drawn from the English-language personalities with the most subscribers and video views on YouTube; the other half were represented by the celebrities with the highest Q scores among US teens aged 13–17, as of March 2014. The results

You Be the Forecaster: Top of the Pop Culture

Claire is a fashion designer for an apparel company that caters to the tween market and is looking for inspiration for the upcoming fall line. She hasn't been the same age as her target market for some time, so she wants to make sure that she is able to speak her customers' language. Claire wonders if what her customers like in terms of music, television, movies, and online media will influence the clothing trends they follow. She decides to immerse herself in the popular culture of the tweens she designs for and see whether inspiration will follow.

Like other creative fields, fashion takes inspiration from the culture around us and is a reflection of the dominant styles and tastes of the times. Consider how Claire can gain inspiration from other forms of culture and how she can reflect the aesthetic of what is popular in her own line.

Cultural Influences: How do cultures influence each other and to what extent do you think other forms of art influence fashion? Are some influences more suited to fashion? If so, which ones and why?

A Matter of Taste: Does Claire need to like the clothes that she designs for her target market herself to be effective as a designer? What is more important, designing for yourself or for your customer? How can she remove her own personal feelings from what she designs in order to best meet her customers' wants and needs?

Coolness: How can Claire help encourage the perception of her brand as cool by the tween market? Are having cool clothes enough, or are there other aspects to a brand that will influence consumers' ideas about its overall coolness?

Types of Popular Culture: Which of the types of popular culture covered in this chapter are the most widespread among the tween market? How can knowing what the target market likes in one type of popular culture help Claire create designs that appeal to them?

Online Media: How do online media differ from traditional media in terms of reach and influence? Which is more credible with a tween audience? As online media becomes more crowded and loses its novelty, what do you think will happen to its influence?

were surprising, with YouTube stars comprising the top five (and six of the top ten) positions. The top five scorers, in order, were Smosh, The Fine Bros., PewDiePie, KSI, and Ryan Higa (Ault, 2014).

The survey also found that YouTube stars scored significantly higher than traditional celebrities across a range of characteristics considered to have the highest correlation to influencing purchases among teens, such as being perceived as more engaging, extraordinary, and relatable than mainstream stars, who were viewed as being smarter and more reliable. Teens reported feeling an intimate and authentic experience with YouTube celebrities, who don't have a team of PR people working to craft their image. Teens also said they appreciated YouTube stars' more candid sense of humor, lack of filter, and risk-taking spirit, which are behaviors that are discouraged in mainstream celebrities, who want to appeal to as broad an audience as possible. However, as celebrity brand strategist Jeetendr Sehdev, who conducted the survey for *Variety*, advises, "If YouTube stars are swallowed by Hollywood they are in danger of becoming less authentic versions of themselves, and teenagers will be able to pick up on that. That could take away the one thing that makes YouTube stars so appealing." Instead, Sehdev suggests that Hollywood encourage its young celebrities to act more like YouTube stars, and that by encouraging unvarnished individualism, studios and networks can increase the appeal of mainstream celebrities among younger demographics (Ault, 2014).

CULTURE AND FORECASTING

It's possible to follow a trend that has a cultural basis from its initial forecast through the chain and ending with the consumer. Each season at Worth Global Style Network (more popularly known as WGSN), forecasters group their trend forecasts into overarching themes based on sociocultural research. WGSN forecasters look at the theories driving each of these trends and share the work of artists of different mediums who are currently examining each of these concepts. The work of these artists shows the emerging aesthetics in each trend category. So seeing what is going on in other forms of art provides confirmation of the trends that WGSN sees for fashion and gives a visual representation of these trends, which the company then shares with their clients. Their clients, the brands and designers who hear the trend forecasts, then translate those concepts into products which consumers choose from and influence each other in the process (WGSN, 2013).

In June 2013, WGSN released its forecast for spring/summer 2015, and one of the three macrotrends was named *Focus*. In the *Focus* forecast, WGSN discussed not only the influence of new technology such as high-definition cameras, but also the work of the artists Ed Atkins and Adeline de Monseignat, who use high definition to create detailed textures in their photographs that can be seen but not touched. The *Focus* trend also connected how "The practices, methods and technology of the Internet are moving into the physical exhibition space. Painters, sculptors and designers produce a new kind of highly textured and poetic expressionism. This is art in the real world, but based on virtual forms" (WGSN, 2014). To the forecaster, the similarities between these different aspects of art and culture are strong indicators of a developing trend that fashion designers can be at the forefront of.

The trend of using high definition in prints caught on early with designers and was spread by popular culture: in its recap of the Resort 2015 collections, *Elle* magazine featured an article on its website featuring "30 Best Resort 2015 Prints" that showed the collections of designers such as Carolina Herrera, Erdem, Cynthia Rowley, and Elizabeth and James, which included high-definition nature prints of florals and birds, and razor-sharp graphic prints from Missoni and Proenza Schouler (Prescod, 2014). Celebrities joined in the trend, such as model Cara Delevingne, who attended the Stella McCartney Resort 2015 collection in a yin–yang printed silk jumpsuit printed in high definition from

McCartney's collection, while Cate Blanchett wore a black dress with a multi-colored floral bodice from the Chanel Cruise 2015 collection at the Australian premiere of *How To Train Your Dragon 2* (Tse, 2014). Department stores such as Macy's then translated the high-definition trend for the junior's market with printed nylon/spandex leggings for their Material Girl brand (macys.com, 2014).

What is important for trend forecasters is to remember that new ideas don't come from the fashion world exclusively, but instead from sources all around. As Andrea Bell, retail and consumer editor at trend forecasting agency WGSN, says, you have to be immersed in all aspects of culture to catch the next big thing:

> A good trend forecaster is constantly aware of the shifts in the marketplace, rumbles in the art world, music, and fashion world. You don't have to be a hipster to get up early and go digging for records at a flea market, but the hunt may lead you to early adopters. Truly immerse yourself in culture and you'll find the common threads that lead to the big pictures. (Wang, 2014)

Chapter Summary

Fashion has much in common with art, music, film, and television, but it just recently has come to be considered one of the creative arts. Much like the way artists in these other areas influence one another, fashion innovation is driven by appropriation, or reinterpreting ideas from others in new and creative ways. Forecasters need to be aware of what is emerging in other areas of art in order to shape their fashion forecasts, because fashion frequently mirrors the arts, and what appeals to people in one branch of the arts will extend to others. Although fashion is a business, what separates it from other product categories is that it is subjective, and consumers don't buy for performance as much as because they like something. This subjectivity means that while some critics will say that fashion can be either in "good taste" or "bad taste" or "in" or "out," that criticism doesn't affect the average person who wears clothing, so whether a trend is adopted and its duration can't be controlled, although through understanding trends, such as how the idea of the concept of "cool" works, it can be predicted. Culture stems from high, low, and popular sources, with popular culture having the most visible and immediate impact on fashion. Traditional forms of media, including magazines, film, television, music, and celebrities have been joined by newer forms of online media such as fashion blogs and social media platforms. However fast the speed of information and communication becomes, forecasters have always had to remain at the forefront of the fashion process to convey that novelty to designers and consumers, and will continue to do so, whatever the medium.

Key Terms and Concepts

Appropriation

Distant opinion leader

Fashion blogs

High culture

Low culture

Popular culture

Viral Marketing

Discussion Questions

Changing Media: What television shows or movies do you remember as having an influence on your fashion sense when you were younger? Are there any shows that you look to now for fashion trends, if so, what are they? How do you watch movies and television shows now—do you watch more in theaters or on televisions with other people, or individually on small screens such as mobile devices? What do you think this means for the spread of trends in the future?

Celebrity Designers: What impact do celebrity designers such as Victoria Beckham and Mary Kate and Ashley Olsen's The Row have on fashion designers who are not celebrities in their own right? Do you think that the trend of celebrity designers is a lasting one, or will it fade away? How can fashion designers make themselves stand out now that they aren't just competing with other trained designers, but instead with actors and musicians?

Fashion and Social Platforms: Do you follow any fashion brands, designers, or retailers on social media? If so, which are the most active and successful at using social media to enhance their brand? What makes a good social media brand? What risks do fashion companies and designers take on when they communicate directly with their customers in such a public way?

Forecasting Activities

Social Media and Brand Image. Look at the websites, Facebook, Pinterest pages, and Twitter accounts for some of your favorite retailers. What is the image they are trying to portray to their customers? Does it match the perception? Is the message consistent across social media?

Star Map. Celebrities appeal to different groups of consumers. What movies, television shows, actors, bands, and singers are influential with college students? Is there a difference between celebrities who are influential with fashion innovators, and those who influence fashion leaders and fashion followers? Map the celebrities most influential for each group and present your findings as a portfolio spread or as a PowerPoint presentation.

The Online Street. Find blogs and websites that report on street fashion (see Resource Pointers). Some focus on the most fashion-forward consumers who create, explore, and discard trends quickly. Others look at fashion—what people at a particular location wear to express self, their lifestyle, and the times. Compare the two types of street fashion reporting to identify:

◆ *global trends*, those visible at several sites simultaneously;

◆ *emerging trends*, those that trickle from avant-garde to mainstream or from one geographical location to another.

What time lags are involved? Are there some street trends too fashion forward for immediate translation? Why?

Resource Pointers

Fashion blogs

Informational blogs
Racked: http://racked.com/
Refinery29: http://www.refinery29.com/

Opinion blogs

BryanBoy: http://www.bryanboy.com/
Man Repeller: http://www.manrepeller.
com/

Street style blogs

The Sartorialist: http://www.thesartorialist.
com/
Street Peeper: http://streetpeeper.com/

Fan blogs

Haus of Rihanna: http://hausofrihanna.
com/
What Kate Wore: http://whatkatewore.com/

PART TWO

FASHION DYNAMICS

> If fashion were a song, color would be the beat.
>
> —Fran Keenan, Saks

6

COLOR FORECASTING

OBJECTIVES

◆ Understand the importance of color as a marketing tool

◆ Describe the process of forecasting color, including color evolution, social and economic trends, consumer preferences, and other influences

◆ Conceptualize the role of color forecasting as a coordinating factor in the apparel supply chain from fiber producer to retailer

◆ Identify the techniques forecasters use to synthesize color direction from signs in the cultural environment

THE LANGUAGE OF COLOR

The human eye can discern 350,000 colors, but the human memory for color is poor. Most people cannot remember a specific color for more than a few seconds (Hope & Walch, 1990). In everyday conversations about color, it is sufficient to refer to a few colors by name—red, yellow, green, blue, white, and black—and add a qualifier—light or dark, bright or dull, cool or warm.

General terms are not sufficient for communicating color information for design and manufacturing. Exact identification, matching, and reproduction of colors requires an effective system with colors arranged in sequential order and identified with numbers and letters. Systems such as this are based on the basic three characteristics of color—hue, saturation, and value (Figure 6.1). **Hue** refers to the color—each color system designates a set of basic colors. Varying the other two characteristics fills out the system. **Saturation** (also called **intensity** or **chroma**) refers to the strength or purity of the color and **value** to the lightness or darkness of the color. The term **tint** applies to any color when white is added. **Shade** refers to colors mixed with black. **Tone** describes a grayed color. Creating a new tint, shade, or tone does not change the designation of the hue, but it does change the value and intensity of a color. Other terms in general usage in discussing color (Shibukawa, 1984) convey variations in value and intensity:

❖ "concentrated" to refer to intense, strong colors;
❖ "deep" to refer to rich, dark colors;
❖ "subdued" for colors neutralized through the addition of black, white, gray, or a color's complement;
❖ "clear" for colors without any neutralizing mix, colors such as the basic colors of the color wheel.

Color systems provide notation systems for the reproduction of colors and guidelines for harmonious color groupings. The **color wheel** (Figure 6.2) is the simplest version of such a system. The **primary colors** cannot be formed by mixing any other colors and are yellow, red, and blue; **secondary colors** are mixed from any two primaries (yellow + blue = green, yellow + red = orange, red + blue = violet). **Tertiary**

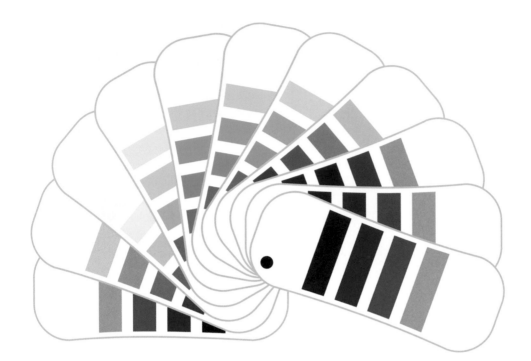

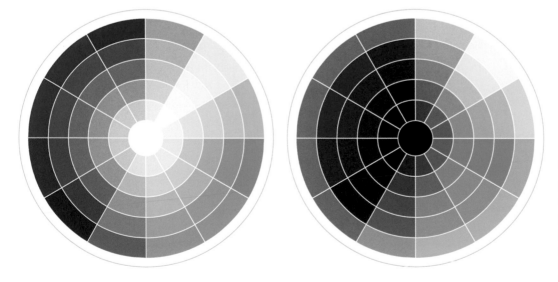

Figure 6.1

The Pantone®
Professional Color
System offers carefully
graded color samples of
different hues and
variations in their value
and intensity.

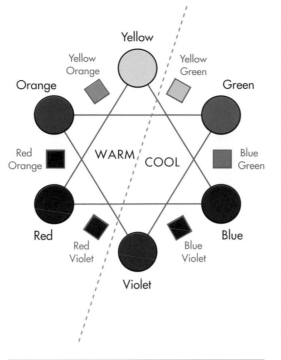

Figure 6.2

Color systems provide guidelines for harmonious color groupings. On the color wheel, colors directly across from each other provide maximum contrast (complements); colors next to each other offer blended color schemes (analogous).

colors are mixed from any one primary color and any one secondary color (yellow + green = yellow-green).

Color experts understand not only the individual colors but also the effect of colors in combination. Because research shows clear patterns of consumer preference linked to value, chroma, and color temperature, forecasters must also consider these relationships (Radeloff, 1991). With this expertise, the forecaster follows the subtle shifts in color trends, develops color stories for combining and coordinating colors, and predicts the significance of the colors for a product category. Relationships on the color wheel help designers select coordinate colors. When a patterned fabric or an ensemble uses colors next to each other on the color wheel, the color scheme is called **analogous**—for example, yellow, yellow-green, and green.

Complementary colors—colors opposite each other on the color wheel (also known as color **complements**)—intensify each other when used in combination even when they are mixed with white, black, or gray. The strong relationship between complements leads to variations: the **double complement** (two sets of complementary colors) and the **split complements** (a color plus the two colors on either side of its complement). Three colors spaced equidistant on the color wheel are called a **triad**—red, yellow, and blue make the primary triad; green, orange, and violet make the secondary triad. An infinite number of color combinations can be developed by varying the value and intensity of the colors (Davis, 1996). Color forecasters are trained experts who can look at colors, assess what they see, and express the qualities of each color in terms of hue, value, and saturation.

THE COLOR STORY

Color grabs customers' attention, makes an emotional connection, and leads them to the product (Figure 6.3). Color is rated as the most important aesthetic criterion in consumer preference (Eckman, Damhorst, & Kadolph, 1990). A 2010 study by Kissmetrics reveals that 85 percent of consumers name color as the primary reason why they buy a product. Even when the basic product stays the same, changing the color gives a sense of something new.

Color consultants help companies decide on the right color story (also known as a color palette)—a group of eight to ten selected colors based on a related theme to sell the product. Forecasts help manufacturers and retailers keep product lines fresh and new while avoiding lost sales caused by presenting products that the consumer is not ready to buy. Color direction means an inclination or tendency toward change in color temperature (warmer/cooler), value (lighter/darker), and intensity (clearer/grayer), or the relative importance of a hue (in/out). A new color is said to be "directional" when it is trendsetting or trend defining ("Color

Figure 6.3
Colorful jackets from
Herno on display at Pitti
W Woman
precollection trade show
in Florence, Italy. Color
grabs customers'
attention, makes an
emotional connection,
and leads them to the
product. Even if the
basic product stays the
same, color gives the
sense of newness.

Forecasting," 2003). For specific clients, forecasters fine-tune general forecasts by selecting particular shades for the target market, product category, price point, and selling venue.

COLOR NAMES

Changing the color of a product keeps the appeal of the new when the product itself does not change much. Color names boost marketing appeal and encourage the shopper to refresh his or her wardrobe. The color forecaster works in the two worlds of color naming—writing product specifications using the notation of particular color systems, and color marketing using color names that coordinate with a theme.

Naming a color for marketing means drawing attention to its attributes by linking the color with the consumer's perceptions. Imagine a light brown "café au lait"—no two people would visualize it the same way. But the theme (a cup of coffee), the season (autumn), the color key (warm), the color family (brown), and the value of the color (light) all are conveyed by the color

name. Even fashion can be captured in a color's name if it recalls cultural references. In the case of "café au lait," the reference is to coffee bars and gourmet coffee as high-fashion concepts—once considered to be a novelty, they have now moved into the mainstream.

Naming colors takes imagination, sensitivity to fashion change across product categories, an understanding of the customer's perception of colors, and the insight to make connections between color and the product's end use. Color description moves from the universal color names (black, white, red, green) to adding qualifiers (light, dark, bright, dull) to "looks like" names. Most color names come from associations in the environment (Eiseman & Herbert, 1990):

- *Natural phenomena*: sky blue, sunshine, grass green, snow white.
- *Flora*: poppy red, moss green, mahogany, orchid.
- *Fauna*: flamingo pink, robin's egg blue, dove gray.
- *Gemstones, minerals, and metals*: amethyst, lapis, amber, slate gray, copper.

- ❖ *Food and drink*: caramel, apricot, champagne, burgundy.
- ❖ *Spices*: cinnamon, paprika, curry.
- ❖ *Dyes*: indigo, cochineal.
- ❖ *Building materials*: brick, adobe, terracotta, bronze.
- ❖ *Locations*: Capri blue, Pompeian red.

Whatever the association, the goal is to depict a mood, paint a picture, and evoke fantasy in the mind of a consumer. Selling with color names dates back at least to the 1960s when green was rebranded as avocado, olive, and lime (Wilke, 1995). Today, the color forecaster, the manufacturer, and the retailer routinely use color names to link fashion change to shifts in the culture—the growing influence of the Hispanic population led to names such as Rosa Roja for red and Mesa Verde for green in palettes. However, color forecaster Fran Suda of Design Options chooses not to name her colors, opting instead for a numbering system, because "Everybody has a different concept of what tomato red is, so if somebody had a bad experience with a tomato red, why should I pay the price?" Suda feels that strategic decisions should be made based on the color itself and not on a name.

COLOR CYCLES

Color cycles refer to two phenomena: the periodic shifts in color preferences and the patterns of repetition in the popularity of colors. Both depend on consumers' desire for novelty—people get tired of what they have and seek something new. There is a time lag between the introduction of a new color or new color direction and its acceptance while people gain familiarity with the idea. Margaret Walch, former executive director of the Color Association of the United States, (or CAUS), identified one such time lag—designer Stephen Sprouse introduced acid shades in the early 1980s, but they were not included in the forecast until 1989 because some colors take longer than

others to become trends. By 1995, yellow-green was in every store from Neiman Marcus to Wal-Mart. A color that had been popular as "avocado" and "olive" in the late 1960s, then declined into a cliché for bad taste by the 1980s, later re-emerged as "kiwi" and "lime" to great popularity. Helped along by new advances in textiles and dyes, the yellow-green family of colors could be reinvented for an audience of young people who did not remember the originals (Morton, 2000). Leslie Harrington, a color consultant working on the CMG (Color Marketing Group) forecast in 2000 (now executive director of CAUS), is credited with her discovery and naming of the sushi-inspired "wasabi green"—a yellow-green that "took off" and stayed popular for years (Scrivener, 2007).

Colors and color palettes move from trendy to mainstream. In time, interest in the colors wanes and then they are replaced by the next new thing. This mechanism means that colors have somewhat predictable life cycles (Danger, 1968; Jack & Schiffer, 1948; Nichols, 1996). It also means that colors that were once popular can be repositioned in a future season—the "harvest gold" of the 1970s became the "sunflower gold" of the 1990s (Nichols, 1996). "French country blue" in the 1980s became new as "periwinkle" in a Provençal palette for 2000. As "Blue Iris," it was named Pantone's 2008 Color of the Year and was selected as the favorite of New York designers for the fall season, according to a Pantone survey. Leatrice Eiseman of the Pantone Color Institute explained that it represented calm in a turbulent year while maintaining a strength and richness because of the purple undertone (Hall, 2008).

The adoption period for a group of colors evolves over a period of 10 to 12 years, reaching its peak in mid-cycle. The color usually appears in fashion, moving quickly to high-end interiors, and then to the rest of the consumer products market.

Beginning with the first color forecast for women's apparel in 1917, the cycles in colors can be charted (Hope & Walch, 1990; Porter, 1994). That first forecast accurately identified the bright purples, greens, and blues, shown by avant-garde couture designer Paul Poiret, which would move into wider use. These colors were appropriated in the short dresses worn by 1920s flappers as a badge of rebellion against traditional women's roles. In the 1930s, Jean Harlow vamped in slinky white dresses for Hollywood films while those hit hard by the Depression preferred soil-resistant brown. In the late 1930s, Schiaparelli mixed art and fashion and introduced "shocking pink"—a radical repositioning of a traditionally pale color symbolizing sweetness and femininity. The years of World War II brought the withdrawal of dyes and pigments from consumer products.

After the war, pent-up demand for fashion was satisfied in the lavish use of fabrics and more vivid color palettes of the New Look by Dior. For less upscale consumers, the postwar period meant the practical, comfortable look of American fashion epitomized by Claire McCardell—bright-colored clothes, mix-and-match possibilities, and styles for a casual lifestyle. The stability of the Eisenhower era (1953–61) was reflected in the popularity of pastels and American favorites, red and navy blue. With the 1960s came fluorescent, acid, and hot colors associated with the youth movement and psychedelic drug experiences. In the 1970s, hippies in denim became fascinated with the authenticity of the American Southwest, beginning the domination of earthy colors associated with the region.

The 1970s ended on a bright note influenced by the punk movement, characterized by bold clothing statements and green and purple hair. The color explosion continued into the 1980s with an upscale pastel phase, the postmodern influence of the Memphis design group based in Milan, Italy on furnishings, and Nancy Reagan's signature red. Lacroix reintroduced Schiaparelli's pink as a fashion color, but because of the brights and neons of the 1960s, the color that had once been considered shocking was now perceived as a soft, bright color. Concerns about the environment made the 1990s the green decade, updating the color symbol for fertility from antiquity. Along with green came the "back to nature colors" of earthy browns such as

"terracotta." Casual looks in classic colors dominated the end of the decade. During the 1990s the fashion industry pushed colors from gray to red and beige to pink, but consumers clung to the safety, simplicity, and chic of black. In the early 2000s, texture merged with color to create newness as special effects from matte to shiny, and glitter to pearl added dimension to color. Predictions of a return to color and color prints that had begun in the late 1990s came true by the mid-2000s.

✦ LONG-WAVE CYCLES

The recurrences of color themes can be traced not just in decades but in centuries. In the Victorian era, Owen Jones chose rich, bright, primary colors for London's Crystal Palace in 1851. He defended his choices saying that these same colors had been used in the architecture of the ancient Greeks. To some color historians, this comment illustrates the cycling of color through history, specifically the periodic return to primary hues. The cycle begins with bright, saturated, primary colors; this is followed by an exploration of mixed, less intense colors; then, it pauses in neutral until the rich, strong colors are rediscovered (Porter, 1994).

Researchers have confirmed a periodic swing (Figure 6.4) from high chroma colors to "multicoloredness," to subdued colors, to earth tones, to achromatic colors (black, white, and gray), and back to high chroma colors. In the period between 1860 and the 1990s, there were four marked color cycles lasting between 15 and 25 years (Darmstadt, 1982, 1985). Other researchers have confirmed the cyclical recurrence of collective color trends (Koppelmann & Kuthe, 1987; Oberascher, 1994). That cycle has been matched to color trends in recent decades (Barry, 1999), as follows:

- ❖ a high chroma phase (e.g., 1972–74);
- ❖ a darkening phase (e.g., 1974–76);
- ❖ a transition to autumnal colors in a brown phase (e.g., 1976–79);
- ❖ a lightening of colors toward beige, off-white, and pastels (e.g., 1979–81);

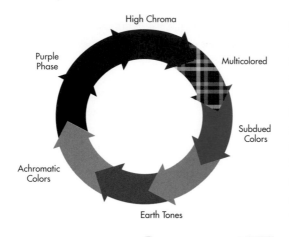

Figure 6.4

Researchers have confirmed a periodic swing from high chroma colors to "multicoloredness," to subdued colors, to earth tones, to achromatic (black, white, and gray), to a purple phase that signals a repeat of the cycle.

❖ an achromatic phase (e.g., 1984–88);
❖ a chromatic phase combining black and white with primary colors (e.g., 1988–91);
❖ a purple phase (e.g., 1992–98);
❖ a return to chromatic colors (e.g., beginning in 1998 and continuing);
❖ an emerging multicolored phase in a revival of pattern including stripes and prints (e.g., spring 2003 and continuing).

Such long-wave oscillations can be observed in color cycles through the decades of the twentieth century.

✦ COLOR CYCLES AND CULTURAL SHIFTS

Color cycles can be sparked by new technology. This happened about 10 years after the opening of the Crystal Palace in the mid-1800s. One of the first synthetic dyes was introduced by the French: a colorfast purple called mauve. The color became the rage—Queen Victoria wore the color to the International Exhibition of 1862—and gave its name to the Mauve Decade. Other strong synthetic dyes for red and green soon followed, allowing for a strong color story in women's clothing. Something similar

happened in the 1950s when the first affordable cotton-reactive dye for turquoise led to a color fad and moved it from eveningwear into sportswear (Hope & Walch, 1990; Porter, 1994). When Apple's first iMac computers were introduced featuring colors of "blueberry, strawberry, grape, tangerine and lime," the traditional high-tech achromatic color palette of black or beige was replaced instantly by colors resembling candy gummy bears. Other products such as cell phones and back-to-school supplies soon followed the iMac's lead (Robinson, 1999).

Economic conditions also disturb color cycles and start new ones. In the depressed 1930s, fabrics and colors were chosen as investments—grays, subdued greens and blues were low-key, could be worn more often, didn't show dirt, thus seldom needed to be cleaned and, therefore, lasted longer. The steep drop in the stock market in 1987 coincided with the eclipse of bright color as the fashion look of the 1980s and the ascendance of Japanese design featuring austere, minimalist black clothing. The terrorist attacks on New York and Washington on September 11, 2001, and an extended economic downturn, ended a growth cycle for luxury goods and slowed consumer spending on apparel. Even the teen market—usually considered recession-proof buyers of apparel—saw a steep decline in purchasing (Greenberg, 2003a). The mid-2000s was a boom time for many who saw their investment in a home increase in value. But high energy prices and a downturn in real estate signaled another crisis period for consumers. When times are uncertain, people respond best to small rather than large change, evolution rather than revolution. According to Margaret Walch of the CAUS, color change slowed beginning in 2002. Instead of big changes, colors shift within color families—for example, pink shifts into lilac (Solomon, 2006).

Color cycles can be associated with social change. A visible cycle was identified by corporate color analyst June Roche in the mid-1980s—the shift between colors associated with femininity and those influenced by men's fashion. She characterized the end of the 1970s as a dark phase in men's clothing with dusty colors that were called elegant, refined, and sophisticated. Use of these typical grayed European colors was new for American women's fashion but coincided with women's entry into fields such as finance, law, and medicine—fields formerly dominated by men. By the mid-1980s, those grayed colors looked dirty, and there was a shift to feminine colors. As a forecaster, Roche asked herself why the feminine colors were popular and how much longer that phase would last (Lannon, 1988). The shift between ultrafemininity and a suggestion of masculinity has been part of the fashion scene since Coco Chanel first introduced women to the concept of borrowing from men's closets in the 1920s.

Color cycles are also associated with nostalgic revivals of looks from previous decades. When the 1970s were revived in the mid-1990s, bright lime green came back with platform shoes, reruns of old television shows such as *The Brady Bunch*, and polyester. The color was not a literal lift from the 1970s, but that decade did provide a directional influence (Winter, 1996). When fashion needs a dose of optimism, look for a revival of 1960s designers such as Mary Quant, Pierre Cardin, and André Courrèges with its miniskirts, color contrasts, and graphic prints, as happened in the spring and fall of 2003 (Bellafante, 2003a) or the pink and green, madras and prints, of a preppy revival a couple of years later (Jackson, 2005).

✦ FORECASTING WITH COLOR CYCLES

When applying a color theory, the color forecaster has to take into account the consumer type and membership in a cultural group. Lifestyles, values, and attitudes all play a part in acceptance or rejection of collective color directions. Although mass media smooths and integrates individual and cultural tendencies, differences between segments remain. Additionally, some consumers are early adopters of fashion change, whereas other more traditional consumers will adhere to traditional colors as color cycles come and go. Applying a color cycle theory takes insight and experience. Complicating

the process further, a color forecaster has more than one color cycle theory to consider.

✧ Long-Wave Color Cycle

No matter the uncertainty about timing, the general long-wave color cycle sequence from high chroma to multicolored, to subdued, to earth tones, to achromatic is helpful to forecasters who sense consumer boredom with the current offerings and seek the next acceptable evolution. For example, multicolor prints became more popular on runways and stores in the mid-2000s, demonstrating a sequence that echoes the long-wave cycle of colors. In 2005 the president of Lilly Pulitzer, talking about his delight in a preppy fashion revival, said: "Fashion has been dark and neutral for about 12 years, so a whole new generation is finally being exposed to these bright-colored styles for the first time" (Jackson, 2005).

✧ Pendulum Swing

Everrett Brown, who introduced the Color Key Program for apparel and paint selection, identified a cycle of approximately 7 years during which the pendulum swings between warm-toned and cool-toned colors (Brown, 1994). Using that theory, a color forecaster in the late 1990s would predict a shift from the orange-based earthy tones of 1998 to "more celestial colors" in cool tones for the turn of the millennium (Crispell, 1997). Color experts saw the life for this prediction extended to the entire first decade of the twenty-first century (Barker, 2007).

✦ SEASONAL CONTINUITY

Some continuity in the color cycle remains regardless of trends. Year after year, fall palettes tend to be darker and less intense than spring palettes. Two perennial returnees every fall are autumn leaf colors, usually in solids paired with plaids and animal prints, along with khaki or tan, often in a safari theme. Every spring some variation of the nautical theme—red, white, and blue—returns along with a citrus or blooming flower scheme (Nelson, 2007; Wrack, 1994) (Figure 6.5).

Figure 6.5

A red-white-and-blue nautical theme is a perennial seasonal color story in the spring.

Individual colors will move in and out more frequently but it will be more important to track color groups, sometimes known as color "families" rather than specific colors (Phillips, 1999). One example of color families classifies colors as:

* *The naturals*—colors derived from sky, landscape, and water.
* *Pastels*—colors lightened with white.
* *Darks*—tones and shades of colors.
* *Brights*—high-intensity colors.

Another group's color families based on the color wheel:

* *Yellows*—true yellow to orange including the range of browns.
* *Reds*—true red to red-violet.
* *Greens*—true green to yellow-green.
* *Blues*—blue-green to blue-violet.

Sorting colors into these groupings clearly shows variation from season to season. Watching these groupings over several years shows a parallel but distinctive evolution for fall and spring seasons.

Today's color forecasts offer a proliferation of shades, and the color forecaster's job is to match color with consumer segments. During the twentieth century, the consumer underwent a color education that has changed visual perceptions. Still, the basic mechanism of color cycles serves the color forecaster well. A new color direction is usually introduced first by a high-profile industry and promoted as a theme. Based on mass marketing, other industries adapt the theme to fit their customers and promote the same set of colors. After a few years, the color direction becomes established; the consumer is ready for a change, and the cycle begins again. While a color trend remains in place, the theme used to promote it evolves—Southwestern colors transmute into a Mediterranean palette and then continue in an Adirondack lodge color story (Kinning, 1994). The colors themselves evolve from season to season. For the forecaster, it is important to monitor consumer response and work through the color families from level to level—from red to a rosy tone to a coral (Tunsky, 1994).

THE COLOR FORECASTING INDUSTRY

Stimulating sales has always been the driving force behind color forecasting. As far back as the late nineteenth century, French textile mills put out color cards, which were then used by American textile companies as a source of ideas and direction (Vanderbilt, 2012). Forecasting for the American consumer began in 1915 with the founding of the Textile Color Card Association of America, predecessor to today's Color Association of the United States (CAUS). Started by a group of manufacturers and retailers trying to keep up with the changing tastes of a consumer-oriented economy, the organization used textile industry specialists to select fashion shades that would be popular in the future. The first forecast was issued for fall of 1917—forty colors presented on cards with custom-dyed silk and wool swatches. The focus of the forecast was women's apparel with basic colors and fashion shades that might build volume sales in the future (Hope & Walch, 1990).

Color marketing intensified after World War II with the increase in demand and availability of consumer goods. Marketers realized that just as color sells apparel, it could be used to promote products across the spectrum of the marketplace. At the same time, the number of lines, size of assortments, and number of stores selling ready-to-wear were expanding. Color provided a way to satisfy many consumers with the same garment. The power of color as a marketing tool combined with increased demand meant that color forecasting assumed even greater economic significance.

By the 1950s, Dayton's Department Store had a small staff watching trends and translating them into apparel (and later home furnishings) to be sold exclusively in their store (Lamb, 1997). The idea of forecasting trends in the marketplace boomed in the years after World War II. **Trend**

merchandising entered the mass market in the early 1980s when trends became a coordinating factor for full product lines that extended beyond a single merchandise category (Nichols, 1996). Today, trend merchandising and color forecasting are an integral part of product development for both hard and soft goods (i.e., from furniture and appliances to fashion and bedding).

Some people claim that color forecasters dictate colors in the current marketplace, but forecasters do not have that power. Color forecasters cannot just say that turquoise will be the new fashion color. Instead, they have to consider the evolution of blue-green over the previous seasons and figure out when the consumer will be ready for a different version.

Financial backing for forecasters comes from manufacturers and retailers who need lead time to develop products for the consumer. Clients for color forecasting services include companies in the apparel supply chain—fiber producers, mills that produce yarn and fabrics, manufacturers of branded merchandise, retailers with private-label operations, and manufacturers who produce apparel in great volume. These clients want to gauge the tastes and preferences of the consumer far in advance of the selling season. Designers of couture collections and the highest priced ready-to-wear lines are more likely to influence color directions rather than follow them. Even so, top designers also subscribe to color-forecasting services as a gauge of mass taste (Lannon, 1988). John Crocco, the creative director for Perry Ellis, calls color forecasts "a self-fulfilling prophecy." He says that if designers choose to follow such forecasts, then they'll be "part of what ultimately becomes the trend. If you don't, you are going to be outside of it" (Marritz, 2011). But if designers disregard a trend and it's a hit, they risk irrelevance, which is something that no fashion company wants.

One potential problem in today's marketplace is how quickly color forecasts can now move from concept to consumer; although palettes are issued 2 years ahead of the fashion season, forecasters are seeing their predictions implemented immediately—actions that may throw off expectations of color evolution (Horton, 2003).

ORGANIZATIONS FOR PROFESSIONAL COLOR FORECASTERS

Color forecasters come to the profession from many backgrounds—textile design, art history, product development, and other fields. Many work independently, consulting on a particular segment of the consumer market. A few consultants work across industry lines developing forecasts for both apparel and interiors. Some color forecasters work for industry trade associations like Cotton Incorporated or the American Wool Council. Others are employed by large fiber producers, fabric manufacturers, or apparel manufacturers. Organizations for color forecasters bring these professionals together to share ideas, inspiration, and resources. Such networking facilitates the overall goal of color forecasting: to establish future color directions for a given population, geographic location, and time as a way for industries in the supply chain to coordinate their efforts.

By joining professional organizations, color forecasters continue to build their skills and expertise, benefit from the different viewpoints and keen vision of others, and promote the professionalism of the field. There are professional organizations for color forecasters worldwide, with membership limited to those who focus on color exclusively or who meet specific criteria. The two leading professional color organizations in America are the Color Association of the United States (CAUS) and the **Color Marketing Group** (CMG).

✦ COLOR ASSOCIATION OF THE UNITED STATES (CAUS)

Leslie Harrington, the executive director of the Color Association of the United States, built her expertise in color forecasting over a lifetime of

Profile: Leatrice Eiseman, Executive Director, Eiseman Center & Pantone Color Institute

Leatrice Eiseman is a color specialist who helps companies make educated color choices for product development and corporate identification. She combines her background in psychology, fashion, and interior design to identify and analyze color trends.

As a Bainbridge Island, WA resident, Eiseman was in the perfect location to discover Starbucks coffee house when it began in Seattle. She was inspired by the idea that rich, deep brown had shifted its identity from earthy and utilitarian to robust and as elegant as espresso. By picking up on the change in attitude, especially among young consumers, she became one of the first forecasters to recognize a trend with staying power that influenced fashion, home decor, and cosmetics for years (Tsong, 2006).

Eiseman has been quoted in *Elle, Vogue, The Wall Street Journal, The New York Times, USA Today*, and has authored seven books on the topic of color—most recently, *Pantone: The Twentieth Century in Color* in 2011. She is a member of the Fashion Group International, the American Society of Interior Designers, the Color Marketing Group Board of Directors, and the Color Association of the United States. Her favorite color is "purple with a warm red undertone," because it is "dynamic and magical—a fabulous color to combine with other hues" and also because it is "the color of creativity—something a color specialist needs a lot of!" ("Pantone," 1998, p. 2).

Similar to musical talent, she believes some people are born with "a wonderful ability to become an interior designer or fashion designer or any area where color is inherent to what they are doing," but that ability must be nurtured by interest and training. Other people with less inborn color ability can learn about color in the same way that people learn to play the piano—by taking lessons and playing for enjoyment. People can hone their color abilities by "reading more about it, observing more, and developing the nerve to venture forth, even if that means making some mistakes."

Flexibility in the use of color is a watchword for Eiseman, who has spent time studying what she calls "crossover colors—these colors are prevalent in nature and can be used in many different ways." They include "all the basics like grays, taupes, aubergine, hunter greens, and navy blues, which are always found in fashion because they combine so well with so many other colors and because our eyes are so accustomed to seeing them." Crossover colors tend to be "part of nature like blue skies." As she explains, "People don't think of sky blue as a neutral color or a basic color, and yet blue in nature is backdrop to a beautiful day." The crossover list has expanded with the addition of the real family of blue-greens because they are a "kind of cusp between the blues and greens." This color family was "really discovered in the 1980s and people have learned to enjoy the color and find that it works with just about every other color in the spectrum."

"Designers are responsible for creating the fashions and putting the colors on those fashions. They are the first ones to be influenced by color cycles because they are so tuned in to what's happening in the world, what's going on about them." Forecasters, too, are looking "further into the future, not just tomorrow or even the next three to six months." To get this forward-looking perspective, she attends trade shows, "where you can see the colors that are being shown and projected for the future." But seeing colors is only the first step. "You have to know your audience. It could be that a color is going to be hot in Europe, but if your demographics embrace a certain area of the country where that color has never done well, even if you think that ultimately the color will happen, it's a little too soon to try it. The bottom line is that you really have to know who your customer is." Cutting-edge colors do "trickle down to the consumer level because the consumer is also looking at the media, new films, and art collections that are traveling around the country."

In addition to her forecast for fashion, Eiseman announces her color forecast for home interiors at an international trade show to an audience of more than 1,000 attendees. She maintains that it isn't crystal-ball gazing but it is attention to lifestyles, social and economic influences, and consumer preferences. She tell clients to "divorce the personal from the professional" when making color decisions (Schlosser, 2005).

Membership in organizations for color professionals is another important part of Eiseman's work as a forecaster. The organizations become a meeting ground for color professionals from "various fields—cosmetics and fashion to automotive and plastics for the kitchen. The color pros discuss things that are happening in the world, the things they expect will be happening in the future, and develop a color palette approximately two years ahead of the current market." After returning to their jobs, the members "may or may not choose to embrace the colors in that palette, but it helps them get a line on what others are doing in other industries and to create a connection between related industries." Ultimately, the connection between different industries "reduces confusion for the consumer shopping for related items because the color palettes are not terribly far apart."

Eiseman advises people interested in becoming color professionals to begin in retailing, where they can "hear what consumers say at point of purchase and how they relate to the colors they are seeing." The retail store is also a good place to study displays because "many of the stores have very talented display people who are really tuned in to how to put colors together." Another training exercise is to be a "comparison shopper, going to Target as well as Bloomingdale's—see the way that merchandise is presented, see some of the support materials like brochures and catalogs. Be a real user of everything that is out there. Most important—look at the big picture, not just a particular segment of fashion but other influences, the big films coming up, the television shows on the horizon, the technological breakthroughs, anything with a color connection. That is what color forecasters do."

Source:
Unless cited in the text, quotes are from author Evelyn L. Brannon interview with Leatrice Eiseman, May 6, 1999.

experience. Working at a paint store in high school and while getting a degree in interior design, she observed not only the customers choosing colors but the sales staff's lack of color knowledge. When the paint company asked her to introduce a computerized color-matching system to dealers and designers in Canada, the job was only supposed to last 6 months; however, Harrington recognized the potential in faux finishing, began appearing on TV demonstrating techniques, wrote a popular book on the topic, and continued to rise in the company. By 1998 she was the director of color and design in the US corporate office of Benjamin Moore Paint. Her assignment to update the entire color line meant keeping the traditional dusty palette, which she called the "heritage colors," and balancing that with brighter colors like fresh greens with a yellow tinge—additions that were controversial at the time, but soon dovetailed with growing consumer interest in the environment and became popular. The updated palette required Harrington to come up with 2,000 color names, a task that she turned into a contest for company employees. She left the company to start her own color consultancy before joining CAUS (Scrivener, 2007). Harrington's story is not unlike that of other color professionals who are members of the oldest forecasting organization in the United States.

The Color Association of the United States issued the first forecast in 1917, focusing on women's fashions. The forecast was aimed at designers and stylists and suggested color grouping just as today's forecasts do. As consumer-oriented marketing accelerated after World War II, more specialized forecasts were developed including:

❖ man-made fibers in the 1950s;
❖ menswear in the 1960s;
❖ home furnishings in the 1970s;
❖ interior and environmental colors, children's clothing, and activewear in the 1980s.

The association also publishes *The Standard Color Reference of America*, a book showing color

standards for wool, cotton, and silk industries in the United States. The original edition contained 106 shades, including those inspired by the colors of nature's flora and fauna, college and university colors, and US Armed Forces shades on silk ribbons. Revised with over ten editions, the number of colors is now up to 191, all printed on silk (Hope & Walch, 1990).

Based in Manhattan, CAUS is a not-for-profit trade association. Members include corporations concerned with apparel, interiors and furnishings, paint, and automobiles, plus designers from all those fields. The cost of membership—several hundred dollars—provides members with exclusive services. Members receive the forecast for one product category each season as a deck of silk-screened color cards, a monthly newsletter, invitations to seminars, consultations including having a collection critiqued, and access to the CAUS archives and research material. The archive includes color swatches for every year in the association's history. CAUS has an internship program for college students (Malarcher, 1995).

CAUS members serve on committees specific to their interests and expertise. When on a committee, the member may serve for many years, providing stability to the process, but there are small changes in the committee makeup over time. The Women's Committee meets twice a year for brainstorming sessions during which they select twenty-five to forty-two colors for women's apparel to appear in the stores 2 years later. The members propose color directions by bringing presentation boards to the meeting. The presentation boards may show pictures of exotic travel locations, evocative images from historical sources, materials gleaned from nature such as bark or wood or stones, or color swatches. Over the course of the meeting, the members reach consensus on the forecast colors. The process involves awareness of the mood of the times, preparation, and discussions where everybody contributes to defining the coming colors. Committees focusing on interiors, menswear, children's wear, and other product categories follow a similar process when deciding by consensus on the forecast colors (Malarcher, 1995).

Color cards from the various committees may contain similar colors which are fine-tuned for a specific market. The classic navy may be light on the children's card, darker on the men's, closer to cobalt blue for interiors, and a more traditional shade for women's (Lannon, 1988). Subtle differences, color evolution, and color combinations are important. If a certain red is in the forecast, its best complement in green must also be there (Malarcher, 1995). It is this level of sophistication and expertise in color that makes the professional's advice valuable (Figure 6.6).

✦ COLOR MARKETING GROUP (CMG)

The Color Marketing Group, an international not-for-profit association based in the Washington, DC, area, was formed in 1962 to provide advanced color information for industries from apparel to automobiles, from health care to corporate identity. Spring and fall meetings are held in North America (with attendees also coming from Australia, Europe, and Japan) to determine color trends globally. Meetings in Europe, Latin America, and the Asia/Pacific Rim help attendees decide on colors specific to their region. As CMG executive director Jaime Stephens explains, these are "true working conferences that result in a tangible work product" (Pelletier, 2007).

Members' job titles range from designer, stylist, and product developer to marketing manager and merchandiser, and the companies they work for range from small independent studios to large corporations. The focus is on color as a marketing tool. Members share information about trends and forecasts because they see the process as translating into profitable business decisions for their companies. In addition to participating in expert panels and workshops, members receive four color palettes a year, a monthly newsletter, and access to the color library.

Figure 6.6

Expert buyers examining samples at the Texworld expo in Paris.

In the CMG, workshops are aimed at the interests and specialties of members (Jacobs, 1994; Verlodt, 1994b). The process begins with forecast workshops for over forty product or end-use categories. The forecast workshops bring together an expert panel of members dealing with the same product category and whose work requires forecasting three or more years before the selling season ("Color Key," 2002).

The fashion industry panel meets in the winter and summer to develop the apparel palette. Eight weeks before the workshops, CMG members send out color samples and their individual color directions forecast to the panel. Using these submissions as a starting point, participants negotiate to determine the set of forecast colors.

A representative from each expert panel participates in a final round of negotiations to determine CMG's palette of new colors for consumer (fashion, residential, communications, etc.) and commercial (retail, hospitality, health care) markets, including individual colors and color combinations.

For members, there are different workshop formats than the experts' panel, including workshops on color directions and how they relate to consumer demographics, the economy, and market research ("Color Forecasting," 2002). The goal of forecast workshops is not to predict specific hues but to indicate color direction. Members work year-round on committee assignments, but meeting schedules depend on the product category. The CMG tracks color by surveying its membership on the use of color in their industries and analyzes findings on an industry-by-industry basis. The result is a kind of continuing scorecard on color use across industries and product categories.

CONSUMERS AND COLOR

As predictors of color preference, categories such as age, ethnicity, income, and gender play a part, but the preference segments are more complex than simple demographics. The Cooper

Marketing Group (Jacobs, 1994) now divides consumers into three categories: color forwards, color prudents, and color loyals. The color-forward consumer enjoys being the first to try a new color but may shop for color ideas at both discounters and upscale department stores. The color prudents are mainstream consumers and wait until a color has more widespread acceptance before buying it. The color loyals play it safe with color, sticking with classic blue or gray instead of choosing fashion colors. Categories like these mirror the bell curve of consumer acceptance from the relatively few innovators and early adopters through mass acceptance to the fashion laggards and apply it to acceptance of color (Figure 6.7). Such mental images can help color forecasters justify their color choices and clarify the fit between color selection, product category, and consumer target.

Only a few consumers are innovative enough to try new colors when they are first introduced. The rest become used to the color over time, perhaps first trying it out in a print or multicolored knit or in an inexpensive accessory or T-shirt. Generally speaking, the more disposable the item, the more experimentation there will generally be with color. As Leslie Harrington of the CAUS says, "If you get tired of a red jacket, you can throw it in a closet. If you buy a red sofa, it's a 365, 24/7 commitment to red" (Vanderbilt, 2012). Color experts forecast when consumers are ready for the new color in certain product categories and price points. However, some critics of the present system see actual research on consumer color preferences as the "missing link" in the process (Diane & Cassidy, 2005). Designers have limited one-to-one contact with consumers, and forecasters' work is more observational and anecdotal rather than scientific. Sales data provide feedback about best-selling colors but not on what was missing from the range. At present, gathering consumer color preferences is not part of the color forecasting process. Similar to other attempts at researching aesthetic choice, color preference research is challenging to design, execute, and interpret and those difficulties may limit its usefulness. Still, if color is a contributing factor

Figure 6.7

The Cooper Marketing Group divides consumers into three categories—color forwards, color prudents, and color loyals. The definitions of these groups correspond to fashion leaders, majority, and laggard segments of a diffusion of innovation curve.

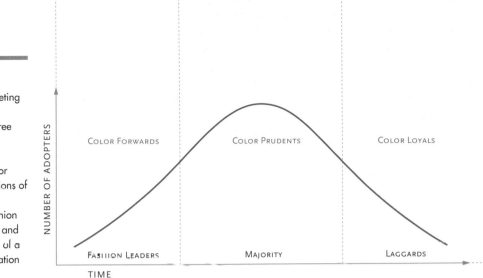

NUMBER OF ADOPTERS

COLOR FORWARDS   COLOR PRUDENTS   COLOR LOYALS

FASHION LEADERS   MAJORITY   LAGGARDS

TIME

to consumers' rejection of products, then collecting preference data could result in higher sales, fewer markdowns, and greater satisfaction.

One independent color forecasting company, Los Angeles-based Design Options, takes consumer preferences into account by shopping the sales racks to see what colors did not sell. "It's not about the new color of the year, it's about what didn't sell so I don't make the mistake of trying to bring something to the forefront that isn't going to sell," says Fran Suda, founder of Design Options. Suda has been in the industry for over 25 years and Design Options produces five different seasonal forecasts for clients: Universal Color, Young Contemporary, Young Men's, Home Fashion, and Kidz. She also produces Power Palettes, which are a tonal overview of an emerging color trend, such as "Beyond Plum," "Red Hot," and "Purple Passion." She credits designer collections with popular priced retailers such as H&M as a major influence, since designers are bringing their color sense to these more accessible collections, and have created a more sophisticated customer.

✦ COLOR SYMBOLS

The power of color comes from its symbolic meaning for people. Colors can represent experiences, emotions, status, and other types of information that are difficult to convey in written or spoken language. However, these associations may vary by culture—brides traditionally wear white for weddings in the United States while brides in China wear red (Feisner, 2001).

Color symbols enter language and appear in pictures and poetry as metaphors—for example, the connection between good fortune and gold at the end of the rainbow. Color communicates emotionally by calling up all kinds of associations of which people are only fleetingly aware (Figure 6.8). Some color symbols are part of a kind of instinctive sense. Red signals arousal because it is associated with blood and fire—signals of danger. Even overlaid with the trappings of modern life, red still gets our attention by evoking ancient responses. Some color symbols have religious origins, such as the depiction of the Virgin Mary in blue as a symbol for truth and justice. Red, the Christian symbol for suffering and regeneration, can be inverted and applied to a "scarlet" woman and the "red-light district." Color can be used for sociological or political reasons as in tribal identification, gang colors, and soldiers' uniforms. Individual colors have symbolic meanings that evolve over time. The Green Man of Celtic mythology was the god of fertility; today we talk about a gardener having a green thumb and green became associated with the environmental movement (Hope & Walch, 1990).

Figure 6.8

Red still gets attention by evoking ancient responses signaling danger. Blue with its cool, calm feeling is the American consumers' favorite color. Color temperature—warm or cool—expresses part of color's language.

Human response to colors can be traced to physiological reactions. Warm colors are associated with activity, cool colors with passivity. Psychologists have recorded immediate and measurable reactions to color, but the total effect depends on the duration of the stimulus. Exposure to red initially results in arousal, but the effect dissipates with continuous exposure over time. Another aspect mitigating the psychological impact of color is the strength of the color—an electric green is more stimulating than a weak, dull red (Hope & Walch, 1990).

✦ FORMATION OF COLOR PREFERENCE

Besides human reaction to color, psychologists are interested in the formation of color preferences. In 1941, Hans J. Eysenck published a study showing a consistent order of color preferences in adults: the first choice was blue, followed by red, green, purple, yellow, and orange. Later research and preference surveys have tended to support the finding of a universal scale of color with a possible biological basis (Porter, 1994). *The Lüscher Color Test*, first published in 1948, links color preference and personality. In this test, the subject is asked to arrange color chips (eight in the short form; forty-three in the full test) in order of preference. The results are interpreted using a key that considers both the meaning of the color and the order of its selection (Lüscher, 1969). These psychological explanations of color point to the power and impact of color, but they are not very helpful to the color forecaster in predicting the success or failure of specific color symbols.

Another approach is to trace the roots of color preference to cultural influence. Some color theorists argue that color transcends cultural and geographic boundaries. To back up this "universalist" view, studies have shown that black, white, and red evoke similar responses in many parts of the world. American researchers compared color words in ninety languages and discovered broad, consistent rules in the cultural evolution of color. They found that the most primitive cultures distinguish only between black and white; if a third color is used, it is always red; the next two colors are yellow and green; then blue is added, followed by all the subtler distinctions (Hope & Walch, 1990).

Color "relativists" argue for a local bias in the development of color terminology. They find that regional and environmental conditions play a major role, citing the observation that the Inuit have more words for white because it is so predominate in their worldview (Hope & Walch, 1990). Author Polly Hope (1990), describes a "color conception of a place" that results from the combination of the natural environment and the indigenous culture. As examples she cites the earth colors, silver, and turquoise of the American Southwest and the lapis blue, gray-green of cacti, and reds and yellows of folk costumes as symbolic of Mexico.

Some color associations combine the universalist and relativist view: blue as a protective color to ward off evil spirits can be found in cultures as disparate as those in the Middle East and Native Americans in the Southwest. With increasing global communication and trade, there will be an inevitable increase in the exchange of color concepts across territorial and cultural boundaries. The color forecaster must constantly investigate the cultural symbolism and the cross-cultural implications of color (Eiseman, 1997).

✧ Preference and Gender

Reported differences exist between men and women regarding their color preferences. In 2011, Kissmetrics created an infographic which cited a number of studies that showed these differences, including a 2003 study conducted by researcher Joe Hallock in which he surveyed 232 people from various demographic groups from twenty-two countries: blue was the top color preference among both men (57%) and women (35%). However, some very interesting differences then surfaced: purple was the second color preference among women, with 23 percent of women indicating it was their favorite color, while 0 percent of men selected it as their favorite. The remaining colors had relatively similar preferences between both men and women. There were slight differences in least favorite color, with 33 percent of women indicating that orange was their least favorite color and 27 percent of men saying that brown was their least favorite color. However, men and women were not so different in this category, as brown was a close second for women as their least favorite color as was orange for men, so both genders expressed a dislike for the two colors, only differing in degrees.

In another study from 2007 cited in the same infographic, doctors Anya Hurlbert and Yahzu Ling demonstrated how men and women differed in their color preferences. Similar to the findings in the Hallock study, blue was the most popular color for both men and women, although differences in preference were found to exist, as women liked colors close to the red end of the spectrum, where pinks are found. Men and women had similar preferences for light and dark colors, although women tended to prefer soft colors, whereas men preferred bright colors. Men were found to tolerate achromatic colors such as white, black, and gray more than women. In a similar study by McInnis and Shearer that was also cited in the infographic, women indicated preferring tints (colors mixed with white) while men preferred shades (colors mixed with black). In a final study, it was found that men do not use the same number of names to specify color as women. Whereas women may differentiate between colors with color names such as "teal," "sky," and "turquoise," to male respondents each of these colors was simply classified as "blue."

✧ Preference and Ethnicity

Surveys tend to support the idea that there is a relationship between color preference and ethnic identity or geographic region. Color trends today span the globe with soft, calming colors from Japan, spicy, earthy tones from Brazil and Latin America, and clean classics from Scandinavia (Buisson, 2007). Some researchers found that African-Americans are drawn to strong, saturated colors in the red, yellow, and brown categories. Hispanics prefer warm, bright colors because those colors stay true in the strong sunlight of Latin America. But variations exist among Hispanics: Mexicans prefer their traditional reds, blues, and blacks; Puerto Ricans like livelier pinks and purples; and Cubans in Florida choose a palette of pastels (Paul, 2002). Immigration can influence a color's popularity. Whereas red is associated with sex and violence in Anglo-Saxon culture, it represents luck and happiness in Asian and Latin cultures. With a more diverse US population, red is more liked today than in the past (Tsong, 2006).

Color preferences can arise from personal experiences—for example, a person's positive or negative reaction to the colors their parents chose for them as children. Color consultants cannot account for these individual differences. Instead they concentrate on broad cultural preferences. Blue is the favorite color for American consumers, especially navy blue. But their second choice varies with age and ethnicity: people over 55 and Asian consumers choose sky blue, people 35 to 55 and Hispanic consumers choose aquamarine, and consumers 13 to 34 and African-Americans choose light blue (Paul, 2002). Blue has global reach—interviews with almost 13,000 consumers in seventeen countries showed that blue is also the favorite color in all of North America, Asia, Europe, South America, and Australia (Soucy, 2005).

✧ Preference and Zeitgeist

Strong cultural preferences can be overtaken by the Zeitgeist. Fashion color symbols arise from cultural norms that have consistent meaning over time—red nails and red lips are powerful sexual signals in all decades dating back to the 1920s. When dye technology permitted making only a few colors, fashion colors persisted for decades and developed deep symbolic associations. Now it is possible to dye any color, and the multiplicity of colors leads to seasonal change and color meanings that are more temporary (Hope & Walch, 1990). In the mid-twentieth century, a single color trend could come to dominate (older people remember the harvest gold and avocado green of the 1960s or mauve and French blue of the late 1970s). But today four or five major color stories emerge at the same time—a reflection of the diversity among ethnic groups and consumer generations. Today's consumer is more eclectic, appreciating "sophisticated" colors (those created by a complex mixture of pigments), offbeat combinations, and color effects like translucence, pearlescence, and metallics (Paul, 2002).

In 2006, forecasters picked yellow as a trend color for the spring/summer 2008 season. Right on time, yellow appeared in store windows on dresses, jackets, shoes, purses, bangles, and headbands. Consumers recognized yellow as the trendy color and sales made it one of the top ten colors for the season. The popularity of yellow came as a surprise to some because people see it as hard to wear. But to forecasters it was a natural pick for the following reasons (Patterson, 2008):

❖ *Evolution of a color family*—Orange and yellow-green had been popular and built an acceptance of that color family. Yellow, between orange and yellow-green on the color wheel, was the go-to color when orange and yellow-green began to wane.

❖ *Symbolic Value*—Yellow provides a psychological lift because it is viewed as warm, cheerful, whimsical, and sunny. For every culture, yellow is associated with enlightenment—a connection of the color with interest in personal philosophy and spiritual search.

❖ *Prior Adoption*—Yellow had been popular on European runways for more than a year in variations from vibrant lemon to softer, easier-to-wear shades like curry and honey, so consumers who had traveled abroad or viewed runway shows online were accustomed to the color and had time to embrace it.

❖ *Zeitgeist*—In gloomy economic times, consumers choose neutrals for big-ticket items but look for fun, optimistic colors for fashion and accessories. A gray sofa with yellow pillows is the right mix for the times. In fashion, yellow mixes for a variety of styles—yellow with black for urban cool, yellow with white for freshness, yellow with

its complement purple for drama, or yellow with blue for relaxed casual—and yellow on an accessory can update an entire ensemble.

Similarly, orange experienced a similar ascent in 2011. *The Wall Street Journal* stated that orange was "out in full force" on the faces of models in the spring 2011 shows who wore graphic orange eye shadow at the Derek Lam show and coral-colored lips, "mirroring the fashion color trend of the season." It wasn't just clothes, says Mikel Cirkus, who heads the Conceptual Design Group at Firmenich, the flavor and fragrance company: there's the Sony Vaio, the new Camaro, both available in orange models, and the "Hugo Boss Orange" label, described as "urban, lighthearted, cool" by the brand. "You're connecting dots here that are traceable" (Vanderbilt, 2012).

✧ Color and Segmentation

Different generations have different preferences. Generation Y prefers bright colors more than baby boomers. Because Generation Y grew up with the Internet and the vibrant colors of virtual worlds, they are more accepting of bright purples and greens when paired with white. Color forecasters must consider the context of colors in terms of meaning and images they inspire in consumers (Buisson, 2007).

Color tends to identify the target market—for example, bold primaries for children's products and trendy or whimsical colors to appeal to teens. With influences from television, toy marketing, and computers, children's preferences tend toward bright colors that adults avoid. When children are asked to rank their top ten favorite colors, they include hot magenta and electric lime, colors that do not appear on the adults' list (Paul, 2002). Some colors declassify a product, extending its appeal to a broad audience; others classify a product as belonging to a specific type of consumer or socioeconomic level (Kanner, 1989). Sensitivity to these multiple meanings enables the color forecaster to target the right colors to the right consumer segment. This segmentation by color preferences makes it important for product developers and marketers to carefully observe the target market—watch consumers in their natural habitat, read what they read, listen to their music, watch their movies, and research their preferences.

COLOR SPECIFICATIONS

Achieving a coherent and comprehensible color story each season begins with the forecast and specification writing. Writing specifications is an essential part of turning ideas and concepts into products. In today's global trade arena, the same color may be fiber-dyed for blending into a sweater yarn, yarn-dyed for use in a plaid shirt, and fabric-dyed for a skirt, all in different countries, but all for the same apparel line. Yet the consumer expects that all the pieces will come together into a coordinated outfit. To satisfy the consumers' expectations, all levels of the supply chain have to communicate precisely and objectively about color.

Apparel product developers have several problems associated with color reproduction. It is difficult to accurately reproduce the same color on different surface textures. Perception of a color can be changed by the amount of color used and by the colors surrounding it. In fabric dyeing, color can be affected by dye quality, mixing, and other manufacturing conditions. Because of the difficulty in exact matching, product developers balance that need against the economic necessity of achieving realistic price points.

Product developers try to resolve the various problems and challenges by writing **color specifications** in a color system, one that identifies the color along with its value (darkness to lightness) and its intensity (bright to subdued). Color systems allow these qualities to be expressed in notation using a number or letter code. Various standardized systems have been developed, but no one system has been universally accepted (Hope & Walch, 1990).

A color forecast is delivered with a set of color cards, fabric swatches, or yarn samples. The designer working with the forecast selects colors for use in the product line and orders additional samples of those colors. A sample of the color helps to communicate the color specification to manufacturing. The two most common systems used in the United States are the **Munsell Color System** and the **Pantone® Professional Color System** (Hope & Walch, 1990).

To color professionals, a color notation system is a precise, scientific language for color identification. For example, in the Munsell System of Color Notation (Munsell, 1998), hue, value, and chroma can describe any color. The Munsell system includes a series of 191 equally spaced hues. Numbers and letters designate each color. Value is designated on a continuum from zero for pure black to ten for pure white. Chroma indicates the degree of difference between a color and a neutral of the same value. The chroma scale starts at zero, but there is no arbitrary end to the scale—light-reflecting materials extend to 20, fluorescent materials to 30. The complete Munsell notation is written symbolically: H(ue) V(alue)/C(hroma). For a vivid red, the notation would read 5R 6/14 (Figure 6.9). For finer definitions, decimals are used—5.3R 6.1/14.4.

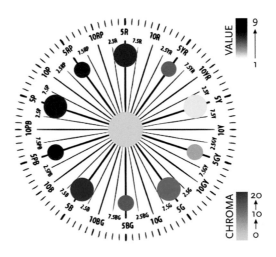

Figure 6.9

The product developer uses the notation of a color system to write manufacturing specifications for the exact color of an item using the code to indicate the hue, value, and chroma.

Pantone develops color standards that allow designers and manufacturers to specify the difference in various pinks using a color code system (i.e., Pantone 12-1107 Pink Champagne and 12-2906 Barely Pink). Beginning with 1,700 hues, the company expanded the range by 56 colors in 1998 (Chirls, 1998a) and by 175 colors in 2002 ("Announcement," 2002) in an attempt to provide a comprehensive mix of colors for fashion, architecture and interior design, and industrial design. Originally organized by groups, the company rearranged the system into color families in 2003 (Gilbert, 2003).

Originally the color swatches were glued to a white backing, but that presented problems: designers couldn't feel the fabric or test it against skin tones and the card and glue made it difficult to obtain an accurate digital reading of the color—the color's spectral fingerprint. Pantone introduced the SMART (sensible, manageable, accessible, relevant, and tough) color swatch card, which consists of a 4- by 8-inch fabric folded into a 4-inch square and shipped in a sealed package that blocks UV rays that might fade the color. The improvements make color selection more precise and easier than the previous system (Tucker, 2007).

Thanks to color matching systems, it's now possible to have a top made in Turkey and a skirt made in Indonesia, and have the two pieces match when they are displayed together in a store in the United States. Laurie Pressman, Pantone's vice president for fashion, home, and interiors, says the reason for color standards is to provide a vocabulary—through swatches, color books, and computer files—to enable Western companies to communicate effectively with their overseas suppliers. "What you have now is so much production shifted to Asia, it's very key to have a standard way to communicate from the design side all the way down through the supply chain."

The problem of color matching is made more complicated by the use of **computer-aided design (CAD)** and other computer-based functions. In the past, a product developer would choose a color and communicate that choice to the mill where dyes would be mixed and the fabric dyed. The mills would submit a **lab dip**, a sample of the color on the correct fabric, for approval by the product developer. The product developer would approve or reject the color based on a visual assessment. Many times the color would not be acceptable, and the process would be repeated until a satisfactory color was achieved or until the mill and product developer agreed that the current version was off but the best that the mill could achieve. In the past, checking for accurate color reproduction has involved having a color stylist visit the manufacturing site to approve the colors or the exchange of color samples between design and manufacturing in a series of approval stages.

With the advent of the Internet, the approval process is moving online. The problem comes in color matching—the onscreen color may or may not match the specified color because it has been altered by the hardware or software used to create it on the monitor (Chirls, 1997). More recently, some manufacturers and retailers with large private-label businesses have invested in technology that improves results and shortens product development schedules. When implemented, all monitors that product developers and the mills use are calibrated to the same color specifications. Color measurement technology is used to determine if the lab dip is within an acceptable range and a visual review confirms it. Even the people doing the visual reviews are tested to ensure that they have the visual acuity to make the decision. Better controls and more specificity allow companies to respond to trends in fashion-sensitive categories like apparel (Power, 2001).

COLOR RELATIONSHIPS ACROSS PRODUCT CATEGORIES

Cycles in color preferences apply across product categories to both hard goods such as automobiles and appliances and soft goods such as apparel and household linens. The timelines differ for each industry because the consumer's replacement rates differ. Industrial products may lag 2 to 5 years behind fashion shades and require modification, but if a color is popular in fashion, it is likely to end up on small appliances and other utilitarian products. People buy clothes more often than automobiles; they redecorate their image more often than their interior spaces. The colors for fashion can show a marked change every 2 years, but the replacement cycle for interior design is between 7 and 12 years (Linton, 1994).

Even to a color consultant specializing in a particular industry, the entire world of color choices is important. Clothing designers look for inspiration in the decorative arts: interior design, architecture, and furniture design. Home fashion designers look for inspiration from apparel and accessories. There is growing cross-pollination between industries regarding color evolution.

In the past, some experts claimed that new trends first show up in the array of colors offered by paint manufacturers (Danger, 1968). Others believed that trends started in the automotive industry because cars require a longer product development cycle (4 to 5 years), and that industry is particularly sensitive to advances in color technologies (Reynold, 1968). Still others expect new color trends to originate in the area of interiors. Today most agree that color trends start with women's fashions, but color trends for interiors occur nearly simultaneously (Craver, 2002). At times, it is an explosion of color in technological gadgets, furnishings, and tableware that precedes the popularity of color in apparel (Graham, 2002). Whatever might have been the case in the past, Jean-Philippe Lenclos' (1994) international survey of color detected a fusing of color fashion across product categories in the mid-1970s. Until that time, color cycles had moved at different speeds in different industries. Subsequently, there was more unification of color trends across product categories.

✦ COLOR IN THE TEXTILE AND APPAREL INDUSTRIES

Color forecasting focuses on a single effect—consumers walking into a store receive a message about the color direction for the season (Figure 6.10). They see apparel and accessories in basic and fashion colors and the related colors in cosmetics. To be effective, the story must be read quickly and be understood easily without verbal explanations. The message conveyed must satisfy many needs and wants—a new look, novel but not intimidating, the promise of complete makeovers, and carefully considered additions to existing wardrobes. The floor must continue to look coordinated even though unsold merchandise from earlier delivery dates hangs in proximity to the newest arrivals. If the coordinating function of color forecasting has worked, colors on the selling floor show an underlying relationship that seems coherent and comprehensible.

✦ COLOR IN CARS

A national poll found that 40 percent of US consumers would switch automobile brands to get their color of choice (DuPont Automotive, 2000). Color in cars is preceded by the establishment of a trend over time expanding to durable and more long-lasting products because customers keep a car for 2 or 3 years when leasing and 5 or more years if they buy (Mateja, 2001). Automotive paints begin in the lab where scientists and engineers create new special effects like pearlescent finishes and test for adhesion and wear. Meanwhile, show cars test the public's reaction to new colors (Hutchings, 2001).

The range of color choices changes with the times, too. Henry Ford was quoted as saying that customers could buy a Model-T in any color they wanted "as long as it's black." In the color explosion of the mid-1950s, the Chrysler Corporation offered a choice of fifty-eight exterior colors either alone or in eighty-six two-tone combinations. Today, we have more color choices than in the earliest era of the automobile but less than in the 1950s. Studies by DuPont between 1959 and 1971 showed a link between popular clothing colors and automobile colors (Hope & Walch, 1990). In 2012, according to the DuPont Automotive Color Popularity Report, the top colors for cars were, in descending order,

Figure 6.10

Consumers walking into a store receive a message about the color direction for the season. This store showcases colors and styles for the resort season with bright, light colors for vacation destinations.

white, black, silver, gray, red, blue, brown/beige, yellow/gold, green and all other colors. The influence of trends is very apparent: silver became the color of choice for cell phones, computers, and home entertainment systems in the early to mid-2000s, leading to its popularity as a car color, while Apple's white iBooks and iMacs helped propel white's prevalence. Even home decor influences car colors, as the earthy browns and beiges that are so popular in homes have led to a rise in their popularity. Both white and black remain top choices worldwide for luxury cars because, just as in fashion, color and price are linked. Color trends extend beyond just the hue of the car, as advances in paint technology that allow manufacturers to use multiple layers to create shimmery silvers, three-dimensional blacks, and pearly whites are gaining in popularity. A new trend is known as "travel," where a color looks very bright from one angle and dark from another, and is starting to spread from neutral tones to bright colors. Another trend that is gaining

popularity is using white primer as a base underneath the paint to make hues of all kinds brighter, so even color values in cars are subject to trends.

✦ COLOR IN INTERIORS

Trends in interior design are defined by a lifestyle concept and its associated colors—such concepts are said to last from 7 to 15 years (Lannon, 1988). Boutique hotels spawn trends for interiors where there has been a pendulum swing from rigorous Modernism to ornamented wood and mosaics, velvet and tapestries, fat sofas and ottomans of a social club—a style that migrated to gated communities in the Sunbelt (Limnander, 2007). The shift reflects consumers' interest away from the obviously mass produced to refined craftsmanship that shows the maker's hand. Even companies that mass produce furnishings and accessories are using advanced technology to introduce variation from piece to piece (Rothman, 2008).

Color trends used to take 3 years to move from the fashion runway to interiors but now the time lag is closer to 6 months (Dowling, 2000) (Figure 6.11). According to forecaster Michelle Lamb, parallels between apparel and home decor are becoming more synchronized—take, for example, the trend in both categories for metallics, neon-flavored yellows (slight green tinge) paired with gray, and skin-tone neutrals ("Trend Guru," 2007). The color family red (from Chinese red to light, bright strawberry and dark, deep cranberry) is a perennial favorite accent for interiors, but even a less popular color like gray (consistently ranked at the bottom of consumers' preference list) becomes fashionable when given a new name like titanium (Pasanella, 2003).

As with the fashion industry, manufacturers and retailers work together closely on developing new looks and directions because color is a primary purchasing consideration. Maison et Objet, the semi-annual home furnishings trade fair in Paris, is influential for new directions. A panel of architects, designers, stylists, and trend forecasters identifies emerging trends for show attendees in a publication and installations (Rothman, 2008). Because the investment in furnishings is generally more than in apparel, consumers feel more restraint in deciding on a change, and even when they decide to change, their choices tend to be rather conservative. Creative teams manage change by experimenting with style innovations and building on those with profit potential (Sykes, 1994).

✦ COLOR IN COSMETICS

Cosmetic colors are the most closely allied to fashion apparel. Fashion periods tend to take on an identifying image, and these changes are paralleled by cosmetics (Hope & Walch, 1990). When sliding-tube lipstick appeared in the 1920s, the flapper had a convenient way to paint her lips bright red. In the 1930s, emphasis shifted to the eyes with the popularity of pale skin and unrouged cheeks. American actresses in the 1940s popularized the image of bright red lips

again and added colored nails. The attention stayed on the mouth until the 1960s, when it shifted again to the eyes. Hippie looks in the 1970s shifted tastes toward the natural look and more beige and earth-toned cosmetic colors. Disco dancing sparked a glittery dress-up phase with eye shadows in metallic colors.

Major cosmetics companies selling in department stores usually have a core group of perennial sellers that stay in the line for years, a smaller group of colors that follow color trends, and seasonal promotion of a fashion color story (Sloan, 1988). Mass product lines, those selling in discount stores and drugstores, may pursue a dual strategy: lagging slightly behind the color trends to attract less fashion-driven customers, and including extreme fashion shades for the fashion-forward customer seeking to satisfy the whim for a trendier image at a moderate price (Wood, 1990).

Professional makeup artists, models, and photographers began to have more influence on trends in cosmetics. Some makeup artists started cosmetic companies based on selling professional lines to the public (Edelson, 1991). The trend now is toward variety where makeup artists create dark and smoky eyes and pale lips for some catwalk shows and the traditional opposite of unaccented eyes and shiny red lips at others—a reflection of the multiplicity of prevalent trends in the 2000s (Fine, 2003). Cosmetic designers predict that this trend will continue as beauty companies look to smaller market niches, style tribes, and specialized groups, eventually producing customized products where consumers participate in designing the products and even the packaging (Siegel, 2003).

International product development companies search for trends and translate them into color formulas, textures, and packaging. Intercos of Milan employs a team of ten trendspotters who travel the world ("Madina," 2002). The company's trend presentations at Cosmoprof, the annual cosmetics trade show in Bologna, are blueprints of what will be new in cosmetics. They serve as a resource for beauty companies who employ trendspotters with titles

Figure 6.11

The forecast of color for interiors, once well behind color in apparel, has closed the time gap, especially for accessories. The change makes it possible for fashion companies, such as Missoni, to create collections for home and fashion in similar color ranges that send a consistent fashion message to consumers.

like "vice president of global lifestyle trend and innovation" (Cooperman, 2001). To highlight the show's forecasting potential, "trendscouting" packages fast-track attendees by identifying the newest products and beauty lines (Epiro, 2008).

Forecasting companies such as Promostyle predict color trends for fashion, interiors, and cosmetics. Cosmetic trends are released 18 months ahead of the season and are presented as four or more stories that predict color, textures, special effects, application techniques, and packaging ("Color Scheming," 2002). Paralleling trends for fashion, cars, and home interiors, new colors in cosmetics feature shimmering and color-shifting effects, intense colors, and new metallic shades from gold to copper. Shimmering effects depend on optically active ingredients that produce color shifts depending on the angle of view. These new ingredients open up the potential for customization cosmetic design (De Guzman, 2007). Makeup colors are influenced by fashion, but sometimes it goes the other way— designer Alber Elbaz finds some of his best colors come from cosmetics "because they've been tested on the face" (Horyn, 2008).

THE PROCESS OF COLOR FORECASTING

Color forecasters are in agreement the majority of the time because they attend the same fabric trade shows in Europe; shop the trendy boutiques and watch street fashion in Europe, Asia, and America; and track the same media. They are members of one or more color associations and collaborate with other members to develop industry color forecasts (Lannon, 1988).

Color forecasters work 18 to 24 months in advance of the season to provide input for the designers' decisions. To work so far ahead, color experts must combine knowledge of color theories and human behavior with acute observational skills. By synthesizing the mood of the times from all the diverse elements of the culture—the economic conditions; happenings in the fine arts; and music, movies, and television

shows that top the charts—color forecasters track trends and recognize new directions. Because color looks different depending on the fabric, color forecasters also stay up to date on new developments in fibers, yarns, and fabrications. To accomplish the task, the forecaster needs a background in the industry, a network of contacts, and the financial backing to travel the globe attending relevant trade shows and shopping the locales where new ideas originate.

✦ SOURCES FOR COLOR IDEAS AND PALETTES

Color forecasters register subtle shifts in consumer preferences, sense when the time is right for a new trend, and pick up directional cues from myriad sources. Color forecasts reflect the mood of the times, both the present and the hints about the future. To forecast color direction, the forecaster must constantly participate in the events that shape the cultural moment and monitor the running commentary of the media. Together, the events and media shape the consumer's preferences and mood. Color stylists look for ideas on the East and West coasts of the United States, in Europe, Latin America, and Asia. Colorists have an eye for the new, the novel, the unique, and the fresh combination. Sources include:

❖ social, economic, and political issues significant enough to affect the thinking, mood, and actions of people (Figure 6.12);
❖ magazines covering fashion, interior design, and entertainment, including those published in Europe;
❖ newspapers, especially features on lifestyle, style, travel, entertainment, and business;
❖ runways in the fashion capitals of Paris, Milan, London, and New York;
❖ trade shows and exhibitions;
❖ the lifestyles of highly visible celebrities in entertainment and prominent role models from other fields;
❖ color schemes featured in films, especially major films with exotic locales, set in stylish

time periods, or featuring distinctive costuming;

❖ styles worn by stars of popular television shows;

❖ the world of music through the club scene, music videos, dance crazes, and the style leadership of stars;

❖ theater, especially productions in which the costuming, set design, or choreography are important elements;

❖ travel destinations that merge new sights and experiences or involve new concepts in the hospitality industry;

❖ street fashion in urban areas, districts associated with the arts, and emerging shopping scenes with small, unique, independent businesses;

❖ flea markets in Paris and London and other inspiring open markets that reflect the character of a specific location and culture;

❖ decorator houses and other showcases for trends in interior design and architecture;

❖ museum shows focusing on artists, collections, archaeological finds, photographers, or artisans, especially those with broad media coverage;

❖ museum shows, auctions, and sales featuring vintage fashion and famous designers;

❖ auctions, especially those featuring the possessions of famous people;

❖ revival of interest in historic periods, especially the architecture, art, and signature looks of those eras;

❖ fads and fashions in cuisine including shopping food markets for food products, produce, and flowers characteristic of the locale;

❖ toys, games, and amusements for different age groups;

❖ new electronic gadgets, computer applications, and breakthrough technologies;

❖ industrial design, graphic design, and package design, because these fields often foreshadow new visual directions.

Consider it a strong directional signal when the same trend is visible during the same time period from multiple sources (Eiseman, 1994). In such cases, trendsetters across industries reinforce the messages, widen the scope, and expand the coverage.

Figure 6.12

Interest in "green" (environmentally friendly) manufacturing revived interest in natural dyes and the softer, more varied color effects they produce.

The color forecaster is always looking for clues to the next new color, the adaptation of basic colors, themes, and directions for color stories. There are some calendar dates that are especially important: the seasonal runway shows and key trade shows. An important trade show for color forecasters is **Première Vision**, an international textile industry fair, held seasonally in Paris (Figure 6.13). Fabric mills make presentations concerning the coming season, show organizers offer their own forecast, and European color and season forecast consultants display in the Hall of Prediction. This show is the crossroads for designers, manufacturers, and forecasters to see the latest in textile developments—a place for scouting and networking. Forecasters combine trips to the runway shows and fabric fairs with shopping the trendiest boutiques and watching street fashion.

The forecaster returns from trips with many new ideas, some of which have to be modified for the American market (Webb, 1994). Two organizing principles help to coordinate the new finds: the color cycle as it has evolved over the previous seasons, and the curve presenting diffusion of innovation across consumer segments. The forecaster adds the new finds to an existing library of ideas. The editing process begins by pinning color samples to a board to study relationships and color groups. At first this process involves a free, open reaction to the colors. As the editing process continues, the forecaster consults the work of previous seasons to maintain the visual rhythm of color evolution. At some point in the process, the forecaster begins to define the themes and concepts that link the colors in a color story. In the final editing stage, the forecaster makes modifications and adjustments based on the client's target consumer, product category, and price point. The final color board for the client provides overall color direction, color stories coordinated around visual themes, and specific color selection.

✦ TECHNIQUES OF TREND ANALYSIS AND SYNTHESIS

The methods used by the Nippon Color and Design Research Institute (NCD) illustrate the critical thinking process required to produce an accurate and justifiable forecast (Kobayashi, 1981).

Figure 6.13
Première Vision, the international textile industry fair in Paris, and its trend displays and presentations are an important stop for trendspotters.

Their approach combines an understanding of the psychology of color and a sense of the spirit of the times. In their system, each color is assessed according to its position on three scales—warm to cool, soft to hard, and clear to grayish. These scales can be represented in a three-dimensional color space with individual colors occupying a unique location. Using this Color Image Scale (Figure 6.14) makes it easier to identify the similarities and contrasts between colors, their relative position to each other, and the color patterns or groupings.

The method visualizes the colors of a season as a pyramid. The broad base represents the colors that are resistant to change. The tip represents the fast-changing fashion colors. The middle represents those colors linked to the image and mood of the times—colors that may persist for 2 or 3 years until the attention of the culture moves on to other interests and concerns. Using this system, it is possible to identify a range of colors from the basic ones accepted with no resistance to the colors that symbolize the times, to the fashion-driven trend colors. Such a balanced method is like taking a snapshot of a color period. It allows the forecaster to create a color assortment for a range of products targeted to different segments along the fashion cycle (Linton, 1994).

For each season, forecasters at the NCD perform a step-by-step trend analysis:

Step 1   **Analysis of current trends.** Forecasters use information from newspapers, magazines, television, and other sources to identify trends.

Step 2   **Analysis of current colors.** Fashion forecasters look at fashion across women's and men's apparel, interior design, and automobiles; identify colors and create swatches of current colors; and use the Color Image Scale to detect relationships.

Step 3   **Image analysis.** Forecasters collect pictures of current images across women's and men's apparel, interior design, and automobiles (sometimes including package design, corporate

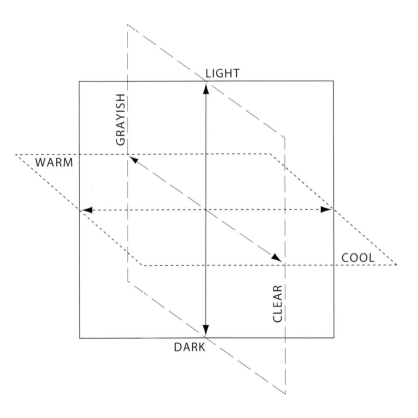

Figure 6.14

The Color Image Scale makes it easier to identify the similarities and contrasts between colors, their position relative to each other, and color patterns.

images, and environmental design) and array them using the categories of the Color Image Scale to detect patterns.

Step 4 **Synthesis of current and emerging lifestyle patterns.** Forecasters look for agreement between the first three steps to develop hypotheses about the direction that lifestyles and consumer tastes are taking.

Step 5 **Patterns in color preferences.** Forecasters use questionnaires and color projection techniques (color-word associations) to explore the psychology of color and consumer preferences. Together with the other steps, this research allows the NCD to identify people's desired images and array them using the same categories as in the other steps.

Step 6 **The forecast.** Forecasters look at the images, themes, and colors to create the forecast. In the presentation, a word or phrase and six to nine colors are identified to capture and communicate each image.

Considerations of political and economic conditions, special upcoming events, and cyclical changes are all part of the final NCD forecast. This comprehensive approach is effective in color planning, product development, marketing, and merchandising. The forecasts can be fine-tuned to identify the volume colors for mass marketing and fashion colors for other niches. The system allows the NCD and clients to compare past results and track shifts in color tastes across seasons.

Although other forecasters may not systematize their methods to the degree achieved by the NCD, their processes are similar. Forecasters (Szwarce, 1994) track the social, economic, and psychological influences on consumers and their reactions. They read all kinds of newspapers and magazines. They travel. They keep up with what is selling at retail. They attend trade fairs and fashion shows. They shop and watch people on the street. Wherever they are, they collect clippings, color swatches, and take photos for inspiration. While preparing a forecast, they organize their observations on boards by product category and color family.

Forecasters work intuitively, discovering techniques that work, refining and reusing them. Some rely on their reading, observation, and networking. Others add qualitative research, including interviews and focus groups with potential customers. Some monitor color on billboards, at automobile shows, and window displays of selected fashion and furniture stores in Paris, London, Tokyo, and New York (Lenclos, 1994). Peclers Paris, a trend forecasting agency based in Paris, begins by spontaneously buying yarns, ribbons, books, and photos based on the staff's experience. At brainstorming sessions, each stylist in the company brings ideas and inspiration. These sessions rationalize the process because they provide a forum for combining instincts, market knowledge, and a sense of fashion's evolution. The process culminates in a color range to guide the company's work with the textile industry and retail clients (Zessler, 1994).

Forecasters may be asked to create a general forecast for an industry, for a product category, or for a more specific purpose identified by a particular client. Whatever the assignment, certain considerations must be factored into the forecast. When forecasting for clients, those considerations become more defined and specific. Forecasters consider the following (Eiseman, 1994; Verlodt, 1994a; Wrack, 1994):

❖ *product life cycle*—some products remain stable; others are quick to change;
❖ *production cycle*—some products can be manufactured with short turnaround times; others involve longer lead times;
❖ *product sensitivity* to external influences such as changing demographics, geographic and cultural conditions, and prices of raw materials—factors that affect all products but have more impact on some;
❖ *design-driven change*—changes in silhouette, fit, pattern, and texture influence product categories differently;

- *product compatibility*—how a product coordinates with other products;
- *sales history*—top-selling colors can be moved into related products;
- *competitors' color choices*—color selection creates distinctiveness and relative advantage;
- *consumers' preferences*, psychological relationship to colors, and economic status;
- *consumers' spending patterns* and confidence in their economic situation;
- *climate* in the regions where the product will be sold, bought, and used.

Taking all these considerations into account, the forecaster identifies stable, classic colors, fashion-driven colors, and new directional colors. For even the most stable colors, the forecaster must calculate the exact shade (Hope & Walch, 1990).

✦ FORECASTS AT THE BEGINNING OF THE PRODUCTION PIPELINE

Large chemical companies make dyes to sell down the production pipeline where coloration actually takes place. More than 6,000 different synthetic dyes are known to exist, and the typical dye producer will offer about 600 in the company's palette. These companies need long lead times for production—typically 4 to 9 months ahead of delivery to the dye house. These long lead times mean that the chemical company needs early warning about color demand so that it can provide the exact shades demanded by fashion. Often forecasting information makes it to the fabric producer but does not flow backward to the producers of the dye materials. Yet, when an order comes in for a particular blue, the company is expected to deliver dye for that exact color. In the past, meeting orders has meant holding high safety inventories in hopes of avoiding a stock-out situation (Dransfield, 1994). Pantone, in an effort to save time in the early stages of product development, partnered with Clariant International, a producer of textile colorants, to assist mills in matching the 1,925 colors in the color portfolio. A joint website provides technical support for mills on dyestuff recipes (Tucker, 2007).

Some dye-producing companies are setting up an early warning system by using fashion experts in Rome, London, Paris, and New York to predict color trends at a generic level—reds are going to be in, for example. These companies also need to know how dark the colors will be because very dark colors can take ten times more dye than pale shades. With this early warning system, a company can concentrate on 250 individual dyes to meet all color requirements for all types of fibers and provide desirable fastness properties. About 20 percent of key dyes are unique and cannot be mixed from other dyes; the rest can. For that large portion of mixable colors, the company depends on the art of the master blender. With the early warning system and partnerships with fabric producers and large textile retailers, the dye producer can be aware of the color forecast in time to meet the demand for fashion-driven colors (Dransfield, 1994).

✦ APPAREL MANUFACTURERS' IN-HOUSE FORECAST

Color decisions begin early in the product development cycle. For designers, a new collection begins with the selection of a color palette. From that first step, it will be from 6 months to nearly a year before those colors appear as a coordinated collection on the runway or in the showroom. The initial decision is critical to success because the eight to ten selected colors signal the personality of the collection. The color story (Figure 6.15) will be combined into prints, yarn-dyed fabrics, and solids and coordinated across jackets, tops, skirts, pants, and dresses into a collection with perhaps 200 separate pieces (Allen, 1985).

Large companies often have a division responsible for developing trend information on colors and styles and reporting to the other divisions involved in product development. Design groups or other executives may carry this responsibility in smaller firms. Wherever the function is located on the organizational chart,

You Be the Forecaster: A Colorful Season

Brennan is the design director for a large manufacturer of knit shirts—mainly T-shirts and polo shirts for both men and women. As design director, Brennan coordinates the efforts of the design staff for several product lines. One of her most important functions is as a color forecaster, because newness and fashion for basic products are tied to color. As the company's fashion forecaster, she scouts trade shows in the United States and Europe and participates in the professional color-forecasting organizations. The company also subscribes to several color-forecasting services.

For Brennan, the color forecast begins when she prepares for a brainstorming meeting with the other forecasters at an international meeting of color professionals. Each participant creates a concept board proposing a direction for colors that will dominate women's fashion 2 years in the future. Together, the group will reach consensus on about twenty-five colors that will be reported to all members of the organization, their companies or clients, and the media. Other industry committees will follow a similar procedure to arrive at a color selection for menswear, children's wear, and interiors.

When Brennan returns to her company, she will synthesize all the information she has gathered, analyze color directions as they apply to her company's line and target consumer, and develop the color story for each of the company's lines.

Brennan will create a concept board suggesting the color direction 2 years in the future. First, she will present her board at a meeting of color forecasting professionals. After they brainstorm together, they will develop a consensus forecast that each can later use with clients. Use the following discussion questions to review and summarize this chapter as you follow Brennan's progress through this process.

Color Ideas: The first stage in color forecasting requires openness to inspiration from a myriad of sources. Review the list of sources for color ideas and palettes in this chapter.

Which sources on the list are most likely to be active and influential at this time? How can Brennan tap into these sources and gather color information as she travels? How can she accomplish this if she works from her home office? What color relationships across product categories will be important in guiding her during this first stage?

Color Cycles: A forecaster must consider more than one kind of color cycle in making color directions understandable.

What looks in current fashion will continue to evolve into the next few seasons? Are these looks part of fashion's historic continuity? How will they influence color evolution? What long-wave oscillations will affect the next few seasons? Is the current cycle bright and saturated, multicolored, muted, earth tones, or neutral and achromatic? What comes next? Is there a cycle related to the influence of men's apparel on women's clothes? Is there a color temperature cycle that will affect the next few seasons? Is there any new color technology that will influence change over the next few seasons?

Color Names and Themes: Communicating color to the trade and to the consumer involves grouping colors around themes that are culturally and socially relevant to the times and naming colors within those themes.

What themes are emerging that would be appropriate for organizing the color story? What sources for color names seem most applicable to the forecast of colors 2 years from now? What elements should Brennan include on the board she takes to the meeting of her professional organization?

Analysis and Synthesis: When Brennan participates in the brainstorming session, she will be involved in a critical thinking process aimed at creating an accurate and justifiable forecast.

What techniques of analysis and synthesis will be in play during the session? When Brennan returns from the meeting and begins working with her clients, what technique of analysis and synthesis will she use?

Figure 6.15

Choosing a color palette for the season, finding inspirational images that set the tone for the collection, and reviewing fabrics are first steps in creating a collection.

executives use forecasts in conjunction with company sales data (see Chapter 10) and in-house color tracking to prepare and present company-specific forecasts. The decision process factors together color forecasts, information about street fashion, fashion collections in the United States and Europe, and reports in trade publications and fashion magazines.

✧ Seasonal Color Story

A design or marketing executive making decisions about color for a product category uses multiple forecasts, including those available from:

❖ professional color organizations like CAUS and CMG;

❖ industry trade organizations like Cotton, Inc.;

❖ textile trade shows like Première Vision;

❖ color companies like Pantone;

❖ for-profit independent color consultancies and services such as Design Options that sell subscriptions to their forecasts.

The Pantone View Color Planner, issued biannually, results from meetings between the company executives and internationally recognized color experts in the fields of women's wear, menswear, and interiors. The meetings take place twice a year in different European cities, in rooms with white walls and sparse furnishings so that nothing competes with the colors that each expert presents as their picks for the upcoming season. Inspiration comes from diverse sources, forecasters bring props such as eggs, paper dolls, and the latest images from the anonymous street "photograffeur" JR to illustrate their findings. "One of our committee [members] came last winter, and he came with a basket full of onions and chopped up all the onions to show how the beauty of the color of an onion is," said publisher and designer David Shah, who runs the Pantone meeting. The resulting forecast provides color names and code numbers for each selection (Hamilton, 2002; Marritz, 2011; Schneider-Levy, 2007; Vanderbilt, 2012).

The availability of multiple forecasts is valuable not because forecasters usually disagree in any major way but because several forecasts tend to verify general color trends. In addition to the color forecasts, the executive will likely subscribe to the services of other forecasters who specialize in textile trends, the fashion scene (see Chapter 8), or in discovering cultural trends (see Chapter 4).

A company often belongs to more than one professional organization and usually sends different executives to the meetings. In that way, the company benefits from having executives active in the workings of the organizations and obtains a multi-lens view of color evolution. When there is time lag between meetings, such as sometimes occurs between the organizations in Europe and America, one company executive may participate in forecasting at the earlier meeting and return to develop the seasonal **colorways**—color groups and combinations. Later, another company executive may participate in the sessions of another color organization, sharing their company forecast with other professionals. In this way, color trends are often shared across national boundaries, organizations, and companies. Forecasters' palettes for a particular season rarely disagree in any major way even if the forecasts are developed independently— perhaps owing partly to the evolutionary nature of the task, and partly to the movement of the forecast through the supply chain (Webb, 1994).

The process of interpreting color forecasts is far from a straightforward task. All forecasts come with a disclaimer saying that they can be inaccurate. After all, a forecast is made when information is incomplete; it cannot be expected to predict the exact future. One complaint about color forecasts is that they include every color. Color forecasters reply that the forecasts indicate the general direction, not an actual color. They become useful only when executives consider color direction in terms of hue, value, and intensity and consider context and usage (Eiseman, 1994).

✧ Color Planning

Even with several color forecasts in hand, the color planning decisions still remain with the executive. The executive edits the information in the forecast for the specifics of a product line

targeted for a particular consumer segment. Upscale, sophisticated markets are likely to relate well to a more European color palette with its subtle, darker, and grayed look. A mass marketer chooses a more immediately understandable color palette that is brighter and more accessible to a broader market segment. For other lines, color decisions depend on the geography, climate, and preferences where the products will be sold or used. Tradition plays a key role in decision making—what is well accepted in society as well as what is typical for a particular manufacturer (Stark & Johnson-Carroll, 1994). By having several forecasts, the executive sees the overall color direction and taps into the expertise of several forecasters when selecting the exact colors for a product line.

Forecasts arrive broken down into ranges of colors—darks, brights, mid-tones, pastels, and neutrals (Calvert, 1994). Women's clothing has the widest spectrum of color among apparel products. Each forecast may include as many as fifty colors. If an executive works with four to six forecasts, that means finding the color undercurrents across 200 to 300 colors. Using these colors as a starting point, the executive will develop five or six ranges of 12 to 20 colors as the in-house color range—75 to 100 colors that allow for several in-store deliveries without repeating a color. This color range will include long-selling colors, perhaps paired in a new color combination. It may recast classic color formulas like spring's recurring red, white, and blue into a newer coral, beige, and teal. Perennial best-selling colors such as black, white, true red, navy, and ivory are so basic that they may not appear in any of the forecasts but still may be used in the product line.

The in-house color range will be applied to fabrics in solid colors and to prints, plaids, and multicolor knit yarns. The newest colors are more likely to appear in the multihued formats (prints and plaids) or in separates that provide an accent to a group. To guide the product development stage, and as a communication tool to the other functional groups in the company, the executive will present the in-house color range in the context of themes and imagery that relate to the target customer (see Chapter 12).

Designers, stylists, and product developers apply forecasts to a line of merchandise specifically for the target customer (Figure 6.16). In selecting colors for a line in a given season, executives make an error if they are:

❖ too brash, overreacting to the forecast by producing a line with fashion-forward colors that do not sell;

❖ too conservative, ignoring the forecast in favor of playing it safe, missing out on hot new colors that catch on with the consumer.

In lines where economies of scale limit changes in silhouette, use of detail, and embellishment, color provides the visual power to attract customers.

Effective interpretation of the forecasts comes with experience of managing color decisions from season to season. After several seasons of brights, the forecast shifts to newness in another color range as the color cycle continues. Brights will still appear in the forecast but will be less dominant than in the previous season. Brights that continue strong in sales figures may be modified to midtones as a transition, allowing the customer to use these new variations with the brights of the previous season (Calvert, 1994). It is never a good idea to leap from one distinct palette to another totally different one.

In the product development stage, executives must go beyond color direction to forecast the significance of the color story and the quality of the trend. Together with the marketers and merchandisers, they must decide specific colors for each item in the line, the coordination of those items within a group, and how many of each item to produce.

✦ FORECASTING AT THE END OF THE PRODUCTION PIPELINE

Retailers take a risk in selecting merchandise because they are predicting future consumer demand. By gathering information from a variety of sources, retailers seek to minimize risk (Kline & Wagner, 1994). Color is a very important part of merchandise selection. As one retailer put it (Noh, 1997): "After years of observing customers selecting one item over another I learned that color was their most important choice—often they selected a style that was not their favorite just because the color was right—but very rarely did they select a style or textile when the color was not what they wanted!"

Information is available for retailers through several channels. Small chains and independent stores use buying offices that provide forecasting information or subscribe to fashion forecasting services. Larger chains rely on their fashion director or corporate buyers who receive the forecast information and fashion subscriptions and disseminate the information to others in the organization. Trade publications such as *WWD* (*Women's Wear Daily*) report on presentations by color consultants at conferences and trade shows across all categories of fashion apparel. Consumer magazines and newspapers carry reports on color forecasting.

Figure 6.16
Designer Sir Paul Smith presents at his work studio.

Chapter Summary

Just as color is central to the heart of a consumer purchase, it is also at the heart of forecasting. Color can be impacted by factors such as value, intensity, tint, shade and tone, and by the various schemes which colors are combined, including analogous, complementary, and others. Color preferences are highly subjective, and can be influenced by symbolism, gender, ethnicity, and region.

Color forecasting has a long history which dates back some 100 years, and since then has gotten more sophisticated, including consumer demographics as well as economics and social factors as considerations. Two of the oldest and most prominent color forecasting organizations are the Color Association of the United States (CAUS) and the Color Marketing Group (CMG). Forecasting is also done by large companies, such as Pantone and Munsell, that produce color standards for designers and manufacturers, as well as small, independent color forecasters such as Los Angeles-based Design Options. Forecasters provide their clients with seasonal color stories consisting of eight to ten colors for different target markets.

The practice of color matching, which is crucial for all manufacturers, has been made easier through color specifications, which remove the subjectivity from color matching and enable designers in one part of the world to know that their products will be made with accurate color matching even though they are being made far away.

While forecasting is widely used in the textile and apparel industries, other industries such as automotive, interiors, and cosmetics also use forecasting as a central part of their product development. Forecasters perform a series of steps in order to accurately assess a color's future popularity, and in addition to developing the palette are also responsible for developing appropriate names for colors. With so many options to choose from, designers and retailers have access to color forecasts that enable them to accurately meet the needs and wants of their target markets.

Key Terms and Concepts

Achromatic
Analogous
Chroma
Color Association of the United States (CAUS)
Color cycles
Color direction
Color Key Program
Color Marketing Group (CMG)
Color palette
Color specifications
Color story
Color wheel
Colorways
Complementary colors
Complements
Computer-aided design (CAD)
Double complements

Hue
Intensity
Lab dip
Munsell Color System
Pantone® Professional Color System
Première Vision
Primary colors
Saturation
Secondary colors
Shade
Split complements
Tertiary colors
Tint
Tone
Trend merchandising
Triad
Value

Discussion Questions

Color Naming: Why do you think color names are important, considering that the color name does not appear anywhere on the product? Which of the environmental associations (natural phenomena, flora, etc.) listed in your text appeal the most to you? Using the color wheel, how would you most accurately describe the colors you are currently wearing? Now, what color names would you give to these same colors to market them most effectively? What is the difference in image?

Color Cycles: What are some colors that are currently gaining in popularity? What are some colors that are losing popularity? Looking at the color trends from recent decades, which type of cycle do you think we are currently in—a high chroma phase, a darkening phase, or another phase entirely? Why do you think this phase is currently popular with consumers? What has sparked this popularity—technology, economic conditions, social change, nostalgia, or something else? What color cycle do you envision becoming popular in the next 3–5 years and why?

Consumers and Color: Consider the following questions if you had to devise an array of colors for a line of (a) T-shirts, (b) bathing suits, and (c) winter coats. What colors would you pick to appeal to color forwards? Color prudents? Color loyals? How would your color choices differ when appealing to men or to women? How would your color choices differ if you were trying to appeal to specific ethnic groups or different generations?

Color Relationships across Product Categories: Which product category (apparel, cars, interiors, and cosmetics) are the most color forward? The most color prudent? Why? What are examples of colors that are very popular in one category but would not be successful in another? What colors are currently popular that you observe in more than one category?

Sources for Color: Where do you get inspiration for the new colors that you purchase for your personal use? Which of the sources (magazines, runways, films etc.) listed in your text do you feel is the most influential? How do you think the various sources might be connected with one another? Which of the various sources can be influenced by fashion brands, and which cannot?

Forecasting Activities

Contrast and Compare Forecasts. Collect color forecasts from several color forecasting services and industry trade groups for the same season (either the current forecast or one for a season just past). Compare and contrast color projections across the several forecasts. Are the color selections similar in terms of hue, value, and intensity? Are the themes, color names, and grouping of colors similar? How closely do the forecasts agree? Where do they diverge? Can the differences between the forecasts be explained by a different focus on product category or target market? Discuss how an executive would make decisions about a product line using these several forecasts.

The Story of Black. Trace black as a fashion color. It has always had an important role in the fashion story. When did it dominate the marketplace? What factors were involved? Which designers became known for the dominant role of black in their collections? What associations make black so popular with consumers? How versatile is black in designs? Forecast the future of black as a fashion color and as a basic color.

Think Local Color. Develop a distinctive "color conception of a place" based on your area of the country. What combination of colors in the natural environment and colors associated with the history of the place symbolize the area's color personality? How are these colors present in the apparel, interiors, architecture, and art of the region? Create a collage expressing this "color conception of a place." Discuss the interaction between fashion colors proposed for national or international use and the distinctive colors of a region. How could local color preferences affect sales of apparel? Is color marketing becoming more or less responsive to local color preferences?

Web of Color. Search for color forecasts on the Internet. Look at sites devoted to fashion, interiors, and automobiles. Sites often have a feature to keep you coming back for periodic updates. Some sites feature a single color and update this color monthly. These sites often have an archive of past issues. Be sure to check the archives for recent color forecasts or directional information. Look at sites that archive designers' runway presentations from past seasons. Set up a personal "favorites" list of color sites that you can check regularly to assist in developing color forecasts.

New Color Search. Play the part of a color-forward consumer. Shop upscale department stores, discounters, and all the retail levels in between looking for new colors that are just beginning to appear in the marketplace. Do the colors differ at the various retail levels? Are the new colors so simple that they can be described in two words, or are they more complex? Can you trace any of these colors back to their cultural roots? Analyze the appeal of these new colors in terms of consumer preference categories such as age, ethnicity, income, and gender. What is your prediction for the future popularity of these new colors?

Resource Pointers

Websites for professional color organizations:

Color Association of the United States: www.colorassociation.com

Color Marketing Group: www.colormarketing.org

Website for color education created by The Society of Dyers and Colourists (SDC): www.colour-experience.org

Websites for trade shows:

Cosmoprof (beauty): www.cosmoprof.com and www.cosmoprofnorthamerica.com

Maison et Objet (home decor): www.maison-objet.com

Première Vision (fabric): www.premierevision.fr

Color forecasting companies:

Cotton Incorporated: www.cottoninc.com

Design Options: www.design-options.com/

Munsell Color System: www.munsell.com

Nippon Color and Design Research Institute, Inc.: www.ncd-ri.co.jp/english/

Pantone: www.pantone.com

The Trend Curve (home decor): trendcurve.com

Online color IQ test:

http://xritephoto.com/ph_toolframe.aspx?action=coloriq

Many a dress of mine is born of the fabric alone.

—Christian Dior

7

TEXTILE FORECASTING

OBJECTIVES

◆ Understand the fiber and fabric product development cycle

◆ Identify the sources of innovation in fiber and fabric product development

◆ Comprehend the role of fiber and fabric trade organizations and fabric councils in disseminating trend information

◆ Connect the relationship between trend formation fibers and fabrics and the product development process

FASHION IN FIBER AND FABRIC

In a retail environment, seeing fashion is not enough. As shoppers walk down the aisles of a store or move among the clothing racks, they reach out to touch the shoulder of a jacket or feel the sleeve of a sweater. This behavior shows the power of touch to connect consumers to textile products (Gladwell, 1996). Fabrics range from slick surfaces like leather and futuristic plastic to softer surfaces like cashmere; from flat weaves to heavy textures like bouclé and the solid structure of flannel to the web-like open structure of crochet. Clothing has been called "the second skin" in recognition of its intimate connection with people's physical and psychological comfort (Horn, 1965). So, it is not surprising that fabrics play such a prominent role in forecasting fashion.

✦ THE FIBER AND FABRIC PRODUCT DEVELOPMENT CYCLE

There are two general categories of fiber: **natural fibers** and **manufactured fibers**. Natural fibers from animals such as alpaca, angora, camel's hair, cashmere, mohair, silk, vicuña, and wool are classified as **protein fibers**. Those from plants such as cotton, linen, ramie, and hemp are classified as **cellulosic fibers**. For manufactured fibers, substances are transformed into fibers as the end product of a process. Manufactured fibers derived from processed plant sources (rayon, acetate, and lyocell) are also classified cellulosic. Other manufactured fibers from chemical compounds (acrylic, spandex, nylon, polyester, and polyolefin) are termed **synthetics**.

In the past, the development cycle for fabrics depended on things such as the growing season for cotton or the shearing season for wool. With the advent of manufactured fibers that can be produced at any time, these earlier seasonal considerations became less important. In today's market the most important consideration is the consumer's willingness to buy, a period that now closely coincides with the use of the apparel. To meet this "in-season" buying trend, merchandising is moving toward continuous delivery of new product throughout the season to keep the selling floor interesting and inviting for purchasers. Stretching back from each apparel purchase is a chain of production that extends to the production of the fiber.

The scheduling of textile development is a critical factor in the introduction of fashion products. The time involved depends on the source of the fiber and the production stages between raw material and final fabric. When production is located offshore, the production cycle involves longer lead times to accommodate transportation from factory to distribution points. The product development process for catalog merchandise and for certain product categories, such as sweaters, starts earlier than for other merchandise sold in retail stores.

The **supply chain** begins with fiber, which is processed into yarn and then into fabric, and ends with **fabric finishing**, including dyeing and printing. Vertically integrated firms control all aspects of the supply chain from yarn to fabric to finishing to apparel. Other firms form strategic alliances between segments of the chain to cooperate in product development, cut lead times, consolidate purchasing, and control inventories. Integrating the supply chain in this way allows companies to plan a 12-month flow of goods. Because today's fashion picture favors a variety of goods at all price points, the emphasis is on **value-added** fabrics—fabrics with special appearance or performance characteristics that will command premier prices over basic fabrics in the marketplace (Chirls, 1998b).

THE PRODUCT DEVELOPMENT PROCESS

✦ FIBER DEVELOPMENT

At each stage in the supply chain, innovation is possible. Fiber producers and mills start projecting fabric trends at least 16 months ahead of the selling season. Fabric, like apparel, goes through stages of development, introduction, selection, and ordering. In the case of fibers and fabric, the customers are apparel design teams who select the fabrics they will use in creating their seasonal collections.

✧ Natural Fibers

Natural fibers have been used for apparel across the millennia. In 1989, Sally Fox reintroduced natural-color cotton, which had a history dating back to the Incas. Organically grown and available in mocha, reddish brown, and sage green, the timing of this innovation matched consumer interest in environmentally sensitive products (Fox, 2003). Today's textile technology continues to refine and expand the properties and uses of natural fibers ("Fibers," 1998). Cotton is moving into high-performance fabrics for activewear because of mechanical and chemical finishing and blending with other fibers. Treatment of linen yarn is increasing its use in knits and weaving techniques, finishes, and blends, which has helped reduce wrinkling. New ways of controlling wool's shrinking and felting properties are making it more useful in knitwear and safe for machine washing and drying.

✧ Manufactured Fibers

Developing new fibers and variations on existing fibers takes a huge research effort and years of work before the innovation is ready for marketing. When new fibers are developed, the US Federal Trade Commission (FTC) designates them with a **generic name** (e.g., nylon, polyester, spandex, and lyocell). Companies that produce and promote the fibers add a trademarked **brand name** (e.g., Invista's brand name for polyester is Dacron, the Accordis trademark for lyocell is Tencel). To be in compliance with the Textile Fibers Products Identification Act, clothing must be labeled with the generic name of the fibers by percentage composition.

Whereas development of a new fiber is rare, novelty in fiber comes about in other ways. The basic properties of a manufactured generic fiber can be altered chemically and physically to obtain different looks and properties. When a variation is distinctive enough, the company will give it a specialty brand name and promote its special properties as a mimic for a natural fiber or because of some other performance advantage. Performance fabrics feature a special attribute such as the ability to regulate body temperature. Novelty in this area comes from making once industrial high-tech applications suitable for apparel.

✦ YARN DEVELOPMENT

Innovation in yarn production focuses on developing products with the fiber blends, finishes, and properties that meet consumer needs (Figure 7.1). Often innovation comes from exploiting the capabilities of weaving looms and knitting machines. Yarn production techniques create differences in:

❖ **texture**—the surface variations from hard and slick to soft and fuzzy, from dull and matte to shimmering highlights and shiny metallic;

❖ **hand**—the way finished fabric feels when handled, and properties such as its ability to recover when stretched or compressed;

❖ **drape**—the way the finished fabric hangs on the body, whether it stands away from the body or clings to the curves.

Each natural fiber—silk, cotton, wool, and linen—involves a unique process to turn fiber into yarn. In contrast, the manufactured fibers begin as solid chips or pellets that are liquefied and extruded through a spinneret. Holes in the spinneret can be engineered to vary in size and shape, and these differences alter the properties of the fiber.

Microfibers are produced when the holes in the spinneret are very small and produce a fiber that is finer than even the finest natural-fiber silk. Generally, these small, fine microfibers make fabrics that are softer and have better drape than the same construction in traditional fibers.

Synthetic fibers are produced as **filaments**—continuous strands. Manufactured fibers can also be textured to create crimp, loop, curl, or coil to increase the bulk, loft, or elasticity of the fiber. They can be spun into yarn in filament form or cut into short lengths that mirror the natural fibers (called **staple length**).

Figure 7.1

The trend at yarn and fabric shows is toward fine-gauge knits and lightweight woven fabrics because they are ideal for layering.

During the spinning process, fibers can be blended together to make the yarn. Blending natural and manufactured fibers offers many possibilities for innovation as the blend also carries the properties of the original fibers but in a new combination. Blending wool with silk, viscose, nylon, ramie, or linen translates the fiber known for warmth into a sheer or lightweight fabric suitable for spring fashions (Holch, 1997). Tencel (a trademarked brand of the lyocell fiber) blended with linen retains linen's aesthetic but adds a softer hand to the fabric (Holch, 1996).

✦ FABRIC DEVELOPMENT

Fabrics used in apparel products are either knitted or woven from natural, manufactured, or blended yarns. **Weaving** is defined as the interlacing of yarns at right angles. The order of interlacing produces patterns called weaves, and each weave has its own characteristics and properties. In **knitting**, yarns are looped together in successive rows—a process that gives more natural stretch to the fabric, although the actual result depends on the fiber content of the yarn and the yarn construction. Variations in the weave or knitting pattern coupled with variations in the fiber content and yarn construction lead to an infinite universe of innovation in fabric structure. Innovation can also be found in new uses for fabrics of different structures. Nike has developed a performance knit employing a new technology called Nike Flyknit ("Nike Engineers Knit for Performance," 2012), in which yarns and fabric variations are precisely engineered only where they are needed for a featherweight, formfitting, and virtually seamless upper and provides a precision fit, creating a feeling of a second skin.

Bonding, crocheting, felting, knotting, and laminating make other fabric structures. Called **novelty fabrics**, such fabrics often appear as accents in a fashion season.

✦ FABRIC DYEING DEVELOPMENT

Color can be added at any stage in fabric production—to the fiber, yarn, or fabric, or to the finished garment (Figure 7.2). In a process specific to manufactured fibers called **solution dyeing**, the color is added to the liquefied fiber before it is extruded as a filament. Manufactured and natural fibers in staple lengths can be dyed as loose fibers before being processed into yarn. Yarn can be colored after production—a method frequently used in the production of woven stripes, plaids, and check fabrics. The fabric can be dyed after weaving in a process called **piece dyeing**—an inexpensive method used most frequently for solid colors. If the fabric is made from two different fibers, it is possible to produce a two-color fabric by adding dyes that are reactive with each fiber to a single dye bath—an inexpensive method called **cross dyeing**. The color can even be applied after the fabric has been made into garments. **Garment dyeing** is used when an apparel manufacturer is trying to match items by dyeing them together. Garment dyeing is also used when an apparel manufacturer wants to manufacture the apparel but conduct consumer testing on colors before committing to delivery. These variations in the dyeing process allow manufacturers to choose the one best suited for their situation and to provide many variations in the effects achieved. Reports on new looks in fabrics frequently include a reference to the way the color was applied or to the effect created.

✦ FABRIC FINISHING DEVELOPMENT

Finishing is used to manipulate the appearance characteristics, performance, or hand of a fabric. Fabric finishing may involve:

- ❖ a *mechanical process* such as passing the fabric between rollers with heat and pressure to create an overall glaze, or abrading the surface with brushes for a suede-like look;
- ❖ a *chemical process* that changes the surface of the fibers, such as acid-washed denim;

Figure 7.2

Colored yarn is used in the production of woven stripes, plaids, and checks.

❖ an *applied finish* that changes the properties of the fabric, such as increasing water repellency.

Finishing techniques allow a fabric to take on many possible looks and properties but they may also increase the fabric price by 10 cents to 50 cents a yard (Chirls, 1996b).

For example, take a basic fabric such as denim—the original fabrication was 100 percent cotton, 14-ounce indigo denim. Breaking in a pair of jeans could take countless wearings and washings. Consumers took finishing into their own hands in the 1970s, soaking jeans in bleach to create a softer, lighter version. Sometimes these do-it-yourself projects resulted in unintended holes in the fabric when the jeans were left in too long or when the concentration of bleach was too strong. Today's controlled finishing processes using stones and enzymes, sandblasting, and abrading mean that new jeans have a well-worn feeling and holes only when that is the intended effect ("Beyond Blue," 1998).

Laser cutting and engraving using lasers such as those made by Trotec laser company add tactile surface interest to fabrics, which provides many design options, since virtually any design can be created with a laser ("Laser Cutting Textiles", 2014). Because the laser beam melts the material, these techniques are particularly suited to thermoplastic synthetics, which results in clean, perfectly sealed edges and no fraying of the end products. Natural fabrics may be cut with a laser printer, but since they are organic, there may be some brown discoloration around the edges.

✦ FABRIC DESIGN DEVELOPMENT

Fabric designers work with color, texture, and light to produce an infinite variety of effects. They manipulate the weave or knitting pattern, surface texture of fabrics, and the color or design printed on the fabric. Fashion seasons (and even eras) are characterized by fabric design. In some seasons, solid colors predominate; in others, texture is the fashion story. Some seasons feature mostly plaids and geometrics; in others, prints become important. Printed fabrics are particularly prone to **boom and bust cycles**—seasons (or even years) when fashion uses few prints alternate with those in which prints are the fashion emphasis (Chirls, 1996a). Of all print categories, florals are the most consistently popular.

Digital printing—preparation of a print design on the computer and using inkjet technology to print the fabric (Figure 7.3)—is currently used for creating accessories like scarves and short yardages for design approval. In the future, the process may be used to customize designs to the shape of garment pieces and the color preferences of individual consumers. This emerging technology may be more cost efficient and widely used for print production in the future ("New Ideas," 2003; [TC], 2003).

✦ TRIMS, NARROW FABRICS, AND FINDINGS DEVELOPMENT

Trims refer to all the items used to embellish and finish a garment. Some are functional—buttons, buckles, belts—but they also serve a decorative purpose. Others are purely decorative such as ribbons, appliqué, beading, binding, and lace. Fashion trends in trim can be a very visible seasonal direction. Lace is a narrow fabric that often headlines a fashion season. Manufacturers develop traditional lace patterns, modern styles with unusual abstract motifs, and hand-made looks. These laces can be modified with lacquering, re-embroidering, flocking, and beading to create new looks (Gilbert, 2002).

Functional items such as elastic, interfacing, thread, and zippers are called **findings**. Even findings can become decorative and trendy at times—for example, when zippers in contrasting colors became a decorative focus in activewear.

Color trends impact trims, narrow fabrics, and findings. If silver is "in," then trims, narrow fabrics and findings will feature this color look. Novelty looks in trim are volatile but, as with

prints, floral motifs are always popular. Once sold in a basic color assortment, the trend today is toward custom color matching of trim to apparel ("Brimming," 1998).

INNOVATION IN TEXTILES

Innovation is driven by consumers' constant desire for novelty, and this desire includes novelty in fabrics and trims. Novelty is a fleeting thing for textile makers. Technology makes it faster to knock off textile products. Companies that want to compete on the basis of original design have to turn out designs quickly because their specialness is quickly diluted by copies (Malone, 1999). Novelty can come from:

- ❖ introducing a new fiber with a unique set of properties;
- ❖ blending several fibers to create a different set of attributes;
- ❖ finishing the fabric in a way that changes the surface or adds functionality;
- ❖ creating a surface texture such as puckered effects, grid patterns woven into the fabric, or beads applied to the surface;
- ❖ coloring the fabric using the latest technology;
- ❖ reviving a handcrafted look.
- ❖ introducing a historical or ethnic source to inspire the texture, structure, or print motif (Figure 7.4);
- ❖ swinging from luxury fabrics to a more casual approach, or the reverse;
- ❖ manipulating fabric by folding, tucking, quilting, and other ways that add volume and dimension;
- ❖ using fabric in an unexpected way counter to rules of appropriateness such as gray flannel for evening wear and velvet for daytime;
- ❖ substituting unexpected materials such as high-tech neoprene for fabric in apparel and accessories;
- ❖ presenting a fiber, fabric, **blend**, or finish as environmentally friendly.

Figure 7.3

Because of developments in digital fabric printers, any photo can now become a fabric print with razor-sharp clarity.

Figure 7.4
Historic or ethnic sources are frequently the inspirations for modern textile prints.

In some fashion seasons, fabrics serve as background and the news is in the way they are cut or colored. Other seasons feature a strong **fabric story**—such as the shine of silk, the cling of matte jersey, the stretch of spandex, the texture of tweed, or fibers that are eco-friendly. Sometimes the focus is on clean-cut minimalism and other times on a strong trim story—the femininity of lace, the handcrafted look of crochet, or the accent of beading. Seasons go by when few prints are featured, and then painterly prints, romantic florals, or bold geometrics take center stage.

Trends in fabric move in the same currents that shape and reshape fashion. Even something as basic as a fiber experiences differing periods of popularity. Natural fibers, once avoided because of care requirements and their wrinkled, rumpled appearance, were lifted by the same wave that heightened the popularity of casual wear. Polyester, a popular fiber choice in the 1970s, became unfashionable in the 1980s but rebounded when it was reinvented as a luxury microfiber. Seen on the runway and in influential fashion stores, in women's wear and menswear, and blended with natural fabrics, the versatile fabric can have the shine of washed silk or the feel of a quality woven, with less weight. A complex manufacturing process makes today's polyester expensive, and difficulties in stitching polyester fabric add to the retail price. The fiber was criticized at one time for being environmentally unfriendly because it was made exclusively from petrochemicals and wasn't biodegradable—although, in its favor, it used fewer care resources and lasted longer than natural fabrics, avoiding the need for frequent replacement. Recent developments have addressed this negative environmental perception; polylactic acid, better known as PLA, is polyester which is derived from 100 percent renewable sources such as corn. Because PLA fiber is derived from annually renewable crops, it is 100 percent compostable, which means that its life cycle potentially reduces Earth's carbon dioxide level, unlike traditional poly fibers known as PET, which currently make up 40 percent of worldwide textile consumption (Farrington et al., 2006).

In the past, polyester's artificial appearance was seen as a negative attribute, but today's fabric designers use its thermoplastic properties to create desirable surface effects. Neil Barrett, who began using polyester at Prada more than a decade ago and still uses it in collections, sums up the fiber's on-trend characteristics: "Polyester gives a technical, clean feel to a garment, with the same modern appeal of a laminated surface" (Sims, 2008).

At the same time that fashion promotes new fibers and fabrics, it also frequently modifies the appearance of basic fabrics. Denim, for example, swings from dark to light colors, heavy to lighter weights, untouched to distressed finishes, crisp to laundered looks. Jean styling touches on Western cuts and details, vintage looks, and edgy street inspiration, depending on the trends. Fashion may favor denim for jeans only (or cut them off for shorts), or expand it into attire like vests, jackets, and dresses. Denim itself is prone to cycles of extreme popularity and then eclipse. In 1999, denim was stronger than it had been in 10 years, partly because it fit the differing tastes and lifestyles of both teens and their parents, and partly because denim was reinvented as fashionable by designers (Schiro, 1999). After a strong cycle led by low-rise cuts, stretch, and decorative treatments, demand for denim diminished in 2003 when consumers began looking for alternative fabrics (Malone & Greenberg, 2003).

Changes in cultural indicators are reflected in fashion choices. When the economy is strong and consumers feel confident, these factors combine to favor upscale clothes in luxury fabrics. During an economic downturn, fashion minimalism (neutral colors, high-quality fabric, and structured tailoring) is offset by embellished looks or cheerful colors to lift the mood.

✦ SOURCES OF INNOVATION

Designers choose fabrics very early in the product development cycle because the attributes of the fabrics are linked to the silhouette and mood of the collection. Some designers have a signature fabric that they

Profile: Product Trend Analysis, Cotton Incorporated

In addition to numerous independent trend forecasting companies, members of the fashion industry also have access to forecasting services provided by Cotton Incorporated. Headquartered in Cary, North Carolina, Cotton Incorporated is funded by US cotton producers and importers and focuses on conducting research and sponsoring promotional activities to increase the popularity of cotton. One major promotional tool is its Cottonworks® Global Fabric Library, which is based at Cotton Incorporated's US marketing headquarters in New York. The library displays approximately 20,000 fabric samples, and acts as a link between mills and clients, with mill name and style numbers used to locate the sales representative and contact information in a directory (Novakovic, 2003).

The second main service that Cotton Incorporated provides is its product trend analysis services. Linda DeFranco joined Cotton Incorporated in 1999 as assistant manager for The Cottonworks® Fabric Library after looking for temp jobs right out of college. Today, DeFranco is the director of product trend analysis at Cotton Incorporated and supervises a team of trend analysts who are tasked with identifying global, cultural, and lifestyle trends which are shown to textile mills, designers, manufacturers, and retailers during Cotton Incorporated's twice-yearly interactive presentations. These presentations guide the design of textiles and silhouettes created by Cotton Incorporated's clients and enable them to plan the colors, fabrics, and styles of their upcoming lines from 18 to 24 months before they are available for purchase ("Biographies: Linda DeFranco," 2014).

The Cotton Incorporated trend forecasting team consists of seven people, with specialists who focus on women's wear, menswear, activewear, and denim. A popular question for the team is where they get their ideas for their forecasts. DeFranco emphasizes that forecasting is a lengthy process and a lot of research goes into each trend forecast. "Market research is a key approach in our department. We also look at what's in stores—what's flying off the shelves and, more importantly, what's not selling. We look at runway shows, research art exhibitions, hotel trends, food trends, designers and collaborations—really everything we can get our hands on to see what the buzz words are, and what people are reading about" (Pfander, 2012).

DeFranco says that research takes three forms:

❖ *Hard facts*—the consumer indicators that are out there for everybody, such as the consumer confidence indicator, housing sales, politics, the big newsmakers that will be affecting the consumer 2 years from the present. These could be an election, the Olympics, or even companies going in or out of business. Forecasting attempts not only to predict how a consumer will be feeling when they walk into a retail store in 2 years' time, but also if they will have the disposable income to purchase new items.

❖ *Observational methods*—through the trained eyes of Cotton Incorporated's trend forecasters, gauging what the consumer will be interested in. Observations are conducted on a global basis: "I send my team all over the world with their cameras, taking pictures, seeing what's going on in the streets of every city you've ever heard of—from Tokyo and Milan to more obscure places like South Africa, Russia, Chile" (Pfander, 2012). Cotton Incorporated feels strongly that fashion trickles up from the streets to the runway, so it is important to see what people are wearing and how they are wearing it in other cultures.

Talking directly with clients—Cotton Incorporated has developed close, long-term relationships with many of its clients, which have resulted in those clients sharing key information with them about what their consumers are asking for. "Sometimes they'll be like, 'My customer is looking for X, Y and Z' and we'll be able to help them choose fabrics or styles, but it also helps us to know, okay, in China, this part of the world, they want to wear their jeans in this certain way. And it helps us when putting their presentations together, because we are a global forecaster, we are not just forecasting for America, we are forecasting for the entire world" ("Linda DeFranco—Trend at Cotton Incorporated," 2014).

Cotton Incorporated trend forecasters combine this research with an analysis of current runway shows and compile their findings into the top five trends that companies need to know each season. Research presentations to clients include guidance on color, fabrics, surface texture, and silhouettes. Clients are provided with a package of 30–40 fabrics to accompany each trend, so, each season, they receive over 120 cotton fabric swatches complete with technical information that they may use for reference and inspiration when creating their collections. In addition to their big seasonal research trend presentation, the forecasters also do smaller, more focused presentations specifically for the denim and activewear markets. Clients can also access photography and video related to each season's trend forecasts at any time online through a members-only website operated by Cotton Incorporated that is available in five languages ("Linda DeFranco—Trend at Cotton Incorporated," 2014).

Cotton Incorporated's product trend analysis team shares its information with its own fabric development team at its Cary, North Carolina, Research Center, which focuses on creating new fabric ideas for weaves, blends, finishes, and coatings for use in both apparel and home markets. "We do not carry the research and development fabrics in the library because that tends to confuse small- and mid-sized clients who need to source fabrics. To develop a fabric a company has to have a 'big pencil'—to get a mill to set up to do something new takes a sizable order of yardage. The research and development staff has their own presentation although there is crossover because we may work with the same clients. For some presentations we would present our conceptual ideas and the research and development staff would follow up with fabrics they have developed" (Novakovic, 2003).

For those who are interested in pursuing a career in trend analysis and forecasting, DeFranco cautions that the competition is fierce: "This is a dream job. Especially if you love to travel, love fashion and are creative" (Zimmerman, 2008). She says that being multidimensional is crucial to being a forecaster, and a well-rounded trend forecaster would be someone who has knowledge of history and of different countries and cultures, and is able to put that all together and look at the world in a unique way. In addition to an education, it is necessary to have an open mind:

> Some trends are much stronger than others, sometimes. The one you thought was minor ends up being huge, and vice versa. But trends are really evolutionary. Things don't just stop. There's a difference between trends and fads. Fads you see coming and you know when they're going to go. But trends, they come back, and of course world events affect everything, but in terms of big macro trends, they don't change so quickly or so frequently. We're a team, too. If it was just me, there could have been some duds in there, but it's a collective group of people with different lifestyles and ages, so we get a good overall view of what's going on (Pfander, 2014).

Sources:

Biographies

Linda DeFranco (2014). Cotton Incorporated Pressroom. http://www.cottoninc.com/corporate/Pressroom/Biographies/Linda-DeFranco.cfm.

"Linda DeFranco – Trend at Cotton Incorporated" (2014). Retrieved from http://cottonuniversity.org/courses/online/linda-defranco-trend-at-cotton-incorporated/1/.

Novakovic, Kathryn (2003, November 10). *Cotton Incorporated Forecast. Presentation at the ITAA Annual Meeting.* Savannah, Georgia. Author Evelyn Brannon telephone interview with Kathryn Novakovic, November 18, 2003.

Pfander, Catherine Blair. (2012, May 24). Cotton Inc's Linda DeFranco Predicts Trends More Than a Year in Advance. NBC New York Thread, NY: http://www.nbcnewyork.com/blogs/threadny/THREAD-Cotton-Incs-Linda-DeFranco-Predicts-Trends-More-Than-a-Year-in-Advance-153732245.html.

Zimmerman, Eilene. (2008, May 11). Roaming the world, detecting fashion. Retrieved from http://www.nytimes.com/2008/05/11/jobs/11starts.html?_r=0.

constantly use season after season, such as Oscar de la Renta's fondness for silk faille and taffeta. Other designers source from several countries. For example, a fall collection of upscale ready-to-wear may draw from Japan for innovative fabrications, Italy for classic wools and silks, and France for embroidery and beading. It may feature a variety of fabric weights and textures, from double-faced cashmere to open weaves to airy gauzes, from structured tweeds and jacquards to soft silk charmeuse, and embellishments from embroideries to lace. Designers are secretive about the fabrics they choose because fabrics contribute so much to the individuality of the collection (Figure 7.5). A few designers become known for their experiments with fabrications—experiments that influence other designers in their selection and use of fabrics.

✦ THE LEADING EDGE OF INNOVATION

High-tech fabrics with novel properties moved from sports gear and rugged adventure wear to high fashion and streetwear. The Material ConneXion, a fabric library for members only in Manhattan, houses a collection of over 3,000 innovative materials, many suitable for apparel. The director explains, "people want to know their textiles are doing more than just covering their body" (Greene, 2002).

Technical fabrics, or **performance fabrics**, can cost up to 30 percent more than non-technical ones but deliver engineered characteristics (characteristics not inherent in the fiber but which are created during manufacturing to improve comfort). Performance fabrics improve the breathability of synthetics, make clothes stain resistant, and enhance a garment's ability to manage moisture or deliver antimicrobial characteristics. A mainstay of activewear, these fabrics are also making their way into travelwear and streetwear. Lycra spandex, an early breakthrough in performance fabrics combined with a successful marketing plan, added stretch to knitted and woven goods. Under Armour, a line of moisture-wicking compression garments designed to be worn under sports uniforms, moved from the athletic field to the gym to the street on the strength of product performance and marketing. Having a workable technology is not enough in the world of apparel; it must be paired with clever marketing that connects the

Figure 7.5

Textiles and unique fabrications can be as much a part of a designer's signature style as the clothing styles themselves.

product to the lifestyle of the consumer (Colman, 2008d).

The goal with performance fabrics is to add engineered characteristics without modifying the look and wearability. Developments include (Peake, 2006):

❧ *body mapping*—providing performance characteristics to specifically targeted areas of the garment rather than to the whole;
❧ *durable performance*—enhanced characteristics are added at the fiber level rather than as a finish so that performance doesn't degrade in use or care and the hand of the fabric is unchanged.

Smart textiles are used in apparel that has some type of mechanical, electrical, or computer capability, and although these technical advancements are impressive, this type of **wearable technology** must also result in comfortable, washable, and practical garments. Nanofinishing in fabrics creates products that change performance characteristics in response to the environment. **Functional textiles** produced by **nanofinishing**—coating the surface of textiles and clothing with nanoparticles—results in apparel that possess one or more desirable properties ("Nanofinishing," 2014). Examples of the types of characteristics that nanofinishing can impart to a fabric include wrinkle resistance, stain repellency, water repellency, UV ray protection, moisture absorption, color fastness, abrasion resistance, fire retardancy, and antimicrobial or self-cleaning properties while remaining durable, breathable, and soft (Wong, et al., 2006). Related to nanofinishing is the process of **microencapsulation**—"a process in which tiny particles or a coating to give small capsules with many useful properties surrounds droplets." Microencapsulated finished fabrics fall under the category of functional textiles. Microencapsulation offers the possibility of producing novel products with many advantages over traditional textile products. The process can impart important new qualities of garments and fabrics, such as enhanced stability and the

controlled release of active compounds which were not possible or cost effective using previous technology (Chinta & Wane, 2013).

Microencapsulation has cosmetic textiles, also known as **cosmetotextiles**. According to the Office for the Standardisation of Textile and Clothing Industries, "a cosmetic textile is a textile article that contains a substance or a preparation that is intended to be released sustainably on to the different superficial parts of the human body, especially the skin, and which claim one (or more) particular propertie(s)" ("Cosmetotextiles," 2012). Typical properties of cosmetic textiles include cleansing, perfume scenting, or change/improvement of appearance. Products that fall into the category of cosmetotextiles include odor-resistant socks, moisturizing gloves, fragrance-infused sheets, and anti-cellulite body shapers ("Cosmetotextiles," 2012).

"Phase change" materials change state (from liquid to solid, and back) to store or release heat with changes in the temperature (Mills, 2007). Outlast® bedding manufacturer uses phase change materials (PCM) technology that was originally developed for NASA. The company has a complete sleep system featuring mattress pads, pillow protectors, pillows, blankets, and comforters each equipped with technology that responds to each person's unique body temperature to balance the microclimate under the covers. These products continuously absorb excess body heat, store it, then release it to maintain a steady, comfortable temperature throughout the night ("Technology," 2014).

Health-care applications may eventually create the largest market for smart textiles, but for now, consumer electronics (cell phones and other personal entertainment and communication devices) is the driving force in the commercialization of smart fabrics. Experts predict that change will be slow for several reasons: retooling of the textile industry will take time, and there are questions about consumer acceptability. Carrying technology on the body and as fashion accessories may not translate to desire for clothing that interacts with the devices or acts as a device itself (Excell, 2007).

✦ GREEN INNOVATION

As a consumer trend, green has reached the tipping point—the point when an idea moves out of special-interest groups and niche markets and into the mainstream—in automobiles, home products, food, and personal care, but fashion has been slower to respond ("Tips," 2007). Environmentalists would say that concern about the ecological impact of consumer decisions is a "trend based on global necessity" (Lipke, 2007). But the connection between green as a consumer value and fashion is a complicated one that begins with the definition of fashion (Figure 7.6).

The basis of fashion is the consumer's constant need for change (discarding clothing before it is worn out for new trendy attire) and conspicuous consumption (status symbols, fitting in, and standing out), whereas environmental ideals focus on reducing ecological harm caused by consumption. The conflict lies between what is good for the environment and what is good for the economy. If people bought clothing and wore it until its useful life ended before discarding (or perhaps recycling) it, the environment would benefit, but it would ruin the economy and be detrimental to quality of life (Lipke, 2008).

The second complication is that the fashion supply chain is long and intricate, which makes it difficult to determine whether a product really is green. To manufacture and retail a green fashion product, a company would have to consider:

* energy consumption and greenhouse gas emissions at each stage of production, distribution, and selling;
* resource selection including materials that are recycled, renewable, organic, and biodegradable;
* the carbon footprint for raw-material extraction and fiber and fabric production;
* the presence of hazardous substances in production;
* alternatives to chemical dyes and wastewater treatment in the dyeing and finishing of textiles;
* the source of packaging materials, transport weight, and disposal;

* social responsibility including political, labor, and human rights issues.

Some textile and apparel companies own their production facilities and can exercise control over production. But most companies work with sourcing partners in a combination of owned and leased facilities, with varying degrees of control.

Consumers seeking to purchase green products can be stymied by the research required to determine what is ecologically sound (Foreman, 2007). "Greenwashing"—false, vague, or misleading environmental claims made by manufacturers in the supply chain and passed on in marketing to consumers—makes sourcing confusing and difficult for companies seeking green solutions. Sometimes there is honest disagreement on what is actually ecologically sound. Bamboo, an eco-friendly material that is gaining popularity in a variety of uses, is an example. It grows quickly without the use of pesticides, but making it into usable fiber requires extensive chemical processing. As Jeff Shafer, the founder of Agave Denimsmith, put it: "Just because something is made from an organic fiber doesn't mean it's great for the environment. You have to think about the entire process, from dyes, to washing, to packaging and printing. It's not that easy to do" (Lipke, 2008).

In order to combat greenwashing, the European Union has created its own ecolabeling system that applies to a large number of products, including textiles. The EU Ecolabel for Textiles, commonly referred to as "the Flower," because the logo features a flower, is both a certification and a marketing tool that promises consumers that the product it is on was made with a limited amount of substances that are harmful to the environment or to health, and reduced water and air pollution. The ecolabel also promises quality assurance in the form of textile shrink resistance during washing and drying, and color resistance to perspiration, washing, wet and dry rubbing, and light exposure. The label can be given to all kinds of textiles, apparel, and accessories, including textiles for interiors, and fibers, yarns, and fabrics ("The EU Ecolabel," 2014).

Figure 7.6
A new group of apparel brands, such as Organic by John Patrick, are made using only environmentally friendly "green" textiles.

Higher raw-material prices and production costs, non-standard sourcing, and the limited availability of some fibers make green products more expensive. Unless consumers are willing to pay a premium price for eco-friendly products, profitability will be elusive (Foreman, 2007). Some fashion industry analysts think that the green trend has passed, but others see it as moving from the fringe to mainstream. Because of the greenwashing in consumer advertising, some people may become disillusioned with green claims.

One answer may be some kind of tracking system paired with consumer access to information. Timberland puts a "Green Index" on its footwear products, which provides information on climate impact, chemicals used, and resource consumption. A New Zealand-based firm, Icebreaker, allows consumers to trace a garment's production history—all the way back to the sheep farm where the wool was grown—on the company's website by typing in a special "Baa Code"—an item code unique to the product (Lipke, 2008). The company's code of ethics is broken down into "Environmental Ethics," "Manufacturing Ethics," and "Animal Welfare."

As innovations continue to enter the market, buying green will become easier for both industry executives at the beginning of the pipeline and consumers. Fibers made from bamboo, hemp, organic cotton, soy (Soya), corn (Sorona), and coconuts (Cocona) are already being marketed. Fabrics made from recycled fiber are finding acceptability based on aesthetics. Première Vision, the influential Paris trade show, added a special section for eco-friendly fibers and fabrics to assist industry executives in sourcing eco-friendly fibers and fabrics (Foreman, 2007).

✦ TRADE ORGANIZATIONS AND FABRIC COUNCILS

Producers of both natural and manufactured fibers band together in **trade organizations** and fabric councils to promote use of their fiber. These groups provide:

- ❖ forecasting information about new developments in fiber and fabric;
- ❖ public relations support for their industry;
- ❖ facilitated fabric sourcing by linking fabric manufacturers using their fiber with apparel manufacturers;
- ❖ research and fabric development activities.

One of the most active trade organizations is Cotton Incorporated (see Profile above), the research and marketing arm for US growers of upland cotton representing cotton mills, knitters, and **converters**. Over the past few decades, consumers have favored cotton for its comfort factor. To maintain that popularity requires a commitment to be competitive—a commitment that includes aggressively promoting the fiber and its uses and supporting research activities to produce new fabric developments ("Looking," 2001). The product development department uses state-of-the-art facilities to create new fabric ideas for apparel and the home. It maintains the Fabricast™ collection of 4,500 cotton or cotton-rich (60 percent cotton or more) **developmental fabrics**—fabrics that could be adapted to the market by designers and manufacturers ("Product Development," 2008). At the February 2008 Première Vision show, Cotton Incorporated introduced trademarked innovations including Storm Denim™ (super water-repellent, breathable), Wicking Windows™ (enhanced wicking with reduced cling and faster drying), and Tough Cotton™ (improved abrasion resistance and fabric strength) ("Cotton Incorporated Presents," 2008).

There is similar promotion and research support for other fibers. Masters of Linen is a confederation of European businesses that brands its products and provides educational and trend information (2003). The American Wool Council is involved in marketing "from fleece to fashion," including monitoring social and fashion trends (2003). The Woolmark Company is the world's leading wool textile organization dedicated to promoting its use. The company, which celebrated "50 Years in Fashion" in 2014, provides trend information on its website (www.woolmark.com) and on its sister website (www.merino.com). Woolmark is also a source for information about knitwear and woven textile innovations, such as its "Cool Wool" campaign which promotes advancements in production of lightweight yarns, making wool an ideal fabric for hotter climates. Woolmark has long been known for its support of emerging designers with its International Woolmark Prize worth $100,000 (www.woolmarkprize.com, 2014). Manufactured fiber companies perform the same functions for their trademarked brands. Invista presents directional trends at its semiannual intimate apparel workshop using trend boards, visuals, fabric swatches, prototype garments, and directional garments purchased in Europe (Monget, 2007).

RESEARCHING SEASONAL TRENDS

Fabric trends emerge before fashion trends because reviewing and selecting fabrics is one of the initial stages of product development. Trends based on textile development follow a diffusion of innovation pattern (see Chapter 2): they are introduced, adopted, and experimented with by more avant-garde designers, then move into more widespread usage, and, finally, cross boundaries into different product categories and different price points.

Fiber producers, yarn and fabric manufacturers, and industry trade organizations play important roles in the diffusion process by informing apparel executives about new innovations in fibers and fabrics. They disseminate information by:

❖ participating in yarn and fabric trade shows (Figure 7.7);
❖ presenting seasonal trend forecasts with themes tied to specific developments in fiber, yarn, fabric, or finishing;
❖ providing designers and product developers with samples of fabrics for in-house presentations, swatching designs, and writing specifications;
❖ providing samples to **fabric libraries** where designers and product developers come to research fabrications and source fabrics from many manufacturers.

Figure 7.7
Fabric trade shows, which may only be attended by members of the fashion industry, are an essential part of researching seasonal trends.

These same companies and organizations work with designers and fabric sourcing specialists to research the potential for new fabrics, including development of **concept garments** (sample garments made to show the potential of the fabrics in apparel). The presentations and consulting activities are designed to help sell more fabric and fiber (Musselman, 1998).

Apparel executives research seasonal trends by attending fairs and trade shows, hearing presentations by companies or trade organizations, visiting fabric libraries, and reading reports in trade publications. Fabrics exhibited at fairs and trade shows are designed for the selling season one year ahead. Visiting one of these shows gives forecasters and apparel executives an overview of the direction fashion is heading in terms of color, texture, and pattern on fabric. Apparel executives who do not travel to the European shows attend shows in New York or Los Angeles. Trend presentations by marketing managers of fiber and fabric manufacturers and industry trade organizations provide a more edited source of information on fabric development. Another way to trace fabric development is in trade publications, which report on the European and American fabric fairs and trade shows and many of the presentations by trade organizations and companies.

✦ PRINT SHOWS

Designers use prints to differentiate their looks from other lines and from knockoffs by fast-fashion retailers and counterfeiters. Some designers hire artists to sit with the seamstresses as they work and hand-paint designs on fabric. Others collaborate with mills or use computer manipulation in-house for experimentation and print development. Today's printing technology enables more complicated designs. The trends that will influence the season come from the runway (Ilari, Socha, & Karimzadeh, 2008).

Directional trends for prints are also evident at shows featuring original artwork from studios specializing in fabric design. The artwork can inspire prints, embroidery, cutout designs, or as beading (Figure 7.8). Held about 15 months ahead

of the selling season, these shows are shopped by retailers with private-label businesses, designers, and converters. Converters specialize in sourcing base fabrics and using contractors to dye, print, and finish them for apparel manufacturers who are unable to meet large minimum orders or who require short lead times. Buyers at the print shows represent many product categories, such as women's wear, children's wear, and menswear. The shows are a place to look for trends in color and pattern and provide an opportunity to buy the original artwork for prints. When a buyer from Marc Jacobs, Target, Nordstrom, or DKNY buys a design, it is taken off display and becomes an exclusive for that company, giving their collection a distinctive look (Hoppough, 2008a).

Identifying trends in prints involves looking for similarities across a season's offerings. For the forecaster, these similarities are likely to occur in the color combination, style of the printer, and finished effect. Trends are frequently expressed in terms of:

- ❖ overall style—folkloric, botanical, or romantic;
- ❖ interpretation—realistic, stylized, abstract, or geometric;
- ❖ scale—small-scale versus large-scale motifs;
- ❖ figure/ground relationships—patterns with proportionately more background showing versus more crowded patterns;
- ❖ reference to art styles such as Art Deco;
- ❖ allusions to artistic effects such as watercolor, pointillism, or collage;
- ❖ complexity—simple versus complicated looks;
- ❖ cultural reference—Asian-inspired or African motifs;
- ❖ historical reference—revival of prints from earlier decades;
- ❖ color story—tropical, sherbet colors, or brights with neutral grounds;
- ❖ motifs—golf, seashells, or animal prints.

Shows like Printsource include seminars on trends presented by a forecasting firm as an introduction to what visitors will see in the exhibition (Hoppough, 2008d).

You Be the Forecaster: Textile Trend Watch

Because businesses now exchange information over computer networks, small entrepreneurial firms in rural or suburban locations can do business with other companies around the world online. This is especially the case when part of the product mix is information itself. Kate is a fabric designer with a small state-of-the-art studio located on an upper floor of a commercial building on the high street of a small town in England. She is considering branching out to include forecasting services as part of her business plan.

Kate and her staff use computer-aided design (CAD) to create fabric designs for clients and transmit their designs electronically. The studio's clients are American corporations that produce fabrics in the United States and in the Far East. To keep current on trends in fabric design, Kate travels to all the European yarn and fabric shows. To guide the work of the studio, Kate develops concept boards using photographs from magazines, swatches of developmental fabrics collected at the trade shows, and other inspiring bits and pieces. For any particular season, Kate develops four or five concept boards, each coordinated around a theme that captures the newness emerging among resources in Europe.

Kate started her business right after design school by working as a freelancer for one company—a contact she made while attending a trade show in Paris. She built the business by adding one or two clients a year and the staff needed to handle that volume of business. With all the news about marketplace turbulence and company mergers and acquisitions, Kate has begun to question the wisdom of depending on a few big clients for business survival. She recently attended a workshop for entrepreneurs in design fields where participants were urged to inventory the attributes of their companies that could be marketed along with design products. Kate realized that her clients value the immediate update information she provides on design directions—information she conveys casually in e-mail correspondence with them.

Putting together her concerns about the business, the marketing suggestions from the seminar, and her access to timely information, Kate decides to diversify her client list and promote her service by launching a Web-based newsletter called *Textile Trend Watch*. Kate plans to report on trends developing in European textile design, project those trends for the US market, and show how the design work from her studio reflects those trends. For the first 6 months, the newsletter will be sent free to a list of US firms Kate found in an industry directory. After 6 months, the newsletter will convert to a by-subscription-only format, but one article and one concept board will be featured each month on a free website. In this way, Kate plans to develop a new profit center for the company while promoting her existing design business.

To attract a loyal readership, the newsletter must be authoritative and filled with leading-edge information conveyed in an interesting, time-efficient format.

Discuss the potential for Kate's idea as a way to review and summarize this chapter. The following questions provide a starting point for the discussion.

Sources of Forecasting Information: What kinds of information on textile development are available? How often should her newsletter be updated? Kate regularly attends European trade shows but how will she gather information that will help her project her findings for the US market? What kind of articles should the newsletter include?

Target Audience (potential readers for the newsletter): What information will clients in the United States find useful and intriguing? Should Kate focus on particular product categories, on price points, or be more comprehensive in her reporting?

Cost/Benefit Analysis: Which trade shows are absolutely key for Kate's new forecasting business? What information can be gathered online or through trade publications? What types of costs would have to be included in Kate's yearly travel schedule and budget (airfares, lodging, and other expenses) to gather the kind of information she needs for the newsletter?

Figure 7.8

Trade shows, such as this one for Printsource, feature the artwork of studios that specialize in textile design. These shows are a good place to research trends in colors, patterns, and motifs.

✦ FABRIC FAIRS AND TRADE SHOWS

Color and fabric trends are the first building blocks for a fashion trend at the twice-yearly fabric fairs and trade shows. Many innovations may be proposed at the yarn and fabric shows, but only a few will coalesce into the trend story for a designer's collection or for the fashion season overall. Trade shows and fairs in Europe and the United States help to coordinate the efforts for the supply chain by concentrating fabrics from many different mills in one location to be viewed in a short time span. Attendees include:

❖ executives in charge of fabric development and purchasing for big-volume apparel manufacturers who are looking for new sources of innovative fabrics;

❖ designers looking for inspiration for their next collection;

❖ forecasters looking for clues to the direction fashion will take in upcoming seasons;

❖ the fashion press.

Apparel executives use these shows to detect developing trends, to identify new resources, for **sampling** (ordering a minimum amount of fabric as a trial order), and to place production orders for fabrics (Figure 7.9).

At the fairs and trade shows, participants also attend seminars and presentations on developing trends in color, fabrics, and fashion presented by forecasters and consultants. Some shows include a display of trend colors and invite participants to clip samples to take with them.

Because costs in terms of time and money prohibit attending all shows and fairs, executives, designers, and forecasters must decide which are most productive. Some choose to attend one show that is the most comprehensive. Others visit one show for spring and another for fall collections (Mazzaraco, 1990). For exhibitors, the show is not only about writing orders on-site but also for attracting buyers to the company's showrooms to write production orders for large quantities.

Dates for the shows are always controversial with sponsors, exhibitors, and attendees. A show too far ahead of the season results in very little

Figure 7.9
Attendees at fabric fairs and trade shows research trends, textile innovations, and new sourcing opportunities.

business and poor attendance. A show too late in the season risks the same result because apparel companies have already placed their fabric orders. A calendar listing show dates is published in trade publications. The calendar allows executives and forecasters to plan which shows to attend for timely trend information. Changes in traditional show dates are usually covered in the trade press. Such changes are likely to increase as the industry continues to adjust the product development schedule in response to the consumer preference for buying in season and the demands of doing business in a global marketplace.

Each show fills a niche in the fashion picture and targets a specific audience with directional information. Shows come and go with shifts in the economy or trends within the industry. To the owner or sponsoring organization, putting on a trade show is a business with income generated from two sources: the exhibitors and the attendees. If the economy causes a drop-off in the number of exhibitors or attendees or if a particular show results in lackluster sales, the owner may decide not to continue the show for the next year. The best way to track shows is through the calendars provided by trade publications. Industry tradition and supply-chain realities combine to ensure the survival of trade shows as a venue for viewing innovations and a sourcing for the upcoming season. Two other shifts in the way the industry works are having an impact on the shows:

* Companies are placing final orders at the last possible date when they feel more confident about style trends.
* Companies are moving away from two seasons a year to more continuous delivery of product to retailers.

These two trends may eventually lead to show sponsors moving from the traditional two shows per year to a more frequent show schedule.

✧ Yarn Shows

Yarn shows provide an overview of the newest fiber blends and finishes designed to deliver improved performance and new textures for innovative styling.

Expofil, a European yarn fair, is held in Paris. The show provides the earliest view of new products and trends for the selling season 15 months ahead. Held biannually, Expofil was linked with Première Vision beginning February 2004, so that each company's buying team could cover one major venue (Murphy, 2003). This show draws exhibitors from Western Europe (primarily from France, Italy, Germany, and the United Kingdom) and includes fiber producers and yarn producers for knitting and weaving. The emphasis at the show is not on basic yarns but on products that push the envelope.

The show's fashion team develops a forum that fills almost 10 percent of the exhibition, where attendees view trends. Structured around three or four themes, and a color-range forecast, the display features several hundred items produced with the exhibitor's yarns grouped by type: flat knit, circular knit, and woven fabrics. Special areas are devoted to trends and materials in home furnishing and to the technical innovations in fibers. The show also publishes the color range, an interactive CD-ROM, and a trend book. Attendees receive a color, fabric, and trend forecast developed in consultation with other trade fairs, fiber producers, fiber promotion associations, and forecasting services such as Trends Union and PromoStyl, plus a 15-minute video presentation by a forward-thinking designer. The seminar program includes presentations on trends in the markets region by region, with emphasis on knitwear and detailed evaluation of consumer segments.

Pitti Filati, a showcase for Italian spinners' natural and synthetic yarns and blends, is held in July and January in Florence. The show features a "research area" with multimedia presentations on the trends that will shape fashion three seasons in the future, complemented by a display of yarns and stitches. Focused on high-end yarns in merino wool, cashmere, and mohair, many participating mills have changed their industrial processes to speed time to market. New yarns have been technologically enhanced (such as adding anti-pilling properties); blended with nylon, cotton, or other fibers to change the hand or attributes; or spun ultrafine. Some alterations in the fabrics relate to global weather changes like milder winters—mills now make wool lighter weight by blending the fiber with silk (Epiro, 2007). In a similar move, another mill **mercerizes** superfine wool, which gives it a texture similar to cotton, a soft hand, and allows colors that are both bright and shiny (and as a value-added feature, the mercerized wool becomes machine washable). While the trend toward lighter, finer, and softer fibers holds steady, many exhibitors bring newness with expanded color palettes. The demand for organic fibers continues to build slowly—one company offers an organic cashmere with fiber sourced from northwest China and colored with dyes approved by the Global Organic Textile Standard (an international industry standard that defines the term "organic" as it applies to the textile supply chain in an effort to improve the credibility of labeling on consumer products) (Olsen, 2008).

✧ European Shows

The most comprehensive and influential show in Europe is Première Vision, held in Paris. Première Vision (or "First Look" in English), a fabric exhibition hosting more than 30,000 visitors from more than one hundred countries, is held twice yearly (February for spring/summer and September for fall/winter) (Borland, 2002b). According to the show's CEO, the venue is "at the top of designers' lists" for finding fabrics that inspire fashion. The show relates its offerings to the cultural trends in the marketplace by adding special display areas for "ethical" textiles, those that are more environmentally friendly (Marsh & Foreman, 2007).

The Première Vision trend forecast highlights the season's direction for weaves, colors, patterns, and surface treatments shown. The forecast begins when textile stylists and forecasters meet in their own countries and then follow up with a meeting in Paris to determine the unifying trends. Eighteen months ahead of the selling season, the show's fashion department produces a color chart and defines the "spirit of

the season"—a forecast that is shown only to exhibitors. The goals of the forecast are to determine major influences, anticipate worldwide trends, and guide creative development. This "guideline for the season" consists of four groups with seven colors per group. The exhibitors combine these insights with the market realities of their own businesses to prepare the fabrics exhibited at the show (Borland, 2002a; "Preparing Season," 2003). The trends identified for Première Vision and the innovative fabrics shown there are widely reported in international trade publications.

Texworld, with 800 exhibitors from 42 countries, runs concurrently with Première Vision and features less expensive textiles for companies on a tighter budget. Attendees may look for trends at Première Vision and then place orders at Texworld, although this show also has a trend forum. Most Texworld exhibitors come from China, India, Turkey, South Korea, Japan, Brazil, and Pakistan, representing the diversity of fabric producers. To assist buyers, the show features on the floor computers with software that helps locate product by type and cost (Foreman & Murphy, 2008).

Another Paris show, Denim by Première Vision, gives attendees ideas for the luxury, high end of the market. Two contrasting looks—the continuing trend for vintage (worn, distressed, washed) and the clean, deep-blue versions—continue to vie for attention in recent shows. Wool blends and double-sided fabrics added novelty. Organic cotton dyed with natural indigo takes longer to make (6 months compared to the usual 2 months) and costs more, factors that limit the fabric to niche lines (Groves, 2008a).

Whereas some fabric shows attract exhibitors from around the world, others focus on specific geographic areas to highlight the distinctive approaches of mills in these locations. Held in Cernobbio, Italy, Ideabiella presents exhibitors from the Italian Biella district twice a year (fall fabrics in September, spring fabrics in March). Attendees select fabrics that will appear in collections the following year. Built on the area's tradition with luxury wools and silks, recent shows featured new fabrications such as a silk–

wool blend with the characteristics of a sports performance fabric ("slippery, supersoft, elastic, and breathable"); cotton–silk double-face fabrics (madras checks on one side and stripes on the other); and linen blends with a slick, shantung finish ("Color-coated," 2008).

Held twice yearly in Hong Kong, Interstoff Asia Essential focuses on innovative fabrics, especially functional fabrics and "eco-textiles" manufactured by mills in China, Japan, South Korea, and Taiwan. The show supports its positioning with a labeling system that identified the raw materials, manufacturing techniques, and finishing processes for exhibited fabrics (Haisma-Kwok, 2008).

✧ Fabric Fairs in the United States

Fabric fairs in the United States provide an opportunity for forecasters and executives to see fabrics from both European and American fabric manufacturers. Each show has its own focus and presents a different facet of the apparel business.

Première Vision Preview show runs in New York before the show in Paris. According to Philippe Pasquet, the CEO of both shows, American designers and buyers looking for European fabrics use the event as part of their development process. However, many of the most innovative fabrics aren't ready for display and won't be shown until Paris. Exhibitors include innovations from the previous season to fill out the show. The parallel show Texworld USA, with its offering of less expensive fabrics from non-European sources, also offers attendees the chance to find something they haven't seen before and to find new suppliers. Many buyers are smaller firms placing small orders (Tucker, 2008).

Material World, held in Miami, showcases exhibitors in categories of yarn, fabric, trim, and information technology. Exhibitors come from Pakistan, Taiwan, China, Korea, India, and the Caribbean Basin and include companies focusing on eco-fabrics. Several exhibitors were product life-cycle management (PLM) consultancies aiming to help apparel companies get a handle on worldwide sourcing and production. These companies allow a designer to put together all the components, including trim, buttons, and packaging, for release to the factory—what are called **full-garment packages** (Hoppough, 2008c).

Las Vegas hosts two parallel shows—Sourcing at MAGIC for fabric and Printsource at MAGIC for original graphics and prints. Exhibitors from as far away as Africa, Bangladesh, and India show wovens, knits, and eco-friendly fabrics for price-conscious customers (Tran, 2008a).

Los Angeles International Textile Show features exhibitors representing fabrics, trims, and finding. Held biannually in April and October, the show's exhibitors emphasize quality and innovation, especially in environmentally sustainable fabrics. Emerging trends included lightweight fabrics for layering partly because of the reduced costs for transportation from the mill and textures like laser cutting, embroidery, waffle weaves, and other treatments that add dimension (Tran, 2008b). Because California has long been known for creativity and as an origin point for trends, forecasters and East Coast textile and apparel executives make this show a destination (Figure 7.10).

✦ PRESENTATIONS

Mills manufacturing couture fabrics show their fabric collections to name designers in the designer's showroom or studio (Holch, 1998). At lower price points, design executives attend "show and tell" presentations structured around trend stories. Each trend story projects a look, mood, and lifestyle across a group of fabrics and illustrates the connection with photos from European runways, sample garments, and concept fabrics (Figure 7.11). Trend stories often include references to historical or ethnic sources of inspiration. The presentations may concentrate solely on fabric developments or merge fabric developments with color, fashion, and print forecasts. Presentations are sponsored by:

- ❖ fiber producers;
- ❖ fabric manufacturers;
- ❖ industry trade associations;
- ❖ forecasting services and consultants.

Figure 7.10
The Los Angeles
International Textile
Show attracts
forecasters because it
provides insight into the
California lifestyle and
the trends that it
spawns.

Figure 7.11
Forecasters use
storyboards to
illustrate the colors,
look, mood, and
fabrics for each trend
story during a
presentation.

European forecasting services such as Trends Union and PromoStyl often bring the same presentations that they developed for European fabric fairs to New York a few weeks later. No matter the sponsor, the presentations are open to the **trade only**, and usually require an invitation or business credentials to attend.

✦ Fabric Libraries

Fabric libraries are collections of fabric swatches and trim samples representing the scope available for a specific upcoming season. The fabrics are usually arranged on large display boards according to styling and intended end-use (tops, bottoms, shirting, etc.). Each sample is referenced with detailed information on fiber content, weight, color range, and fabric manufacturer. Some fabric libraries are maintained by trade organizations and represent the current fabrics from many mills and converters. Because swatches are updated seasonally, these fabric libraries are helpful when apparel-design teams are looking for inspiration or for locating new fabric sources.

Some design consultants, museums, fashion schools, and designers maintain fabric libraries of historical fabrics, embroideries, and trims. Tag Sale, with an inventory of about 300,000 pieces (mostly swatches but also vintage clothing), provides a textile design resource with clients like Michael Kors, Ralph Lauren, and J.Crew. Customers stop by the archive to buy swatches from bins labeled "Asian," "Paisleys," "Nauticals," "Animals," to name just a few, paying between $250 and $450 per swatch. Fifteen field agents collect fabrics worldwide to add to the inventory. Tag Sale owners claim that it is no longer a question of vintage as a trend but rather which vintage era is trending up—they predict that designs from the 1950s through the 1970s will be nostalgic for boomers and new to younger consumers. Other vintage and antique textile design resources include (Dyett, 2007):

- ❖ T.D.G. (Textile Design Group)—4 million swatches;
- ❖ Andrea Aranow Textile Documents— specializes in elite, museum-quality designs;
- ❖ Vintage Loft—specializes in beading and embroideries.

Because mills often collect swatches of their fabrics for a given season on a card, poster, or in a book, these collections become a record of fashion trends for that time. These swatch collections are now avidly collected because of their value in charting style changes and because they represent a resource for today's designers seeking inspiration.

Chapter Summary

Textiles play a significant role in consumer purchase behavior, and innovation can occur at each stage of the product development process—fibers, yarns, fabric structures, fabric dyeing, finishing and design as well as trims, narrow fabrics, and findings. Sources of innovations include the category of performance textiles, and developments that have been made to improve textiles' environmental impact. Trade organizations and fabric councils such as Cotton Incorporated work to promote use of particular fibers through trend forecasts and new products. Seasonal print trends are shared with industry members and designers at print shows, yarn shows, and fabric shows in the United States and Europe, at presentations, and in fabric libraries.

Key Terms and Concepts

Blend
Boom and bust cycles
Brand name
Cellulosic fibers
Concept garments
Converters
Cosmetotextiles
Cross dyeing
Developmental fabrics
Digital printing
Drape
Fabric finishing
Fabric libraries
Fabric story
Filaments
Findings
Finishing
Full-garment packages
Functional textiles
Garment dyeing
Generic name
Hand
Knitting
Manufactured fibers

Mercerize
Microencapsulation
Microfibers
Nanofinishing
Natural fibers
Novelty fabrics
Performance fabrics
Piece dyeing
Protein fibers
Sampling
Smart textiles
Solution dyeing
Staple length
Supply chain
Synthetics
Technical fabrics
Texture
Trade only
Trade organizations
Trims
Value-added
Wearable technology
Weaving

Discussion Questions

Understanding Fiber: What characteristics do you associate with fibers such as cotton, silk, linen, wool, or polyester? What types of garments do you think of when you think of these fabrics? How do you think changing a garment's fiber content impacts its perception?

Innovation: As we have read, much of the innovation in textiles comes from athletic companies such as Nike Flywear. Why do you think that the athletic industry is so influential? What are some other non-fashion related industries that use textiles extensively?

Influences: How do you feel that the environmental movement will continue to influence the textile industry? Do you think environmentalism will impact natural or synthetic fibers more? What other major issues might influence textile development?

Forecasting Activities

The Leading Edge of Fibers and Fabrics. Visit the websites of innovative textile manufacturers to obtain information about developmental fabrics—the newly developed innovations that provide special characteristics or properties. Brainstorm possible product categories for these fabrics. What traditional fabrics will these new developmental fabrics replace? What traditional fabrics will be enhanced by pairing them with these developmental fabrics? What consumer audience is likely to see the value-added benefits in these developmental fabrics and be willing to pay more for those benefits?

Fabrics in the News. Collect reports on runway shows for a particular season from either trade publications or fashion magazines. Glean all the news about fabric and trim from each article, and compile a profile of the important fabric news for that season. Repeating the process over several seasons will reveal directional trends for fibers, fabrics, and trims.

A Trend by Any Other Name. Collect reports on trend stories presented by fiber producers, fabric manufacturers, trade organizations, and forecasting services for a given season using trade publications and websites. The trend stories will have different names, but there will be correspondence between the various forecasts. Identify the distinctive themes presented for this season. Relate these themes to product categories, consumer segments, and price points.

Resource Pointers

Websites for professional color organizations:
Color Association of the United States: www.colorassociation.com
Color Marketing Group: www.colormarketing.org
Website for color education created by The Society of Dyers and Colourists (SDC): www.colour-experience.org

Websites for trade shows:
Cosmoprof (beauty): www.cosmoprof.com and www.cosmoprofnorthamerica.com
Maison et Objet (home decor): www.maison-objet.com
Première Vision (fabric): www.premierevision.fr

Color forecasting companies:
Cotton Incorporated: www.cottoninc.com
Design Options: www.design-options.com/
Munsell Color System: www.munsell.com
Nippon Color and Design Research Institute, Inc.: www.ncd-ri.co.jp/english/
Pantone: www.pantone.com
The Trend Curve (home decor): trendcurve.com

Online color IQ test:
http://xritephoto.com/ph_toolframe.aspx?action=coloriq

In fashion you are supposed to hate what you have loved before. I cannot do that.

—Jean Paul Gaultier

8

THE LOOK: DESIGN CONCEPTS AND STYLE DIRECTIONS

OBJECTIVES

◆ Differentiate between the three modern eras of fashion and understand the influence of each era on contemporary fashion

◆ Examine the concept of style tribes as a way of affiliation

◆ Describe the skills and abilities required of forecasters on a global fashion scale

◆ Identify the online sources of information available to forecasters

◆ Understand the fashion calendar and the interactions that create directional information

◆ Compare the countries that are influential design centers and recognize their signature styles

◆ List the skills and abilities required of forecasters on a global fashion scale

◆ Identify trends, analyze visual and symbolic core concepts, and synthesize directional information for clients

TREND MULTIPLICATION

In his book *The Empire of Fashion*, Lipovetsky (1994) identified three modern eras in fashion. The first began in the 1860s, lasted for one hundred years, and established the organization of the high-end fashion industry that is still in place today. The second began in the 1960s with the ready-to-wear revolution and shifted the emphasis of fashion from the mature consumer to the youth movement (Figure 8.1). The third era began in the late 1980s and has lasted until the present day, and is known for having many different kinds of looks which are all in style at the same time and for the extreme diversity in designers' signature styles.

Lipovetsky's divisions are a convenient way to view change. Organizing observations into a timeline and characterizing each segment allows the observer to see the shape of change, and the antecedents and consequences of change become more apparent.

✦ THE FIRST ERA OF MODERN FASHION

From the 1860s to the 1960s, Paris was known as the center of innovation; it set the annual trends and was followed by the rest of the world. In the early years of the era, Charles Frederick Worth, the first couturier, established the system that is still used today when he set up a fashion house, began showing designs prepared in advance, changed styles frequently, and employed models to show the clothes to clients. Paris's influence on the fashion world continued for decades. Organized fashion shows on fixed dates began after World War I, an innovation that coincided with France's need for fashion as an export and the influx of professional buyers from the United States and other countries in Europe. Professional buyers, through a fee arrangement with the designers, acquired models for manufacturing at lower prices in their own countries.

The absolute dictatorship of fashion designers over their clientele was undermined in the 1920s.

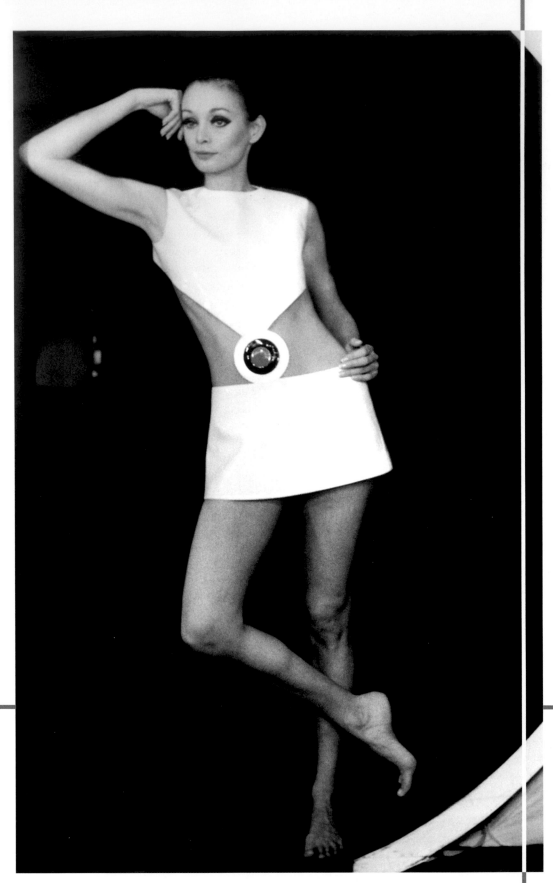

Figure 8.1

The second era of fashion began in the 1960s with a tilt toward youthfulness and the ready-to-wear revolution. Pierre Cardin was an innovative designer and marketer.

Early in the decade Coco Chanel popularized "the poor look" of simple dresses, jersey suits, sweaters, cloche hats, and pants. Jean Patou introduced the sportswear approach to fashion, which he described as follows: "I have aimed at making [my clothes] pleasant to the eye and allowing absolute liberty of movement." These looks replaced the elaborate fashions and constricting stays that kept women sedentary with a new aesthetic ideal for the modern woman—slim, active, athletic. Chanel's "poor look" and Patou's sportswear were also much easier to imitate, thereby opening up fashion to more consumers.

Daytime dress became more comfortable and functional, but evening fashion continued to be the epitome of seductive femininity. This fracturing of looks played out in ever more varied forms. A woman could choose to be sexy, or dress like a "schoolgirl" in black dress with white collar and cuffs, or adopt the look of a professional woman in a tailored suit, or of a sporty woman in trousers and a sweater set. After the 1920s, the unity of a single fashion message disappeared; disparate and sometimes opposed looks shared the stage. Fashion gained transformative power as it became possible to manipulate appearance to express one's self, personality, and individuality—to change the way a woman viewed herself and how other people saw her. Instead of issuing strict commands, fashion began to offer a diversified set of options inviting the consumer to choose.

✦ THE SECOND ERA OF MODERN FASHION

The ready-to-wear revolution coincided with a tilt toward youthfulness and novelty as ideals. A two-tiered fashion system emerged with couture focused on masterpieces of execution and ready-to-wear focused on improving manufacturing technology and trend-driven merchandising. Pierre Cardin showed a ready-to-wear line at the French department store Printemps in 1959, opened the first ready-to-wear department in 1963, and was the first to sign licensing agreements with ready-to-wear

manufacturers. In 1966, Yves Saint Laurent created the first ready-to-wear line conceived on its own terms and not as an adaptation of **haute couture**. Emerging new designers like Mary Quant focused exclusively on ready-to-wear. During this second era, because of licensing contracts that put their name on merchandise, designers became brand names for a variety of products from apparel to fragrance, accessories to home decor.

The emergence of youth as an ideal brought with it new emphasis on the values of individual expression, spontaneity, and the humor of stylistic collages and juxtapositions. Good taste and the distinctions of class were identified with the "old" order. The cult of youth became intrinsically linked with the cult of the body. Instead of following the latest fashion dictates closely, the consumer became more autonomous. "In" was not defined by aspirations for status or social position but by being "in the know." Clothes could be casual as long as they conveyed a youthful, liberated, and individualized image.

✦ THE THIRD ERA OF MODERN FASHION

The defining characteristics of the third era of modern fashion are diversity in acceptable looks and a blurring of the line between what is "in" and "out" of fashion. Today, all styles are legitimate—pared-down modernism and sexy vamp looks, short and long, tight and loose, "down-and-out" distressed fabrics and refined chic, sneakers and stilettos exist simultaneously. During the first two eras of modern fashion, following trends as defined by designers, the press, and merchants was important in presenting an appropriate image to the world. In the third era of modern fashion, a broad range of alternative looks became acceptable and people became less inclined to define "appropriate" in any definite terms.

The seeds of the current era of fashion can be seen in the 1920s when fashion began to fracture into multiple looks and in the 1960s when individualism and consumer autonomy encouraged a proliferation of fashion alternatives. Gone were the days of unitary trends passed from haute couture to the rest of the world. Instead, the fashion world fragmented into multiple trends from multiple centers of creation and popularized by mass media. During the two earlier eras of modern fashion, the distinction between "in" and "out" of fashion was highly defined. The loss of this distinction can be seen as a shift between fashion—the following of an accepted norm that fluctuates over time—and style—the pursuit of a personal, individualistic look outside of time-based oscillations (Polhemus, 1996).

The growing autonomy of the consumer and the rejection of fashions touted by designers and the press mean that, today, few new styles achieve quick adoption. The pressure for instant assimilation has disappeared. For consumers, the concepts of following trends and being a fashion victim are one and the same (Polhemus, 1996). The wish to avoid both designations has driven consumers toward individualized selection and mixing of influences. The result of these forces is that while the pace of fashion introduction and the translation of styles into all price points have increased, the speed of adoption has slowed down (Lipovetsky, 1994). Instead of following fashion dictates and trends, consumers filter from the many options and choose those that fit their individual aesthetic. Ironic mixtures of styles and influences define today's fashion. There is no longer one single fashion; there are many fashions.

Barbara Vinken (2005) builds on Lipovetsky's **analysis** by identifying a hundred years of fashion—from Worth to Saint Laurent, with Schiaparelli and Chanel as the high points—when haute couture expressed **modernity** and dictated fashion. Beginning in the 1980s, she terms the new era "postfashion" where creative direction comes from *prêt-à-porter* (ready-to-wear), the dictatorial power of the couturier is broken, and fashion becomes a coproduction between the designer and the people who wear the clothes. The aesthetic shifts from fashion as art to fashion as commentary, which fragments and recombines symbols of affluence and poverty, beauty and ugliness.

The idea of fashion as a coproduction between designer and consumer corresponds with the rise of peer-based sources of information. Consumers began to reject the artificial scripts of top-down marketing in favor of "new media" such as the Internet and consumer-generated content. The "old media" was comprised of print media or television and depended on controlling the message and mass marketing, but the new media appealed to a fragmented set of subcultures, each with its own interests (Popcorn, 2005). The new tastemakers became aficionados of a cultural niche who reviewed available products and reported their opinions on **blogs** (a term that comes from combining the words "Web logs") and special interest websites—a fan-to-fan form of communication that bypassed traditional gatekeepers (Leeds, 2006).

✧ Style Tribes

Substituting for the distinction between "in" and "out" in the third era of modern fashion is the distinction of "belonging to" a group, a cluster of like-minded and like-living people. Adopting an appearance style is a marker of membership in a **style tribe** (Polhemus, 1996). Steampunk, a subculture based on a time-traveling fantasy world, is one part retro-romantic and one part technology. Devotees read Jules Verne and H. G. Wells and are interested in outdated transportation systems such as zeppelins (blimps) and steam locomotives, vaudeville stage performances, and the Victorian Age. Unlike hip-hop and Goth, which seem threatening to outsiders, steampunk may be bizarre, but its quaintness attracts a following. The aesthetic expresses a desire for formality, refinement, and ritual—adherents attend tea parties and time-traveler balls. The style incorporates music, film, design, and fashion. The look fuses current fashion with neo-Edwardian touches like a gentleman's waistcoat and paisley bow tie and extends to a brass-encased iPhone. For women, the look is built on corsets, bustles, crinolines, and parasols. Favored designers include

Figure 8.2

The look of the steampunk style tribe is instantly recognizable, and aspects have trickled up into mainstream dress.

Alexander McQueen and Ralph Lauren. Emerging in the early 1990s as a taste in literature, steampunk has grown into a worldview supported by its own Internet culture, handmade clothing designers, and retailers (La Ferla, 2008b) (Figure 8.2). Group membership as conveyed by a "uniform" is not a new idea—hippies of the 1970s dressed to convey their unmaterialistic value system (Wintour, 1998b). Although the appearance style of this group has blurred into a stereotype, there were actually separate style tribes within the hippie look, including the flower child, African-influenced styles, groups with a political agenda, and others.

Style tribes can be found in the subcultural groups that give rise to street fashion. A version of the same phenomenon is at work when the social clusters in a high school can be recognized by the cultural uniform they wear—rebels, skateboarders, or preps (Sullivan, 1998). People in technological or creative fields often evolve a "uniform" look, even down to the preferred brand names for each item (Figure 8.3).

Figure 8.3

Steve Jobs, founder of Apple, was known for his signature black turtleneck, a look that was adopted by others in the tech field.

Occupational clusters, groups sharing a special interest from stock car racing to bird-watching, cliques with the same taste in fashion and decor—all of these and many more are style tribes.

Designers act as style tribe leaders when they present a consistent signature style that appeals to consumers who share that aesthetic and not to others. Designers such as Maison Martin Margiela, Comme des Garçons, Alexander McQueen, and others have a signature style recognizable to even a casual observer.

Some specialty stores and brands appeal directly to style tribes through their selection of merchandise and the design of their bricks-and-mortar and online stores. Department stores and specialty retailers such as the Gap appeal to a broad spectrum of shoppers, but some specialty stores create teen-friendly shopping environments and websites focused on specific teen subcultures. The goal is to "allow [teens] to be part of the brand and image" (Weitzman, 2001) (Figure 8.4).

✧ The Role of the Forecaster

The explosion of the number of trends in this third era of modern fashion creates a more cluttered information environment for today's fashion forecaster. Because consumers' decisions are less restricted by social rules, buying behavior is more difficult to predict. In this third era of modern fashion, a "triple logic" is in effect (Lipovetsky, 1994):

- ✤ the logic of aesthetics;
- ✤ the logic of industrial clothing manufacturing;
- ✤ the logic of consumers acting on individual taste.

It is the fashion forecaster's job to sort out the workings of this triple logic. The forecaster appreciates and understands the aesthetics demonstrated in designers' collections and in street fashion. While appreciating the art, the forecaster edits away the theatrical trappings to discover the wearable clothes underneath.

Figure 8.4
Once the exclusive style of upper-class Ivy Leaguers, the preppy look was appropriated as a status symbol and lifestyle statement. Capitalizing on this style tribe's aesthetics, Ralph Lauren's Rugby stores offer head-to-toe preppy looks for men and women.

"Wearable" relates both to the industrial logic of being reproduced at lower price points and satisfying the needs of consumers' lifestyles. Clothes that are wearable for one consumer are impossible for another. The forecaster's understanding of aesthetics, manufacturing, and what is considered wearable from the consumer's point of view forms the basis of each season's forecast.

Fashion forecasting requires three competencies:

❖ proficiency in researching fashion developments using the tools of environmental scanning;
❖ the ability to identify the visual and symbolic core concepts within and across collections;
❖ the expertise to analyze the match between fashion developments and the marketplace and to synthesize an actionable forecast for a client.

Information is gathered in the research phase from many sources, such as fashion shows and trade events, as well as fashion news from print, broadcasting, and online channels. These sources are sifted for **core concepts** or trends. Core concepts are culturally expressive ideals that are endlessly reinterpreted across seasons, years, and decades. Trends can be identified when they are recognized as similarities across information sources. Next, trends are analyzed to determine the potential match with consumer profiles. The consumer profile must go beyond demographics such as age or gender to the subtle differences in personal philosophy as expressed in lifestyle, group membership, preferences, and taste (Polhemus, 1996). Finally, the elements are assembled into an actionable forecast by product category, price point, and retail concept. An actionable forecast is plausible and detailed enough to support executive decisions on design (the logic of aesthetics and manufacturing) and assortment planning (the logic matching style and price to consumer lifestyles).

THE FASHION MAP

As fashion insiders, forecasters have a fashion map of the marketplace—a mental map of the locations where innovations are likely to be glimpsed early, the supply chain of the textile/apparel industry, and the retail conduit to consumers. Fashion insiders also have another fashion map—the schedule of seasons and shows. When consumers shop for winter coats or summer swimsuits, fashion insiders are seasons ahead in their thinking. Forecasters use these fashion maps to organize their observation of directional information. Because innovations rarely apply to the entire marketplace, information must be tagged for the appropriate price point, category, and classification. In this way, forecasters turn random bits of data into useful information for decision support.

✦ FASHION GEOGRAPHY

Fashion leadership no longer belongs exclusively to the French couturiers. Today, the fashion world is global with design centers in many countries. However, some design centers have special cachet. They are made distinctive by their design heritage and by the aesthetic that they represent (Hastreiter, 1997).

✧ French Luxe

French fashion traces its roots to haute couture, one-of-a-kind showpieces made by skilled dressmakers for a particular client. In the first half of the twentieth century, fashion was dominated by French designers. The first years of the century, *la Belle Époque*, represents the high-water mark for class-conscious extravagance with ribbons, laces, flowers, feathers, and jewels. Haute couture, with its focus on artistry and workmanship, has continued as a tradition of French fashion and filters down to luxury labels of Paris ready-to-wear (Figure 8.5). With the **Chambre Syndicale**, French fashion's governing board, and support from the French government, designers made Paris the fashion capital for luxury.

Profile: David Wolfe, Creative Director, The Doneger Group

David Wolfe began his career in 1959 in Ohio and went on to become one of Europe's leading fashion illustrators: "European ready-to-wear styles were becoming interesting to American designers and retailers, and there was a hunger for this kind of information. [Forecasters] were like foreign correspondents, only for fashion" (Zimmerman, 2008).

Wolfe switched from illustration to the fashion forecasting industry in the late 1960s at I.M. International, one of the first fashion forecasting and consulting firms, then with The Fashion Service, a company he founded and managed prior to joining Doneger in the 1990s. Today, Wolfe is an avidly sought-out public speaker, and his expertise is so renowned that he was called to testify before the US House of Representatives Subcommittee on Courts, the Internet, and Intellectual Property in Washington, DC on the topic of fashion design protection in 2006.

Unlike many forecasting services, Doneger began as a traditional buying office but morphed into a fashion merchandising and trend-forecasting organization, positioning itself as the "one-stop shop" for retailers, manufacturers, and designers. Doneger Group currently publishes runway reports, retail/street reports, color and design concepts and directions, directional beauty themes, and fabric reports to provide its subscribers with up-to-the-minute information in all things beauty and fashion-related (Casabona, 2007; "Corporate Information," 2014; Moin, 2006, 2008).

The Doneger Group's staff of twenty forecasters brings global market trend analysis to the fashion industry in presentations, consulting, and publications. The division has over 400 subscribers. When adding to the staff, Wolfe says, it is "a red flag to me when I'm hiring someone who says 'my whole life is fashion.' You have to be interested in much more than fashion. You have to understand the world if you are going to understand what people want to wear" (Zimmerman, 2008).

Wolfe's perspective on fashion comes from observing change over time. He thinks fashion is changing more slowly now than it did when he began his career. According to Wolfe, in the fashion business, "It's no longer a seasonal game. It's an evolutionary process these days" (Lockwood, 2013). He sees style today in a holding pattern where most consumers, male and female, are content with the familiar, although that is partly the fashion industry's fault: "We're stuck in retro. We're standing with one foot in the past and one foot in the future" (Lockwood, 2013). However, he is optimistic about the future: "The newness is coming from science and technology, not from a design studio" (Cisco, 2014).

Wolfe (1999) characterizes most of the twentieth century as about upward style mobility—"No matter where you were on the economic or social strata, you looked up, up, up." But a few decades ago fashion began to look downward to the street for inspiration. He even goes further back in tracing the shift: "I think Levi Strauss invented the garment that was the watershed turning point in fashion. He's responsible for the entire downward dressing spiral."

For Wolfe (1998), the shift in the latter half of the twentieth century toward an anything-goes-anywhere way of dressing had negative economic consequences for the fashion industry. As he puts it, "If we can redefine appropriate apparel for different occasions, different lives, different ages—we are going to sell a lot more. I think we are going to see people reestablishing some rules because it is too difficult to get dressed in the morning if you don't have rules. Rules make it easier, not harder." That doesn't mean that consumers will give up comfort and casual clothes, but he thinks fashion is "starting to chart a trend toward dressing up again—back toward not uncomfortable formality but appropriateness."

As for trends, Wolfe (1999) thinks they work differently now. When he started in the business, "all you had to do was pick out the right person to copy." In those times a trend started as an idea "and it rippled out, and rippled out, and rippled out, and eventually everybody made a bit of money from it." Today he divides trends into "macro" and "micro" categories. "Macro trends are the big, big ideas that affect everybody, in every walk of life, in every price point, every gender—those are the big deals, the real trends." The micro trends are "those cute little ideas that fashion editors love, and fashion stylists love, and the display people love—because they are a great way to communicate excitement to each other in the fashion industry, to get our ideas across." Because of the short life span of these micro trends, people in the industry can make "a little bit of money, intensely for a very, very short period of time, but a nanosecond later, it's over."

As a forecaster, Wolfe goes back to look at the forecasts he made a decade before to see how things actually worked out. Technology will change what clothes are made from (like high-performance fabrics), the way clothes are made (laser cutouts for decoration and fused seams rather than sewn), clothes themselves (pockets designed for take-along electronic gadgets), and the way the industry communicates with the customer (pinpointing individual customers with electronic messages about new merchandise).

In the mid-2000s Wolfe declared, "There is no fashion mainstream any more. Instead of mainstream there are a thousand little branches all going at different speeds. It's almost as if the consumer has become a solo player in the marketplace. And that makes it hard to plan mass movements of merchandise" (Horyn, 2005). In a presentation entitled "The Big Picture: Spring 2014 and beyond," he said that although there are plenty of trends to talk about, if something is a real trend, it lasts longer than a season. Some of the trends he saw on the horizon included modern graphic stripes, expanded color palettes, unnatural materials (see-through plastic, rubber, vinyl), ultralight fabrics, shifting silhouettes, and familiar items in unexpected colors and materials (Lockwood, 2013).

Encouraged by televised fashion shows, reality shows like *Project Runway*, and museum displays of Paris collections, Wolfe sees the public's interest in fashion insider information growing in much the same way people became fascinated with show business information in the 1990s (Poggi, 2007).

Sources:
Cisco (2014, January 15). Internet of everything: Fashion and technology with David Wolfe. Retrieved from YouTube. Creative Directors. Retrieved from Doneger.com.
Lockwood, Lisa (2013, March 15). Doneger's David Wolfe serves up spring 2014 trends. Retrieved from wwd.com.

Figure 8.5
French fashion is known for its focus on artistry and workmanship, a tradition that can be traced to its roots in haute couture.

Louis Vuitton has been one of France's most important design houses since its founding in 1854. After many successful years with American Marc Jacobs at the helm, the company received great accolades for hiring French designer Nicholas Ghesquière as artistic director of Women's collections after Jacobs resigned. "Louis Vuitton has always incarnated for me the symbol of ultimate luxury, innovation and exploration. I am very honored of the mission that I am entrusted with, and proud to join the history of this great Maison. We share common values and a vision. I can't wait to join the team. Together we will build the future of the brand while preserving its precious heritage" ("Louis Vuitton and Nicholas Ghesquière," 2013).

✧ American Sportswear

When the Nazis occupied Paris during World War II, the United States was cut off from Paris's influence and American fashion came into its own as the center of sportswear design (Brubach, 1998; Tapert, 1998). Sportswear presented an alternative tradition by substituting practicality and casual comfort for virtuoso cut, custom fabrics, and embellishment. American sportswear has its roots in mass-produced clothes such as jeans and off-the-rack clothes from the department store. Whereas French couture focused on artistry, American sportswear focused on the changing lifestyles of women. Claire McCardell, an American designer of the 1940s, is credited with offering women a more casual, active, and less constricted view of what a modern woman should wear. The look of American fashion was fully established in the 1970s with the emergence of Halston's simple but sophisticated cuts, Calvin Klein's minimalism, Ralph Lauren's idealized nostalgia, and Donna Karan's career woman wardrobe (Alfano, 2003). Today, American sportswear is a paradigm—luxurious without being ostentatious, styled for women who want clothes that make sense (Figure 8.6). This paradigm has spread around the world as casual, sporty, unconstructed styles. In the opinion of *Vogue* contributing editor Andre Leon, there are five designers in the United States "that you always

look to for excitement": Marc Jacobs, Michael Kors, Ralph Lauren, Oscar de la Renta, and Carolina Herrera, but he also acknowledges the talent of younger designers such as Mary Kate and Ashley Olsen of The Row:

> Mary Kate and Ashley are very, very solid designers in the American mainstream of the fashion world. And they work hard, and they research. They're very serious about their craft, and it's about the luxury and the understated quality of what they do. It's not about fireworks. It's about a kind of classical American tradition of maybe a cable-knit sweater or just a—even a cashmere cape, you know, like a poncho you'd wear on a plane in first class. (Young & Hobson, 2013)

✧ British Edge

The high point for British fashion came in the 1960s when young people rebelled against the repressive English class system, bent on self-expression in music and clothing. This was the first wave of street fashion to make its way into mainstream fashion. Mods and Carnaby Street, Mary Quant and the Biba boutique showcase for young fashion still echo in today's fashion world. British art schools that nurtured the talents of Alexander McQueen, Stella McCartney, and Matthew Williamson continue to graduate designers who fill London boutiques with ironic, hip, and radical fashion (Trebay, 2002d). British fashion tends to take center stage when the accent is on youthful fashion and translation of street fashion (Figure 8.7). Fashion is so important to Britain's economy that Samantha Cameron, wife of the Prime Minister and British Fashion Council ambassador, described it as the "most successful of our creative industries" — bigger than film, music, and advertising (Friedman, 2014). British fashion is far more encompassing than London, particularly with the popularity of Scottish fashion designers such as Christopher Kane, whose brand is a part of the Kering luxury group, and Jonathan Saunders, who has done lines for Target and Topshop in addition to his own ready-to-wear collection.

Figure 8.6

American sportswear, with its roots in mass-produced clothing, offers practicality that fits with an active lifestyle.

Figure 8.7

British fashion came into its own with the street fashion of the 1960s and continues to be thought of as youthful, whimsical, and hip.

✧ Italian Ease

From small family-run artisan mills to multimillion-dollar factories, Italian fashion developed from a tradition of fine fabrics from the Como, Biella, and Prato regions, and leather from Tuscany. Italian design was influential in the 1950s when the Fontana sisters created fashions for Hollywood actresses like Elizabeth Taylor and Gina Lollobrigida (Feitelberg, 2003). Italian design resurfaced in the 1970s when designers such as Giorgio Armani, Gianni Versace, Roberto Cavalli, and Missoni moved to center stage. In the 1990s, designers such as Prada and Dolce and Gabbana and the resurgence of the Gucci brand further popularized Italian fashion with consumers all over the world. The Italian look has always been a blend between quality and design—softer, more textured, and less hard-edged than French fashion (Figure 8.8).

Italian fashion is in the process of change with a younger group of designers finally emerging to carry on the legacy of older designers such as Valentino and Armani. Previously, Suzy Menkes, head fashion reporter and editor for the *International Herald Tribune*, was known for asking, "Can anybody name me one Italian designer under the age of 50?" (Hindin-Miller, 2014) at each Milan fashion week, and now young designers such as Julian Zigerli and Massimo Giorgetti are succeeding with encouragement from established designers. Milan-based *Elle* stylist Nicolò Milella says new Italian labels have found success because of the designers' strong personal images, and immediately recognizable branding: "The designers are great personalities, they're online, available, always around in the right places, fun to be with, friendly and cool," he says. "Everybody wants to be friends with them, and buying their pieces is a sort of way of getting into their friendship circle" (Hindin-Miller, 2014).

✧ Japanese Cut

The radical modernism of the Japanese designers such as Issay Miyake, Rei Kawakubo, and Yohji Yamamoto emerged in the 1980s offering a sculptural alternative to the heavy French structures and the softer Italian styles. The Japanese designers relied on high-tech fabrics and finishes and unusual cuts and wrapping effects (Figure 8.9). Their innovations sparked the movement toward deconstruction and minimalism that continues to influence fashion.

Japan is especially known for its streetwear, and men's streetwear in particular. Since the end of World War II, Japan has had an ongoing fascination with American culture, and like the style tribes found on the streets of Shibuya and Harajuku, many Japanese brands derive inspiration a very specific aspect of American culture, which they interpret from their own unique perspective, with their version often surpassing the original in terms of quality and style (Harris, 2013). The brand Bounty Hunter was originally founded as a toy company in Harajuku in 1995, and expanded to include T-shirts and hoodies which infuse American punk, rockabilly, and motorcycling culture. Another example is J.S. Homestead, which reinterprets vintage American pieces by mixing in modern basics and details in their designs (Harris, 2013).

✧ Belgian Individuality

Ann Demeulemeester, Martin Margiela, Walter Van Beirendonck, and Veronique Branquinho all trace their fashion roots to Antwerp. The first of the Belgian designers came to prominence in the 1980s. Their work is defined by structural cuts and tailoring in a deconstructed mode (Figure 8.10). The work of Belgian fashion designer Dries Van Noten was highlighted in the fashion capital of Paris with the exhibit "Inspirations" that was held at the Musée des Arts Décoratifs from March to November of 2014 ("Dries Van Noten," 2014). Younger designers emerging from Belgium include Jean-Paul Lespagnard, who presented his spring/summer 2014 collection in Paris, and Bernhard Willhelm, who has designed costumes for theater plays and music stars like Bjork (Martorelli, 2013).

Whereas some of the traditional roots of fashion are still visible in the collections shown in Paris, London, Milan, and New York, the design world is much more complex these days

Figure 8.8
Italian fashion is known for the rich, luxury fabrics of wool and silk and for high-quality workmanship with a softer edge than that of French fashion.

Figure 8.9
Japanese designers introduced a radical modernism—sculptural, unusual cuts, and voluminous silhouettes.

(Foley, 1998). The city where a designer is based is less restrictive than it used to be—designers of many nationalities work in all the fashion centers and designers show in multiple capitals in a single season. Each season new designers emerge and established designers change houses. The same designer may create their own lines plus lines for other houses. The forecaster must revise the fashion map every season. Clients, buyers, and journalists arrive at the shows in Paris, London, Milan, and New York with expectations based on the visual signature of each capital. And, no matter where they show, designers are categorized in part by their creative origin.

✧ Fashion Weeks for Ready-to-Wear

Fashion weeks consist of runway shows in each of the four fashion capitals—New York, London, Milan, and Paris. Although not as costly as couture, **designer ready-to-wear** clothing is still expensive, luxurious, and beautifully executed. Whereas a couture outfit may be made only once or, at most, a few times, designer ready-to-wear is reproduced in the hundreds or thousands. The designers walk a fine line between playing it safe and getting little press coverage and going over the top with offbeat looks that fail in the stores. Designers in this category get lots of press coverage and their successes and failures are recorded on the scorecard kept by the press.

Some collections leap forward into the fashion future, while other collections work and rework a concept season after season or refine favorite themes over and over. Trends reported in the press often begin here when editors notice underlying similarities across designers' collections, when a designer presents an outstanding collection with a unifying theme, or when an item stars in many shows and becomes newsworthy. A magazine editor, fashion director, or forecaster setting out to cover the collections in a single season would choose between hundreds of shows presented by established and emerging designers and by design houses and brands. Covering the shows means assessing each in terms of the line's history and the spirit of the times, identifying emerging or continuing trends across shows, and spotting the standout outfits that can be used to illustrate the trends (Figure 8.11).

The ready-to-wear shows for fall/winter occur in February/March and spring/summer in September/October. The actual dates, placement of shows within the schedule, and logistics depend on negotiation between the show organizers (Chambre Syndicale de la Haute Couture for Paris and Chamber of Fashion for Italy).

Costs for a runway show can run to as much as $750,000 (or even $2 million for the most extravagant shows). Although important clients and celebrities are invited to the shows, the real aim is to attract fashion editors' interest and sell to store buyers. If the right people don't see the presentation, the investment in a show is wasted (Murphy, 2001a, 2002a).

In each fashion capital a coordinating group arranges the schedule so that key shows don't overlap—British Fashion Council, Council of Fashion Designers of America, Camera Della Moda (Milan), and Fédération Français de la Couture (Paris). In New York, designers check with Ruth Finley, publisher of the Fashion Calendar, for possible conflicts before scheduling. Her calendar, with a current subscription price of $425 per year, has been keeping track of shows since 1941 (Wilson, 2007c).

Further complicating the schedule is the overlap between showing the line and beginning development of the future season. Fashion week can clash with fabric shows like Première Vision in Europe. Some designers leave immediately after their shows and fly to Paris to view the latest in fabric development. Others send members of their design team to Première Vision, attend other fabric shows where dates do not conflict with fashion weeks, or buy fabrics from company representatives or **showrooms** ("PV," 2002).

The schedule for shows in the fashion capitals will continue to be a controversial issue because the dates must accommodate the requirements of designers, who need time to develop their lines; the merchants, who must place orders; and

Figure 8.10
Belgian designers are known for structural cuts, tailoring, and a modern deconstructed look.

Figure 8.11

Covering fashion weeks means seeing hundreds of shows in the four fashion capitals and identifying trends emerging from the multitude of images.

the press, who must photograph and present the fashion news to the public. The fallout from decisions about timing reverberates down the supply chain to manufacturers of fibers, fabrics, trims, and findings.

In addition to the designers who stage runway shows, other designers participate in **trade shows** or showroom events. Satellite trade shows for accessories are set to precede, coincide, or follow each fashion week. Each trade show in each city fills a niche and targets specific retailers. For example, the Paris trade show Atmosphère features designers who are fashion forward and directional and targets retailers with smaller fashion boutiques. For designers, showing in this trade show is often a stepping-stone to international import markets. Merchants and journalists must find time in a hectic schedule of runway shows to also cover the trade shows.

An alternative is to see the shows online. Companies specialize in covering runway shows on subscription and no-fee sites. StyleSight provides 2 million images from the latest designer runway shows to subscribers who pay $15,000 per year for access (Jana, 2007), and

Style.com has photos of runway collections available for viewing within hours of each show. Still, it is unlikely that television or online will replace seeing the shows in person because the runway pictures cannot convey the total experience (Braunstein, 2001).

Travel doesn't have to end with the last Paris show. Journalists and buyers can continue on to cover fashion weeks in Australia (especially strong for swimsuit styling), São Paulo (Brazil), Berlin (Germany), and Copenhagen (Denmark). These second-tier cities are especially valuable to retailers looking for unique lines for their stores and to journalists and forecasters taking a more global look at fashion concepts (Huntington, 2001). Each city adds its own flavor to the fashion picture. The Nordic Fashion Association (Sweden, Norway, Iceland, Finland, and Denmark) aims to become the leader in the combining of fashion, healthy living, and sustainable energy (Groves, 2008b). Fashion week in Berlin highlights the city as an emerging creative hub (Drier & McGuinness, 2007). New fashion weeks are being added constantly. Ann Watson, fashion director of Henri Bendel, attends many and explains: "Fashion has become so global that more and more countries are using fashion weeks as a way to unleash the creativity in their cultures." Many of these emerging fashion capitals pay fashion journalists to travel to their shows (Wilson, 2008d).

✧ Los Angeles Fashion Week

Los Angeles is considered a secondary fashion city when compared to New York, London, Milan, and Paris, but its fashion district rivals New York's in size, it has a reputation for originating trends, and it has a skilled workforce (Menkes, 2003a; Oblena, 2003). Los Angeles Fashion Week is mounted as a centralized event organized by 7th on Sixth (the same group that organizes New York shows) and features both women's and men's lines. Suzy Menkes (2003), reporting for the *International Herald Tribune*, defined the "L.A. look" as more upbeat and colorful than New York with three facets: a "quirky indie spirit," a "gritty, cool side," and a "vintage style that had been building since the 1970s." Another feature of California fashion is celebrity lines—stars from movies, music, and television moonlighting as designers (Chammas, 2008).

✧ Men's Ready-to-Wear

Designers with both women's wear and menswear lines often show a mix of the two on the catwalk. However, there are designated biannual fashion weeks for menswear in London, New York, Milan, and Paris—January for fall/winter and June for spring/summer (Ageorges, 2003). Because of its history with traditional menswear fabrics and design, Milan is usually considered the most important of these events. To the uninitiated, menswear doesn't seem to change much from season to season, but the changes are just more subtle. Trends for menswear fashion are defined by the style (traditional or modern), the attitude (cool, hip, or edgy), the fit, including the length of the jacket, the width of the lapels, the placement of the collar notch and buttons, the number of buttons, pocket and vent details, and fabric color and pattern. Traditional looks feature full tailoring while modern styles are lighter, softer, and less constructed (Gellers, 1999).

✧ Couture

Made-to-measure for the most discriminating clients in the world, haute couture features the finest fabrics, embroideries, and workmanship in fashion. Style changes introduced in couture include the replacement of full crinoline by the bustle (Worth), the little black dress (Chanel), and the New Look (Dior), and many more (Milbank, 1985). In 1929, there were 91 couture houses with a clientele of 20,000. When designer ready-to-wear exploded in 1967, the number of couture houses plummeted from 37 to 19. Today, fewer than a dozen houses cater to about 500 people who can pay up to $80,000 for a dress (Horyn, 2007). According to Suzy Menkes of the *International Herald Tribune*, the future of haute couture is not threatened by the cheapness of "fast fashion"—superwealthy women will always want the best in creativity and craftsmanship—but couture is threatened by time because few women will fly to Paris, participate in multiple fittings, and wait 6 weeks for delivery (Menkes, 2008a).

Clients may pay as much as $20,000 for a couture suit from a major house. In return, a client gets a suit made by hand from scratch exclusively for her. The fabrics will be exquisite, the garment will be fitted to her figure (requiring up to seven fittings), tailored and lined for a flawless silhouette (silk suits are sometimes lined with cashmere), and decorated and embroidered by master artisans. A jacket may take 130 hours of skilled labor to produce, and a ball gown 300 hours or more. The result is a light, virtually weightless garment—an effect that can't be reproduced in machine-made clothing (Rubenstein, 1998). Karl Lagerfeld explains that the couture package includes more than the clothes: "Couture is about service, the salon, the vendeuse, the box, the way the clothes are wrapped and presented to the client" (Horyn, 2003a).

Haute couture shows are held in Paris after designer ready-to-wear for the same selling season—January for spring and July for fall/winter collections. Because haute couture is made-to-order for specific clients, it does not require the lead time for manufacturing that ready-to-wear clothes do. Houses showing couture collections are not all based in Paris. If designers can meet the criteria set by the Chambre Syndicale, then they are allowed to participate.

Shows not on the official couture calendar, "off-calendar" shows, feature new couturiers hoping to attract clients and make the leap onto the couture calendar in the future. Luxury jewelry firms often unveil collections during couture weeks because the clientele overlaps (Socha, 2003).

The death knell for couture has been sounded many times, given the prices, shrinking number of couture houses, and small client base. But beginning in the mid-1990s with John Galliano at Dior, interest in couture revived. Journalists point to the commercial demands of ready-to-wear as a limiting factor on creativity, while couture is a creative undertaking. Although it may be a cliché to say that couture is a fashion "laboratory" for design, it is true that looks from couture collections do spin off into ready-to-wear (Horyn, 2002). Hollywood stylists looking for the perfect runway dress for their clients help swell the client base for couture (Horyn, 2007).

A couture line loses money for a designer, but owners feel that costs are justified given the promotional boost the attention brings to fragrance, licensed lines, and ready-to-wear. Because it can be experimental, couture is directional for fashion themes, references to designers and eras of the fashion past, ethnic influences, silhouettes, fabrics, and colors.

✦ FASHION OFF THE RUNWAY

Established designers will always be on the runway, but the chaos of fashion week and the overcrowded schedule (100 or more shows in each of the fashion capitals) sometimes swamp smaller designer labels and those of emerging talents. Designers who choose not to present their collections on the catwalks save the huge costs in time, money, effort, and distraction, but they also miss out on the visibility, magazine attention, and coverage on television and the Internet. Instead, these designers invite stores and magazines to come to the showroom or send them lookbooks (photographs of the line). Showroom visits provide a chance for designers to present their point of view more completely than they can in a runway show (Wilson, 2002).

The costs of a runway show during fashion week also do not make sense for well-established brands who sell their apparel at a moderate price point like Jones Apparel Group, Liz Claiborne, Guess, and St. John (Lockwood, 2003). Citing the shift in emphasis at the shows from retailers to the press, mainstream brands would rather focus on presenting the line to retailers in the showroom and using advertising to stimulate consumer interest.

✧ Showrooms

When a forecaster, magazine editor, or retail buyer talks about scouting the market, he or she often refers to visiting the showrooms of designers, manufacturers, and entrepreneurs in the Fashion Center (also known as the Garment District) of New York City. The Fashion Center has the highest concentration and greatest diversification of apparel resources. Open on weekdays throughout the year, the Fashion Center allows a fashion professional to discover new trends and new resources. Not only a district for seeing apparel lines, the businesses run the gamut from agents for European fabric houses to suppliers for trimmings, belts, buttons, and other findings.

✧ Boutiques

Emerging designers newly graduated from school or from apprenticeships as assistants to well-known designers need a retail showcase. They find it by opening small boutiques in fashion's capital cities. These shops are usually found in arty, edgy, fashion-forward enclaves clustered with the boutiques of other designers, vintage apparel stores, bars, and restaurants. SoHo in New York was one such neighborhood starting in the 1970s, but it evolved into today's showcase for European and American brands. When that happens, the avant-garde multibrand specialty stores and new designers migrate to emerging areas like the Meatpacking District (west of Ninth Street in the West Village), NoLIta (north of Little Italy), and Alphabet City (avenues A, B, C, and D in the East Village) (Caplan, 2001; Ozzard, 2001).

One of the original fashion neighborhoods, London's Carnaby Street, once the focus of Mod fashion in the 1960s, degenerated to selling cheap tourist souvenirs until it became a retail magnet for denim brands, but it wouldn't attract fashion-forward customers without independent boutiques and chic cafés. The retail mix includes unbranded stores (stores owned and stocked by brands but selling specialty products like vintage or limited-edition lines) and concept stores (stores selling cult sneakers, street-inspired looks, or secondary lines by name designers). The real estate management company that owns the properties actively recruits small, innovative retailers by offering competitive rents, store fixtures, and short leases (Jones, 2007a).

New designers also find a showcase in multibrand specialty stores with a reputation for discovering design talent. In the specialty stores, the fashion is often mixed with an in-store café, gallery space for art, objects, fashion, and accessories in a unique retail concept (Raper & Weisman, 1998). One such stop in Paris is Colette on the chic Rue St. Honoré (Figure 8.12). The store also features art exhibits, magazines and books, and a café (Jackson, 1998). Sarah Lerfel, who runs the store, puts it this way: "We want to surprise our customers and show them things that they shouldn't necessarily find elsewhere. We want to open our doors more to the independents and support creativity" (Murphy, 2002b). Fashion-forward boutiques can be found in major cities worldwide— Dover Street Market in London and New York, Corso Cuomo in Milan, Verso in Antwerp, Podium Concept in Moscow—and upscale resort destinations (Fraser-Cavassoni, 2008). Frequented not only by customers but also by the fashion press and forecasters, the visual presentation, product mix, and styles are directional for trendspotters.

Figure 8.12
Multibrand specialty stores like Colette in Paris have a reputation for discovering design talent and showcasing trends.

◇ Trade Shows

Almost every week of the year, somewhere in the world there is an apparel trade show. There are trade shows for:

❖ all categories of apparel—women's, men's, and children's;
❖ categories of accessories;
❖ niche and specialty categories such as ecologically conscious vendors;
❖ private-label manufacturers;
❖ special sizes—plus sizes and petites.

Trade shows are centered on selling fashion but they also showcase new design talent and identify trends for specific product categories, price points, and target audiences. Seminars at the shows provide a venue for networking among apparel executives and for discussion of issues that have an impact on the apparel industry.

New York trade shows coincide with the line releases by manufacturers—January (summer), late February to early March (early fall merchandise known as Fall I), late March to early April (fall merchandise known as Fall II), August (holiday and/or resort), and November (spring merchandise). These shows (e.g., Fashion Coterie, and Designers & Agents) allow buyers from around the country to see a wide range of lines. The trade shows feature name designers' lines, lines by young designers, and international contingents from Brazil, Australia, South Korea, and Turkey.

The shows are especially important for independent stores because they offer a chance to see many lines and select merchandise that differentiates the independents from the large department store chains. As one buyer puts it: "The items [we look for] really have to be one of a kind with maybe a technical aspect of great fabric, and also something that's not carried by everyone" (Larson, 2003b). Buyers use the New York trade shows to place orders for immediate delivery and to order for the upcoming season. For many buyers, the shows offer a chance to crystallize trends into specific lines and items customized for their location and customer. For buyers and forecasters, the trade shows offer a way to get an overview of seasonal trends in a more convenient and concentrated way than the alternative, canvassing individual showrooms.

◇ Regional Markets

Serving the same purpose for buyers who do not come to New York are the **regional markets** around the United States, located in Atlanta, Dallas, Chicago, San Francisco, Los Angeles, Denver, Miami, and other regional centers. Regional market centers lease space to manufacturers and sales representatives who carry multiple lines in permanent showrooms and for seasonal shows.

Planned to make buying easier and more convenient for smaller department stores and specialty stores, these marts have evolved as sites where merchandise aligns closely with the needs and preferences of different regions. Manufacturers use regional markets to test the direction of lines and to test the market response to items. Entrepreneurs in the middle price points often begin by showing at regional marts to test the viability of their design direction. Forecasters and buyers for large department store chains use regional markets to explore local market trends that may not show up in national buying patterns.

In addition to the well-known designers and apparel manufacturers showing at regional markets, such shows provide a showcase for designers working far from the runways on the fringes of the market. One such trendsetting concentration for contemporary clothing is in southern California. Working outside the fashion establishment, these designers specialize in the "California look"—body conscious and active looks that display a gym-toned body, ethnic-inspired looks, and ironic combinations not usually thought to be compatible. The result is inexpensive contemporary clothing, sophisticated junior wear, and more directional clothes than traditional bridge and career clothes lines. Aimed at independent stores making "smallish buys," these lines epitomize trends toward seasonless fabrics and a casual lifestyle (Steinhauer, 1998).

✦ STREET FASHION

Street fashion is synonymous with youthful experimentation, with subcultures from cliques to gangs, with the impulse to provoke attention, comment, or reaction (Koda, 2002). Consumers become their own fashion stylists when they take available clothing resources and mix, restyle, and customize items in individualistic and expressive ways. "Street fashion can afford to make mistakes, to change its mind overnight, because it's cheap or on sale or found on the curbside like an orphan," explained artist Ruben Toledo (2002). But the trip from street to mainstream may take decades, as it did with hip-hop style—beginning with the music, the look that appropriated items from Tommy Hilfiger and Ralph Lauren collections, to lines such as Phat Farm targeted at hip-hop audiences (Greenberg, 2003c). On a similar trajectory, vintage began its evolution from secondhand discards to street fashion to celebrity icons in the 1970s when consumers mixed finds from flea markets, resale shops, and the family attic. Today, vintage is an industry with trade shows, auctions for couture designs, famous shops in the fashion capitals (like Decades and Lily et Cie in Los Angeles and Resurrection in New York), small shops in nearly every city, and online shops and auctions. Consumers continue to put together unique looks with vintage pieces but today they have to compete with designers shopping for inspiration and celebrity stylists shopping for clients (Hirschberg, 2000).

Although innovative street looks sometimes influence designer collections, for some apparel categories—juniors, contemporary, and denim—virtually all trends derive from street looks. Street looks are influential for casual streetwear and directional for other age groups and categories (Figure 8.13). To research trends, companies send designers to locales expected to furnish inspiration.

The reputation of Tokyo teens for creating and exploring trends led to "cool hunt" tours—a fashion consultant charges $800 a day to guide design teams to top boutiques where tastemakers shop. The design tourists spend $20,000 or more on clothes and accessories to inspire the next season. Some save time by shipping the finds to factories in China where

Figure 8.13

Miu Miu uses old-school street art in this urban-influenced collection.

they are resized for the American and European customer, manufactured, and shipped to stores (Rowley & Tashiro, 2007).

Any city where the focal point for youth is on playful experimentation with fashion can provide trend information. Likely locales feature small, local, non-traditional companies; vibrant street life centered on underground music culture, cafés, and clubs; and shops experimenting with new retail concepts. The retail concepts mix apparel, decorative accessories for the home, and vintage finds in displays reflective of the tastes of the proprietor.

Additional sources for information on street fashion come from forecasting firms, street fashion blogs, websites, and trade shows. Forecasting firms scout for images and supply companies with pictures and video. Trade shows bring together small firms with direct ties to street influences.

Some influences from the street are translated directly into manufacturers' lines if the target consumer is likely to identify with the source and is ready to adopt the innovation. But some influences from the street are too raw or too advanced to move directly into the mainstream. These influences instead trickle up from the street to mainstream, eventually appearing in a modified version. Over time, street influence may have a more general effect in inspiring a shift in mood or emphasis.

TREND IDENTIFICATION, ANALYSIS, AND SYNTHESIS

Forecasters work for clients as consultants and within corporations. The yearly agenda for a trend forecaster might look like this (Schweiss-Hankins, 1998):

❖ travel to Europe to shop key cities, attend international trade shows, and purchase samples—two to four trips per year;

❖ travel to trade shows in cities around the United States—six to eight per year;

❖ travel to attend fabric previews and markets—two to four per year;

❖ purchase trend predictions and color services—four to ten per year;

❖ subscribe to fashion magazines and trade journals to stay up to date on trends and industry news;

❖ attend presentations by fabric mills and other key suppliers;

❖ attend meetings of professional organizations such as color forecasting groups.

The purpose of all this activity is to organize observations, present findings, and suggest ways to implement these ideas into merchandise targeted toward the customer.

The forecaster sifts through the information using a process called **abstracting**, which consists of identifying underlying similarities (or differences) across ensembles and design collections (Fiore & Kimle, 1997). The differences and similarities are frequently expressed as:

❖ the *totality of the look*—minimalist versus extravagant, feminine versus masculine, sexy versus refined;

❖ the *theme or mood*—survivalist versus gothic romanticism;

❖ a *swing* in fashion's pendulum—from flared to narrower legs, from functional to frilly;

❖ the *proportions* of the apparel pieces—hem length or in-seam length for pants, placement of the waistline, width or fullness of the garments;

❖ the *silhouette*—tubular shift, hourglass, blouson, or wedge;

❖ *point of emphasis*—shoulders, bust, waist, derrière, or legs;

❖ the *fit*—body hugging, body skimming, body conscious, or loose;

❖ a *specific detail*—collar, pocket, lapel, waistband treatment, sleeve, or cuff;

❖ *exaggeration in the details*—the size, shape, color, texture, or pattern at the neckline or hem or on the collar, pockets, or belt;

You Be the Forecaster: From the Runway to Main Street

Lauren began her career in retailing where her flair for fashion led to a position as fashion director for a sixteen-store chain in the Midwestern United States. The stores target young women with trendy, fashion-forward apparel presented in a lifestyle concept that covers categories from prom dresses to casual, weekend clothes. As fashion director, Lauren's function is to translate the season's fashion story into one specifically targeted to her store's customers, location, and price points.

Lauren begins by gathering information about trends from the runways, showrooms, and streets. She attends seasonal shows at the Apparel Mart in her part of the country, always looking for new resources to set her stores apart from others in the same market. She also attends trade shows in New York and Los Angeles and researches fashion trends in Europe one or two times each year. From these activities and sources, she synthesizes all the emerging trends into an overall fashion story, seasonal theme, and merchandising direction for the stores. She communicates her findings to the buyers and other executives in the corporate offices in a seminar using visuals of runway shows, store windows, and street fashion. She repeats the seminars for sales associates at each store in the chain at the beginning of the new season just as the new merchandise begins to arrive in the stores.

Lauren's role expanded when the chain decided to launch a private-label line. The goal was to make the selling floor distinctive with fashion products not available at any other stores. The chain contracted with a product development company that would handle all the design and production of the products. Lauren became the fashion link between the two companies. Now, on her trips in the United States and Europe, she looks for fashion ideas that can be adapted for the private-label line.

Use the following questions to review and summarize Lauren's approach.

Information Gathering via Travel: Lauren does not have a large budget for travel, but she can make one trip to Europe and two trips within the United States. When should she go? What should she plan to accomplish on these trips?

Information Gathering Online: To augment her travel, how can she use the Internet in her information gathering?

Merchandising the Store: Stores need a constant influx of merchandise to keep the look fresh and exciting but the selling floor mustn't look disorganized. How can both requirements be met? Lauren's stores use a lifestyle concept carrying everything from casual clothes to prom dresses. How can she use trend merchandising in each of these categories?

- a *specific trim*—beading, embroidery, appliqué, lace, or cording;
- a *specific finding*—buttons, zipper, or snaps;
- a *fabric type*—woven or knit, napped, or metallic;
- *fabric finishing*—gradation in color dyeing, slashing, or abrading;
- a *specific fabric*—transparent fabrics, velvet, or jersey;
- a *color story*—the rise of a dominant color scheme, a shift in mood, or a narrative that ties together the color trends.

The trend may be reported within a product category—dresses or suits —or across categories.

The ability to recognize similarities between garments and between collections is useful in many fashion careers (Fiore & Kimle, 1997):

- Designers, product developers, and buyers abstract across the garments in a group and the groups in a collection so that a visual theme or aesthetic connects the items.
- Sales representatives and marketing executives abstract across the product line to recognize points to be emphasized in selling the line.
- Fashion journalists abstract across multiple collections to identify patterns in the seasonal offerings and visual and symbolic core concepts that can be translated into editorial features.
- Forecasters abstract across multiple collections and across time to identify patterns that indicate fashion change and direction.

✦ CORE CONCEPTS

Forecasters are readers of signs and interpreters of meaning. To recognize core concepts when they appear on the runway and in the street, a forecaster must be familiar with the visual sources and the symbolic meanings of fashion. That means understanding the meaning for the originators of the look and for those who appropriate the look for their own use. It is this deep understanding of signs and symbols and how they are used to create meaning that makes the forecast more accurate, meaningful, and actionable.

Designers are inspired by a myriad of influences from new fabrics to travel experiences, art movements to popular culture, street fashion to the spirit and style of a **muse**—a woman who embodies the ideal look for that designer. Identifying the core concept in an apparel ensemble, a group, a collection, or a season is more than just analyzing the tangible form. It involves active processing of the intangible attributes—references to past fashions or to ethnic costume, sensuous or sexual connotations, and imaginative and expressive aspects. It is the juxtaposition of familiar symbols with exotic ones that creates a *frission*—a signal of something new and different (Craik, 1994).

Some core concepts recur over and over in fashion. Each reappearance contains something new, along with traces of all that has come before. These perennial core concepts can be categorized as follows:

Concepts Referencing the Past. Vera Wang's favorite kind of research is buying vintage dresses and swatch books of rare fabrics and embroideries. She explains, "I find an idea, then I study it, evolve it … you always have to take it to another level" (Talley, 1998). She is one of many designers who are influenced by fashion from the distant and not-so-distant past.

Concepts Referencing Ethnic Sources. Middle Eastern, Asian, Latin, and African cultures have inspired fashion. However, some of the results have been controversial, with some critics seeing African regalia on white models as politically incorrect and on black models as patronizing. Critics locate the fault in a "detached view" that tries to "simulate" a look instead of integrating or synthesizing it into something "authentic" to its time and place (Spindler, 1997). Still, references to ethnic sources continue in collections as homage to the creativity of naïve artists and as shorthand for the symbolic values of naturalness and authenticity.

Concepts Related to Sexuality. Fashion watchers have long identified the outsider sensibilities of prostitutes as a source of fashion innovation (Field, 1970; Simmel, 1904). Stiletto heels, rouge and lipstick, red nail polish, and women smoking cigarettes all began in the subculture of prostitutes and spread to other classes. Expressions of sexuality go with the attitudes of living outside accepted norms and dressing the part with clothes, hairstyles, makeup, and accessories. The specifics are linked to the time—Carole Lombard in a white bias-cut dress in the 1930s, or Kate Moss in a transparent slip dress in the 1990s. Today's fashion picture includes all the symbols for seduction, including partial nudity, red lips and nails, stiletto heels, and the colors red and black. One of the great contrasts for a collection or a season is gradation between lady-like looks and the vamp (a seductress) or tramp (the fallen woman). Another contrast that recurs nearly every season is a contrast between masculine and feminine gender symbols. A man's watch on a slender female wrist, a military uniform stylized for women,

a tuxedo, oxford shirt with a tie—when a woman borrows from a man's wardrobe, the effect is a sexy, slightly subversive look.

Concepts Referencing Sports. American sportswear grew out of fashions designed for an active lifestyle that included playing sports and being a spectator at sporting events (Figure 8.14). Today, all categories of sports from skateboarding to motocross to extreme sports are referenced in collections for casual and streetwear. Famous brands have usurped many of the looks originated by small manufacturers of outdoor gear as apparel for participants in extreme sports. Some consumers favor the authentic sports apparel that they use as multifunctional pieces for recreation and work. Other consumers are satisfied with the active look in name brand lines ("City Slickers," 1998).

Concepts Referencing Appropriateness. Sometimes referred to as "uptown chic" versus "downtown hip," the concept means that some styles connect with certain places and attitudes. An uptown girl wears a jacket, silk T-shirt, and carries a Hermès bag. A

Figure 8.14

Playing sports or just wanting an athletic look keeps consumers buying styles associated with sports from tennis to motocross.

downtown girl wears black jeans, white cotton T-shirt, and high-tech sneakers. Designers tend to relate to one sensibility or another. Labels like "preppy" or "bohemian" reference the establishment, classy and conservative versus the unconventional and rebellious.

Avant-Garde Concepts. Labeled "artsy" by some, original, creative, individual, and surprising innovations are not usually praised or accepted. Avant-garde designers frequently have a point of view that comments on the issues of the day (Betts, 1998). Few really avant-garde styles are sold or worn. However, these ideas sometimes have a long-lasting impact on fashion. Examples include Rudi Gernreich, Paco Rabanne, André Courrèges, and Pierre Cardin in the mid-1960s, as well as Japanese and Belgian designers in the 1990s. Designers who work in the space between art and commerce appeal to the individualists and intellectuals among fashion insiders. Their appeal to a larger public is negligible. Their work often references architecture. Other style points include intricate draping, wrapping, and pleating, asymmetry, unconventional fastenings, unusual fabrics, and sculptural effects.

The Concept of Modernity. The term "modernity" refers to the aesthetic that emerged with technological innovations such as the automobile, telephone, plastics, synthetic dyes, and man-made fibers, and with mass media and entertainment such as the movies. Collections with modernity as a theme strenuously avoid any reference to past fashion. Instead, they focus on sleekness, banishment of frills, functional details, and performance and technical fabrics.

The Concept of Postmodern. Postmodern culture is associated with an emerging global economy, fragmentation in society, extreme eclecticism in the use of signs and symbols, unease with the consequences of modernity, and fluidity in social identities. Collections with a postmodern inclination focus on mixing symbols from different cultures and times or on the protective function of clothing. As designer Jil Sander puts it: "We don't know what the future will bring. We're confused and almost feel lost in our mass consumer society with its global information system" (Cooper, 1998). The design response is to create clothing that is a mad mix of all that has gone before or that functions as a utilitarian personal habitat.

As previously mentioned, abstracting involves recognizing the symbolic and visual core concepts in a garment, a collection, or a season. But the forecaster must go beyond merely recognizing the core concepts to putting them in the perspective of fashion evolution. The forecaster's job is to predict which core concepts represent trends and how those trends are likely to play out in the future.

Whether the forecaster is working inside a company or as a consultant, the reporting from all the travel, observation, and interpretation is a trend presentation. If the company creates branded or private-label lines, the audience will include product developers. If the company is a retailer, the audience will include buyers who select from the lines of national brands of those products that match the trends. Marketing, promotion, and sales staff will attend so that they can present the merchandise within the context of trends. The attendees should leave the presentation understanding how the current trends fit with the company's identity and the customer's lifestyle.

✦ DIFFERENT DESIGNERS WITH THE SAME DESIGN CONCEPT

Designers are presumed to be creators and originators. Their goal is to build a recognized branded image that consumers identify with and feel loyal to. They work independently and cloak their collections in secrecy until they are revealed on the catwalk. How then do designers in a given season so often end up with similar design concepts, themes, and moods for the season?

✧ Zeitgeist

The usual answer to this question is Zeitgeist—trends are a part of the spirit of the times (see

Chapter 1). Listen to designers talking in the same buzzwords about a given season's style, fabrics, and fit. Tomas Maier, designer for Bottega Venata, said that he "got a click on the armor" while visiting a museum. Then how does one explain the articulated sleeves in the Jil Sander show and the chain mail looks in Karl Lagerfeld's designs for Fendi in the same season? Each season some inspiration clicks for designers, "independently but somehow in unison" (Trebay, 2003a).

Synchronicity can also partly be explained because designers attend the same fabric trade shows and those trade shows feature the directions anticipated by leading forecasting agencies (Freeman, 2002).

Designers do inhabit the same cultural strata—read the same periodicals, attend the same parties, know many of the same people, and know which movies and plays are "hot" topics of conversation among the media elite. Because designers are experiencing the same cultural current, it is only natural that these influences will foreshadow fashion change and lead to some similarities in the collections.

✧ Designer's Designer

A few designers in each era are highly original talents who experiment with new design directions. Paul Poiret, Coco Chanel, Madeleine Vionnet, Charles James, Christian Dior, Yves Saint Laurent, and André Courrèges were such designers in their eras. Christian Lacroix's 1987 debut with his pouf skirts and madcap mixes of color and pattern introduced something new and directional. The emergence of Japanese designers in the late 1980s played an influential role in setting the design agenda for the early 1990s. Beginning in the late 1990s, Ann Demeulemeester, Martin Margiela, and Helmut Lang played this role. Recently, Isabel Toledo has been held in this regard. These are the designer's designers—the ones who influence other designers.

Today's version of the breed creates clothes appreciated by only the most intellectual of the fashion insiders, but they exert tremendous influence on other designers following their lead.

Suzy Menkes (2003a, 2008b), fashion doyenne of the *International Herald Tribune*, pointed out one such designer: Azzedine Alaïa. She challenged observers to "take any look at the collection that the designer showed in Paris in January and you could find its double offered for the autumn-winter season" on other runways. Whether it is "homage or just copycat designing," Menkes sees the designer as exceptionally influential for other designers.

✧ Trial Balloons

Each collection and each season is a learning experience for a designer. The designer sends out a collection and gets feedback from the press, the professional buyers, and the clients. Plans for the next season's collection mix design influences with the response to the designer's most recent collections, and the reaction of press and merchants to the most recent collections of other designers.

Couture designers are in the business of innovation, but ideas evolve over time. Revolutionary revisions like Dior's New Look in 1947 and Courrèges' future-oriented modernism in the 1965 collection are rare. Instead, new fashions first make their appearance as trial balloons, as tentative explorations of a new direction or a new look. Couture is a low-risk way to try out an idea and to judge the reaction, because the designer makes only one sample for the runway and custom-makes any that sell rather than committing to larger-scale production (Freeman, 2002). When Yvan Mispelaere, couture designer for Féraud, showed girlish collections, his ideas did not catch on except with Marc Jacobs, who showed very similar looks the season after. Part of the pressure to copy comes from the necessity to produce several collections a year—a pressure that translates into a designer finding ideas wherever he or she can (Horyn, 2001).

When an idea debuts, the designer more fully exploits the new approach in subsequent collections. Meanwhile, others have recognized the innovation, transposed it, developed variations, and amplified it. All these modifications are individual acts of creation based on that initial seed. Together they coalesce into a trend recognizable across collections in a given season. These similarities arise because designers must assert their individuality within the constraints of what their competitors are doing and the spirit of the times (Lipovetsky, 1994).

✧ Knockoffs

The designers' aesthetic is translated to lower price points in three ways:

- ❧ the **counterfeit**—a close copy passed off as authentic (Figure 8.15);
- ❧ the knockoff—a close copy of another company's original but one that does not carry the originator's label;
- ❧ an interpretation of the look—an adaptation that attempts to mimic the aesthetics, not copy the style exactly.

Counterfeiting is big business and is increasing exponentially, according to the Counterfeiting Luxury Report conducted by the UK legal firm Davenport Lyons. According to the firm's findings, it has become increasingly acceptable for consumers to own counterfeit merchandise, and nearly two-thirds of respondents indicated that they were proud to have bought fake luxury clothing, footwear, watches or jewelry, and were willing to boast about it to friends and family—a worrying shift in consumer behavior. Counterfeiting, a crime of theft, also damages company reputation, affects sales, and reduces the value of intellectual property like trademarks ("Analysis," 2007). Direct transmission of runway shows, digital photography, the Internet, and other new technologies are making the job of the counterfeiter easier (Murphy, 2000).

Copying is a deeply ingrained historical practice in the fashion industry. An article in the *Saturday Evening Post* from 1963 states flatly that design "piracy is not the exception in the industry, it dominates it," and illustrates the point with a running industry gag, "At least I changed the buttons" (Poling, 1963). Some designers, even those with big names, copy other designers (Agins, 1994). Ralph Lauren was found

Figure 8.15

Even small-business entrepreneurs, such as designers and boutique owners, can be targets for knockoffs.

guilty and fined by a French commercial court for "counterfeiting" a long, sleeveless tuxedo dress from Yves Saint Laurent's fall 1992 couture collection (Betts, 1994; Ingrassia, 1994). Legal cases are being brought to protect ownership of the way a product looks or is presented under the definition of **trade dress**, a form of trademark infringement (Young, 1998). In these cases, the firm with an original design is attempting to prevent others from trading on its reputation, image, and customer's goodwill by presenting similar goods. Trade dress is an expansion of the trademark law that refers to the design or appearance of a good or service. However, these cases are hard to win when the product is apparel. When children's clothing manufacturer Samara Brothers sued Wal-Mart for copying its line using trade dress, they lost because they could not prove that consumers connected the distinctive look of their line with its origin (their company) (Davczyk, 2000). Trademark law grants use of a particular mark to identify a particular company and its products. Ownership of a trademark is justified because it minimizes consumer confusion about the origin of a product and preserves the goodwill the company has established with that consumer. A word, term, symbol, or device can be trademarked.

The design for Levi's pocket, first trademarked more than 100 years ago, has become the front line for legal battles. The company has filed more trademark infringement lawsuits than any other large corporation in order to remove copies from stores (Barbaro & Creswell, 2007). Shoe designer Christian Louboutin has filed a series of lawsuits against high-profile companies such as Yves Saint Laurent in an attempt to protect its use of red-lacquered outsoles on women's dress shoes as its own trade dress (Burchart, 2013). In September 2012, a court ruled that Louboutin's use of red soles had a secondary meaning that consumers recognized as a trademark, but the court extended protection only to shoes that had a contrasting, non-red upper – monochromatic red shoes with a red upper and a red outsole were not protected and any shoe designer could sell them.

For companies that specialize in knockoffs— the translation of high-priced fashion into cheaper versions—technology has speeded up the process. Simonia Fashion, founded in 1980, is one of hundreds of companies copying runway looks for fast-fashion retailers. Seema Anand selects a look from the shows covered online at Style.com, e-mails the picture to her factory in Jaipur, India, and delivers the knockoff months ahead of the designer version (sometimes in as little as 14 days). The company maintains a showroom in New York and has sales of $20 million, about 80 percent in knockoffs for private labels for department stores like Bloomingdale's and Macy's and chains like Forever 21 (Wilson, 2007b).

Runway designers aren't the only ones being knocked off. Dana Foley and Anna Corinna started their partnership as sellers at a flea market and turned their eye for updating vintage into a fashion company with a store on the Lower East Side in New York and one on Melrose Avenue in Los Angeles with $20 million in annual sales. When Paris Hilton wore a Foley & Corinna flowery dress (price: $400) on *David Letterman*, a fast-fashion chain began selling a $40 copy. The designers went from "under the radar" to publicized for being knocked off—not a plus when customers returned originals, preferring instead the copies. What can these entrepreneurs do? Nothing legally, since clothing designs are not protected as intellectual property. "We would kick people out of the store who we knew were knocking us off," Ms. Foley said. "One guy spit at Anna's feet when she wouldn't let him buy a dress. He said, 'But I could copy Marc Jacobs!'—like it was a compliment" (Wilson, 2008a).

Top designers like Nicole Miller and Diane von Furstenberg, president of the Council of Fashion Designers of America (CFDA), have tried to amend copyright laws to provide 3 years' protection for designs of apparel, handbags, footwear, belts, and eyeglass frames and would establish penalties for those who copy (Ellis, 2007), an effort backed by the American Bar Association, but so far no standards have been established (Lynch, 2008). The problem is how to define knockoffs versus trends (looks seen everywhere simultaneously, which are in the public domain). Further blurring occurred when name designers created "cheap chic collections" for mass marketers and fast-fashion chains (Wilson, 2007d). Although most players agree that original ideas deserve protection, designers and manufacturers disagree on how to do it. Manufacturers expect higher costs for research into design ownership, higher legal fees, and delays delivering apparel to stores (Wilson, 2008b). But for designers, timing is the key issue—when knockoffs of potentially best-selling designs arrive in retail stores before the designers' own creations, they lose sales.

✦ TREND DYNAMICS: LABEL, COATTAIL, AND FLOW

Of the many ideas on the runway, only a few are adopted by consumers and become a trend. In the first 100 years of modern fashion, this adoption came from designers' clients. Some fashion counts from that period show that only one-tenth of runway designs were produced for clients (Lipovetsky, 1994). The rest were neglected, forgotten, and replaced by a new crop of proposed fashion ideas in the next season. The gatekeeper role initially played by clients was taken over by merchants and by the fashion press. Merchants now decide which fashion ideas will be available to consumers, which will be made in small numbers, and which in volume. The fashion press defines trends by deciding which of the many ideas on the runway will be promoted in the pages of trade publications, newspapers, and fashion magazines.

In the past, collections could be categorized as either "editorial" (providing a hook for telling a story or creating a fantasy) or "retail" (wearable, targeted for a consumer segment). Now, the press and the merchants tend to be in sync on the looks that will be tested further in the marketplace (Socha, 1998b). Editors know that readers buy from the pages of the magazine and that everything shown must be available at retail price. Both magazines and stores cover established designers and new talents. More than ever, editors and store executives share information—key fashion stores invite editors to see what they are buying and creating in private-label merchandise for a season, and store fashion directors carefully analyze the press's approach. Designers have to be realistic about appealing to both the needs of retailers and the press.

Trends, once identified, must be given a name, label, or slogan that can be used as a popular identifier (Meyersohn & Katz, 1957). If the name is synchronous with the spirit of the times, original, and catchy, it will speed the trend on its way. With the labeling comes a surge in interest. This surge of interest catches the attention of people in the industry who recognize the potential of the trend and rush to produce it in their own lines. This phenomenon is called the coattail effect. Popular at first with a relatively small sphere of "fashionistas," the trend will pass from group to group across social boundaries of age, income, and lifestyle—a process called flow.

✦ TREND ANALYSIS AND SYNTHESIS

Many variations of apparel styles are available in the marketplace simultaneously. Almost all are "marked" with meaning. An unmarked apparel item is the most generic of its kind. When color or styling is added, the apparel becomes a marker for some identity. Think of a white T-shirt. How many meanings can be attached to a simple white T-shirt depending on the way it is worn, its fit, what it is paired with, and the occasion when it is worn? People are symbol users and apparel offers a stage for that ability.

Each person must make decisions about what styles to pluck from the marketplace for personal use. These decisions include those about hair, cosmetics, clothing, and accessories. Being anti-fashion or no-fashion is as much a decision as being fashionable. People make these decisions every day when they dress. Because the decisions are based partly on demographics, lifestyle, and situation and partly on personality and taste, a certain consistency emerges for each individual—a personal signature style.

People in all likelihood are a member of a style tribe because of where they live, how they make a living, or how they choose to spend their leisure time. Groups evolve a way of dressing that signals the group's identity and aesthetic code.

Because there exists an almost infinite universe of style variations, the possibilities for individual expression and group identification are also infinite. Yet, people's styles can be classified into general categories. Combining styles under an umbrella definition makes it possible for designers to act as style tribe leaders, specialty stores to develop retail concepts that appeal to certain customers and not to others, and marketers to target specific consumer audiences. Marketers call these classification schemes **consumer segmentation** (see Chapter 9).

Analysis and synthesis are the two faces of forecasting. In **analysis**, a phenomenon is dissected to achieve a more complete understanding of its components. **Synthesis** is a creative reintegration of the parts. In fashion forecasting that means:

* an accurate reading of the trend in all its subtle aspects;
* matching the trend with the consumer profiles most likely to adopt it initially;
* matching the trend with the product category, price point, and retail concept most likely to complement it.

Finally, the forecaster hypothesizes about what it will take to energize and accelerate the flow of the trend across consumer segments.

Chapter Summary

Fashion has evolved rapidly in the modern era of fashion, which spans from the mid-nineteenth century to the present. Although each development can be tied to a certain time period, the impact of those innovations is still applicable in today's fashion industry. Today, forecasters and fashion consumers have more access to information than ever before in the form of blogs and other online resources. This access provides insight to subcultural groups such as style tribes as well as up-to-the-minute fashion show images and industry information, which requires forecasters to analyze and synthesize the vast amount of information available to them into core concepts which become wearable trends. As our global society becomes increasingly more connected, the influence of modern fashion capitals such as Britain, France, Italy, Japan, Belgium, and the United States are complemented by the increasing influence of secondary fashion capitals with their specialty markets. While inspiration can come from anywhere, and designers who have their finger on the pulse of the Zeitgeist may often have similar ideas, the industry is currently trying to protect designer trademarks and trade dress from piracy in the form of counterfeit or knockoff merchandise, but guidelines for such protections have not yet been set.

Key Terms and Concepts

Abstracting	Modernity
Analysis	Muse
Blogs	Postmodern(ism)
Chambre Syndicale	Regional markets
Consumer segmentation	Showrooms
Core concept	Style tribe
Counterfeit	Synthesis
Designer ready-to-wear	Trade dress
Haute couture	Trade shows

Discussion Questions

The Modern Eras of Fashion: How do you think the fourth era of modern fashion will be characterized? What developments in society and technology will influence fashion in the next 10 years and how will they influence it?

Style Tribes: What style tribes have you seen in person before? What traits do you think a style tribe such as punks has in common with a more organized group that shares a common aesthetic such as a sorority? What clothing cues do members of each group who don't know each other use to recognize one another?

Influential Designers and Countries: Who are your favorite designers and what country are they from? Do their signature styles reflect the influences that their home countries are known for? Which country's signature style is your favorite overall and why?

Core Concepts: Which core concepts (e.g., the past, ethnic sources, or sports) do you reference the most frequently in your own style? Why do you prefer those concepts over others, and how do you feel they represent your personality?

Counterfeiting: Do you own any counterfeit merchandise? Do you think there is anything wrong with buying counterfeit products? How do counterfeit goods impact designers and brands? What do you think would happen to the price and the prestige level of your preferred brands if counterfeit merchandise was totally eliminated from the marketplace?

Forecasting Activities

Business Breakthroughs and Classic Designers. Investigate the design and marketing of fashion by influential designers like Paul Poiret, Jean Patou, Coco Chanel, Elsa Schiaparelli, Pierre Cardin, and Yves Saint Laurent to discover practices that were revolutionary in their time but are now commonplace ways of doing business. What revolutionary ways of doing business today will become accepted practice in the future?

Systematic Updates. Develop a bookmarked list of websites related to fashion—sites on designers and their collections, online fashion magazines, sites promoting trade shows, blogs, and sites associated with fashion reporting (see Resource Pointers for suggestions). Group the sites according to when they are updated—daily, weekly, monthly. Read these sites on a regular basis for increased knowledge of fashion and trend identification.

What's a Copy? Monitor fashionista.com and counterfeitchic.com for reports of knockoffs. Both sites feature side-by-side photographs of originals and copies. What defines an original? How can it be described in obtaining (future) copyright protection?

Editing the Avant-Garde. Using online sources that report on fashion, capture images from two or three of the most avant-garde collections from couture and ready-to-wear (see the Resource Pointers at the end of this chapter for suggestions). Mentally strip away the theatrical aspects of the garment. Are there wearable clothes underneath? What styles from these avant-garde collections could be reproduced at lower price points for consumers? What types of consumers are likely to relate to the aesthetics of these fashion looks?

Fashion Capitals. Read Internet coverage on each of the fashion capitals—Paris, Milan, London, and New York—to analyze the visual signature (see Resource Pointers). Does each fashion capital have its own style niche? Which designers epitomize each fashion capital? Which designers are outside the tradition of each fashion capital? What are the aesthetic commonalities between designers of the same nationality—American, French, Italian, British, Belgian, German, and Japanese? What cultural factors contribute to these commonalities?

Deconstructing a Designer's Core Concepts. Select a designer and deconstruct the visual and symbolic core concepts in the most recent collections. Prepare a presentation board showing the original source referenced in the collection and the translation of that source by the designer. Compare to other designers referencing similar sources.

Resource Pointers

Online fashion show sources:
www.firstview.com

The Moment (fashion, design, food, travel blog)

New York Times: www.nytimes.com/pages/fashion/index.html

On the Runway
www.style.com/vogue

www.WWD.com

Fashion magazines and news:
www.businessoffashion.com

www.fashiontelevision.com

www.hintmag.com

www.lucire.com

www.racked.com

www.refinery29.com

www.videofashion.com

Fashion week calendars:
www.infomat.com

www.mbfashionweek.com

Fashion search engines:
ShopStyle: www.shopstyle.com

Style Hunter: www.stylehunter.com

Portals for fashion information:
www.fashion.com

www.fashioninformation.com

Fashion Infomat: www.infomat.com

Fashion Week Daily:
www.fashionweekdaily.com

Note: For vintage clothing sites, see Resource Pointers in Chapter 3.

PART THREE

MARKETPLACE DYNAMICS

> I am in the fashion business but I feel when I design I'm in the business of trying to figure out what people want and why they want it. One of the main reasons that I do work in the fashion industry is because I'm intrigued about why people choose certain clothes to reflect their mood.
>
> —*Stella McCartney*

9
CONSUMER RESEARCH

OBJECTIVES

◆ Recognize the relationships between consumer research and product development, brand awareness and loyalty, and retailing

◆ Distinguish the connection between consumer research and forecasting

◆ Compare the methods for answering questions about consumers' preferences for new products and marketing initiatives

◆ Outline current views on demographics and consumer segmentation and their relationship to forecasting consumer demand

BUSINESS BEGINS AND ENDS WITH THE CONSUMER

Every forecast begins with the customer—by observing their adjustments to the marketplace and noting the unexpected ways customers adjust the marketplace to their lifestyles and preferences. Consumer research figures importantly in decisions about product development, brand marketing, and retailing.

Product development had traditionally been production driven—a "push" system because fiber, textile, apparel manufacturers, and retailers pushed products through the system toward the consumer. Consumer choice was limited to a predetermined merchandise mix. To succeed, a company competed against the consumer's reluctance to make a purchase and against other producers in the same category. Advances in production technology made it faster and more efficient to produce more products. The "push" system shaped retailing—new styles were introduced seasonally, selling first at full retail price, and then closed out in a flurry of markdowns at the end of the season. In this system consumers participated only when they made a purchase, and that decision was reported in the sales figures.

As apparel executives realized that shoppers were more knowledgeable, demanding, and independent than ever before, attention shifted to a "pull" system—consumers' demands began to pull those products that they wanted to purchase through the fiber, textile, and apparel product development process and into retail stores. By the late 1980s, the apparel market was described as "consumer driven" in recognition of this principle. Manufacturers had to shift from products that could be made conveniently in volume to products shaped by consumer input. In such an environment, only a continuous flow of consumer information can shape a product. Consumer research became a priority as a way to tap into shifting consumer preferences. Product development has become a team activity that assimilates the expertise of consumer researchers, marketers, merchandisers, and production people. Conducting studies, translating consumer input into specifications, and delivering product pretested with consumers became the new paradigm as talking to customers replaced trying to second-guess them.

Evolution toward a demand-activated system had four waves (Lewis, 1996a):

❖ *The First Wave: Building an Information Infrastructure.* The first wave began in the early 1980s when large companies began experimenting with information technologies and building the infrastructure for a "pull" system.

❖ *The Second Wave: Time Efficiencies and Inventory Reduction.* Quick Response (QR) manufacturing initiatives characterized the second wave with emphasis on efficiencies, cost reduction, reduced cycle times, and inventory reduction through shared communication between firms in the supply chain.

❖ *The Third Wave: Focusing on the Consumer.* By the mid-1990s, leading companies were in the third wave, focusing on the consumer as the "center of the universe," partnering with other firms in the supply chain to deliver maximum response to consumer needs, and reaping the benefits in increased market share and profitability.

❖ *The Fourth Wave: Markets of One.* The fourth wave arrived when suppliers defined "markets of one" and segmenting down to the individual level (Pine, Peppers, & Rogers, 1995). With this approach, supply chain partnerships deliver not just replenishment of desired products in a timely way but actually anticipate consumers' needs and develop new products to satisfy them. The demand-activated "pull" approach places more emphasis on creating, producing, and delivering the right products for consumers.

Together the second and third waves emphasized timely stocking of goods, a continuous flow of information, and accelerated schedules. During this phase, response time between an order to a manufacturer and delivery to a retailer's distribution center shrank from a few months in the 1970s to a few weeks by the 1990s. New team approaches required the breaking down of functional departments and the updating of computer networking capabilities within companies. Partnerships between textile producers, apparel manufacturers, and retailers created challenges. Coordinating development schedules and facilitating the information flow between partners meant faster product development and manufacturing and continuous release of new products. The characteristics of the second and third waves highlight the need for reliable and valid forecasting of consumer demand.

Relatively few products sell in mass numbers, and many others have limited appeal, making them, until recently, non-commercial. These niche products can now be profitably marketed via the Internet because the location of producer and buyer are irrelevant and the aggregation of many small sales leads to profit. Even the line between producer and buyer blurs when consumers participate in the design of the products. Bloggers specializing in one of the many niches become sources of information, even functioning as trendsetters when they attract enough readers. With more access to products, consumers become more experimental in seeking products that help personalize and customize their world (Williams, 2007).

The appeal of personalizing choice and customizing purchases extends from food to music, TV to fashion. In restaurants, customers are choosing multiple small plates—such as tapas, sushi, dim sum, and appetizers—rather than the traditional entrée so they can enjoy multiple tastes across several dishes. Music playlists are personalized on iPods, and DVR, on-demand service, and services such as Hulu or Netflix and Redbox make television and movie watching possible at the viewer's convenience (Severson, 2007). Apparel companies are overturning traditional business practices to involve customers in product creation:

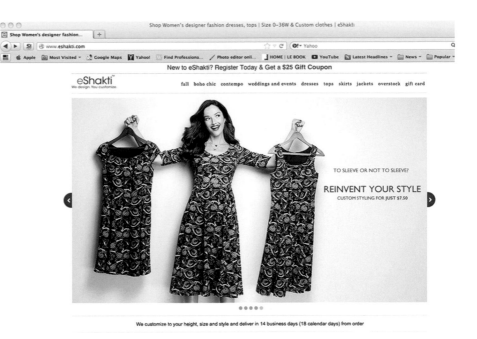

Figure 9.1

eShakti, a mass-customization online women's retailer, specializes in clothing from sizes 0 to 36W. The company offers custom styling and sizing on almost all its products, and each style is cut to order.

❖ Design-it-yourself footwear allows wearers to customize the style, color, and fit of their athletic shoes and the practice is moving into fashion footwear (Olson, 2007).

❖ The chains American Girl, Build-A-Bear, and Color Me Mine pottery studios have popularized the concept of interactive customer design and that concept has been applied to eShakti, a mass-customization online women's retailer founded in 1999 that specializes in clothing from sizes 0 to 36W. The company offers custom styling and sizing on almost all its products, and each style is cut to order (Figure 9.1), which keeps warehouse costs low. Founder B. G. Krishnan emphasizes the importance of consumer research: "In terms of fashion design, we present a unique look, based on choice of fabric, colors and hand-embellishments and our trendy styling. What helps us maintain our competitive advantage is the research we do as well as the customer advisory body that previews and post-reviews our products from time to time."

❖ The company Threadless runs design competitions in an online social network where members offer ideas for T-shirts, vote on which ones are best, and then order them for $15. A company with no designers, models, sales force, or retail distribution increases revenue at the rate of 500 percent each year, keeps costs low, and never faces markdowns. Every shirt sells out because the community members decided what they wanted in advance (Chafkin, 2008).

THE VOICE OF THE CONSUMER

The opportunity to build consumer satisfaction comes each time the individual considers a purchase (Figure 9.2). To succeed, manufacturers and retailers must make clear the connection between the consumer, the product, and the situation. One approach is to bring the voice of the consumer into product development. The process begins with a series of questions:

❖ What creates customer acceptance?
❖ What are the consumer's expectations?
❖ Is the product competitive on desired attributes?
❖ Does the product surprise customers with exciting attributes?

Figure 9.2
The opportunity to build brand loyalty comes whenever a consumer considers a purchase.

When a company focuses on delivering quality, the effort is only worthwhile in terms of sales and **brand loyalty**—purchase and repurchase of the brand again and again—if consumers understand and appreciate the value-added attributes. The process continues with a series of questions about consumers' perception of quality:

* Does the product over- or under-deliver expected attributes?
* How will quality influence performance or appearance?
* Does the customer really appreciate the differences in quality?

The voice of the customer is translated by a multifunction product development team into operational terms—specifications, process planning, and process control.

It sounds easy—just ask customers what they expect from products and have product developers write specifications to fit those responses. But a list of product attributes is not enough. Even with a list, it is a leap to assume that the more an attribute is present, the more satisfied the customer. When asked, consumers attempt to generate a rational, socially acceptable explanation for behavior or preferences (i.e., reading and following care labels, careful prepurchase searches for value) even when these behaviors are really a minor part of decision making.

Some attributes are expected but do not significantly contribute to customer satisfaction (e.g., buttons are expected to stay on, seams are expected to hold together). Others are desirable and customers say they make an important contribution to satisfaction (i.e., ease of care, accurate labeling). And yet others, the unspoken motivators, are exciting attributes consumers do not expect but that increase customer satisfaction when they are present (e.g., design details for a "good" price, flattering colors, novelty embellishment) (Snyder, 1991). More important than a list of attributes is an understanding of the dynamics of consumer/product/brand interactions—the consumer of products is really a consumer of images, of products *as* image. The trick to anticipating consumer demand is

discovering what "bonds" a consumer to a product (Pine, 1993).

The product may be right, but if the experience of buying it is not, consumers will not buy. Recreational shopping—browsing and window-shopping, leisurely visits to the mall for fun—has been crowded out of the American schedule by other activities. Retail has polarized into the minimal-service, wide-selection warehouse formats and the high-end, entertainment format stores. Conventional department stores are left in the middle.

Ninety-four percent of US Internet users also shop online (a figure slightly lower than Britain, Germany, Japan, and South Korea). Purchase of fashion is second only to books with these shoppers who value 24/7 access and convenience. Although they were at first reluctant to participate, designers and luxury brands have now found a consumer base for their collections at sites that specialize in exceptional customer service, same-day delivery, and free returns (Horton, 2008a). Consumers are savvy about selecting the preferred experience— one that is functional, fulfills the need, and is value-oriented versus one that is creative, emotional, and "high touch," where the experience is more important than the price.

Spending behavior can be classified into four types (Seckler, 2002c):

* *Impulse buying,* often associated with the thrill of the hunt at off-price retailers or online auction sites such as eBay.
* *Routine purchases* at mass merchants that provide pricing and convenience.
* *Lifestyle-based shopping* at retailers that carefully define the target audience.
* *Custom products* (made-to-order products) or personalized services.

Findings from a survey of more than 2,000 female respondents with minimum household income of $35,000 (a figure that was balanced in order to be representative of census data) showed how shoppers discriminate among shopping alternatives. In the category of casual clothes, department stores and discounters each

Profile: Kate Spade New York

Kate Spade New York is a brand that experienced massive levels of popularity in the 1990s, only to find that it had not kept pace with the changing nature of fashion and was in danger of becoming irrelevant by the mid-2000s. By 2005, the brand was down to only $84 million in net sales, and in 2006, Kate Spade sold her brand to Liz Claiborne, Inc. (which eventually changed its name to Fifth & Pacific) (Mellery-Pratt, 2013). Then, something extraordinary happened: its management team, led by chief executive officer Craig Leavitt and chief creative officer Deborah Lloyd, and guided by the consumer research the brand conducted, completely turned the company around. In just 5 years, the company has jumped from $126 million in net sales to finishing 2013 with approximately $750 million in net sales (Mellery-Pratt, 2013).

Craig Leavitt intended to have a career in politics, but his plans changed when he was recruited by the Bloomingdale's executive training program, but he still draws on his past in his current role as CEO of Kate Spade: "I do think there are a lot of parallels [between politics and fashion] because in the end, being in our industry, it's about understanding what the consumer wants, and hopefully, in politics, it's about understanding what your constituents want," he said. "In the end, it's so much about working and understanding people and what they're trying to accomplish" (Craig, 2013).

It is this understanding of Kate Spade's target customer that is the core of its turnaround. Upon joining Kate Spade, one of the first things Deborah Lloyd did was hire the Redscout branding firm, which conducted 3 months of consumer research, including photographing all the women it could find carrying Spade bags in New York and Los Angeles in order to create a collage that personified the Kate Spade customer (Timberlake, 2011). Their research did not end with simple observation; the company became dedicated to pursuing understanding of their customers' preferences for categories as diverse as books and hotels. The brand defines its ideal customer's personality as "culturally curious, quick, playful, spirited and chic" (Lazarus, 2014). The resulting customer profile determined by this in-depth research was extremely precise. "[The Kate Spade woman] lives in a ten-floor walkup, but has champagne glasses. She doesn't take hours doing all of her holiday cards perfectly, she has a glitter party with her friends," said chief marketing officer Mary Beach (Mellery-Pratt, 2013). Their customer research also resulted in their brand positioning: that "Kate Spade inspires you to lead a more interesting life" (Lazarus, 2014).

This position has formed the basis for three key strategic decisions that changed the company's direction and made it into the powerhouse it is today. These three strategies were product category expansion beyond handbags, a multi-channel approach that includes both direct-to-consumer and wholesale businesses, and international expansion (Mellery-Pratt, 2013).

Kate Spade's experience with customer research really benefited the company when it came time to develop the new brand Saturday, which was designed to meet the wants and needs of a younger customer than that of the Kate Spade brand. According to Kyle Andrew, SVP and brand director for Kate Spade Saturday, "We know the Saturday consumer acts differently than older consumers who shop at Kate Spade New York. Our target customer lives online, is addicted to social media and wants access to information very quickly and easily" (Fiorletta, 2013).

Further research on Saturday's target customer was collected through in-house studies and focus groups, and indicated that younger shoppers do not require as much personal service as the typical Kate Spade customer. As Andrew says, "Shoppers at Kate Spade New York, a luxury brand, want a high degree of service from in-store associates. They want to be looked after and treated well, and seek suggestions from store associates. Saturday brand consumers, however, are more independent and move faster throughout the store" (Fiorletta, 2013). The brand met these consumer presences by merging its website and brick-and-mortar store and by replacing paper signage with in-store iPads that have all of the information a consumer could want about a product. Not only does this action make the retailer more responsive to its target customer, but it also saves them a lot of money by avoiding printing costs (Fiorletta, 2013). By staying constantly attuned to its consumers' wants and needs, analysts predict that Kate Spade will reach the $2 billion mark for net sales in just a few years.

Sources:
Craig, Victoria (2013, December 17). Kate Spade's CEO: What it takes to make a brand sparkle. Retrieved from Fox Business.

Fiorletta, Alicia (2013, April 5). Tablets help Kate Spade Saturday optimize brand experiences. Retrieved from Retail Touchpoints.

Lazarus, Nancy (2014, March 26). Kate Spade's CMO: "The customer has a voice and so do we." Retrieved from mediabistro.com

Mellery-Pratt, Robin (2013, November 26). Can Kate Spade become a $4 billion business? Retrieved from Business of Fashion.

Timberlake, Cotten (2011, February 24). Kate Spade's got a brand new bag. Retrieved from Bloomberg Businessweek Magazine.

attract more than 30 percent of shoppers, whereas specialty stores and online/catalog sources split another 30 percent. When shopping for dresses, suits, and eveningwear, department stores are the clear choices with more than 40 percent choosing this option; specialty stores were second with almost 20 percent. Department stores, specialty stores, and discounters were about equal as sources for intimate apparel and accessories. In all categories except casual apparel, which stayed the same, Internet/catalog gained share over the previous year's figures ("How," 2008).

Research keeps manufacturers and retailers in touch with consumers as part of business planning and decision making. Consumer research falls into two general categories: qualitative and quantitative. In **qualitative research**, the researcher listens to consumer talk or observes consumers in natural settings and reports findings as descriptions of consumer types or categories of behavior. In **quantitative research**, the researcher conducts surveys or experiments with a group of consumers—the sample—in hopes of understanding something about a larger group—the population with similar characteristics—and reports results in numerical data.

Consumers under age 25 are frequently the focus of qualitative and quantitative research because they have tremendous spending power, show greater interest in fashion than other age groups, and are influential in establishing trends. This is not to say that people's personalities change drastically and they lose interest in fashion; with age comes more life experience and new responsibilities which result in a change in our needs and values that in turn impact our buying behavior. Henrik Vejlgaard (2008) sums up this change in values as we age like this: "at age 30, a woman will be interested in new clothes; at 40, she will be interested in new clothes for her children; at 60, she will be interested in the new beauty products for 'mature women'; and at 80, she will be interested in hearing aids in the most trendsetting design" (p. 77). Although young consumers readily participate in market research, some critics see them (especially teens) as a vulnerable population that can be exploited by researchers and the companies that employ them. "Youths don't always understand the deeper implications of marketing studies and experiments—they don't necessarily get why they are drawn to certain products," contends journalist and author Alissa Quart (Seckler, 2003a). She is not the first to criticize the merchandising of teen culture. The PBS Frontline documentary *The Merchants of Cool* argued that turning teen culture into popular culture denied teens' ability to authentically express themselves and create their own lifestyles (Goodman & Dretzen 2001). But given the constantly evolving and contradictory consumer, research offers one of the few windows manufacturers and retailers have into understanding what customers want and why they want it.

✦ ASKING "WHAT" AND "WHY" QUESTIONS

Qualitative research is used to ask "what" and "why" questions—questions that probe the consumer's relationship to a style, product, product category, or the marketplace. Such research falls into two general types: interviews and observation.

Focus groups are used to interview small groups of consumers. For a deeper understanding of consumer motivations, researchers use a lengthy one-on-one **depth interview**. In both focus groups and depth interviews, researchers (often psychologists or psychotherapists) use **projective techniques** to allow people to reveal themselves in non-threatening ways. Participants may be asked to select a picture that corresponds to their feelings about a product, brand, or shopping situation. Or, participants may create a collage representing the personality of a brand and then discuss how they feel about the brand and how they imagine the brand feels about them. In this way, people can project deeply held emotions through visual imagery, making it accessible for discussion (Masterson, 1994).

For some researchers, consumers' actions speak louder than words. Consumers cannot always verbalize what they do and why they do it. And consumer actions can contradict responses given in an interview or on a survey. Observation allows researchers to study consumers' behavior directly.

✧ Focus Group Research

Focus groups are a method of research based on informal, uncensored talk about products in a group interview setting. Designed to help companies become more responsive to consumer needs and wants, focus groups help companies become more competitive. Successful focus group discussion elicits consumer perceptions, opinions, beliefs, and attitudes as they relate to the product.

Urban Outfitters and Anthropologie are specialty chains that are owned by the same company but target different audiences (Figure 9.3). Urban Outfitters targets adults 18 to 30 years old with apparel, accessories, and home decor. This audience was described by the company as "the upscale homeless" because they left their parents' homes to live in dorms or apartments. Anthropologie's customer is older—a 30- to 45-year-old woman with a husband, family, and a home. Both chains carry branded and private-label products and sell through multiple channels: catalogs, websites, retail stores. The company uses regular focus groups to find out what customers like about the stores and the products. As one executive explained: "We believe the customer is the only

(a)

(b)

Figure 9.3

Urban Outfitters and Anthropologie are owned by the same company but target different audiences. Urban Outfitters (a) targets 18- to 30-year-old adults—an audience described by the company as "the upscale homeless" because they have left their parents' homes to live in a dorm or an apartment. Anthropologie (b) targets an older customer—30 to 45 years old—with a husband, family, and home. The company uses focus groups to find out what customers like about the stores and the products.

real vote that counts, and we listen to them regularly. We do get feedback, and we're able to respond to that feedback" ("Urban," 2007).

When Nike wanted to explore the future direction of track apparel (and by extension ideas for women's activewear) the company sent a designer and a merchandise manager to conduct a 2-hour focus group with eight Oregon State University female track athletes. The eight runners were asked to discuss the comfort and design of their favorite running gear and to react to prototype garments ("Nike Focus Group," 2008). The focus group researcher uses the interviews to identify all the reasons that motivate acceptance or rejection of a product. Then the researcher can generalize from those ideas to the ideas in the population. But the researcher will not be able to estimate how many people hold those views (McQuarrie & McIntyre, 1988).

The **focus group moderator** works with the company sponsoring the research to develop a set of questions to serve as a guide to the discussion. Focus group participants are recruited, usually by a market research firm

that maintains a database of consumer contacts, and participants often receive a monetary incentive for participation. Participants must meet a set of guidelines defined by the sponsoring company. Usually these guidelines involve age, gender, income level, and recent apparel-purchase activity.

A focus group interview consists of eight to twelve participants who are typical customers of the brand that meet with the moderator in a specially designed room equipped with audio and video recording equipment (Figure 9.4). The participants are told that the session is being recorded for later analysis. Often the client views the sessions through a one-way mirror. The research may include multiple groups at different locations. Although it involves extra expense, some focus group research merits interviews in different parts of the country to determine if consumers hold different views depending on location.

Moderators need a way to break the ice so that participants feel free to talk about feelings and experiences. Some groups begin with participants sharing stories about their latest

Figure 9.4

Focus groups can provide apparel companies with consumer insights that can't be observed from sales reports.

shopping trip, the nicest sales associate they ever met, or their favorite outfit. Sometimes participants are asked to assemble a collage illustrating who they are or their relationship to the product and share it at the beginning of the session. Such activities help reduce a group's inhibitions about talking about feelings and lifestyle practices.

To help the discussion along, the moderator often introduces a stimulus. The stimulus may be storyboards for ads, mock-ups of packaging, video clips of styles or shopping environments, or actual products. Reacting to these stimulus items organizes and directs the discussion in ways that elicit information of interest to the sponsor. In focus group research, the best information related to consumer satisfaction comes not from asking consumers to describe the kinds of goods they want to buy, but from asking instead about their experiences engaging in a consumption activity (i.e., shopping for gifts, buying and wearing career clothes). In analyzing focus group research, each element mentioned has equal status—the attribute mentioned more often is not more important than any of the others. The interviews offer the chance to collect reactions to proposed products and information on the ways that consumers allocate resources, as well as evaluate outcomes and develop expectations. Using the context information— how people buy and use the goods—and the concrete personal and environmental elements present in the product talk generates a set of tangible and intangible product attributes that are important to consumers (Fennell, 1991). Focus groups are moving out of the traditional conference room setting and going online. Wet Seal, a California-based brand, created a social networking community where teens can create designs, vote on the designs, tag (add keywords and associations), share, and purchase outfits. Over one million designs were created in the first few months of the network, and the site generated a 10 percent increase in revenue for the company (Corcoran, 2008c). The social networking sites now provide the voice of the consumer to the company—a function once filled by traditional focus groups.

Focus groups are a useful tool in understanding consumers, but findings should not be accepted without skepticism. If one or more people dominate a group, only their opinions will be reflected in the findings. Focus groups in one location may not reflect the tastes of other geographic regions. And consumers are fickle—an honest opinion given at one point in time may change by the time the merchandise reaches the stores.

Focus groups are not designed to seek consensus but to extract the maximum information from a group that is diverse in many ways, even though participants come from a specific **consumer segment** based on age, gender, income level, and recent purchase behavior. The analysis of the interviews often leads to identification of naturally occurring niche markets and the less tangible attributes that attract customers.

✧ Consumer Anthropology

Research helps companies understand motivators within a product category or the more specific motivators to buy a particular brand. When people cannot verbalize what they think, observing actual behavior provides rich data on the meanings attached to brand choice (Levin, 1992). Harvard professor Gerald Zaltman uses depth interviews to look deeply at the psychology of an individual in search of more universal insights. He asks interviewees to bring images or pictures that describe feelings on a given topic. One consumer brought a picture of a rain forest to depict shopping in department stores, explaining that both are dense, crowded, and involve facing the unknown. Another brought a picture of a military tank to represent shopping because driving a tank gave her control, protection, and increased security from the manipulations of the store. By conducting many interviews, researchers tap into "that messy stew of memories, emotions, thoughts, and other cognitive processes we're not aware of or can't articulate" (Bowers, 2003b).

Other in-depth interviews use the consumer's residence as the stimulus for discussion. The researcher and consumer chat about preferences and choices while videotaping a consumer's closets and medicine cabinet. In another approach, the researcher shops with the consumer to observe preferences and shopping behaviors (Seckler, 2002b).

Some researchers rely on video to bring the consumer's behavior alive for companies. They may videotape consumers at the mall or at a bar after work, or they may use video to capture interviews at schools or offices. Some researchers give cameras to consumers and ask them to create a videotape of their experiences with products.

A company called Envirosell analyzes consumers' in-store shopping behavior using cameras that look like those used for security. "Trackers," or researchers, observe and note the time consumers spend in shopping activities. Using the trackers' notes and annotated tracking sheets, the company analyzes how much time a person spends looking at displays, scanning tracks, or reading labels. Because the company has been conducting studies for years, researchers are able to trace shifts in consumer behavior, such as how much less time consumers are spending on each shopping trip (Underhill, 2000). As Underhill explains, "We are not particularly interested in the actions of an individual but we are interested in establishing patterns" (Steigerwald, 2007).

Even luxury stores are installing video technology in stores to monitor shopping patterns. By observing traffic entering the stores and at certain locations within the stores, researchers can determine "conversion rates"—the shoppers who buy versus those who fail to make a purchase. These observations allow retailers to gauge the effects of advertising, marketing, and changes in merchandise on sale as benchmarks for future planning. Because the luxury stores are especially concerned about ambiance, observation equipment is getting smaller and more discreet so that it is completely concealed from shoppers (Moin, 2003c).

As mentioned in Chapter 2, "cool hunting" was the term applied in the late 1990s to looking for emerging trends by observing the most fashion-forward young people. Cool hunters,

recruited from the **consumer cohort** of cool kids, roamed the streets looking for the next new thing. In time, some companies concluded that the expenditure was not justified given that the trends identified tended to be fads rather than those that create demand across consumer segments. Rather than relying solely on cool hunting, companies made the practice part of a more inclusive research approach (La Ferla, 2002). But companies still found that observing consumers on the street gave a better reading than the runway shows did on emerging trends. Companies began sending their own people to observe the street scene in places like Tokyo, Paris, Brazil, Italy, and Australia (Feitelberg, 2003b; Rozhon, 2003).

One design director uses the Internet to observe teen customers. She goes to content sites, shopping sites, and teen movie home pages. By checking out the online polls, questions in advice columns, product reviews, and posts by teens, she "see[s] what's being said, get[s] into their heads, and see[s] how they're getting their feeling across" (Bowers, 2003a). Such observations help this executive to understand the teen generation—a generation that is different from her own now and different from the way she was as a teen. With that understanding, she can position her company's products for the preferences and mindset of today's teen.

Brands and retailers are quickly adopting user-generated content—from blogs to social networking to video like those used on popular sites such as Facebook and YouTube. Some sites, like Keep.com, focus on **social shopping** (users bookmark, share, and blog about their favorite products). Brands are adding social shopping to their own websites or establishing a branded presence on Web destination sites like Stylehive.com and Pinterest.com. A number of sites allow shoppers to design or customize products. These efforts offer apparel executives a listening post for consumers' opinions and attitudes toward styles, product categories, and shopping (Corcoran, 2007b).

Interviews and observational techniques capture consumers' worldview and natural language (the way they actually talk about styles, products, and shopping). Consumer anthropology becomes a catalyst for quantitative research to determine how many people feel the same way.

✧ Relational Marketing

Companies communicate with consumers through different media. Each type of media serves a different purpose (Sloan, 1991):

❖ *Preference media*, such as advertising on TV and in print, attempts to win new users for a brand.
❖ *Behavior media*, such as promotions in stores or direct marketing, attempts to spur action in potential or infrequent users.
❖ *Relationship media* talks directly to the company's current, active customers.

Building a "learning relationship" with customers means building an ongoing, interactive connection that encourages collaboration on how to meet consumers' needs. In **relational marketing**, each company develops ways to interact directly with customers. One way to interact with consumers is on the website using a technique called **collaborative filtering**. This is how companies such as Amazon or iTunes make their suggestions for products their users may be interested in. Collaborative filtering is unlike consumer segmentation, which tries to determine the shared likes and dislikes of people with the same demographic or lifestyle characteristics—single, young, urban professional or married, suburban housewife, for example. Instead, collaborative filtering starts with a person making selections or rating suggestions. After about fifteen choices, the software begins to match its recommendations to the person's tastes. It does this by comparing the choices made by this individual with the choices thousands of others have made, some who have the same taste in books, movies, and fashion. The user "educates" the filter by grading the recommendations it makes. In time, the filter becomes a powerful communication tool between the company and the user—the

consumer benefits by receiving customized recommendations that reduce search time and the company learns about customer's preferences and about the group of others who share the same preferences. The central idea is that what you like is much more predictive of your future purchases than where you fit into a segmentation scheme. One of the benefits of collaborative filtering is that as the consumers' tastes change, the filter picks up on the differences (Gladwell, 1999).

Research reveals a difference between stores that consumers "shop most frequently" and the stores they are most loyal to. In a survey of 3,000 consumers nationwide, people shopped most frequently at retailers that competed on lowest everyday prices but reported being more loyal to retailers that gave "value for the money" in an environment of wide selection and customer service. Customer reward programs played a significant role in generating loyalty. With loyalty comes recommendation of that retailer to others—the word-of-mouth endorsement so powerful in consumer culture (Silveman, 2008). In another survey of more than 19,000 consumers, 21 percent could be classified as "advocates" for a particular retailer—consumers who recommend the retailer to others, increase their purchases from the retailer when new products are offered, and stay with the retailer when other stores sell an identical product. Advocates can be recruited by providing a unique experience through some combination of quality, store atmosphere, and assortment. Advocates of mall-based specialty apparel chains bought 32 percent more from their favorite retailer compared to non-advocates (Corcoran, 2008a).

Retailers are using relational marketing when they identify their best customers, offer them preferred customer cards, and promote the use of the cards with discounts on purchases. With the cards, companies can track purchases and discover consumer preferences. Some companies take it further and alert customers via e-mail, text, or phone when something new in their preference range arrives or when a special promotional event is likely to be of interest (Figure 9.5).

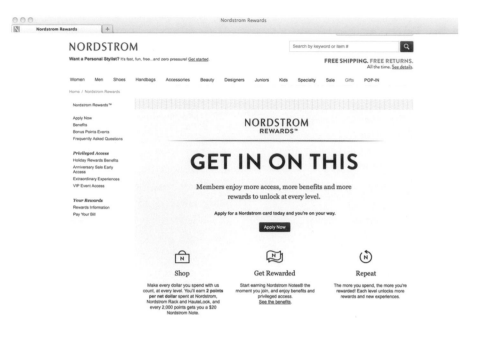

Figure 9.5

Programs such as Nordstrom Rewards encourage relationships and build brand loyalty.

Building direct-to-consumer relationships depends on multiple contacts and follow-up, but marketers feel the effort is important to increase brand loyalty and as a way to justify premium prices. As one apparel executive put it, "Every customer we have is our focus group" (Socha, 1998a).

✦ ASKING "WHAT" AND "HOW MANY" QUESTIONS

The qualitative phase of testing provides the product development team with data on the way consumers view and operate within their marketing environment. The quantitative phase centers on determining the incidence of those responses in the population. Traditionally, marketers have used large-scale surveys to provide answers about the size and preferences of consumer segments.

✧ Surveys and Panel Studies

Survey research asks a set of questions to a group of people at one point in time. The purpose of a survey is to investigate consumer attitudes and opinions. Surveys are a relatively inexpensive way to tap into consumers' views on products, shopping habits, and information sources.

Surveys can be used to track changes among consumer segments. The CEO of Première Vision felt that something was changing in the menswear market—"The speed of evolution was changing and we wanted a closer look"—and commissioned a study of 8,000 men in eight countries—China, France, Germany, Italy, Japan, Spain, the United Kingdom, and the United States. Findings showed a shift in men's self-image from strong and daring to sexy, elegant, and romantic, and a growing interest in purchasing their own clothes rather than having clothing purchased for them by the women in their lives (Hoppough, 2008b).

Surveys can even be used to probe the connection between self-image and purchasing. An online poll of 2,000 women, one-quarter earning more than $250,000, found that 51 percent view shopping as a hobby. When these luxury shoppers need to chase away the blues, 37 percent buy handbags, 21 percent prefer jewelry, and 16 percent splurge on shoes. Half of the women in the study spend more than $5,000 on clothing and accessories each year. Luxury shoppers especially value uniqueness as a way to distinguish themselves from others, define a personal style, and express their creativity. In pursuit of those aims, they actively seek out one-of-a-kind items and waiting lists for specialty items and limited-edition products (Bell, 2008).

Not all research findings can be taken at face value. Surveys are only a snapshot of a particular point in time and may not provide directional information in a fast-changing marketplace. Further, what consumers say in answer to survey questions and their actual behavior may be very different. Confidence in the findings of a survey depend on:

❖ the size of the sample—larger samples are preferred;

❖ how closely the participants' profile matches the consumer segment of interest;

❖ stimulus items (garment prototypes or illustrations) are carefully selected to elicit responses useful to decision makers;

❖ the statistically calculated confidence level for the specific study (usually included in the research firm's report and expected to be 95 percent or higher).

A **panel study** asks questions of a group of people over time in order to track changes in consumer attitudes and opinions. Tina Wells, CEO and founder of Buzz Marketing Group, divides her company's 9,000 "buzz spotters" in twenty countries into four groups or tribes—techies, preppies, alternatives, and independents—based on a profile that includes fashion, entertainment choices, lifestyle, favored shopping locations, and other identifiers ("Forecasting Trends," 2008).

The NPD Group collects purchase information from a panel of more than 3.5 million consumers across a broad spectrum of product categories including fashion (apparel and footwear), home decor, toys, entertainment, and consumer technology. The panel data, along with custom studies (studies designed to focus on a more specific set of questions), provide "a window into the marketplace" that helps clients like Wal-Mart identify market trends ("Wal-Mart," 2007). The NPD FashionWorld's AccuPanel tracking data on apparel purchasing and consumer preference show which features and styles are "gaining traction in the

marketplace." Take something as mundane as wrinkle resistance in menswear: in terms of preference, 51 percent of men seek out this feature for what they wear to work. Sales of wrinkle-free garments continue to rise at the rate of 2 percent each year. Apparel manufacturers and retailers respond to such directional information by increasing the offering of wrinkle-free items such as dress shirts, pleated pants, and even a washable suit (Nolan, 2007).

Some firms specialize in panel research on specific consumer segments. The Zandl Group tracks fast-moving teen and young adult consumers. Sometimes results can be surprising or even counterintuitive. When the safety of products produced offshore made news, the Zandl Group asked 100 out of 500 young people on a panel of "thought leaders" how the problems would affect their buying (Figure 9.6). Responding within 2 hours—fast turnaround for consumer research—these mostly twenty-somethings took the opposite tack to the majority by rejecting any appeal to "buy American." Focusing on apparel, they wanted to buy from companies that they knew did not use sweatshop labor regardless of the country of origin (Seckler, 2007b).

Even though surveys and panel studies have significant drawbacks, the techniques will continue to be a popular way to take snapshots of current market conditions. The panel study, with its potential to track changes through time, provides more directional information for forecasting. Surveys, panel studies, and the statistical quantification they provide continue to be an important element in understanding consumer preferences and behavior.

✧ Research in Malls

Malls sometimes include a consumer research facility where studies are conducted for companies. The study sponsor identifies particular characteristics for participants, usually demographic categories such as gender, age, and income. Personnel from the research company intercept customers in the mall, ask them some preliminary questions to verify that they meet the sponsor's requirements, and invite them to

Figure 9.6

Irma Zandl, president of the Zandl Group, in the Brooklyn loft that serves as headquarters for the trend analysis firm.

participate in a study. Participants are usually offered a small incentive, such as free lunch at one of the mall's restaurants or a gift. Customers who agree to participate are taken to the research facility where they may be interviewed, asked to provide opinions on products, or complete survey questionnaires. By conducting studies at mall-based consumer research facilities in different geographic areas, companies gain insight into consumer preferences and how they differ according to location.

One of the main drawbacks to **mall intercept research** is time. It may take several weeks to design the study, negotiate with the research sites, distribute the research materials, and run the studies. Suppose it takes a month before data are available; that time horizon may be too long in a fast-paced competitive environment. The quality of the data depends on how high the standards of the research facility are in regard to recruiting participants, administering the research, and analyzing the data. Because a research facility works for many companies, it must keep each sponsor's data confidential.

✧ Style Testing

Computer-aided design (CAD) and the Internet make it possible to incorporate a research phase in the product development process. **Style testing**—pretesting styles with consumers—can aid in early identification of "winners" and "losers" (styles with such low consumer interest that they can be eliminated from further development). A fashion scout can see a new design in Europe and send a photo of it to corporate headquarters where a prototype design can be developed using CAD; the design is then submitted to consumer testing and results are tabulated—all within 24 hours (Potts, 1990).

The push to reduce time in the concept-to-market process means that apparel executives have less time to make assortment decisions and it increases the risk that the wrong products will arrive in stores faster than ever. Involving consumers in the product design process can help guide decisions and perhaps reduce excessive markdowns. Whether pretesting colors, patterns, new products, or styles, consumer input can help manufacturers and retailers make key decisions before committing to supplies, production, and inventory. Consumer views can be accessed directly through focus groups, Web-based consumer panels, and social networking sites. Add to that the ability to gather information indirectly in every consumer interaction—in the store, through catalogs, online. Together these data allow apparel executives to probe beyond consumers' needs to their preferences, which are the input for product design. At present, most retailers have little if any contact with consumers during the product development process ("Outlook," 2008).

✧ Shopping Simulation

In a traditional survey, consumers answer questions posed by a researcher and may give responses that seem more socially acceptable than their actual behavior. Moving the research onto the computer as simulated shopping trips can help eliminate this bias because consumers are less likely to identify what is being tested (Rickard, 1993). On the computer, the participant navigates through several shopping trips, each of which includes different prices and products. During the simulated shopping trips, consumers browse shelves, choose items by touching the screen, take a closer look at the item, and either "buy" the product or return it to the shelf. Computer simulation technology offers researchers another tool for discovering consumer preferences and projecting the potential market for products.

✧ In-Store Testing

In surveys, a small sample of consumers is asked questions about their intention to purchase and the results are inferred to be representative of the actual behavior of a larger population. Such a projection is not necessary when research is conducted in a natural in-store environment. Sales are a clear measure of behavior, whereas attitudes or intention to buy are not.

In-store research takes several forms:

❖ *Showcase and Laboratory Stores*—Some manufacturers operate specialty stores as laboratories to test the viability of new products (Gordon, 1990). Designers and manufacturers create **showcase or laboratory stores** that are museums to the product and offer a chance to present their entire line. Although primarily a billboard for the brand and an educational environment for retailers on the latest in visual merchandising, the stores also serve a research purpose. The stores are a place for the manufacturer to gather intelligence about what consumers want, which products in the line are heating up and which are cooling down, and which packaging and promotional initiatives are most effective (Fitzgerald, 1992). When Nike wanted to understand the female customer, the company opened up a women-only boutique. The store was located in Newport Beach, California, because the area has a high concentration of fitness-conscious shoppers. Because the purpose of the store was to gain insight into what the consumer wanted, data was collected on sales, and sales associates encouraged shoppers to complete questionnaires. The information was funneled to the product-development team and to other stores carrying Nike products for women (Feitelberg, 2001).

❖ *Test Stores*—Specialty store chains selling store labels designate certain stores as test sites. Any store in the chain may be designated as a test store for a particular time period. The test store is cleared of merchandise and reset with test merchandise. Then, business continues as usual—consumers are completely unaware that a test is under way.

❖ *Test Merchandise Groups*—A less extensive approach is to plant test groups of merchandise with ordinary merchandise. When product developers monitor sales information from these test sites, the company can fine-tune sales potential by optimizing the selling price and color assortment. They can also discover items that often are sold together as input for promotions and visual merchandising.

❖ *Pop-Up and Concept Stores*—**Pop-up stores** are retail stores that are in place for a limited time period. Small as a kiosk or large as a boutique, these stores are partly public relations efforts and partly testing grounds for new merchandise, line extensions, and new product concepts. **Concept stores** are specifically situated in areas where trendy customers shop and are stocked with test merchandise. Sales identify the colors, patterns, styles, and embellishments that appeal to the most fashion-forward shoppers—an indicator of emerging and developing trends. In December 2010, Kate Spade New York created a pop-up shop in the shape of an igloo in Bryant Park that was a big hit (Figure 9.7).

✦ CONSUMER SEGMENTATION

Consumer segmentation attempts to discriminate between types of consumers based on a set of variables. The variables can be demographic (age, sex, income, and ethnicity), psychographic (lifestyles, personality, and preferences), or a combination. Apparel executives—product developers, marketers, and merchandisers—use consumer segmentation to position styles, products, brands, and retail formats in the marketplace. A critical issue is deciding which set of variables will produce the clearest and most accurate picture.

Consumer research can be used to develop a consumer segmentation scheme. Suppose a jeans company acquired a new brand and wants to know how the consumers for this new brand differ from other brands it owns. Focus groups, observational techniques, surveys, or panel studies could be used to clarify this issue. The company would want to avoid **cannibalizing** its current brands—that is, shifting buyers from its current brands to the new brand. Instead, the company wants to give the new brand a unique position that attracts new consumers and increases the company's profits. Results from the research will be used by product developers, marketers, and merchandisers to reach that goal.

Consumer segmentation can also be used in designing research. Suppose a contemporary dress firm wants to be "trend right" for the coming season. Advertising positions the company as fashion forward, but sales figures

Figure 9.7
Kate Spade New York created a pop-up shop in the shape of an igloo in Bryant Park that featured holiday products and gifts.

show that the majority of sales come from more mainstream designs. The company plans a two-tier fashion assortment with trendy styles to attract consumers and less trendy variations for more conventional consumers who nevertheless bond with the company's image. The company employs a research firm to style-test the line. Questions researchers and company executives must answer in planning consumer research include:

* What ages and income levels should be consulted?
* Are there communities or subcultures (style tribes) that tend to be trend indicators for the rest of the country?
* Should participants include only fashion-forward customers?

Today, consumer research blends attention to consumer types with attention to the way a consumer interacts with the brand or uses the product. Depending on the situation, the consumer may use a different set of criteria each time they make such a decision. Complicating the picture is the fragmentation of markets into smaller and smaller niches. Not long ago, a trend moved from a few fashion-forward consumers to the mainstream, or the majority of consumers. Most trends today move within niches; few are picked up by the majority of consumers (Haber, 2007b). So now, more than ever, forecasters and other fashion industry professionals must pay careful attention to the definitions of market niches. To create desirable products, select appealing assortment, and aim promotion campaigns, a company must focus on small, sharp consumer segments—affluent twenty-something men living in Miami rather than affluent men between the ages of 20 and 35 living anywhere in the United States. Not only must the segments be precisely drawn, they need to be redrawn frequently using consumer research techniques. Traditionally, segmentation research for a brand or retailer is done every 2 to 3 years; however, because consumers' tastes are now so fluid, it may be necessary to conduct segmentation seasonally. To make the effort

worthwhile, the image of the target consumer must be part of product development and merchandising. One company goes so far as to put a picture representing the typical consumer on the wall of the conference room and referring to her by name (fictitious) during planning discussions ("Outlook," 2008).

Because consumer research is expensive, apparel management will never have all the information they need to make decisions. But with careful attention to research design, the dollars spent on information gathering can pay off by increasing sales. Whether the goal is to define a market, create optimal strategies for existing brands, position brands and products, or identify gaps in the market for new product opportunities, the steps are the same:

* Define the situation using data and findings from past research efforts.
* Use qualitative and quantitative research to collect consumer-defined attributes of the product, the search and purchase experience, and the experience of using the product.
* Map the preference patterns using consumer segmentation.

The resulting "maps" of the market by consumer type help marketers and forecasters identify the microsegments in the market that are directional for the future. Being just ahead of these trends is an excellent place to be when making decisions about product development, marketing, and merchandising.

The terms "consumer segment" and "**target audience**" have thus far been used in a general way to mean that certain people are more likely than others to adopt an innovation at a particular time in the diffusion process. For marketers, these terms have a more precise meaning. A target audience is that slice of the population most likely to be attracted to the tangible and intangible attributes of a product, company image, or service. Defining the target audience takes discipline. It is much easier to think that every person between the ages of 25 and 45 will want a particular product or identify with a certain image. However, attempting to hit a target audience that's too inclusive results in creating indistinct, unfocused, generic merchandise without differentiation from other similar products in the market. Achieving differentiation means presenting a product in a way that highlights how it is different and better than other products of its type.

Traditionally a target audience would be defined as one or more consumer segments, each with certain demographic characteristics such as age, gender, ethnicity, and income. Then, the marketing executive develops a positioning strategy (Ries & Trout, 1986), a unique marketing approach that:

❖ appeals directly to that target audience;
❖ differentiates the product from all others in the category;
❖ positions the product in the minds of the consumers as desirable for purchase (Figure 9.8).

Segmentation strategies based on **demographics**—consumer characteristics such as age, gender, marital status, and occupation—are no longer sufficient because consumer attitudes and behavior are not driven primarily by demographics. Consumers can behave in unexpected ways—for example, when very affluent consumers combine luxury branded goods from specialty stores and basics from discount retailers. Shifts in consumer behavior mean that the traditional way of doing business whereby manufacturers propose new products, identify targets for those products through a segmentation study, and develop a positioning strategy is too simplistic for today's marketplace.

Psychographics—consumer psychology plus demographics—help identify a consumer segment by shared values, attitudes, preferences, and behaviors (Piirto, 1991). Psychographics evolved from groundwork laid in the late 1950s when characteristics such as personality traits, attitudes, and motives were used to identify consumer clusters. By the mid-1960s, non-demographic segmentation was becoming a keystone in marketing strategy. Today, marketers view the value system embedded in each individual—the consumer's culture—as having more impact than demographics.

(a)

(b)

Figure 9.8

(a) Eileen Fisher, whose designs have a distinctive look positioned to appeal to women of a certain age with flattering, modern styling (b).

The consumer's culture can overrule demographic classifications. High-income households consider brand quality to be more important than do consumers at lower income levels. Yet consumers of all income levels who tend to be trendsetters or opinion leaders show a far greater preference for quality than even high-income families (Kelly, 1994). Health-, fitness-, and nutrition-conscious consumers comprise a relatively small but influential segment of consumers in all demographic categories. Although they may be of different ages and come from various income ranges, they are more alike than different when it comes to choosing products that enhance and support their image of themselves as healthy and fit. Positioning becomes more actionable when it is built on both the "whos"—demographics—and the "whys"—psychographics—of consumer behavior (Rueff, 1991).

Geodemographics links geography and demographics to show the clustering of similar people in a neighborhood (Edelson, 2003). Census data on age, income, ethnicity, and other categories are "smoothed out" to create an identity, label, and affluence rating for a neighborhood. The resulting clusters are useful for pinpointing locations for new stores or malls, to target mailings of catalogs, and to reveal insights about consumer preferences. The fragmentation of markets in the 1980s meant that products and services had to be targeted not to a mass market but to submarkets identified by combinations of demographics and geography.

In the early 1970s, a college professor and entrepreneur used cluster analysis and census data to create zip code clusters (Weiss, 1988). The concept behind the analysis is that neighborhoods geographically separated may be more similar to each other than those nearby. For example, the demographic makeup of college towns and the preferences of the residents are similar no matter where in the country they are located. These college towns are more like each other than they are like other towns in their vicinity. Using this logic, the company Claritas merged US Census data with credit card, mail-order sales, television

viewing, subscription, and other purchasing information to create PRIZM (Potential Rating Index by Zip Market)—a system sorting all the zip codes in the United States into neighborhood types. Each type can be profiled by demographics, lifestyle, media usage, and preference for make of car, food, and other products. The data are updated each year (Levanas, 1998). PRIZM currently has sixty-six defined consumer segments, and each is very clearly portrayed (Edwards, 2007). For example, one segment, the Young Digerati, "are tech-savvy and live in fashionable neighborhoods on the urban fringe. Affluent, highly educated, and ethnically mixed, Young Digerati communities are typically filled with trendy apartments and condos, fitness clubs and clothing boutiques, casual restaurants and all types of bars—from juice to coffee to microbrew." Some of the lifestyle and media traits of this group are that they "shop at Bloomingdale's, travel to Asia, read Dwell, watch Independent Film Channel and [drive the] Audi A3."

Claritas was one of the first companies to make geodemographic information useful to marketing executives, but it has been joined by others so that today's executive can choose among competing firms. Each company offers its own version of clustering and its own interpretation of the resulting clusters.

Today, a company is not restricted to buying geodemographic analysis from one of the research firms—the technology is now available on their employees' laptops. While the basic technology linking Census data and mapping has been around since the 1960s, the software did not become available on the personal computer until the mid-1990s (Freed, 1994). At that time, companies began to sell the basic mapping software at a relatively low price, planning to make money by selling updated packages of geographic, economic, and demographic data. With the software, an analyst can map competitor locations, areas of dense population, neighborhoods with high income and high-traffic roads, and other information to support strategic marketing decisions.

Geodemographics is useful to forecasters in pinpointing the markets where hot trends begin and in mapping their potential diffusion. Geodemographics can identify the towns and neighborhoods that are teen-poor (under 4 percent of the population is aged 14 to 17) and those with higher concentrations for teens, areas that are attracting young adults, and those where boomers are migrating (Sutton, 1993). These patterns signal retail growth potential for some stores and product categories and a mismatch for others. Because the United States is heading for a more diverse population by the end of the twenty-first century, one way to forecast the future is to identify and monitor locations where diversity already exists (Allen & Turner, 1990). Geodemographics allows forecasters to locate diverse neighborhoods where consumption patterns today may anticipate those that will develop in other locales as the future unfolds.

✦ GENERATIONAL COHORTS

Similarity in patterns of consumer behavior have been traced to **generational cohorts** who share the same "age location" in history and a collective mindset (Strauss & Howe, 1991). In this view, group membership is involuntary, permanent, and finite—from birth on, all members encounter the same events, moods, and trends at similar ages, giving each cohort a distinct biography and a peer personality. Individuals in the cohort may agree with the values and viewpoints of their generation or spend a lifetime battling against it; either way, membership in the cohort shapes their relationship to people and products. Using this typology, five generational cohorts are currently active consumers (Gronbach, 2008).

✧ The G.I. Generation

Born between 1901 and 1924, the G.I. generation lived through the Great Depression in their youth and fought in World War II (1941–45) as young adults. Consumption is mostly limited to daily maintenance and health care. Their purchasing tends to be through their boomer caregivers.

✧ The Silent Generation

Born between 1925 and 1945, the silent generation came of age during the 1950s and fought in the Korean War (1950–53). This group got its name from a 1951 *Time* magazine article because of their lack of ambition and overly cautious nature (Zernike, 2009). This group's purchasing centers on delaying aging and remaining independent, eating out, and shopping for a bargain.

✧ The Baby Boom Generation

Born between 1946 and 1964, the children in this generation were the result of a post-World War II baby boom. Boomers were the first TV generation and fought the first televised war, in Vietnam. Instead of bonding to fight the war as the G.I. generation had, some boomers bonded to protest the war and evade service. This is the generation of Youthquake, the Summer of Love, Woodstock, and Earth Day. They can be subdivided into an older cohort who were the flower children and hippies of the late 1960s and early 1970s and a younger cohort who became the yuppies (young urban professionals) of the early 1980s. The boomers control much of the nation's wealth and retire at the rate of one every 8 seconds. Whereas their purchase of cars and apparel is slowing, boomers value products that make life easier or save time.

✧ Generation X

Born between 1965 and 1980, this generation experienced a higher risk of being children of divorce (almost twice as often as boomers) and grew up as latchkey kids and as members of blended families due to remarriage. Boomers experienced the euphoria of Youthquake, whereas Generation X-ers were labeled "slackers" for their pragmatic approach, sense of social distance, and falling expectations. The first computer generation, Gen X consumers are experienced shoppers, fond of popular culture, and cynical about media manipulation. A small generation (9 million fewer than boomers), these consumers don't respond to conventional media and are difficult to target in the fragmentation of the Internet.

✧ Millennial Generation, Generation Y

Born between 1981 and 1995, this generation's parents are mostly boomers. The size of this generation almost equals boomers and surpasses them in purchasing—Gen Y purchasing is at 500 percent compared to their parents when adjusted in dollars. Attentive to cyberspace, fickle in their tastes, and expecting the best, this group favors brands and retailers with strong ecological or humanitarian records (Tran, 2008d).

This is the generation that is rethinking everything about how young people choose to spend their time and money and taking the fashion industry with them, because a major shift is in progress. Retail analyst John Morris, who is employed with BMO Capital Markets, says that his regular focus groups with teenagers about what trends they find most appealing are technology- not clothing-related. "You try to get them talking about what's the next look, what they're excited about purchasing in apparel, and the conversation always circles back to the iPhone 6," he said (Harris & Abrams, 2014). Demographers aren't precise in placing dividing lines between generations but Gen Y probably ended in 2000 and a new generation, yet to be officially named (but some analysts are referring to it as Generation Z), is being born.

The apparel marketer must be savvy about targeting consumers by generational cohort. If it is true that the mainstream (a majority of all consumers) no longer exists, each American generation spanning roughly 20 years, encompassing millions of consumers, and shaped by unique cultural conditions, provides its own mainstream with specific needs, wants, and aspirations.

Identifying generations in other cultures helps forecasters and other fashion professionals understand and define global marketing opportunities. China is likely to become the largest retail economy and the spending power will be in the hands of the "only child" generation—profiled as urban, educated, ranging from late teens to early thirties, with rising disposable incomes. The Chinese who are part of this generation grew up during boom times, embrace fashion, and enjoy spending money on themselves. Wherever a company does business, a generational view can provide insights into the marketplace (Lowther, 2008).

✦ LIFESTYLE SEGMENTS

Psychographics was extended in the early 1970s by the introduction of research into lifestyles (Piirto, 1991). In that time, society was being remade by young people who dropped out rather than get married and start families and careers, and by women who began choosing careers over traditional homemaker roles. Lifestyle research was an attempt to understand the changing social order. The framework for such studies is Attitudes, Interests, and Opinions (AIO)—how consumers spend their time, what interests are important to them, how they view themselves and what opinions they hold about the world around them. A typical lifestyle study will survey consumers and then sort them into categories, such as "soccer mom" for stay-at-home matriarchs.

Today, lifestyle segments form a foundation concept for product development, marketing, and merchandising. A lifestyle message has become a key strategy for apparel brands. Vendor shops in department stores present the company's products as a recognizable, coordinated concept carried out in products, accessories, display fixtures, mannequins, construction materials, and ambiance ("One-stop Shops," 1998). Consumers recognize products and presentation as belonging to their group and gravitate toward those brands.

✦ LIFE STAGES

Similarity in patterns of consumer behavior can be traced to the life stage of the consumer. Consumption priorities alter depending on the stage of life and the accompanying tasks and challenges. Using life stages as a framework, the forecaster can predict shifts in what consumers do with their discretionary dollars.

Adults at every life stage blend all three kinds of consumption, but each life stage puts a different priority on the elements in the combination. A young couple starting life together and beginning careers will put emphasis on acquiring possessions and defining their image as individuals and as a family. Spending focuses on a car, a media center, and a home or an apartment with furnishings. Financial security dampens the need for acquiring possessions but fuels the satisfaction of personal, entertainment, and convenience needs through the purchase of services. Spending focuses on season tickets to the theater or sporting events, travel, restaurant meals, and professional services such as custom clothing, personal shoppers, lawn maintenance, and interior design services. With gratification of the need for possessions and services, the consumer shifts emphasis to altruistic activities such as charity work or mentoring others, personally meaningful experiences, and life-enhancing pastimes.

The life stages represent consumption of different products and the pursuit of different kinds of experience. Although the stages are related to maturing, consumers at all ages participate in each kind of spending. Only the emphasis shifts and, with it, the consumer's discretionary spending.

Consumer segmentation is possible because patterns build up from individuals with certain demographic and psychographic characteristics, representatives of a certain lifestyle segment, and confronting a specific life stage. The individuals blend into groups and into larger consumer segments based on shared characteristics (Piirto, 1991). The consumer segmentation strategies for the twenty-first century reflect the new realities of consumer behavior—there is still an underlying similarity among consumers who gravitate to a particular style or image, but that similarity is complex and multifaceted. Forecasters use cohort membership, lifestyle, and life stage to project potential acceptance or rejection of trends and styles.

✧ Consumer Segmentation and Forecasting

The demographics have already been written about the future consumer. By 2025, the oldest baby boomers will be 79 years old, the oldest

Gen X-ers will be eligible for Social Security, and the Gen Y generation will be in their thirties. Three demographic trends will shape the future:

1   If current trends continue, the population of the United States is projected to rise to 438 million in 2050, from 296 million in 2005, with 82 percent of the increase attributed to immigrants arriving from 2005 to 2050 and their US-born descendants, according to projections developed by the Pew Research Center (Pew Research, 2008). Of the 117 million people added to the population during this period, 67 million will be the immigrants themselves and 50 million will be their US born children or grandchildren, putting pressure on natural resources and making people question the impact of products and services on the environment.
2   The nation's senior population will more than double in size from 2005 through 2050, as the baby boom generation enters the traditional retirement stage. The number of working-age Americans and children will grow more slowly than the elderly population, and will comprise a smaller share of the total population.
3   The Latino population, already the nation's largest minority group, will triple in size and will account for most of the nation's population growth through 2050. Hispanics are projected to make up 29 percent of the US population in 2050, compared with 14 percent in 2005 (Pew Research, 2008).

✧ Consumer Generations

The oldest American generations—the G.I. and silent—are past their consuming prime. Their concerns center on health, well-being, and maintaining independence. The boomers continue to consume some categories of products (entertainment and travel), but purchases of apparel and cars are down and not likely to rise significantly; they will pass their peak of consumption when the majority of them are past 50. Still, they control much of the nation's personal wealth and will influence the generations that follow them as that wealth is passed down. Gen X consumers are buying products appropriate to their life stage at expected rates, but will never reach boomer levels because this generation is smaller than the ones surrounding it. Gen Y has surpassed boomers in generational size and is consuming at 500 percent the rate of boomers (adjusted dollars, age for age). Apparel sales spike as each segment of this generation seeks mates, but they are fickle in tastes and prefer retailers and manufacturers with good records on ecological and humanitarian issues (Gronback, 2008).

Designers, merchandisers, and marketers will continue to focus on generational cohorts because the symbols and images that a generation grows up with give them a recognizable sense of style and influences purchasing throughout the life cycle. But today, five living generations are influencing and communicating together. According to Marshal Cohen, chief industry analyst at the NPD Group, "The last time you had this level of communications was [early in the twentieth century] when all generations lived together in one house." Other generations find the G.I. and silent generation admirable. Boomers are known to have rapport with millennials (Seckler, 2008c). Boomer moms and millennial daughters often shop together, vacation together, and text message each other several times a day. In a switch, the millennial is considered to be the savvy shopper, and one research firm says young adults influence 88 percent of household purchases including apparel. Traditional thinking says that the same styles and labels cannot be sold to two different age groups—if the older group wears it, the edge is off for the younger customer. But some brands and retailers are breaking those rules (i.e., Vera Bradley, Tory Burch, Scoop NYC, and others) (van Dyk, 2008).

Two cohorts will help define the marketing landscape: the "New" American Dream and the First Globals (Zogby, 2008). The American Dream has traditionally been defined by prosperity and upward social mobility. Younger members of the silent generation, boomers, and older members of Gen X are joining to redefine it as less material, more spiritual—two out of

three adults can be included in this group. The First Globals are younger people who see themselves as citizens of the world. They travel, study abroad, and expect to live some part of their lives outside the United States. Both these trends surfaced in the mid-1990s and continue to accelerate.

✧ Diversity

When there is a more diverse population, understanding ethnic groups becomes more important. According to the Selig Center of Economic Growth ("African-American Consumers," 2013), the buying power of African-American consumers is currently $1 trillion and is forecast to reach $1.3 trillion by the year 2017, which makes this demographic group influential in style and consumer trends. However, the demographic is marketed to as a single entity. A think tank, Future Focus 2020, released a study of 1,000 African-American consumers segmented by lifestyle, income level, aspiration, and preferences that identified ten distinct groups, from avid churchgoers to urban trendsetters ("Strength," 2008).

Marketing to ethnic groups is more complex than it first appears. Hispanics are not a single marketing segment, but represent seventeen Latin American countries, Puerto Rico, and the Caribbean. Racially, Hispanics can be white, black, Indian, or a multiethnic mix. Because cultural patterns and traditions vary widely among these countries, marketing to Hispanic consumers can be challenging (Lane, 2003). The picture is just as complex for Asian consumers. Although the Asian population as a whole tends to skew younger, Japanese- and Chinese-Americans have a sizeable baby boomer population, a hint that these groups have been in the United States longer, may be more fully assimilated, and may have preferences more similar to those of the mainstream consumer. Whereas Asian consumers' preferences and shopping behavior may vary depending on country of origin, the value patterns are similar, with a strong emphasis on traditional family life (Wellner, 2003b). Arab-Americans are currently the fastest growing niche market in the

Figure 9.9

Runway fashion designers are catering to the needs of affluent Muslim consumers by offering high-end hijabs and other Islamic styles.

multicultural mix of American marketing (Figure 9.9). Additionally, the mixed-race or multiethnic consumer represents an understudied consumer segment—one in sixteen Americans under the age of 18 is of mixed ethnic background (Ambardar, 2008).

Diversity is increasing in the United States overall, yet some areas will not change much. California is one of the most diverse states, but Maine's white population is currently 92.5 percent, although its non-white population did increase by 37 percent in the years 2000–10. Religious diversity is increasing with immigration from India, Pakistan, and the Middle East (mostly Hindus and Muslims), as well as China, Japan, and other Asian countries (increasing the number of Buddhists). However, many of these immigrants settled in California or the major cities in the Northeast or Midwest. These patterns may lead to very diverse and heterogeneous regions and a complex marketing picture (Orndoff, 2003).

✧ Fashion and the Consumer

Women. Michael Silverstein, a senior partner and managing director at Boston Consulting Group,

sees a global shift to "the female economy" by 2028 when women will earn more than men and become even more demanding consumers starved of time and looking for convenience in shopping. He bases his hypothesis on responses to an online survey of 11,000 women and interviews with individuals—a process he plans to continue for 10 years with annual updates. Between 66 and 70 percent of the women surveyed are optimistic that they will be better off in five years regardless of the overall economy (Seckler, 2008b).

Men. Genevieve Flaven, managing partner of France-based fashion intelligence consultancy Style-Vision, sees a shift away from gender correctness and strict dress codes for men to greater variety in expression of male personalities. She predicts more diversity, particularly in men's accessories, and more personal and creative choices in work and casualwear. Already visible in Japan, the United States, the United Kingdom, and Latin America, the shift is not as strong in Europe, India, and China ("Statistics," 2008).

Trends. David Wolfe, creative director at Doneger Group, sums it up: "Nobody swallows

You Be the Forecaster: Extending the Line

Caleb is a marketing executive with a successful menswear designer line. The brand has an established name and a winning fashion concept that it wants to extend through the launch of a women's wear line—a much more volatile and risky market. The lure for such a strategy is the market potential, at least twice as big as menswear. However, the risks are big, too. The women's wear market is more competitive and more trend driven than menswear. Where four collections a year is customary in menswear, women's wear requires six to eight. Costs for fabrics, sampling, models, and photographers are all higher. The formula for success in menswear—high-quality tailoring and a rational, practical way of dressing—does not translate easily to the faster-paced women's wear business. Although the quality and simplicity of the menswear approach to dressing appeals to career women, women have more experience with change, newness, and self-expression in clothes.

Some menswear designers made the crossover, but even some of those had difficulties initially. Caleb's company plans to build the next big mega brand with multiple lines spanning the apparel market. The first step is an extension in women's wear. If the new line is to succeed, the company must learn about this new target audience, find out how to position its brand in this new market, and use the findings to project the company's future.

Use the following questions to review the chapter and summarize the route Caleb might take to get the answers his company needs.

The Conceptual Map of Consumer Preferences: The company needs a picture of the potential match between the company's line and consumer expectations. What are the consumer's expectations for the brand? What are the most desirable attributes of products in this category? What exciting or surprising attributes of the product or brand will attract consumers initially? What attributes will turn consumers into brand-loyal customers? How sensitive is this consumer segment to quality issues?

Research Strategy: Initial answers to these questions may come from women who are already buying from the men's line. The next step is to map out a research plan to gather continuous information about consumers' wants and needs. How will information be gathered: In focus groups? By using observational techniques in the marketplace? In mall intercept studies? Through relational marketing? Through surveys or panel studies?

Reducing Risks: Before rolling out a complete line and placing full production orders, executives will need data on consumer reaction to proposed styles. How will these tests be conducted: In-store testing? As stimulus items in focus groups? As images in a computer poll of consumers nationwide?

Identifying the Consumer Segment: What must an apparel manufacturer understand about customers in order to meet their needs, wants, and expectations? Develop a checklist of the information needs of an apparel executive who must forecast directions in consumer preference patterns into the future.

a trend whole any more" (Haber, 2007a). Designer Francisco Costa argues that rather than seasonal or industry-wide trends, there are trends for each fashion house as part of its recognizable aesthetic signature. As early as 2005 David Wolfe was saying, "There is no fashion mainstream any more. Instead of a mainstream there are a thousand little branches all going at different speeds. It's almost as if the consumer has become a solo player in the marketplace" (Horyn, 2005).

✦ CUSTOMIZATION AND PERSONALIZATION

Mass production develops standardized products for a stable, homogeneous market where the goal is efficiencies of sale. If it is true that consumers want *what* they want, *when* they want it, the *way* they want it, then the time has come for **mass customization**. Mass customization is an alternative strategy to mass production's "one size fits all" and couture's "one of a kind." The idea is to deliver a unique, personalized, or customized product on a mass basis at a cost competitive with mass production (Bathory-Kitsz, 1996).

Mass customization takes advantage of the technological advances in manufacturing and communication to facilitate a one-to-one marketing strategy (Anderson et al., 1998). Mass customization was never envisioned as replacing mass production. Rather, the two will coexist and evolve with improvements in manufacturing and communication technologies.

Customization, when it does away with standard sizes, has produced higher levels of participation than expected. Lands' End predicted that its custom-fit chinos would appeal to heavy or short people or people who cared intensely about perfectly fitted casual clothes— perhaps 10 percent of customers. Instead, 40 percent of all chino and jeans sales on the company's website were custom orders.

Customers enter their measurements and characteristics on the website, a computer program analyzes the information and calculates the dimensions of the pants, and the order is manufactured and shipped in 2 to 4 weeks for a price that is comparable to mass-produced products (Tedeschi, 2002). Personalized and customized wear has become commonplace for athletes, as promotional campaigns for entertainers and their fans, and for gifts and company identity programs. Consumers have taken design matters into their own hands with handmade accessories, redesigned vintage, and modified thrift-store finds. Online companies like threadless.com engage users in the design process. The Intimacy lingerie store begins with stocking the broadest range of bra sizes, adds a 30-minute fitting appointment, and personalizes the fit with alterations to create a personalized product and purchase experience (Bowers, 2008). A few companies, such as eShakti, have fully implemented the consumer-designed, custom-sewn garment (also known as made on demand—MOD).

Individually produced garments may carry higher costs, but consumers are generally willing to pay more for customization (Figure 9.10). Mass customization represents future opportunities for the apparel industry. But there are obstacles, such as delays in the development of appropriate technological linkages or imaging systems, the capital investment required to implement the strategy, and the learning curve when companies and consumers encounter new ways of conducting business. The payoffs for mass customization, however, include higher customer satisfaction, stronger loyalty to the brand, the ability to gather more information about the consumer, and the potential for better forecasting because of the relationship between the core consumer and the company (Zimmermann, 1998b).

(a)

(b)

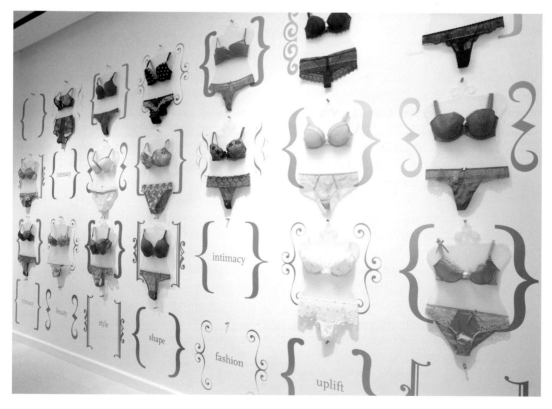

(c)

Figure 9.10

The customization and personalization of products for a specific consumer comes in many forms: (a) a Fendi baguette customized by artist Jeff Koons; (b) the made-to-measure section for men in Prada offers customized belts; (c) Intimacy, an Atlanta-based lingerie retailer that makes personalized fitting and alterations part of its business plan.

Chapter Summary

In today's marketplace, the consumer is king, and apparel and retail companies take their consumers' opinions very seriously. Through a variety of techniques including focus groups, survey research and panel studies, and in-store testing, apparel and retail companies use market research to define and meet their customers' needs. Consumer segmentation allows companies to narrow their focus through use of demographics, psychographics, and geodemographics to reach just the right target audience for the brand. Demographic groups such as the baby boomers and the millennials, as well as ethnic groups such as the Latino market or the African-American market, all influence the products and services that everyone purchases, and changes in these markets will continue to influence changes in product development. Recent developments in technology have impacted the influence of trends, and with the advent of mass customization of apparel, consumers can get exactly the fit and style they are looking for, if they are willing to pay for it.

Key Terms and Concepts

Brand loyalty

Cannibalizing

Collaborative filtering

Concept stores

Consumer cohort

Consumer segment

Demographics

Depth interview

Focus group

Focus group moderator

Generational cohort

Geodemographics

Mall intercept research

Mass customization

Panel study

Pop-up stores

Projective techniques

Psychographics

Qualitative research

Quantitative research

Relational marketing

Showcase or laboratory stores

Social shopping

Style testing

Survey research

Target audience

Discussion Questions

What generational cohort are your parents members of? Your grandparents? What products and brands are they loyal to, and why? How do you think their age impacts the products and services they purchase regularly?

Brand Loyalty: What loyalty programs do you belong to? What types of communication do you receive from them? What kinds of special offers do you receive? Have you ever chosen one brand or retailer over another because you wanted to get points or other membership benefits? What does the retailer know about you because of your purchase behavior?

Mass Customization: Have you ever ordered any customized products? If so, why did you want a one-of-a-kind item? What kinds of products are best for customization? Were there any downsides to ordering a custom item, such as additional wait time?

Forecasting Activities

Social Shopping. Monitor the user-generated content on a fashion-oriented website. The site does not have to be associated with a brand or retailer. What are people talking about most frequently? What topics or ideas generate the most heat (interest, passion, excitement)? How would you characterize the users? What activities do they engage in—tagging, sharing, blogging? Now monitor another site. What are the similarities or differences? What recommendation would you make to a company that wanted to glean insights into consumer preferences from similar sites?

Filter Training. Find a website that promises personal recommendations for a taste-based product like books, movies, or fashion. Train the filter to your own set of preferences. Use the site for a month, and observe how well the filter seems to know you. Does it offer any surprising recommendations or ones you would not have found on your own? What can go wrong to throw off the filter (like buying presents for others from this website)? Is there a way to correct these inputs? What do you see as the future for this technology?

Customization Online. Using a search engine, locate three sites that offer customized beauty, clothing, or accessories. Analyze the offers by comparing prices and quality with mass-produced products. What is the time lag between order and delivery? What kind of information must a customer provide? What is your assessment of the likely success or failure of these sites?

Researching the Generations. Use the generational names as keywords in a database search. What kinds of information are available on generational cohorts? Select one generation, and collect several recent articles. Analyze how the observations in the articles relate to the design and sales of apparel products. Use the articles to analyze the spending patterns for possessions as a sign of accomplishment and identity, the purchase of services, and the search for meaningful experiences for a generational cohort. Try to project the spending patterns for this generational cohort at the next life stage.

Research Reports. Locate a published report of a consumer segmentation study in marketing journals or apparel trade publications. Select a product category and analyze the connection between the types of people profiled in the study and that product category. Is the category likely to rise or fall in popularity? Is the market for the product category increasing or decreasing? Should the product category be repositioned to target a different consumer audience? Is this branch of fashion going at a different speed than others?

Resource Pointers

Envirosell, a behavioral market research and consulting company, featuring articles about the company and their methods: www.envirosell.com

Websites related to mass customization:
eShakti: www.eshakti.com
J. Hilburn custom men's shirting and
    suiting: http://jhilburn.com/
Lands' End: www.landsend.com

Fashion social networking sites:
Glam: www.glam.com
MyStyleDiaries: www.mystylediaries.com/
SugarScape: www.sugarscape.com

Brands with social networking space:
Wet Seal: www.wetseal.com

We have to know where the customer is going, and get it to her before she gets there.

—Kenneth Cole

10

SALES FORECASTING

OBJECTIVES

◆ Establish the role of sales forecasting in linking supply and demand

◆ Identify the basic techniques of sales forecasting

◆ Summarize new developments in sales forecasting practices

◆ Demonstrate the link between computer technology and advances in sales forecasting practices

SALES FORECASTING IN CONTEXT

Whether in marketing, sales, finance, production, or distribution, a professional working with short-term sales forecasts needs perspective and context to guide decision making. Quarterly sales figures are small slices of larger cycles (Figure 10.1). Understanding those cycles helps a professional modulate decisions

with some recognition of the bigger picture and what is likely to happen next. Notice how the line representing sales level reflects ups and downs of seasonal variation. But that does not explain the variation completely. The line representing sales level also reflects the influence of the medium-term cycle. For example, at a jeans company, this line could represent the seasons when denim is a strong fashion story versus seasons when it is not. Finally, notice how the line responds to a long-term cycle like a strengthening or weakening economy. The sales level line shows the interaction of short-, medium-, and long-term cycles.

✦ THE PRODUCT LIFE CYCLE

A product progresses through a series of predictable stages called a life cycle, from the point when it is merely a concept to the end of its time in the marketplace (Figure 10.2). For marketing executives, this concept has strategic and tactical implications (Bolt, 1994; Levitt, 1986). For new products, the **product life cycle** provides a preview of the stages and duration that can be expected. For existing products, the recognizable stages in the product life cycle indicate what could happen next. The stages of the product life cycle are:

❖ *Development stage* —This stage begins when a company identifies a market opportunity; product ideas are researched, screened, and developed to satisfy the needs of a target market; and decisions on pricing are made. During this stage, investments are made, but no revenue is generated.

❖ *Introduction stage*—Successful introduction depends on whether the product has been tested and is acceptable to the target market, marketing activities have been correctly integrated, and the launch is timed properly. The goal is to entice the consumer to try the product. During this stage, sales will begin and increase in volume, or the product will fail.

❖ *Market development stage*—A product may survive introduction because it is novel or

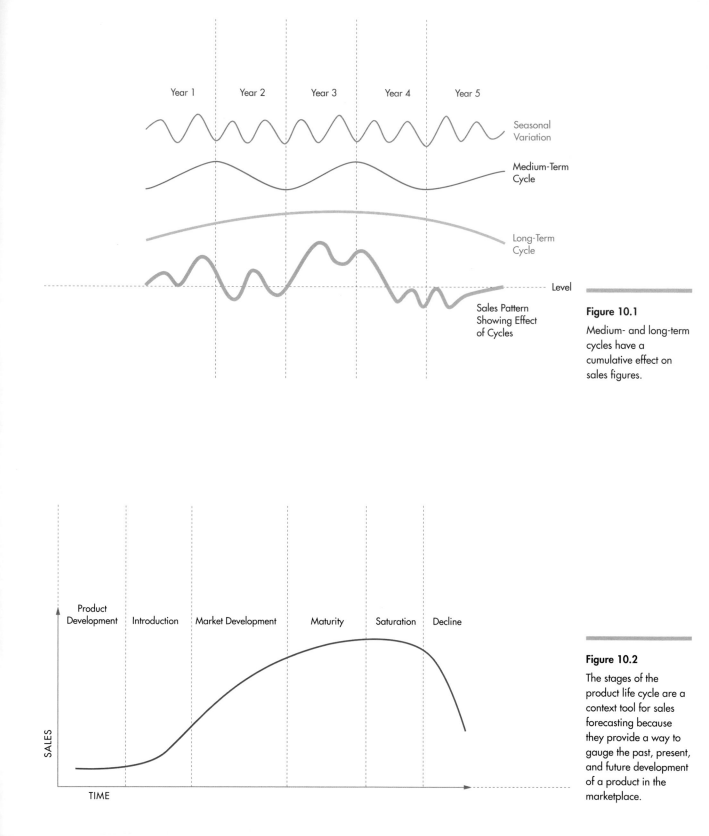

Figure 10.1

Medium- and long-term cycles have a cumulative effect on sales figures.

Figure 10.2

The stages of the product life cycle are a context tool for sales forecasting because they provide a way to gauge the past, present, and future development of a product in the marketplace.

unique, but to continue to sell it must provide a bundle of tangible and intangible attributes that satisfy consumers enough to generate repeat sales or recommendations to others. The company must convince the consumer to prefer this product and this brand. Sales gain momentum as information spreads through advertising, promotion, and word of mouth.

❖ *Exploitation stage*—During this stage, a market-oriented company will seek to extend sales beyond the initial target market to other segments and open new distribution channels as a way to extend the market and promote sales volume.

❖ *Maturity stage*—Variations and versions of the product become widely available. Competition between brands increases and prices decline. At this point, supply catches up with **demand**. Demand can be characterized as expansion—new customers buying for the first time—and replacement or repeat demand—users replacing the product with the same or similar product.

❖ *Saturation stage*—Expansion demand disappears as competitors attempt to take market share from each other using sales promotion activities. Because so much product is available, a "sameness" becomes apparent and brand preference weakens. New substitute products appear and lure customers away. Most companies realign their marketing mix to extend this stage as long as possible.

❖ *Decline stage*—All products eventually decline because consumers' needs, wants, or habits have changed, substitute products have appeared, and the product attributes have degenerated. Some companies withdraw the product at this stage and introduce a replacement product. If not, the decline stage sees a strong downward trend in sales volume, with most sales of the repeat type.

Risk exists at every stage of the product life cycle, but especially at the beginning. In the mid-2000s, Urban Outfitters fielded a resident merchant and design team based in London to monitor European trends. Reacting quickly to emerging trends was deemed an advantage over the usual practice of most companies that send a team several times a year for a week's shopping trip. In 2005 Urban Outfitters noticed a strong trend in Europe toward a silhouette change. John Kyees, Urban Outfitters' corporate financial officer, explained:

> Every season, there are differences in micro fashion changes, and those might be color palettes, prints, length of skirts, or rise in denim jeans. About every 10 to 12 years, there's a silhouette change. And that's what I would describe as a macro change. The last time it occurred was in the early '90s—the fashion moved from the silhouette of an inverted triangle to a silhouette of a triangle.
>
> ("Urban Outfitters," 2007)

To help the audience visualize the difference, he described the inverted triangle as a big top over a skinny bottom like leggings or a tight pant, and the triangle as tighter top over a larger shape on the bottom like a tiered skirt. The team saw in Europe signs of a pendulum swing back to the inverted triangle shape and predicted its arrival in the United States in 6–9 months.

Urban Outfitters invested in the silhouette shift for 2006 merchandise, but the chain struggled with sales that year. As Kyees described the problem: "Normally, we would be able to adjust to a micro trend, but a macro trend is a little harder to adjust." Although the new silhouette was selling in Urban Outfitters' European stores, it wasn't in the United States. When "the silhouette doesn't work, it doesn't matter what the color is. It doesn't matter whether she likes the top. If it doesn't work with the whole package, then she's not going to buy it." Although the company still expected to see the silhouette break through in the United States, they were unsure about the timing and how to help the consumer transition through the change ("Urban Outfitters," 2007).

Time spent attempting to predict the shape and duration of a new product's life allows a more measured approach to production and merchandising and creates lead time for planning competitive moves. Looking at a product's place in the product life cycle provides lead time to develop ways to extend stages and indicates when a product should be phased out. Attention to the stages of the product's life cycle provides a background of expectations against which sales volume can be viewed and projections for the future made (Shearer, 1994).

✦ THE BUSINESS CYCLE

When evaluating sales figures, the forecaster uses a process known as **decomposition** to take into account underlying factors that may be influencing the pattern (Shearer, 1994). The sales figures may reflect an underlying trend toward increasing or decreasing sales, seasonal variation, and the existence of medium- and long-term cycles such as the **business cycle**. The business cycle refers to the cyclical nature of the economy as it passes through the rising and falling phases of prosperity and stagnation. The decomposition process attempts to disentangle trend, seasonal, and cyclical effects to gain a clearer picture of the current situation and a glimpse of future directions.

The cyclical nature of the national economy was first recognized in the nineteenth century and economists have debated the existence and causes of this cycle ever since. A business cycle that rises and falls every 4 to 5 years is common in most of the developed nations of the world. A shock to the system such as an oil embargo and higher oil prices can deepen a recession, whereas lower prices can soften a downturn. Even though these shocks increase or decrease the amplitude of the business cycle, the cycles are still present. Government policy attempts to counteract cyclical movement in the economy, but as long as the underlying causes remain and these causes are not fully understood, the business cycle will continue to be a factor that should be considered in sales forecasting.

✧ The Apparel Cycle

Although there is general agreement that the sales of durable goods are cyclical, there is less agreement on the existence of an apparel cycle. Some experts agree that there is an apparel cycle but disagree about the length of the cycle. An economist for a marketing research firm (Moin, Edelson, & Tosh, 1996) sees 18- to 24-month expansion periods followed by 6- to 12-month contraction periods. In his view, only two apparel cycles since 1948 have been fashion driven and both occurred during the 1960s. Demographics, pricing, or the general business cycle accounts for the others (Steidtmann, 1996). A CEO of an apparel firm sees the cycles of hot apparel sales followed by a cooling-off period in 3- to 5-year intervals. Others argue that swings in apparel sales are tied to the overall health of the economy and job security. Still others see sales driven not by apparel cycles but by life cycle stages—as the median age of the population rises and priorities shift away from fashion-driven purchasing. Some observers suggest that business and apparel cycles are flattening out with fewer peaks and valleys (Moin et al., 1996). When an issue is this controversial, the best approach for forecasters is to monitor the business and apparel cycles, develop ways to predict the timing and amplitude of the cycles, and plan a corporate response. The first step is to understand why cycles happen.

One reason cycles exist is because of the lag between changes in demand and response to that change. Consider the executive watching sales figures for an indication of change in demand level (Shearer, 1994). The figures are naturally variable, and it may be some time before the executive recognizes an increase in demand and responds to it (Figure 10.3). Meanwhile, the increased demand will begin to pull down inventory levels. At some point, the executive will see the disparity between demand and inventory and increase production. In time, production will build back inventory to the level of demand. If there were no random variations to obscure this point from the executive's view and if actions could be enacted immediately, cycles would disappear because the executive would be able to synchronize demand, inventory, and production. However, when the executive decides to cut back production, another lag between change and response is likely. During that time, production continues to build inventory and inventory levels rise above demand. Once again production is cut back, inventory falls below demand, and another cycle commences. In the worst-case scenario, these cycles apply not to a single company but to the industry, and the effect ripples down the supply chain to industries providing materials and components. Industries dependent on consumer taste are more prone to this kind of cycle.

✧ Consumer Confidence as an Indicator

Inventory levels in key industries within the economy signal phases of the business cycle. Commentators and analysts also look at other factors as indicators of turning points in the business cycle. Levels of retail sales and consumer expenditures are often mentioned as factors. Analysts watch two indexes of consumer confidence (Weiss, 2003):

❖ The *Consumer Confidence Index* (CCI) from the Conference Board, a non-profit business research organization. The CCI uses five questions and a mail survey of 5,000 households. The first two questions deal with the current state of business (called the Present Situation Index), and the other three ask consumers to consider conditions 6 months into the future (called the Expectations Index).

❖ The *Index of Consumer Sentiment* (ICS), managed by the Survey Research Center at the University of Michigan. The ICS uses a phone interview to ask five questions about consumers' confidence in making big-ticket purchases.

The surveys break down results to highlight demographic (but neither survey reports findings by race or ethnicity) and geographic differences.

The idea behind consumer confidence as an indicator is that there is a relationship between economic conditions and consumer behavior. Specifically, consumers are more willing to buy when they expect economic conditions in the future to be favorable to their own well-being (Figure 10.4). As the chief economist for a financial rating company put it: "Consumer confidence figures are really a measure of how we feel about ourselves. If consumers are worried, Main Street retailers better get worried, too" (Weiss, 2003). One of the key factors influencing consumer

Figure 10.3

The natural and expected ups and downs of sales can mask a change in demand. The time it takes an executive to recognize the change and respond contributes to the start of another cycle.

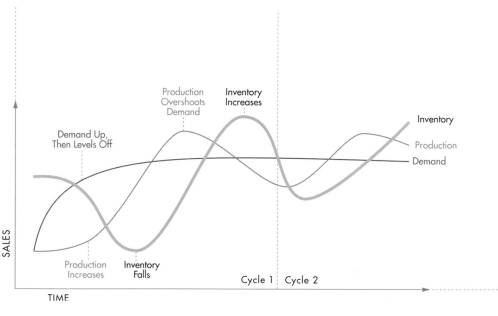

Figure 10.4

Measures of consumer confidence reflect Americans' optimism or pessimism about their economic well-being in the present and future. Retailers and manufacturers watching these indexes assume that consumers are more willing to buy when they expect economic conditions in the future to be favorable.

sentiment is employment—when employment numbers are high, consumer confidence tends to be too; but when unemployment is high, consumer doubts about the economy and their financial future pull consumer confidence down.

If consumer confidence is down, manufacturers anticipate that consumers will spend less overall, shift spending to other categories, postpone purchases, or become more sensitive to price. When anticipating a downturn in consumer confidence, companies are more likely to turn to price promotion.

Like many economic issues, predictability based on consumer confidence is controversial. Some people question whether consumers respond to actual economic conditions or to news about economic conditions. These people argue that consumer confidence is overly influenced by the media's reaction to political, social, and economic issues and to stock market fluctuations. A study by Cotton Incorporated ("Confidence," 1998) shows only a weak correlation between consumer confidence levels and spending for apparel.

✧ Leading Indicators

Forecasting techniques tend to be stronger in predicting trends than in recognizing and anticipating cycles (Shearer, 1994). The **leading indicator** approach attempts to overcome this problem. Forecasters begin with a set of economic factors likely to signal a turning point in the business cycle—factors such as interest rates, housing starts, and consumer confidence. The factors are chosen because of their importance to overall economic health, their history of being in sync with the business cycle, and the quick release of the figures for use in analysis. Forecasters construct a set of time-series techniques representing the factors and then take a weighted average to produce a final leading indicator that can be charted. If well constructed, the peaks and troughs of the leading indicator will anticipate those seen in sales by 6 to 12 months (Figure 10.5).

This kind of analysis is more useful in anticipating the turning points in the business cycle and less useful in predicting the amplitude of the upswing or downswing. Because all industries are tied together in the national economy, leading indicators constructed by the government can be helpful in putting sales forecasting in a larger context. The government's leading indicators are frequently discussed on national and business news broadcasts and reported in business and trade publications.

Figure 10.5

If well constructed, leading indicators predict what sales will be like 6 to 12 months in the future.

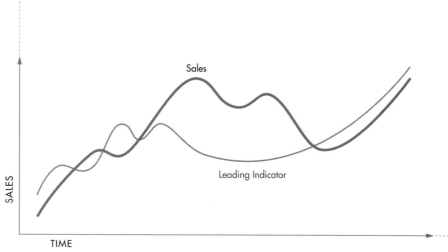

✦ THE FASHION SYSTEM

In the marketplace, consumer shifts may correlate with changes in tastes, lifestyles, immigration, or technological developments, shifts in the prices of raw materials, and other such factors. A system such as this is an example of **self-organized criticality** because the changes form a dynamic that can be understood only from a holistic viewpoint, one that considers the entire system, not just the individual elements. Fashion, like many systems, can be characterized as a mass of intricately interlocking subsystems, just barely on the edge of criticality, with avalanches of all sizes rippling through and rearranging things. Such a system is always poised on the edge—just as the fashion system is always poised on the edge of change. Self-organized criticality, like the phase transitions at the edge of chaos, offers an intriguing visualization that allows executives to explore fashion as a non-linear system and question the role of fashion forecasting in the future.

There is a lot of apparel already in production in a pipeline when an innovation in fabrication, color, or styling can emerge unexpectedly which may have no effect, create a small avalanche of interest, or even set off a huge chain reaction that changes the entire system.

When consumers begin to experiment with a new lifestyle component or **consumer confidence** shifts, the change ripples through the system. A new movie, music video, or Vine introduces street fashion to a larger audience and a kind of "information contagion" passes the look from one individual to another, from one social group to another.

Buyers and sellers behave like agents in a complex system because they interact with each other, sharing information by word of mouth (Figure 10.6). Through self-selection, some buyers cluster around certain products or styles, forming patterns of preference. When an innovation enters the system, it may disappear almost immediately or some agents may adopt it and spread news of the innovation to others. On occasion these activities reach a critical mass and set off a chain reaction of decisions, resulting in a "hit" (Farrell, 1998). What appears to be an occurrence of many people simultaneously coming to the same decision really started with a single innovation that built in popularity as networks formed and patterns of interaction emerged. This occurrence, or hit, can be a random event that was not initiated by the actions of some coordinating outside force. A hit moves through a social system, creating new preference structures and networks. Some hits are so powerful that they fundamentally change the relationships between agents, dissolving some connections and forging others.

Early in the twenty-first century there was a push to create "connectedness" between workers inside the company, suppliers, and customers (Levy, 2003). Retailers attempted to create an up-to-the-minute continuous flow of sales information by installing point-of-sale (POS) scanners in retail stores (Fisher et al., 1994). Although this seemed like a logical move toward real-time marketing, there were some unanticipated benefits. The availability of POS data made it possible to identify smaller market niches. Flexible manufacturing made it possible to produce smaller quantities of products efficiently enough to earn a profit. Together with global competition, faster product development, and attempts to give consumers exactly what they wanted, these forces unleashed a proliferation of products. The increase in new products meant that each one had a shorter lifetime. The result was that there was little or no **sales history** on which to base forecasts. POS data is **aggregated** (summarized and combined by categories), making it even more difficult to forecast demand for the many individual products or stock-keeping units (SKUs).

Forecasting is relatively easy, straightforward, and accurate for products with long life cycles and steady sales. However, the fashion apparel business is one of the most volatile because it creates products that are new, highly seasonal, or have short life cycles. In such situations, forecasts become increasingly inaccurate. Errors in sales forecasting result in two kinds of losses:

Figure 10.6

The marketplace is viewed as a complex system because buyers and sellers network with each other, share information, and form groups and alliances without an outside force coordinating the activity.

❖ **markdowns**, when retailers have unwanted goods remaining at the end of a selling period, goods that must be sold at a discounted price, even if that sale price results in a loss;

❖ **stockouts**, when sales on more popular items are lost because merchandise is not in stock at the time when consumers request it.

The downturn of the US economy just after the turn of the twenty-first century pushed apparel companies to focus on inventory control and sales forecasting. Big-volume brands invested in computer systems to forecast demand so that they could keep inventories low. This approach was complicated by a trend among retailers to buy closer to the season, giving manufacturers little room for mistakes. For basic styles expected to sell at full price, the strategy was core replenishment—keep retailers in stock on these stable sellers. The fashion items that created excitement in the stores were viewed as "one-hit wonders" and not restocked. For the styles between these extremes, companies tracked retail sell-through of goods on a daily basis by style, color, and stores, reacting quickly on items that started to trend upward. Reacting quickly was not easy for brands importing merchandise because of the long lead times when compared to domestic manufacturing ("Vendors," 2001).

Fast fashion is a term used to describe practices employed by several large global retailers in which merchandise assortments are adapted to "current and emerging trends as quickly as possible" (Sull & Turconi, 2008). Fast fashion differs from the traditional retail calendar with its fall and spring seasons, instead relying on a steady flow of new merchandise for consumers. The main reason for the rapid rise of fast-fashion retailing is technological advancements that have greatly reduced the product development cycle. The product development process traditionally took large retailers 6 months or more from concept to completion; now, however, thanks to computer-aided design (CAD), product development has been compressed from 6

months into 6 weeks, and in some cases as few as 2 weeks ("Fast Fashion," 2005). Fast-fashion retailers have grown more rapidly than the apparel industry as a whole while taking market share from traditional retailers. They also have had a superior fiscal performance to that of other sectors of the retail industry (Sull & Turconi, 2008).

Fast-fashion retailers produce a large number of designs, which are shipped in continuous small deliveries so that new merchandise is regularly on the showroom floor. These garments are shipped in groups of twelve to sixteen collections each year, which is a stark contrast to the traditional retail calendar that consists of fall and spring collections. While many traditional retailers rely on outsourcing production to a network of global contractors and subcontractors, fast-fashion retailers such as Zara are vertically integrated and own their own production facilities, a setup which provides total control; Zara can design, manufacture, and ship a new garment to its stores and have it on display in just 15 days from start to finish (Ferdows, Lewis, & Machuca, 2004). Producing so many styles for such a large number of stores necessitates having massive production facilities. Inditex makes approximately 840 million garments per year for Zara and its other brands (Hansen, 2012). Despite the large number of garments it manufactures, Zara's production facilities are extremely flexible. Unlike the majority of retailers that limit changes in orders to 20 percent once the season has begun, Zara lets its retailers change 40–50 percent of their orders, which allows them to avoid overproduction and, ultimately, markdowns (Ferdows et al., 2004).

Because of the constant turnover of styles, fast-fashion retailers have transformed the traditional retail calendar from a biannual delivery schedule to one with many more frequent deliveries. In response to the pressure placed on them by fast-fashion companies, one traditional department store retailer, JC Penney, entered the fast-fashion landscape by opening "boutiques" in several of its stores for the brand extension MNG by Mango. The boutiques, which are about 1,500 square feet and are highlighted from other departments through the use of Mango's distinctive lighting and decor, have merchandise deliveries once every 2 weeks. After its launch, the brand's performance was impressive: MNG by Mango is three times more productive than any of JC Penney's other contemporary brands (Alva, 2011).

Sales forecasting has an impact on every apparel executive's profession whether they help develop the analysis, read and act on the reports, or merely react to the result of overestimating or underestimating sales. For this reason, apparel professionals need a basic understanding of the traditional approaches to sales forecasting and the leading-edge technologies making real-time marketing a reality in the apparel industry.

For retailers, software for assortment planning—assistance in deciding which stock-keeping units will be offered in each store, on what date, and in what quantities—is helping pinpoint local preferences and match them to products. Instead of being confined to store square footage and sales velocity, the latest software considers customer size and color preferences, lifestyle, and local weather. For example, if fashion dictates a big denim season, the software identifies those clusters of stores likely to benefit from the trend and those that will not, like New York City where stores do better with career styles. Manufacturers use similar tools to "recap information early on, to see what's selling [at the wholesale level] and maybe make drop decisions earlier than in the past, and do substitutions more easily," according to Debbie Beer-Christensen, associate director of wholesale systems at Phillips-Van Heusen Corp (Corcoran, 2008e).

SALES FORECASTING CONCEPTS

People sometimes confuse the **sales forecast** with the **sales plan** (Mentzer & Moon, 2005). The sales forecast is a projection of expected demand given a set of environmental conditions. Quantitative and qualitative methods are used to develop the sales forecast. A sales plan is the managerial strategy designed to meet or exceed the sales forecast. The sales plan defines goals and provides motivation for sales levels that meet or exceed the base—the underlying sales forecast. Managers sometimes make the mistake of skipping or ignoring sales forecasting and set the sales plan goal at 5 percent or 10 percent higher than last year's sales. Unless environmental factors such as growth in the industry, market share, or consumer demand favor that increase, no amount of motivation or promotion will make the sales plan happen. The measure of accuracy for the sales forecast is the difference between the forecast and what actually happens. The best way to improve forecasting accuracy is to review actual sales figures against the sales forecast for the same time period. Differences between the two must be explained in terms of variation in the environmental conditions or problems with assumptions underlying the forecast. In this way, executives build a better understanding of how environmental factors have an impact on sales.

Sales forecasts have a specific time horizon and are usually updated quarterly. Many executives in a firm need access to the sales forecast, including:

* marketing managers planning promotion, pricing, and channel placement for individual products and product lines;
* sales managers developing the sales plan by geographic territory or sales force deployment;
* financial managers projecting costs, profit levels, and capital needed to operate;
* production managers planning and scheduling labor and equipment, and ordering raw materials;
* distribution managers planning the logistics of getting products from production sites to retailing venues.

Sales forecasting requires access to three kinds of information. First, forecasters need *internal*

Profile: Brian Tully, Senior Vice President, Global Operations at Lanier Clothes, a Division of Oxford Industries, Inc.

Lanier Clothes is a leading menswear manufacturer which designs and markets branded and private-label men's suits, sportcoats, suit separates, and dress slacks that are sold in national chains, department stores, specialty stores, specialty catalog retailers, and discount retailers across the United States. The company uses the strategy of brand tiers by producing multiple brands, each with its own design signature, price point, and target market. Each of Lanier Clothes' brands corresponds with the standard department store categories of "good," "better," and "best" pricing tiers. Company brands include:

❖ Arnold Brant Collection, upscale luxury tailored clothing (Lloyd & Palmieri, 2007);

❖ Ben Sherman, an iconic British label known for its cool factor and association with rock musicians, selling at the bridge-level price point (Collins, 2007; Lipke, 2006);

❖ Geoffrey Beene, tailored clothing for men and boys at the better price point ("Five Year," 2009);

❖ Kenneth Cole, tailored clothing with modern contemporary styling;

❖ Billy London, retro-mod look for younger customers;

❖ Docker, traditional styling at the moderate price point.

In addition to its private labels, Lanier also produces clothing for branded clients such as Stafford, Lands' End, Alfani, Structure, and Kenneth Roberts. Tully explained that the motivation for the company to balance its private-label operations with branded lines arose because Lanier Clothes had been "more negatively impacted by the trend toward [casual] than any other division [in Oxford Industries]," because total sales for tailored clothing "has been pretty consistently a downward trend. The real key has been increasing market share every year. Becoming more branded is definitely a strategy—it gives you a stronger identity in the marketplace" (1999).

Lanier Clothes currently produces more than 2 million pairs of pants and 2.5 million coats annually. With manufacturing operations in seven countries, a design studio for unique fabrications in Italy, and a design/product development and sample department in the United States, the company employs state-of-the-art planning tools to manage their business. Additionally, they collaborate with retailers to manage stocks of the company's products down to each individual store and stock-keeping unit.

Along with the challenges of any fashion business, such as short selling seasons and difficulty in predicting consumer preferences for color and style, Lanier Clothes must manage a complex supply chain for a complex product—each style comes in multiple colors and sizes. Sizing for tailored clothing is more detailed than for other apparel categories—dress shirts are sized by separate neck and sleeve measurement, tailored clothing by chest measurement and coat length, and pants by waist and in-seam measurement. John Baumgartner, Chief Information Officer and Senior Vice President of Oxford Industries, explained the scope of the company's challenge: "For just one pant style with four different color options, we might be managing a combined SKU count of more than 100" ("Supply Chain," 2009).

In the late 1980s, Oxford Industries started to explore upgrading corporate planning functions through internal reviews and working with a consulting firm to determine how investments in information technology could increase operational efficiency. Tully has seen changes in the way sales forecasting is done since he joined the company in 1978. "The way technology allows people to do more—a function of being able to collect the data and format the data." Specifically, in the past executives "had less time to forecast because so much time was spent collecting the data." Now that it is easier to gather results, the emphasis has shifted from acquisition to analysis. "Technology has been wonderful in giving us great tools to play 'what-if' with, but people have to understand the market and what the numbers should be. It takes a sense of the business (which you only get by time and involvement) to recognize when the numbers aren't right or when you want to look at them in a different way" (1999).

The company implemented JDA Demand software to improve forecast accuracy. Baumgartner cites an example of how the planning system works: A key customer's seasonal forecast didn't agree with the company's on a particular style—the retailer predicted higher demand. In a meeting to reconcile the forecast, the retailer decided to begin the season with a moderate buy and monitor results to determine which forecast was more accurate. "In that situation, our forecast to produce less product turned out to be more accurate, and the retailer agreed to use our forecast for the remainder of the season. Without our ability to offer a statistically sound forecast, we would have manufactured at least 10 percent to 15 percent more product, forcing the retailer to eventually mark it down" ("Supply Chain," 2009).

According to Tully, in the forecasting process, the "starting point is historical data—how has [the company] done with this customer in the past, how has [the company] done with this style in the past." Insights from historical data are blended with input from the retail partner on what's going on with the customer base. The numbers get adjusted based on the judgment of company executives with years of experience, who "look at the numbers and add a more qualitative or expert opinion." That opinion takes into account "consumer confidence, macroeconomics issues, what's happening in the marketplace, and what's happening with competitors" (1999).

As Danny Halim, vice president of supply and manufacturing solutions at JDA, sees it ("Supply Chain," 2009): "Demand planning is not just about figuring out how much of a product will sell, but taking the style/color/size complexity and aggregating that up so you can look at demand by product line or geographic region or distribution channel. At the same time, you need to be able to look in the other direction and see demand in a very granular way, down to the store level." Tully explains that the apparel executive looks at a number of seasons at once with "different levels of granularity" in the forecasts. A forecast that looks at a selling season farthest in the future will be "at a very high level," such as the total number of units for a particular season. The forecast of the closest season to the selling period will break the total units into product categories, such as "how many suits, how many sportcoats and a breakdown by customer." For the next season the forecast shows a breakdown by style. For the current selling season, the company gets "point-of-sale history every week showing how you actually stand."

"New products are the roughest things to forecast," says Tully (1999). "On fashion, it's really just a matter of looking at history. The only tool we have is what we have done in the past that is similar. Will the color behave like a similar fashion color in the same product? Will this new style behave like one in a similar rollout? If you can find something similar [to the new product], that can help, but you can still get burned in both directions." Whether forecasting for "a new product or a new target customer or a new channel of distribution, it is very difficult to forecast growth and the expert opinion becomes crucial."

Sources:

Collins, J. (2007, August). Ben Sherman goes back to its roots. *License*, 10(7), 52–54.

Five year licensing renewal for Oxford Industries and Geoffrey Beene, LLD (2009, July 28). Reuters. Retrieved August 30, 2009, from www.reuters.com. Lanier Clothes (2014). Retrieved October 26, 2014, from www.lanierclothes.com.

Lipke, D. (2006, December 11). At Ben Sherman consolidating collection; Brit brand to sell single collection in U.K. and U.S. markets in effort to create unified premium image. *Daily News Record*, p. 3.

Lloyd, B., & Palmieri, J.E. (2007, June 11). At Oxford impacted by tough clothing sales; President of Arnold Brand label resigns but retains financial interest; Oxford remains committed to line. *Daily News Record*, p. 4.

Supply chain didn't fit after apparel company changed its business model (2009, March 27). *Logistics & Supply Chain Strategies*. Retrieved August 30, 2009, from www.supplychainbrain.com.

Tully, Brian (1999, June 11). Phone interview.

data on sales volume and marketing actions such as changes in pricing, promotional efforts, or channels of distribution. Second, they need information on *future plans* for marketing and product distribution. Finally, they need *external data* relevant to their market and information on general economic, political, and cultural conditions.

The internal data allow the forecasters to group data in different ways to evaluate recent and past performance (Bolt, 1994). Some of the basic ways to group data for analysis are by:

❖ *Sales volume*—Determine the relative contribution each product or product group makes to the company's revenue by comparing sales for that product or group to total sales volume.

❖ *Sales volume by geographic area*—Break down sales by geographic area (such as by sales territories) and compare actual sales to potential sales given the demographics and retail climate in each area.

❖ *Sales volume by time period*—Discover seasonal effects and the result of price changes, promotions, and advertising on sales by comparing fluctuations in sales against a timescale.

❖ *Sales volume by **sales channel***—Discover which sales channels are most profitable by comparing sales performance by type of distribution and retail venue as a guide to increasing or decreasing reliance on each channel.

Viewing sales volume through these various lenses, the forecasters correlate the effect of past decisions on sales and market share.

The quality of the forecast depends on how precisely sales are tracked. Company executives decide whether to track sales by:

❖ stock-keeping unit (individual products by color and size);
❖ individual product;
❖ product family (related items).

The company executives also decide how to aggregate sales data—daily, weekly, or monthly. Setting these levels for analysis depends on the prior experience of the company, the product profile, and the volatility of the marketplace.

The sales forecast is a projection of expectations given past performance and what is known about future marketing efforts. These projections will be inaccurate unless they are corrected to take into account external data such as the expectations for the economy and the effects of the product life cycle. Putting sales projections in context improves forecasting accuracy.

STRATEGIC DATA PARTNERSHIPS

In the past, each segment of the apparel industry, from fabrics and apparel manufacturers to retailers, developed its own forecasting and planning. Manufacturers overproduced the number of styles they made in order to provide a "safety" stock to meet unpredictable demand, and both manufacturers and retailers shared the costs of keeping these products in inventory. As the season progressed, shortages of hot-selling items could not be restocked and excess items were marked down. Levels of safety stock were necessary to ensure delivery dates and to reduce uncertainty about demand.

The apparel industry acts like a **retail supply chain** with integrated forecasting and planning. Retailers share responsibility for forecasting and planning with their vendors. Manufacturers share forecasts with suppliers of components such as fabric, findings, and trim.

Technology makes collaborative forecasting possible (Power, 1998). The necessity of keeping safety stock is reduced when manufacturing becomes more agile and efficient because products are produced closer to delivery dates. Better forecasting practices reduce uncertainty about demand and that further reduces the need to carry inventory. By reducing the two reasons for carrying inventory—as safety stock, because of uncertainty about demand—the apparel supply chain saves on inventory costs and gains dollars for technology investment.

The vision of real-time marketing in the twenty-first century is emerging with the following characteristics:

❖ active, continuous processing of up-to-the-minute information about consumers, competitors' actions, and the dynamics of the marketplace;
❖ quick reaction to opportunities by adjusting the flow of goods or changing prices and promotion strategy;
❖ connection through secure global communications networks.

As previously mentioned, the introduction of point-of-sales (POS) scanners allowed marketers to capture sales data as it happened, which could be tabulated weekly (or more frequently during peak periods) and shared with vendors through electronic data interchange (EDI). The vision for EDI was as a conduit for forecasting data between vendors and retailers. Instead, it became an excellent way for retailers to transmit electronic versions of standard business documents such as purchase orders and invoices. The standard formats did not allow for the capture of other information relevant to forecasting.

Today, traditional EDI is augmented by **extranets**—private networks that enable users outside a company to access information using Internet-based technology. Extranets allow retailers and manufacturers to share information, create joint forecasts, and monitor results.

✦ AUTOMATED REPLENISHMENT SYSTEMS

In an **automated replenishment system**, a retailer and a manufacturer collaborate on a system to share critical sales forecasting information (Hye, 1998). The goal is more precise forecasting and improved in-stock positions in stores. In this kind of collaboration, manufacturers gain access to retailers' information about promotion plans, store openings, local events, and other factors that have an impact on forecasts. Retailers gain access to order status and are alerted to any problems in production or distribution as it affects delivery time. Additionally, partners can share more subtle information, such as insights about how sales in one department may spur increased sales in a related department—information with significant impact on forecasts.

Retailers are demanding more of manufacturers, especially large companies with significant information technology investments. JC Penney depends on a VF Corporation software system called Retail Floor Space Management to analyze differences in climate, demographics, and historical sales patterns and suggest the best product assortments for more than 1,000 stores. The goal of this kind of collaboration is to avoid under- or overstocking, improve customer service, and increase sales. VF Corporation established itself as a leader in vendor-managed inventory in the early 1990s with a system that analyzed daily inventory for each retailer's stores and each stock-keeping unit using forecasts of sales, planned promotions, shipping lead times, and changes in retail floor space. This early version of "collaborative planning, forecasting, and replenishment" (CPFR) was credited as helping double VF's Wrangler jeanswear brand in the decade when it was introduced (Bacheldor, 2003). After acquiring brands targeting surfers, skateboarders, and other outdoor enthusiasts, the company has positioned itself as a "lifestyle" apparel company. VF Corporation's supply chain includes more than 800,000 SKUs (numbers that identify each product it makes in all divisions), ships to approximately 47,000 retailers, produces

products in more than 1,600 factories, purchases fabrics from over 100 wholesalers, and trim from nearly 3,000 suppliers. With each acquisition, VF converted the supply management to their systems. "Humans have a real habit of getting into habits. Because a color was once popular, there is a tendency to stay with it, even though demand has gone down. [The software] doesn't have any habits," according to Ellen Martin, vice-president of supply chain systems (McAdams, 2007).

Nygård International, a manufacturer of women's moderate and bridge apparel, developed a high-level automated replenishment system (Zimmermann, 1998c). The Nygård approach is based on the idea that retailers do 80 percent of their business on 20 percent of their products. Nygård combines highly automated production with an extranet for EDI transactions with suppliers and customers such as Dillard's. The company's response to orders is so quick that retailers need no inventory except what is on the sales floor, and out-of-stock situations on fast-selling items are virtually eliminated. In some cases, orders received at Nygård in the morning are shipped within 24 hours. The manufacturer accomplishes this feat by having a constant accurate picture of its inventory position with retailers and suppliers. Using POS data, the system identifies slower-selling items and generates an alert to reduce production on those items. The system is further augmented with a customer database system to provide more accurate information about the women who purchase Nygård apparel. This information is used to make decisions about new products.

Nygård combines technology with knowing his target market—baby boomer customers who are frequently overlooked by other companies. Peter Nygård plans to visit all 330 Dillard's stores over the next several years to talk with his customers because, as he says, "Designing isn't worth anything unless it sells" (Sewing, 2007).

Some companies are even converting lost sales into customer service opportunities. In its automated replenishment system, Duck Head Apparel allows retailers to enter an item missing from the sales floor into the POS system as a sale. A ticket is generated and the item is shipped from Duck Head's distribution center directly to the customer in 48 hours (Zimmermann, 1998a).

✦ CATEGORY MANAGEMENT

Category management is another collaborative strategy between manufacturers and retailers. In category management, the manufacturer provides expertise in a category including trends, fit, silhouettes, and finishes and makes recommendations on merchandising assortment, display, and inventory controls in that product category on a store-by-store basis. Whereas the store retains control and often modifies the suggestions, the manufacturer acts as a specialist in forecasting to keep the right flow of merchandise going to the selling floor. The exchange of sales data allows the vendor to pinpoint emerging trends and restock accordingly.

More manufacturers have the potential to participate in category management because more companies own multiple brands in a product category through mergers and acquisitions. VF Corporation owns several jeanswear brands—Lee and Wrangler for department stores, Rustler and Rider priced for mass-market channels. With several denim brands, the company can position each for a different target consumer and different retail channels. VF Corporation differentiates the brands in image, pricing packaging, placement, and presentation (Ozzard, 1996). The **brand tiers** or a multiple-brand strategy enable the company to cover more of the market. Because VF Corporation has a multiple-brand strategy in the denim business, a corporate infrastructure of EDI, and automatic replenishment programs, the company is in position to partner with top retail accounts in category management.

As these collaborative efforts to create a retail supply chain strategy become more common, so do advances in forecasting software. New software packages can produce forecasts for each SKU, categorized by type of product, location, and channel of distribution. The software determines which methods produce the best forecast by analyzing demand data (historical sales data), testing multiple methodologies, and comparing forecasts to actual results. The system is designed to adjust forecasts to consider the impact of holidays and sales. Picking the best forecast for product, consumer type, region, and channel of distribution is possible because of advanced mathematical modeling, artificial intelligence, and advanced computing technologies. EDITD is an online resource for merchandising professionals, available by subscription, that provides several forecasting services, including market analytics that enable members to compare their own product assortment offerings by SKU with those of their competitors. Their system allows members to view competitors' new stock, discount activity, entry and exit prices, and the number of options available in their stock, which allows subscribers to benchmark their own product assortment against that of their competition.

SALES FORECASTING METHODS

To be of value, the POS data a company collects in large-scale databases must be reduced to meaningful proportions using conceptual and statistical frameworks. Yet many managers have a limited background in sales forecasting and are daunted by the many statistical techniques that can be used. Selecting which techniques are appropriate for a particular situation can be confusing. To begin to pierce that confusion, managers can view these techniques as falling into three broad categories (Mentzer & Moon, 2005):

❖ **Time-series techniques**—A common forecasting task is to predict sales for the next 12 months based on sales of the past 36 months. **Time-series forecasting** are quantitative techniques—that is, they use values recorded at regular time intervals (sales history) to predict future values.

- **Correlation or regression techniques**—Another common forecasting task is to predict the increase in sales given some marketing action such as a sales promotion or advertising campaign. In this case, correlation or regression techniques are used to compare how a change in one variable (e.g., advertising effort) causes a change in another variable (e.g., sales volume).

- **Qualitative techniques**—Changes in sales volume may result from the actions of the company or from other factors such as actions by competitors and economic conditions. Time-series techniques cannot foresee and regression techniques cannot account for changes in demand patterns and other relationships that affect sales volume. Instead **qualitative techniques** (also called subjective and judgmental techniques) call on the expertise of people inside and outside the company to adjust the forecast to account for these factors.

The three categories include many different sales forecasting techniques—there are about sixty different time-series techniques alone. However, managers need to understand only a few basic techniques—all the others are variations of the basic group. Sets of quantitative management tools are now available as software packages so that managers can manipulate data in spreadsheets and databases on their desktops instead of having to request an analysis from the management information staff. Because the software performs the calculations, managers can shift their focus to understanding the reasoning behind the mathematics.

✦ TIME-SERIES TECHNIQUES

Time-series forecasting looks only at patterns in sales history and projects those patterns to make a forecast. Time-series techniques look at one or more of the following patterns (Figure 10.7):

- **level**, the horizontal sales history as if demand was stable with no trend, seasonality, or noise in the sales data;

- **trend**, the continuing pattern of increasing or decreasing sales represented as a line or curve;

- **seasonality**, a yearly pattern of increasing or decreasing sales that corresponds to the season;

- **noise**, the part of sales fluctuations that appears random and cannot be explained because the pattern has not occurred consistently in the past.

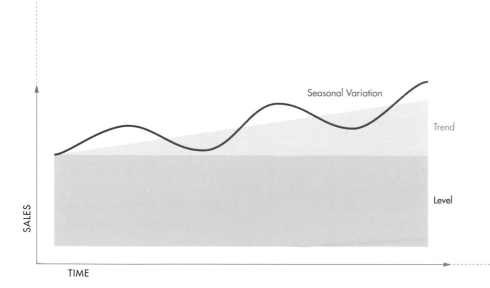

Figure 10.7

Sales data can be dissected into the components of level, trend, seasonality, and noise.

All time-series techniques can be classified either as **open-model time-series (OMTS)** or **fixed-model time-series (FMTS)** techniques.

Open-model time-series techniques first analyze the time-series to determine the components, then build unique models, and forecast the time-series into the future. Using OMTS forecasting techniques has a number of drawbacks: the method requires training, considerable analysis time, and many periods of sales history, and results vary in accuracy with the skill of the user. Thus, the OMTS techniques have limited use in sales forecasting (Bolt, 1994).

FMTS techniques are simpler and less expensive because they require less data storage. Due to the fact that they adjust quickly to changing sales conditions, these techniques are appropriate for short-term forecasting. FMTS begins with the idea that the forecast for next month's sales is the average of all past sales. The average "dampens" out fluctuations caused by noise, trend, and seasonality. So, the average does a good job of identifying the level but ignores two important patterns—trend and seasonality.

Improvements in calculating the average can improve the forecasting power of FMTS techniques (Mentzer & Moon, 2005):

❖ *Moving Average*—The forecaster can improve the forecast by using only the most recent data to calculate the average rather than using all previous data. To do that, the forecaster must decide how many periods of sales data to use in making the forecast. If the forecaster chooses too many, the moving average and the ordinary average for all time periods are practically the same. If the forecaster chooses too few, the moving average projects sales for the next period equal to sales for the last period.

❖ *Exponential Smoothing*—Exponential smoothing can provide a way to improve on the moving average by weighting the most recent sales period more heavily in the forecast while decreasing weights for the older periods at an exponential rate. A number of additional techniques have been developed to fine-tune the exponential smoothing technique and increase sensitivity to trend and seasonality.

FMTS techniques are useful if changes in the overall level of demand, trend, and seasonality are fairly regular. FMTS techniques do not take into consideration the impact of outside factors such as price changes, sales promotions, or economic activity.

✦ CORRELATION OR REGRESSION TECHNIQUES

Missteps in apparel at Wal-Mart can be traced to overreliance on internal data and to the exclusion of external trend data. The company has a huge volume of information in their databases but lacks "strong knowledge about what happens with the competition and with consumers' mind-set," according to an industry analyst. In contrast, the competition (Target and Kohl's) have done a better job of blending internal and external trend data for decisions about fashion products (Power, 2007).

Correlation or regression techniques look at the relationships between sales and outside factors. Outside factors include marketing-mix changes such as price changes, advertising, and promotion. The analysis helps researchers see the effects of relevant factors such as whether sales decline after implementing a price increase or if sales increase in the time period just after the launching of an advertising campaign.

Correlation or regression techniques are also used to investigate the relationship between sales volume and economic or demographic shifts. In that case, the analysis allows researchers to see if a decline in consumer confidence in the economy has led to decreasing sales or to determine whether, as consumers age, their purchasing patterns change.

To understand these types of problems, the forecaster needs datasets that include past history on each factor and sales volume. By comparing outside factors and sales volume, the forecaster seeks to discover whether a relationship exists and, if so, its strength. That relationship then can be used to forecast sales under similar situations in the future.

Therefore, unlike time-series techniques, correlation or regression techniques provide a "broad environmental perspective for forecasting sales" (Mentzer & Moon, 2005, p. 12). The drawback to these techniques is that they require large amounts of data and are most useful when the time horizon is more than 6 months.

✧ Government Sources for Data

Some of the data needed for correlation and regression techniques comes from the government. Government data provide a comprehensive statistical picture of life in the United States. The government specializes in socioeconomic characteristics of the US population, including age, race, gender, educational attainment, labor-force status, occupation, income, and much more. Other countries do the same. Sales forecasters use this information to put past, current, and expected sales into the larger context of economic life. For forecasting purposes, the following government information is particularly important:

- ❖ *The Census Bureau*—The US Census is conducted every 10 years and is the basis for the yearly updates by private data companies. The Census Bureau publishes the *Current Population Reports* series, which contains long-range projections of the population by age, sex, and race.
- ❖ *The Consumer Expenditure Survey*—This survey provides data on the full range of household expenditures by age group, income, and household type.
- ❖ *The Bureau of Labor Statistics (BLS)*—Every other year, the BLS projects the size and characteristics of the labor force and growth projections for various industries and occupations.

✧ Additional Sources of Data

Non-profit organizations such as trade associations and consumer groups are good sources of information. Consider not only associations in the apparel industry but also others with relevant information about consumer spending trends. For example, the National Association of Realtors publishes studies on home-buying activity.

With the coming of the information age, more companies began specializing in collecting and selling data from **syndicated surveys**—surveys conducted by a group of sponsors who are interested in the same topic and who share costs and results. Such surveys focus on media use, market studies, and other research efforts. Companies that run such surveys publish directories describing the studies that are available and their cost.

The cliché "timing is everything" holds true for forecasting data. Government surveys are valuable because they track trends over time and are conducted in a consistent way year after year. However, the most up-to-date numbers come from private sources. The forecaster must decide whether to use the no-frills, relatively inexpensive government sources or the quick but sometimes costly private sources.

✦ QUALITATIVE TECHNIQUES

Quantitative techniques are predicated on the idea that patterns in sales figures from previous time periods will repeat. If a forecaster doubts that assumption, qualitative techniques provide another forecasting tool. They tap into the expertise of people in the organization. Qualitative techniques are especially useful when:

- ❖ fine-tuning forecasts derived from quantitative techniques;
- ❖ forecasting for new products when historical data are not available;
- ❖ forecasting long range (see Chapter 4) or at the corporate level.

Forecasts derived from quantitative techniques are useful beginning points, but they are usually "adjusted" using some subjective or judgmental approach.

✦ In-House Expert

Sometimes, adjusting a quantitative forecast comes down to a key employee with the knowledge, information resources, and skill to see beyond the numbers and into the dynamics of the marketplace. Such an "expert" has a deep understanding of the market, the consumer, product quality, and other environmental factors that have an impact on sales. The in-house expert uses this expertise to fine-tune the forecast, sometimes on a product-by-product basis. The value of such an employee cannot be overestimated. However, there are drawbacks. The loss of such an employee can be catastrophic to a company's forecasting efforts because the expertise of this person is difficult to transmit to a replacement. In addition, using one in-house expert introduces the bias inherent in a single viewpoint.

✦ Executive Committee

An alternative to the single in-house expert is to involve groups of executives, salespeople, or outside experts. One approach is to convene a sales forecasting meeting with executives from each functional area in the company: from finance, marketing, sales, and production and distribution. These executives use the sales forecasts generated with quantitative techniques as a take-off point. Then, the group works to arrive at a consensus on needed adjustments to the sales forecast.

Instead of executives, another approach taps into the front-line experience of salespeople to produce or adjust sales forecasts. These are the people closest to the customer and who have the responsibility to generate sales volume. Again, the process begins with sales forecasts generated with quantitative methods. The task for the group is to fine-tune those initial forecasts.

✦ Polling Experts

Meeting to adjust the sales forecast is not always practical. For forecasts with a longer time horizon, a polling process replaces the meeting format. This is also a good approach when forecasting involves new products for which no sales data exist. More time allows for the involvement of experts either within or outside the company in adjusting the quantitative forecasts. Frequently these experts are polled in a process called the **Delphi method**, a "wisdom distillation tool" ("Just the FAQs," 1995).

The goal of Delphi is to generate "best guess" scenarios that represent the consensus of the experts. Usually participants do not know who the other respondents are—a procedure that removes the bias of group dynamics. Participants provide written responses to some question or issue. These responses are summarized and shared with the other participants. In subsequent "rounds," the participants refine and clarify the issues in a series of responses.

✦ Polling and Retailing

Chain retailers targeting teens must be especially sensitive to shifting trends. Because these chains stock merchandise from many manufacturers, they must be aware not only of style shifts but of shifts in the brands that are selling. One retailer who learned this the hard way was Kohl's, which chose to increase the presence of its private brands from 30 percent in 2007 to over 50 percent in 2011 and up to 54 percent by 2012 despite the fact that consumers had been clearly telling the company that they didn't like the private/exclusive label merchandise in stores for years. The result was a drop in customer satisfaction: the percentage of shoppers who indicated they felt that "Kohl's has the brands they prefer" declined each year to 7.8 percent in 2011 from 10.8 percent in 2007. In November 2013, Kohl's announced they would begin re-emphasizing national brands, including Nike and Levi's instead of its own store brands (Cheng, 2013).

✦ Handling Bias in Qualitative Techniques

The main problem with qualitative forecasting is the potential to introduce bias into the process. Some typical situations where bias may present problems are:

❖ when executives, salespeople, and experts use information they already have rather

You Be the Forecaster: Data on Demand

Breanna started as a manufacturer's representative calling on small accounts and regional store chains. She was promoted last year to national sales manager for a manufacturer specializing in activewear. The company recently merged with a former rival to form a company with several brands—one at the better price point sold through specialty stores, two moderate lines targeted to department stores, and one line sold through mass marketers. With these brand tiers in place, the company is investigating new collaborative ventures with top retail accounts, including category management and automated replenishment.

Breanna's laptop gives her access to the company's data warehouse with years of sales history available for analysis. During her rise through the company, she has taken advantage of the company's liberal policy on professional development. As technology changed, she attended seminars on forecasting software and other courses to update her skills. Breanna's analysis skills are important to succeed in her position, but just as important is her experience and knowledge of the market.

For about a month Breanna has been noticing a trend in the sales figures from the Northeast—sales are markedly higher for sportswear in brighter colors. She knows that fashion is moving away from neutrals and toward a more colorful palette. Still, traditionally the Northeast is a region thought to favor a more traditional color range. She wonders: What is driving these sales in the Northeast region?

Use the following discussion questions to summarize this chapter and review the possibilities open to Breanna.

Data Needed to Answer the Question: Does Breanna need sales volume reports by SKU, individual products, or product families (apparel groups or lines)? Or, would it be more helpful to look at sales by salesperson or distribution channel? Or, is the answer really one of location, in which the revenues should be broken down by city within the region? The need of a sales manager for data is interactive—as Breanna examines the situation, should she focus on more detailed information about a particular salesperson, a particular store, or a particular product?

Analysis Needed to Answer the Question: Can this question be answered with quantitative methods? What will time-series analysis disclose? Will Breanna learn anything helpful from correlation or regression analysis? Are there any qualitative methods that could be used to answer the question?

Technology: How can technology assist Breanna in her quest for an answer? What technology assistance should her company invest in so that it can capitalize on the sales forecasting process?

Modeling: If Breanna discovers a model—a pattern of spending, a profile of a consumer—that relates to the popularity of color in sportswear, what then?

than seeking out additional information that may enhance their decision-making ability;

❖ when participants bring corporate political agendas to the table along with their expertise;

❖ when participants do not have the skills or abilities to process very complex issues.

The first situation can be corrected by supplying market research and other information to the people involved. For the others, if forecasters are aware of these drawbacks and take steps to alleviate the problems as much as possible, qualitative techniques can increase the accuracy of sales forecasting.

✦ FIGURING OUT SALES FORECASTING

A skiwear company is an extreme example of what most apparel companies face (Fisher et al., 1994). Demand for fashion skiwear is dependent on factors that are hard to predict—weather, fashion trends, and the economy (Figure 10.8). The marketplace for skiwear is volatile and seasonal—the peak retailing season lasts only 2 months. Because the company's products are nearly all new each year, sales forecasting is a challenge. The skiwear company has to speculate on potential sales, not just produce to meet orders. The company has the added complications of having to book production capacity and deal with a more complex supply chain.

After several internal attempts to work on the sales forecasting problem, one company hired a group of consultants to figure out how to improve forecasting (Fisher et al., 1994). Even though the company had shortened its product development process, it still needed an edge.

The company persuaded twenty-five of its best retail customers to place orders early. This early information helped pinpoint which individual styles in the line were likely to be the most popular. However, there were still two issues: the company was having problems with stockouts and markdowns, and about half of its production was still based on risky, speculative demand forecasts.

Figure 10.8

Skiwear offers a forecasting challenge because demand depends on factors that are hard to predict—weather, fashion, and the economy.

The skiwear manufacturer was already using a "buying committee" to adjust quantitative forecasts. This group of company managers met to make consensus forecasts for each item in the line. The results were not impressive, as some parka styles outsold the original forecast by 200 percent and others sold less than 15 percent of the original forecast. The consultants revised the "buying committee process." Instead of a single consensus forecast, each member made an independent forecast for each style and color. This shift made each executive responsible individually for the forecasts. Although disturbing to members at first, time showed some interesting implications for forecasting. In the group setting, some people tended to dominate the meeting and the "consensus" forecast was heavily influenced by their views. With each individual forecasting for each style and color, some styles produced obvious high levels of agreement; on others, there was little or no agreement. As sales data came in under the new forecasting system, it became clear that when buying committee members' individual forecasts were in close agreement, they were also accurate forecasts. This finding gave the company a way to sort those styles likely to be forecast accurately from those with high levels of uncertainty. Even forecasting for items with high levels of uncertainty could be improved dramatically by adjusting the forecast using the early order data from retailers.

Within several seasons, the consultants and company executives had evolved a workable combination of forecasting and production planning that practically eliminated markdowns and stockouts. The company replaced highly speculative forecasts of demand with forecasting in carefully thought-out stages. When individual forecasts by company executives were in agreement on particular styles, those styles were scheduled for production far ahead of demand. The company used fast and flexible manufacturing for the more unpredictable styles because it could use market signals such as early season sales to synchronize supply and demand. By blending expert in-house judgment, expertise from its retail customers, and sales data, the skiwear company solved a difficult sales forecasting problem.

✦ BLENDING QUANTITATIVE AND QUALITATIVE TECHNIQUES

The factors that influence a sales forecast can be classified as controllable and uncontrollable (Bolt, 1994). Controllable factors include marketing actions and operating practices. The uncontrollable factors are either direct—those that have an obvious and immediate effect on sales—or indirect. Uncontrollable factors with a direct effect on sales include actions of competitors, access (or loss of access) to channels of distribution, and government regulations. Indirect factors either exert an influence on sales in the mid-range forecast or indicate long-term shifts. Uncontrollable factors with an indirect effect on sales are stages in a product life cycle or shifts in the preference characteristics of the target market for the mid-range forecast. The uncontrollable factors with the longest time horizon are changes in the country's economic situation (cost of living, rate of inflation, currency exchange rates) or in social, political, and cultural aspects (Figure 10.9). A sales forecast rests on a given set of environmental factors— the uncontrollable factors. Although uncertainty is always present in any forecast, accuracy improves if environmental factors are researched and weighed as part of the forecasting process.

Each forecasting method—time-series, correlation or regression, and qualitative techniques—has its purpose and brings advantages and disadvantages. The techniques are complementary. Time-series techniques generate a forecast based on sales history and are used to identify and forecast trends and seasonal patterns. The main advantage of time-series techniques is that they pick up quickly on changes. Correlation and regression analyses take external factors into consideration but they do not identify trends or seasonality. Because correlation and regression require more data, they are not useful for picking up quickly on shifts. Qualitative techniques do what time-

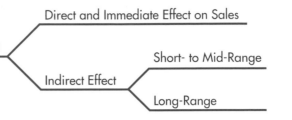

Figure 10.9

The factors that influence a sales forecast can be classified as controllable or uncontrollable and can be visualized in a tree diagram.

series, correlation, and regression cannot—they deal with changes in the business environment for which there is no historical data. The best practices for sales forecasting indicate the use of time-series forecasts for an initial projection, and correlation or regression analysis to provide a broader perspective on environmental factors. Then, qualitative methods can be used to "adjust" or fine-tune the quantitative forecast.

DATA MINING

When data migrated from paper to digital storage on computer, a new era in data analysis and forecasting began. Improved computer technology made it possible to collect and store more and more data. The use of scanners to collect sales data moved analysis away from a retrospective viewpoint to more dynamic, real-time analysis. Companies began to accumulate vast storehouses of historical data about consumer transactions. Corresponding improvements were made in software to organize, summarize, and analyze the information. Today, improvements are extending database technology into a process called **data mining**. Data miners search through vast stores of data to ("An Introduction," 1997):

❖ answer business questions too time-consuming to answer using traditional methods;
❖ discover patterns hidden in gigabytes of data;
❖ find predictive information experts miss because it lies outside of their expectations.

Data mining uses statistical techniques and models to reveal previously invisible relationships that can be used in decision making and forecasting. Data mining requires a **data warehouse**—a system for storing and delivering massive quantities of data. The amount of data that can be stored today is mind-boggling: computers known as "Large Hadron Collider" computers can store 15 petabytes a year of data, which is equivalent to about 15,000 years' worth of your favorite music (Harford, 2014). A data warehouse organizes information from many databases into a single system (Figure 10.10). The databases may include consumer shopping behavior, demographics, and attitudes; sales history, promotion and pricing data; competitor actions; and any other information categories that are deemed relevant to decision making.

The data warehouse is useless unless an executive can efficiently retrieve data to use in decision support. A data warehouse is extensively indexed and specifically designed to answer business questions with a fast access time. High-powered software for data manipulation sits on top of the data warehouse and allows the user to "slice and dice" the data in almost any imaginable way. Together, the data warehouse and data manipulation software provide a flexible executive information system (EIS) (Dhar & Stein, 1997).

In data mining, the software sorts through the data warehouse to discover patterns and then builds models based on those patterns to predict behavior. A pattern is an event or combination of events that occurs more often than random chance would dictate. A model is a description of how the pattern came to exist based on historical

DATABASES
Consumer Shopping Behavior
Demographics
Consumer Attitudes
Sales History
Promotion Information
Pricing Data
Competitor's Actions

DATA WAREHOUSE   ANALYSIS SOFTWARE   EXECUTIVE'S DESKTOP

Figure 10.10
Data warehouse system.

data and can be used to make predictions about new data (Chan & Lewis, 2002).

Modeling falls into two types: supervised and unsupervised. Unsupervised modeling techniques are either classification or regression. *Classification* predicts group membership—the output is categorical, having only a few values (for example, brand loyal versus brand changers or trendy versus mainstream versus laggards). *Regression* predicts a specific value from among values that are continuous (for example, the dollars that will be spent on a shopping trip). Supervised modeling techniques include association and clustering. *Association* looks for affinity groupings such as items that are usually purchased at the same time. *Clustering* sorts a diverse group (such as Hispanic customers) into subsegments based on the similarity of members to each other (perhaps by the state of residence or age group). To make clusters meaningful, the data miner must recognize the underlying pattern of similarity and attach the appropriate identifiers. Commercially available data mining software provides a selection of modeling tools (Chan & Lewis, 2002).

Apparel manufacturers and retailers have huge amounts of consumer data flowing in daily from many different sources including stores and e-commerce sites. Data mining helps executives to learn about customers' buying habits, gain insights into their preferences, create one-on-one relationships with them, encourage consumer loyalty, and promote future sales. Any apparel company can use data mining to analyze customer patronage behaviors (how often people shop, when they are likely to shop, and what they usually buy at the same time) or life stage,

and use the resulting models to trigger promotions, adjust menus on websites or visual merchandising in stores, or fine-tune merchandise assortments (Peterson, 2003).

One of the newest uses for data mining is in "merchandise optimization," which means deciding when to mark down merchandise and by what percentages. By looking at historical results and using sales forecasting techniques, the executives can determine a "natural demand" for items. Even new items without sales histories can be analyzed by using similar products sold in the past. As one retailer using the software explained: "We were prepared to mark down the merchandise 30 percent, based on gut instinct, inventory levels, and the product's life cycle, but the software recommended the company 'hold steady' on prices. We followed the analytics-driven suggestion and reaped extra dollars" (Moin, 2003b).

Limited Brands has several different store concepts targeting different customers. For data mining, the company looks to ask "any question on any data at any time." Typical questions might inquire about which impulse items work best near checkout or how many and what kind of customers purchase only those items on sale. Data mining allows a company to be proactive by helping executives anticipate what consumers want. Data mining consolidates decision making by addressing what happened in the past (reporting), what is happening now (description), what might happen (prediction), and what can happen (anticipation) (Clark, 2002).

As an example of data mining in practice, take the case of a marketing director for a retail catalog hoping to entice the customers of similar catalogs to switch their purchases to her catalog. She knows all about her customers—age, gender, credit history, and buying patterns. She wants to target customers who buy often and spend more than $100 on each order. Naturally, the competition is unlikely to share their proprietary information on customer transactions. The answer is to create a model using known information about current customers. Suppose that data mining reveals that 98 percent of the customers who order from every catalog and spend at least $100 make over $60,000 per year, live in urban areas, and watch HGTV (Home and Garden Television). This model gives the marketing director a way to selectively target new customers.

As another example, consider the mass-market apparel company that test-markets styles before making a production commitment. The company knows the demographic information on their customers, transaction information on current and past sales, and their own marketing plans. Collecting sales information at each test site provides enough data for modeling. Using data mining, an executive can take the test-market information, identify the characteristics of consumers who respond to the styles, compare that model to the overall market, and predict the potential for those styles to succeed.

Online retailers use collaborative filtering (basing recommendations for future purchases on customers' rating of previous purchases) to drive sales. Data mining software finds links between past decisions and the potential of future sales. Barneys New York, an upscale chain, increased online sales by 10 percent using the technique for targeting e-mails to customers. The software examined the price most likely to

produce a buying decision, the time of day and day of week when purchases were made, the style and product attributes most preferred (i.e., organic fabrics). By weighing those factors, the software determined the likelihood that a particular customer would open the e-mail message and click through to buy the product (Taub, 2008).

If senior managers see data mining as a magic business booster, they are likely to be disappointed. Building a model is helpful only if it identifies actions that are possible and reasonable. Suppose that data mining models the customer for custom-made suits as between 40 and 50 years old and the owner of a sports car or a luxury car. Unless the company can reach that segment with the right message, the model is useless (Elliott, 1998). Data mining is best viewed as a move toward steady improvement and, occasionally, toward providing an extra competitive edge on a project, with a customer, or for a particular time period. Data mining is just a more sophisticated analysis technique. It cannot replace experience with the business and knowledge about the market. Users still must decide how to interpret the models and how to implement decisions that increase sales revenues (Small, 1997).

One of the drawbacks of data mining may be the insatiable appetite of marketing people for more information and more new analysis tools. Some see this as a vicious circle where "discovering" a correlation unleashes another round of data gathering and investigation. As data mining software becomes more accessible, one spin-off will be a requirement for greater statistical literacy among executives (Schrage, 1997).

Chapter Summary

While it may seem that due to the unpredictability of the fashion system, forecasting is a nearly impossible endeavor, sales forecasting is possible: the same patterns emerge again and again, but never in exactly the same way. By understanding forecasting and taking advantage of the tools available, apparel industry executives can make well-educated estimates for their merchandise assortment, thereby minimizing risk of lost sales dollars through markdowns or stockouts. Through analysis of internal and external data combined with quantitative and qualitative forecasting techniques, apparel executives can create an effective merchandise assortment in accordance with each item's product life cycle. Business and the apparel industry are highly cyclic, and are highly impacted by factors such as consumer confidence, and an economic indicator known as the leading indicator. The field of data mining has further allowed apparel industry members to better target their customer, through practices such as automatic replenishment and category management, which enables companies to best meet their customers' needs.

Key Terms and Concepts

Aggregated
Automated replenishment system
Brand tiers
Business cycle
Category management
Consumer confidence
Correlation or regression techniques
Data mining
Data warehouse
Decomposition
Delphi method
Demand
Extranets
Fast Fashion
Fixed-model time-series (FMTS)
Leading indicators
Level (in time-series forecasting)

Markdowns
Noise (in time-series forecasting)
Open-model time-series (OMTS)
Product life cycle
Qualitative techniques
Retail supply chain
Sales channel
Sales forecast
Sales history
Sales plan
Seasonality (in time-series forecasting)
Self-organized criticality
Stockouts
Syndicated surveys
Time-series forecasting
Time-series techniques
Trend (in time-series forecasting)

Discussion Questions

Sales Forecasting. How does a product's position on the product life cycle impact its sales forecast? As a retailer, what size of orders would you place for a product at each stage of the life cycle and at what stage would you stop ordering the product? How does the business cycle impact how retailers order merchandise?

Retail Supply Chain. How are the fortunes of the members of the retail supply chain connected? How might something at an early stage of the chain such as an increase in cotton prices impact all of the different members in the chain? How might something at the end of the chain such as a retailer going out of business impact the other members?

Data Mining. How many frequent shoppers clubs, such as Sephora's Very Important Buyer's program, are you a part of? What online retailers do you shop regularly? Based on the types of e-mails and other promotional offers you receive from these companies, what information do you think these companies know about you? Do you like it when you receive targeted marketing such as discounts and promotions for products you have purchased in the past? Why or why not?

Forecasting Activities

Statistical Treasure Hunt. The US government collects an amazing array of statistics related to the economic condition of the country. Look at the sites listed in the Resource Pointers section at the end of this chapter. Select one or more statistics that might help explain fluctuations in apparel sales. Making decisions such as this is the first step in using correlation or regression to provide a broad environmental perspective on sales volume.

Product Life Cycle Detectives. Fashion is always evolving and changing. Create a snapshot of this moment in fashion time by creating a presentation picturing apparel and accessory products in each stage of the product life cycle. What's coming? What's "in" now? What's reached its peak in popularity and started declining? What's out of fashion?

Look and Listen. Pick a business news website and monitor it for a month. What breaking news on the health of the economy would be helpful to apparel executives in putting sales figures into a larger context of economic activity? What reports on government statistics would be helpful in understanding and interpreting sales history?

Click and File. Begin a Pinterest or other online file on data mining. Run keyword searches on the Internet and on business and industry databases. Although you may not understand everything in the articles, pay special attention to examples related to the textile and apparel industries. Beginning an online file is the first step toward self-education about this emerging technology.

Resource Pointers

Dismal Scientist: www.economy.com/ dismal/

Economic Statistics Briefing Room: www. gpoaccess.gov/indicators/index.html

EDITD merchandise assortment software: http://editd.com/

Fedstats: www.fedstats.gov

United States' Bureau of Labor Statistics: http://www.bls.gov/home.htm

United States' Census Bureau: http://www. census.gov/

United States Consumer Expenditure Survey: http://www.bls.gov/cex/

PART FOUR

FORECASTING AT WORK

> What is the right path? I know which is the right path; it's that path which gives you the final result in the store.
>
> —*Giorgio Armani*

11

COMPETITIVE ANALYSIS

OBJECTIVES

◆ Identify the connection between acquiring and analyzing forecasting information and applying the insights to competitive situations

◆ Relate the steps of competitive analysis from question-forming and information-gathering to analysis and reporting

◆ Outline the ethical and legal issues involved in information gathering

COMPETITIVE ADVANTAGE

The goal of competitive analysis is to provide a company or an individual with **competitive advantage**. Competitive advantage occurs when there is a lack of balance in the marketplace so that one company is favored over another. To sustain competitive advantage, a company must anticipate the actions and reactions of rivals (Amit, Domowitz, & Fershtman, 1988). Examples of competitive advantage can be having a faster **speed to market**—the ability to get products in stores quickly—or excellent replenishment systems that prevent stockouts, or a very close connection with a target market. BCBGeneration, the "little sister" line of BCBG targeted to millennial shoppers, is priced 30 percent lower than BCBG and has a competitive advantage over other similarly priced startup lines because of its connection to the label (Figure 11.1). Generation's competitive advantage comes from the sharing of information about production of key items such as dresses, sweaters, and rompers, which gives it expertise that newer brands don't have. Annette Schatz, executive vice president and general manager of Generation, says, "We have a lot of institutional knowledge around something that could be hard. We do share all that information across all the brands" (Trahn, 2014).

Digital communication brings with it a shift in the factors that contribute to competitiveness (DuMont, 1997). Instead of low value-added activities, the industry is moving to strategies based on agility, faster response times, and demand-activated production (Figure 11.2).

Analyzing a rival company's position opens up several opportunities (Gelb et al., 1991):

❖ outsmarting the competition by exploiting their weaknesses;
❖ avoiding surprises that may upset a company's strategic plan;
❖ imitating the competition in search of a better way to do the task or a better way to make decisions;
❖ recognizing as early as possible when a company is on the wrong path and cannot compete in a particular market;
❖ identifying a new niche where the company can be competitive.

Analysts categorize these as informational, offensive, and defensive opportunities (Prescott & Smith, 1989): *informational* because a company's executives need an overall understanding of their industry and their

FUNCTIONS	OLD	NEW
DESIGN	Runway Shows Status Appeals	Demand-Activated Product Development Mass Customization
DEVELOP	Low-Cost Labor Mass Production Long Production Runs	Partnerships Networks
DISTRIBUTION	Efficiency with Volume Dynamic Management	Speed
RETAIL	Real Estate Location Superior Service Reputation	Convenience Entertainment Online Access

Figure 11.2
The transformation of the textile and apparel industries means shifting from low value-added activities to strategies based on agility, faster response times, and demand-activated production.

competitors; *offensive* because competitive analysis attempts to discover where competitors are vulnerable and what actions can be taken to capitalize on that temporary advantage; *defensive* because competitive analysis involves thinking ahead about competitor moves that could threaten the firm's position in the market.

✦ FASHION BRANDS AND COMPETITIVE ADVANTAGE

Branding is a competitive strategy—a way of targeting customers with a coherent message. Building a brand requires substantial investment by a company that must pay off to justify supporting the brand with advertising and promotion. The payoff for brands meeting or exceeding consumers' expectations is called **brand loyalty**—purchase and repurchase of the brand again and again (Friedman, 1996). Consumer research tracks how much a brand is worth using surveys, panel studies, and focus group interviews.

Creating a distinct **brand image** means identifying a set of tangible and intangible characteristics across a collection or product line and promoting that image to customers (Carpenter, 1998). A relevant brand image begins with a vision that invites the consumer to enter a world, participate in a lifestyle, and express a certain style. Think of the consistent point of view carried across the products, visual merchandising, and advertising of designer Ralph Lauren. No matter the product category or price point, there is an unwavering brand identity that the consumer can read. Successful brands have high recognition and an emotional connection with consumers (Gobé, 2001). To consumers, possessing the products is connected to identification with the brand image.

When brand identity is defined, advertising and promotion become keys to building **brand recognition** and loyalty. Positioning entails emphasizing the differences between a brand and the competitors' products (Ries & Trout, 1986). Promotion and advertising help consumers recognize the product and the experience of possessing that product. Advertising works in two ways: it builds brand awareness over time, and it grabs attention for a particular season line or item. The most successful apparel advertising campaigns today project an aspirational environment and replay the imagery over and over (Parr, 1996). A brand definition that strikes a chord with the public and allows for consistent reinforcement through multiple messages lays the foundation for brand building.

Brand building also involves distinctive visual merchandising. Visibility is boosted for a brand when the product is showcased in an **in-store shop**—a section devoted to a single brand with display and signage supporting the brand identity. Also important is point-of-sale identification such as packaging, hangtags, and signage.

When successful, branding results in a consumer's identification of a brand name with a reputation for style and quality and a unique niche in the marketplace. But according to Isabelle Harvie-Watt Clavarino, chief executive officer of Havas Media Group, brand loyalty is almost nonexistent in today's marketplace: its 2013 Meaningful Brands Index revealed that "the majority of people worldwide wouldn't care if 73 percent of brands disappeared tomorrow." The company's online survey of 150,000 consumers indicated that in order to get repeat purchases from customers, it is necessary today to create a series of values around a brand that contribute to people's lives, such as making them feel better, smarter, more organized or benefiting a community. Brands with higher meaning have higher consumer attachment: "People expect brands to positively impact their lives or the life of their community today and that's just a basic fact" (Zargani, 2013). Competitive analysis enables companies to regulate brand image and positioning according to changing conditions and to innovate when new opportunities arise. One such opportunity was the emergence of lifestyle brands—a strategy that requires multiple lines of coordinating products supporting the brand image (Larson, 2003c).

In earlier eras, Anne Klein, Yves Saint Laurent, and Pierre Cardin all licensed their names to other product lines. What is the

Profile: Ruth Stanat, President and Chief Executive Officer, SIS International Research

Ruth Stanat founded SIS International Research in 1984 to consult on strategic planning, market research reports, and market expansion or business development studies, and to provide customized tracking for competitive intelligence. Before starting the firm, she was vice president of strategic planning for Chase Manhattan Bank, senior planning officer of the Mars Corporation, and she held senior marketing and strategic planning positions with International Paper Company, Spring Mills, Inc., and United Airlines. She is a charter member of the Society for Competitive Intelligence Professionals and serves as a member of the organization's board of directors.

Stanat's book *The Intelligent Corporation* (1990) explained the concept and implementation of "corporate intelligence networks"—a central depository stocked by cooperating individuals who gather, analyze, and disseminate information to support decision making. Technology may have changed since the book came out, but Stanat discovered in a follow-up study that "the companies who were early adopters of the concept gained a competitive edge in the marketplace." Another thing that has changed is the time it takes to build a corporate intelligence network—in 1990 she estimated that it took 5 years for the system to evolve; in 2004 it is possible to "build a corporate intelligence network in 12 to 18 months." According to Stanat, "the information must be not only synthesized and analyzed, but interpreted in terms of impact on the business."

During the years 1990 to 1993, Stanat traveled to more than eighty countries and expanded SIS International Research to 120 countries in Asia, Europe, Latin America, and the Middle East. Since then she has written two books on business development and market expansion. *Global Gold—Panning for Profits in Foreign Markets* (1998) is a guide to success in international markets with contributions from over thirty authors from around the world. In this book Stanat segmented countries into three categories:

❖ "I"—Countries that value individualism, are consumer driven, have mature markets and infrastructure, and produce products that are designed for the comfort, safety, and preferences of the consumer.

❖ "We"—Countries with a strong sense of group decision making in business and family matters where the expertise of elders is held in high esteem.

❖ "They"—Countries with a long-standing heritage and sense of nationalism where companies and consumers make decisions within the context of traditional cultures and the country's heritage.

The book also features Stanat's insights on the cultural and business fine points for each country or region, a key to establishing and maintaining relationships over time.

When asked about textiles and apparel, Stanat pointed out the global nature of the industry, saying, "That makes intelligence-gathering even more critical." As she sees it, "the real challenge is in the increasing velocity of world trade as third-world countries come up to speed very quickly and are no longer third-world countries."

Stanat's third book, *Global Jumpstart—the Complete Resource for Expanding Small and Mid-Sized Businesses* (1999), grew from monitoring the success and failure of companies throughout the world. The book helps "global pioneers" research markets to minimize the risks of expansion. As she says in the book, "business research and market-intelligence gathering provide insurance policies against being blindsided when entering foreign markets." Knowing the local customs, consumer attitudes, government policies, and local competitive conditions is the key to success.

Is competitive intelligence a new idea? Not according to Stanat, who points out that Dutch traders in the fifteenth century used information to exploit markets and fuel their global expansion. Japanese trading companies were set up in part to gather information about foreign markets. Although the style may differ depending on the culture—Asians, for example, do information gathering through word-of-mouth networks—companies of all kinds monitor their own businesses and their competitors. "We've formalized it in the United States and exported it to Europe." As the effort continues, Stanat sees risks increasing with "more computer fraud and more hacking into the global intelligence network."

For those seeking a career in competitive intelligence, Stanat recommends spending time abroad and becoming fluent in a second language (Stanat speaks French and German). "It is hard to do business with other cultures without a level of understanding," she says, and because of this she recommends undergraduate or graduate study in Asian or Latin American Studies. Her son, Michael, clearly followed his mother's advice: his own book, *China's Generation Y: Understanding the Future Leaders of the World's Next Superpower*, was published in 2005. The company has diversified recently by launching webinar services on global market issues such as the Middle Eastern market, and, by 2012, had conducted research in over 120 countries for over fifty industries with key regional research hubs in London, Toronto, and Mexico City. SIS International Research celebrated its thirty-year anniversary in 2014.

Sources:

Author Evelyn Brannon's interview with Ruth Stanat, February 26, 2004.

Boyett, J. H., & Boyett, J. T. (2001). *The guru guide to the knowledge economy.* New York: Wiley.

Stanat, R. (1990). *The intelligent corporation.* New York: AMACOM.

Stanat, R. (1998). *Global gold—Panning for profits in foreign markets.* New York: AMACOM.

Stanat, R. (1999). *Global jumpstart—The complete resource for expanding small and mid-sized businesses.* New York: Perseus Books.

SIS International Concepts sismarketresearch.com.

difference between these brands and today's brands such as Tory Burch, Vera Bradley, and Lilly Pulitzer? A powerful brand name with a generic image taps into the consciousness of a broad consumer population and then extends out to fill more and more product niches with its branded merchandise to create a lifestyle brand (Ozzard & Seckler, 1996). Beginning with products at the designer, bridge, and better levels plus accessories, footwear, jeanswear, fragrance, hosiery, eyewear, activewear, intimate apparel, handbags, and leather goods, some expand into additional niches such as children's wear, bed linens, and products for the home. Unlike earlier versions of this strategy, today designers exercise more control over the design, marketing, advertising, and distribution of products using their brand name. They tend to view these arrangements as collaborative partnerships rather than just revenue sources.

Some brands focus on a lifestyle concept and produce products in many categories based on a designer's name, a retailer identity such as J. Crew, or an idealized lifestyle such as Bohemian or preppy. These brands depend on an image people can buy into and express by possessing the products. The forecasting challenge is determining how much core product to make and how to stay flexible enough to take advantage of a rising trend or a surprise bestseller. Follow-up to both situations requires a strong infrastructure in sourcing, manufacturing, and distribution.

Brand names signal a level of fashion, taste, and style to consumers. In the fashion industry, there are different kinds of brands. **Store brands** are products developed and merchandised through the company's own stores and the stores carry no other brands—UNIQLO, Banana Republic, Madewell, and Victoria's Secret. **Private-label brands** are brands owned by retailers and merchandised through that retailer's stores along with the brands of other companies—The Original Arizona Jean Company for JC Penncy and INC International Concepts at Macy's. **National brands**— Splendid, Guess, Nike—and **designer name brands**—Marc Jacobs, Rodarte, Stella McCartney—are sold to retailers through the wholesale market, and carried by many retailers who often compete in the same market area. These traditional definitions have changed as national and designer name brands open their own freestanding retail stores and private-label brands achieve the prominence of national brands.

Value includes styling, durability, quality fabrics, and consistent fit. Brands build customer loyalty by delivering excellent value regardless of price point—high, low, or medium. Like many luxury designers, Joseph Altuzarra's collaboration with Target featured his aesthetic at a low price point, yet his high-end sales did not suffer because he had customer loyalty (Figure 11.3). To the consumer, a brand name represents familiarity, consistency, and confidence in performance. In surveys, consumers report a willingness to pay extra for brands they prefer because brands deliver more than non-brands (Lewis, 1995). Because brand names are associated with so many desirable attributes, they also act to simplify purchase decisions, saving time and adding convenience to the shopping experience. Brand names when linked with lifestyle, self-expression, and aspirations epitomize intangibles that are desirable to the consumer.

✦ THE RETAIL LANDSCAPE

✧ Department Stores

Department stores emerged at the turn of the twentieth century from neighborhood collections of independently owned shops. The department store format brought everything the customer wanted under one roof. The next shift occurred when the department store moved out of downtown locations and into malls. The mall can be viewed as a much bigger department store with specialty stores acting like departments in that larger store. Department stores got into trouble in the mid-1990s because they did not adapt to meet the needs of the emerging customer: a two-wage-earner,

Figure 11.3
Joseph Altuzarra's collaboration with Target gave him name recognition among consumers for his lower-priced line without sacrificing his luxury customers.

educated, younger family who found department store shopping unappealing and too time consuming. Specialty stores did a better job of providing the kind of merchandise consumers wanted, and also the kind of environment they wanted to purchase it in. Combining shopping and entertainment appealed to a consumer trying to get more out of every experience (Figure 11.4). Shoppers today can shop 24/7 in a blurring of online and brick-and-mortar venues. Nanette Lepore and Bloomingdale's cooperated in a "magic window" experience—shoppers try on an outfit and the dressing room mirror takes a photo that can be sent to a cell phone, e-mail address, or social network. Friends seeing the image can offer opinions, which are displayed on the mirror as if it was a computer screen. When websites began, catalogs and department store assortments were merely displayed. But as websites evolved in sophistication, stores needed to match or improve on the online experience. Customers living outside big cities now have the opportunity to find and buy emerging designers, vintage, luxury brands, and fast fashion. Fashion blogs, social networks, and fashion search engines provide fashion information for the new "extreme shopping" experience (Corcoran, 2007c).

Department stores are at a crucial point in their existence. Department store sales have declined steadily since January 2001 when seasonally adjusted sales were more than $19.9 billion. In January 2014, that figure had sunk to less than $14.2 billion. The difference is even wider when inflation is taken into account: when adjusting for inflation, in January 1999, department stores had sales of almost $26.7 billion (in 2013 dollars), almost twice their sales in January 2014. This decline has occurred at the same time as retail sales overall have risen. The main reason for this decline is non-store sales, which include Internet sales. Internet sales rose by 6.5 percent from January 2013/14, while department stores sales declined by 5.7 percent during that same time. Another source of competition is specialty clothing stores, which grew by 1.2 percent during this same year (Kurtzleben, 2014). But retail stores are not going away just yet. Moody's Investor's Service predicts that online sales of apparel and footwear

Figure 11.4
New technology such as "virtual dressing rooms" makes a shopping experience more entertaining for consumers.

as a percentage of total retail sales will rise to about 16 percent by 2016, while online retail sales in general are expected to grow 14 percent annually during this time period (Young, 2014). Retail stores are a crucial part now of an online logistics chain that allows consumers to see, feel, and try on the products they have researched online.

The changing retail landscape, increased competition, and the threat of consolidation through acquisition by major players such as Macy's, has made this the most challenging sector of retail. Proactive department store retailers are embracing new technologies to help them retain current customers while attracting new ones. Hudson's Bay and Lord & Taylor stores are experimenting with sending digital notifications to consumers' smartphones as they are shopping through a partnership with Swirl in-store beacon marketing platform. Michael Crotty, Hudson's Bay and Lord & Taylor executive vice president and chief marketing officer, says, "When we see how consumers are interacting with mobile devices, it is not hard to believe that they will get very comfortable with and really appreciate targeted messages when they walk into a retail environment" (Moin, 2014).

✧ Catalogs

Catalogs gained popularity at a time when busy customers wanted to be able to shop any time of the day or night. For the retailer, catalogs aimed at two audiences: current customers and potential customers. Catalogs can work as a brand builder, to generate store traffic, and as a profit center (Dean, 1998). The chief reason people shop using catalogs is convenience, but other reasons include access to special sizes and brand loyalty based on previous experience with the catalog's merchandise.

When retailers also have a catalog, they get an early reading on new styles, colors, and accessories because merchandise appears in the catalog before reaching the store. Finding out what's working and not working 30 days ahead

of store POS data allows companies to react more quickly ("Urban," 2007). Aside from sales, catalogs allow companies to build consumer databases showing who responded, what they bought, and where they live. Tracking returns helps identify consumer satisfaction with quality, fit, and fabrication. Databases derived from catalog sales have a much greater level of detail than that captured at point-of-sale in stores. Patterns in this data can be directional for deciding where to locate new stores as well as for targeting customers' style preferences.

Although it is easy to imagine that catalogs are a dying industry, they are still very relevant; retailers sent 11.9 billion catalogs in 2013, according to the Direct Marketing Association. Catalogs have changed to fit today's customer, with fewer pages and merchandise descriptions, and larger photos and lifestyle images. Retailers find that consumers use catalogs for inspiration, and as a reminder to visit their website. Catalogs have a high return on investment, costing less than $1 each to produce and distribute, but a typical average return for each catalog mailed is about $4 in sales (Holmes, 2014).

J.Crew, which began as a catalog retailer and now has over 300 stores, still sends out 40 million catalogs each year. The company combines its catalog sales numbers with its Internet revenues, since they feel the two are so closely intertwined. Some companies who experimented with dropping their catalogs saw their online sales quickly fall and therefore reinstated their catalogs, while others, like Express, who had never been catalog retailers before, launched new catalogs. "Our 20-something customer makes little delineation between channels. She or he enjoys viewing our catalogue online, in her mailbox or on the phone, so we make sure our fashion is always available no matter where our customers want to view it," Express CMO Lisa Gavales said. "That said, we haven't seen any virtual viewing work as well as a good, old-fashioned paper catalog" (Fox, 2012).

✧ Online Shopping

When fashion first arrived on the Internet, forecasters doubted it would grow to today's levels of sales or popularity. They pointed to consumers' need to see, touch, and try on as a limiting factor. High-speed Internet access, website improvements, and liberal return policies have overcome those issues for many consumers. Sites offer experiences not available in stores—at Timberland.com shoppers can design their own footwear and a detailed chart helps consumers from Asia and Europe to convert sizes. Enlarging, spinning, rotating, and zooming images replaces touch for shoppers (Barbaro, 2007a).

A global online survey revealed that fashion is second only to books for Internet shoppers. Fashion is growing faster online than any other e-commerce category. Customers in the United States, the United Kingdom, Germany, South Korea, and the Scandinavian countries have been the earliest adopters of online fashion. Online, any consumer can command the same selection and service as a celebrity client—a designer dress can appear on a retailer site 24 hours after the runway show, be delivered in New York or London on the same day, and be worn by the buyer 5 months before the line appears in stores. Labeled the "trend of the quick consumer" (Horton, 2008b), this almost instant connection is being exploited as a marketing strategy through partnerships between designer lines and online retailers such as the "Little-A-Like" capsule collection of mother and daughter outfits that Elisa Sednaoui created for online retailer Yoox.com for summer 2014.

The current online interactive environment includes blogging, social networking, and sites built with user-generated content. Users at these sites represent a new shopper category, the "conspicuous cyber consumer" (Harkin, 2008). Fashion sites take many forms including (Figure 11.5):

❧ *Multibrand sites* (also known as collection sites) such as Net-a-Porter.com set up online stores for designers and luxury brands and act as an international portal for fashion consumers. Sometimes a designer will create an exclusive collection for the site, but the merchandise is usually the same as that carried in stores. Some multibrand sites have entered partnerships with social networks to create members-only shopping clubs (Horton, 2008b).

❧ *Fashion-focused search engines* such as Polyvore.com make finding fashion easier online because a keyword search for "pumps" will bring up only shoes. Fashion search engines like Glimpse.com and ShopStyle.com are more visual than the traditional search engines such as Google and include spreads that look like magazine pages. When the shopper clicks on an item they are directed to a store site for the sales transaction (Corcoran, 2007a).

❧ *Review sites* such as Bag Snob on Snobessentials.com aggregate product recommendations and reviews to help consumers find desirable merchandise quickly.

❧ *Blogs* such as Lolomag.com where a fashion fan becomes a journalist by sharing discoveries and suggestions with readers—a form of peer-to-peer recommendation.

❧ *Social shopping sites* such as Keep.com sign up users who browse the site and bookmark a wishlist of items, a digital wardrobe that can be "shopcasted" to friends and other users. Each participant has the opportunity to become a maven, connoisseur, or fashion curator whose advice and taste is trusted by other consumers (followers). This form of peer recommendation helps consumers sort through the huge number of choices in the market (Harkin, 2008).

❧ *Social consciousness sites* (also called ethical sites) such as Ethixmerch.com provide access to green brands, especially those not readily available in stores outside metropolitan areas.

❧ *Bricks-and-mortar retailers* such as Macy's, Nordstrom, and Bloomingdale's use their corresponding websites as part of a competitive strategy and to promote

Figure 11.5

Websites make online shopping easier and more interactive, with some characteristics of shopping with friends. Fashion blog The Cut (a) shares fashion finds, and retail sites like Casadei (b) are constantly becoming more creative in their presentation.

(a)

(b)

traditional shopping. To do this, store websites seek to align the online and in-store experiences to build customer loyalty. *Magazine-associated sites* such as *Vogue*, *Elle*, *Marie Claire*, and *Lucky* offer links to purchase products featured in the current month's ads, fashion features, and user-generated sections for sharing photos and ideas (Aspan, 2007).

Because the marketplace is in a constant state of evolution, the seeds for the next innovation in shopping venue or shopping experience already exist. Forecasters use competitive analysis techniques to:

❖ recognize shifts in retail formats, evaluate their potential impact, translate the potential to their clients, and assess problems and threats that may derail the innovation;

❖ assist clients in repositioning their businesses to be more in tune with the changing marketplace;

❖ assist entrepreneurs, small companies, and spin-off lines in finding the optimal entrance strategy into a business niche;

❖ assist clients in matching consumer segments, products, and services.

Selfridges, a London department store, is such a success story of repositioning that it is a stopover for American store executives when they are in Europe. Once considered dowdy, Selfridges is now "ultra-cool" in design, amenities (with fourteen food and drink options, a body-piercing salon, and Europe's largest beauty hall), and styles. The store revamped its way of doing business and now rents sections to vendors who design and stock their own space; focuses on name brands rather than private label; and offers a merchandise mix from bicycles to books, tattoos to designer brands. The store has become a magnet for tourists as well as for Londoners, a destination known for its retailing mixed with a sense of theater (Rozhon, 2003).

DEFINING COMPETITIVE ANALYSIS

In today's competitive marketplace, it is important to track news about the industry and about a company's current and potential partners and competitors. Forecasting information is useful only when it can be applied to decision making about the future. The success of a company's decisions rests not only on what action it takes but also on the actions of its competitors. An executive must have information about fashion change and competitors in order to decide on short-range **tactics** and long-term strategies. Combining forecasts with competitor information makes it possible to formulate actionable decisions.

Competitive analysis (or **competitive intelligence**) means using public sources to develop a detailed and accurate view of the market environment, both trends in the industry and what the competition is likely to do. The goal of competitive analysis is to take the pulse of companies whose actions may have an impact on decision making. A climate of fast-paced technological development and an international marketplace increase the importance of competitive analysis (Carr, 2003).

Competitive analysis is a continuous process of collecting information from published sources, public government documents, and interviews ("Frequently," 1998). It does not mean gathering proprietary information in illegal or unethical ways. Competitive analysis scans can be customized to capture news about companies considered to be industry leaders as a way to measure operations against the best practices. The scan can also be customized to focus specially on companies that are allies or **direct competitors**. As it is impossible to gather all the information needed, any gaps are identified and, where possible, filled in by reasoning during the analysis stage. The analysis makes the information useful to executives as support for planning and decision making.

Competitive analysis shares commonalities with other forecasting activities because it also involves data gathering, analysis, and interpretation. Competitive analysis takes into account past and current situations as part of a proactive stance toward business challenges and opportunities. It can be applied to planning tactics—scoping out seasonal direction and planning short-range strategy. Or it can be used to forecast the competitor's **mid-range strategies** 2–5 years ahead and applied to more long-range **strategic planning** to gain competitive advantage and ensure business survival and long-term growth. The tactical approach means focusing attention on a particular project or the implementation of a current business strategy. A strategic approach means having a longer time horizon and a more comprehensive view. Tactical, mid-range, and strategic planning require an ongoing flow of information about the industry, business climate, and competitive situation (Prescott & Smith, 1989).

Competitive analysis offers two benefits: it *confirms* what the company thinks it knows, and it *warns of change* in cases where having the right information is crucial. The potential benefits of using competitive analysis are not restricted to large corporations. Companies of every size benefit from competitive analysis (McGonagle & Vella, 1990):

❖ *Large apparel companies*—Corporations with **brand tiers**—several brands for similar products but at different price levels—or brand extension—multiple product lines from eyeglasses to apparel to towels based on lifestyle concepts—use competitive analysis to monitor and control their own activities. Jones Apparel Group, VF Corporation, Ralph Lauren, and PVH use a multibrand, multichannel strategy. For these large companies, it is vital that senior management have the best information about the different brands within their own

company in comparison to rival companies. Competitive analysis is important in making far-reaching decisions about business strategy.

❖ *Mid-sized apparel companies*—To survive in business, mid-sized apparel companies must sustain and strengthen current markets and look for new opportunities. In a climate of acquisition, mid-sized companies may seek to acquire other companies as part of their growth plans or they may be the targets of an acquisition. Competitive analysis benefits these mid-sized companies by identifying market threats and opportunities.

❖ *New business*—Entrepreneurs, whether designers, manufacturers, or retailers, need to identify potential backers with deep pockets to finance the first critical years of establishing the company's name and market niche. Business start-ups require competitive information for solid business planning and to justify investment to venture capitalists.

Large corporations frequently have a staff dedicated to gathering and analyzing information about competitors. Companies also hire consultants for specific projects. Most are members in the Strategic and Competitive Intelligence Professionals (SCIP), a professional association for consultants and corporate employees.

There are four parts to a competitive analysis system: question forming, information gathering, data analysis, and communication of results ("Curriculum," 1998). The first steps in competitive analysis are things a professional already does—attending trade shows, reading the trade and business press, and networking with others in the industry. The next step is becoming more systematic and continuous at gathering and analyzing competitor information ("Curriculum," 1998).

You Be the Forecaster: Competitor Alert

Adrienne's company develops and produces knit sportswear under its own brand name and for other companies' private-label ventures. In this very competitive category, the players constantly change as one company acquires another and new brands emerge to satisfy niche markets. Awareness of the competitive environment has always been important to the company, but a new CEO has decided to give this effort higher visibility and more emphasis. Adrienne has been given the responsibility of developing an in-house competitive analysis team. The CEO wants the team to provide a constant flow of information about the company's direct competitors and conduct monthly strategy sessions with the corporate executives from product development, merchandising, marketing, and sales.

Adrienne's first step is to map the competitive environment. She interviews executives in the company to identify competitors and their position relative to her company and within the industry. She pays special attention to the sales staff and implements a message board which is available only to company employees where they can share information and insights on shifts in competitors' positions.

She extends her interviews to include vendors (companies who sell fabrics, findings, and trims to her company and to others in the same category) and business-to-business customers (the retailers who buy from her company). While Adrienne conducts interviews, her assistant compiles files on each competitor including financial information, marketing initiatives, personnel bios, and any other publicly available documents. With this background, Adrienne will draw a relationship map for her company and for its competitors. These maps will disclose the strategies each company is using and provide the basis for ongoing competitive analysis.

Acquisitions by companies continually rewrite the relationship maps. Sales channels that were once secure business for the company are now being challenged. Adrienne and her staff are looking at ways to improve their analysis techniques and increase competitive awareness among all employees. It is important that each executive in the company participate in the process of competitive analysis both to enrich the information pool and to sharpen the company's competitive edge.

Competitive Advantage: What is competitive advantage? How is competitive advantage built for brands? What is the competitive advantage/disadvantage for department stores, specialty stores, catalogs, online stores, and shopping channels on television?

Environmental Scanning: How can Adrienne use media scans to gain the information she needs for decision making? How can teams collaborate on finding the relevant bits and pieces of information to support forecasting? How can an executive or team build customized sets of trends based on media scans?

Question Forming: What decisions or issues are the focus of Adrienne's competitive analysis? Do they involve regulatory, technological, or competitive environment changes on the horizon? Fashion direction, marketing, and promotional strategy?

Competitors: The direct competitors are obvious. Are there any indirect competitors who should be considered?

Probable Uses of the Analysis: Is the analysis likely to be used as informational, offensive, or defensive? What kinds of decisions will depend on the analysis—tactical or strategic or both?

Priorities for Information Gathering: List the kind of information Adrienne needs; then set priorities about which kinds of information to gather. What methods will be employed in gathering this information? What ethical or legal issues might be involved?

Analysis Model: Which analysis model—competitive environment, market scan, competitor profile, or management profile—will be most helpful to decision makers? What methods of data analysis will be used?

✦ QUESTION FORMING AND INFORMATION GATHERING

The first step in competitive analysis is to identify the issues or decisions that will become the focus of the process. Issues may involve changes in the regulatory, technological, or competitive environment. Decisions may involve fashion direction, marketing, and promotional strategy. By listing the kind of information they need for decisions, professionals set priorities and structure information gathering in categories—what is critical, relatively important, or merely nice to know. Because there will not be time or resources to gather all the information, the search will concentrate on the critical and important categories (Heath, 1996b). There will always be more questions than can be answered given time and money constraints. Finding the high-priority questions is an essential first step. One industry employee uses a technique he calls "the five whys"—for questions that seem important, ask "why" five times. Through this process, questions get dropped or refined to the point until there are three to five questions that are of genuine interest to decision makers (Rosenkrans, 2003).

The quest for information uses four sources (Heath, 1996b):

❖ Published sources, including information in newspapers and magazines, trade publications, government documents, company reports, investment and financial publications, press releases and presentations by company executives at conferences.
❖ **Fieldwork**, or direct observation and interviews with employees, suppliers, customers, and experts.
❖ **"Soft information"** from the popular press, television shows that mention the company or product, and industry rumors.

In-house sources such as the sales force, customer service, technical support, and other front-line workers who know before managers about the competitors' newest products and plans (Heath, 1996a).

Companies leave paper trails whenever they take actions such as hiring or firing people, buying supplies, opening new plants, or expanding their distribution channels. Companies must deal with local, state, and federal governments in undertaking actions, and that makes government sources a good place for basic information on finances, plant size, and regulatory issues.

Competitive analysis can be undertaken for a specific project and have a specific end date. But companies that use competitive analysis most successfully monitor information by category and frequency (Prescott & Smith, 1989):

* continuous monitoring of general industry trends and technological development;
* continuous monitoring of marketing, sales, and financial information on key partners and competitors;
* periodic monitoring on a weekly, monthly, or seasonal basis of partners' and competitors' organizational goals, customer profiles, services, and channels of distribution;
* occasional monitoring of public and international affairs, human resources, general administrative structure, and other business practices as changing situations require.

Continuous, periodic, and occasional monitoring can be focused on a specific goal—to keep tabs on the competitive environment, changes in the marketplace, the actions of a direct competitor, or the management style of a company as it influences decisions.

It may seem strange to monitor not only the competition but also **business-to-business partners**—firms closely allied with the company as suppliers or customers. However, competitive analysis can be a way to pick up on signals that promote better understanding between firms that do business with each other. Missing signals from business partners can be costly when it leads to a disruption in either the supply or the demand side of a business. Partner firms are probably also doing business with others, and part of achieving total quality management is finding out if a competitor is doing a better job in terms of products or services (Fuld, 1992). Monitoring business partners provides an early warning of changes or shifts in alliances that can have long-term effects on the business.

✧ Competitive Environment Scan

A professional makes decisions contingent on the decisions of counterparts at competing firms. That is, they must anticipate the effect a decision will have on their own company and the likely response from competitors (Zajac & Bazerman, 1991). A competitive environment scan provides the background for those decisions. Depending on the company's needs, the scan can be updated on either a continuous or a periodic basis. The purpose of this scan is to locate general information on an industry and the relative position of the companies in that industry. This type of scan will include information on industry size, market share by company, and trends in the industry.

Trade magazines such as *Women's Wear Daily* (or *WWD*) usually publish one issue a year as an overview of an industry. These issues provide helpful background data and suggest ways to organize information on the industry—perhaps by size of companies, product categories, or geographic location. Tracking back a few years using these special issues provides directional information on the industry and highlights issues and trends that are of perennial interest and those just emerging. Other sources for industry overview information include:

* US Department of Commerce and other government sources;
* reports prepared for investors;
* private analyst publications such as Deloitte, KPMG, Moody's or Valueline;

- databases of magazine and newspaper articles on the industry and the companies in the industry such as Infotrac, Lexis Nexis, or Business Source Complete;
- trade associations that conduct surveys of industry practices.

Investor reports may be obtained free through databases compiling company profiles and from brokerage firms seeking new investors. The newspaper and magazine articles contain data on companies in the industry and often include the names of experts who can be contacted for interviews for more detailed information.

Some companies compile a company history on each of their key partners and competitors (Fuld, 1985). The company history includes a chronology of the company's activities, including acquisitions of other firms, name changes, and major changes after a new chief executive officer (CEO) or management team was installed. Trade magazines often profile one company per issue, and these profiles are a good first step in compiling a company history. By adding articles on the company from other newspapers and magazines and a recent annual report from the company, the executive has the sources needed to compile a timeline for the company and a company history.

✧ Market Scan

Companies have a good idea who their direct competitors are but often fail to consider indirect or hidden competitors. Direct competitors sell the same general product to the same customers in the same distribution channels. **Indirect competitors** are those that offer alternatives that may redirect a customer away from making a purchase. Using competitive analysis techniques to develop a market overview promotes a more comprehensive answer to questions about who the firm's competitors are now and in the future.

All companies going after the same target customer with products that can be substituted for each other or competing for that customer's discretionary spending are competitors. Customers may decide to change brands, trade up or down in terms of quality and price, substitute a different product, or shift spending to another category of goods at any time. The purpose of a market scan is to identify trends, shifts in consumer preferences, and changes in competitor strategies that may have an impact on the firm in the short and long term.

Figure 11.6

Executives need a detailed profile of their direct competitors including shopping the line as it is presented to the customer.

The scan begins with an overview of the size of the market and expected growth rates for key customer segments—age range, income levels, geographic concentration, and lifestyle (Figure 11.6). Government documents from the Census Bureau are a good starting point. Business and industry databases provide articles projecting growth or contraction of market segments and reports on lifestyle surveys covering the market segments. Important directional information includes consumer preferences for styling, fabrications, and brands. Suggestions that consumer preferences vary by regions of the country or by ethnicity indicate that different strategies must be formulated for each region or group.

The scan continues with the identification of key brands and estimates of their market share: for example, comparing how brands may vary in terms of pricing, styling, fashion, and fabrication. Other comparison factors may be whether brands use different distribution channels, if companies vary in their marketing and promotional strategy, or an estimation of the strength of brand identity for each company. Breaking down the key brands into the smallest possible segment by product line produces a better, more finely tuned picture of the market.

Companies that are looking ahead strategically will analyze potential threats. Possible threats include emerging companies with a novel approach to attracting customers, shifts in consumer preferences or lifestyle, and reallocation of consumers' discretionary spending away from apparel products and toward another category such as home decor, entertainment, or travel. If there are threats, there are also untapped opportunities in this market.

Market reports are available from market research firms, publishing companies specializing in marketing, and consultants. Market reports can cost thousands of dollars and may go out of date quickly. Companies that conduct their own market scan and update it periodically will be in a better position to evaluate competitive moves by rival firms and to position their own products and company to gain competitive advantage now and in the future.

✧ Competitor Profile

Companies need a detailed profile of their direct competitors, including a breakdown of each product line by design, quality, distribution, packaging, marketing, and promotion. Supplementing the breakdown with figures about costs associated with each aspect is helpful, but such information is among the most difficult to obtain. Sometimes historical data can be used to trace developments up to the current time and to hypothesize about future directions (Schlossberg, 1990). Important insights can result from an understanding of the **corporate culture** in the competing firm. Even details such as how offices are allocated or the frequency of meetings suggest how the company functions internally, how employees relate to each other, and how decisions are made. The popular website The Business of Fashion, run by British editor Imran Amed, feels that corporate culture is so important to an apparel company's success that it published *The Companies & Culture Issue*, a special print issue featuring articles on Victoria Beckham, Hermès, and Rick Owens, complete with a Company Culture Guide to coincide with the launch of its own Business of Fashion Careers (www.businessoffashion.com).

To provide decision support, a competitor profile should include the following (Gelb et al., 1991):

* overview and history of the company;
* a breakdown of product lines including sales figures and pricing;
* an overview of the company's marketing strategies, including defining and developing new target customers;
* an overview of corporate strategy on issues such as technology and research and development;
* a financial analysis of the company, including costs, profits, and overheads;
* information on international strategies in terms of marketing and production.

In addition to a company history, companies must be aware of announcements about new products, price changes, new promotional initiatives, personnel changes, plant openings or closings, and openings of new distribution centers. Even ads for the company's products indicate the competitor's positioning strategy in different markets. Information about the company in the trade press, as well as business and industry databases, fills out the profile (Martin, 1992).

Government data, public documents, and investor reports help assess the financial health and market share of a competitor. Some computer databases such as the US Securities and Exchange Commission's EDGAR database require only entering the company name to locate this information. Many companies overlook internal sources of competitor information such as the sales staff and suppliers who can discuss sales levels, floor space, or other details about how the competitor is doing business.

An effective way to organize information in a competitor profile is to use three categories: (1) what competitors say about themselves; (2) what other competitors say about them; and (3) what third parties such as reporters, suppliers, and customers say about them. Evaluating each of these categories separately gives a much clearer picture and raises more interesting questions than combining them (McGonagle & Vella, 1990).

Gathering information for competitive analysis is a creative process. One professional suggests looking for information close to where the company or the corporate division has its headquarters (Schlossberg, 1990). Many apparel companies have showrooms or sales offices in fashion centers such as New York, but others are headquartered where the company was founded, often in small and mid-sized cities. When a large company is headquartered in a smaller city, that company is big news and will be covered extensively in the local press. For information on those firms, instead of going to national sources, check local sources first. For example, read the website for the local paper in the city where the corporate headquarters are located.

Another creative and frequently overlooked source of information on competitors is employment ads in trade publications and newspapers. In describing themselves to potential employees, companies frequently provide insights about new initiatives in the company. Perhaps the company is changing computer-aided design (CAD) systems or expanding the number of designers. In either case, the ad may signal that more emphasis is being placed on product development than in the past. Similarly, employment ads that mention expansion plans, new equipment, or other changes are helpful in developing a profile that anticipates the competitor's strategy (Fuld, 1988).

One competitive analysis professional suggests focusing on the competitor's relationships with other companies such as partners, vendors, or advertising agencies. Some of these relationships are public, but others may be undisclosed or less obvious; some will be formal alliances, but others will be informal. Information about public companies will be readily available, but information about privately held companies will be more difficult to find. When a company collaborates with another, it will disclose information to the business partner—for example, a manufacturer and retailer who work jointly on assortment and inventory issues or a manufacturer who contracts with companies in other countries for sourcing fabrics and production services—and look to that partner business for information that may not be available from the company itself. For example, a company may protect information about product development, but its partner company may announce the ways that the two companies are cooperating—thereby disclosing the information of interest. Use information on formal and informal alliances to create a map because companies give away their strategic plans by forming these relationships (Mockus, 2003).

The more detailed the profile of the competitor, the more helpful it is in supporting tactical and strategic decision making. The profile on a key competitor should be continuously updated to provide the most up-to-the-minute picture of the competitive situation. Only with such detailed and current information can a company recognize a competitive advantage and act on the opportunity.

✧ Management Profile

The corporate culture of a rival firm may give it some sort of competitive edge. A new CEO may come to a company with the experience of what worked and what did not work at other firms, along with a mandate to increase profits, such as when J.Crew hired former Gap CEO Mickey Drexler. A firm might change from a chain-of-command system to a functional team approach to product development. A competitor based in another part of the country could seek to acquire a new entrant into the market, such as when Seattle-based Nordstrom acquired the Chicago-based online men's styling service and online retailer Trunk Club for $350 million (Elejalde-Ruiz, 2014). Today's rising young executive may be tomorrow's president of a rival firm. In all these cases and many more, the management styles and backgrounds of executives at a rival firm are essential to understanding the situation and predicting what comes next. Competitive analysis includes profiling key decision makers as a way to anticipate and explain their strategic moves.

Occasionally a trade publication, business magazine, or newspaper will profile a corporate officer, focusing on his or her successes, management style, and financial acumen. Television cable channels that focus on business sometimes offer interview programs with administrators who have become prominent in an industry. Other sources for collecting management profiles include articles in trade publications and newspapers about an executive's promotion, "who's who" directories for business and industry, and brief biographies in annual reports and convention materials when a well-known industry speaker is on the program.

In the case of a firm's president or CEO, chances are that the person has been prominent in business news about the industry prior to assuming the position (Figure 11.7). A search of databases using the executive's name or that of his or her former company may provide articles in which they were interviewed about a range of issues. Another source of information comes from interviews with colleagues and coworkers who discuss how this administrator approaches business decisions.

Attending trade shows and conventions that feature representatives from rival firms on the program offers the chance to gain insight on the direction the firm will be taking in the future. There is usually a question-and-answer session and the responses during this period can be more revealing than the prepared remarks.

Assembling a profile of a senior manager's education, work history, philanthropic interests, and management philosophy requires time, patience, and creativity. But such a profile opens a window into the behavior and customary approach of a key decision maker in business situations—a critical piece of information in a competitive environment.

✦ ETHICAL AND LEGAL ISSUES

Information can be so valuable that some individuals will go to illegal lengths to obtain or share it for personal gain. The former vice president of investor relations for Carter's children's clothing pled guilty in 2012 to conspiracy to commit securities and wire fraud in connection with an insider-trading conspiracy primarily involving Carter's stock. He gave private company information to hedge funds and a hedge fund consultant "in exchange for friendship, reciprocal stock tips about other public companies and future business and networking opportunities," and traded on the information himself to make money (Vardi, 2013).

Industrial espionage occurs when someone breaks the law to collect data. Examples of industrial espionage include "hacking" into a company's computer to steal files, stealing

Figure 11.7

In addition to running her company, Diane von Furstenberg has been president of the Council of Fashion Designers of America (CFDA) since 2006.

samples from a trade show display, or entering a firm's plant or distribution center surreptitiously to spy on operations.

At trade shows such as Utah's Outdoor Retailer market, guarding against industrial espionage is top priority because so many new and innovative products are revealed to the industry for the first time. Trade show organizers do their best to prevent spying with posted rules against unauthorized photography on the back of admission badges and through background checks of attendees and the creation of a special hotline to report suspected photography and spying incidents. Even though there is security provided by the event organizers, some companies with proprietary merchandise hire their own security to guard against counterfeiters (Winslow, 2013).

Some information-gathering activities are not illegal but are considered **unethical practices**. Examples of these kinds of activities include misrepresenting a person's identity to extract information from a firm's employees, and giving a competitor's employee an employment

interview solely to debrief them about the other company's operations. Other activities fall in a gray area—not illegal but questionable, such as going through a competitor's trash when it has been put on the curb for pick-up. Cautious companies guard against this form of intelligence gathering by shredding all documents before discarding.

Competitive analysis professionals and the managers they work with need to be clear about the ethical boundaries of information gathering. The president of the Strategic and Competitive Intelligence Professionals (SCIP) suggests using "the Mommy Rule"—"If your mother saw you, would she approve?" Others call it the *"60 Minutes* Rule" to remind people to consider how they would explain themselves if they had to do it on a television news magazine show such as *60 Minutes* (Wheatley, 2003).

Although there are no government regulations on competitive intelligence gathering and there is no licensing system for practitioners, most people in the field voluntarily abide by a code of ethics such as that published to members by SCIP. Common sense and a sense of fair play will guide the actions of most executives, but there are some activities to avoid (Murphy & Laczniak, 1992; Paine, 1991):

- purposeful searches for confidential business information or classified government information;
- covert surveillance;
- obtaining information under false pretenses, deceit, or misrepresentation;
- encouraging other professionals such as bankers and lawyers to leak confidential information;
- seeking information in ways that interfere with a person's privacy.

Illegal or unethical practices are unnecessary in order to conduct successful competitive analysis because there are so many public sources of information and computer databases that make obtaining information easier than in the past.

✦ METHODS OF DATA ANALYSIS

Competitive analysis is different from market research. Strictly factual information such as the organizational structure of a company or the location of distribution centers requires very little analysis. The information on general industry trends, potential competitors, and technological developments requires more extensive analysis to determine the short- and long-term implications for a company (Prescott & Smith, 1989).

Having gathered the information is only the first step. Next, the analyst must evaluate the information for **reliability**—the first clue to consider is the original source and the credibility of that source. **"Disinformation"** results from inaccuracies in published articles, from people misrepresenting their knowledge or expertise, and from countering moves by competitors seeking to protect their secrets. The only protection from inaccurate information is to check and double-check information using multiple sources. Another source of inaccuracy is

related to the timeliness of information; since facts in a magazine story are already months old, and those in a book may be years old, they may already be obsolete by the time they are read. Researchers must keep in mind that events can change quickly.

The next step is organizing the information using an outline of key topics (see the earlier discussion of scans and profiles for organizational structures) and making inferences about what it means. There are many forms of analysis, and they may be performed by a team or by an individual analyst. The most frequently used methods include the following.

✧ Strengths–Weaknesses–Opportunities– Threats (SWOT) Analysis

Look at a competitive situation and analyze the company's strong and weak points and strategize about possible challenges and possible opportunities. For example, Tory Burch, after working in marketing and public relations for several designer firms, saw an opening for a lower-priced brand in the contemporary fashion category (Figure 11.8). Rather than focus on apparel, the plan called for launching a complete retail concept with a boutique and fifteen product types from shoes to umbrellas, swimwear to handbags, dresses to shoes. The successful line now consists of more than 1,000 styles (20 percent are repeats of signature items that are updated for the season). But the company faces the challenge of keeping their team together, dealing with competition from brands like Nanette Lepore, Diane von Furstenberg, and others, and oversaturation as the company grows. As Tory Burch says, "Our customer doesn't want to see herself coming and going" (Agins, 2008).

✧ Scenario Planning

Researching and writing scenarios is a way to investigate the way the competitive environment can evolve. Viewing several alternative futures allows executives to incorporate this long view in their strategic planning. The non-profit group Forum for the Future collaborated with Levi Strauss & Co. to envision how "climate change,

Figure 11.8

Tory Burch saw an opening for a lower priced, contemporary brand but rather than focus on apparel, launched a complete retail concept—a boutique with fifteen product lines.

resource shortages, population growth and other factors will shape the world of 2025 and the future of the fashion industry within it" (Forumforthefuture.org, 2010). Working with forty industry experts, four plausible scenarios were created for the *Fashion Futures 2025: Global Scenarios for a Sustainable Fashion Industry* project. The four scenarios were:

1   *Slow is beautiful*—A world of political collaboration and global trade where slow and sustainable is fashionable.
2   *Community couture*—Where high-tech systems deliver for the speed-obsessed global shopper.
3   *Techno-chic*—Where resource crises constrain consumption in a world focused on local communities.
4   *Patchwork planet*—A world of fast consumption in global cultural blocs.

For each of the four scenarios, a unique profile was created that responded to each of the following statements: (1) "The world is …," (2) "Fashion is …," (3) "The fabrics we wear are …," (4) "We get our clothes …," (5) "Clothes are made …," (6) "We care for clothes …," (7) "When we have finished with clothes …," (8) "The industry is sustainable through …," and (9) "Successful fashion businesses are …" to create an in-depth description of what the apparel industry might look like in the year 2025. The authors of the project were careful to caution that scenarios are not predictions, but instead tools to imagine what the world could look like, with the end-goals of stimulating new ideas, including challenges and opportunities and testing strategies for robustness.

✧ Content Analysis

Content analysis involves extracting significant data from the sources and classifying it by topic and reliability. Content analysis condenses the information into meaningful clusters that can be evaluated to determine their implications. Technology has made content analysis very easy;

many types of software are available that can conduct content analysis on interview or focus group transcripts, documents, websites or news articles, anything that can be transcribed or read can be analyzed. One such product is WordStat by Provalis Research, which provides content analysis of open-ended responses, interviews, or focus group transcripts and allows the user to extract themes and trends from their data (www.provalisresearch.com, 2014). Other companies that produce data analysis software include Atlas.ti, NVivo, and MAXQDA, so it is possible to choose the best fit for a company's needs from among many options.

✧ Pattern Recognition

Look for patterns in the information—an apparel company hiring more designers may be changing strategies; a division that was barely mentioned in last year's annual report but is prominent in this year's probably means that the division's status has changed within the company. Having background and historical information makes it more likely that the analyst will spot an emerging pattern in the data.

✧ Information Gap Analysis

Anomalies are data that do not fit expectations. **Outliers** are cases or facts that are unexpectedly high or low in value. **Omissions** are missing reasons for an action or a business decision. These unanticipated gaps in the information gathered during a competitive analysis may be mistakes or misunderstandings or they may be significant clues. It is important to recognize anomalies, outliers, and omissions, and diligently search for an explanation. Ignoring these gaps may lead the analyst to incorrect conclusions.

It is important during the analysis phase to keep the information separate from conclusions. Experienced analysts organize the information first, then draw conclusions, and, finally, check to see that they have enough data to support each conclusion. If a conclusion lacks support, it is dropped until additional information confirms it (McGonagle & Vella, 1990).

✦ FROM COMPETITIVE ANALYSIS TO COMPETITIVE ADVANTAGE

Competitive analysis assists executives in corporate-level planning by identifying the nature and intensity of competition in the industry, the characteristics of the dominant firms, and projections for the future size of the market. Competitive analysis assists executives at the business-planning level in developing a competitive strategy and in making the frequent tactical decisions required to compete effectively in a marketplace (McGonagle & Vella, 1990). Competitive analysis contributes to the overall planning and forecasting functions by justifying projects, priorities, and actions, and by generating new ideas about how to solve problems or take advantage of opportunities.

In addition to these basic uses of competitive analysis, there are other more sophisticated applications:

❖ *Shadow market planning*—The goal in **shadow market planning** is to have one or more people in a company be so familiar with a competitor that they can answer "what if" questions about that competitor's strategy on a current and continuous basis. They accomplish this task by regularly monitoring the elements of a competitor's marketing efforts to such an extent that they can put themselves in the competitor's place (McGonagle & Vella, 1990).

❖ *"Best practices" benchmarking*—**Benchmarking** means comparing a company with other firms considered "best" in terms of efficient operations. In "best practices" benchmarking, the firms chosen for comparison may not even be in the same industry. Lex Wexner of Limited Brands was asked by a market analyst which retailers he used as benchmarks for Victoria's Secret. He replied: "The two we talk about most are Apple and Starbucks. We learn most from them. VS and Apple should be like cousins" (Moin, 2007) (Figure 11.9).

❖ *Competitive benchmarking*—In **competitive benchmarking**, the firms chosen for comparison are the company's direct competitors. A set of specific measures such as capital investment, productivity, and product quality is used to create a side-by-side comparison of how the company fits into the competition with other firms (Ghoshal & Westney, 1991).

❖ *Sensitization*—The goal of **sensitization** is to shake up a company's assumptions about its place in relationship to competitors. Sensitization uses information about competitors to build a sense of urgency in a company by alerting executives to gains by competitors or an emerging challenge from a new company (Ghoshal & Westney, 1991).

❖ *Reverse engineering for products*—**Reverse engineering** means purchasing and dismantling a product to determine how it was designed and constructed. The purpose of this process is to estimate the costs and evaluate the quality of the product to determine how to produce a more competitive product. Beyond the product itself, reverse engineering may involve the way the product is packed or shipped or the way it is manufactured. For certain types of products, such as computer software, reverse engineering is illegal.

❖ *Reverse engineering for services*—Customer satisfaction is essential to business success in today's market. If a rival firm has a reputation for better service from sales associates, fulfillment of phone orders, or some other service component, that service can become the target for competitive analysis. The process involves profiling the steps and attributes of the service and comparing it to current practices in the industry. For example, after the success that non-apparel retailers such as Best Buy experienced with in-store pickup of online purchases, Moody's Investors Service recommended that apparel retailers offer their own customers the same option for faster delivery service (Young, 2014).

(a)

(b)

Figure 11.9

An analyst asked Lex Wexner of Limited Brands what companies he used in benchmarking his retail chain Victoria's Secret (a) and he cited Apple computer stores (b) but didn't elaborate. What attributes of product, store ambience, marketing, or corporate culture do these companies share?

Any corporate program of competitive analysis involves both quantitative and qualitative data. Few professionals have the full range of skills to accomplish competitive analysis. A much better approach is to see competitive analysis as a shared responsibility among employees. Today's computer networks make this easier to accomplish. Whatever the approach, competitive analysis is an important part of forecasting and planning—a process that involves employees at all levels and in all job categories. To be effective, competitive information must be communicated widely throughout the company using formal reporting methods such as memos and newsletters, along with less formal methods such as intranet sites, e-mail, and bulletin boards (Fuld, 1988).

Chapter Summary

All firms want to get, and keep, a competitive advantage in the marketplace, but with the retail landscape in constant change, it can be difficult to hold on to consumers' brand loyalty. Competitive analysis allows companies to stay aware of their position in the market as well as keep an eye on what their competitors are doing so that they can continually innovate in order to stay ahead of market changes. Competitive analysis can be conducted by all sizes of companies and for any length of time to assist in the planning process. Methods include competitive environment and market scans or competitor and management profiles, but information gathering should never cross the line into unethical or illegal activities. Data analysis such as SWOT analysis, scenario planning, content analysis, pattern recognition, and information gap analysis enables professionals to take the information they have obtained, use it to make an actionable plan that takes unforeseen events into account, and establish a competitive advantage among industry members.

Key Terms and Concepts

Anomalies

Benchmarking

Brand image

Brand loyalty

Brand recognition

Brand tiers

Branding

Business-to-business partners

Competitive advantage

Competitive analysis

Competitive benchmarking

Competitive intelligence

Content analysis

Corporate culture

Designer name brands

Direct competitors

Disinformation

Fieldwork

Indirect competitors

Industrial espionage

In-store shop

Mid-range strategies

National brands

Omissions

Outliers

Private-label brands

Reliability (of information)

Reverse engineering

Secret shopper

Sensitization

Shadow market planning

Soft information

Speed to market

Store brands

Strategic planning

Tactics

Unethical practices

Value

Discussion Questions

Competitive Advantage: Think of some of your favorite apparel and retail brands. What competitive advantages do you think they possess? Consider some apparel and retail brands that you used to love, but no longer do: how did they lose their competitive advantage? What gaps exist in the marketplace currently that a new company could fill and have their own competitive advantage?

Competitive Analysis: How might developing the ability to conduct a competitive analysis benefit you in your career? How could you apply such knowledge about other companies at your job? How could you use such information when conducting a job search?

Unethical Practices: What risks do apparel professionals take when they engage in unethical practices? Why do you think executives might take such risks? Do you think it is now easier or harder to hide obscure unethical behavior?

Forecasting Activities

Styles on the Net. Choose something specific to shop for—apparel, accessories, or shoes. Read blogs, use fashion search engines, visit fashion-focused social shopping sites, multibrand sites, store, and magazine sites. Compare the information found at each kind of e-fashion site. Where did you find the most helpful information? The most fashion-forward suggestions? Which sources of information are you likely to use for future purchases?

Be a "Secret Shopper." Fieldwork is one way to gather information about a competitor's business—shop their stores and wear their product. Pick a specialty store chain as a "client" for competitive analysis. Then, take on the role of a "**secret shopper**"—a person who appears to be just a customer but who is actually noting the operational details of a business. Compare the product, visual merchandising, pricing, and service at two or more of your client's competitors. Prepare a chart comparing the stores. Conclude with ways your "client" can meet or surpass the competition.

Competitive Analysis Start-Up. Start a competitive analysis Pinterest file on the apparel industry. Begin with a file for material on the total industry. Add files for two or three major companies. Develop a one-page company history on the major companies in timeline form showing the development of the company, its brands by product category and price, and quotes taken from recent articles about the company's direction in the future.

Help-Wanted Ads. Using the classifieds section of *WWD* and the Careers pages of major apparel and retail companies, collect employment ads for positions in the apparel industry in product development and design, production, quality control, sales, visual merchandising, advertising and promotion, buying, and retail management. When you have a collection of ads, examine what they reveal about companies. Compare ads across companies: How do the ads reflect the corporate culture of each firm? What specific information do the ads reveal about the company structure? Are there any hints about changes in the way that the company is doing business?

CEO Profile. Select a company in which you are particularly interested. Find out the name of the president or CEO of the firm. Use database searching to locate profiles of the company and the CEO. Some databases contain not only the text of print articles but also transcripts of media interviews. The interviews are particularly helpful in developing a CEO profile. Using several articles or interviews, compile a profile that includes:

◆ background information on the executive's early life, education, and career path;

◆ the situation when the CEO stepped into this position, the challenges faced, actions taken, and the outcome;

◆ information about the executive's style of management and philosophy of business.

Complete the profile by selecting several recent quotes by the executive that suggest the probable direction the firm will take over the next year.

Resource Pointers

For industry profiles:
www.apparelmagazine.com
2025 Fashion Futures:
www.forumforthefuture.org

Moody's: www.moodys.com
Strategic and Competitive Intelligence
Professionals (SCIP): www.scip.org
Women's Wear Daily: www.wwd.com

> Data is very important, but you have to be good at reading the data in an emotional way.
>
> —*Mickey Drexler, J.Crew CEO*

12

PRESENTING THE FORECAST

OBJECTIVES

◆ Introduce the guidelines for performance, effective visuals, and the use of audiovisual equipment

◆ Establish the purpose and characteristics of trend reporting

◆ Explore traditional and leading-edge presentation techniques and the role of technology

TREND REPORTING

The role of a fashion forecaster is to identify, develop, and present fashion directions in fabrics, colors, and styles and put them into the context of the culture and lifestyles of the consumer. The forecaster explains what is happening, why the trend is developing, and who is leading the trend. Fashion forecasting is a resource for product development, merchandising, marketing, and retailing executives (Figure 12.1). Trend reporting helps these executives interpret fashion change by relating new directions to brand or store strategy.

Trend reporting begins by describing the appeal of a trend through labeling. The label may refer to:

❖ a look—retro, minimalist, Japanese influence;
❖ the mood or spirit—youthful, sophisticated, playful;
❖ a lifestyle message;
❖ a tie-in with a celebrity;
❖ a target market—urban youth, working women, early retirees;
❖ a brand image or designer's name;
❖ a concept—career casual, investment dressing, mix-and-match;
❖ the source of inspiration, whether historical or ethnic—*la Belle Époque*, Moroccan;
❖ a pop-culture influence such as a hit movie or television series.

Trend reporting continues the labeling process by describing the basic elements of the trend:

❖ *fabric*—fiber content, functional attributes, texture, pattern;
❖ *color*—hue, value, intensity, color schemes;
❖ *silhouette*—shape of the garment, hemline, coordinating elements of the total ensemble;
❖ *details* and design features;
❖ *subtleties* of fit, proportion, and coordination.

The description may also include attributes such as the size category (juniors, misses, plus size, petites), price category (designer, bridge, better, moderate), and the season (fall/winter, spring/summer, cruise).

Describing the trend is only the first step in trend reporting. The forecaster must also provide a trend map detailing the stage in development and probable scope of each trend.

(a)

Figure 12.1a and b

At shows such as Première Vision, product development, merchandising, marketing, and retailing executives receive the latest trend information.

(b)

✦ TREND MAP

The **trend map** identifies which trends are just emerging, continuing to build, or declining. The theories about fashion dynamics (see Chapters 2 and 3) and the product life cycle (see Chapter 10) provide frameworks for these observations. The trend map allows the apparel executive to make merchandising decisions (Figure 12.2). Continuing trends form the core business targeted to mainstream customers. Exit strategies must be devised for clearing merchandise associated with declining trends. Emerging trends represent the opportunity to test the potential product and get in on the ground floor of "the next big thing."

✧ Quality of the Trend

The trend map draws distinctions between **major trends**—those that will appeal to large groups of consumers—and **minor trends**—those with niche appeal to small groups of consumers (Perna, 1987).

Major trends are fabrics, colors, styles, and looks that are likely to move into the mainstream. These trends have already been tested in the market and continue to receive support in terms of sales and media coverage. They represent volume-sales potential. Minor trends have more limited sales potential because they are too avant-garde, too distinctive, or too complex to appeal to a broad audience. However, these trends have potential for regional sales or through specialty retailers with target customers who like the look. Minor trends often appear at the top of the price range or at the bottom. Fads often play out as interesting and fun minor trends (Figure 12.3).

✧ Potential of the Trend

The trend map must indicate the quality of each trend. Some items, styles, or looks are **trial balloons**—designer experiments to gauge the effect and potential of a new idea (Perna, 1987). These trial balloons are likely to be commented on by fashion insiders and the media but will not receive support from most retailers. Occasionally, a trial balloon has strong, instantaneous appeal because it is the perfect statement mirroring the spirit of the times (see Chapter 1 for a discussion of the Zeitgeist). In those rare instances, the item or look suddenly sells out quickly. The initial restricted availability and strong reaction (sometimes fueled by media coverage) combine to drive the popularity of that item.

Figure 12.2

Calvin Klein designer Narciso Rodriguez in front of one of his trend boards.

Some items, styles, or looks represent **embryonic trends**—that is, trends in the very first stages of development (Perna, 1987). Perhaps a trial balloon in one season is further developed and given more prominence in the next season. The trend has not yet developed, but the look is poised to take off; fashion insiders are tracking its development, but the public is largely unaware of its existence.

If fashion innovators and fashion-forward retailers adopt a specific look, it is called a **directional trend** (Perna, 1987). For more mainstream companies, directional trends offer the opportunity to introduce avant-garde concepts by featuring the trend in promotions, through visual merchandising, or in fashion shows. Although most customers will end up buying merchandise associated only with major trends, the directional trends bring excitement and a feeling of forward motion to fashion.

✧ Interactions with Other Product Categories

It is important for the trend map to establish relationships between classifications:

- ❖ skirt length and pants styles influence shoe design and height of heels;
- ❖ style and design of ready-to-wear clothing influence hosiery;
- ❖ outerwear coordinates with the style and fit of dressy and casual looks;
- ❖ the structure and fit of apparel relates to the styling of innerwear and vice versa;
- ❖ accessory stories closely parallel the fashion story, tapping into the same design inspiration;
- ❖ makeup and hairstyles coordinate with apparel styles.

✧ Estimating the Relative Strength of Trends

Based on an understanding of the marketplace and fashion dynamics, the forecaster estimates the **timing of a trend**—how soon the trend will "hit," and how long it will continue. In addition to timing, the forecaster must estimate the **scope of a trend**—how big it will be, and how broad an impact it will have on markets. Recommendations indicate the relative strength of various trends and the kind of investment in product development and merchandising that they merit (Perna, 1987).

Figure 12.3

A trend map not only covers the merchandise category of direct interest to the audience but also points to other product categories where the trends will be influential. Trends for apparel parallel those for shoes, accessories, legwear, jewelry, and cosmetics.

Profile: Lidewije Edelkoort, Edelkoort and Trend Tablet

Lidewije "Li" Edelkoort has been called the "grandmother of trend forecasting." Her first job was as a junior buyer for a department store in the Netherlands, but only a few years later she went to Paris to work as a consultant. Prior to starting Trend Union in 1986, she worked at another famous French forecasting company, Nelly Rodi. Today, she works in Europe, the United States, China, and Australia studying and presenting lifestyle trends, which Edelkoort considers to be the way people are *acting*.

Edelkoort employee Philip Fimmano says that trends are embedded in society, and are patterns that repeat themselves. The company likens the way trends work to a radio, broadcasting short-term trends of 6–18 months, mid-term trends of 3–5 years, and long-term trends of 5 to 10 or 15 years in duration. The duration of a trend can impact industries differently: for example, short-term trends influence fashion in the form of retailers meeting consumer demand for metallics such as bright silver in shoes and accessories, while mid-term trends impact designers who work one year in advance to create their collections, and textile designers who work even farther ahead than that. Long-term trends are what Edelkoort particularly focuses on; these are lifestyle trends that affect areas such as the automotive, paper, and education industries.

Companies come to a trend forecaster because they want to have information about what is going on in the future, designers want inspiration, and manufacturers want to fit a product to the market. To give the best possible service to her clients, Edelkoort has developed its "Seven Virtues of Trend Forecasting," which are guiding principles for the company's forecasts. These include:

* *Purity*: Stay true to who you are.

* *Restraint*: A frame within which to work.

* *Generosity*: Always give your utmost.

* *Integrity*: Never sell out.

* *Patience*: Redo until it is right.

* *Kindness*: Keep things positive.

* *Respect*: Respect those around you.

These values guide the focus of the company and its forecasts. For example, the value of restraint is exemplified through structuring forecasts with one umbrella concept under which all trends are expressed, and by using only clear and precise language in its books. The value of integrity is demonstrated in that the company does not look to external sources—all forecasts are produced internally by Edelkoort's fifteen employees in its Paris bureau. Occasionally, integrity may also mean that Edelkoort has to fire one of its clients if the client tries to pressure them to say or do something they don't feel is true, but this is very rare. Patience is shown in that trends can take time to evolve, and the whole staff will redo a presentation even at the last minute as new evidence becomes available, because they are professionals.

It is just as important to keep in mind what forecasting is not, in order to understand the process. At Edelkoort, forecasting is not one's personal taste. Trends don't belong to anyone, they are merely observed as evidence of the way people live. Fimmano puts it this way: "We are not owners of our ideas, just custodians of them." Trends aren't *predicted*—the information that is acquired by the forecaster is *proposed* by the forecaster to the client. This is because forecasters do not create trends. Even if a forecaster says that something is going to be blue, black, and red, and it's in all of the stores, if people don't like it, they won't buy it.

At Edelkoort, trend forecasting uses both the left and right sides of the brain in a holistic approach, and the process involves intuition, which is likened to a muscle that must be constantly worked through steady research, never-failing curiosity, reading, and always watching. Once the intuition is formed, results must be made understandable and visible to clients. In order to stimulate their intuition, forecasters at Edelkoort take time to leave the office to travel and to attend seminars and various fashion weeks. Travel is crucial to their job to understand aesthetics and different approaches, to get out of their comfort zone, and to counter the negative effects of technology, which in their opinion has canceled out a lot of intuition.

At the start of each season, the team at Edelkoort has a meeting where each member shares their abstract thoughts, images, things they bought on trips and other inspirations. At one such meeting, Edelkoort brought a shiny pebble she found on the beach, and that in turn led to a "polished" theme that was presented. Team members don't look online or in magazines at this stage; they rely on their real-life experiences, considering themselves to be a nomadic company. "Our work is 24 hours a day," says Fimmano. Once the team has their idea, it is refined over a 6-month period. In addition to travel, forecasters use Edelkoort's enormous library of digital images and the book collection it has maintained since 1986. Edelkoort has employees known as "Iconographers," who look for images full-time in the company archives. The team embraces books, documentaries, and film as sources for inspiration. "Not just showing images on the first page of Google," says Fimmano, Edelkoort's forecasters dig deep for their source material.

In their books and presentations, Edelkoort strives for perfection. They consider their work to be about editing—extracting something to its purist form. After an initial compilation of up to 4,000 images, the content is then edited down to only 200 pages of the best visuals. Colors are edited down from an initial 600–700 references to a final presentation of only 60–70 colors, based on what Edelkoort's colorists feel will look freshest in 2 years' time. All colors are presented through fabric swatches, not Pantone reference numbers, because materials inspire them. Throughout the entire process, the team always has a plan B, because although things don't always work out at the time, they may resurface later. "A good idea is always going to remain a good idea," says Fimmano.

Fimmano says that at Edelkoort life is like a family, with Li at the center, and employees feel respected and loved. Even though the Edelkoort employees represent all different shapes, sizes, and nationalities, they respect each other's abilities, and take care to identify what tasks each person is good at, so no one on the team is expected to be good at everything. They even have lunch together every day. This close connection is crucial because Fimmano says employees need to be in an environment where they are constantly happy and inspired.

The hard work of the team is produced in several different publications such as their trend books, which describe trends in colors, fabrics, shapes, and styles for members of the textile and fashion industries, as well as interior design, beauty and wellness markets. Titles include *Colour Forecast*, *Pattern Beauty*, *Activewear*, *Men's Colour*, *Lifestyle Forecasting Book*, and the *Well-Being Bible*. Edelkoort also has produced *Bloom*, a horticultural magazine and the first of its kind, since 1998.

Sources:

Presentation by Philip Fimmano, Edelkoort Exhibits to the International Textile and Apparel Association, November 14, 2014.

Presentation by Sophie Carlier, Manager, at Trend Union offices, June 2014.

http://www.edelkoort.com/

✦ TREND BOARDS

Trend boards identify the mood or spirit of each trend and its thematic focus, then fuse visual and verbal elements into a vivid image. The best combine an evocative theme, the visual development of the theme in fashion, and the verbal flourish that engages the viewer's psyche.

✧ Classical Jazz

The forecaster may recognize a pattern among suits on fashion runways around the world—classical styling but with just a touch of the unconventional in fabrics, design details, and colors. The forecaster creates a presentation board to convey this trend by creating a collage of examples by many designers and adding the phrase "Classical Jazz." The phrase captures perfectly the idea that designers are improvising on a classic silhouette in the same way that jazz musicians improvise on a classic tune.

✧ Desert Drama

Movies such as *The Great Gatsby* with Leonardo DiCaprio have been known to inspire fashion and beauty trends. Imagine that the biggest movie coming out next year features a love story set in the 1930s where the lovers make a long trek through the desert. The costumes inspire an interest in the clothes worn by liberated women of the 1930s who were explorers, pilots, photographers, and foreign correspondents. The

fashion forecaster reports this direction on a trend board juxtaposing stills from the movie, ravishing photographs of the sculptural shapes of sand dunes, and new fashions. He ties together the inspiration and the look in the phrase "Desert Drama."

When designers, manufacturers, and retailers pick up on the trend, each is likely to recast the theme slightly to reflect their own customers' interests and sophistication. For example, a mainstream department store may pick up on the adventurer theme and the neutral color scheme from "Desert Drama," pair it with a promotion of rugged, functional casual clothes, and call it "Entering Neutral Territory." The underlying trend information is present, but the theme has been translated in a way that gives the user an opportunity to craft an image.

Coming up with the concept is a high form of communication, one that involves many levels of meaning. Fashion forecasters must be masters of this form of communication. Finding themes that capture the essence of a trend is a creative challenge for the forecaster. The themes may be inspired by something occurring in the culture—in science, current events, fine arts, performance arts, sports, or popular culture. Or, the inspiration may come from travel destinations and ethnic influences. Trends often resonate with past fashion periods, and the words and images of those times are used to convey the connection.

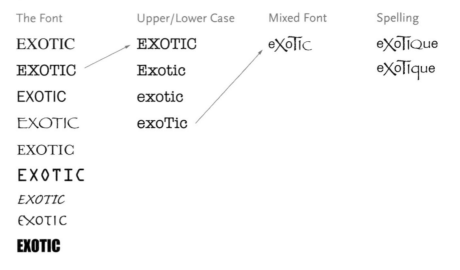

Figure 12.4

The fonts selected for titles and labels convey the theme of the trend board.

The theme, once identified, becomes the unifying force. The typeface, graphics, borders, and background color are selected to further the theme. Computer-generated type avoids the amateurish effect of hand lettering. Experimenting with the typeface—upper case and lower case, effects such as bold letters, and other techniques—connects the message of the text with the theme (Figure 12.4). Photographs, sketches, fabric swatches, and color palette are all coordinated to the theme. If color names are used, the names relate to the theme. For example, colors associated with the jazz theme might be red hot, blue note, and brass, while colors in a trend story about the influence of China on fashion might have names such as lacquer red, jade, and Ming blue.

The layout of the trend board controls how the viewer sees and comprehends the content (Figure 12.5). Forecasters use every design device to keep the eye of the viewer moving within the borders of the trend board. The best trend boards have a focal point with all the items arranged to move the viewer's eye on a path around the board. The first step is to decide on orientation, either portrait for vertical layouts or landscape for horizontal layouts. If the space is divided into half in both directions, the focal point becomes the center of the layout. This is less interesting visually than a layout that divides the space into an uneven number of units. Dividing the space into thirds in both directions provides flexibility—choose any one of four possible focal points—and makes the layout more dynamic and arresting visually. Arrangement of images and text on the board usually follows one of the classic patterns:

- *band*—balance content in a column against white space;
- *axial*—a tree shape with trunk (like band) but with added branches;
- *group*—a collage of touching or overlapping images to create a composite image;
- *grid*—like a newspaper layout with columns, pictures in columns, or pictures spanning two or more columns;
- *path*—similar to group but with dynamic movement from image to image to guide the viewer's eye.

Weak trend boards fail to use a strong focal point or organize images so that the viewer's eye is captured by the visuals. They direct the viewer's eye away from the images. "White space" (unfilled portions of the board) allows the viewer's eye to rest, but too much space can detract from the interest in the images.

Forecasters use trend boards at every stage in the forecasting process. Trend reporting begins

LAYOUTS FOR TREND BOARDS

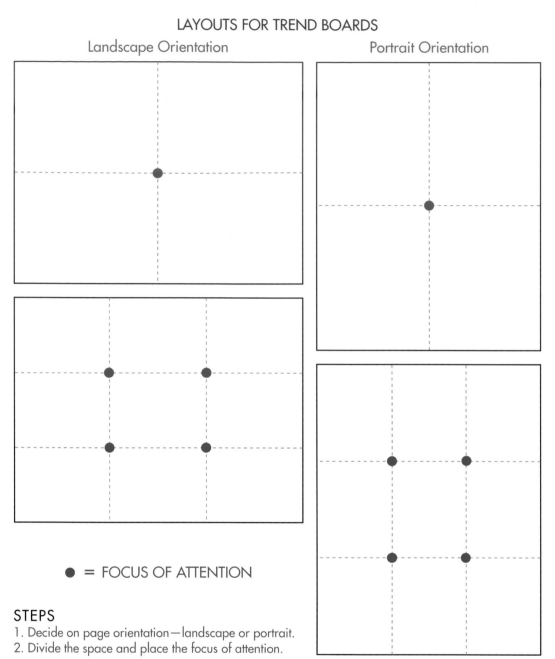

Landscape Orientation

Portrait Orientation

● = FOCUS OF ATTENTION

STEPS
1. Decide on page orientation—landscape or portrait.
2. Divide the space and place the focus of attention.

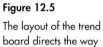

Figure 12.5
The layout of the trend board directs the way the viewer's eye takes in the content.

Figure 12.6

Forecasters scout for new developments in fibers, yarns, blends, and fabrics at international trade shows and then report their findings in trend presentations.

with new developments in fibers, yarns, blends, and fabrics (Figure 12.6). Color forecasters use trend boards to communicate the seasonal color forecast. Fashion directors working for manufacturers and buying offices working for retailers use trend boards to report on fashion trends from the runway and the streets.

Design teams translate trend boards into **concept boards** that guide line development (Chase 1997; Tain, 1997). Having a visual concept of the fashion direction helps in the editing process when the design team selects the ideas that have the strongest potential to succeed in the marketplace. The strength of that potential rests on reading fashion—projecting a consistent image within each coordinated group and across the groups that make up the line.

Concept boards are used in selling apparel internally to the manufacturer's sales force and externally to retail buyers. Sometimes a single concept board is used to convey the source of inspiration, the color and fabric story, the styling, pricing, and key specifications in a visual way. Other companies opt to use one board for the color story, one for the trend story, and another

to suggest visual merchandising options. The boards facilitate communication between the buyer and seller. As one accessories executive put it: "When [buyers] see the boards, it all clicks" (Feitelberg, 1998b).

PRESENTATION TECHNIQUES

The traditional way to communicate trend information is in a meeting. The forecaster speaks to the group using many types of visuals—trend boards, slides or video of runway shows, sample garments, fabric swatches or short yardage, and color chips—to illustrate the trends and drive home points. The technical mastery of all possible visual techniques is beyond one person, but the fashion forecaster coordinates artists, graphic designers, and video production staff in developing the elements of the presentation.

Designing a fashion presentation means:

❖ *describing* the trend so well that the audience can recognize it;

- ❖ *analyzing* the trend so that the audience understands how it functions;
- ❖ *showing* the trend in its natural habitat so that the audience participates vicariously in its discovery.

Forecasters begin by defining the goals of the presentation and the experience to be shared by the presenter and the audience—the needs and wants of the audience, their probable level of interest, and their level of knowledge. The goal of the presentation becomes the standard for selecting appropriate graphics, techniques, and technology.

Effective communication depends on clarity. Clarity is not the same as simplicity. Fashion forecasting involves complex relationships that can only be explained by presenting many examples. Oversimplification or "dumbing down" the information can make it meaningless. Instead, effective presentations focus on a particular message and make it clear through organization and the careful application of display and dissemination techniques. Making a few important points is better than clouding the communication by attempting too much in a limited timeframe.

✦ SPEAKING ABOUT FASHION

To be effective, the forecaster needs public speaking ability. Performance issues such as tone of voice and gestures can make or break a presentation.

◇ Narrative Drive: Beginning, Middle, and End

Aggressive research and brilliant analysis of fashion trends can come to nothing if the presentation is lackluster. Research and analysis transform data into information, but the fashion forecaster must also be a performer interacting with the audience. Ideas are exciting only if they are communicated with power and assurance (Flacks & Rasberry, 1982).

The audience is on the side of the speaker. They come to the meetings with high hopes of spending an entertaining interlude learning new things. They also come with the distractions of their business and personal lives and the fear that they may be wasting time attending this meeting. It is up to the speaker to engage the audience immediately in a shared experience with a strong introduction.

It is common for speakers to focus too much on the body of the speech—the main points, the actions that must occur, the recommendations—at the cost of preparing a compelling beginning. Yet it is this beginning that familiarizes the audience with the style of the speaker and sets the tone of the presentation.

It is a myth that a good presentation begins with a joke. It is also a mistake to begin a speech with an apology: "I'm sorry I'm late," "I hope you will bear with me because I have a cold," "I haven't had time to prepare for this occasion because I was rushing to complete the trend boards." These openings turn audiences off. Such openings also cause the audience to focus on mistakes and on the presenter's nervousness (Flacks & Rasberry, 1982).

Instead, a good opening acknowledges the purpose of the meeting, sets the stage for the body of the speech, and captures the audience's attention. For example, surprise the audience with several examples of fashion behavior that seem unrelated and show a connection. Or, bring the audience into the data-gathering experience by showing a street scene with a variety of people wearing looks that relate to the trends in the presentation. Or, enlighten the audience by showing the parallel between fashion behavior and something else happening in the culture such as a new dance craze or direction for interior design. Brief clips of interviews with consumers who are very pleased or very displeased with the state of fashion set the tone for a lively session. It is not difficult to find a creative and colorful way to begin a trend report. All it takes is brainstorming and a commitment to getting off on the right foot with the audience.

Speakers are frequently advised to "tell them what you're going to tell them, tell them, and then tell them what you told them." This is good advice. Hearing is not as effective as reading for the transfer of knowledge. By repeating the main points three times in different ways, the presenter allows the audience to take in and process the meaning. Presenters often introduce the topic and provide a brief overview—a kind of teaser that will keep the audience looking forward to the unfolding of the ideas and information in the talk. Then, they proceed in an organized way to the core presentation using variety and change of pace to maintain interest. The final repetition comes in the conclusion of the presentation.

The ending is just as important as the beginning of a speech. The goal of the conclusion is to drive home key points, motivate action, and leave the audience inspired and energized. The conclusion is not tacked on but flows smoothly from the core presentation. Perhaps the speaker returns to the images used at the beginning of the speech and elaborates on the content and meanings; or the conclusion could be a flash summary of the key trends. Whatever the content of the conclusion, there are several pitfalls to avoid. Some presenters attempt to present new information in the conclusion—a problem for the audience because there is not time for processing the ideas. Other presenters tell the audience that they are going to stop and then proceed on for several more points and several more minutes—a technique that irritates listeners. The audience needs a clear signal that the speech is over. The most poised presenters stop talking, smile, and pause, all the while maintaining eye contact with the audience, and either ask for questions or leave the podium if no question-and-answer session is scheduled.

✦ Visuals with Impact

Trend boards are only one form of visuals used by forecasters. Actual trend boards can be used in a presentation or the trend board can be photographed either by conventional or digital camera and reproduced in sizes ranging from postcard to poster. The trend board's images become part of computer-generated slide shows.

In a short presentation of 10 to 30 minutes, it is difficult to find the time to show a video, but a short video segment can add realism to a presentation. Videos of runway shows and street fashion give the audience the feeling of seeing trends firsthand. When trends tie into larger cultural issues, video clips help the audience see the bigger picture. In addition, videos of interviews either with consumers or with designers enliven a presentation.

PowerPoint slides are the foundation of many presentations, but the results are often amateurish and obscure and can oversimplify the content (Tufte, 2003). Visual impact improves when presenters follow a few guidelines by (Reynolds, 2008):

* keeping the color choices simple, limiting the number of colors to three or four for the whole presentation;
* avoiding complex screen patterns and ready-made templates;
* creating a "master slide" with the color scheme, page design, and design elements such as bullets, and using that custom template consistently throughout the presentation;
* improving the readability of the text by using a large, easy-to-read font and making the contrast between background and text strong—dark on a light background or light on a dark background;
* following the K.I.S.S. principle in designing each slide: Keep It Simple and Short;
* using appropriate clip art and importing graphics (photographs and sketches in digital form) to enhance the presentation.

Avoid the overused PowerPoint look of bullet points unless no other option will convey the information. Instead, use the best photographs and other quality visuals with the minimum text.

Keep the lights on and make a connection with the audience. Use eye contact. Whenever possible, use a small, unobtrusive remote to change slides so that the speaker is not tied to the computer during the presentation and transitions are seamless.

Visuals should not overpower the speaker or the content. The first task is finding the best, most representative visuals; the next is writing clear and compelling titles that are easy to read. Whether on a trend board or a computer-generated slide, a visually pleasing layout helps convey the message. When visuals are integrated carefully into the organization of a presentation, they add appeal and make the content more accessible to the audience.

✧ Speaking with Confidence

Most people, even experienced speakers, get stage fright. After all, the speaker has lots to think about:

- ✤ the content of the speech;
- ✤ the comfort of the audience, including acoustics, temperature, or distractions;
- ✤ the attention level of the audience;
- ✤ whether the speech is running too long or too short.

The best remedy for stage fright is good preparation so that the speaker is completely fluent with the content, visuals, and order of presentation. Actors swear by rehearsal and so should speakers. Too often, the last-minute rush to complete preparations deprives the speaker of time for practice. If a speaker is convinced that he or she has something worth listening to, then that confidence has a magnetic effect on the attention of the audience.

Stage fright just before getting up to speak is normal. A slight case of nerves gets the mind and body sharply awake and ready for a challenge. Excessive nervousness may come from worries about whether the audience will like the speaker. Skilled presenters shift the focus away from the personal by asking instead whether the audience will understand the trends. If the speech is well researched and thought out, the answer will be yes. With this realization comes confidence.

Nervousness sometimes results in shallow breathing. Taking slow, deep breaths before arising to speak means that the body has stored enough oxygen to provide the energy required to begin talking. After that, the momentum of the narrative and the importance of the points will carry the talk forward.

The audience is most comfortable when the presenter talks in a relaxed but energetic way. The style should be conversational. By speaking to different parts of the room during the talk and maintaining eye contact with the audience whenever possible, the presenter draws more people into the content. Make points with gestures that are appropriate to emphasize points. If the speaker enjoys the presentation and gets involved with the content, the audience will, too.

A professional forecaster is also a professional communicator. Polishing these skills is just as important as any other aspects of the job. There are excellent books on the topic for those who prefer to learn on their own. There are also classes and seminars for those who like group-learning situations. There are organizations for people who want to continuously improve their abilities through practice with helpful feedback from fellow members. Finally, there are vocal coaches who work with people one-on-one to overcome problems and improve their comfort levels with public speaking.

✧ Equipment Management

Ask any teacher, salesperson, or lecturer about what can go wrong during a presentation, and he or she will talk about equipment problems—the presentation fails to load on the computer, carefully chosen fonts change when the presentation meets a different computer, an embedded video refuses to play, or a projector does not focus the images on the screen. Even an easel that is the wrong size or too light to hold a trend board can cause problems.

A trend report has some built-in problems and solutions in terms of equipment. The forecaster may use actual trend boards in the presentation. Even if there is no easel, trend boards can be propped up against a chair or even against the wall and the talk can proceed. If trend boards have been inserted into a computer-generated slide show, both a computer and a projector are required. The most common problem in this situation is failing to have the proper cables to join the equipment together. Whatever the equipment, here are some tips for the fashion forecaster who travels and must present in unfamiliar surroundings:

❖ *Call ahead*—Check with the presentation sponsor well ahead of the date of the talk. Discuss the equipment available, size of the room, and technical assistance.

❖ *Come equipped*—If there are any doubts about equipment and location, bring equipment along. Laptop computers and projectors are all made to travel. Equipment can often be rented if the presentation is in a metropolitan location. All equipment should include cables, power cords, and extension cords.

❖ *Carry backup*—If the presentation is on the hard drive of a laptop computer, carry a duplicate on a flash drive or saved to "cloud" storage or Dropbox. If possible, carry two copies of any video that will be used in the presentation—one embedded in the presentation, one as a DVD.

❖ *Leave a paper trail*—Regardless of the equipment, plan to distribute printed copies of the key points to the audience. It is a courtesy to provide paper for notes and a reminder of the key points. Computer-generated slide shows offer a convenient way to accomplish this task because they allow the presentation to be printed out six slides to the page. Some speakers have the handout on the chairs prior to the arrival of the audience. Others pass them out before the beginning of the talk. With notes in hand, even if all the equipment fails, the speaker and audience have a joint reference point and the talk can proceed.

Whenever possible, an experienced speaker will scout the room ahead of time, rearranging the equipment in a way that suits the presentation's content and the audience. Sometimes a room is not set up for a meeting until a few minutes before the time to begin, but if there is time, a little practice in the space where the presentation will take place helps build confidence. Finally, although visuals are an important element of a trend report, the most important part is the speaker and the insights and information he or she is there to share. An experienced speaker does not let equipment (or equipment problems) stand between the messenger, the message, and the audience.

✦ NEW PRESENTATION TOOLS

Today, trend boards and other presentations can be completely computer generated. Graphics can be captured into the computer from websites, scanned in, copied, and transferred from digital cameras. Images can be manipulated with software packages that crop, resize, shift colors, alter focus, and create many other special effects. Text can be added in different fonts, sizes, and colors. Original graphics can be created with drawing and painting programs. Styles, colorways, and textile designs can be illustrated with computer-aided design teams, manufacturers, and retailers' routine.

Although this sounds like a great advance, not all problems have been eliminated. Computer hardware and software for such graphic-intensive uses are expensive. Graphics take up a lot of storage space. Decisions must be made about the resolution (the number of pixels horizontally and vertically that make up the graphic) depending on the image, the scanner, and the computer. The higher the resolution, the more memory is required to store the graphic. Without sophisticated color-calibration software and color matching between the original color of the images, how they appear on the computer screen and how they look printed out require compromise or careful trial-and-error experimentation. Because all the problems are not worked out, most forecasters use a combination of traditional and computer-based techniques.

Nowadays multimedia presentations of forecasting information arrive on websites. Many of the design principles for creating presentations can be transferred to the design of a website. Software packages and books are available to guide users in designing websites. Websites can incorporate short video clips and sound bites along with text, graphics, and photographs.

Additionally, websites offer the opportunity for interactive participation by visitors and feedback through e-mail. Taking full advantage of these possibilities awaits a new wave of fashion forecasting professionals.

AVOIDING FORECASTING TRAPS

No matter the technical proficiency of the presentation or the charisma of the presenter, only the quality of the content matters. There is no science of forecasting that can guarantee predictions. However, the forecasting frameworks (Chapters 2, 3, and 4), the multiple viewpoints generated by the various forecasting disciplines (Chapters 5 through 11), the blending of quantitative and qualitative approaches, and the collaboration of teams help avoid forecasting traps. Here are some guidelines for evaluating the quality of forecasts.

✦ AVOIDING TRAPS IN FORECASTING METHODS

People believe that forecasters work based on gut instinct. Instead, they use a number of methods depending on the forecasting task.

✧ Time Horizons, Limitations, and Assumptions

Strategic business decisions rely on forecasts. To use forecasts appropriately, it is necessary to understand the purpose and limitations of each forecasting method. Because economic conditions fluctuate widely over time, economic forecasts are short-range projections based on assumptions about the future. Demographic forecasts have a longer horizon because the underlying trends in mortality, fertility, and migration rates rarely change quickly or dramatically. Assumptions in economic forecasts are often derived from demographic forecasts. Focus groups only show the range of responses to an issue with hints about the whys. Focus groups are not projections of who or how many

people will feel the same way. As these brief examples illustrate, all forecasting methods have time horizons, built-in assumptions, and limitations. Using the methods incorrectly or interpreting them without consideration of the limitations results in faulty forecasting.

✧ Connecting the Dots

The forecaster's job is to see connections between dissimilar phenomena—to connect the dots (Mahaffie, 1995; Russell, 1989). The danger is in making a broad jump to the wrong conclusion using faulty assumptions. Examine the social or technological developments that are associated with the forecast. Step back and consider the "real world" constraints of human nature and economic realities. Be sure the linkages between intermediate steps make sense and are supported by evidence.

✧ Statistics as Truth

People put faith in statistics because numbers carry the promise of precision and accuracy. But using statistics to size up a situation requires a deep understanding of statistical methods and care in interpreting findings. The careful forecaster does not manipulate statistics to make a point or leave out data that tend to disconfirm a hypothesis. Instead, the forecaster looks for all possible explanations and facts with bearing on the interpretation. Anyone relying on a statistical forecast should understand the methods in at least a general way and be willing to ask questions until he or she is comfortable with the analysis and the findings.

✦ AVOIDING TRAPS IN THE FORECAST

Operating in the realm of the future, forecasters must still measure their predictions against real-world experiences.

✧ Lack of Imagination and Insight

Forecasts can be too conservative, missing some interesting possibilities. Consider the implications of the forecast on other, related fields and estimate the effects on other products and market segments (Mahaffie, 1995). Extend the forecast to include potential spin-offs from the change. Early closure or narrow thinking can doom a forecast to limited usefulness. Of course, some possibilities (e.g., the end of the organization, the phasing out of a product line) can be so daunting that they are difficult to consider.

✦ Excessive Optimism

Overly optimistic forecasts fail to consider the "downside risk" associated with the shift, change, or innovation (Mahaffie, 1995). These upbeat views are easy to listen to and pleasant to contemplate. However, failure to consider limiting factors—those conditions likely to inhibit or deflect the forecast—can lead to overestimating the impact of the change.

✦ Hidden Agendas

Forecasters are often pressured to find evidence supporting the client's preconceived ideas. **Normative forecasting** is done on purpose to motivate people to take actions toward some desirable result. If it is recognized and labeled appropriately, there is no problem (Mahaffie, 1995). But normative forecasting is not identical to nor a substitute for detached, objective forecasting about the future.

✦ Estimating Speed and Time

Some forecasts overestimate the speed at which an innovation will spread through society. Diffusion of innovation occurs in two steps, with early adopters increasing the visibility of the new style and opinion leaders endorsing the style within their social groups. It takes time for the first stage of impersonal, media- and marketer-based influence and the second stage of word-of-mouth to build so that a new style becomes a mass fashion. Evaluate the plausibility of the timing based on clues in consumer research and cultural indicators.

✦ AVOIDING TRAPS IN TREND ANALYSIS

Whether the forecaster is dealing with ideas and concepts or facts and figures, he or she must focus on analysis techniques that will produce the most accurate predictions possible.

✦ Anecdotal Evidence versus Statistical Analysis

The passion for trends in media coverage leads to stories based entirely on anecdotes. These stories make interesting points but are only directional if backed up by well-designed research studies or population data (Russell, 1989). The existence of the story alerts the forecaster to an emerging issue, but prediction requires more. Trend analysis comes down to evaluating the evidence—both qualitative and quantitative—supporting the trend. If stories abound but there is little other valid backing for the trend, use caution when acting on the predictions.

✦ Wish Fulfillment versus Reality Check

Consumer research often reports on the unmet longings of people and translates these into trends. However, these "wishes" must be submitted to a reality check to fine-tune predictions (Russell, 1989). Sometimes consumer wishes are mere nostalgia for a simpler life or some other projection that may be impossible to satisfy. Still, such clues may provide the basis for an effective ad campaign, promotional effort, or a revised list of store services.

✦ Two Sides of the Coin

Every trend has two sides—the trend and the countertrend (Popcorn, 1991). Trend analysis includes investigating both since the two sides of the trend can be interpreted for different market segments. The clever forecaster takes these trend dynamics into consideration and the clever marketer makes profit on both the trend and the countertrend.

The Generational Lens

Every forecaster would be wise to use a generational lens to examine trends and make predictions (Russell, 1989). Cohorts of consumers move through predictable life stages that influence purchasing priorities. The preferences of consumers often reflect those formed at a particular age, and these preferences persist throughout the life cycle. Generational cohorts develop a personality and a style that mark their consumption behavior. For all these reasons, the age structure of the American population and the changes in that structure are fundamental building blocks for accurate predictions.

Influential Segments

If key market segments such as "working women" and the "older baby boomers" fail to accept a trend, it has virtually no chance of becoming a major trend. Even so, acceptance by these two groups does not guarantee a trend's success, because the absolute population numbers are too small and because these groups have specific preferences that may not be reflected in the overall population. Acceptance by key consumer segments is necessary but not sufficient for a trend to succeed.

Trends in Collision

Consumer trends are not easy to sort out. Rarely are there clear-cut moments when one trend ends and another begins (Letscher, 1994):

Overlapping Trends. Changes in one area have carryover or overlap to others. The classic example of overlap came with the adoption of the miniskirt in the mid-1960s and the subsequent increase in pantyhose sales, from 10 percent of the market to 80 percent of the market in less than 2 years.

Offsetting Trends. Regarding offsetting trends, one set of lifestyle changes may be congruent, another incongruent with an innovation. For example, smaller families and the desire for a convenient shopping experience would appear to work against warehouse club and wholesale outlets, but the desire for low prices and wide selection made them destinations that offset these negatives.

Discontinuity. Some events cause discontinuity in a trend so that it changes course, merges with another trend, or terminates. The event may be the introduction of a new style, a change in consumer priorities, or an economic upturn or downturn. Recognizing the event is the first step. The astute forecaster works out these potential interactions as part of the forecast or recalibrates the forecast as events unfold.

Fads versus Trends

Companies make money on short-term fads and on long-term trends. The trick is to be able to distinguish between them early on to determine entrance and exit strategies (Letscher, 1994). A trend is supported by multiple lifestyle changes, presents clear long-term benefits to the consumer, and parallels changes in other areas. The more adaptable an innovation is, the more likely it will be a trend, because it can be modified for broader audiences. A trend is a basic theme in society (e.g., the increase in popularity of yoga). It can be expressed in many ways (e.g., wearing yoga pants as casualwear instead of jeans, fashion shows featuring yogawear) (Figure 12.7). As one apparel executive put it, "It's not going to be so much about trends any more," because people are more interested in their lifestyles. They will ask instead, "Is this trend fitting in with my lifestyle?" (Hammond, 1999). If the innovation is more unidimensional, it is more likely a fad.

"Fringe" versus "Mainstream"

Forecasters and journalists often spotlight fringe products, services, and looks that tend to be exaggerated, extreme, or impractical—the kind of things avoided by mainstream American consumers. These innovations have the potential to become mainstream trends only if they have a desirable set of tangible and intangible benefits and can be modified and expressed in different ways to appeal to a broader public (Letscher, 1994).

Specificity versus Direction

Especially in fashion but also in other forecasting fields, it is impossible to have control over or access to all variables that impact on change.

Figure 12.7

Yogawear companies such as Athleta use fashion shows to demonstrate the function and style of their line.

You Be the Forecaster: Communicating a Vision

Megan is a new hire at a forecasting company who is tasked with synthesizing her managers' research into a presentable forecast. By taking the data that her managers have collected, she can translate the information it contains into concepts that can be communicated to clients in a format that is both educational and entertaining.

If she makes the right connections and presents her forecast in a clear and concise manner, Megan can help her firm's clients be on the cusp of an emerging trend that they can capitalize on for profit.

Using the data her managers gathered, Megan compiled and synthesized the data and then organized it using various presentation techniques into a themed forecast.

Organizational Schemes and Structures: Which of the organizational schemes do you think are most effective for conveying a trend? Which of the organizational structures do you think are most influential when Megan is trying to persuade a client to adopt a particular viewpoint?

Trend Reporting: How do labeling, trend maps, and trend boards help forecasters such as Megan organize information into easily communicable ideas for clients? What do you look for in a label or map or board to engage and hold a viewer's interest?

Presentation Techniques: What can Megan do to make her presentation go as smoothly as possible, in terms of speaking, visuals, and equipment?

Forecasting Traps: What common forecasting traps are you prone to when presenting your own ideas? How can Megan keep aware of these traps when writing and delivering her presentation in order to avoid making them? What types of criticism is she vulnerable to if she falls into any of these traps?

Recognizing this situation, a careful forecast will be as objective and comprehensive as possible while pointing out missing details. Such forecasts only show direction and the probable characteristics of change, not the specifics of how those variables will actually interact (Mahaffie, 1995).

✦ AVOIDING TRAPS AS A FORECASTER

A forecaster's reputation is a valuable possession, one that is built over time as clients learn to rely on the expertise and honesty of a professional.

✧ Don't Oversell Accuracy

Forecasts are based on assumptions. If those assumptions are within historical trends and inside normal limits, the forecast is said to be "reasonable." Careful forecasters present alternative futures—a set of scenarios showing low, medium, and high impact from the projection. If the forecaster stamps one of the scenarios as "likely," then that is the forecaster's interpretation based on expertise and experience. Reasonable forecasts may be inaccurate if other factors not initially considered turn out to be important. Likely forecasts may not happen because unexpected outcomes sometimes do occur. The only real gauge of forecasting accuracy is to include "milestones" in the forecasts—points where the forecast can be evaluated and adjustments made (Mahaffie, 1995; "What Is a Forecast," 1995).

✧ Don't Oversell Expertise

Forecasting is too multifaceted for any one person to master. Encourage the use of integrated forecasting so that factors associated with fashion change, consumer behavior, cultural shifts, and competitive position can be correlated for decision support. No single forecasting discipline has the answer, but each serves a complementary function.

Chapter Summary

Presenting the forecast to an audience is the last stage of a long process. Forecasters constantly gather data from multiple sources, and read between the lines to recognize patterns that emerge from that data. Trend reporting includes trend maps, trend boards, and the presentation. Presentation techniques involve effective speaking, visuals, and equipment management. Even experienced forecasters can fall prey to some of the most common forecasting traps, but by staying mindful of those traps, they can easily be avoided.

Key Terms and Concepts

Concept boards
Directional trend
Embryonic trends
Major trends
Minor trends
Normative forecasting

Scope of a trend
Timing of a trend
Trend boards
Trend map
Trial balloons

Discussion Questions

A forecaster is preparing for a presentation on seasonal fashion change. Design, merchandising, and marketing executives will be in the audience. Use the following questions to summarize the chapter and review the steps a forecaster would use in preparing and presenting trend information.

Data Gathering and Pattern Recognition: What are data for a trend presentation and how are they gathered? What two ways of thinking about data aid in pattern recognition?

Transforming the Data into Knowledge: What is information design? How can data be organized in a way that creates knowledge? What is interaction design? Why is it important? What is sensory design? What does sensory design have to do with the fashion forecaster's job of presenting fashion trends?

Trend Reporting: Why is labeling a trend important to communicating a trend? What is the difference between major and minor trends? How is the quality of a trend assessed? What are the attributes of a good trend or concept board? What stages are involved in the development of the theme for a concept board?

Presentation Techniques: How can a fashion forecaster improve the performance aspects of the presentation? What are the attributes of a good visual presentation?

Forecasting Activities

Basic Training. Use websites First View (www.firstview.com), www.style.com, or WWD.com to look at the designer collections for last season. These websites give you a chance to come to your own conclusions without commentary or analysis from others. Select two designers with very different approaches to fashion. Comb through their collections looking for trial balloons and embryonic, major, and minor trends. Develop a brief presentation explaining fashion change as experimentation and illustrate the talk using these two designers' work.

Turn of Phrase. Clip clever headlines from fashion stories and ads in magazines and trade journals. Analyze the inspiration and connections captured in these turns of phrase. Hear the rhythms as you read the headlines. Try revising them using your own concepts and ideas. Writing such headlines is a skill that can be cultivated. The first stage in developing the skill is awareness and the rest is practice.

Trends on Board. Develop trend boards in class. Collect a large number of clippings from catalogs and magazines. Brainstorm possible themes that unite the elements. Choose a phrase that captures the theme. Develop a text style that works with that theme. Use care and craftsmanship to complete the board either using collage methods (cut and paste) or compositing using graphics software. Display the trend boards in class and discuss the content and the techniques of actually making a trend board.

Resource Pointers

Presentation tips:

Garr Reynolds: http://www.garrreynolds.
com/preso-tips/

Presentation Zen (Garr Reynolds' blog): www.
presentationzen.com

GLOSSARY

A

Abstracting The process of identifying underlying similarities or differences in individual elements and interrelationships across products and design collections.

Achromatic Pure neutrals such as black, white, and gray.

Aggregated The term for point-of-sale data when figures on individual products or stock-keeping units (SKUs) are summarized and combined by categories.

Analogous Color combinations made from closely related colors adjacent on the color wheel.

Analysis The phase in forecasting when a trend or phenomenon is dissected to achieve a more complete understanding of its components.

Anomalies In information analysis, data that do not fit expectations.

Appropriation To take inspiration from another person or culture's style or look and interpret it for one's self.

Automated replenishment system A collaborative effort between a retailer and a manufacturer involving vendor-designed assortment plans and automatic shipping to keep stock at optimum levels.

B

Backlash When negative opinion of a trend leads to consumers refusing to adopt it and it dies out.

Benchmarking In competitive analysis, comparing a company with other firms considered to be the best in terms of efficient operations.

Blend A combination of two or more natural, synthetic, or manufactured fibers in a single yarn or fabric to provide desirable attributes.

Blogs Journal-type entries, sometimes from consumer to consumer, sometimes from company to consumer, that provide information and opinions in the form of web logs; a new style of information transfer that bypasses traditional media gatekeepers and the time lag involved in media production.

Boom and bust cycles Periodic swings in popularity between times when an item is "in" and "out" of fashion.

Brand image A distinct set of tangible and intangible characteristics that identify a brand to a target customer.

Brand loyalty The degree to which a customer purchases and repurchases a brand again and again.

Brand name The trademarked and proprietary name a company uses to promote its products through advertising, labeling, and other marketing initiatives.

Brand recognition The degree to which consumers are aware of a brand name and brand image.

Brand tiers A strategy in which a company owns multiple brands in a product category and positions each for a different target consumer and different retail channels, differentiating between the brands in image, pricing, packaging, placement, and presentation.

Branding A competitive strategy that targets customers with products, advertising, and promotion organized around a coherent message as a way to encourage purchase and repurchase of products from the same company.

Bubble up (also known as the **trickle-up theory**) A chain of events beginning with street-style innovation, picked up and popularized through media, disseminated to street kids in other locales, and finally finding its way into a designer's collection.

Business cycle The cyclical nature of the economy as it passes through the rising and falling phases of prosperity and stagnation.

Business-to-business partners Firms closely allied as suppliers, manufacturers, or customers.

Buzz The way trends spread through the media; the excitement about something new, and a feeling of being "in the know" because of insider information.

C

Cannibalizing When buyers shift from a company's current brands to a new brand they introduce, hurting sales of existing brands.

Category management A collaborative strategy between a retailer and a manufacturer in which the manufacturer acts as a specialist in forecasting, keeping the right flow of merchandise going to the selling floor; provides expertise in a category, including trends, silhouettes, and finishes; and makes recommendations on merchandising assortment, display, and inventory controls in that product category on a store-by-store basis.

Cellulosic fibers Natural fibers from plants like cotton, linen, ramie, and hemp.

Chambre Syndicale The governing board of the French fashion industry.

Change agents The small group of innovators who begin the diffusion process by spreading trends visually and verbally to others in their group.

Chase and flight (also known as the **trickle-down theory**) The idea that fashion change is triggered by imitators who chase the status markers of the elite in a drive toward upward social mobility; flight because the elite respond by flying away toward new forms of differentiation.

Chroma (see **saturation**)

Classic An item or style that is introduced, gains visibility, generates multiple purchases or replacement purchases, and reaches a plateau level of widespread acceptance that persists over a long time period; an item or style that delivers at least the core attributes desirable to the consumer while avoiding extremes in styling.

Coattail effect (also known as the **bandwagon effect**) The phase in the life cycle of a trend when it catches the attention of people in the industry who recognize the potential of the trend and rush to produce it in their own lines.

Cohort(s) A group of consumers who share preferences and demographic characteristics—the basic unit of consumer research.

Collaborative filtering A process that allows a person to train software by making a series of selections; the software then is able to match its recommendations to the person's tastes by comparing the individual's choices with those of thousands of others.

Collective selection The idea that individuals in large numbers choose among competing styles, those that "click" or "connect" with the spirit of the times, thereby forming a feedback loop between the fashion industry and the consumer—a feedback loop moderated by aesthetic trends and social-psychological processes.

Color Association of the United States (CAUS) Based in Manhattan, a not-for-profit trade association formed in 1915 to provide color forecasting to members, including corporations and designers concerned with apparel, interiors and furnishings, paint, and automobiles.

Color cycles Periodic shifts in color preferences and the patterns of repetition in the popularity of colors.

Color direction An inclination or tendency toward change in color temperature (warmer/cooler), value (lighter/darker), and intensity (clearer/grayer), or the relative importance of a hue (in/out).

Color Key Program A system developed to assist in coordinating paint colors and apparel based on whether a color has cool or warm overtones.

Color Marketing Group (CMG) An international non-profit association formed in 1962 to provide advanced color information for industries from apparel to automobiles, from health care to corporate identity, and based in the Washington, DC area.

Color palette The eight to ten colors selected during the initial design phase that signal the personality of the collection.

Color specifications Color notation written according to a system that allows the designer or product developer to indicate the specific hue (color), value, and intensity for a product.

Color story (see **color palette**)

Color wheel The simplest version of organizing color into a graphic form that helps designers form harmonious color groupings and specify colors.

Colorways Color groups and combinations used for an item, ensemble, or group within a line.

Compatibility An estimate of harmony between the innovation and the values and norms of potential adopters.

Competitive advantage A situation in which, for a period of time, there is an asymmetry in the marketplace that favors one company over another.

Competitive analysis The process of using public sources to develop a detailed and accurate view of the market environment—both trends in the industry and what the competition is likely to do.

Competitive benchmarking In competitive analysis, comparing a company with its direct competitors on a set of measures such as capital investment, productivity, and product quality.

Competitive intelligence (see **competitive analysis**)

Complementary colors A color scheme formed from colors directly across from each other on the color wheel.

Complexity A gauge of the difficulty faced by a consumer in understanding and using the innovation.

Computer-aided design (CAD) Computer hardware and software designed to assist the designer in creating and presenting design concepts.

Concept boards Collections of clippings, objects, fabrics, color chips, and other items arrayed on a stiff cardboard foundation and used in the product development stage to coordinate the efforts of the design team or to present visual concepts to the manufacturer's sales force and retail buyers.

Concept garments Sample garments made to show the potential of developmental, performance, or other innovative fabrics in apparel.

Concept stores Stores stocked with test merchandise and specifically sited in areas where trendy customers shop—sales become indicators of emerging and developing trends.

Conspicuous consumption The behavior of the upper strata of the social system who display wealth by participating in an extravagant lifestyle, including the acquisitions of homes and furnishing and the wearing of apparel made by expensive modes of production and using costly materials; originally used to refer to the lifestyle of the wealthy around the turn of the twentieth century.

Conspicuous counter-consumption The practice of status denial, as when people with wealth and status choose to dress down.

Conspicuous leisure An attribute of the upper strata of the social system that does not have to work for a living and can participate in an extravagant lifestyle of travel, entertainment, and the pursuit of pleasure.

Consumer adoption process The mental process used by individual consumers in deciding between adopting or failing to adopt an innovation.

Consumer cohorts Groups of consumers who share similar demographic and psychographic characteristics.

Consumer confidence An index of consumer feelings of economic well-being, used to predict future consumer expenditures and turning points in the business cycle.

Consumer segment A portion of the population identified by demographic characteristics such as age, gender, ethnicity, and income.

Consumer segmentation The practice of dividing the total population into homogeneous (the same or of a similar type) groups that can be targeted with products and product promotion.

Contagion The transmission of trends from person to person, similar to the spread of a virus such as the flu.

Content analysis A method of analyzing information involving extracting significant data from source material, classifying it, and noting patterns and regularities in the data.

Converters Companies that specialize in sourcing base fabrics and using contractors to dye, print, and finish them for apparel manufacturers unable to meet large minimum orders or who require short lead times.

Core concept Ideas, themes, or connections that reoccur frequently and act as grouping variable for forecasting reports.

Corporate culture The personality of a company, including the way it does business, its relationship to consumers, its style of communications, and the way the company operates internally.

Correlation or regression techniques Statistical techniques for comparing how a change in one variable (e.g., advertising effort or some outside factor) causes a change in another variable (e.g., sales volume).

Cosmetotextiles A textile product that contains a substance or a preparation for release on different parts of the human body, such as the skin, and with one (or more) desirable properties.

Counterfeit The term for a product that is a close copy of a designer's product and is passed off as authentic.

Countertrends Trends that contrast with another prevailing set of trends, both of which offer opportunities for businesses because of the contradictory aspects of human behavior.

Cross dyeing A piece dyeing process that produces multiple colors in a blended fabric when dyes that are reactive with each fiber are used in a single dye bath.

Cultural drift Directional pointers for the way society is moving.

Data mining The ability to search through vast stores of data to answer complex business questions, discover patterns in databases, and find predictive information that lies outside experts' expectations.

Data warehouse A system for storing and delivering massive quantities of data.

Decomposition The process of breaking down a pattern to analyze the underlying factors of influence.

Delphi method A method of polling used to elicit expert input using a process that combines brainstorming and debate to generate ideas, clarify complex issues, and reach consensus.

Demand An expansion of orders resulting from an influx of new customers buying for the first time or replacement or repeat purchases by users.

Demographics Consumer characteristics such as age, gender, marital status, and occupation.

Depth interview A research technique in which a researcher interviews a single consumer at a time in a lengthy dialogue aimed at discovering the meaning products or brands have for that consumer.

Designer name brands Brands based on the aesthetic taste and reputation of a known designer; these products are developed by the designer's firm or through licenses, sold to retailers through the wholesale market, and carried by retailers who often compete in the same market area.

Designer ready-to-wear Expensive, luxurious, and beautifully executed clothes manufactured using mass-production techniques and, therefore, not as costly as couture.

Developmental fabrics Newly developed innovations in fiber, yarn, or finishing that provide special characteristics or properties and that are presented for consideration to designers and manufacturers.

Diffusion curve A visualization of diffusion of innovation as a bell curve showing the progressive participation of consumers, beginning with innovators and early adopters, proceeding to majority adoption, and concluding with laggards.

Diffusion process The process by which innovations spread within a social system, including the kind of consumers participating in each stage.

Digital printing Preparation of a print design on the computer that is printed to fabric using inkjet technology.

Direct competitors Companies that sell the same general product to the same customers in the same distribution channels.

Directional trend The stage of trend development when fashion innovators and fashion-forward retailers adopt the look, style, detail, accessory, or other fashion idea and public awareness of the idea begins to build.

Disinformation In competitive analysis, inaccuracies in published articles, from people misrepresenting their knowledge or expertise, and from countering moves by competitors seeking to protect their secrets.

Dissonance A stage in the consumer adoption process that occurs after purchase when the consumer questions the adoption decision and seeks reassurance.

Distant opinion leader The idea that celebrities and popular culture serve as a source of new meanings and as a conduit to transmit those meanings to consumers.

Double complements Color combinations consisting of two sets of complementary colors.

Drape The way the finished fabric hangs on the body—whether it stands away from the body or clings to the curves.

E

Economic risk The risk of performance problems after the purchase, the risk that the purchase price may reduce the ability to buy other products, or the risk that the price will fall after purchase.

Embryonic trends The first stages of trend development when a look, style, detail, accessory, or other fashion idea is poised to take off, fashion insiders are tracking its development, but the public is largely unaware of its existence.

Enjoyment risk The risk of becoming bored by the purchase or not liking it as much as expected.

Environmental scanning A method of systematically tracking and analyzing trends using media sources.

Erogenous zone The idea that any part of the female body may become the focus of erotic attention and that fashion change is partly powered by the shifting of this zone.

Extranets Business-to-business private networks for transactions and collaborative forecasting between manufacturers and their suppliers, manufacturers and retailers.

F

Fabric finishing Processes used to manipulate the appearance characteristics, performance, or hand of a fabric, including mechanical or chemical techniques and the application of films to the fabric surface.

Fabric libraries A collection of seasonal fabric samples where designers and product developers come to research fabrications and source fabrics from many manufacturers.

Fabric story The seasonal trends in fabrics including texture, fabric properties, prints, novelty fabrics, and trims.

Fad A trend of short duration that is introduced, gains rapid visibility and acceptance among a relatively small contingent of consumers, and fades quickly because it is not supported by corresponding lifestyle changes.

Fashion A style that is popular in the present or a set of trends that have been accepted by a wide audience.

Fashion blog Commentary by fashion mavens or professionals available on the Internet and inviting comments and dialogue with readers.

Fashion counts A method for researching fashion change that consists of finding a suitable source for fashion images, sampling the images in a systematic way, applying a standardized set of measurements or observations to each image, and analyzing the data to reveal patterns of fashion change.

Fashion cycles The idea that there exist discernible cyclical patterns in fashion that recur over time.

Fashion leaders People to whom others look for advice about clothes or other aesthetic products; also known as **opinion leaders**.

Fast fashion Retailers and manufacturers who organize their firms to deliver new styles in weeks instead of months (as in traditional firms), keep inventories very lean, rarely repeat styles, but are able to capitalize on the fast-changing trends.

Fieldwork A method of data gathering involving observation and interviews.

Filament A continuous strand of man-made or manufactured fiber as it comes from the spinneret or a continuous strand from the unwound cocoon of a silk moth.

Findings Functional items on apparel such as elastic, interfacing, thread, and zippers.

Finishing (see **Fabric finishing**)

Fixed-model time-series (FMTS) A set of statistical techniques that begins with the idea that the forecast for next month's sales is the average of all past sales.

Flow The process that occurs when a trend passes from a relatively small group of fashion-forward consumers to other groups across social boundaries of age, income, and lifestyle.

Focus group(s) A qualitative method of research based on informal, uncensored talk about products in a group interview setting.

Focus group moderator The research professional who leads the focus group discussion using a schedule of questions previously agreed to by the client.

Forecasting The process of anticipating future developments by watching for signals of change in current situations and events, and applying the forecasting frameworks to predict possible outcomes.

Full-garment package The term for a company's offer to handle production from spinning, knitting or weaving, dyeing, finishing, and garment production.

Functional textiles Textiles that have a purpose other than just aesthetics, such as sun protection or antimicrobial properties.

G

Garment dyeing The process of applying color after the fabric has been made into garments.

Gatekeepers People or groups that filter the innovative ideas proposed by designers and street fashion and determine which will be disseminated widely and which will be discarded—a role played today by journalists, manufacturers, and retailers.

Generational cohorts Group of consumers who share the same "age location" in history and a collective mindset.

Generic name The common name given to a new fiber when it is developed by the Federal Trade Commission (e.g., nylon, polyester, spandex, and lyocell).

Geodemographics An approach to consumer segmentation that links to consumer lifestyle and preferences with geographic location.

H

Hand The way finished fabric feels when handled, including properties such as its ability to recover when stretched or compressed.

Haute couture Extravagant, high-priced clothing that shows off the ultimate level of dressmaking design and skill, and which is made to order for specific clients; also known as couture.

High culture Events, activities, directions, and trends derived from the fine and performance arts.

Historic continuity The concept that fashion is a steady evolution of styles, including the continual recurring of symbolism and elements of decoration.

Hue The color itself in a color system.

Hype Awareness and excitement about an innovation created through the purposeful efforts of public relations executives.

I

Idea chain A set of linked events that move a phenomenon from a subculture to the mainstream or a graphic representation of that moment.

In-depth interview (see **depth interview**)

Indirect competitors Companies that do not sell the same or similar products but offer alternatives that may redirect a customer away from a purchasing situation.

Industrial espionage Information-gathering activities that involve breaking the law to collect competitive data.

Influentials Change agents who are recognized by others for their abilities to adopt and display innovations and who tend to establish the standards of dress for others in the social group.

Information cascades The process that occurs when a fashion leader acts to adopt or reject the innovation; frequently others imitate the action, beginning a cascade of decisions either positive (all individuals in the group adopt the innovation) or negative (all reject the innovation).

Innovation Something new submitted to the public's attention for approval and adoption.

Innovators People who adopt new product innovations relatively earlier than others in their social group.

In-store shop A section of a department store devoted to a single brand with display and signage supporting the brand identity.

Intensity (see **saturation**)

K

Knitting The process of forming fabric by looping together yarns in successive rows.

Knockoff The practice of copying designs from higher-priced lines into lower-priced lines either as line-for-line copies or as close facsimiles, but without labeling the result with originator's label.

L

Lab dip A sample of a specified color on the correct fabric submitted for approval by the product developer.

Labeling A name, label, or slogan that acts as an identifier for a trend and serves to connect the trend to the spirit of the times in an original and catchy way.

Leading indicators A statistically weighted set of economic factors likely to signal a turning point in the business cycle—peaks and troughs of the leading indicator anticipate those seen in sales by 6 to 12 months.

Legitimation An optional stage in a consumer's adoption process during which the consumer seeks additional information about the innovation.

Level (in time-series forecasting) The horizontal line showing sales history as if demand was stable with no trend, seasonality, or noise in the sales data.

Long-term forecasting A forecasting timeline sufficient for decisions related to repositioning or extending product lines, initiating new businesses, reviving brand images, or planning new retail concepts.

Low culture Events, activities, directions, and trends derived from local special-interest groups outside of mainstream awareness.

M

Major trends A distinction applied by a forecaster when a trend is expected to have broad public appeal.

Mall intercept research Market research conducted for a client using consumers recruited from shoppers in a mall who satisfy the requirements of the client.

Manufactured fibers Fibers derived from chemically processing plant sources or made synthetically from chemical compounds.

Manufacturing cycle In apparel planning and scheduling, a rolling forecast where long term is usually 12 months, but can be as short as 6 months to as long as 18 months.

Markdowns Unwanted goods remaining at the end of a selling period that must be reduced in price in order to sell.

Mass customization The process of delivering a unique, personalized, or customized product using mass-production techniques and at a cost competitive with mass production.

Mass market theory (see **trickle-across theory**)

Mavens People with knowledge about some aspect of lifestyle, a passion for newness, and the desire to share their interest with others.

Megatrend A trend so fundamental that it indicates a critical restructuring of culture.

Memes Self-replicating ideas—advertising slogans, catchy bits of dialogue from television or a movie, a product, look, or brand—that move through time and space without continuing support from their original source.

Mercerize A yarn or fabric treatment that increases strength, luster, and dye affinity.

Microencapsulation Through the use of tiny particles, a process which imparts new qualities to garments and fabrics, such as enhanced stability and the controlled release of active compounds.

Microfibers Fibers produced when manufactured fibers are extruded through very small holes in the spinneret to produce fabrics that are softer with more drape.

Microtrends Distinction applied by a forecaster when a trend is expected to be limited to a small, specialized group of consumers.

Mid-range strategies Business approaches focused on actions 2 to 5 years ahead.

Modernity A stage in the evolution of culture and associated aesthetic that emerged with technological innovations such as the automobile, telephone, plastics, synthetic dyes, and man-made fibers and with mass media and entertainment such as the movies.

Monosocial Individuals who would rather stay among people like themselves.

Munsell Color System A color specification system that includes a color atlas, the *Munsell*

Book of Color, with about 1,600 chips arranged in equal steps of hue, value, and chroma (intensity or saturation) and a notation for each.

Muse A woman—often a client or employee of the design house or a celebrity—who embodies the ideal look for a designer.

N

Nanofinishing The process of coating the surface of textiles and clothing with nanoparticles, which results in apparel that possesses one or more desirable properties such as wrinkle resistance.

National brands Brands developed and promoted by manufacturers who sell to retailers through wholesale channels.

Natural fibers Fibers that originate from animals (alpaca, angora, camel's hair, cashmere, mohair, silk, vicuña, wool) or plants (cotton, linen, and hemp).

Noise (in time-series forecasting) The part of sales fluctuations that appears to be random and cannot be explained because the pattern has not occurred consistently in the past.

Normative forecasting Forecasting done on purpose to motivate people to take actions toward some desirable result, rather than as a detached, objective forecasting about the future.

Novelty fabrics Fabrics formed through processes other than weaving or knitting, including bonding, crocheting, felting, knotting, or laminating.

O

Observability In the consumer adoption process, the degree of visibility afforded an innovation.

Omissions In information analysis, missing facts or reasons for an action or business decision.

Open-model time-series (OMTS) Techniques (e.g., Box Jenkins) that first analyze the time-series to determine the components, then build unique models and forecast the time-series into the future.

Opinion leaders Individuals who are influential on the attitudes and decision making of people in their social circle.

Outliers In information analysis, cases or facts that are unexpectedly high or low in value.

P

Panel study Research that asks questions of a group of people over time in order to track changes in consumer attitudes and opinions.

Pantone® Professional Color System A color specification system that includes a color atlas, *The Pantone Book of Color* (1990), with 1,225 colors identified by name and color code.

Pendulum swing Refers to the periodic movement of fashion between extremes.

Perceived risk The imagined potential consequences of purchasing something new and novel.

Performance fabrics High-tech fabrics originally developed for industrial, active sports, or rugged outdoor usage, which are adapted to use in high fashion and street apparel.

Piece dyeing Fabric dyed after weaving but before other apparel manufacturing processes.

Planned obsolescence The idea that products are designed to wear out so that consumers are pushed back into the marketplace to purchase replacements or substitutions.

Point-of-sale (POS) data Information captured at the time of sale—the starting point for sophisticated sales forecasting techniques.

Polysocial Individuals who mix and mingle among a wide variety of people and places.

Pop culture/popular culture Events, activities, directions, and trends—derived from advertising, magazines, movies, television, music, and other media and popularized by celebrities—that serve as a source of inspiration for consumer purchasing.

Pop-up stores Stores in place for a limited time period as a public relations effort or to test new merchandise, line extensions, and product concepts.

Positioning A unique marketing approach that appeals directly to a specific consumer segment in a way that differentiates the product from all others in the category.

Postmodern(ism) A stage in the evolution of culture and an aesthetic associated with an emerging global economy, fragmentation in society, extreme eclecticism in the use of signs and symbols, unease with the consequences of modernity, and fluidity in social identities.

Première Vision An important trade show for color and textile forecasters held in Paris.

Primary colors The fundamental colors in a color system from which all other colors are mixed.

Private-label brands Brands owned by retailers and merchandised solely through the retailers' stores.

Product life cycle A series of predictable stages from the development of a product until it disappears from the marketplace.

Projective technique A consumer research technique where consumers draw a picture, assemble a collage, or in other indirect ways communicate their view of the marketplace, which can then be interpreted by psychologists, sociologists, or anthropologists.

Protein fibers Natural fibers from animals such as alpaca, angora, camel's hair, cashmere, mohair, silk, vicuña, and wool.

Psychographics Aspects of lifestyles, consumer preferences, and consumer psychology that are used to identify a consumer segment by shared values, attitudes, preferences, and behaviors.

Q

Qualitative research An approach to research based on ethnography, case studies, and phenomenological studies in which human experiences are observed in a natural setting and described or explained using the natural language, categories, and frameworks of the subjects.

Qualitative techniques A set of techniques that are used to tap into the expertise of people inside and outside the company to adjust the quantitative forecast to account for environmental factors; also called subjective and judgmental techniques.

Quantitative research An approach to research that uses experimental methods or surveys to collect data on a sample in order to generalize the finding to a population.

Quick response A strategy that seeks to shorten product development cycles and make other adjustments to make apparel manufacturing agile and responsive to market demand.

R

Regional markets Centers that lease space to manufacturers and sales representatives who carry multiple lines in permanent showrooms and for seasonal shows.

Relational marketing A marketing strategy based on building a "learning relationship" with customers—an ongoing, interactive connection that encourages collaboration between a company and its customers on how to meet consumers' needs.

Relative advantage The perception that an innovation is more satisfactory than items that already exist in the same class of products.

Reliability (of information) The trustworthiness of information as measured by the credibility of the source.

Retail supply chain The linked segments of the apparel industry, especially when those segments share integrated forecasting and planning.

Retro fashion The revival of a look or style from a former period but not exactly in the same form or with the same companion elements or for the same use or occasion.

Reverse engineering A way of gaining competitive information by purchasing and dismantling a product to determine how it was designed and constructed.

Reverse ostentation (see **conspicuous counter-consumption**)

S

Sales channel A particular form of retailing or category of retail distribution.

Sales forecast A projection of expected demand given a set of environmental conditions, which is developed using quantitative and qualitative methods.

Sales history Data on products in terms of which sold and in what quantities.

Sales plan A plan that defines goals and provides motivation for sales levels that meet or exceed the sales forecast.

Sampling In product development, ordering a minimum amount of fabric as a trial order.

Saturation (also called **intensity** or **chroma**) The strength or purity of a color.

Scenario A technique used by futurists consisting of a series of stories or summaries that describe the evolution from the present situation to one or more possible futures.

Scope of a trend The forecaster's estimate of how important a trend will be and how broad an impact it will have on markets.

Scouts Individuals who are adept at recognizing the potential and power of a subcultural style and transmitting it into the fashion system.

S-curve The cumulative form of the diffusion curve; interlocking sets of S-curves can be used to represent the spread of an innovation from one consumer segment to another or from one company to another.

Seasonal color analysis An idea promoted in the 1980s to help consumers select the "right" colors to enhance their personal coloring and avoid the "wrong" colors, in which color groupings were named for the four seasons and varied in undertone (warm or cool) and saturation (clear, bright, and vivid versus subdued and less intense).

Seasonality (in time-series forecasting) A yearly pattern of increasing or decreasing sales that corresponds to the season.

Secondary colors A set of colors mixed from two primary colors.

Secret shopper A person who appears to be just a customer but who is actually noting the operational details of a business for the purpose of competitive research.

Self-organized criticality The state of a system in which change is constant, the components of the systems are barely stable, and the next change in the system may have no effect or set off a catastrophic chain reaction.

Sensitization A strategy that intends to shake up a company's assumptions about its place in relationship to competitors by using information to build a sense of urgency about competitive challenges.

Shade A color mixed with black.

Shadow market planning A technique in competitive analysis in which one or more people in a company are so familiar with a competitor that they can answer "what if" questions about that competitor's strategy on a current and continuous basis.

Short-term forecasting In the fashion industry, the process that begins 2 to 3 years before the arrival of merchandise in the retail store, a process that allows the segments of the textile/apparel pipeline to coordinate seasonal goods around looks that can be communicated to the customer through the press and stores.

Showcase or laboratory stores Stores where mega niche and lifestyle (also known as 3-D) brands can present their entire line as a billboard for the brand, an educational environment for retailers on the latest in visual merchandising, and a research site for gathering intelligence about what consumers want, which products in the line are heating up and which are cooling down, and which packaging and promotional initiatives are most effective.

Showroom The part of a designer's or manufacturer's facility where buyers and the press come to see the seasonal line.

Simultaneous adoption theory (see **trickle-across theory**)

Smart textiles Fabrics that change performance characteristics in response to the environment.

Social risk The risk that the consumer's social group will not approve of an innovative purchase.

Social shopping Social networking websites specifically adapted for shared online shopping experiences including finding, designing, commenting on, and purchasing products.

Soft information Information from the popular press, television shows that mention the company or product, and industry rumors.

Solution dyeing A process specific to synthetic and manufactured fibers whereby the color is added to the liquefied fiber before it is extruded as a filament.

Speed to market A retailer's ability to get products in stores quickly, which gives them a competitive advantage.

Split complements Based on a simple complement; a color combination that includes a color and the two colors on either side of its complement.

Staple length The relatively short lengths of a fiber either from natural sources or cut from the filament form of synthetic or manufactured fibers.

Status float phenomenon (also called the **trickle-up theory**) The view that higher-status segments with more power imitate those with lower status and that status markers float up (rather than down) the status pyramid.

Stockouts Situations when merchandise is not available at the time when consumers request it, resulting in lost sales.

Store brands Brands developed and merchandised through a company's own stores.

Strategic planning A business approach that focuses on gaining competitive advantage and ensuring business survival and long-term growth—planning with a long time horizon and a more comprehensive view.

Strategic windows A strategy that involves timing the firm's product offerings to the customer's readiness and willingness to accept and adopt those products.

Style testing Pretesting styles with consumers to identify "winners" and "losers" early enough in the product development cycle to enable styles with low consumer interest to be eliminated from further development.

Style tribes A group that has adopted a distinctive style of dress as a marker of membership, providing satisfaction of the dual drives to fit in and stand out.

Subcultures Groups that invent or adopt specific aesthetic codes that differentiate them from other subcultures and from the mainstream.

Supply chain The linked functions that begin with a fiber that is processed into yarn, then into fabric, and ends with fabric finishing, including dyeing and printing.

Survey research A method of data gathering in which consumers are asked to answer a set of carefully designed questions about themselves, attitudes toward shopping, opinions of products and services, and other issues of interest to the researcher.

Syndicated surveys Surveys conducted by a group of sponsors who are interested in the same topic and who share costs and results.

Synthesis The phase in forecasting when the forecaster achieves a creative reintegration of the parts of a trend or phenomenon and projects future directions.

Synthetics Manufactured fibers derived from processed plant sources (rayon, acetate, and lyocell) and chemical compounds (acrylic, spandex, nylon, polyester, and polyolefin).

T

Tactics Business approach that focuses on seasonal direction, planning short-range strategy, and current business matters.

Target audience A consumer group identified by demographics and psychographics as most likely to be attracted to the tangible and intangible attributes of a product, company image, or service.

Target market A slice of the population more likely than others to adopt an innovation at a particular time in the diffusion process or be attracted to the tangible and intangible attributes of a product, company image, or service.

Tastemakers Celebrities, models, fashion stylists, and fashion leaders who increase the visibility of an innovation and make it acceptable to mainstream consumers.

Technical fabrics (see **performance fabrics**)

Tertiary colors Colors mixed from one primary color and one secondary color.

Texture The surface variations of fabric from hard and slick to soft and fuzzy, including effects produced by interaction of light and the surface (dull or shiny).

Thinking inside the box An approach to problem solving used when it is relatively easy to gather relevant information and apply traditional methods to discover the solution.

Thinking outside the box An approach to problem solving used when problems are so difficult that traditional methods do not work; a holistic approach that looks at the problem from multiple viewpoints and seeks to recognize patterns and relationships.

Time-series forecasting Quantitative techniques that use values recorded at regular time intervals (sales history) to predict future values.

Time-series techniques Quantitative methods of arraying sales history data with the goal of predicting future sales levels.

Timing of a trend The forecaster's estimate of how soon the trend will "hit" and how long it will continue.

Tint A color to which white is added.

Tone A grayed color—a color plus gray.

Trade dress A form of trademark infringement that allows owners to protect ownership of the way a product looks or is presented and to prevent others from trading on their reputation, image, and customers' goodwill.

Trade only Events and venues open only to those in the textiles and apparel industry including trade shows, forecasting presentations, and fabric libraries.

Trade organizations Groups formed by producers of both natural and manufactured fibers to promote use of their fiber by providing forecasting information, public relations support, and fabric sourcing for apparel manufacturers.

Trade shows Expositions open only to people in the industry that are centered on selling fashion but also showcase new design talent and identify trends for specific product categories, price points, and target audiences.

Trend Identifiable similarities across information sources related to styles, details, or other aspects of appearance characterized by a building awareness of this new look and an accelerating demand among consumers.

Trend (in time-series forecasting) The continuing pattern of increasing or decreasing sales represented as a line or a curve.

Trend boards Collections of clippings, objects, fabrics, color chips, and other items arrayed on a stiff cardboard foundation and used to identify the mood or spirit of each trend and its thematic focus.

Trend initiators Things a consumer reacts to either positively or negatively, such as political, economic, sociocultural, or technological initiators.

Trend map Part of the forecaster's task, a framework that identifies which trends are just emerging, continuing to build, or declining.

Trend merchandising In-store merchandising using trends as a coordinating factor for full product lines which extend beyond a single merchandise category.

Triads Color combinations with three colors equally spaced on the color wheel—the primary triad is red, blue, and yellow; the secondary triad is orange, green, and violet.

Trial balloons Designer experiments presented to merchants, the press, and the public to gauge the effect and potential of a new idea.

Trialability In the consumer adoption process, an evaluation of the ease of testing out the innovation before making a decision.

Trickle-across theory (also known as **simultaneous adoption theory**) A theory that holds that fashion information trickles across horizontally within social strata rather than vertically across strata because mass media and advances in manufacturing allow access to fashion ideas by consumers in all socioeconomic groups simultaneously.

Trickle-down theory (see also **chase and flight**) A theory that holds that fashion spreads downward through the class structure from the fashionable elite—the rich and socially prominent—to the lower classes.

Trickle-up theory (see **status float phenomenon** and **bubble up**)

Trims All the items used to embellish and finish a garment, whether functional—buttons, buckles, belts—or decorative—appliqué, beading, binding, and lace.

U

Unethical practices Information-gathering activities that are not illegal but involve misrepresentation.

V

Value (in color) The lightness or darkness of the color.

Value (competitive) Includes styling, durability, quality fabrics, and consistent fit.

Value-added Fabrics with special appearance or performance characteristics that will command premier prices over basic fabrics in the marketplace.

Viral marketing A type of Internet marketing designed to encourage customers to try a software product, share it with the people they know, and thereby propagate the product on behalf of the company that created it—a digital form of word-of-mouth advertising.

W

Wearable technology Textiles that incorporate electronic technologies into the apparel or the fabric of the apparel.

Weaving The process of forming fabric by interlacing yarns at right angles in patterns called weaves; each weave has its own characteristics and properties.

Z

Zeitgeist Generally translated as the "spirit of the times."

BIBLIOGRAPHY

10 ways Project Runway Changed the Fashion Industry. (2012, September 27). Fashionista. http://fashionista.com/#!/2012/09/10-ways-project-runway-changed-the-fashion-industry#1.

Abell, D. F. (1978). Strategic windows. *Journal of Marketing, 42,* 21–8.

About Twitter, Inc. (2014). Twitter. https://about.twitter.com/company.

Adrian, 1903–1959. (2014). The Museum at the Fashion Institute of Technology. http://fashionmuseum.fitnyc.edu/view/people/asitem/items$0040:5573/0?t:state:flow=07f208ad-2d40-4873-8b84-835fbd62350d.

African-American consumers are more relevant than ever. (2013, September 19). Nielsen. http://www.nielsen.com/us/en/insights/news/2013/african-american-consumers-are-more-relevant-than-ever.html.

Ageorges, D. (2003, June 27). Paris men's fashion week set to begin. The Age. www.theage.com.

Agins, T. (1994, August 8). Copy shops: Fashion knockoffs hit stores before originals as designers seethe. *The Wall Street Journal,* A1, A4.

Agins, T. (1995, February 28). Out of fashion: Many women lose interest in clothes, to retailers' dismay. *The Wall Street Journal,* A1.

Agins, T. (2008, February 5). Tory Burch fashioned a business model first. *The Wall Street Journal* (Eastern Edition), B1.

Alabi, M. (2013, September 30). Ed Hardy: From art to infamy and back again. http://www.cnn.com/2013/09/04/living/fashion-ed-hardy-profile/.

Alfano, J. (2003, May). The best of American fashion: What's right now? *Harper's Bazaar,* 88, 90.

Allen, J. (1985). *Showing your colors.* San Francisco: Chronicle.

Allen, J. P. & Turner, E. (1990, August). Where diversity? *American Demographics,* 34–8.

Allenby, G. M., Jen, L., & Leone, R. P. (1996). Economic trends and being trendy. The influence of consumer confidence on retail fashion sales. *Journal of Business & Economic Statistics,* 14, 103–12.

Alter, J. (1992, October 5). The cultural elite. *Newsweek,* 30–4.

Alva, M. (2011, January 24). Foreign apparel chains invade U.S. with "fast fashion" strategy speed trumps cost for Zara, H&M and others, challenging local stores. *Investor's Business Daily.* http://news.investors.com/business/012111-560596-foreign-apparel-chains-invade-us-with-fast-fashion.htm?p=full.

Ambardar, R (2008, January). Advertisers and changing demographics—Do marketers know who they're selling to? *World & I 23.1.* Business Index. Retrieved September 6, 2008, from Alabama Virtual Library.

Amed, I. (2011, October 3). The business of blogging: The Sartorialist. http://www.businessoffashion.com/2011/10/the-business-of-blogging-the-sartorialist.html.

American Wool Council. (2003). http://www.sheepusa.org/.

Amit, R., Domowitz, I., & Fershtman, C. (1988). Thinking one step ahead: The use of conjectures in competitor analysis. *Strategic Management Journal, 9,* 431–42.

An introduction to data mining. (1997) Pilot software [Web], 11 pp. Retrieved September 16, 1997, from www.santafe.edu.

Analysis: Keeping it real. (2007, August 10). *In-Store,* 9.

Anderson, L. J., Brannon, E. L., Ulrich, P. V., & Marshall, T. (1998). Toward a consumer-driven model for mass customization in the apparel market. Unpublished working paper of the National Textile Center, Auburn University, Auburn, AL.

Announcement. (2002). Retrieved August 1, 2002, from www.pantone.com.

Aspan, M. (2007, August 21). The Web way to magazine ad sales. *The New York Times.* www.nytimes.com.

"Audience" (2014). Curbed Network. http://curbednetwork.com/audience.

Ault, S. (2014, August 5). Survey: YouTube stars more popular than mainstream celebs among U.S. teens. Variety. http://variety.com/2014/digital/news/survey-youtube-stars-more-popular-than-mainstream-celebs-among-u-s-teens-1201275245/.

Bacheldor, B. (2003, May 26). New fashion—100-year-old apparel manufacturer VF is overhauling its IT architecture to keep up with changing times. *Information Week.* Retrieved August 7, 2003, from Business & Industry Database.

Back to the 50s. (1972, October 16). *Newsweek,* 78–9, 81.

Baker, J. (2013, October 30). Top 20 flannel shirts for fall retrieved. WhoWhatWear. http://www.whowhatwear.com/fall-fashion-trend-flannel-plaid-shirts-shopping-2013.

Banks, L. (2013, August 26). How to tell the fashion future? *The New York Times.* http://www.nytimes.com/2013/08/27/fashion/how-to-tell-the-fashion-future.html?pagewanted=all&_r=0.

Banner, L. W. (1983). *American beauty.* Chicago: University of Chicago Press.

Barbaro, M. (2007a, May 15). Clothing shoppers finding the right fit online. *International Herald Tribune,* 11.

Barbaro, M. (2007b, December 2). Meteorologists shape fashion trends. *The New York Times.* Retrieved December 2, 2007, from www.nytimes.com.

Barbaro, M. & Creswell, J. (2007, January 29). Levi's turns to suing its rivals. *The New York Times.* Retrieved January 29, 2007, from www.nytimes.com.

Barker, B. (2002, July 30). Inside the Inditex empire. *Women's Wear Daily,* 10–11.

Barker, O. (2007, January 3). These people color your world. *USA Today,* 01D.

Barry, E. (1999, February/March). The color guard. *Metropolis,* 60–5, 99, 101.

Bass, F. M. (1969, January). A new product growth model for consumer durables. *Management Science, 15,* 215–27.

Bathory-Kitsz, D. (1996, January/February). "Tea. Earl Grey. Hot.": Mass customization presents major opportunities and major threats. *Consumer Goods,* 13–14, 16, 18.

Beckett, W. (2007, June 27). Doneger's Wolfe predicts minimalism will last. *Women's Wear Daily,* 8.

Behling, D. (1985/1986). Fashion change and demographics: A model. *Clothing and Textiles Research Journal, 4*(1), 18–23.

Bell, J. (2008, February 4). The luxe life. *Footwear News,* 24.

Bellafante, G. (2003a, February 12). In an age of anxiety, dodging adulthood. *The New York Times.* Retrieved February 13, 2003, from www.nytimes.com.

Belleau, B. (1987). Cyclical fashion movement: Women's day dresses: 1860–1980. *Clothing and Textiles Research Journal, 5*(2), 15–20.

Berger, J. (2013). *Contagious: Why things catch on.* New York: Simon & Schuster.

Betts, K. (1994, September). Up front: Copy rites. *Vogue,* 148, 154.

Betts, K. (1998, September). Some nerve. *Vogue,* 614–21.

Beyond blue denim/Lifestyle Monitor. (1998, May 12). *Women's Wear Daily.* Retrieved June 17, 1998 from www.cottoninc.com.

Bikhchandani, S., Hirshleifer, D., & Welch, I. (1992). A theory of fads, fashion, custom, and cultural change as informational cascades. *Journal of Political Economy, 100,* 992–1026.

Binkley, Christina. (2010, February 4). Which stars sell fashion?—As Oscars approach, designers vie to dress celebrities who will inspire viewers to shop; When star power won't translate into sales. *Wall Street Journal* (Eastern edition), D1. Retrieved using ProQuest.

"Bio" (2014). Patricia Field. http://patriciafield.com/pages/bio.

"Biography" (2014). http://www.thesartorialist.com/biography/.

Bird, L. (1995, September 6). Tired of T-shirts and no-name watches, shoppers return to Tiffany and Chanel. *The Wall Street Journal,* B1.

Bishop, S. (2014, October 22). Personal communication.

Blair, Elizabeth, (2013, September 17). Forecasting fashion trends. www.npr.org.

Blumberg, P. (1975). The decline and fall of the status symbol: Some thoughts on status in a post-industrial society. *Social Problems, 21*(4), 480–97.

Blumer, H. (1969, Summer). Fashion: From class differentiation to collective selection. *Sociological Quarterly, 10*(3), 275–91.

Bolt, G. J. (1994). *Market and sales forecasting: A total approach.* London: Kogan Page.

Borland, V. S. (2002a, February). Spring ahead. Textile World [online]. Retrieved from http://www.textileworld.com/Issues/2002/February/Textile_News/Spring_Ahead.

Borland, V. S. (2002b, December). Creativity rules at Premiere Vision. Textile World [online]. Retrieved from http://www.textileworld.com/Issues/2002/December/Knitting-Apparel/Creativity_Rules_At_Premiere_Vision.

Borrelli-Persson, Laird (2014, September 13). How '80s pop artist Keith Haring continues to influence the fashion world. http://www.vogue.com/slideshow/1444377/pop-keith-haring/.

Bourne, Leah (2012, March 22). The "Mad Men" fashion effect. Forbes.com. http://www.forbes.com/sites/leahbourne/2012/03/22/the-mad-men-fashion-effect/.

Bowers, K. (2003a, February 13). Oiling the teen machine. *Women's Wear Daily,* 8–9.

Bowers, K. (2003b, March 19). Subliminal messages. *Women's Wear Daily,* 3.

Bowers, K. (2008, February 4). Intimacy expands its fit philosophy. *Women's Wear Daily.* Retrieved February 4, 2008, from www.wwd.com.

Bowles, H. (1998, November). Trend trekker. *Vogue,* 190.

Branch, J. (2008, September 18). In the name of fashion, embracing a trend. *The New York Times.* Retrieved September 18, 2008, from www.nytimes.com.

Brannon, E. L. (1993). Affect and cognition in appearance management: A review. In S. J. Lenon & L. D. Burns (eds.), *Social science aspects of dress: New directions* (pp. 82–92). Monument, CO: International Textile and Apparel Association.

Braunstein, P. (2001, February 26). Strutting the cyber catwalk. *Women's Wear Daily,* 18.

Brenninkmeyer, I. (1963). *The sociology of fashion.* Sirey.

Brenninkmeyer, I. (1973). The diffusion of fashion. In G. Wills & D. Midgley (eds.), *Fashion marketing: An anthology of viewpoints and perspectives* (pp. 259–302). London: Allen and Unwin.

Brimming with trimmings. (1998, May). *Body Fashions Intimate Apparel, 28*(5), 18.

Britten, R. (2007, September 18). Flashy and tailor-made: Rag trade blogs. *International Herald Tribune,* 23.

Brown, E. (1994). Designer of distinction. In H. Linton (ed.), *Color forecasting* (pp. 136–45). New York: Van Nostrand Reinhold.

Brown, R. (1992). Managing the "S" curves of innovation. *Journal of Consumer Marketing, 9*(4), 61–72.

Browne, A. (1994, September). Revival of the fittest. *Bazaar,* 130, 136.

Brownfield, P. (2002, October 30). "Girls Club" is canceled by Fox. *Los Angeles Times.* http://articles.latimes.com/2002/oct/30/business/fi-fox30MO.

Brownie, B. (2014, January 28). Why fashion isn't cool. *The Guardian.* http://www.theguardian.com/fashion/costume-and-culture/2014/jan/28/1.

Brubach, H. (1994, February 20). Style: Cut above. *The New York Times,* 67.

Brubach, H. (1998, May 3). Style; Spectator sportswear. *The New York Times.* Retrieved May 5, 1998, from http://www.nytimes.com/1998/05/03/magazine/style-spectator-sportswear.html.

Buisson, J. (2007, April). Color trend forecast. *Coatings World, 12*(4), 47–49.

Burchart, T. (2013, January 30). Christian Louboutin v. Yves Saint Laurent—No end to their trademark battle over the color red? http://www.lexisnexis.com/legalnewsroom/intellectual-property/b/copyright-trademark-law-blog/archive/2013/01/30/christian-louboutin-v-yves-saint-laurent-the-trademark-battle-for-the-color-red-may-continue.aspx.

Calvert, D. (1994). Textile design and apparel. In H. Linton (ed.), *Color forecasting* (pp. 190–2). New York: Van Nostrand Reinhold.

Caplan, D. G. (2001, May 31). Do you know your ABC's? *Women's Wear Daily,* 4, 17.

Cardin, M. M. (Producer), & Charney, N. (Director). (1992). *Christian Dior: The legend* [Video]. New York: VideoFashion, Inc.

Cardwell, Diane (2011, August 7). Waiting hours to see the McQueen exhibit, in a line not unlike a runway. http://www.nytimes.com/2011/08/08/nyregion/alexander-mcqueen-exhibition-at-metropolitan-museum-of-art-draws-thousands.html?_r=0.

Carman, J. M. (1966). The fate of fashion cycles in our modern society. In R. M. Hass (ed.), *Science, technology and marketing* (pp. 722–37). Chicago: American Marketing Association.

Carpenter, D. L. (1998, May). Return on innovation—The power of being different. *Retailing Issues Letter,* 1–5.

Carr, M. M. (ed.), 2003. *Super searchers in competitive analysis* (pp. 141–56). Medford, NJ: Cyber Age Books.

Casabona, L. (2007, April 16). A prominent presence: Walking the show floor with Abbey Doneger. *Women's Wear Daily,* 18.

Caughey, J. L. (1978). Artificial social relationships in modern America. *American Quarterly,* 30, 70–89.

Celebrity influentials. (2008, October 6). *Women's Wear Daily.* Retrieved October 6, 2008, from www.wwd.com.

Chafkin, M. (2008, June). The customer is the company: Threadless churns out dozens of new items a month—With no advertising, no professional designers, no sales force, and no retail distribution. *Inc., 30*(6), 88–96.

Chammas, S. (2008, March 3). Designers dressing up. *Los Angeles Business Journal, 30*(9), 41.

Chan, C. & Lewis, B. (2002). A basic primer on data mining. *Information Systems Management, 19*(4), 56–60.

Chase, R. (1997). *CAD for fashion design.* Upper Saddle River, NJ: Prentice Hall.

Cheng, A. (2013, November 4). Kohl's shift back to name brands such as Nike draws upgrade. *The Wall Street Journal Marketwatch.* http://blogs.marketwatch.com/

behindthestorefront/2013/11/04/kohls-shift-back-to-name-brands-such-as-nike-draws-upgrade/.

Chinta, S. K. & Wane, P. P. (2013, May). Use of microencapsulation in textiles. *Indian Journal of Engineering, 3*(7).

Chirls, S. (1996a, November 12). Prints make fast break for spring. *Women's Wear Daily,* 12.

Chirls, S. (1996b, June 11). Sales on rise, but profits stall. *Women's Wear Daily,* 12.

Chirls, S. (1997, June 24). Pantone out to keep colors real as they connect with the Internet. *Women's Wear Daily.* Retrieved May 12, 1998, from www.pantone.com.

Chirls, S. (1998a, July). Pantone broadens its palette. *WWD/Global,* 32.

Chirls, S. (1998b, June 23). TDA told: Price squeeze goes on. *Women's Wear Daily,* 9, 11.

City slickers. (1998, January). *Sportstyle, 20*(1), 43.

Clark, K. (2002, November). From data to decisions. *Chain Store Age,* 62, 68–69.

Coddington, Grace (2009). In *The September Issue.* Roadside Attractions Films.

Coelho, P. & McClure, J. (1993). Toward an economic theory of fashion. *Economic Inquiry, 31,* 595–608.

Collier and Fuller (1990), *Choose Change.* London: Flamingo Research, as cited in Brownie, 2014.

Colman, D. (2008a, April 3). For a leather jacket, any cause will do. *The New York Times.* Retrieved April 3, 2008, from www.nytimes.com.

Colman, D. (2008b, May 8). Stripes that are seen, not heard. *The New York Times.* Retrieved May 8, 2008, from www.nytimes.com.

Colman, D. (2008c, May 29). Penny pinching looks great. *The New York Times.* Retrieved May 29, 2008, from www.nytimes.com.

Colman, D. (2008d, August 7). Muscling into the mainstream. *The New York Times.* Retrieved August 7, 2008, from www.nytimes.com.

Color-coated: An air of optimism takes hold at Ideabiella with pops of color ranging from sky blue to chocolate. (2008, February 18). *Daily News Record,* 18.

Color forecasting. (2003). Retrieved May 17, 2003, from www.colormarketing.org.

Color key. (2002, February). *DWC Magazine.* Retrieved September 3, 2002, from www.dwcdesignet.com.

Color scheming. (2002, March). *Soap, Perfumery, & Cosmetics,* 23.

Confidence in consumer confidence? Tread carefully, look closely. (1998, March). *Textile Consumer.* Retrieved June 17, 1998.

Cooper, N. (1998, September). Maximum security. *Vogue,* 256.

Cooperman, J. (2001, March). Color guard. *WWD Magazine,* 68, 70, 72.

Corcoran, C. T. (2007a, April 26). New ways to find fashion online. *Women's Wear Daily,* 9.

Corcoran, C. T. (2007b, May 16). Shopping online now more social. *Women's Wear Daily,* 8.

Corcoran, C. T. (2007c, September 1). Tech's the ticket. *Women's Wear Daily,* 14.

Corcoran, C. T. (2008a, January 17). Shoppers love stores who love them. *Women's Wear Daily,* 17.

Corcoran, C. T. (2008b, June 11). Shoppers envision store of the future. *Women's Wear Daily.* Retrieved June 11, 2008, from www.wwd.com.

Corcoran, C. T. (2008c, August 13). Wet Seal's teen social. *Women's Wear Daily.* Retrieved August 13, 2008, from www.wwd.com.

Corcoran, C. T. (2008d, September 10). Vivienne Tam bags fashionable computer. *Women's Wear Daily.* Retrieved September 10, 2008, from www.wwd.com.

Corcoran, C. T. (2008e, October 8). Retailers assort for customer wants. *Women's Wear Daily.* Retrieved October 8, 2008, from www.wwd.com.

"Corporate". (2014). http://www.corporate.r29.com/.

"Corporate Information." (2014). The Doneger Group [website]. Retrieved http://www.doneger.com/web/231.htm.

Cosmetotextiles market takes off. (2012, July 23). http://www.knittingindustry.com/cosmetotextiles-market-takesoff/#sthash.TaDJx5GZ.dpuf.

Cotton Incorporated presents trend forecasts, textile innovations and sourcing expertise at Première Vision. Cotton Incorporated. Retrieved February 19, 2008, from www.cottoninc.com.

Covert, J. (2007, February 7). Kohl's to sell Elle-branded clothing. http://online.wsj.com/news/articles/SB117081646201400432?mg=reno64-wsj.

Cowles, C. (2012, June 8). Dynasty costume designer Nolan Miller is dead. http://nymag.com/thecut/2012/06/dynasty-costume-designer-nolan-miller-is-dead.html.

Craik, J. (1994). *The face of fashion: Cultural studies in fashion*. London: Routledge.

Craver, R. (2002, July 9). Participants at High Point, N.C. *Knight Ridder Tribune Business News*. Retrieved October 11, 2002, from Business and Industry Database.

Creative woman's world. (1971, June). *Family Circle*, 8.

Crispell, D. (1997, December). Pre-millennial purples. *American Demographics*. Retrieved May 5, 1998, from www.demographics.com.

Crow, D. (2007, February 3). Special search engines bring a buzz to bloggers. *Sunday Business* (London). Retrieved February 3, 2007, from Business Index.

Crupi, Anthony. (2009, July 2). TV's a more effective ad medium than Web. http://www.adweek.com/news/television/tvs-more-effective-ad-medium-web-99775?page=1.

Cunningham, Bill. (2010) In *Bill Cunningham New York*. Zeitgeist Films.

Curriculum modules for educational programs. (1998). Society of Competitive Intelligence Professionals. Retrieved September 17, 1998, from https://www.questia.com/library/journal/1P3-574973/forecasting-color-demand-at-ciba-geigy.

Currid, Elizabeth (2007). *The Warhol economy*. Princeton, NJ: Princeton University Press.

The cycle. (2003, February). *Women's Wear Daily*, 15.

Danger, E. P. (1968). *Using colour to sell*. New York: Gower.

Darmstadt, C. (1982). Farbige Rassungen für Bügerhauser des Historismus und les Jugendstils unter hertigen Aspekten. Unpublished doctoral dissertation, Dortmund University, Germany.

Darmsadt, C. (1985, June 6). Farbe in der Architektur ab 1800. *DBZ, 743–748*.

Dash, M. (1999). *Tulipomania*. New York: Three Rivers Press.

Daswani, K. (2008, June 30). The details matter. *Women's Wear Daily*. Retrieved June 30, 2008, from www.wwd.com.

Davczyk, S. (2000). Aesthetic functionality in trade dress: Post-secondary aesthetic functionality proposed. *Commercial Law Journal, 105*(3), 309–31.

Davis, A. P. (2013, December 5). Will getting rid of "fashion bloggers" return fashion week to its former glory? Retrieved from The Cut.

Davis, F. (1991). Herbert Blumer and the study of fashion: A reminiscence and a critique. *Symbolic Interaction, 14*(1), 1–21.

Davis, M. L. (1996). *Visual design in dress* (3rd ed.). Upper Saddle River, NJ: Prentice Hall.

Dean, B. (1998, January). Measuring catalog effectiveness. *WWD/DNR Specialty Stores*, 4, 6.

Defining moments. (2007, April 9). *Women's Wear Daily*, 28.

De Guzman, D. (2007, May 14). Painting the market red. *ICIS Chemical Business Americas*, 28–9.

The descent of the "Wally" dress. (1931, August 19). *Life, 13*(6), 57.

de Paula, M. (2012, December 21). Top 10 most popular car colors. www.forbes.com.

Detouzos, M. (1997). *What will be: How the new world of information will change our lives?* New York: HarperCollins.

Dhar, V. & Stein, R. (1997). *Seven methods for transforming corporate data into business intelligence*. Upper Saddle River, NJ: Prentice Hall.

Diane, T. & Cassidy, T. (2005). *Colour forecasting*. Oxford: Blackwell.

D'Innocenzio, A. (2001, February 26). Frenetic fashion cycle confuses consumers and stores. Fox News. Retrieved February 27, 2001, from www.foxnews.com.

Direction is in the eye of the beholder. (1999, April 19). *Discount Store News*, A10.

Dokoupil, T. (2008, March 6). Revenge of the experts. *Newsweek* (Web exclusive). Retrieved March 6, 2008, from www.newsweek.com.

Doonan, S. (2009, August 5). Hardy har har har! Reality's go-to gaudy couturier. http://observer.com/2009/08/hardy-har-har-har-realitys-goto-gaudy-couturier/#ixzz3Flui6CB6.

Dougherty, S. & Hoover, E. (1990, July 30). Pages: John Naisbitt and Pat Aburdene reap profits as mega-prophets. *People, 57*.

Dowling, M. (2000, August 1). Merchandising: Fashion dressing up home. *Catalog Age*. Retrieved May 21, 2003, from www.catalogagemag.com.

Dransfield, A. (1994, Spring). Forecasting color demand at Ciba-Geigy. *Journal of Business Forecasting*. Retrieved May 6, 1998.

Drier, M. & McGuinness, D. (2007, July 9). The Wild West. *Women's Wear Daily*, 2S.

Dries Van Noten – Inspirations (2014). http://www.lesartsdecoratifs.fr/francais/mode-et-textile/expositions-70/actuellement-447/dries-van-noten-inspirations/.

Dubroff, J. (2014, September 24). Taylor Swift and Cara Delevingne: Reigning Queens of Style. http://www.vanityfair.com/style/photos/2014/09/taylor-swift-cara-delevingne-queens-of-style#.

Duff, C. (1994, February 11). Six reasons women aren't buying as many clothes. *The Wall Street Journal*, B1, B3.

DuMont, S. R. (1997, February 1). The global textile/apparel industry meets the digital revolution. Paper presented at the World Economic Forum, Governors for Textile and Apparel, Davos, Switzerland.

DuPont Automotive. (2000). Silver, other "techno colors" drive 21st century consumer. *Paint & Coatings Industry, 16*(2), 70–4.

Dyett, L. (2007, August 27). The one to swatch. *Daily News Record,* 154.

Eckman, M., Damhorst, M. L., & Kadolph, S. J. (1990). Toward a model of the in-store purchase decision process: Consumer use of criteria for evaluating women's apparel. *Clothing and Textiles Research Journal, 8*(2), 13–22.

Edelson, S. (1991, July 19). Painting the town with MAC. *Women's Wear Daily*, 16.

Edelson, E. (2003, May 8). Consumers to designers: You're not the boss of me. *Women's Wear Daily*, 8–9.

Edelson, S. (2008, May 9). Meatpacking District in flux. *Women's Wear Daily*, 4.

Edwards, C. (2007, February 5). Marketers need complex maps. *Advertising Age, 78*(6), 17.

Eiseman, L. (1994). Color forecasting: Crystal ball or educated choice? In H. Linton (ed.), *Color forecasting* (pp. 148–58). New York: Van Nostrand Reinhold.

Eiseman, L. (1997). All about color. Pantone. Retrieved May 12, 1998, from www.pantone.com.

Eiseman, L. & Hebert, L. (1990). *The Pantone book of color*. New York: Abrams.

Elejalde-Ruiz, Alexia. (2014, August 14). Nordstrom paying $350 million for Chicago's Trunk Club. http://www.chicagotribune.com/business/breaking/chi-nordstrom-trunk-club-20140814-story.html.

Elliott, C. (1998, June 1). Trends: Give your data a workout. *Internet Week*, 32.

Ellis, K. (2007, April 26). Copyrighting a dress: Congress mulling bill to protect designers. *Women's Wear Daily*, 1.

Engel, P. (2013, May 23). Women in a poor West African country are force-feeding themselves for beauty's sake. http://www.businessinsider.com/women-force-feeding-in-mauritania-2013-5?op=1#ixzz3A9PG6OzW.

Epiro, S. (2007, June 26). Mills cautions heading into Pitti Filati. *Women's Wear Daily*, 10.

Epiro, S. (2008, March 28). Cosmoprof catering to key buyers. *Women's Wear Daily*, 5.

The EU Ecolabel for Textiles factsheet. 2014. http://ec.europa.eu/environment/ecolabel/documents/factsheet_textiles.pdf.

Excell, J. (2007, September 3). Smart textiles: A cut above. *The Engineer*, 20.

Fahey, L. & Randall, R. M. (1998). What is scenario learning? In L. Fahey & R. M. Randall (eds.), *Learning from the future* (pp. 3–21). New York: Wiley.

Faith Popcorn's BrainReserve Trend Forecast for 2008. (2008, January 2). Retrieved January 2, 2008, from Internet Wire.Business Index.

Farrell, W. (1998). *How hits happen*. New York: Harper Business.

Farrington, D .W. Lunt, J., Davies, S., & Blackburn, R. S. (2006). Poly(lactic acid) fibers. *Biodegradable and Sustainable Fibers*, 191–220.

Fast fashion and supply chain management. (2005, July 29). *Just-style Global News*. Retrieved from Lexis Nexis database.

Feisner, E. A. (2001). *Color studies*. New York: Fairchild.

Feitelberg, R. (1996, February 22). Girls will be boys: Unisex looks. *Women's Wear Daily*, 22–3.

Feitelberg, R. (1998a, June 25). Designers told: Vary the vision. *Women's Wear Daily*, 10.

Feitelberg, R. (1998b, August 17). Trend boards make everything click. *Women's Wear Daily*, 10.

Feitelberg, R. (2001, December 13). Sport report: Breaking out of the boardroom. *Women's Wear Daily*, 8.

Feitelberg, R. (2003, February 10). Italian fashion legacy at heart of FIT exhibit. *Women's Wear Daily*, 20.

Feitelberg, R. (2003b, February 20). Taking it from the streets. *Women's Wear Daily*, 12.

Fennell, G. (1991). The role of qualitative research in making what the consumer wants to buy. In R. H. Holman & M. R. Solomon (eds.), *Advances in consumer research* (Vol. 18, pp. 271–79). Provo, UT: Association of Consumer Research.

Ferdows, K., Lewis, M. A., & Machuca, J. A. D. (2004, November). Rapid-fire fulfillment. *Harvard Business Review*, 82(11), 104–10.

Fibers: The foundation of fashion. (1998, June 23). *Women's Wear Daily*, 1–31.

Field, G. A. (1970). The status float phenomenon—The upward diffusion of innovation. *Business Horizons*, 8, 45–52.

Fine, A. (2003, April). Beauty's queens. *WWD/BeautyBiz*, 22–6.

Fiore, A. M. & Kimle, P. A. (1997). *Understanding aesthetics for the merchandising and design professional*. New York: Fairchild.

Fisher, M. L., Hammond, J. H., Obermeyer, W. R., & Raman, A. (1994, May/June). Making supply meet demand in an uncertain world. *Harvard Business Review*, 72(3), 83–9.

Fitzgerald, K. (1992, January 27). Marketers learn to "just do it." *Advertising Age*, 63(4), S-7.

Flacks, N. & Rasberry, R. W. (1982). *Power talk*. New York: Free Press.

Flugel, J. C. (1930). *The psychology of fashion*. London: Hogarth.

Foley, B. (1998, July 8). The dating game: Calvin joining Helmut with a September show. *Women's Wear Daily*, 1, 14.

Forecasting trends: Who defines the "new black." (2008, January 3). Talk of the Nation (NPR transcript). Retrieved January 3, 2008, from www.npr.org.

Foreman, K. & Murphy, R. (2008, February 12). Recession fears seen impacting Paris textile shows. *Women's Wear Daily*, 16.

Fox, M. (2012, May 24). Why retail catalogs survive, even thrive, in the Internet age. *USA TODAY Money* [online]. http://usatoday30.usatoday.com/money/industries/retail/story/2012-05-28/catalogs-in-the-internet-age/55188676/1.

Fox, S. (2003). Innovation in the field. Retrieved May 30, 2003, from www.foxfibre.com.

Fox, S. (1984). *The mirror makers: A history of American advertising and its creators*. New York: Vintage.

Fraser-Cavassoni, N. (2008, February 24). Checking the racks around Europe. *International Herald Tribune*, 11.

Freed, J. C. (1994, August 14). Spreadsheets beware, demographic mapping is here. *The New York Times,* 8.

Freeman, H. (2002, June 19). Trend spotting. The Age. Retrieved May 23, 2003, from www.theage.com.

Frequently asked questions. (1998). Society of Competitive Intelligence Professionals. Retrieved June 8, 1998, www.scip.org.

Friedman, A. (1996, December 6). A blueprint for brand licensing. *Women's Wear Daily,* 14.

Friedman, M. (2014, March 16). Denim overalls are making a comeback— as chic fashion options. http://www.nydailynews.com/life-style/fashion/denim-overalls-making-comeback-chic-fashion-options-article-1.1719684.

Friedman, V. (2014, September 16). What does "British" style really mean? Retrieved: http://www.nytimes.com/2014/09/17/fashion/london-fashion-week-simone-rocha-christopher-kane-thomas-tait.html?_r=1.

Fritjers, P. (1998). A model of fashion and status. *Economic Modeling, 15,* 501–17.

From stupidity to greed, why business is bad. (1988, October 18). *Women's Wear Daily,* 1, 4–6.

Fuld, L. M. (1985). *Competitor intelligence: How to get it; how to use it.* New York: Wiley.

Fuld, L. M. (1988). *Monitoring the competition.* New York: Wiley.

Fuld, L. M. (1992). Achieving total quality through intelligence. *Long Range Planning, 25*(1), 109–15.

Furchgott, R. (1998, June 28). For cool hunters, tomorrow's trend is the trophy. *The New York Times,* 10.

Gelb, B. D. (1997). Creating "memes" while creating advertising. *Journal of Advertising Research, 37*(6), 57–9.

Gelb, B. D., Saxton, M. J., Zinkhan, G. M., & Albers, N. D. (1991, January/February). Competitive intelligence: Insights from executives. *Business Horizons, 34,* 43–7.

Gellers, S. (1999, December 15). Defining modern for the moment. *Daily News Record,* 15–16.

Get the "Mad Men" Look (2012, March 22). http://www.forbes.com/pictures/elid45gdg/get-the-mad-men-look/.

Ghoshal, S. & Westney, D. E. (1991). Organizing competitor analysis systems. *Strategic Management Journal, 12,* 17–31.

Gilbert, D. (2002, October 22). Solstiss: Fashion's lace machine. *Women's Wear Daily,* 10.

Gilbert, D. (2003, May 13). Pantone rearranges its rainbow. *Women's Wear Daily,* 20.

Gladwell, M. (1996, November). The science of shopping. *The New Yorker,* 66–75.

Gladwell, M. (1999, October 4). The science of the sleeper. *The New Yorker.* Retrieved February 26, 2002, from http://www.gladwell.com.

Gladwell, M. (2002). *The tipping point.* Boston: Back Bay Books.

Gobé, M. (2001). *Emotional branding: The new paradigm for connecting brands to people.* New York: Allworth Press.

Goldsmith, R. E., Flynn, L. R., & Moore, M. A. (1996). The self-concept of fashion leaders. *Clothing and Textiles Research Journal, 14*(4), 242–8.

Goldwert, Lindsay (2012, September 17). Kate Middleton's Prabal Gurung dress sells out in under an hour; MyHabit site sold $1,995 dress for $599. *New York Daily News.*

Goodman, B. & Dretzen, R. (Producers), & Goodman, B. (Director). (2001, February 27). *The Merchants of Cool.* Boston: WGBH.

Gopnik, A. (1994, November 7). What it all means. *The New Yorker,* 15–16.

Gordon, I. J. (1994). *The Delphi method.* A publication of the United Nations University Millennium Project Feasibility Study (Phase II).

Gordon, M. (1990, August 31). Levi's to open stores to test merchandise. *Women's Wear Daily,* 13.

Grad student and banker accused of being spies. (1998, October 13). *Opelika-Auburn News,* A7.

Graham, D. (2002, September 13). Black magic. *The Halifax Herald Limited.* Retrieved January 21, 2003, from www.herald.ns.ca.

Greco, J. (1994, February). Name that trend … and sell! *Writer's Digest,* 40–1.

Green, P. (1998, August 24). Perfume futurist is a "trend trekker" with a nose for what's new. *Star Tribune,* 03E.

Greenberg, J. (2003a, February 18). Times are changing. *Women's Wear Daily,* 14.

Greenberg, J. (2003b, February 19). The show must go on. *Women's Wear Daily,* 10–11.

Greenberg, J. (2003c, April 10). Keeping it real. *Women's Wear Daily,* 4.

Greene, J. (2002, August 20). Fibers and fabrics get active. *Women's Wear Daily,* 13.

Grigoriadis, V. (2014, March). Slaves of the red carpet. *Vanity Fair.* http://www.vanityfair.com/hollywood/2014/03/hollywood-fashion-stylists-rachel-zoe-leslie-fremar.

Grimberg, J. (2013, October 17). Fashion's fortune teller: Three questions for a top trend forecaster. www.style.com.

Grimond, G, Lloyd, I., St Clair, K., & Willis, R. (2014). Influence in fashion. http://moreintelligentlife.com/content/lifestyle/rebecca-willis/influence-fashion.

Gronbach, K. (2008, June 2). The six markets you need to know now. *Advertising Age,* *79*(22), 21.

Groves, E. (2008a, June 12). PV's denim show grows in second edition. *Women's Wear Daily.* Retrieved June 12, 2008, from www.wwd.com.

Groves, E. (2008b, August 6). Scandinavians form fashion association. *Women's Wear Daily.* Retrieved August 6, 2008, from www.wwd.com.

Haber, H. (2007a, January 10). Forecasting fall. *Women's Wear Daily,* 19S.

Haber, H. (2007b, March 7). Fashion's new segmented society. *Women's Wear Daily,* 6.

Haché, Kat. (2014, July). Andreja Pejic on coming out as transgender, and why this was her moment—EXCLUSIVE. Bustle. http://www.bustle.com/#/articles/33508-andreja-pejic-on-coming-out-as-transgender-and-why-this-was-her-moment-exclusive.

Haisma-Kwok, C. (2008, April 1). Green leads Interstoff Asia. *Women's Wear Daily,* 11.

Hall, C. (2008, January 31). A season of change; the top 10 Pantone colors chosen by New York designers for Fall 2008. *Women's Wear Daily,* 12.

Halpern, A. (2010, September 8). Meet trend forecaster Nina Stotler. http://nymag.com/thecut/2010/09/trend_forecaster_nina_stotler.html.

Hamilton, W. L. (2002, January 10). Seeing the future in all its hues. *The New York Times.* Retrieved January 10, 2002, from www.nytimes.com.

Hammond, T. (1999). A new twist. *WWD/WWD-MAGIC* 26.

Hansen, S. (2012, November 9). How Zara grew into the world's largest fashion retailer. *The New York Times.* http://www.nytimes.com/2012/11/11/magazine/how-zara-grew-into-the-worlds-largest-fashion-retailer.html?pagewanted=all&_r=0.

Harford, T. (2014, March 28). Big data: are we making a big mistake? *FT Magazine* [online]. http://www.ft.com/cms/s/2/21a6e7d8-b479-11e3-a09a-00144feabdc0.html.

Harkin, F. (2008, February 19). The luxury world after Web 2.0. *The Financial Times,* 14.

Harris, E. A. & Abrams, R. (2014, August 27). Plugged-in over preppy:.

Teenagers favor tech over clothes. *The New York Times* [online]. http://www.nytimes.com/2014/08/28/business/less-prep-more-plugs-teenagers-favor-tech-over-clothes.html.

Harris, J. (2013, January 13). The 50 greatest Japanese brands of all time. Complex. http://www.complex.com/style/2013/01/the-50-greatest-japanese-brands-of-all-time/.

Hastreiter, K. (1997, December). The world war of fashion. *Paper,* 64.

Heaf, J. & Cochrane, L. (2014, April 15). How Mad Men changed the way men dress. http://www.theguardian.com/fashion/2014/apr/15/mad-men-changed-way-men-dress-don-draper.

Heath, C. & Heath, D. (2007). *Made to stick: Why some ideas survive and others die.* New York: Random House.

Heath, R. P. (1996a, September). The competitive edge. *Marketing Tools.* Retrieved September 17, 1998, from www. demographics.com.

Heath, R.P. (1996b, October). The wonderful world of color marketing today. Retrieved May 5, 1998, from www.demographics. com.

Heine, Christopher (2014, February 2). JCPenney isn't drunk tweeting the Super Bowl—It's wearing mittens; Stunt causes buzz and goads Kia Motors and Doritos. http:// www.adweek.com/news/technology/jc-penney-isnt-drunk-tweeting-super-bowl-its-wearing-mittens-155437.

Henken, K. (2014, August 16). Andrea Bell of WGSN. FBA 360. https:// fashionaccelerator360.com/blogs/andrea-bell-wgsn.

Higham, W. (2009). *The next big thing: Spotting and forecasting consumer trends for profit.* Kogan Page.

Hindin-Miller, I. (2014, January 13). Is Milan finally seeing a young designer renaissance? http://www.businessoffashion. com/2014/01/is-milan-finally-seeing-a-young-designer-renaissance.html.

Hirschberg, L. (2000, September). New old thing. *Harper's Bazaar, 473–9,* 551.

Hirschman, E. C. (1980). Innovativeness, novelty seeking, and consumer creativity. *Journal of Consumer Research, 7,* 288–95.

Hirschman, E. C. & Stampfl, R. W. (1980). Roles of retailing in the diffusion of popular culture: Microperspectives. *Journal of Retailing, 56*(1), 16–36.

Holch, A. (1996, November 26). Tencel's variety show. *Women's Wear Daily,* 11.

Holch, A. (1997, February 4). Wool blends bloom for Spring '98. *Women's Wear Daily,* 9.

Holch, A. (1998, July 14). A luxury buying. *Women's Wear Daily,* 16–17, 19.

Hollander, A. (1994). *Sex and suits: The evolution of modern dress.* New York: Kodansha International.

Holmes, E. (2014, April 16). Why online retailers like Bonobos, Boden, Athleta mail so many catalogs. *Wall Street Journal Online.*

Holmes, S. (2014, March 11). Meet the woman responsible for the viral "First Kiss" video. http://www.elle.com/news/lifestyle/first-kiss-video-melissa-coker-interview.

Honorary Clio Winner: Patricia Field (2013, May 13). http://www.adweek.com/sa-article/honorary-clio-winner-patricia-field-149267.

Hope, A. & Walch, M. (1990). *The color compendium.* New York: Van Nostrand Reinhold.

Hope, P. (1990). Fashion: Geography of color. In A. Hope & M. Walch (eds.), *The color compendium* (p. 127). New York: Van Nostrand Reinhold.

Hoppough, S. (2008a, January 28). Fresh prints. *Daily News Record,* 32.

Hoppough, S. (2008b, February 18). Survey says: An exclusive PV study reveals new insight into the buying behavior of the modern man. *Daily News Record,* 16.

Hoppough, S. (2008c, April 14). Want fries with that? From product life-cycle management to organics, if you wanted it, Material World had it. *Daily News Record,* 23.

Hoppough, S. (2008d, April 28). Printsource: Get whisked away. *Daily News Record,* 20.

Horn, M. J. (1965). *The second skin.* Boston: Houghton-Mifflin.

Horton, D. & Wohl, R. (1956). Mass communication and para-social interaction. In G. Gumpert & R. Cathcart (eds.), *Inter/ Media* (pp. 32–55). New York: Oxford University Press.

Horton, O. (2003, March 12). End of road for seasonal trends? *International Herald Tribune.* Retrieved March 12, 2003, from www.iht.com.

Horton, O. (2008a, February 19). Online fashion shopping finally comes of age. *International Herald Tribune.* Retrieved February 19, 2008, from www.iht.com.

Horton, O. (2008b, February 20). Fashion e-commerce finally comes of age. *International Herald Tribune*, 11.

Horton, R. L. (1979). Some relationships between personality and consumer decision making. *Journal of Marketing Research, 16*, 233–46.

Horyn, C. (2001, March 13). How the offbeat slips into mainstream fashion. *The New York Times*. Retrieved August 11, 2001, from www.nytimes.com.

Horyn, C. (2002, July 23). As the Dow falls, couture turns contrarian. *The New York Times*. Retrieved August 11, 2002, from www.nytimes.com.

Horyn, C. (2003a, January 26). Karl Lagerfeld's understated mastery. *The New York Times*. Retrieved January 26, 2003, from www.nytimes.com.

Horyn, C. (2003b, February 10). Little-known stars jazz up the opening act. *The New York Times*. Retrieved February 10, 2003, from www.nytimes.com.

Horyn, C. (2005, January 4). The lady's gone, but don't look for a tramp. *The New York Times*. Retrieved January 4, 2005, from www.nytimes.com.

Horyn, C. (2007, October 18). The coming of the X-frocks. *The New York Times*. Retrieved October 18, 2007, from www.nytimes.com.

Horyn, C. (2008, June 19). Conspicuous by their presence. *The New York Times*. Retrieved June 19, 2008, from www.nytimes.com.

How the survey was done. (2008, June 30). *Women's Wear Daily*. Retrieved June 30, 2008, from www.wwd.com.

Huntington, P. (2001, July). Fashion's second circuit. *WWD/Global*, 16.

Hutchings, H. V. (2001, November 5). The hot hue of the future is being decided now. *Automotive News, 76*(5956), 4–6.

Hye, J. (1998, April 8). Wal-Mart and Sara Lee: Collaborating on the Internet. *Women's Wear Daily*, 16.

"Iconoculture." (2007). CEB Iconoculture Consumer Insights. https://iconoculture.com/.

Ilari, A., Socha, M., & Karimzadeh, M. (2008, January 22). New technologies give prints pop. *Women's Wear Daily*, 16.

Indvik, Lauren (2011, May 16). 5 Best Practices for fashion retailers on Facebook. http://mashable.com/2011/05/16/fashion-brands-facebook/.

Ingrassia, M. (1994, June 6). A not-so-little black dress. *Newsweek, 72*.

Isbecque, D. (1990). Personal color analysis. In A. Hope & M. Walch (eds.), *The color compendium* (p. 242). New York: Van Nostrand Reinhold.

Jack, N. K. & Schiffer, B. (1948). The limits of fashion control. *American Sociological Review, 13*, 731–8.

Jackson, J. (1998, October). Crazy for Colette. *Bazaar, 128*.

Jackson, K. (2005, August 18). What's pink and green and worn all over? *The Boston Globe*. Retrieved August 18, 2005, from www.boston.com.

Jacobs, D. L. (1994, May 29). The titans of tint make their picks. *The New York Times, 7*.

Jana, R. (2007, November 26). Trend: Runway edge. *Business Week, 2*.

Jesella, K. (2007, May 10). The collarbone's connected to slimness. *The New York Times*. Retrieved May 10, 2007, from www.nytimes.com.

Jimenez, G. C., Murphy, J., & Zerbo, J. (2014). Design piracy legislation: Should the United States protect fashion design? In G. C. Jimenez & B. Kolsun (eds.), *Fashion Law: A Guide for Designers, Fashion Executives, and Attorneys* (2nd rev. ed.). New York: Bloomsbury.

Jones, N. (2007a, May 24). Carnaby gets its cool back. *Women's Wear Daily, 44S*.

Jones, N. (2007b, July 12). A fashion model? Britain looks to set "gold standard" for improved treatment. *Women's Wear Daily*, 12.

Jones, R. A. (2002, February 27). Doneger: Casual cools? *Women's Wear Daily*, 12.

Jones, R. A. (2003, March). In with the old. *WWD Magazine, 42*, 84–5.

Jorgensen, D. L. (1989). *Participant observation: A methodology for human studies*. Newbury Park, CA: Sage.

Just the FAQs, Ma'am. (1995, May). *Marketing Tools*, 61–2.

Kaiser, S. (1990). *The social psychology of clothing*. New York: Macmillan.

Kaiser, S. B., Nagasawa, R., & Hutton, S. S. (1995). Construction of an SI theory of fashion: Part 1. Ambivalence and change. *Clothing and Textiles Research Journal, 13*(3), 172–83.

Kanner, B. (1989, April 3). Color schemes: Shades of meaning. *New York Magazine, 22*(14), 22.

Kania, J. (1998). Customer-driven scenario planning. In L. Fahey & R. M. Randal (Eds.), *Learning from the future* (pp. 264–84). New York: Wiley.

Karimzadeh, M. (2006, September 12). Youth isn't everything: Brands chase boomers with power to spend. *Women's Wear Daily*, 1.

Katz, E. & Lazarsfeld, P. (1955). *Personal influence*. New York: Macmillan/Free Press.

Kauffman, S. (1995). *At home in the universe*. Oxford: Oxford University Press.

Keith Haring's 54th Birthday. http://www.google.com/doodles/keith-harings-54th-birthday.

Keller, E. & Berry, J. (2003). *The influentials*. New York: Free Press.

Kelly, K. J. (1994, June 20). "Consumer culture" overrules income. *Advertising Age, 65*(26), 4.

Kermouch, G. (2002, November 11). A therapeutic passion for fashion. *Business Week*. Retrieved November 12, 2002, from MasterFILE Premiere Database.

King, C. & Ring, L. (1980). Fashion theory: The dynamics of style and taste, adoption and diffusion. In J. Olson (ed.), *Advances in consumer research* (Vol. 7, pp. 13–16). Ann Arbor, MI: Association for Consumer Research.

King, C. W. (1963). A rebuttal to the "trickle down" theory. In S. A. Greyer (ed.), *Towards scientific marketing* (pp. 108–25). Chicago: American Marketing Association.

Kinning, D. (1994). Colourcast services. In H. Linton (ed.), *Color forecasting* (pp. 174–8). New York: Van Nostrand Reinhold.

Kissmetrics. (2010). How do colors affect purchases? https://blog.kissmetrics.com/color-psychology/.

Kletter, M. (2003, February 18). Under the influence. *Women's Wear Daily*, 20.

Kline, B. & Wagner, J. (1994). Information sources and retail buyer decision-making: The effect of product specific buying experience. *Journal of Retailing, 70*(1), 75–88.

Knight, K. (2013, October 13). 30 ways to wear a flannel shirt. http://keltiecolleen.buzznet.com/photos/30waystowearaflannel/.

Knight, M. (1999, February 15). Steve Rifkind, coach of the street teams. *Daily News Record*, 34.

Koda, H. (2010). In *Bill Cunningham New York*. Zeitgeist Films.

Koski, L. (2013, August 5). Leandra Medine on the rules of man repelling. Retrieved: http://www.wwd.com/eye/people/leandra-medine-on-the-rules-of-man-repelling-7075799.

Kroeber, A. L. (1919). On the principle of order in civilization as exemplified by changes of fashion. *American Anthropologist, 21*, 235–63.

Kobayashi, S. (1981, Summer). The aim and method of the color image scale. *Color Research and Applications, 6*(2), 93–107.

Koda, H. (2002, October 27). Street style sashays and bobs down the ages. *The New York Times*. Retrieved Septmber 7, 2009, from www.nytimes.com.

Koppelmann, U. & Kuthe, E. (1987). Präferenzwelen beim Gestaltungsmittel Farbe. *MarkeintAFP, 2*, 113–122.

Kuczynski, A. (2007, October 21). Coming up clover. *The New York Times*. http://www.nytimes.com/2007/10/21/style/tmagazine/21kuczynski.html?pagewanted=print&_r=0.

Kurtzleben, Danielle. 2014, February 13. The decline of department store sales. US News.com.

La Ferla, R. (2002, July 7). Once hot, now not, hunters of cool are in a freeze. *The New York Times,* ST6.

La Ferla, R. (2003, January 21). To Hollywood, and designer-watching. *The New York Times.* Retrieved January 21, 2003, from www.nytimes.com.

La Ferla, R. (2006, December 21). When the runway is paved. *The New York Times.* Retrieved December 21, 2006, from www.nytimes.com.

La Ferla, R. (2007a, May 10). Faster fashion, cheaper chic. *The New York Times.* Retrieved May 10, 2007, from www.nytimes.com.

La Ferla, R. (2007b, July 12). The knitting circle shows its chic. *The New York Times.* Retrieved July 12, 2007, from www.nytimes.com.

La Ferla, R. (2008a, January 31). The newly uptight. *The New York Times.* Retrieved January 31, 2008, from www.nytimes.com.

La Ferla, R. (2008b, May 8). Steampunk moves between 2 worlds. *The New York Times.* Retrieved May 8, 2008, from www.nytimes.com.

La Ferla, R. (2008c, September 18). Shop locally: General Tso's shopping spree. *The New York Times.* Retrieved September 19, 2008, from www.nytimes.com.

La Ferla, R. (2008d, July 8). Forget gossip, girl; the buzz is about the clothes. http://www.nytimes.com/2008/07/08/fashion/08gossip.html?pagewanted=all&_r=0.

La Ferla, R. (2010, March 3). Film and fashion: Just friends. *The New York Times* [online]. http://www.nytimes.com/2010/03/04/fashion/04COSTUME.html?pagewanted=all.

Lamb, M. (1997). *Trend* 101. Available from www.trendcurve.com.

Lane, L. (2003, April 21). Marketing to Hispanics is complex, but essential. *DSN Retailing Today, 42*(8), 8, 28.

Lannon, L. (1988, March). Swatch watch. *Savvy,* 40–43, 100–1.

Larson, K. (2003a, February 12). Moderate makers race the clock. *Women's Wear Daily,* 4, 14–15.

Larson, K. (2003b, March 5). New venues, raw nerves. *Women's Wear Daily,* 10.

Larson, K. (2003c). Charron on Claiborne: Diversification is key. *Women's Wear Daily,* 4.

Laser Cutting Textiles. (2014). Trotec Laser website. http://www.troteclaser.com/en-US/Materials/Pages/Textiles.aspx.

Laver, J. (1937). *Taste and fashion.* New York: Harrap.

Laver, J. (1973). Taste and fashion since the French Revolution. In G. Wills & D. Midgley (eds.), *Fashion marketing* (pp. 379–89). London: George Allen, Irwin.

Leeds, J. (2006, September 3). The new tastemakers. *The New York Times.* Retrieved September 3, 2006, from www.nytimes.com.

Leland, J. (2000, January 1). How the future looked in 1899. *Newsweek, 106,* 109.

Lencek, L. (1996). *Nothing to hide: History of the bathing suit* [Video]. TLC/Australian Film.

Lenclos, J. (1994). Atelier 3D Couleur: Trends, signs, and symbols. In H. Linton (ed.), *Color forecasting* (pp. 36–59). New York: Van Nostrand Reinhold.

Letscher, M. G. (1994, December). How to tell fads from trends. *American Demographics.* Retrieved July 22, 1998, from www.demographics.com.

Levanas, T. (1998, January 1). You are what you buy—that's the premise of "clustering." *Gannett News Service.* Retrieved February 16, 1999, from www.elibrary.com.

Levenbach, H. & Cleary, J. P. (1981). *The beginning forecaster: The forecasting process through data analysis.* Belmont, CA: Lifetime Learning.

Levin, G. (1992, February 24). Anthropologists in adland. *Advertising Age, 63*(8), 3, 49.

Levitt, T. (1986). *The marketing imagination.* New York: Free Press.

Levy, S. (2003, April 28). The connected company. *Newsweek,* 41.

Lewis, R. (1995, November 8). What's a brand worth? *Women's Wear Daily,* 10–11.

Lewis, R. (1996a, May). Power to the consumer. *Women's Wear Daily/Infotracs,* 5.

Lewis, R. (1996b, October 31). Observations: The 3-D brands: Creators of dreams and dollars. *Women's Wear Daily* (Section II), 34.

Lieber, Chavie. (2014, September 30). Veteran Reporter Teri Agins on how celebrities have stolen the fashion spotlight.http://racked. com/archives/2014/09/30/teri-agins-hijacking-the-runway-celebrity-fashion.php.

Limnander, A. (2007, November 4). Club house. *The New York Times.* Retrieved November 4, 2007, from www.nytimes.com.

Linton, H. (1994). *Color forecasting.* New York: Van Nostrand Reinhold.

Lipke, D. (2007, April 2). The greening of menswear. *Daily News Record,* 13.

Lipke, D. (2008, March 31). Is green fashion an oxymoron? How an industry driven by disposable trends and aesthetic whims can reconcile itself to an era of conservation. *Daily News Record,* 12.

Lipovetsky, G. (1994). *The empire of fashion.* Princeton, NJ: Princeton University Press.

Lloyd, B. (2007, November 12). Champion aims younger with new ads: Print, outdoor and viral campaign is designed to draw connection between activewear and streetwear. *Daily News Record,* 8.

Lockwood, L. (2003, February 7). The no-shows. *Women's Wear Daily,* 16.

Loftus, M. (1999, June 7). An industry to be tied. *U.S. News & World Report,* 46.

LOLO (2014). "About." LOLO Magazine. http://lolomag.com/about/.

Looking at Cotton Inc.'s roots. (2001, October 2). *Women's Wear Daily,* 12.

Louis Vuitton and Nicolas Ghesquière. (2013, November 5). http://us.louisvuitton.com/ eng-us/articles/louis-vuitton-and-nicolas-ghesquiere.

Lowe, J. W. G. & Lowe, E. D. (1984). Stylistic change and fashion in women's dress: Regularity or randomness? In T. C. Kinnear (ed.), *Advances in consumer research* (Vol. 11, pp. 731–4). Provo, UT: Association of Consumer Research.

Lowther, B. (2008, February 19). It's all about me. *Women's Wear Daily,* 6.

Loyer, M. (2002, March 9). Trend-spotting: New spins on old techniques. *International Herald Tribune* (Special Report), 9.

Lüscher, M. (1969). *The Lüscher color test.* New York: Random House.

Lusher, Adam (2012, March 8). Fashion's dark secret; Celebrities paid to sit in front rows at shows, designer says. *The Ottawa Citizen,* D7. Retrieved through Proquest.

Lynch, A. & Strauss, M. D. (2007). *Changing fashion.* Oxford: Berg.

Lynch, M. (2008, August 12). AVA backs anti-knockoff law. *Women's Wear Daily.* Retreived August 12, 2008, from www.wwd.com.

Macys.com (2014, October 5 – access date). Material Girl juniors' printed leggings. http://www1.macys.com/shop/product/ material-girl-juniors-printed-leggings?ID=1323 180&CategoryID=21561#fn=sp%3D1%26 spc%3D225%26ruleId%3D%26slotId%3D1.

Madina Ferrari of Intercos with an exclusive look at her 2003 trend forecast. (2002, March). *WWD/Beauty Biz,* 44–5.

Mahaffie, J. B. (1995, March). Why forecasts fail. *American Demographics.* Retrieved July 22, 1998, from www.demographics.com.

Majewski, L. & Bernstein, J. (2014) *Mad world: An oral history of new wave artists and songs that defined the 1980s.* Harry N. Abrams.

Makridakis, S. G. (1990). *Forecasting, planning, and strategy for the 21st century.* New York: Free Press.

Malarcher, P. (1995, Winter). Coloring the future. *Surface Design Journal,* 20–1.

Malone, S. (1999, January 12). Speed: The upsides and the downsides. *Women's Wear Daily,* 12–13.

Malone, S. (2002, December 26). They will rise again. *Women's Wear Daily,* 10.

Malone, S. & Greenberg, J. (2003, May 8). Denim's Downturn. *Women's Wear Daily,* 3.

Marin, R. & Van Boven, S. (1998, July 27). The buzz machine. *Newsweek,* 22–6.

Marketing (2003, June 11). *Women's Wear Daily.* Retrieved July 7, 2003, from Business & Industry Database.

Marritz, I. (2011, February 10). The business of color: Company sets fashion trends. www.npr.org.

Marsh, E. & Foreman, K. (2007, November 21). New horizons. *Women's Wear Daily,* 6B.

Martin, J. S. (1992). Building an information resource center for competitive intelligence. *Online Review, 16*(6), 379–89.

Martorelli, M. (2013, December 18). Top 5 young Belgian designers.

Masters of Linen: Mission. (2003). Retrieved November 11, 2003, from www.mastersoflinen.com.

Masterson, P. (1994, March 14). Brands seek subconscious boost. *Advertising Age, 65*(11), 29.

Mateja, J. (2001, September 21). Ford designer keeps close eye on fashion. *Chicago Tribune.* Retrieved October 17, 2001, from Newspaper Source Database.

Mazzaraco, M. (1990, May 15). SA: Trekking to Europe for fabric direction. *Women's Wear Daily,* 16, 18.

McAdams, J. (2007, March 12). Synchronized stock: Many acquisitions later, apparel giant VF runs a best-of-breed supply chain. *Computerworld, 41*(11), S10.

McCarthy, J. (2014, February 13). Instagram registers 15x more engagement than Facebook: L2. http://www.luxurydaily.com/instagram-registers-15x-more-engagement-than-facebook-l2/?intcid=inline_link.

McCracken, G. (1988a). Consumer goods, gender construction, and a rehabilitated trickle-down theory. In *Culture and consumption* (pp. 93–103). Bloomington: Indiana University Press.

McCracken, G. (1988b). Meaning manufacture and movement in the world of good. In *Culture and consumption* (pp. 69–89). Bloomington: Indiana University Press.

McGonagle, J. J. & Vella, C. M. (1990). *Outsmarting the competition: Practical approaches to finding and using competitive information.* Napierville, IL: Sourcebooks.

McMurdy, D. (1998, January 12). Corporate fortune-tellers. *Maclean's,* 33.

McQuarrie, E. F. & McIntyre, S. H. (1988). Conceptual underpinnings for the use of group interviews in consumer research. In M. S. Houston (ed.), *Advances in consumer research* (Vol. 15, pp. 580–6). Provo, UT: Association of Consumer Research.

Medina, M. (2007, January 2). Hidden potential; a vintage dealer's old-fashioned accessories finds are surprisingly au courant. *WWD Accessories Supplement, 193,* 12.

Meltzer, M. (2013). Costume designers for TV have a big impact on fashion.

Memo Pad: The sartorialist.com. (2007, September 5). *Women's Wear Daily,* 22.

Menkes, S. (2003a, March 18). Azzedine Alaia, all copy the king. *The International Herald Tribune.* Retrieved March 18, 2003, from www.iht.com.

Menkes, S. (2003b, April 8). Making a splash in Los Angeles. *International Herald Tribune.* Retrieved April 8, 2003, from www.iht.com.

Menkes, S. (2008a, January 28). "No season, no reason"—but gorgeous clothes. *International Herald Tribune.* Retrieved January 28, 2008, from www.iht.com.

Menkes, S. (2008b, March 3). Only one master. *International Herald Tribune,* 16.

Mentzer, J.T. & Moon, Mark A. (2005). *Sales forecasting management: A demand management approach.* Thousand Oaks, CA: Sage.

Merriam, J.E. & Makower, J. (1988). *Trend watching: How the media creates trends and how to be first to uncover them.* New York: Amacom Books.

Mete, F. (2006). The creative role of sources of inspiration in clothing design. *International Journal of Clothing Science and Technology,* 18(4), 278–93.

Meyersohn, R. & Katz, E. (1957). Notes on a natural history of fads. *American Journal of Sociology, 62,* 594–601.

Michaud, H. A. (1989). *Integrated forecasting, scheduling, and planning: Generic model.* Wilmington, DE: Dupont Information Systems.

Millbank, C. A. (1985). *Couture: The great fashion designers.* London: Thames & Hudson Ltd.

Miller, C. C. (2008, September 9). Fashion designers go online for latest trends. *International Herald Tribune, 17.*

Mills, B. (2007, March). Profiles of leading technical apparel fabric suppliers. *Just Style.* Retrieved March, 2007, from www.just-style.com.

Mockus, D. (2003). Do you really know what the competition is doing? *The Journal of Business Strategy, 24*(1), 8–10.

Modis, T. (1992). *Predictions.* New York: Simon & Schuster.

Moin, D. (2003a, February 21). The mini: Better or worse. *Women's Wear Daily, 11.*

Moin, D. (2003b, April 16). "Optimizing" mark-downs by computer. *Women's Wear Daily, 8.*

Moin, D. (2003c, July 9). High tech meets high fashion. *Women's Wear Daily, 13.*

Moin, D. (2006, November 6). Doneger group at 60: Adapting is key. *Women's Wear Daily, 18.*

Moin, D. (2007, October 17). "No regrets" for Wexner: Chief of Limited Brands glad to be out of apparel. *Women's Wear Daily, 1.*

Moin, D. (2008, February, 25). Doneger acquires Directives West. *Women's Wear Daily, 29.*

Moin, D. (2014, July 28). Hudson's Bay Co. Technology Grabs Shoppers. *Women's Wear Daily.*

Moin, D., Edelson, S., & Tosh, M. (1996, March 25). Charting the cycles: Predictable patterns meet chaos theory. *Women's Wear Daily, 1,* 14–15.

Monget, K. (2007, November 19). Invista creates new video workshop format. *Women's Wear Daily, 6.*

Morton, J. (2000, October). *Quirks of the color quest.* Retrieved May 18, 2003, from www. colormatters.com.

Mower, S. (1996, February). A question of taste. *Bazaar, 161-2,* 208.

Munsell, A. H. (1976). *Munsell book of color.* Baltimore, MD: Munsell Color/Macbeth.

Munsell, A. H. (1998). *Munsell system of color notation.* Retrieved July 6, 1998, from www. munsell.com.

Murphy, P. E. & Laczniak, G. R. (1992). Emerging ethical issues facing marketing researchers. *Marketing Research, 4*(2), 6–11.

Murphy, R. (2000, June 18). France, Italy to fight fakes, coordinate fashion calendar. *Women's Wear Daily, 2,* 12.

Murphy, R. (2001a, July 30). No slow down here: Designers jam Paris RTW show schedule. *Women's Wear Daily, 1,* 18.

Murphy, R. (2001b, August 1). H&M's Rolf Eriksen: Steering fashion fashion country by country. *Women's Wear Daily, 1,* 7.

Murphy, R. (2002a, February 25). Designers, press say Paris calendar is too busy. *Women's Wear Daily, 6.*

Murphy, R. (2002b, November 13). Colette cuts power brands. *Women's Wear Daily, 2.*

Murphy, R. (2003, May 28). Expofil, PV entwine shows. *Women's Wear Daily, 13.*

Musselman, T. (1998, March) Clear on the concept. *Apparel Industry Magazine, 59*(3), 46–50.

Naisbitt, J. (1982). *Megatrends.* New York: Warner.

Naisbitt, J. & Aburdene, P. (1990). *Megatrends 2000.* New York: Morrow.

Naisbitt, J. & Brealey, N. (1996). *Megatrends Asia.* New York: Simon & Schuster.

Nancarrow, C., Nancarrow, P., & Page, J. (2002). An analysis of the concept of cool and its marketing implications. *Journal of Consumer Behavior, 1*(4), 311–22.

Nanofinishing in textiles. 2014. Retrieved from http://www.nanowerk.com/spotlight/ spotid=912.php#ixzz36imocXXK.

Nelson, K. (2007, November 8). Perfect for prowling. *The New York Times.* Retrieved November 8, 2007, from www.nytimes.com.

New colors 2002. (2001). Retrieved June 11, 2001, from www.pantone.com.

New ideas for digital textile printing expand technological possibilities. (2003). Retrieved May 29, 2003, from www.cottoninc.com.

The next files: Industry predictions. (2003, July 14). *Daily News Record.*

Nichols, P. (1996, May). Shades of change. *American Demographics.* Retrieved May 25, 1998, from www.demographics.com.

Nike engineers knit for performance. (2012, February 2012). http://nikeinc.com/news/nike-flyknit.

Nike focus group meets Beaver Track. (2008, March 3). *Oregon State Women's Cross Country* [online]. http://www.osubeavers.com/ViewArticle.dbml?DB_OEM_ID=30800&ATCLID=207852333.

Nippon Color and Design Institute. (1994). Color and image forecasting. In H. Linton (ed.), *Color forecasting* (pp. 25–31). New York: Van Nostrand Reinhold.

Noh, M. (1997). Fashion forecasting information and timing for product development and merchandise selection. Unpublished master's thesis, Auburn University, Alabama.

Nolan, K. (2007, May 21). Performance features the fabric of men's work wear. *Retailing Today, 46*(8), 18.

Nystrom, P. (1928). Character and direction of fashion movement. In *Economics of fashion*. New York: Ronald Press.

Oberascher, L. (1994). Cyclic recurrence of collective color preferences. In H. Linton (ed.), *Color forecasting* (pp. 66–77). New York: Van Nostrand Reinhold.

OBEY x Keith Haring limited edition collection. (2012). Urban Outfitters blog. Retrieved February 5, 2015, from http://www.blog.urbanoutfitters.com/blog/obey_keith_haring.

Oblena, L. (2003, March 29). D&A presents style mavens of the West Coast. Fashion Windows. Available www.fashionwindows.com.

Olsen, K. (2008, June 24). Pitti Filati mills focus on color, organics. *Women's Wear Daily.* Retrieved June 24, 2008, from www.wwd.com.

Olson, E. (2007, December 2). If the shoe fits, wear it. If not, design one that does. *The New York Times.* Retrieved December 2, 2007, from www.nytimes.com.

O'Neill, J. (1989, September). Forecasting—Fact or fiction? *Textile Horizons, 9*(9), 26–8.

One-stop shops/Lifestyle Monitor. (1998, July 2). *Women's Wear Daily,* 2.

Orndoff, K. (2003, January/February). Assessing American diversity. *The Futurist, 37*(1), 22–6.

Our story. (2014). http://instagram.com/press/#.

Outlook from WWD/DNR CEO Summit. (2008). New York: Kurt Salmon Associates.

Ozzard, J. (1996, May 8). VF's brands serve a broad market. *Women's Wear Daily,* 12.

Ozzard, J. (2001, April 17). A space race: Emerging NYC areas can still be found. *Women's Wear Daily,* 1, 16.

Ozzard, J. & Seckler, V. (1996, September 19). Fashion revolution: The 3-D mega niche. *Women's Wear Daily,* 1, 6–9.

Pacanowsky, M. (1995). Team tools for wicked problems. *Organizational Dynamics.* Retrieved February 22, 1999, from www.elibrary.com.

Paine, L. S. (1991). Corporate policy and the ethics of competitor intelligence gathering. *Journal of Business Ethics, 10,* 423–36.

Pallay, J. (2007, February 12). A crowded street: As streetwear is disseminated into the mainstream, what will become of an underground movement? *Daily News Record,* 96.

Pantone Color Institute biographies. Retrieved June 10, 1998, from www.pantone.com/bios.html.

Parr, K. (1996, October 31). The image makers. *Women's Wear Daily,* 16.

Parsons, J. L. (2002). No longer a "frowsy drudge": Women's wardrobe management: 1880–1930. *Clothing and Textile Research Journal, 20*(1), 33–44.

Pasanella, M. (2003, May 1). The uncolor solution. *The New York Times,* D1, D4.

Pasnak, M. F. D. & Ayres, R. W. (1969). Fashion innovators. *Journal of Home Economics, 61*(9), 698–702.

Patterson, J. (2008, May 8). Sunny, cheerful and upbeat, the season's trend color is hot stuff. *Orlando Sentinel.* Retrieved June 15, 2008, from EBSCO.

Paul, P. (2002, February). Color by numbers. *American Demographics, 24*(2), 30–6.

Peake, G. (2006, May 22). The 4 big buzzwords. *Daily News Record,* 37.

Pelletier, S. (2007, October 1). For the love of color. *Association Meetings.* Retrieved October 1, 2007, from Business Index.

Perna, R. (1987). *Fashion forecasting.* New York: Fairchild.

Pesendorfer, W. (1995). Design innovation and fashion cycles. *American Economic Review, 85*(4), 771–92.

Pesendorfer, W. (2005). Second reply to Coelho, Klein, and McClure. *Econ Journal Watch, 2*(1), 42–6.

Pesendorfer, W. (2004). Response to "Fashion cycles in economics." *Econ Journal Watch, 1*(3), 455–64.

Peterson, K. (2003, June). Mining data at hand. *Chain Store Age, 79*(6), 36.

Pew Research Social & Demographic Trends Project February 11, 2008. U.S. Population Projections: 2005–2050. By J. S. Passel and D. Cohn. http://www.pewsocialtrends.org/2008/02/11/us-population-projections-2005-2050/.

Phelan, H. (2012, April 20). 10 eco-friendly fashion brands we can get behind. Retrieved: http://fashionista.com/2012/04/10-eco-friendly-fashion-brands-we-can-get-behind.

Phillips, L. (1999, June). 2001: A color palette. *American Demographics,* 18–19.

Piirto, R. (1991). *Beyond mind games: The marketing power of psychographics.* New York: American Demographics.

Pine, B. J. (1993). *Mass customization: The new frontier in business competition.* Boston: Harvard Business School Press.

Pine, B. J., Peppers, D., & Rogers, M. (1995, March–April). Do you want to keep your customers forever? *Harvard Business Review, 73*(2), 103–14.

Poggi, J. (2007, February 5). Retail experts expect more consumers to tune into fashion weeks. *Women's Wear Daily,* 34.

Polegato, R. & Wall, M. (1980). Information seeking by fashion opinion leaders and followers. *Home Economics Research Journal, 8,* 327–38.

Polhemus, T. (1994). *Streetstyle: From sidewalk to catwalk.* London: Thames and Hudson.

Polhemus, T. (1996). *Style surfing.* London: Thames and Hudson.

Poling, J. (1963, September 21). Piracy on 7th Avenue. *Saturday Evening Post,* 28–34.

Pollard, K. & Scommegna, P. (2014, April). Just how many Baby Boomers are there? Population Reference Bureau. www.prb.org.

Popcorn, F. (1991). *The Popcorn report.* New York: Doubleday.

Popcorn, F. (1997). *Clicking.* New York: HarperCollins.

Popcorn, F. (2005, December). Cultural relevance: CEOs must go beyond marketing to embed their products in the culture. *Chief Executive,* 35.

Porter, T. (1994). Color in the looking glass. In H. Linton (ed.), *Color forecasting* (pp. 1–9). New York: Van Nostrand Reinhold.

Postrel, V. (2003). *The substance of style.* Harper Perennial.

Postrel, V. (2010, September 11). Fashion as art. *The Wall Street Journal* [Online]. http://www.wsj.com/articles/SB10001424052748703453804575479902076411376.

Potts, M. (1990, April 15). Purchasing power. *The Washington Post,* H1.

Power, D. (1998, March 4). Executives taking new look at role of technology. *Daily News Record,* 3.

Power, D. (2001, February 7). Target's color story. *Women's Wear Daily,* 22.

Power, D. (2007, August 15). Analysts call for Wal-Mart to tap external trend data. *Women's Wear Daily,* 9.

Preparing season. (2003). Retrieved May 23, 2003, from www.premierevision.fr.

Prescod, Danielle (2014, June 16,). 30 best resort 2015 prints. http://www.elle.com/fashion/trend-reports/30-best-resort-2015-prints#slide-1.

Prescott, J. E. & Smith, D. C. (1989, May–June). The largest survey of "leading-edge" competitor intelligence managers. *Planning Review, 17,* 6–13.

Press. (2014). https://about.pinterest.com/en/press.

Press information. (2014). https://www.tumblr.com/press.

Pressler, M. W. (1995, February 19). From riches to rags? Grunge's flop, other trends wear on the apparel industry. *The Washington Post,* H1, H7.

PV, runway overlap brings headaches. (2002, December 17). *Women's Wear Daily,* 9, 11.

Radeloff, D. J. (1991). Psychological types, color attributes, and color preferences of clothing, textiles, and design students. *Clothing and Textiles Research Journal, 9*(3), 59–67.

Raper, S. & Weisman, K. (1998, May 27). Paris: The boutique boom. *Women's Wear Daily,* 40, 44.

Record, J. (2014). In *Oh you pretty things: The story of music and fashion.* London: BBC.

Reynold, W. H. (1968, July). Cars and clothing: Understanding fashion trends. *Journal of Marketing, 32,* 44–9.

Reynolds, G. (2008) *Presentation Zen.* Berkeley, CA: New Riders.

Rick Owens Paris fashion week show took runway diversity to a whole new level. (2013, September 26). *The Huffington Post.*

Rickard, L. (1993). Goodyear test-drives the Visionary shopper for market research. *Advertising Age, 64*(45), 24.

Ries, A. & Trout, J. (1986). *Positioning: The battle for your mind.* New York: McGraw-Hill.

Robertson, T. S. (1971). *Innovative behavior and communication.* New York: Holt, Rinehart and Winston.

Robertson, T. S., Zielinski, J., & Ward, S. (1984). *Consumer behavior.* Glenview, IL: Scott Foresman.

Robinson, D. E. (1958, November/December). Fashion theory and product design. *Harvard Business Review, 36*(6), 126–38.

Robinson, D. E. (1975, November/December). Style changes: Cyclical, inexorable, and foreseeable. *Harvard Business Review, 53*(6), 121–31.

Robinson, G. (1999, November 22). Apple sows seeds for colorful new world. *The Baltimore Sun.* http://articles.baltimoresun.com/1999-11-22/entertainment/9911220004_1_bright-colors-imac-pantone.

Rogers, E. M. (1962). *Diffusion of innovations.* New York: Glencoe.

Rogers, E. M. (1983). *Diffusion of innovations* (3rd ed.). New York: Free Press.

Rose, M. M. (2002, October 7). Hollywood Reporter. Saks dresses up promo deal with Fox's "girls." http://business.highbeam.com/2012/article-1G1-93027583/saks-dresses-up-promo-deal-fox-girls.

Rosenkrans, W. (2003). Pattern recognition. In M. M. Carr (ed.), *Super searchers in competitive analysis* (pp. 141–56). Medford, NJ: Cyber Age Books.

Rothman, S. (2008, February 7). Putting trend spotters on the spot. *The New York Times.* Retrieved February 7, 2008, from www.nytimes.com.

Rowland, K. (2014). In *Oh you pretty things: The story of music and fashion.* London: BBC.

Rowley, I. & Tashiro, H. (2007, May 7). Testing what's hot in the cradle of cool. *Business Week,* 46.

Rozhon, T. (2003). The race to think like a teenager. *The New York Times.* Retrieved August 7, 2003, from www.nytimes.com.

Rubenstein, H. (1998, April). Why does this dress cost $30,000? *InStyle,* 195.

Rubinstein, R. P. (2001). *Dress codes: Meanings and messages in American culture.* Boulder, CO: Westview.

Rueff, R. (1991, February 4). Demographics won't find the bull's eye. *Advertising Age, 62*(6), 20.

Runyan, R.C., Noh, M., & Mosier, J. (2013). What is cool? Operationalizing the construct in an apparel context. *Journal of Fashion Marketing and Management, 17*(3).

Russell, C. (1989). Lifestyles of the ordinary and anonymous: A guided tour of the real American market. Paper presented at the Consumer Outlook conference, New York City.

Ryssdal, K. (2012, June 8). Costume designer Nolan Miller's influence on fashion. http://www.marketplace.org/topics/life/costume-designer-nolan-millers-influence-fashion.

Sahadi, J. (2005, January 7). Fashion's future is a 6-figure job. Retrieved January 7, 2005, from www.cnnmoney.com.

Sally Fox: Innovation in the field. (2003). Retrieved May 30, 2003, from www.foxfibre.com.

Sapir, E. (1931). Fashion. In R. A. Seligman (ed.), *Encyclopedia of the social sciences* (Vol. 6, pp. 139–41). New York: Macmillan.

Sauers, J. (2012, February 8). How fashion blogger BryanBoy became a front-row fixture. http://observer.com/2012/02/bryanboy-new-york-fashion-week-anna-wintour-karl-lagerfeld-marc-jacobs/#ixzz3FcYRcGAt.

Schiro, A. (1998, May 5). Sign of autumn: "Watch for falling hemlines." *The New York Times.* Retrieved May 5, 1998, from www.nytimes.com.

Schiro, A. (1999, February 2). Denim turned every which way but loose. *The New York Times,* B10.

Schlossberg, H. (1990, March 5). Competitive intelligence pros seek formal role in marketing. *Marketing News, 24,* 2, 28.

Schlosser, J. (2005, June 27). How I make decisions. *Fortune, 151*(13), 106.

Schneider-Levy, B. (2007, May 7). Color theory; Pantone offers the fashion industry an inside view on the spectrum of color trends. *Footwear News,* 12.

Schrage, M. (1997, June 30). Data mining in a vicious circle. *Computerworld,* 37.

Schrank, H. L. (1973). Correlates of fashion leadership: Implications for fashion process theory. *Sociological Quarterly, 14,* 534–43.

Schweiss-Hankins, D. (1998, November 20). Retail fashion programs and fashion trends. Paper presented at the Annual Meeting of the International Textiles and Apparel Association, Dallas, TX.

Scrivener, L. (2007, April 1). They colour your world. *Toronto Star.* Retrieved April 1, 2007, from EBSCO.

Seckler, V. (2002a, March 11). The luxury squeeze: Wealthy have less, wannabes in waiting. *Women's Wear Daily,* 1, 4.

Seckler, V. (2002b, August 21). Trend spotters play it safe. *Women's Wear Daily,* 8.

Seckler, V. (2002c, June 26). Coping with consumers' choices. *Women's Wear Daily,* 9–10.

Seckler, V. (2003a, January 24). Quart-ing teenagers. *Women's Wear Daily,* 2, 13.

Seckler, V. (2003b, February). Research: Too much red for one brand to own it. *WWD/Global,* 8.

Seckler, V. (2003c, February 21). The mini: Better or worse. *Women's Wear Daily,* 11.

Seckler, V. (2003d, April 16). Angling for an edge with youths. *Women's Wear Daily,* 10.

Seckler, V. (2007a, January 31). Trying new identities on for size. *Women's Wear Daily,* 7.

Seckler, V. (2007b, September 26). Who's buying into Americana? *Women's Wear Daily,* 16.

Seckler, V. (2008a, February 20). For apparel brand loyalists, the fundamental things apply. *Women's Wear Daily,* 22.

Seckler, V. (2008b, August 20). Q&A: What women want. *Women's Wear Daily.* Retrieved August 20, 2008, from www.wwd.com.

Seckler, V. (2008c, September 17). Staying on top of generations in flux. *Women's Wear Daily.* Retrieved September 17, 2008 from www.wwd.com.

Sedghi, A. (2014, February 4). Facebook: 10 years of social networking, in numbers. http://www.theguardian.com/news/datablog/2014/feb/04/facebook-in-numbers-statistics.

Severson, K. (2007, December 5). Is the entrée heading for extinction? *The New York Times.* Retrieved December 5, 2007, from www.nytimes.com.

Sewing, J. (2007, January 11). The Nygard comfort zone. *The Houston Chronicle,* 1.

Shearer, P. (1994). *Business forecasting and planning.* New York: Prentice Hall.

Sherman, L. (2014, September 9). Jenny Packham spring 2015 ready-to-wear. http://www.style.com/fashion-shows/spring-2015-ready-to-wear/jenny-packham.

Shewfelt, R. L. (2014, May 5) How the Met gala became such a starry night. https://ca.celebrity.yahoo.com/blogs/celebrity-news/-how-the-met-gala-became-such-a-starry-night-122800333.html.

Shibukawa, I. (1984). *Designer's guide to color 2.* San Francisco: Chronicle.

Siegel, H. (2003, December 1). Five X 5. *WWD/BeautyBiz*, 58–61.

Silverman, D. (2008, June 30). A delicate balance. *Women's Wear Daily*. Retrieved June 30, 2008, from www.wwd.com.

Simmel, G. (1904). Fashion. *International Quarterly, 10*, 130–55.

Simon-Miller, F. (1985). Commentary: Signs and cycles in the fashion system. In M. R. Solomon (ed.), *The psychology of fashion* (pp. 71–81). Lexington, KY: Heath/Lexington.

Sims, J. (2008, May 10). Silk or synthetic: Today's polyester has a luxurious sheen perfectly suited to high fashion. *The Financial Times*, 7.

Sinnreich, A. & Gluck, M. (2005, January 29). Music & fashion: The balancing act between creativity and control. In Ready to share: Fashion & the ownership of creativity, a Norman Lear Center Conference.

Sloan, P. (1988, October). Makeup: The hue and dye. *Savvy*, 94–6.

Sloan, P. (1991, December 16). Bozell rewires media strategy. *Advertising Age, 62*(53), 12.

Small, R.D. (1997, January 20). Debunking datamining myths. *Information Week*, 55.

Snyder, R. (1991, January). Interview with John Wittenbraker, Vice-President, ARBOR, a Philadelphia Market Research Company. *The Communicator, 26*(1), 6–7.

Socha, M. (1998a, June 8). Differentiate or die—product. *Women's Wear Daily*, 10, 14.

Socha, M. (2003, July 2) Fish and fowl mix: Paris couture week inject more RTW. *Women's Wear Daily*, 1, 4.

Socha, M. (1998b, May 8). Runways to aisles, picks stick. *Women's Wear Daily*, 12.

Socha, M. & Ozzard, J. (2000, April 14). Building buzz, one by one. *Women's Wear Daily*, 14, 16.

Solomon, W. (2006, March 31). New colors springing up: There really is a "they" who decide what's hot for the season. *The Morning Call*. Retrieved July 21, 2008, from EBSCO.

Soucy, C. (2005, April). Hues you can use: Understanding color. *Jewelers Circular Keystone, 176* (4), S48.

Spindler, A. (1997, June 3). Taking stereotyping to a new level in fashion. *The New York Times*. Retrieved May 5, 1998, from www.archives.nytimes.com.

SPRZ NY. (2015). Uniqlo.com. http://sprzny.uniqlo.com/us/.

Stark, S. & Johnson-Carroll, K. (1994, July). Study finds color choices far from random. *Bobbin*, 16, 18.

Statistics: The style counsel. (2008, April 8). *Brand Strategy*, 58.

Steidtmann, C. (1996, October 31). The future of fashion. *Women's Wear Daily* (Section II), 35.

Steigerwald, B. (2007, December 8). Opinion: How we shop. *Pittsburgh Tribune Review*. Retrieved December 9, 2008, from EBSCO.

Steinhauer, J. (1998, February 24). The Los Angeles contemporary look. *The New York Times*, Retrieved May 5, 1998, from www.archives.nytimes.com.

Stoefel, K. (2014, September 5). Here is Anna Wintour using a flip phone in 2014. http://nymag.com/thecut/2014/09/here-is-anna-wintour-using-a-flip-phone-in-2014.html.

Strauss, W. & Howe, N. (1991). *Generations: The history of America's future, 1585 to 2069*. New York: Morrow.

Strength in numbers. (2008, January). *Black Enterprise, 38*(6), 53.

Strugatz, R. and Yi, D. (2014, June 12). Incomes keep soaring for fashion's top bloggers. WWD. http://www.wwd.com/fashion-news/fashion-features/incomes-keep-soaring-for-fashions-top-bloggers-7726536?full=true.

Sull, D. & Turconi, S. (2008, July). Fast fashion lessons. *Business Strategy Review, 19*(2), 4–11.

Sullivan, R. (1998, August). Teen tribes. *Vogue*, 217–24.

Sutton, S. M. (1993, March/April). Honing in on the hottest markets. *Monitor, 23*(2), 34–7.

Swash, R. (2011, September 3). Who is Mr Street Peeper? http://www.theguardian.com/fashion/2011/sep/13/blogging-new-york-fashion-week-autumn-2011.

Sykes, S. A. (1994). Color forecasting and marketing for home furnishings. In H. Linton (ed.), *Color forecasting* (pp. 1–9). New York: Van Nostrand Reinhold.

Szwarce, D. (1994). A colorful experience. In H. Linton (ed.), *Color forecasting* (pp. 138–45). New York: Van Nostrand Reinhold.

Tain, L. (1997). *Portfolio presentation for fashion designers.* New York: Fairchild Books.

Talley, A. L. (1998, July). Style fax. *Vogue,* 26.

Tanaka, J. (1998, March 2). Futurism—the trendiest profession. *Newsweek,* 14.

Tapert, A. (1998, September). The American comfort class. *Bazaar, 474,* 550.

Tapp, Alan, & Bird, Sarah (2008, Spring). Social marketing and the meaning of cool. *SMq, 14*(1), 18–29.

Taub, E. A. (2008, May 19). Guessing the online customer's next want. *The New York Times,* C6.

[TC]2 and digital printing. (2003). Retrieved May 29, 2003 from www.tc2.com.

Technology (2014). http://www.outlast.com/en/technology/.

Tedeschi, B. (2002, September 30). An online success for Lands' End. *The New York Times.* Retrieved January 11, 2003, from www.nytimes.com.

Thomas, B. (2007, December 17). Beyond the business suit. *Daily News Record,* 14.

Thompson Smith, S. (2007, September 6). NYC lights up in style. *The News & Observer* (Raleigh, NC). Retrieved August 26, 2008, from EBSCO.

Tips from eco-style pioneers. (2007, April 2). *Daily News Record,* 18.

Toledo, R. (2002, October 27). Trend spotting at the street parade. *The New York Times,* SR17.F.

Trahn, K.T.L. (2014, April 30). BCBGeneration eyes Millennials. WWD.

Tran, K. T. L. (2008a, March 4). Price pressure builds at sourcing shows. *Women's Wear Daily,* 19.

Tran, K. T. L. (2008b, April 8). Focus shifting closer to home at L.A. textile show. *Women's Wear Daily,* 12.

Tran, K. T. L. (2008c, April 8). Slow ride: A number of fashion designers are stepping back from the disposable world of fast fashion, instead focusing on a more eco-conscious, long-term approach. *Women's Wear Daily,* 18S.

Tran, K. T. L. (2008d, July 2). Retailing's sweet spot: Stores look to lure millennial generation. *Women's Wear Daily.* Retrieved July 2, 2008, from www.wwd.com.

Trebay, G. (2001, August 21). A mother lode of old inspiration. *The New York Times.*

Trebay, G. (2002a, August 6). If you can't stand the heat, get out of the suit. *The New York Times.* Retrieved August 9, 2002, from www.nytimes.com.

Trebay, G. (2002b, October 2). Workwear that says peekaboo, you see me. *The New York Times.* Retrieved January 11, 2003, from www.nytimes.com.

Trebay, G. (2002c, October 9). Smoky. Hot. Crowded. Inspirational. *The New York Times.* Retrieved January 11, 2003, from www.nytimes.com.

Trebay, G. (2002d, November 19). London: The town that would be king again. *The New York Times.* Retrieved January 11, 2003, from www.nytimes.com.

Trebay, G. (2003a, January 4). A search for men's fashion starts at the lost and found. *The New York Times.* Retrieved January 14, 2003, from www.nytimes.com.

Trebay, G. (2003b, March 8). Fashion diary. *The New York Times.* Retrieved March 8, 2003, from www.nytimes.com.

Trebay, G. (2007, September 29). Al Gore's fashion forecast. *The New York Times.* Retrieved September 29, 2007, from www.nytimes.com.

Trend guru shares color design forecast at Las Vegas market. (2007, August 3). *Furniture World Magazine.* Retrieved August 2, 2007, from www.furninfo.com.

True Blood costume designer Audrey Fisher interview on dressing Sookie & The Gang. (2014, June 20). http://www.realstylenetwork.com/fashion-and-style/2014/06/true-blood-costume-designer-audrey-fisher-interview-on-dressing/.

Tse, R. (2014, June 23). Resort 2015 is already making the rounds: The 10 best celebrity style looks so far. http://www.fashionmagazine.com/scene/red-carpet-society/2014/06/23/resort-2015-celebrity-style/.

Tsong, N. (2006, September 28). Forecasters on the lookout for the next big color. *The Seattle Times*. Retrieved September 28, 2006, from Newspaper Source Database.

Tucker, R. (2007, March 7). Pantone takes steps to save time, money. *Women's Wear Daily*, 16.

Tucker, R. (2008, July 22). N.Y. textile fairs manage growth in difficult time. *Women's Wear Daily*. Retrieved July 22, 2008, from www.wwd.com.

Tufte, E. (2003). *The cognitive style of Powerpoint: Pitching out corrupts within.* Cheshire, CT: Graphic Press.

Tunsky, P. (1994). Pat Tunsky, Inc. In H. Linton (ed.), *Color forecasting* (pp. 179–80). New York: Van Nostrand Reinhold.

Turk, R. (1989, December 3). Fashion taboos are yielding to "anything goes." *Birmingham News*, 18E.

Underhill, P. (2000). *Why we buy: The science of shopping.* New York: Simon & Schuster.

Urban Outfitters at Lehman Brothers Retail Seminar. (2007, May 1). *Fair Disclosure Wire*. Retrieved May 1, 2007, from Business Index.

Vanderbilt, T. (2012, April 27). Sneaking into Pantone HQ: How color forecasters really decide which hue will be the new black. www.slate.com.

van Dyk, D. (2008, March). The Millennials. *Time*, 55–69.

Vardi, N. (2013, December 3). Feds target apparel-industry insider trading ring. Forbes.com. http://www.forbes.com/sites/nathanvardi/2013/12/03/the-apparel-insider-trading-ring/.

Vasilopoulos, V. (1998, March 2). Kiton, Brioni Windsor some, lose some at Sotheby's. *Women's Wear Daily*, 1.

Veblen, T. (1899). *The theory of the leisure class.* New York: Macmillan.

Vejlgaard, H. (2008). *Anatomy of a trend.* New York: McGraw-Hill.

Vejlgaard, H. (2013). *Style eruptions.* Confetti Publishing Inc.

Vena, J. (2010, February 25). Rihanna 'Rude Boy' video director 'wasn't trying to rip anybody off'. http://www.mtv.com/news/1632688/rihanna-rude-boy-video-director-wasnt-trying-to-rip-anybody-off/.

Vendors take control, put reorders at risk with lean inventories. (2001, August 8). *Women's Wear Daily*, 1, 4–5.

Venkatraman, M. P. (1991). The impact of innovativeness and innovation type on adoption. *Journal of Retailing, 67*(1), 51–67.

Venkatraman, M. P. & Price, L. (1990). Differentiating between cognitive and sensory innovativeness: Concepts, measurement and their implications. *Journal of Business Research, 20*, 293–315.

Verlodt, P. (1994a). Beyond the crystal ball. In H. Linton (ed.), *Color forecasting* (pp. 159–64). New York: Van Nostrand Reinhold.

Verlodt, P. (1994b). Color marketing group. In H. Linton (ed.), *Color forecasting* (pp. 32–5). New York: Van Nostrand Reinhold.

Vesilind, E. (2007, July 18). Retailers zero in on chic L.A. shopping spots. *Women's Wear Daily*, 14.

Vinken, B. (2005). *Fashion zeitgeist.* Oxford: Berg.

Walker, R. (2007, July 8). Mass appeal. *The New York Times*. Retrieved July 8, 2007, from www.nytimes.com.

Wallendorf, M., Belk, R., & Heisley, D. (1988). Deep meaning in possessions: The paper. In M. S. Houston (ed.), *Advances in consumer research* (Vol. 15, pp. 528–30). Provo, UT: Association of Consumer Research.

Wal-Mart and Sam's Club select The NPD Group for consumer panel data. (2007, June 28). *Wireless News*. Retrieved June 28, 2007, from Business Index.

Wang, C. (2013, December 6). Fashion Week will become even more exclusive, may start banning bloggers. Retrieved from *Refinery29*.

Wang, L. (2014, June 10). Role call | Andrea Bell, retail editor and trend forecaster. http://www.businessoffashion.com/2014/06/role-call-andrea-bell-retail-editor-trend-forecaster.html.

Wasson, C. R. (1968, July). How predictable are fashion and other product life cycles? *Journal of Marketing, 32*, 36–43.

We tried Banana Republic's version of Kate Middleton's Issa engagement dress – here's how it looked. (2013, August 14). *Huffington Post Style*.

Webb, A. L. (1994). Timing is everything. In H. Linton (ed.), *Color forecasting* (pp. 203–6). New York: Van Nostrand Reinhold.

Weisman, K. (2008, February 6). Skate and surf wear goes mainstream. *International Herald Tribune*. Retrieved February 6, 2008, from www.iht.com.

Weiss, M. J. (1988). *The clustering of America*. New York: Harper and Row.

Weiss, M. (2003, February). Inside consumer confidence surveys. *American Demographics, 25*(1), 22–9.

Weitzman, J. (2001, March 16). "Tribal" looks lead teen retailers. *Women's Wear Daily*, 21.

Wellner, A. S. (2003a, April). The next 25 years. *American Demographics, 25*(3), 24–7.

Wellner, A. S. (2003b, November). Inside Asian generations. *American Demographics, 22*(11), 11.

WGSN. (2014). *Macro Trends – Spring / Summer 2015: Focus*. http://www.wgsn.com/storage/vol10/wgsn/en/micro/Art_Dept/2013/Macro_ss15/pdfs/WGSN_SS15_MACRO_TRENDS.pdf.

What is a forecast? (1995, December). *American Demographics*. Retrieved July 22, 2008, from www.demographics.com.

Wheatley, M. (2003, May 22). Turning data into decisions. *Supply Management, 8*(11), 22.

Wicks, A. (2012, September 12) Harper's Bazaar launches ShopBazaar. Retrieved: http://www.wwd.com/media-news/fashion-memopad/the-bazaar-boutique-6274703.

Wilke, M. (1995, October). The reluctant shopper in the pink. *American Demographics*. Retrieved May 5, 1998, from www.marketingpower.com.

Will cigars stay hot? How to track the trend. (1997, July 21). *Newsweek, 59*.

Williams, R. (2007, April). The long tail: the new retail paradigm? http://business.highbeam.com/437094/article-1G1-163063872/long-tail-new-retail-paradigm-due-technological-advances.

Williamson, C. (2011, February 20). Andrej Pejic: Who's that boy? *The Telegraph*.

Wilson, C. (2014). *Let's talk about love: Why other people have such bad taste*. New York: Bloomsbury Academic.

Wilson, E. (1985). *Adorned in dreams*. Berkeley: University of California Press.

Wilson, E. (2002, November 11). Show business: Designers prosper without the runway. *Women's Wear Daily*, 1, 6.

Wilson, E. (2003a, April). Fashion supernova. *WWD Magazine*, 78–79.

Wilson, E. (2003b, April). Reality bites back. *WWD Magazine*, 80.

Wilson, E. (2003c, July 9). Designer fall outlook: Brighter skies ahead and more deals, too. *Women's Wear Daily*, 1, 8.

Wilson, E. (2007a, March 29). Somehow it feels old hat. *The New York Times*. Retrieved March 29, 2007, from www.nytimes.com.

Wilson, E. (2007b, September 4). Before models can turn around, knockoffs fly. *The New York Times*. Retrieved September 4, 2007, from www.nytimes.com.

Wilson, E. (2007c, September 8). Fashion's calendar girl of 1941 and 2007. *The New York Times*. Retrieved September 8, 2007, from www.nytimes.com.

Wilson, E. (2007d, September 9). The knockoff won't be knocked off. *The New York Times*. Retrieved September 9, 2007, from www.nytimes.com.

Wilson, E. (2007e, November 1). Is this it for the It bag? *The New York Times*. Retrieved November 1, 2007, from www.nytimes.com.

Wilson, E. (2008a, March 13). When imitation's unflattering. *The New York Times*.

Retrieved March 13, 2008, from www.
nytimes.com.

Wilson, E. (2008b, May 21). Simply irresistible. *The New York Times.* Retrieved May 21, 2008, from www.nytimes.com.

Wilson, E. (2008c, May 29). Dress for less and less. *The New York Times.* Retrieved May 29, 2008, from www.nytimes.com.

Wilson, E. (2008d, September 8). The sun never sets on the runway. *The New York Times.* Retrieved September 8, 2008, from www.nytimes.com.

Winslow, Ben. (2013, July 31) Guarding against industrial espionage at the Outdoor Retailer's Expo. Fox 13, Salt Lake City.

Winter, D. (1996, September 1). Uh, oh: Colors and fabrics of the '70s are making a comeback. *Ward's Auto World, 32,* 38–41.

Wintour, A. (1998a, July). Letter from the editor. *Vogue,* 22.

Wintour, A. (1998b, August). Letter from the editor: Clans and cliques. *Vogue, 50.*

Wolcott, J. (1998, August). Tanks for the memories. *Vanity Fair, 68,* 70, 73–4, 76.

Wolfe, D. (1998, January). The state of fashion 1998. Paper presented at the annual meeting of the National Retail Federation, New York.

Wolfe, D. (1999, January). The state of fashion 1999. Paper presented at the annual meeting of the National Retail Federation, New York.

Wong, Y. W. H., Yuen, C. W. M, Leung, M. Y. S., Ku, S. K. A., & Lam, H. L. I. (2006, March) Selected application of nanotechnology in textiles. *AUTEX Research Journal, 6*(1), © AUTEX. http://www.autexrj.com/cms/zalaczone_pliki/1-06-1.pdf.

Wood, D. (1990, August 10). Fashion vs. natural looks: Two ways to pick a palette. *Women's Wear Daily,* 8, 10.

Wood, M. (2014, March 5). No longer clashing, wearable tech embraces fashion. *The New York Times.* http://www.nytimes.com/2014/03/06/technology/personaltech/no-longer-clashing-wearable-tech-embraces-fashion.html?_r=0.

Wrack, K. S. (1994). Shopping is in-depth market research. In H. Linton (ed.), *Color forecasting* (pp. 181–8). New York: Van Nostrand Reinhold.

Young, A. B. (1937). *Recurring cycles of fashion 1760–1937.* New York: Harper and Row.

Young, A. B. (1966). *Recurring cycles of fashion, 1760–1937.* New York: Cooper Square Publishers.

Young, R. & Hobson, J. (2013, September 5). *Vogue's* Andre Leon Talley on the state of American fashion. Here & Now. http://hereandnow.wbur.org/2013/09/05/andre-leon-talley.

Young, V. M. (1998, September 14). Copycat suits increase with competition. *Women's Wear Daily,* 20–1.

Young, V. M. (2014, July 1). Moody's: Stores still needed as online traffic grows. WWD.

Zajac, E. J. & Bazerman, M. H. (1991). Blind spots in industry and competitor analysis: Implications of interfirm (mis)perceptions for strategic decision. *Academy of Management Review, 16*(1), 37–56.

Zargani, L. (2013, August 2). Examining the challenges, importance of building brand loyalty. WWD.

Zernike, K. (2009, March 7). Generation OMG. *The New York Times.* http://www.nytimes.com/2009/03/08/weekinreview/08zernike.html?pagewanted=all&_r=0.

Zessler, I. (1994). Peclers Paris. In H. Linton (ed.), *Color forecasting* (pp. 195–202). New York: Van Nostrand Reinhold.

Zimbalist, K. (1998a, April). Fashion conspiracy. *Vogue,* 154, 164.

Zimmerman, E. (2008, May 11). Roaming the world, detecting fashion. *The New York Times.* Retrieved May 11, 2008, from www.nytimes.com.

Zimmermann, K. A. (1998a, April 4). Duck head shifting into automatic. *Women's Wear Daily,* 20.

Zimmerman, K. A. (1998b, December 9). Mass-produced for individual looks. *Women's Wear Daily,* 24.

Zimmermann, K. A. (1998c, March 18). Nygard's quick response: Paperless and profitable. *Women's Wear Daily,* 20.

Zogby, H. (2008). *The way we'll be: The Zogby Report on the transformation of the American Dream.* New York: Random House.

Zogby, John (2010, July 8). How the recession has changed America's spending. http://www.forbes.com/2010/07/08/recession-spending-pew-opinions-columnists-john-zogby.html.

IMAGE CREDITS

INDEX